D1490632

Office Procedures for the 21st Century

SEVENTH EDITION

Sharon Burton
Brookhaven College
Dallas County Community College District
Dallas, Texas

Nelda Shelton
South Campus Tarrant County College District
Fort Worth, Texas

PEARSON
Prentice
Hall

Upper Saddle River, New Jersey 07458

Library of Congress Cataloging-in-Publication Data

Burton, Sharon.
    Office procedures for the 21st century / Sharon Burton, Nelda Shelton. —7th ed.
        p. cm.
    Rev. ed. of: Procedures for the automated office. 6th ed.
    ISBN 0-13-230857-6
    1. Office practice—Handbooks manuals, etc. 2. Secretaries—Handbooks, manuals, etc.
    I. Shelton, Nelda. II. Burton, Sharon. Procedures for the automated office. III. Title.
        HF5547.5.J45 2007
        651.3—dc22

2006021058

Editor-in-Chief: Vernon R. Anthony
Senior Acquisitions Editor: Gary Bauer
Editorial Assistant: Dan Trudden
Marketing Manager: Leigh Ann Sims
Marketing Coordinator: Alicia Dysert
Managing Editor—Production: Mary Carnis
Manufacturing Buyer: Ilene Sanford
Production Liaison: Denise Brown
Full-Service Production and Composition: Heather Willison/Carlisle Publishing Services
Manager of Media Production: Amy Peltier
Media Production Project Manager: Lisa Rinaldi
Director, Image Resource Center: Melinda Patelli

Manager, Rights and Permissions: Zina Arabia
Manager, Visual Research: Beth Brenzel
Manager, Cover Visual Research & Permissions: Karen Sanatar
Image Permission Coordinator: Kathy Gavilanes
Senior Design Coordinator: Mary Siener
Cover Design: Lisa Klausing
Cover Image: Background image: Jupiter Images; Left to right: Jupiter Images; Deborah Jaffe, Jupiter Images; LWA/Dan Tardif, Jupiter Images; Eric Audras, Jupiter Images; Paul Taylor, Getty Images
Interior Design: Wanda España
Printer/Binder and Cover Printer: Quebecor World

Photo Credits: Cover: Getty Images, Inc., Paul Taylor; Jupiter Images – Nonstock, Deborah Jaffe; Jupiter Images – PhotoAlto, Eric Audras; Jupiter Images - Image 100; Jupiter Images - Blend Images, LWA/Dann Tardif; Jupiter Images - Comstock Images, Comstock; Chapter 1 Opener: Getty Images Inc. - Image Bank, Gordon, Larry Dale; Figure 1-1: Corbis Digital Stock; Figure 1-2: PhotoEdit Inc., Deborah Davis; Figure 1-4: Texas Instruments Incorporated; Figure 1-9: PhotoEdit Inc., David Young-Wolff; Figure 1-10: Getty Images Inc. - Image Bank, AJA Productions; Figure 1-12: PhotoEdit Inc., David Young-Wolff; Chapter 2 Opener: Getty Images Inc. - Stone Allstock, Zigy Kaluzny; Figure 2-4: Corbis/Bettmann, Jose Luis Pelaez, Inc.; Figure 2-5: Getty Images – Stockbyte; Figure 2-7: Getty Images – Stockbyte; Figure 2-8: PhotoEdit Inc., Bill Bachmann; Chapter 3 Opener: Getty Images Inc. - Stone Allstock, Laurence Dutton; Figure 3-8: PhotoEdit Inc., Kayte M. Deioma; Chapter 4 Opener: Getty Images, Inc. – PhotoDisc; Figure 4-1: Corbis/Bettmann, Jose Luis Pelaez, Inc.; Figure 4-5: Dorling Kindersley Media Library; Chapter 5 Opener: Getty Images, Inc. – Taxi, Michael Krasowitz; Figure 5-3: PhotoEdit Inc., Frank Siteman; Figure 5-5: Getty Images, Inc.- Photodisc, Craig Brewer; Chapter 6 Opener: Photolibrary.Com; Figure 6-1: PhotoEdit Inc., Michael Newman; Figure 6-5: PhotoEdit Inc., Jonathan Nourok; Figure 6-6: PhotoEdit Inc.; David Young-Wolff; Chapter 7 Opener: Index Stock Imagery, Inc., Eric Kamp; Figure 7-1: United Parcel Service; Figure 7-6: Xerox Corporation; Figure 7-7: Danita Delimont Photography, Bill Bachmann; Figure 7-8: Getty Images, Inc.- Photodisc., Spike Mafford; Chapter 8 Opener: Corbis RF; Figure 8-9: AP Wide World Photos; Figure 8-10: PhotoEdit Inc., Michael Newman; Chapter 9 Opener: Getty Images Inc. - Stone Allstock, Peter Cade; Figure 9-1: PhotoEdit Inc., Bill Aron; Figure 9-7: Stock Boston, Jim Pickerell; Figure 9-9: PhotoEdit Inc., Gary Connor; Figure 9-12: Getty Images - Photodisc; Chapter 10 Opener: Getty Images - Photodisc, EyeWire Collection; Figure 10-1: Jupiter Images Picturequest - Royalty Free, Stockbyte; Figure 10-7: PhotoEdit Inc., Myrleen Ferguson Cate; Figure 10-8: Chris Usher Photography & Associates, Inc.; Figure 10-9: Alamy Images, Harry Mole; Chapter 11 Opener: Getty Images Inc. - Stone Allstock, Rainer Grosskopf; Chapter 12 Opener: Getty Images, Inc. – Taxi, Chabruken; Figure 12-3: The Stock Connection, Ron Solomon; Figure 12-7: Getty Images, Inc.- Photodisc, Jack Hollingsworth; Figure 12-8: Getty Images/Digital Vision; Figure 12-10: Getty Images, Inc.- Photodisc., Jacobs Stock Photography; Figure 12-11: Jupiter Images - FoodPix - Creatas - Brand X - Banana Stock – PictureQuest; Figure 12-12: Corbis/Stock Market, Tom Stewart; Chapter 13 Opener: PhotoEdit Inc., Lon C. Diehl; Figure 13-2: Masterfile Corporation, Jon Feingersh; Figure 13-7: Bruce Laurance; Figure 13-8: Getty Images - Digital Vision; Chapter 14 Opener: Getty Images - Photodisc, Eyewire; Figure 14-1: Photolibrary.Com; Figure 14-2: Photolibrary.Com; Figure 14-3: Omni-Photo Communications, Inc., Frank Siteman

Pearson Education Ltd.
Pearson Education Singapore, Pte. Ltd.
Pearson Education Canada, Ltd.
Pearson Education—Japan

Pearson Education Australia PTY, Limited
Pearson Education North Asia Ltd.
Pearson Educación de Mexico, S.A. de C.V.
Pearson Education Malaysia, Pte. Ltd.

10 9 8 7 6 5 4 3 2 1
ISBN 0-13-230857-6

Brief Contents

Contents

Preface

Welcome to the seventh edition of *Office Procedures for the 21st Century* by Sharon Burton and Nelda Shelton. This text/workbook is a leader in the office administration market because of its relevant, accurate, and comprehensive treatment of office procedures. This text uses a proven system to teach students concepts and procedures and to assure they develop the hands-on skills they will need to be successful in today's digital office. The concise presentation has been especially effective with students who need to develop office skills quickly. In this edition, we have increased coverage of the communication and human relations skills required to be effective in today's work environment. We have also emphasized critical thinking, sound reasoning, ethical decision making, efficient use of technology, and high productivity throughout the book.

Success in today's competitive, diverse, and global business environment requires office professionals to be on the cutting edge of the latest office procedures. Even though job titles and functions may vary from company to company, most organizations rely on common office tasks and basic office procedures to keep operations running smoothly. This text addresses the skills, strategies, and techniques needed to perform the common office procedures employed in any business.

The seventh edition continues to facilitate acquisition of the basic office procedures by upgrading levels of thinking from knowledge to comprehension and, finally, to application. After completing this course, you should be able to:

- Understand the role of organizational structures, your supervisor's role, and your role.
- Demonstrate teaming and collaboration and personal and interpersonal skills to develop effective working relationships.
- Prepare for your employment search.
- Prioritize, plan, and manage for results.
- Use the telephone effectively.
- Prepare written communications and distribute processed information.
- Consider the most cost-effective method for mailing.
- Set up and maintain files.
- Perform basic financial tasks.
- Schedule appointments, maintain calendars, and receive visitors.
- Plan meetings and conferences.
- Make travel arrangements.
- Prepare for future professional challenges.

The goal of this latest edition of *Office Procedures for the 21st Century* is to stimulate your thinking, build your functional skills, provide you with useful step-by-step suggestions for improvement, and become a valuable on-the-job reference once the course is done. The information included in this edition will benefit you whether you are new to an office environment or are more experienced and need to update your office skills.

Key Features of the Seventh Edition

Effective communication skills related to teamwork, collaboration, and interpersonal skills are emphasized throughout.

The **early focus on the employment process** is intended to help you begin planning your job search and developing your resume.

ETHICAL★ISSUES ◄ A **focus on ethics** has been provided throughout each chapter to help you think critically about ethical dilemmas or difficult situations related to the office environment.

Instruction boxes offer tips on how to perform specific office tasks.

Stop 'n Check

What travel information can you easily access from the Internet?

_____

_____

_____

◄ **Stop 'n Checks** are located after key concepts that challenge you to recall and think critically.

Quick Tips

HAVE YOU BLOGGED LATELY?

What is a blog? A **blog** is a shortened term for *Web log*, a Web site that is updated on a regular basis, structured in reverse chronological order so the most recent posted information is listed first, typically with a strong personal perspective. Blogging could be called another way of meeting online at your convenience.

Companies may use blogs to ask questions of their customers about changes in products, announcements about new products, requests for comments or opinions about ideas affecting their business, etc. If your company has a blog, as an office professional you might be asked to monitor the blog and report to your manager new comments. Visit www.blog.com and browse the blogs. You will see blogs from businesses to personals.

◄ **Quick Tips** cover strategies and information on rarely emphasized concepts.

 The **Student Data CD** provides discussion questions, on-the-job situations, workshops, and most forms needed for the end-of-chapter assignments.

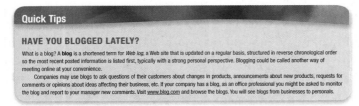

◄ **Student working papers** are packaged with each book at no additional cost.

Expanded Exercises and Application Material

End-of-chapter assignment material has been reorganized and expanded into two sections: Review of Key Concepts, which features exercises that support concept retention and develop critical thinking skills, and Building Your Office Skills, which focuses on developing practical problem-solving skills that can be used immediately on the job.

Concept Review and Reinforcement

- **Review of Key Concepts** provides a quick review of the key concepts organized by learning objective that will help you prepare for quizzes and tests.

- **Key Terms** with definitions for study or review

- **For Your Discussion** provides a set of thought-provoking questions designed to get you to think about the key chapter concepts in ways you must explain, describe, or define.

Building Your Office Skills

- **Exploring the Workplace: *Activities*** allows you and team members opportunities to research the latest trends in office procedures and related concepts. This section is great for critical thinking, as well as improving your communication skills.

- **Developing Critical Thinking Skills: *Problem Solving on the Job*** presents a minimum of four situations which offers opportunities for applying critical thinking skills to realistic office-related problems.

- **Using the Web: *Research Activities*** offers opportunities to build investigative skills and to use Internet resources in real-world office-related situations.

- **Get Tech Wise** offers opportunities to use common technology features efficiently and effectively to achieve specific goals.

- **Improving Your Writing Skills: *Workshops*** provides a review of rules relating to punctuation, capitalization, number usage, and grammar in the form of exercises.

- **Simulation: *In the Office at Supreme Appliances*** has been expanded with applications to allow you to serve first as an intern on a part time basis and then later to become hired as an administrative assistant. By completing these applications, you will learn how to handle multiple tasks following instructions and independently manage your time while adhering to organizational constraints of time and resources. You will have many opportunities to practice procedures related to the chapter concepts by using forms and documents that are used in a typical office.

- **Building Your Portfolio** encourages the creation and maintenance of a portfolio of suitable documents completed as chapter assignments. This portfolio of your work will be helpful in demonstrating to employers that you have the type of skills and experience that they are looking for.

Changes in the 7th Edition

Since the first edition, the authors have focused on using a proven format that helps students build their office skills quickly. The seventh edition contains many updates and enhancements that will be helpful to students to assist them in transferring their knowledge to the workplace, including the following:

- New topics have been added, such as mission statements; investigative, periodic, and informational reports; office security; Web conferencing; and presentation skills.

- Additional terminology has been added, including *basic knowledge skills, constructive criticism, hard skills, integrity, soft skills, blog, Web conferencing, extemporaneous speaking,* and *podium panic.*

- Opportunities are provided for students to recognize the important role personal qualities play in the office environment, and activities have been enhanced to help them develop their attitudes and interpersonal skills that are in demand by employers. Additional information about effective work habits, self-management skills, and communication skills are provided in the Instructor's Manual.

- Critical thinking is continually stressed throughout the text. For example, activities that require critical thinking are found in the following:

  - Stop 'n Checks
  - For Your Discussion questions
  - Developing Critical Thinking Skills: Problem Solving on the Job
  - Exploring the Workplace: Activities
  - Using the Web: Research Activities
  - Simulated applications

  Additionally, new situations are presented in the Improving Critical Thinking section to help students understand their personal responsibility as it relates to ethical issues regarding their working relationships and their organization's resources.

- The end-of-chapter assignments actually allow students to practice tasks that help them to become familiar with basic office procedures. These activities are built on a skill-focused framework to reinforce the learning outcomes.

- The simulation, Supreme Appliances, has been expanded to allow students to experience working as an intern in Chapters 1 and 2; in Chapter 3 on the job search, the simulation addresses applying for and being employed as a fulltime employee in the marketing department.

- Supreme Appliances provides a wide variety of applications throughout the text, which offers experience in related fields such as banking and payroll.

- Opportunities have been added to help students build their teaming and collaborative and interpersonal skills. Examples include the international project in Chapters 11 and 12 and a presentation in Chapter 13. The end-of-chapter assignments, such as the Improving Critical Thinking and Exploring the Workplace, have been enhanced to include directions for students to work collaboratively. Additional information about teaming and collaboration is provided in the Instructor's Manual.

- Specific suggestions have been given in every chapter on how to build a portfolio from the results of students' assignments.

Supplemental Resources

FOR THE INSTRUCTOR

All instructor resources are available on the Instructor's Resources CD (IRCD), or you can download them from the Instructor Resource Center at www.prenhall.com. Register once and gain access to instructor materials for all of your Prentice Hall textbooks.

Instructor's Manual The instructor's manual includes detailed chapter teaching tips and strategies, discussion points, additional assignments, and Web links. A sample syllabus, which can be customized easily to a course, is included. The syllabus represents best practices in creating a syllabus and includes components that cover student responsibilities and completion schedules. Answers to discussion questions, simulated applications, workshops, and chapter quizzes and exams are included. Suggested solutions to improving critical thinking skills are also provided.

Chapter Quizzes and Exams Use the 14 chapter quizzes to pretest or posttest students and use the four major exams to measure student learning.

Electronic Test Generator This computerized test generation system gives you maximum flexibility in preparing tests. It can create custom tests and print randomized versions of a test at one time, as well as build tests randomly by chapter, level of difficulty, or question type. The software also allows online testing and record keeping, and you can add problems to the database.

Instructor Resources CD (IRCD) The IRCD contains the Instructor's Manual with Test Item File, Prentice Hall Test Gen, and the PowerPoint Lecture Presentation Package.

PowerPoint® Slides More than 480 slides provide lecture points to guide discussion.

JWA Human Relations and Interpersonal Skills Videos JWA Videos on human relations and interpersonal communication topics are available to qualified adopters. Contact your local representative for details.

Newsletter A twice-yearly newsletter brings teaching tips, additional class activities, and trends in the workplace. The newsletter will be sent directly to the instructor's e-mail address.

Online Course Support

OneKey Distance Learning Solutions: Convenience, Simplicity, Success
Ready-made **WebCT** and **Blackboard** online courses! If you adopt a OneKey course, student access cards will be packaged with the text, at no extra charge to the student. OneKey courses include Research Navigator, a premium online research tool.

Research Navigator
This is a premium research tool.

FOR THE STUDENT

Student Resources CD Packaged in the book, this CD contains the files needed to complete assignments in the textbook.

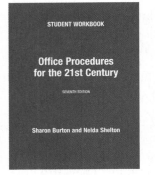

Office Procedures for the 21st Century Student Workbook This workbook contains the working papers needed to complete assignments in the textbook. It is packaged at no additional cost with purchase of a new textbook. Additional copies can be purchased online at www.prenhall.com. (ISBN: 0-13-232235-8)

Companion Web Site: Go to www.prenhall.com/burton This companion Web site is ideal for additional classroom practice and for use in distance learning courses. It is available 24/7 and includes chapter outcomes, multiple choice questions, true-false questions, and links to other relevant sites on the Internet.

Acknowledgments

No author can produce a textbook without the contributions of many outstanding professionals. First and foremost, we warmly thank Lucy Mae Jennings for her original work on the first two editions of *Procedures for the Automated Office*.

For the seventh edition, we gratefully appreciate the following reviewers for their excellent comments and constructive suggestions:

Ruth Levy, Westchester Community College

Jan Kehm, Spartanburg Technical College

Barbara Brown, Southwestern Community College

Roxanne Gunner, Boise State University

Tommie Nash, Gwinnett Technical College

Judie Golden, Mission College

Marjory Wooten, Lanier Technical College

Dianne Campbell, Athens Technical College

Joe French, Southwestern Technical College

Carnella Hardin, Glendale College

Additionally, we are grateful to the following professionals who contributed excellent suggestions that were incorporated into the sixth edition:

Wanda Shelton, Applications Consultant; Microsoft® Certified—Master Level, Tarrant County College District

Nancy Stacy, Lead Business Analyst, Origin Technology

Janice M. Brown, Hewlett-Packard Company

Shelly M. Duke, Branch Manager, Kelly Services

Lisa Stone, MOS Certified, Nortel-Business Prime

Cathy Gaona, Corporation Safety Secretary, Printback, Inc.

Monica Morales, Administrative Assistant, Brookhaven College

Kelly Murray, Supervisor, Administration & Budgets, Burlington Northern Santa Fe

Cathy Moore, MOS Certified, Administrative Assistant, Ameriserve

Doris Youngman, Insurance Coordinator, Florida Sports and Orthopaedic Medicine, Palm Harbor, Florida

We thank students and teachers who continue to recognize this text as outstanding and one that builds office skills as well as the personal qualities and interpersonal skills employers demand of their employees.

If you would like to provide feedback, we invite you to do so. Send your comments and suggestions to Sharon Burton at sburton@dcccd.edu or Nelda Shelton at nelda.shelton@tccd.edu.

Office Procedures
for the 21st Century

chapter

1

Understanding the Changing and Challenging Office

chapter **outline**

Your Company

Know Your Company
Mission Statement
Ethics in Business
Organizational Structure

You and Your Manager

Your Role

Job Titles
Office Support Functions
Telecommuting
The Office of the Future

Your Work Space

Ergonomics

International Employment

learning **outcomes**

When you have completed this chapter, you should be able to:

- Describe the purpose of a company mission statement.

- Explain the purpose of a company code of ethics.

- Define and explain the classifications of authority.

- Explain the importance of developing a good working relationship with your manager.

- Explain the role of the office professional.

- Identify common office support functions.

- Define the elements of appropriate ergonomic design in the workplace.

The age of electronics is here. Smaller, faster, and wireless is the name of the game. The twenty-first century office is high-tech; office procedures are changing rapidly and are influenced greatly by these technological changes. Today's office professional must possess a broad array of both technical and interpersonal skills. To keep pace with changes, this means the office professional must be committed to lifelong learning. The future promises to be an exciting one!

The purpose of this chapter is to help you understand how you will contribute to today's changing and challenging office. You will study how your role supports the company, its mission, and your manager by the functions you perform and the work space you use.

Throughout the remainder of this text, the words *manager* or *supervisor* will be used to refer to persons at all levels of management, and *office assistant*, *administrative assistant*, and *office professional* will be used to refer to support personnel.

Your Company

To project the image that you are a professional who knows what is going on in your company, you must first spend some time getting to know all about the business. Look beyond the job you are required to do and keep abreast of company happenings.

KNOW YOUR COMPANY

Knowing about your company allows you to leave the impression with others that you are knowledgeable and can be a source of reliable information. Much of this information is available in annual reports, files, and the company intranet system. Your experiences and inquiries will also increase your knowledge. Remember, you represent your company's image (see Figure 1-1).

FIGURE 1-1 • You represent your company's image.

You should know the answers to the following questions:

- Is my company a national or international company?
- Where are its various plants or offices located?
- Who are the top executives?
- What products does my company sell or manufacture or what services does it provide?
- Who are my company's competitors?
- How does my company rank in its industry?
- Is my company publicly or privately owned?

Learn as much as possible and stay informed about your company's progress. Showing interest in learning about the business can enhance your advancement within the company.

MISSION STATEMENT

A **mission statement** presents the goals, strategic intent, and business direction for a company. Having a mission statement can be one of a company's most important plans. By affirming the company's primary goals, this statement assures that everyone in the company is working toward the same objectives. Common elements found in mission statements are concern for public image; quality; commitment to survival, growth, and profitability; identity of customers, markets, and services; a statement of company philosophy; and the traits that set the company apart from its competition. Each company's mission is different.

If your company has a Web site, the mission statement usually appears on it. For example, Ben & Jerry's (Figure 1-2) shares its mission statement online (www.benjerry.com). Notice that the mission statement (Figure 1-3) is divided into three parts—product, economic, and social—and that these "three parts must thrive equally in a manner that commands deep respect for individuals in and outside the company and supports the communities of which they are a part."

ETHICAL★ISSUES

ETHICS IN BUSINESS

In addition to mission statements, companies also develop codes of ethics. **Ethics** is defined as a person's motivation based on his or her ideas of right

FIGURE 1-2 • Ben & Jerry's ice cream factory located near Waterbury, Vermont.

OUR MISSION STATEMENT

Ben & Jerry's is founded on and dedicated to a sustainable corporate concept of prosperity. Our mission consists of 3 interrelated parts:

Product Mission

To make, distribute & sell the finest quality all natural ice cream & euphoric concoctions with a continued commitment to incorporating wholesome, natural ingredients and promoting business practices that respect the Earth and the Environment.

Economic Mission

To operate the Company on a sustainable financial basis of profitable growth, increasing value for our stockholders & expanding opportunities for development and career growth for our employees.

Social Mission

To operate the Company in a way that actively recognizes the central role that business plays in society by initiating innovative ways to improve the quality of life locally, nationally and internationally.

Central To The Mission Of Ben & Jerry's is the belief that all three parts must thrive equally in a manner that commands deep respect for individuals in and outside the company and supports the communities of which they are a part.

FIGURE 1-3 • Ben & Jerry's mission statement.
Reprinted with permission of Ben & Jerry's.

and wrong. A **code of ethics** (also called a *code of business conduct*) is a set of rules governing the behavior of all members of an organization. The code of ethics calls for high standards of honesty, objectivity, diligence, and loyalty. Companies are concerned about issues of ethical and socially responsible behavior of all their employees. These issues range from the management person who pads his or her expense report to the office assistant who takes office supplies home for his or her children to use as school supplies. The overall view is that everything costs someone something. Behaviors that violate the company's code of ethics usually end up costing the customer.

Companies are also concerned with public confidence. The code of ethics is a way to assure the public the company is concerned and is addressing ethics with its suppliers, customers, and employees. This same code gives the employee direction concerning expectations of the company regarding his or her behavior on the job. For example, Texas Instruments, Inc., a world leader in the semiconductor industry based in Dallas, Texas (Figure 1-4), has developed a code of business conduct. A portion of that code is presented in Figure 1-5.

ORGANIZATIONAL STRUCTURE

When beginning your employment, it is important that you understand the classifications of authority used by management within your organization's structure. There is a wide variety of ways to structure jobs within an organization. Organizational structure emphasizes people-to-people relationships. Automated/electronic office concepts in organizational structure are centered on the flow of information and the communication needs for decision making,

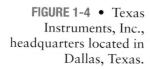

FIGURE 1-4 • Texas Instruments, Inc., headquarters located in Dallas, Texas.

Stop 'n Check

1. What is the purpose of a mission statement?

2. What is the purpose of a code of ethics?

and they involve a systems approach to organizational structure. Regardless of the approach used, **chain of command** (the direction authority flows; also called **line authority**), authority, and responsibility must be established.

Classifications of Authority

The distinction among managers in terms of authority and responsibility is expressed as *levels of management.* Most organizations have three common divisions: top level, middle (intermediate) level, and supervisory (operating) level. The higher the level of management, the more responsibility and decision-making power the manager has. The lower the level of management, the more responsibility the manager has for day-to-day functions. Top-level management usually consists of the president or chief executive officer (CEO) and vice president(s). Middle-level management typically is comprised of the division heads, sometimes called regional heads, or area heads or chiefs. Supervisory-level management generally consists of the department heads or functional managers (see Figure 1-6).

The two most common types of organizational structure are line organization and line-and-staff organization.

Line Organization

The oldest and simplest organizational structure used by management is **line organization.** In line organization, authority flows vertically down within the organization delegated from top management to middle management.

The Code of Business Conduct contains principles that have long been part of TI's values and ethics statements. Certain behaviors have been specifically included in this Code of Business Conduct in recognition of the growing interest that investors have in the conduct of publicly-held companies, their employees, and their directors. The public has every right to know what TI standards are in these areas. Furthermore, the public legitimately expects TIers to know and adhere to the standards of conduct. This Code of Business Conduct is intended to comply with New York Stock Exchange listing standards. Employees should refer to the section entitled Compliance Procedures, Policies and Rules for guidance on complying with this Code of Business Conduct. No provision of this Code of Business Conduct may be waived for any director or executive officer without approval of the TI Board of Directors and appropriate public disclosure.

- We do not take any role in any outside concern that would adversely influence our TI responsibilities. When faced with a potential conflict, we communicate with supervisors and others to implement safeguards and take steps to prevent such a conflict from materializing. We make full disclosure and withdraw ourselves from discussions and decisions when our personal interest appears to interfere with TI's business interests.
- When exchanging business courtesies, meals and entertainment, we avoid activities that could create even the appearance that our decisions could be compromised.
- We respect the rights and property of others, including their intellectual property, and only accept their confidential or trade secret information after we clearly understand our obligations as defined in a non-disclosure agreement or similar document. We protect and preserve TI assets, including TI business opportunities and intellectual property, for TI's benefit and not for our personal benefit.
- We compete fairly without collusion or collaboration with competitors to divide markets, fix prices, restrict production or allocate customers.
- We assure that those who seek to do business with TI have fair opportunities to compete for our business.
- We provide full and accurate information for use in internal and external reports.
- We keep records that are verifiably accurate.
- More items are listed. . . .

FIGURE 1-5 • Partial code of ethics from Texas Instruments, Inc.
Code of Business Conduct, Texas Instruments Incorporated, www.ti.com. Reprinted with permission.

Line authority allows supervisors to supervise employees immediately below them in the organizational structure. The middle managers are in charge of specific activities, and they in turn delegate authority to lower-level managers or supervisors who are in charge of employees carrying out their operational duties. Supervisory level managers are usually charged with the responsibility to give orders, hire, terminate, and take disciplinary action. They make the majority of these decisions and direct line personnel to achieve company goals. See Figure 1-6 for an example of line organization.

FIGURE 1-6 • Top-, middle-, and supervisory-level management with line organization structure and arrows showing flow of authority.

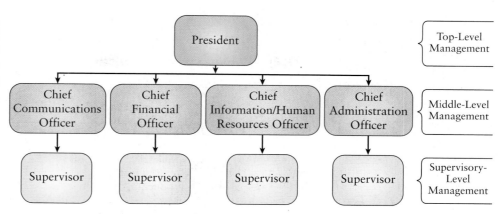

The advantages and disadvantages of the line organization are as follows:

Advantages

- The structure of the organization is easily understood.
- Employees have direct accountability to their superiors.
- Each worker has a clear-cut place.

Disadvantages

- Each supervisor has large areas of responsibility.
- The organization is more structured, thus less flexible.
- The flow of communication and information is often restricted.
- The ability to transfer employees to where they are most needed is limited.

Line-and-Staff Organization

Another common management organizational structure is called a line-and-staff organization. As its name implies, the **line-and-staff organization** contains both line positions and staff positions. **Line positions** are those directly involved in the day-to-day operations such as vice presidents, production supervisors, or department heads. Employees who hold **staff positions** do not actually produce the product or service, but do contribute to the company's overall mission. When a CEO, vice president, or manager is responsible for several areas, he or she must rely on others' expertise. In these cases, knowledge specialists are available to provide advice. An example of a staff position might be a *legal advisor* who would provide legal advice as needed to the CEO, vice president(s), or supervisor(s). Staff positions serve the organization by indirectly supporting line functions and by providing advice and knowledge to other individuals in the chain of command. See Figure 1-7 for an example of line-and-staff organization.

The advantages and disadvantages of line-and-staff organization are as follows:

Advantages

- Line personnel have freedom from performing specialized tasks.
- Staff has flexibility to pursue unique projects.
- Expertise is available to line personnel.

FIGURE 1-7 • Line-and-staff organizational structure with bolded lines showing line authority and thin lines showing staff authority.

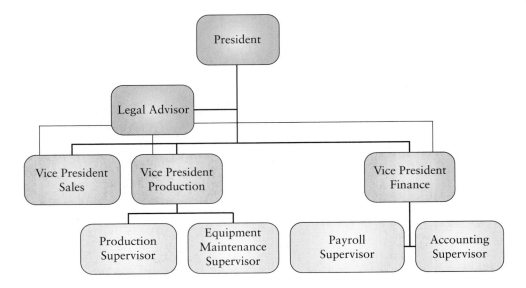

Disadvantages

- Line employees do not have a clear understanding of the staff manager's duties.
- Problems arise if staff managers with line duties contradict the line manager.

Participatory Management

Organizations today, in an effort to increase productivity and to meet competition, are focusing more on using participatory management. **Participatory management,** put simply, is forming project teams to bring together employees with the talents needed to work on a specified project. This management style is in contrast to the traditional line-and-staff management style. Employees are invited to work in smaller units within large organizations and are encouraged to communicate with different levels of management. Employees are asked for input about their areas of responsibility and frequently are brought together in conferences to discuss problems and offer solutions. Under participatory management, each employee reports to someone in the formal structure, but while on a team working on a specific project or problem, each team member has equal authority even if the team is made up of a project director, an office assistant, an accountant, and a custodial employee.

You should be aware that opportunities to participate in project teams and other forms of participative decision making may exist where you are employed, and you should accept your responsibility in making valuable contributions.

Stop 'n Check

1. Identify the three levels of management

   a. _____

   b. _____

   c. _____

2. What is the difference between line and line-and-staff organization?

   _____

   _____

What role does the office assistant play in the company's overall mission? Your role will be to support the person in whatever line or staff position your supervisor holds. By doing this successfully, you will be contributing to the company's overall mission. You must understand, however, that organizational structures and job titles vary from company to company. You must begin by recognizing the chain of command and the management style used in your organization. To do this, you need to understand how authority has been established. Studying the company's organization chart (discussed in the next section) will reveal what you need to know.

Organization Chart

An **organization chart** is a graphic illustration of the formal structure of an organization. To understand an organization chart, look for lines of authority, the existing division of work (into what may be called *divisions*, *departments*, *teams*, *units*, or some other appropriate title), and the relationship of the work groups to each other. If an organizational manual exists, a description of the division of work and the positions shown on the organization chart will be given in the manual or will be located on the company's intranet. The titles shown in an organization chart may be expressed as either functions or positions, but the form chosen should be used consistently throughout. Figure 1-8 shows an example of an organization chart for a single company division. Functions that occupy the same level of management should be shown on the same horizontal line, as illustrated by the Vice President Sales and the Vice President Production in the organization chart in Figure 1-7. The bold lines indicate line authority. The thin (sometimes broken lines) lines indicate staff authority.

As an office assistant, you might be asked to create an organization chart. Organization charts may be created using the chart feature of Microsoft® Word or by using a software program such as OrgPlus™ from HumanConcepts dedicated to automatically generating charts.

FIGURE 1-8 • Organization chart for Supreme Appliances Marketing Division.

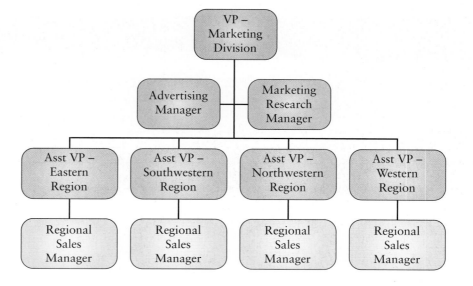

You and Your Manager

Building a good relationship with your manager is necessary if you want to be recommended for promotion, to obtain raises, and/or to be given key assignments. To accomplish any or all of these, you must receive good performance evaluations. How well you do your job depends on this. Your principal job is to see that your manager succeeds at his or her job (see Figure 1-9). By doing so you are contributing to the company's mission through the work you do. Other benefits are gained as well because this positive relationship creates a positive work environment for you.

FIGURE 1-9 • A loyal and supportive relationship between manager and office professional is important.

Stop 'n Check

Take a few moments and list the qualities you expect from an ideal supervisor.

_____

_____

_____

_____

_____

Adapt to Your Manager and Your Job

✔ Each time you are assigned to a new manager, learn his or her priorities, preferences, and work habits.

✔ Adjust your schedule to that of your manager. After you are well acquainted with your manager, perhaps you can make helpful suggestions, provided you have thought an idea through carefully. But do not attempt to change your manager. Keep in mind the only person you can change is yourself.

✔ Admire and respect your manager, and do what you can to build his or her morale.

✔ Refrain from expressing your manager's opinions. Everything that goes on in your office should be kept confidential.

✔ Refrain from giving your personal interpretation of a company policy. That is your manager's job.

✔ Be careful not to give away secrets inadvertently to your friends and coworkers, your manager's counterparts, or competitors.

✔ Be loyal. Loyalty (being devoted or true to one thing or person) is rated as one of the most desirable traits that an office professional can possess. It means that you support a person and his or her ideas and actions.

Your Role

You should understand your role in the company because you will be expected to contribute to the company's overall mission. You will be successful on the job by acquiring the necessary skills and putting them to use efficiently. Make sure you are current on such areas as the common job titles in your field. Be prepared to answer questions such as: What are the office support functions I will be required to do? What is the possibility of working from home? What is the long-range prospect for office positions in my field in the future? What will tomorrow's office be like?

JOB TITLES

As office support roles become more diversified, job titles are also changing. Although some of today's office professionals are still called *office assistant, clerical assistant, secretary, senior secretary,* **executive secretary,** or *administrative secretary,* titles are changing.

The most common job titles reported by members of the International Association of Administrative Professionals (IAAP) in a 2005 survey (see http://www.iaap-ha.org) are *administrative assistant,* 30 percent; *executive assistant,* 18 percent; *executive secretary,* 6 percent; *office manager* or *supervisor,* 5 percent; and *secretary,* 5 percent. More than one fourth (26 percent) of those surveyed have a wide range of titles, commonly including terms such as *coordinator, administrator, specialist, associate,* or a title denoting specialized business types or functions such as legal, accounting, medical, and human resources. See the table below showing current job titles.

Previous Job Titles	Current Job Titles
Office assistant, clerical assistant, clerk typist	**Administrative assistant**
Secretary or senior secretary	Executive secretary or secretary
Executive secretary, administrative manager	**Office manager** or supervisor

Usually a job title that includes the word **administrative** denotes a higher level of responsibility than the word *assistant* does. **Assistant** is a generic term that is being used more and more to denote an employee who performs all types of basic office functions. **Executive assistant** denotes an office professional who works for one or more managers. A **receptionist** is a person who supports management at all levels and usually greets the public and answers the phone.

OFFICE SUPPORT FUNCTIONS

Typical office support functions range from routine to managerial functions. These functions fall into five categories: routine, technical, analytical, interpersonal, and managerial.

- **Routine functions:** require minimal *original* thinking; include essential skills, such as filing (document storage and retrieving with emphasis on electronic record keeping), photocopying, coordinating direct mailings, and keeping logs.

- **Technical functions:** require judgment and advanced office skills, such as a high level of document preparation and proficiency using various software applications, including spreadsheets, databases, project management, and presentations (creating and presenting); maintaining multiple schedules and calendars; handling messages and correspondence (with voice mail, e-mail, and regular postal mail); and maintaining computer files, directories, and databases.

- **Analytical functions:** require critical and creative thinking and decision-making skills, such as creating and analyzing reports, planning meetings and special events, working closely with vendors and suppliers, and making decisions regarding equipment purchases.

Start Off on the Right Foot

Face it! It costs a company a lot of money to find the right office professionals, train them, and keep them motivated enough to remain working with the same company. So, it's crucial that the company start off on a positive note with new employees. Here's what many companies do on Day 1 to ensure a good start with their new office professionals.

- ✔ Let new office professionals see the big picture by discussing the company's mission and purpose.

- ✔ Take a skills inventory of all new employees so the company can place them in positions where they will be productive.

- ✔ Connect new employees to a work team that depends on their professional skills.

- ✔ Acquaint new office professionals with their new surroundings and new coworkers.

- ✔ Assign each office professional a volunteer mentor whom he or she can rely on to answer questions, give support, and supply encouragement.

- ✔ Make new office professionals feel welcome as valued members of the staff.

It may sound simple enough, but it takes good management to make it a reality.

- **Interpersonal functions:** require judgment, analytical (decision-making), and people skills, such as coordinating a team project.
- **Managerial functions:** require planning (analytical), organizing (analytical), measuring (analytical), and using Internet/intranet and communications for research, interviewing, orienting, supervising, and motivating other staff (interpersonal communication); examples include budgeting, staffing, evaluating personnel, and problem solving.

TELECOMMUTING

More and more companies are offering office personnel the opportunity to work from home or other remote locations connected to the office via computer called **telecommuting** (see Figure 1-10). The same work completed in

---

Your Role and How to Be Successful in the Office

1. Be efficient—organize work, manage time, maintain desirable attitudes, and set priorities.
2. Know how to use application software.
3. Know procedures for preparing and processing written communications—composing letters, processing incoming and outgoing mail, and preparing reports.
4. Understand concepts of equipment-oriented procedures—sending and receiving e-mail; using an electronic calendar, voice mail, local area networks, online databases, and computer-assisted retrieval; understanding and using multimedia technology; assisting with teleconferencing and desktop publishing; and managing electronic files.
5. Know procedures and guidelines for dealing with people (customer service)—face-to-face in the office, in meetings, over the telephone—and for making appointments and travel arrangements.
6. Use office electronics—computers, copiers, scanners, and fax machines—for effective job performance.
7. Use published sources, databases, and the Internet for research.
8. Understand filing and records control—filing procedures, rules, systems, supplies, equipment, retention, storage, and retrieval.
9. Understand how banking services are related to office procedures.
10. Know the importance of a job campaign and ways to launch a successful one.
11. Recognize career opportunities and job mobility in the office and office-related occupations.
12. Reinvent your skills to be ready to meet your company's changing needs.

Stop 'n Check

List the five office support functions.

a. _____

b. _____

c. _____

d. _____

e. _____

FIGURE 1-10 • More and more employees are choosing to work from home.

the office can be done at these remote locations using phones (or cellular phones), fax machines, computer hookup (by modem, broadband access, or wireless technology), printers, scanners, voice mail, e-mail, instant messenger, laptop, and handheld computers.

One question commonly asked by telecommuters is, "How will my manager or supervisor know I am working if he or she cannot see me working at my desk?" The obvious answer is the telecommuter's workload is measured by the amount of work submitted on time or ahead of time. Here are a few of the questions that should be answered before agreeing to telecommute.

- Am I expected to work specified hours? This time should be defined.
- Who will provide the equipment needed for my home office?
- Who will pay for the supplies used? The phone?
- How often will I be required to contact the office?
- How will work be submitted? How often? When?

Virtual Office

The Internet and a growing list of breakthrough telecommunication services have made today's world smaller and more accessible. An increasing number of managers are abandoning the problems and politics of corporate life in favor of working independently. By doing so, the need for full professional assistance with a variety of support responsibilities is provided by **virtual assistants (VAs)** with just the click of the mouse. Virtual assistants are independent entrepreneurs. They work from their fully equipped home offices to assist other entrepreneurs or companies with the following tasks:

- desktop publishing
- Internet research
- event planning and reminder services
- word processing
- travel arrangements
- technical writing and grant proposal writing
- bookkeeping
- marketing support

Communications are generally by, but not limited to, e-mail, mail, fax, telephone, and file and diskette transfer. The entrepreneur or company avoids insurance, payroll tax, and Occupational and Safety Health Administration (OSHA) issues that employees bring and pays only for "time on task," or by project. Because VAs save companies or independent entrepreneur's money, are available beyond a nine-to-five schedule, work only when needed, and require no office space and no equipment, their popularity is growing.

Virtual assistant opportunities are growing so fast that VAs have founded their own International Virtual Assistants Association (IVAA). You may obtain more information about this organization from the Web site www.ivaa.org.

THE OFFICE OF THE FUTURE

What will the office of the future be like? The prospects for the employment of office personnel look very positive. More than 184,000 administrative assistant and secretarial positions will be added in the United States between 2002 and 2012, representing growth of 4.5 percent according to the U.S. Department of Labor, as reported by the IAAP.

Here is what the futurists tell us:

- Mobile offices allowing employees to work from anywhere will become more common.
- Internet research, desktop publishing, computer training, and Web site maintenance will play a larger role in the office professional's job function.
- Web-based conferencing services will continue to provide employees with real-time access to meetings, thus reducing the need to travel.
- Telecommuting will increase.

As companies continue to outsource work outside the United States, job markets will shrink. The need for education will determine how well workers will advance. The U.S. Census Bureau reports that a worker over eighteen years of age and holding a bachelor's degree will earn nearly twice as much as a worker over eighteen with a high school diploma.

Your Work Space

With most Americans spending 70 percent of their waking hours at work, the office environment should be as safe, healthy, comfortable, and productive as possible. Then why don't we feel more at home in the workplace? The answer is we have traditionally been expected to conform to the workplace. However, workers have not conformed as management expected. One reason has been that as computer technology advanced and more office workers began using computers, problems of user comfort arose. Because of the physical and medical problems that have developed, an entire market of products has evolved that supports computer workstations. Office furniture and computer accessories designed for comfort, including halogen task lights, mouse pads, ergonomic keyboards, monitor arms, ergonomic chairs, wrist rests, and adjustable seating and reception desks, are all available.

ERGONOMICS

With such emphasis being given to the development of computer products and the work environment, the field of ergonomics evolved. **Ergonomics** is the science of fitting the workplace to meet the physical and psychological needs of the employee. Everything that affects the worker must be taken into consideration—computer workstation, décor, furniture, lighting, work space, air quality, heating and cooling, acoustics, and equipment placement.

Computer Workstation

You should position your computer, monitor, keyboard, and mouse pad to avoid stress or strain on your body (see Figure 1-11). This placement is crucial to your good health. What seems to be only a minor problem can become a major one when allowed to go unchecked for months and sometimes years.

Computer screen glare or a copyholder that does not adjust presents additional problems. Complaints arise about eyestrain, backaches, and

FIGURE 1-11 • Correct posture at the keyboard.

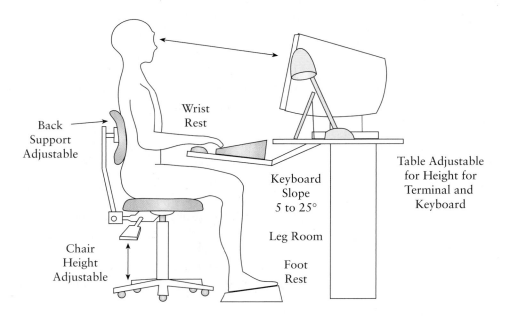

Back Support Adjustable

Wrist Rest

Chair Height Adjustable

Keyboard Slope 5 to 25°

Leg Room

Foot Rest

Table Adjustable for Height for Terminal and Keyboard

FIGURE 1-12 • A wrist pad in front of your keyboard and on your mouse pad decreases the chance of getting carpal tunnel syndrome.

headaches. The greatest complaint of office professionals has been screen glare. Long hours at the computer can also lead to repetitive motion illnesses, the most common of which is **carpal tunnel syndrome**, a wrist ailment typically caused by incorrect alignment of hand and wrist. A wrist pad placed in front of the keyboard to rest hands when not keyboarding and a wrist pad attached to the mouse pad to rest the wrist when using the mouse helps to alleviate this problem (Figure 1-12). Workers also have to cope with "computer squeal," a high-frequency, barely detectable squeal that some computer terminals emit. This problem can cause anxiety, headaches, and nausea.

Décor

Colors that blend tastefully should be used throughout each office area. The color scheme should be harmonious, but contrasting colors should be used to break the monotony of look-alike stations. The colors in your work environment can affect health and productivity as much as a supportive chair. Psychologists know color can affect a person's mood, efficiency, and perception of time, temperature, and noise. Most office planners agree cool tones are best for tasks requiring high levels of concentration; large areas of yellow, bright green, bright red, and dark brown can have negative effects on workers.

Furniture

Office furniture manufacturers have designed modular furniture to carry out the office landscape concept. Modular furniture consists of separate components that can be fitted together in various arrangements to meet the user's needs. If the worker's duties change, creating a need for a change in working surface, the modular furniture can easily be rearranged.

The chair is one of the most important pieces of furniture in the office. A poorly designed or maladjusted chair can be a major contributor to poor circulation and stress on the spine, back, and neck. When selecting a chair, consider the following:

- The seat should be slightly wider than your hips and thighs.
- Most modern chairs can be pneumatically adjusted. You sit on the chair and a pneumatic lever located under the seat allows you to adjust the seat up or down.
- The chair back should be adjustable up and down and forward and back to adjust to your size.
- These seat adjustments allow you to adjust the seat to ensure good circulation in your legs and feet.
- If you are moving from desk to desk in your workstation, you should have a chair with a five-pedestal base. This type of base helps to keep the chair from turning over as you move.

When equipment is set up correctly, the keyboard should be placed at a comfortable height that allows the arms and wrists to move without strain. The monitor should be placed behind the keyboard, positioned so the worker can look slightly down at the screen. Improper positioning of the monitor can increase glare and affect the worker's posture and productivity. Office professionals who require bifocal glasses often complain of neck problems caused by the angle they must hold their head to see the screen. If you wear

Stop 'n Check

Place a check mark in the appropriate column to determine if your workstation is ergonomically correct.

	Yes	No
• Does the size of the seat fit your shape?	_____	_____
• Is the chair height adjustable?	_____	_____
• Does the chair support your lower back?	_____	_____
• Can you adjust the seat to tilt downward and upward?	_____	_____
• Does the chair have a five-pedestal base?	_____	_____
• Is your keyboard placed at a comfortable height that allow the arms and wrists to move without strain?	_____	_____
• Is the monitor placed behind the keyboard, positioned so that you can look slightly down at the screen?	_____	_____
• If you wear bifocals, do you adjust your chair so your neck is not strained when looking at the monitor or so you can look down to view the monitor?	_____	_____
• Is your work surface adjustable?	_____	_____

Ergonomic Tips

1. Give support to your lower lumbar region of your back to avoid fatigue and stress on the spine.

2. Use wrist pads to reduce the risk of carpal tunnel syndrome.

3. Tilt the seat forward to decrease muscle strain and back pressure and improve blood circulation.

4. Use a copyholder to minimize head and eye movement and avoid neck strain.

5. Elevate your feet to take the strain off the legs and back.

6. Tilt the monitor so you are looking down into the monitor rather than up.

7. If you use a laptop at your desk, place your laptop on the desk and consider getting a separate monitor or an add-on pointing device and keyboard.

8. If you fly a lot and use your laptop, you should use the tray table in front of you. Try to keep your wrists straight and your elbows at a 90-degree angle.

9. Even if you use a laptop for casual use, apply all the rules for it that you would apply for a desktop computer.

10. To avoid end-of-workday aches, pain, or fatigue, stand up and stretch every 20 minutes for 20 seconds.

bifocals, you should wear reading glasses to correct this problem or make certain you can look down to view the monitor. Refer to Figure 1-11 showing correct positioning of the equipment and the user.

Work surfaces and chairs should be adjustable. Disk drives should be within easy reach of the worker.

Creating a good ergonomic working arrangement is important to protecting your health. Every situation is different, and if you can't seem to get your arrangement to feel right or you are confused about how to arrange your workstation so it is ergonomically correct, you should seek professional advice.

International Employment

More and more companies are moving their operations outside the United States to take advantage of a cheaper labor market. **International employment** offers employees the opportunity to work abroad. You might have noticed many of the products you purchase are made outside the United States. Our government has also signed trade agreements with other countries that make it easier for U.S. companies to do business with those countries. One example is our agreement with Mexico and Canada—the **North American Free Trade Agreement (NAFTA)**. This agreement has allowed companies to move to Mexico or Canada, resulting in goods flowing freely across U.S. borders.

If you consider working abroad, you will see many similarities to employment in the United States from required skills to job titles. For instance, some job titles are the same as in the United States; others are only slightly different, as you can see from the following list:

- receptionist
- secretary
- administration assistant
- medical secretary

- team secretary
- PA (personal assistant) or PA to general manager
- secretary/commercial assistant
- medical transcriptionist

The following are examples of positions for which you might be qualified. The announcements appear exactly as they are advertised. Notice the skills required, the wording of the ads, and difference in spelling.

Working overseas is not for everyone. Careful thought and planning should go into making this decision. Here are some of the questions you might ask yourself before considering international employment.

Office Manager

London, UK

An assistant to a busy property developer/entrepreneur with good organizational skills. The successful candidate will be proficient in Excel and Word, be numerate, have good telephone manners, plenty of initiative and self motivation. If you want a challenge and enjoy working alone contact . . .

Secretary

France

Truly international team seeks English mother tongue member. Working at a high level for this household name you will use plenty of initiative as well as your basic secretarial skills. As part of the team you will organise the travel and internal and external meetings of 5 vice-presidents and have the experience and confidence to work autonomously when necessary. Spoken French is important, other languages are useful. Word and Power-Point are vital.

Secretary/Office Co-Ordinator

Mt. Colah
Australia

Small firm of architects in Mt. Colah requires the services of an all rounder. Duties include reception, general office duties and bookkeeping including payroll. Experience with Word and Excel essential. Minimum 2 years experience in a similar position and driver's license is necessary. Salary negotiable depending on experience. Please fax resume to . . .

Stop 'n Check

Complete the following assessment to evaluate your interest in international employment by placing a check mark in the appropriate blank.

	Yes	No
1. Am I fluent in more than one language?	_____	_____
2. Do I really like to travel and consider it exciting?	_____	_____
3. Do I understand and embrace diversity in other cultures?	_____	_____
4. Have I researched and visited international centers where I live?	_____	_____
5. Do I have or have I begun to develop a resume for working overseas?	_____	_____
6. Do I know how to research countries, work eligibility requirements, customs, regulations, and foreign companies over the Internet or at the library?	_____	_____
7. Have I previously worked on international projects through volunteer work or my college course work?	_____	_____

With more and more companies establishing offices in countries outside the United States, the office professional may be offered new employment challenges. What if your company advertised a position in Mexico, Canada, Spain, Japan, or South America? Would you be up to the challenge? Businesses are coping with massive changes that are occurring as a result of ever-increasing market internationalization. One of these changes is offering its personnel opportunities to work abroad.

Quick Tips

KEEPING ABREAST OF YOUR CHANGING AND CHALLENGING OFFICE

- Read all company news e-mails, newsletters, bulletins, or flyers to keep "in the know."
- Always display a willingness to learn.
- Keep current by reading professional periodicals
  - *Officepro* (published by International Association of Administrative Professionals)
  - *The Information Management Journal* (published by the

Association of Records Managers and Administrators)
- *Business Week*
- *Fortune*
- *U.S. News & World Report*
- *Newsweek*
- *The Wall Street Journal*
- *PC Magazine*
- *PC World*
- *Home Computing*

Concept Review and Reinforcement

Review of Key Concepts

OUTCOME	CONCEPT
1. Describe the purpose of a company mission statement.	A mission statement defines for employees the company's goals, strategic intent, and business direction.
2. Explain the purpose of a company code of ethics.	A code of ethics is a set of rules governing the behavior of all members of an organization. The code of ethics calls for high standards of honesty, objectivity, diligence, and loyalty.
3. Define and explain the classifications of authority.	Line organization is where authority flows vertically down within the organization. Supervisors control employees immediately below them and usually give orders, hire, terminate, and take disciplinary action. Where line managers use staff specialists to assist them, the organization's structure is called a *line-and-staff organization*. Staff managers usually do not have authority. They supply information or expertise to specific line managers in an advisory capacity by making recommendations. Participatory management is forming project teams to bring together employees with the talents needed to work on a specified project. Employees are asked for input about their areas of responsibility and are brought together to discuss problems and develop solutions.
4. Explain the importance of developing a good working relationship with your manager.	Building a good relationship with your manager is necessary to be recommended for promotion, to obtain raises, and/or to be given key assignments. To accomplish any or all of these, you must receive good performance evaluations. Your principal job is to see that your manager succeeds at his or her job. By doing so you are contributing to the company's mission through the work you do.
5. Explain the role of the office professional.	You should understand your role in the company because you will be expected to contribute to the company's overall mission. You should be familiar with current job titles such as *administrative assistant*, *executive assistant*, *executive secretary*, *office manager* or *supervisor*, and *secretary*; be ready to telecommute if asked; or become a virtual assistant to assist entrepreneurs with such tasks as desktop publishing, Internet research, event planning and reminder services, word processing, travel arrangements, technical writing and grant proposal writing, bookkeeping, and marketing support. You should be knowledgeable about the office of the future, Internet research, desktop publishing, computer training, Web site management, and the likely increase in mobile offices allowing office professionals to work anywhere.
6. Identify common office support functions.	Routine functions: require minimal *original* thinking; include essential skills such as filing (document storage and retrieving with emphasis on electronic record keeping), photocopying, coordinating direct mailings, and keeping logs. Technical functions: require judgment and advanced office skills, such as a high level of document preparation and proficiency using various software applications, including spreadsheets, databases, project management, and presentations (creating and presenting). Analytical functions: require critical and creative thinking and decision-making skills, such as creating and analyzing reports and planning meetings and special events.

Interpersonal functions: require judgment, analytical (decision-making), and people skills, such as coordinating a team project.

Managerial functions: require planning (analytical), organizing (analytical), measuring (analytical), using Internet/intranet and communications for research, interviewing, orienting, and supervising.

7. Define the elements of appropriate ergonomic design in the workplace.	Ergonomics is the science of fitting the workplace to meet the physical needs of the employee in office layout, décor, furniture selected, and position of the computer and monitor. Long hours at the computer can lead to repetitive motion illnesses, the most common of which is carpal tunnel syndrome. When selecting a chair, consider the following: The seat should be slightly wider than your hips and thighs; make sure you can adjust the seat up or down; the back should be adjustable; for your safety you should have a chair with a five-pedestal base; make sure the keyboard is placed at a comfortable height and allows your arms and wrists to move without strain; make sure the monitor is placed behind the keyboard, positioned so that you can look slightly down at the screen; if you wear bifocals, be sure to adjust the chair or seat so your neck is not strained when looking at the monitor or can look down to view the monitor. Your work surface should also be adjustable.

Key Terms

Administrative. Term that denotes a higher level of responsibility than *assistant*.

Administrative assistant. Current job title replacing *office assistant*, *clerical assistant*, or *clerk typist*.

Analytical functions. Require critical and creative thinking and decision-making skills, such as analyzing reports and making decisions regarding equipment purchases.

Assistant. Generic term used to denote an employee who performs all types of basic office functions.

Carpal tunnel syndrome. Wrist ailment typically caused by incorrect alignment of hand and wrist when using the computer keyboard.

Chain of command. The direction authority flows in a company's management/employee organization; also called *line authority*.

Code of ethics. Set of rules governing the behavior of all members of an organization. The code of ethics calls for high standards of honesty, objectivity, diligence, and loyalty; also called *code of business conduct*.

Ergonomics. Science of fitting the workplace to meet the employee's physical and psychological needs.

Ethics. Person's motivation based on his or her ideas of right and wrong.

Executive assistant. Newer job title replacing titles such as *office assistant*; denotes an office professional who works for one or more managers.

Executive secretary. Newer title replacing *secretary* or *senior secretary*.

International employment. Opportunity for employees to work abroad.

Interpersonal functions. Job functions that require judgment, analytical (decision-making), and people skills, such as coordinating a team project.

Line-and-staff organization. Organizational structure containing both line positions and staff positions, where line managers use staff specialists to assist them; however, staff positions lack the authority to make final decisions.

Line authority. Management style that allows supervisors to supervise employees immediately below them; also called *chain of command*.

Line organization. Oldest and simplest organizational structure used by management.

Managerial functions. Job functions that require planning (analytical), organizing (analytical), measuring (analytical), and motivating (interpersonal communication) skills; examples include budgeting, staffing, evaluating personnel, and solving problems.

Mission statement. Created by management to define the goals, strategic intent, and business direction for a company to ensure everyone in the company is working toward the same goals.

North American Free Trade Agreement (NAFTA). Agreement that eliminates trade barriers with Mexico or Canada, resulting in goods flowing freely across U.S. borders and some U.S. companies expanding operations into those countries.

Office manager. New job title replacing *executive secretary* or *administrative manager*.

Organization chart. Graphic depiction of the formal structure of an organization.

Participatory management. Management style in which employees are invited to work in smaller units within large organizations and are encouraged to communicate with different levels of management for problem solving.

Receptionist. Job title for a person who supports management at all levels; a receptionist usually greets the public and answers phones.

Routine functions. Job functions that require minimal original thinking; includes essential basic skills such as filing, photocopying, and keeping logs.

Staff positions. Position where the manager works in an advisory capacity to line managers.

Technical functions. Job functions that require judgment and advanced office skills, such as a high level of keyboarding and proficiency with various software applications.

Telecommuting. Office personnel working from home or other remote location connected to the office via computer.

Virtual assistants (VAs). Job title for those who provide full professional assistance with a variety of support responsibilities in home offices, such as desktop publishing, Internet research, event planning and reminder services, word processing, travel arrangements, technical writing, grant proposal writing, and marketing support.

For Your Discussion

Retrieve file C1-DQ from your student data disk. Save the file by keying your last name at the beginning of the file name; for example, Henderson-C1-DQ. This naming convention is to be used throughout the text. Saving your file in this manner will avoid overwriting the original file.

DIRECTIONS

Enter your response after each question or statement.

1. Discuss how the role of the office professional relates to the company's mission statement.

2. Describe how the office professional applies ethics on the job.

3. Explain the difference between line authority and staff authority and compare the advantages and disadvantages of each.

4. What is meant by *participatory management,* and how does it affect the organizational structure?

5. What is the purpose of the organization chart?

6. What is meant by *chain of command* in relation to classification of authority?

7. List five ways you can build a good relationship with your manager.

8. Describe the five basic office support functions. Include in your discussion examples of each function.

9. Discuss the advantages and disadvantages of telecommuting and having a virtual office.

10. Describe the ideal ergonomically correct office. Include office layout, décor, furniture, and computer equipment.

Building Your Office Skills

Exploring the Workplace: *Activities*

When saving files for exploring the workplace, save the file by keying your last name at the beginning of the filename, such as Henderson-C1-EW1 (activity number).

1. Read an article in a business periodical (such as the *Wall Street Journal, Business Week, U.S. News & World Report,* or *e-Business Advisor*) concerning one of the following topics and summarize findings in memo format to your instructor; include your source.

   a. Mission statement

   b. Changes in organizational structure

   c. Virtual assistants

   d. International employment

   e. Telecommuting

2. As a team or with a partner, select a company in your area to visit and identify the company's organizational structure.

   a. Obtain a copy of the company's organization chart and be prepared to present your findings to the class.

   b. If the company you selected does not have an organization chart, ask for a copy from a friend's or relative's company. Be prepared to discuss your findings with the class.

3. Look in the newspaper and locate at least three job titles used in your area for office positions for which you are now qualified or for which you may in the near future be qualified. Using a memo format, list the office support functions discussed in the chapter required for each job title. For example, *administrative assistant*—identify specific analytical, interpersonal, and managerial functions. Include the source of your information.

4. As a team select an office in which one team member works or set up an interview with someone in an office to evaluate the office layout, décor, furniture, and computer arrangement to determine if the office is ergonomically meeting the physical and psychological needs of the employee. Create a set of questions using the list shown in the Stop 'n Check on page 20. Write a memo to your instructor about your findings. Include in the memo your questions, answers, and a table that outlines the items evaluated and whether they met or did not meet the specifications mentioned in this chapter. Identify the department and title of the person you interviewed. Do not include the company or the person's name. Should you have difficulty finding an office, ask your instructor about using an office at the college.

Developing Critical Thinking Skills: *Problem Solving on the Job*

Introduction

These situations are designed to help you develop one of the most important workplace skills identified by employers—thinking skills. Developing these skills requires that a person

- think creatively by generating new ideas;

- make decisions by specifying goals and constraints, generating alternatives, considering risks, and evaluating and choosing the best alternatives;

- solve problems;

- learn by using efficient learning techniques to acquire and apply new knowledge and skills; and

- reason by discovering a rule or principle underlying the relationship between two or more objects and apply it when solving a problem.

You will learn more about developing critical thinking skills in Chapter 3.

Each chapter has at least four case studies in which you will be asked to generate new ideas, evaluate and choose the best alternative, recognize problems, and devise a plan of action. Be specific in your responses.

Retrieve file C1-OJS from your student data disk. When saving files for Developing Critical Thinking Skills, save the files by keying your last name at the beginning of the filename and adding the situation number, such as Henderson-C1-OJS1 (situation number).

Directions

Enter your response after each situation.

1. **Mission statement.** Cindi, an administrative assistant, has worked for the Army/Air Force Exchange Service

(AAFES) for five years and has just completed her performance evaluation. The one area for improvement revealed in her review session is to demonstrate ways in which she could support the mission of the organization. Although Cindi earned 7 out of 10 on the rating scale, she wanted to improve her rating on the next performance review. The mission statement for AAFES is: "To provide quality goods and services at competitively low prices and generate earnings to supplement appropriated funds for military morale, welfare, and recreation (MWR) programs." Why is it important for Cindi to understand the organization's mission statement? Cindi's goal is to receive a higher rating on her next performance review. How can she demonstrate her support for the organization's mission to receive a higher rating?

2. **Company's structure.** The late 1980s saw a sharp decline in worker confidence in business because of the restructuring and downsizing of companies. Recent scandals such as Enron and WorldCom have produced further decline in confidence. How can a company's mission statement, code of ethics, organizational structure, classification of authority, and organization chart help improve consumer and employee confidence? Be sure to include a response for each item listed in the question.

3. **Telecommuting.** David Morgan accepted the opportunity to telecommute and work from his home. His company provided all the office equipment and paid for a dedicated fax/phone line with voice mail and all his office supplies. He agreed to do the same work at home that he was doing in the office. He was to have all his work completed and submitted by Friday of each week. Friday was the only day he had to report to the office each week, and on that day he was busy with conferences and meetings after turning in his work. Jana, one of David's coworkers, called him several times during an eight-week period to ask business questions but was never able to speak with him. Jana reported this to David's manager and commented she thought David was traveling more than working. Was Jana correct in reporting David? If so, why; if not, why not? What were some of the assumptions Jana made? What do you think motivated Jana to do what she did? What do you think David's manager said to Jana? What do you think David's manager said to him?

4. **Chain of command.** Your company has a manufacturing plant in Mexico City. You do not have to communicate with this plant to do your job, but Chikondi, whose office is next to yours, is required to communicate daily with the office in Mexico City to clarify and resolve problems. Chikondi speaks Spanish fluently and has established a successful working relationship with those in the Mexico City office. Milan, another office assistant, resents all the laughing and talking Chikondi does. She complains that she can't do her work because of it. She tells you she plans to go to Chikondi's supervisor and complain, and if she doesn't get results at that level of authority, she will go to a higher level. She has asked you to support her should the supervisor ask any questions. What would you say to Milan about your involvement? What would you recommend Milan do if the situation is disturbing her work? What do you think Milan's supervisor's response will be? To Chikondi? What do you think the supervisor would say if Milan went over his or her head to a higher authority if the problem was not resolved?

Using the Web: *Research Activities*

The World Wide Web, also known as the Web, comprises a vast collection of documents stored in specialized computers all over the world. These computers are linked to form part of a worldwide communication system called the Internet. When you conduct a search, you direct your computer's browser, such as Netscape or Microsoft® Internet Explorer, to go to Web sites where documents are stored and retrieve the requested information for display on your screen. The Internet is the communication system by which the information travels.

A *search tool* is a computer program that performs searches. A *search method* is the way a search tool requests and retrieves information from a Web site.

In your searches, you will use any one or all of the following popular tools:

- Yahoo, known as a directory search, uses both subject and keyword search methods. Choose a subject search when you want general information on a subject or topic.

- Google searches for information through use of keywords, such as "office trends" and responds with a list of references or hits. Choose a keyword search method to obtain specific information as its database is substantially larger and more current than that of a directory search, such as Yahoo.

If you are new to searching the Web, follow this general procedure:

- Connect to the Internet via your browser (Netscape or Internet Explorer).

- In the browser's location box, type the address (URL) of your search tool choice. Press Enter. The Home Page of the search tool appears on your screen. The addresses for two popular search tools are:

- www.yahoo.com
- www.google.com

- Type your query in the address box at the top of the screen. Press Enter.

- The matching references are displayed on your screen. The references returned are called *hits* and are ranked according to how well they match your query.

- Use this style to reference all Web sites:

  If author is identified: Author(s). [Date]. *Title*. Retrieved (date) from [Host, business, agency, program]: [URL]

  If no author is identified: Document title or name of Web page. Retrieved [date] [URL]

  In each chapter, you will find several Web activities to add to your knowledge of the chapter content and understanding of the search process and to help improve your search skills. When saving files for using the Web, save the files by keying your last name at the beginning of the filename, such as Henderson-C1-WebA (to identify the activity).

A. You have been asked to give a presentation. You have always wanted to travel and see the world; therefore, you have decided to locate information about working abroad. Present the results of your search in outline form for approval.

1. Enter the following keywords, including the quotation marks and the plus sign, to help narrow your search: "international + employment"

2. Locate an ad for a position in a foreign city and country where you might like to work. Locate information about the U.S. Embassy, living overseas, warnings posted regarding working abroad, language requirement, and other interesting information. Summarize or print any information you could use in your presentation.

3. Outline the information to be included in your presentation.

Tip: Use the outline feature of your word processing software to present the information.

B. You are to locate one mission statement and one code of ethics.

1. Select a company(s) you would like to search. Here are some suggestions to begin your search.

   www.yum.com (owners of KFC, Taco Bell, Pizza Hut, A & W, Long John Silvers). Look for words such as "responsibility" or "supplier code of conduct."

   www.gm.com (General Motors Corp.). Look under "The Company," then "Corporate Responsibility."

   www.aa.com (American Airlines). Look under "About Us," then "Customer Commitment."

   www.dellcomputer.com (Sells Dell computers). In the search box, type "mission statement." Look under FAQ (frequently asked questions).

2. After locating your mission statement and code of ethics, highlight the text, copy it, and paste it into a memo to your instructor. Outline the steps you went through to locate the mission statement and the code of ethics. Be sure to include the URL where you located each.

Tip: Highlight, copy, and paste the URL as well.

Get Tech Wise: *Ergonomically Designed Furniture, Supplies, and Equipment*

Research online or visit an office supply store and locate three items from this list of ergonomically designed office supplies, furniture, and equipment. Then, research two additional ergonomically designed items that are not in the list. Describe how each item is ergonomically designed and identify the brand, cost, item's use, physical impairment it helps correct, and any other information of importance you find. Write your report in memo format to your instructor. Include each URL if researched online or the store name and location if you visited an office supply store. When saving files for Tech Wise, save the files by keying your last name at the beginning of the filename, such as Henderson-C1-Tech.

Anti-glare monitor filters	Ergonomic staplers
Wrist and keyboard pads	Adjustable desks
Task chair, pneumatic, armless	Ergonomic footrests
Ergonomic pens and pencils	Ergonomic keyboards and mouse

Improving Your Writing Skills: *Punctuation Workshop*

Introduction

To enhance your writing skills, workshops such as grammar, capitalization, and punctuation are provided. Each chapter includes an exercise(s) based on rules provided in the Appendix. This appendix is an office professional's condensed guide to language usage. Before completing a workshop exercise, spend some time reviewing the specific rule(s) and examples in the Appendix that are identified in the workshop.

Retrieve file C1-WRKS from your student data disk. Save the file by keying your last name at the beginning of the filename; for example, Henderson-C1-WRKS.

Simulation: *In the Office at Supreme Appliances*

Supreme Appliances

INTRODUCTION TO SUPREME APPLIANCES

Welcome to Supreme Appliances, Inc. You are presently completing an internship and have been hired as an administrative assistant to support Amanda Quevedo, vice president of the Marketing Division. Your internship is a part-time job in which you will receive supervised practical training in the office technology field. The internship is closely related to your academic and career goals and will serve as a precursor to professional employment. You will be closely supervised by your mentor, Amanda Quevedo, in an apprenticeship-like relationship until you complete your internship. This internship provides you with academic credit as well as hourly pay.

Ms. Quevedo will delegate tasks to be completed, supervise your work, and evaluate your performance. You have completed your orientation for interns and are beginning your first official day.

The assignments you receive will help you build skills that are similar to the ones you will face in today's office. At times you will be given assignments that will require you to use initiative or that may require clarification or additional information. While employers notice employees using initiative, as an intern you will need to ask for additional information to complete the assignment. It's much better to ask for additional detail and complete the work accurately and in a timely manner than to complete a task and do it wrong and have to do it again.

Before you begin your tasks, note the following information about your company. Supreme Appliances, Inc., sells both large and small home appliances. It also manufactures its own line of refrigerators, stoves, freezers, and dishwashers. Henry Pippen serves as president of Supreme Appliances, Inc., and his administrative assistant is Kirk Lawrence.

The company address is:

14 Shady Lane
Rochester, NY 14623

The marketing division measures and analyzes market potential and assists in short- and long-range forecasting. The division's organization chart is shown in Figure 1-8.

From the chart, you can see the vice president supports divisions in four regions: Eastern, Southwestern, Northwestern, and Western. Each region is supported by a sales office. In addition to these regions, Supreme has two manufacturing plants.

Staff Managers

Yolanda Johnson, Advertising Manager
Beth Morgan, Marketing Research Manager

Assistant Vice Presidents of the Marketing Division

J. R. Rush, Eastern Region, Extension 6534

Thomas Strickland, Southwestern Region, Extension 6535

Sid Levine, Northwestern Region, Extension 6536

Karen Baxter, Western Region, Extension 6537

Most of the communications are with the four regional sales offices and the two manufacturing plants.

Managers of Regional Sales Offices

Joanna Hansen, Eastern Region, 85 Jefferson Street, Boston, MA 02116-5508

John Reddin, Southwestern Region, 1508 Commerce Street, Dallas, TX 75201-4904

Mary Anderson, Northwestern Region, 803 N.W. Everett Street, Portland, OR 97209-3313

Kyle Rhodes, Western Region, 1400 Lincoln Street, Denver, CO 80203-1523

Managers of Manufacturing Plants

Raymond Jones, Southwestern Manufacturing Plant, 2600 W. Vickery Boulevard, Fort Worth, TX 76102-7105.

Eugene Harrison, Western Manufacturing Plant, 3509 Mission Street, San Francisco, CA 94110-5429.

Your office uses a network system that connects all of the offices and plants. Therefore, you will be able to communicate with all the appropriate personnel throughout the organization.

Your job will entail prioritizing office tasks; composing letters and e-mails; processing incoming and outgoing mail; handling the telephone; planning meetings and conferences; welcoming visitors; keyboarding other documents, such as agendas and meeting notes; scheduling appointments; and making travel arrangements.

On occasion, you will be asked to assist the office support staff in other offices to help handle the workflow.

Application 1-A

Organization Chart

Supplies needed: Plain paper or Microsoft® Word, Figure 1-8, information about Supreme Appliances

Ms. Quevedo has asked you to create two files of the Marketing Division's organization chart—one file with titles only (for Ms. Quevedo) and one file with titles followed by names (for your reference). Since you are a new intern, she believes the organization chart with titles and names will help you and other new employees identify management personnel.

- Use Figure 1-8 to create the organization chart and the information provided in this simulation.

- In your first copy, do not include any personnel names, include only job titles. Save the file by keying your last name at the beginning of the file; for example Henderson-C1-AP-A1. Print a copy according to your instructor's directions.

- In your second copy, add each person's name using the information about Supreme Appliances. Save this file as (your last name)-C1-AP-A2. Print a copy according to your instructor's directions.

- Use Microsoft® Word to create the chart. To successfully complete the following steps, you must have the Organization Chart Word 2003 feature installed on your computer. If you have questions about the availability of this feature, check with your instructor. If you do not have access to Word, use a ruler to create the boxes.

  1. Open Word. Make sure a blank document screen displays.

  2. Click on the Insert menu and select Picture.

  3. Click on Organization Chart.

  4. In the first highlighted box of your chart type VP –Marketing Division.

  5. To add the two boxes for the second level, highlight the VP – Marketing Division box, then click on Select, Level, Insert Shape, Assistant. One box will be added. Repeat the steps for the second box. Key the Advertising Manager and Marketing Research Manager's titles.

  6. Key in the appropriate titles for the third level. See Step 9 to delete a box.

  7. To add each box on the fourth level under each Assistant Vice President, click on the first Vice President to the left to select it, then click on Select, Branch, Insert Shape. Key the appropriate title. Repeat this step for each of the other three boxes you need to add to the fourth level.

  8. To decrease the size of the chart, click inside the chart until the outside square appears around the chart, (called fillhandles) then click on the circle (handle) at the top left corner and drag the chart down and to the right to the desired size. Reverse this procedure to enlarge it.

  9. If you need to remove a square, click on the square until the round handles appear; then press the Delete key.

  10. Add names to title in the chart to create the second chart.

  11. Ms. Quevedo will need copies of this file to take to a meeting next week.

Application 1-B

Company Information, Mission Statement, Code of Ethics— Inserting Files

Supplies needed: C1-AP-B1, Mission Statement; C1-AP-B2, Code of Ethics; C1-AP-B3, Supreme Appliances company information; plain paper.

Retrieve file C1-AP-B1 from your student data disk. Three new employees have been added to the Marketing Division. Ms. Quevedo plans to meet with them to welcome them to the division. She asks you as her new intern to attend as well because she will be discussing the company's mission statement, code of ethics, basic information about the company, and the important role each employee plays. She has given you three files to combine into one file.

1. Insert file, C1-AP-B2, the code of ethics file a double space below the mission statement. Although you could copy and paste the information, you are to practice inserting files into documents. Do not copy and paste any of the documents. Use the Insert, File command to insert the files.

2. Delete the centered heading, SUPREME APPLIANCES and change Code of Ethics to all capital letters.

3. Center in all caps and bold the heading, **COMPANY INFORMATION**, a double space below the code of ethics.

4. Insert the file, C1-AP-B3, containing the Supreme Appliances' company information, a double space below the code of ethics.

5. Make any spacing changes that are necessary.

6. Change the font to Times New Roman, font size 12, for the entire document.

7. Save and name the file (your last name)-C1-AP-B1.

Application 1-C

Self-Assessment: Office Support Functions

Supplies needed: Form 1-A, Self-Assessment: Office Support Functions. Forms are provided in the forms packet accompanying your text. This form is also provided on your student data disk.

Retrieve file C1-AP-C1 from your student data disk.

The Human Resources (HR) department has asked all full-time office support staff to complete an office skills self-assessment. The purpose of the assessment is to identify which office support functions each person believes he or she needs to improve. Ms. Quevedo has asked you to participate in this training effort as well. Complete the self-assessment by placing a check mark in the box by each area in which you feel you need improvement.

Building Your Portfolio

INTRODUCTION TO CREATING YOUR EMPLOYMENT PORTFOLIO

Finding the right job for you in today's competitive job market can sometimes be difficult. You have to do more than what is expected of you to make a lasting impression during an interview. During your study of office procedures, you will be creating sample documents that can present your skills to an interviewer much better than words. You will be creating your employment portfolio, chapter by chapter, so you can show an interviewer the quality of work you are capable of producing.

WHAT IS AN EMPLOYMENT PORTFOLIO?

An employment portfolio is a collection of samples of your *best* work arranged in an attractive binder or file folder—whatever you choose—that will demonstrate your organization, writing, and critical thinking skills. Remember the key word is *best*. You would not want to include any work that has errors, is unattractive, or is unclear to the reader. For example, an organization chart you have created using Microsoft® Word is a great example showing your ability to use the special chart feature in the word processing software. Other samples of your work may include a resume, cover letter, and completed application form, all of which will be taught in Chapter 3.

WHAT IS THE PURPOSE OF THE PORTFOLIO?

The collection presents your abilities in a much stronger, more positive way than your describing the work you are capable of doing. Its purpose is to build confidence in your skills, knowledge, and abilities in the interviewer's mind.

The following suggestions may help you in preparing a portfolio:

- **Make your portfolio speak for you.** If your employment portfolio is clean, complete, and carefully organized, that's how you will be judged. If it's unique, colorful, creative, and imaginative, that, too, is how you will be judged. So, too, will you be judged if your folder or binder is messy, incomplete, and haphazardly put together. Before giving your portfolio to someone else for evaluation, consider whether it reflects how you want to be presented.

- **Attend to the mechanics of the portfolio.** Make certain the folder containing your documents is the kind specified and that it is clean and attractive. In the absence of any specification, use a pocket folder, which is an inexpensive means of keeping the contents organized and secure. Put your name and address on the outside cover. Organize the material inside as requested. And submit it on time.

  - **Include exactly what is requested.** If your instructor wants three finished copies, that's the minimum your portfolio should contain. If an employer wants to see five samples of different kinds of documents, be sure to include five samples.

  - **Add supplemental material judiciously.** If you believe supplemental documents will present you in a better light, include that too, but only after the required material. If you include extra material, attach a note to explain why it is there. Supplemental documents might include letters, graphics, diagrams, or spreadsheets that suggest other useful dimensions of your thinking and abilities.

  - **Include perfect final documents.** Show that your own standard for finished work is high. Final documents should be printed on high-quality paper, be carefully proofread, and follow common formats.

  - **Demonstrate growth.** The signal value of portfolios is they allow you to demonstrate how a finished document came into being. Consequently, your instructor may ask for drafts to be attached to final documents, the most recent on top, so he or she can see how you followed revision suggestions and how much effort you invested.

To build such a record of your work, date every draft of each document.

- **Demonstrate work in progress.** It may be that you present partially finished work that suggests future directions and intentions. Both your instructor and future employer may find such preliminary work valuable. When you include such tentative drafts or incomplete work, be sure to attach a note explaining why it's not quite finished.

- **Attach a table of contents.** For portfolios containing more than three documents, attach a separate table of contents. For those containing only a few papers, embed your table of contents in the cover letter. For this class, create a table of contents listing chapter number and name.

- **Include a cover letter.** The cover letter represents your most recent assessment of the work you completed, serving two primary purposes: (1) as an introduction explaining the portfolio's contents and (2) as your self-assessment of the quality of the work. Based on your instructor's directions, your cover letter may be completed after Chapter 6 or at the end of this class.

Adapted from *The Blair Handbook* (5th ed.), by Toby Fulwiler and Alan R. Hayakawa. Prentice Hall, 2006, pp. 226–267.

1. Beginning with Chapter 1, with the help of a team member or your instructor, select the best work from the following:

   - Exploring the Workplace: Activities. Explain what you were to do in the activity, your approach to completing the activity, what you learned from the activity, and how you can apply the results of the activity to your own employment.

   - Simulation: In the Office at Supreme Appliances. Include the two organization charts you created.

   - Get Tech Wise. Include the report on ergonomically made equipment and supplies available to prevent health problems in the office.

2. Make certain that you include the question, situation, or an explanation of what your assignment was so an interviewer could tell what work you were required to do and what your final response or document looks like.

As you complete the assignments in each of the chapters, keep in mind the document(s) you will want to showcase in your portfolio as it will represent YOU!

chapter **outline**

learning **outcomes**

When you have completed this chapter, you should be able to:

- Describe the five basic workplace skills an office professional needs to be successful.

- Describe the basic knowledge skills an office professional needs in the workplace.

- Describe the ten personal qualities needed in the workplace.

- Describe the eleven interpersonal skills needed in the workplace.

- Describe how to display ethical behavior in the workplace.

- List the human relations questions you should ask yourself before considering international employment.

Business and industry representatives are becoming more and more concerned about the gap between the workplace skill requirements for entry-level employment and the workplace skill levels of most entry-level applicants. Employers are finding most applicants possess adequate **hard skills**, also called *technical skills*, but many applicants lack what is often referred to as *soft skills* necessary for success on the job. These human relations **soft skills** include **personal qualities** such as being responsible, being dependable, being a self-starter, having a positive self-esteem, being sociable, exhibiting self-management, displaying integrity/honesty, projecting a pleasant personality, showing your human side, and projecting a professional image. Soft skills also include **interpersonal skills** (interaction with others), which you will learn about later in this chapter, such as participating as a team member, teaching others, interacting with customers, demonstrating leadership ability, negotiating agreements, and respecting diversity. Employers are looking for all these skills in entry-level applicants.

You should understand there is a great deal of difference between **employment** (having a job) and **employability** (possessing the qualities necessary to maintain employment). Possessing excellent human relation skills, both personal and interpersonal, will enable you to project an image of professionalism that will cause you to be viewed as an asset to your company. When you lack these soft skills, often "having a job" can be temporary.

The purpose of this chapter is to emphasize the two areas of human relations soft skills employers are most concerned about employees possessing—personal qualities and interpersonal skills. In this chapter and throughout this text, you will learn more about the soft skills necessary to succeed in today's office.

Identifying Five Basic Workplace Skills

Research by the Secretary's Commission on Achieving Necessary Skills in 1991 identified certain basic workplace skills as necessary to be successful in the workplace. Even though these skills were identified years ago, employers today are still emphasizing the importance between having these skills and performing successfully on the job. In Figure 2-1 you will notice five basic workplace skills, six basic workplace knowledge skills, and ten personal qualities required for job success. Although the purpose of this chapter is to focus on soft skills, which include both personal qualities and a variety of interpersonal skills, a review of all the skills is necessary because each one is important.

RESOURCES

You must be skillful in locating and managing resources. Managing resources involves identifying, organizing, planning, and allocating resources. Examples of **resources** are time, money, material and facilities, and human resource management. You will learn more about time management in Chapter 4.

INFORMATION

You must be skillful in managing **information.** Managing information means acquiring, evaluating, organizing, maintaining, interpreting, and communicating. You must also use computers to process information. You will learn more about developing these skills in Chapters 6 and 7.

FIGURE 2-1 • Workplace skills necessary to succeed in today's office.

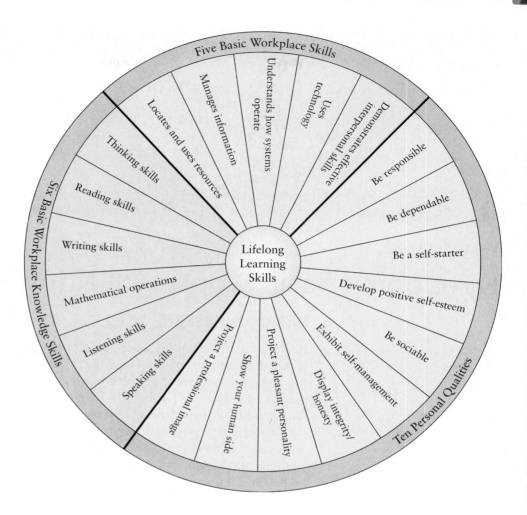

Five Basic Workplace Skills

Manages information
Understands how systems operate
Uses technology
Demonstrates effective interpersonal skills
Locates and uses resources

Thinking skills
Be responsible

Reading skills
Be dependable

Writing skills
Lifelong Learning Skills
Be a self-starter

Mathematical operations
Develop positive self-esteem

Listening skills
Be sociable

Speaking skills
Exhibit self-management

Project a professional image
Display integrity/honesty

Show your human side
Project a pleasant personality

Six Basic Workplace Knowledge Skills

Ten Personal Qualities

SYSTEMS

You must understand how social, organizational, and technological systems work and operate effectively within them. This means monitoring and correcting performance and often improving and designing simple systems. You will learn about operating and managing mail systems in Chapter 7 and setting up and managing filing systems in Chapter 8.

TECHNOLOGY

You must be able to work with a variety of technologies, which involves selecting procedures, tools, or equipment, including computers and related technologies. You should understand the intended use of the **technology** and the proper procedures for its setup and operation as well as how to maintain and troubleshoot problems. Look for the Get Tech Wise section at the end of each chapter for an opportunity to learn about or practice some of these skills.

INTERPERSONAL

You must be able to work with others. More information about these workplace skills will be discussed later in this chapter, and additional information regarding these topics will be emphasized throughout the textbook.

Stop 'n Check

List the five basic workplace skills.

a. _____

b. _____

c. _____

d. _____

e. _____

Developing Basic Workplace Knowledge Skills

BASIC KNOWLEDGE SKILLS

Basic knowledge skills such as thinking, reading, writing, performing mathematical operations, listening, and speaking are also identified in Figure 2-1 as important workplace skills. A basic mastery of these skills is required to obtain any job. You learned how to read, write, and complete mathematical operations in classes devoted to developing these skills while you were in primary and secondary schools and in college classes.

Listening, speaking, and thinking skills were developed by using these skills in all classes. Employers have expressed that more emphasis should be placed on developing listening, speaking, and thinking skills prior to entering the workforce. They say most employees do not listen carefully, do not have a good command of the English language, and cannot demonstrate it through their speaking skills, nor can they think through even simple problems to obtain a solution. This chapter emphasizes how you can improve your thinking skills. Listening and speaking skills will be discussed in depth in Chapters 5, 6 and 13. Now let's begin by focusing on developing stronger thinking skills.

THINKING SKILLS

How could any office professional not possess thinking skills? Of course, everyone possesses thinking skills. The term **thinking skills** refers to the degree to which a person can use these skills to arrive at a decision or develop a viable solution to a problem.

Your supervisor may expect you to use your ability to think of new creative ideas, make decisions, solve problems, visualize abstractly, or just know how to learn or reason. An office professional should develop these skills and know when to use each one. Take a moment to review the following list of ways you may be required solve a problem on the job.

Creative thinking	Generate a new idea.
Decision making	Specify goals and constraints, generate alternatives, consider risks, and evaluate and choose best alternatives.

Problem solving	Recognize problems and devices and implement a plan of action.
Visualizing	Organize and process symbols or other items.
Knowing how to learn	Use efficient learning techniques to acquire and apply new knowledge and skills.
Reasoning	Discover a rule or principle underlying the relationship between two or more objects and apply it to solve a problem.

How should you go about developing better thinking skills? The best way is to use these skills every time an opportunity presents itself. Here are some basic steps you can use to begin.

1. Gather all the information about the problem.
2. Determine what you know about the problem already that might be helpful in forming a solution.
3. Determine if more information is needed and where to get it.
4. Outline all possible solutions, whether right or wrong.
5. Analyze each solution, discarding those you know are wrong and narrow your choices to two or three when possible.
6. Identify the pros and cons for each solution.
7. Select the best solution among the choices.

Here is an example of how these steps might work.

Example problem:

You work as an office assistant in the security department. This department oversees the employee parking facilities. Your supervisor has received many complaints that the employee parking lot is too small. Your supervisor will add the expenditures in this year's budget to solve the problem. He has asked you to chair a committee to study the problem and present to him the committee's ideas and recommendation(s). See Figure 2-2.

By applying the steps laid out in Figure 2-2 when you are faced with a problem, you can improve your ability to think logically and systematically. As with other skills, knowing the process and practicing are the keys to success.

Developing Personal Qualities

When you accept a position with a company, management expects you to do the best job you can and to get along with everyone to the best of your ability. Remember that your contribution is essential to a smooth-running, productive, and efficient office. By upholding a high standard of personal qualities, you will demonstrate excellent human relations skills to those around you, and your role will become a central one on the office team (see Figure 2-3).

QUESTION TO BE RESOLVED	ANALYSIS AND/OR ACTION
1. Gather all the information about the problem.	• Need measurements • Need someone to measure
2. Determine what you know about the problem already that might be helpful in forming a solution.	• Measure the perimeter of the parking lot—someone must do. • Measure a compact car, a sedan, an SUV, and a van—someone must do. • Determine how many entrances and exits are available—there are two entrances and two exits. • Determine how many parking spaces are available now—someone must count. • Determine the number of handicapped parking spaces and the sizes—someone must count. • Determine if there are any reserved spaces and, if so, how many—someone must count. • Determine the condition of the surface of the parking lot—someone must evaluate.
3. Determine if more information is needed and where to get it.	• We may need a survey conducted of those who presently use the lot and those who would use the lot if more spaces were available. • We need to research local regulations (zoning, traffic, and building) that might affect plans to restripe or expand the lot. There may be other questions.
4. Outline all possible solutions without ruling any out at this point because of cost or practicality.	• Purchase land and build a second lot. • Offer incentives such as close reserved parking for carpooling. • Restripe lot using space according to sizes of vehicles. • Offer free or subsidized passes for public transportation.
5. Analyze each solution, discarding those you know are unworkable, and narrow your choices to two or three if possible.	• Discard purchasing second lot. Budgets have been cut in all areas and money is tight or has already been designated for more important projects. • Conduct the survey to have a more accurate use of the lot. • Resurface and restripe the lot according to the common automobile, SUV, and van sizes and in compliance with local regulations.

(continued)

QUESTION TO BE RESOLVED	ANALYSIS AND/OR ACTION
6. Identify the pros and cons for each solution.	**Survey**: **Pros:** More information will allow us to be more accurate in our recommendation. **Cons**: Cost, time, and who will conduct it, tally, and report findings—gather this information. **Resurface and Restripe:** Would allow more spaces without expensive expansion. **Cons:** Cost, time, contractor, or maintenance—gather this information.
7. Select the best solution among the choices.	**Recommendation:** • Complete a survey to determine usage. • Resurface and restripe according to vehicle size. • Offer incentives for carpooling and using public transportation.

FIGURE 2-2 • Problem-solving questions to address and analyses and/or actions to take.

Stop 'n Check

1. List below the ideas you would not have thought of from the example in Figure 2-2. What do you think caused you to miss these ideas?

_____

_____

_____

_____

2. Identify the thinking skills mentioned in this section.

_____

_____

_____

BE RESPONSIBLE

Responsibility means accepting the assignment of duties. When you accept a position, you are being entrusted with and assigned many duties to be performed. You are expected to perform these duties to the best of your ability. To be responsible, you must answer to someone for your actions, and on the job this means your supervisor. Displaying responsibility is one of the key human relation skills. You will learn more about responsibility in Chapter 14.

FIGURE 2-3 • Personal qualities needed to project a professional image.

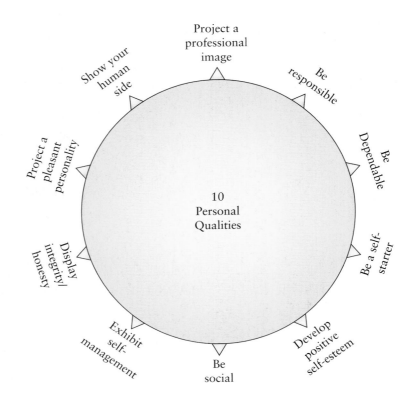

BE DEPENDABLE

Dependability means being consistent and reliable in your behavior. For instance, you would display dependability by having an excellent attendance record and by being prompt in arriving at work each morning and in returning on time to your workstation after breaks and lunch. Dependability helps create a desirable office atmosphere.

Each employee in your office depends on every person being there. When someone is absent, no matter the reason, or is late returning from lunch or a break, someone in the office must cover for that person. When someone is covering for another individual, that someone is not getting his or her own work completed. Hostile feelings can grow quickly toward any person who does not carry his or her workload and is not dependable.

BE A SELF-STARTER

A **self-starter** takes the initiative to begin a task for which he or she is responsible. Don't wait for your manager to ask you to do something—be observant and anticipate what you are expected to do without having to be told.

When you finish your work, ask if you can help someone else. Everyone feels overworked and underpaid, and when someone sits idly by while others are swamped, a negative attitude toward the person who is not busy builds. You can't just say, "It isn't my job," because it is your job to help anyone at any time you are not busy. You are paid to work a full day's work, and you should project the image of always wanting to help when help is needed.

DEVELOP POSITIVE SELF-ESTEEM

Self-esteem is the opinion you have of yourself. The following list identifies some of the concepts that affect your self-esteem.

- the value you place on yourself as a person
- the opinion you believe others hold of you
- your strengths and weaknesses
- your social status and how you relate to others
- your independence and your ability to be independent

Low self-esteem is when you view one or more of these items negatively, which results in a poor self-image. **High self-esteem** is just the opposite and causes you to be confident, sure of yourself, and possess a good attitude toward your ability to succeed. Having positive self-esteem is critical to your living a happy life both at home and in the workplace. A person who is self-confident relies on the correctness of his or her own judgment and competence in spite of the discouragement and influence of others. A confident person maintains composure, which is a feeling of calmness and tranquility, and exhibits poise, which denotes ease and dignity of manner. Here are some ways to become confident:

1. Believe in yourself and your ability to take on new and challenging assignments. Tell yourself you can do any task given you. When you have a problem, you can always ask for help.

2. Do not expect to control the circumstances under which you work; they are beyond your control. You can remain in control of your reactions, however. Don't overreact to minor problems. Just say to yourself "This too shall pass," and do your best.

3. Accept that the business world is demanding and fast-paced. Take one thing at a time. To cope with a heavy workload, proceed with assurance and keep your cool.

4. Be patient, take time to distinguish between fact and fiction, and withhold judgment until you have all the facts.

5. Accept criticism; in fact, welcome it. Use it as a tool to help improve your skills and knowledge.

6. Develop a sense of humor. Laugh at yourself and laugh with others. Do not take yourself or your problems too seriously.

BE SOCIABLE

Sociability demonstrates understanding, friendliness, adaptability, empathy, and politeness in group settings. Some employees develop social bonds with certain coworkers. You may find others with whom you work who have interests similar to your own and because of these similar interests you will become closer and friendlier toward them. You should, however, strive to be friendly toward each person in your work group (see Figure 2-4). A pleasant smile and an acknowledgment of each one as you work will continually show others that you are a friendly, pleasant coworker.

FIGURE 2-4 • Being social among your coworkers helps develop a positive office environment.

Always take part in office get-togethers such as birthday celebrations, lunches, or holiday celebrations. Your attendance and participation is part of your belonging to the office group and showing your desire to support one another.

EXHIBIT SELF-MANAGEMENT

Self-management means that you set personal goals, monitor your progress, assess yourself accurately, and exhibit self-control. Your goals may be for self-improvement in certain areas, attempting something new, or working on a problem you might have.

When you are faced with difficult situations in the workplace, you should always exhibit self-control. You know yourself better than anyone else; therefore, if this is an area you need to work on, set self-management goals to develop the ability to react as you should in stressful situations. When you are in a tense situation, stop and think before you speak. Give yourself time to analyze the reaction of others to what you might say. This time can allow you to organize your thoughts and response, help you develop the desired attitude, and avoid reacting inappropriately.

You should seek to cultivate attitudes and traits that will contribute to your success. When you succeed in displaying an appropriate attitude or trait in a difficult situation, you will be able to apply that experience in coping with the next difficult situation. You will learn more about self-management in Chapter 4.

DISPLAY INTEGRITY/HONESTY

Integrity and honesty mean the same thing—being sincere and trustworthy. No one wants to work with someone who does not possess these characteristics. The lack of these characteristics can lead to termination of employment. Just as you set these standards for yourself, you should expect the same standards from everyone with whom you work. Integrity encompasses sound moral or ethical principles, fairness, honesty, sincerity, and the courage to stand up for these moral precepts. Strength of character and integrity are among the most important traits a person can possess.

PROJECT A PLEASANT PERSONALITY

Personality is what you are, the sum of all your mental, physical, and emotional experiences. Everyone's personality is affected by the experiences of daily living. Psychologists tell us that one's personality is formed early in life, yet at no time is one's personality completely fixed. Changes in personality take place gradually, but they do occur; therefore, personality development or improvement is possible.

Projecting a pleasant personality is easy when things go right. To be successful in business, you must be able to:

- Maintain composure when things go wrong.
- Say "no" tactfully when you must.
- Soothe the feelings of an irate customer or coworker.
- Be considerate and tolerant of someone who is inconsiderate of you.
- Exhibit poise under extreme pressure.
- Be patient and try to understand people with different personalities.

SHOW YOUR HUMAN SIDE

A friendly smile and cheerful "Good morning" may be classified as ceremonial language, but they are highly desirable when they are coupled with sincerity and an optimistic approach to life. Take the initiative to speak first; call others by name. Make an effort to get acquainted with as many coworkers as possible.

Try to be the coworker you would want everyone else to be. Here are some tips to reach that goal:

- Be pleasant, courteous, responsive, and understanding.
- Listen attentively when someone is talking with you.
- Be responsive to what is going on around you.
- Treat others as you wish to be treated.
- Avoid being condescending when giving instructions.
- Suggest rather than command; request rather than demand.
- Show consideration for others in all the things you do, both large and small.
- Be thoughtful; for instance, stop at the office professional's desk when you must go in to see his or her manager.
- When you must interrupt someone, time the interruption so that the person is at a stopping point when you ask for his or her attention.
- Respect the rights of others.
- Do not discuss religion, money, morals, personalities, or politics in the office. Knowing what not to say is as important as knowing what to say.
- Gain the trust of others by never talking about anyone. Be especially careful not to make remarks about coworkers.

- Be polite enough not to pry into personal affairs; avoid asking personal questions.
- When you are talking, take the time to say exactly what you intend to say, but be tactful.
- Think and then speak; otherwise, your statements may come out wrong and place you in an embarrassing position.
- Be cooperative and do more than is expected of you.
- Be generous, but not to the point of punishing yourself.

Remember that little things do count. You can create a pleasant, businesslike atmosphere for you and your manager by your rapport with the employees at all levels and with outsiders who come to your office or call on the telephone. Be consistent, not moody, as you show your human side. In addition to creating a pleasant atmosphere, your thoughtfulness will help you enjoy your relationships with others.

PROJECT A PROFESSIONAL IMAGE

What is professionalism? **Professionalism** is aspiring to meet the highest possible standards of your profession rather than a set of minimum requirements. Notice the picture in Figure 2-5 in which the administrative assistant has agreed to present a PowerPoint presentation. Embrace these opportunities rather than shying away from them.

First impressions are everything, and the first impression you want to make is by projecting a positive professional image. A professional image reflects:

- an educated and skilled employee
- a team player who contributes valuable ideas
- a polished individual whose appearance and communication style are "professional"

FIGURE 2-5 • Take advantage of every opportunity to show your knowledge and skills.

- a person who can solve problems and integrate ideas
- a person who takes pride in each piece of work he or she produces
- an employee who works for the betterment of the organization and is not self-serving
- a person who takes pride in his or her career and who has aspirations for the future
- an employee who manages assignments by applying quality standards
- an employee who is willing to work hard and accept new and more challenging responsibilities
- an employee who is willing to learn and grow professionally
- one who seeks to learn about professional organizations such as the International Association of Administrative Professionals (IAAP) (You learned about this organization in Chapter 1, more details will be given in Chapter 14.)

Sir Walter Scott said, "Success or failure is caused more by mental attitude than by mental capacity." You should approach life and your job with a positive attitude. Periodically take inventory of your needs and your accomplishments. Set new goals and keep reaching. Your rewards will be many, including physical vitality, an alert mind, and an optimistic attitude toward life.

Stop 'n Check

Rank the 10 personal qualities in order with the most important listed first and the least important last.

a. _____   f. _____
b. _____   g. _____
c. _____   h. _____
d. _____   i. _____
e. _____   j. _____

Developing Interpersonal Skills

To be an effective office professional, you must be aware at all times each person you meet, whether customer or coworker, is forming an image of the organization, your manager, and you. You must rely on your business personality to communicate effectively with everyone you come in contact with in your business activities.

You cannot depend on knowledge, skills, and abilities alone for success in your job. Your performance as an effective office professional and your happiness on the job will be closely linked to your ability to communicate and to get along with people. This in turn will depend on your understanding the importance of interpersonal skills. Let's consider what happened to an office assistant named Violeta.

Violeta was one of several office assistants at a large travel agency in downtown Denver. The manager and assistant manager were discussing which of the office assistants should be promoted to office manager to replace the present office manager who had been promoted to travel agent after she received her certification. The manager mentioned that Violeta should be selected for the office manager position. He stated that she had less experience than the other four office assistants and had adequate technical skills, but she would make a great office manager. The assistant manager said he thought that Anita would make a better office manager. Anita knew more about the computer system being used and had several years of experience with the travel agency. The first manager said, "I agree about Anita's technical skills and experience, but I have personally seen Violeta resolve several difficult problems. She has terrific people skills and works really well with customers as well as the rest of the office staff." The assistant manager said, "Yes, you are right. Let's promote Violeta. We can keep Anita in mind as our second choice."

Situations like this happen all the time in the workplace. Often a person is promoted simply because he or she has good interpersonal skills combined with adequate technical skills. You should strive to display good interpersonal skills at all times. Do not depend solely on your technical skills and knowledge, even if they are superior skills.

Interpersonal skills are not just getting along with people, however. These skills are more than that. Here are some of the interpersonal skills to help you succeed in the workplace. Figure 2-6 shows how you can improve your

FIGURE 2-6 • Improving your interpersonal skills one step at a time can help to achieve a professional image.

A professional

Cope with change

Keep confidential information confidential

Respect diversity

Embrace constructive criticism

Negotiate effectively

Exercise leadership

Offer exceptional customer service

Teach others

Learn to work with difficult people

Recognize individual differences

Be a team player

interpersonal skills by working on one skill at a time. The reward is projecting a professional image.

BE A TEAM PLAYER

In every company, management expects each employee to be a productive worker whose efforts contribute to the goals and objectives of the organization. You and your manager should be working for common goals and functioning in harmony with others in the organization.

If you will think in terms of what you can contribute rather than of what you can get, you will find it easier to do the right thing at the right time. You may perform much detailed work, but you need not feel subservient. On the contrary, you should feel that you are part of a team. **Teamwork** means collaboration with another employee(s) assigned a task or goal for which the team must be cooperatively working together to arrive at a solution or recommendation (see Figure 2-7). Teamwork ranks with communication and trust as components for a good relationship with your manager. Communication is highly important; keep your manager informed. Because your role is to assist, do everything possible to assist your manager in being successful. You will learn more about communication in Chapter 6. Here are some helpful ways you can be a team player:

- Take full responsibility for your part of the workload and for the problems that arise within the scope of the team's work.

- Study your part of the assignment but ask for help from other team members when necessary.

- Give helpful criticism when necessary but do so diplomatically. Criticize the work not the person. It is better to say "The introduction needs . . ." rather than "You left out . . . in your introduction."

- Share the praise and other rewards for accomplishment even though you are the most deserving.

FIGURE 2-7 • Office professionals working as a team.

Stop 'n Check

A variety of skills are required to be an effective team member.

1. Using the list of ways you can be a team player just shown, which item do you think is most important?

_____

_____

2. Explain why you chose this item.

_____

_____

_____

- Strive for excellence and be enthusiastic about being on the team.
- Make others feel important.
- Be courteous and show respect, but be yourself.
- Let your personality sparkle just enough for others to be glad they had a chance to work with you.

RECOGNIZE INDIVIDUAL DIFFERENCES

To deal effectively with others in the workplace, it is necessary to recognize that people have different capabilities, needs, and interests. These different capabilities, needs, and interests are referred to as **individual differences.** The purpose of learning and understanding about individual differences in personality types is to help you build a better working relationship or establish rapport with others. Author Andrew J. Dubrin offers the following suggestions for dealing with different personality types in *Human Relations: Interpersonal Job-Oriented Skills* (Pearson Prentice Hall, 2007). These suggestions are restricted to readily observable aspects of personality.

1. When relating to a person who appears to be neurotic based on symptoms of worry and tension, be laid back and reassuring. Attempt not to project your own anxiety and fears. Be a good listener. If possible, minimize the emphasis on deadlines and the dire consequences of a project's failing. Show concern and interest in the person's welfare.

2. When relating to an extraverted individual (one with an outgoing, friendly personality), emphasize friendliness and warmth and provide a stream of chatter. Talk about people more than ideas, things, or data. Express an interest in a continuing working relationship. These people can put together creative ideas and plans.

3. When relating to an introverted individual, move slowly in forming a working relationship. Do not confuse quietness with lack of interest. Tolerate moments of silence. Emphasize ideas, things, and data more heavily than people. Introverted people may get upset if you borrow a stapler and forget to return it.

4. When relating to a person who is open to experience, emphasize information sharing, idea generation, and creative approaches to problems. Appeal to his or her intellect by discussing topics of substance rather than ordinary chatter and gossip.

FIGURE 2-8 • To deal effectively with others in the workplace, it is necessary to recognize people have different capabilities, needs, and interests.

5. When relating to a person who is closed to experience, stick closely to the facts of the situation at hand. Recognize the person prefers to think small and deal with the here and now.

6. When relating to an agreeable person, just relax and be yourself. Reciprocate with kindness to sustain a potentially excellent working relationship (see Figure 2-8).

7. When relating to a disagreeable person, be patient and tolerant. At the same time, set limits on how much mistreatment you will take. Disagreeable people sometimes secretly want others to put brakes on their antisocial behavior.

8. When relating to a conscientious person, give him or her freedom and do not nag. The person will probably honor commitments without prompting. Conscientious people are often taken for granted, so remember to acknowledge the person's dependability.

9. When relating to a person of low conscientiousness, keep close tabs on him or her, especially if you need the person's output to do your job. Do not assume because the person has an honest face and pleasing smile he or she will deliver as promised. Frequently follow up on your requests, and impose deadlines if you have the authority. Express deep appreciation when the person does follow through.

10. When relating to a person with a high propensity for risk taking and thrill seeking, emphasize the risky and daring aspects of activities familiar to you. Talk about a new product introduction in a highly competitive market, the latest technology available, skydiving, bungee jumping, or race car driving. Risk takers desire situations that involve thrill seeking. The decisions they make because of this propensity can affect their performance on the job.

The more you recognize certain personality types and how they are different or similar to your type personality, the better you will be able to relate to them and find it easier to work with them in harmony.

LEARN TO WORK WITH DIFFICULT PEOPLE

No matter how congenial you are, how much a team player you are, how nice and cooperative you are, you will encounter people with whom it is difficult to interact effectively. While some employees who are difficult to work with perform their jobs well, other difficult people do not perform well on the job or interfere with the job performance of others.

Many types of difficult people have been identified. Some are bullies, gossips, gripers, naggers, dictators—the list could go on. Here are a few common types and some suggestions on how to cope with them.

The Bully

The **bully** uses intimidation to gain control by making others angry or afraid. The bully tries to push all your buttons by yelling, name calling, sarcasm, mocking, putting down, belittling, embarrassing, or negativity to cause these reactions in others.

Coping

- Think only about the positive attributes of the bully—what you like about him or her when he or she is not bullying.
- Look him or her straight in the eye. Using a calm, normal voice and "I" and not "you" words, say exactly what you don't like about his or her behavior. For instance, "I do not like it when people raise their voice at me. I feel as if I am being treated as a child. I am not a child. I am an adult and want to be treated as such."

Gossips

Gossips go from person to person spreading negative rumors about others whether true or not and trying to set one person against the other. They look for people who will listen and agree with them. They feel open to use anyone's name who listens to them and say such things as "I just talked to Jo and she told me . . ." It makes them feel powerful.

Coping

- When the gossiper begins telling his or her rumor, break into the conversation and say something positive about the person or situation.
- Each time the gossiper resumes by saying "Yes, but . . .," break in again and give a positive statement about the person or situation. Gossips dislike talking to people who always find the good in others or in situations.
- If you refuse to listen, sooner or later the gossips will get the message.

Know-it-all

Know-it-alls believe they are the experts. They have opinions about everything, but when they are found to be wrong, they pass the buck or become defensive.

Coping

- Deal with them on a one-to-one-basis, not in a group setting.
- Check the facts, be sure they are correct, then state your facts.
- Do not put down the know-it-all.
- Give the person a way out so he or she can save face.

Backstabber

Backstabbers will try to get you to discuss a problem or situation in which you are involved. They appear to befriend you and encourage you to talk freely. Later they go to the person or supervisor with whom they know they can cause the most damage to you, and they repeat what you told them, often embellishing the information. They want to discredit you to others.

Coping

- Do not retaliate by talking about the backstabber. You may appear to be the backstabber, not him or her.
- Stay away from the backstabber—as far as you can in all professional matters. Build alliances with people you know you can trust. When someone mentions what they heard the backstabber say about you, just say "Oh, that's Mr. B. He has never forgiven me for my last promotion. I don't know what the problem is. He won't let me talk to him about it. I just ignore him."
- Always think before you speak. Don't say anything to anyone in the office you wouldn't want repeated.
- Keep an accurate record of what happens. If the backstabber is your boss, you need accurate verification of what was said—date, time, conversation, and anyone else who heard it.

Blamers

Blamers never solve their own problems. When faced with a problem, they think someone else caused it—the supervisor, a group member, or you.

- Attempt to get the blamer to answer the question, "Whose responsibility was it for (whatever the problem is)?" Answering that question gets to the heart of the problem.
- Remind the blamer he or she must take ownership of his or her actions. Life is a matter of choices. Who made the choice?

Difficult people tend to bring out the worst in us. Many know how to "push our buttons" to cause us to react emotionally, to cause us distress, or simply to create tension. Here is a plan to follow to help you deal with these difficult situations.

1. Do not react emotionally; stand back and take a look at the situation. If you do not have to respond immediately, take time to write down everything in as much detail as possible.
2. Analyze the behavior of the difficult person. Identify exactly what was said that caused you to feel threatened or upset. What do you believe motivated the person to make the statement or to create the situation?
3. Analyze your behavior and emotional response (e.g., anger, frustration, disappointment).
4. Decide exactly what behavior—all or part—you believe you must acknowledge and respond to and why.
5. Define all the ways you might respond.
6. Decide on a plan: What will you say (making sure you form the statements using "I" and not "you," where will you say it, and when will you say it?
7. Imagine how the person might respond.

Chapter 10 covers a related topic—dealing with difficult callers.

TEACH OTHERS

Often the opportunity will arise on the job for you to help others learn new techniques, processes, software, equipment, or other new skills. Seize every opportunity to volunteer when the need arises to help others learn. Office personnel who work together and learn from one another create an atmosphere that eliminates stress, offers solutions in times of crisis, and prevents work bottlenecks when someone is absent. Here are some helpful hints to successfully teach others:

- Be patient; not everyone learns at the same rate.
- Recognize that some learn by doing rather than just being told.
- Don't overwhelm the learner; teach in short segments.
- Always review when you begin and summarize when you end a session.
- Don't view others' learning as a threat to your job.

OFFER EXCEPTIONAL CUSTOMER SERVICE

Exceptional customer service is helping customers, clients, or coworkers with a willingness to put their needs first to help resolve their problems. Some of these skills are:

- Smile and be friendly.
- Offer to help before being asked.
- If you can't help, locate someone who can.
- If the person is upset, let him or her vent frustration and then show empathy and understanding.
- Go the extra mile above and beyond what would normally be expected of you.

These highly desirable skills will promote your professional image and the customers-first image of the company. Customer service does not mean just offering excellent service to those customers outside your business; it also means you see each person within your organization as a customer as well and treat him or her as such.

EXERCISE LEADERSHIP

Exercising **leadership** means communicating clearly and effectively your position on certain matters, persuading or convincing others, and responsibly challenging existing procedures and policies when necessary. A good leader shows self-confidence and intelligence, follows the rules, stands behind his or her word, is trustworthy, and has a sense of humor.

It has been said that good leaders are made, not born. If you have the desire and willpower to become a leader, your chances of attaining that goal will improve by developing effective leadership skills. Good leaders develop through a never-ending process of self-study, education, training, and experience. Remember, power does not make you a good leader; power just means you are the boss. A good leader influences employees to want to do a good job by leading rather than just bossing people around. You will learn more about leadership in Chapter 14.

NEGOTIATE EFFECTIVELY

According to the U.S. Department of Labor, **negotiating** means exchanging ideas, information, and opinions with others to work toward agreements to formulate policies and programs and/or arrive jointly at decisions, conclusions, or solutions. A good negotiator:

- thinks before he or she begins. Do your homework so you will know the other's side and then develop a plan and write it down. Know the minimum and maximum for which you are willing to settle.
- is ready to compromise. Identify the benefits of your offer. Even getting a little of what you want makes you a winner.
- displays excellent people skills. You must observe the other person and be ready to adjust to his or her personality.
- is a good listener. Develop the habit of summarizing what the other person says to make sure you understand his or her intent.

EMBRACE CONSTRUCTIVE CRITICISM

Constructive criticism is the process of offering one's opinion about the work of another. The criticism should involve both positive and constructive comments and offer the comments in a friendly manner rather than an oppositional one. Some people tend to take criticism negatively; we should embrace constructive criticism, even welcome it because it can help us improve. Here are some guidelines on how to give constructive criticism and how to accept it.

Follow these guidelines to give constructive criticism:

1. Be genuine. Criticism is only constructive if the person giving it truly means to help the person receiving it and feels it is important.
2. Always give criticism in private.
3. Don't sound threatening. Avoid statements that start with "I think you should," or "You have to," or "You had better." It would be better to say, "Let's take a look at what has been happening and see if, between the two of us, we can work out a solution. What do you think?"
4. Focus on the problem, not the person.

To receive constructive criticism:

1. Welcome the criticism. See it as a way for you to improve.
2. Listen carefully to the criticism; restate the criticism when necessary.
3. Focus on the problem, not the person giving it.
4. Understand it can help improve the interpersonal relationship between you and the person giving the criticism.

RESPECT DIVERSITY

What is diversity? **Diversity** refers to the variety of experiences and perspectives that arise from differences in race, culture, religion, mental or physical abilities, heritage, age, gender, sexual orientation, and other characteristics. Offices today are diverse. Keep these thoughts in mind about diversity.

- Our workforce is becoming more diverse.
- Employers consider diversity to be sound business practice because it allows them to better serve a wide range of customers.
- Your employer is bound by state and federal law to ensure that no employee suffers discrimination and that he or she is allowed to progress to his or her full potential.
- Diversity is not just cultural diversity which may or may not be identified by physical characteristics. It encompassers less-visible differences such as religion and sexual orientation.
- Sensitivity to the differences of others is essential. Learn about these differences in order to help build good working relationships.
- People have more similarities than differences. Recognize that we all want good health, peace, and security for ourselves and our families.
- Respect, tolerance, and goodwill are the keystones to enjoying the rich diversity of our world.

As an office professional, you must be knowledgeable about diversity in the workplace and embrace it.

KEEP CONFIDENTIAL INFORMATION CONFIDENTIAL

Whatever management system you work for, you will always have to practice discretion when it comes to confidential information.

Refrain from repeating your manager's opinions. In fact, most activities that take place in your office should be kept confidential. To gain the trust of your organization, your manager, and your coworkers, do not discuss, mention, or refer to company business outside your office.

When there is an upcoming company announcement and you are aware of it, keep it confidential. Company announcements should come from management.

Be careful not to give away confidential information to your friends and colleagues or to your company's competitors. Sometimes just one isolated fact obtained from you is all the information that a competitor needs. Confidential information is often given away without intent. For example, you may be very proud of where you work and the decisions made by management. As a result, you discuss this information with new acquaintances at a social event. When this happens, you never know where the information will be shared, with whom, and how it will be used. When it comes to sharing company information, use good judgment and discretion at all times.

COPE WITH CHANGE

People resist change because they want to continue to be in control of what is happening. They seem to have a natural inclination to do so. But changes do come in our lives, and they come sooner than we expect them. Changes in the office are brought about rapidly today because:

- Technology is being continually updated.
- Competition is now increased because companies are competing in a global marketplace.

Stop 'n Check

1. List any interpersonal skills you plan to improve.

    a. _____

    b. _____

    c. _____

2. Date you will assess your improvement: _____

- Businesses are **restructuring**—in other words, making changes within the organization to meet competition. They are restructuring by combining or eliminating functions and by **downsizing,** which means reducing staff by eliminating jobs and sometimes whole departments and divisions.

- Increased government involvement affects business activities.

Regardless of where you work, you will experience change. Anticipate change and realize it is a constant. Expect to use new equipment and new software, experience several new job assignments, and shift priorities during your career. Welcome change and view it positively. You will learn more about coping with change in Chapter 14.

Displaying Ethical Behavior

ETHICAL ★ ISSUES

Every office professional must display ethical behavior to be viewed as a professional. **Ethical behavior** is behavior that conforms to accepted professional standards of conduct. You learned in Chapter 1 that ethics are a system of deciding what is right, or more right, in a given situation. Ethics involve your values and what you believe to be the right way you should live your life; therefore, you behave in ways that display these values.

Many questionable employee practices are common in the workplace. Here are some examples of situations of questionable behavior:

- doing something unethical based on a request by your manager—for example, shredding documents

- altering information on documents

- not reporting incidents, such as accidents in a manufacturing company

Without rules, good ethical practice becomes ambiguous. Codes of ethical practice, as you learned in Chapter 1, are an increasingly popular tool for reducing that ambiguity. Codes of ethics can be effective depending on whether the organization supports them and how employees are treated when they break the code. In the end, as an employee you have the responsibility to do the right thing based upon your own judgment and personal principles. Additional information about ethical behavior will be discussed throughout the text.

Stop 'n Check

Identify two additional examples of unethical situations.

a. _____

b. _____

International Human Relations

If you should decide to work in an office in a country outside the United States, you have several things to consider. Among the questions you might ask yourself are the following:

- What general traits are expected of an overseas worker?

  You must be ready and willing to change, possess a sense of adventure, have a desire to be challenged, be open-minded, be patient, and above all, be flexible.

- What type of adaptation and coping skills must I possess?

  You must be emotionally stable, be able to cope with stress, be prepared for culture shock, have a sense of humor, and be observant and willing to make adjustments when needed.

- What intercultural communication skills must I possess?

  You must have tolerance, sensitivity, good listening skills, and good non-verbal skills, and you should possess a second language.

- What traits and skills must I possess personally to be effective in an office?

  You must be independent, self-reliant, resourceful, persistent, versatile, organized, loyal, and energetic. You must possess leadership skills, good verbal communication skills, and a commitment to working overseas.

- What skills will enable me to understand and appreciate different social and political cultures?

  Take the time to read articles on what is happening socially and politically in the country in which you are interested. Research the Internet to learn about the leaders, political parties in power, famous musicians, movie stars, and sports figures. Identify common customs for greetings, gift giving, and meetings. Locate the nearest U.S. consulate office to obtain current information for U.S. workers.

Professional and technical expertise alone is not enough when working overseas. You must embrace the characteristics listed previously to deal with problems of global survival. You could see many things you aren't used to, such as poverty, war, and ecological destruction. You must rely on your inner strength to continue to develop those human relations skills necessary to be successful when working in an international environment.

Quick Tips

ACKNOWLEDGE THE UNIQUE SPELLING OF A SUPERVISOR OR COWORKER'S NAME

- Make certain you know the correct spelling and pronunciation of coworkers', supervisors', and clients' names.

- In written correspondence—for example, on a "While You Were Out" note—use the accent mark; for instance, José González.

- When typing a document, use Microsoft® Word symbols. Go to Get Tech Wise toward the end of this chapter to practice using inserting accent marks and other symbols in Word.

Concept Review and Reinforcement

Review of Key Concepts

OUTCOME	CONCEPT
1. Describe the five basic workplace skills an office professional needs to be successful.	Research by the Secretary's Commission on Achieving Necessary Skills in 1991 identified these basic workplace skills as necessary to be successful in the workplace: • resources • information • systems • technology • interpersonal
2. Describe the basic knowledge skills an office professional needs in the workplace.	Basic skills such as reading, writing, performing mathematical operations, listening, and speaking are required to obtain any office job, along with these thinking skills: • creative thinking that generates new ideas • decision making that specifies goals and constraints, generates alternatives, considers risks, and evaluates and chooses best alternatives • problem solving that recognizes problems and devises and implements a plan of action • visualizing to organize and process symbols or other items • knowing how to learn to acquire and apply new knowledge and skills • reasoning to discover a rule or principle underlying the relationship between two or more objects and to apply it when solving a problem
3. Describe the ten personal qualities needed in the workplace.	Personal qualities are: 1. Be responsible. 2. Be dependable. 3. Be a self-starter. 4. Develop positive self-esteem. 5. Be sociable. 6. Exhibit self-management. 7. Display integrity/honesty. 8. Project a pleasant personality. 9. Show your human side. 10. Project a professional image.

4. Describe the eleven interpersonal skills needed in the workplace.

Interpersonal skills are:

1. Be a team player.
2. Recognize individual differences.
3. Learn to work with difficult people.
4. Teach others.
5. Offer exceptional customer service.
6. Exercise leadership.
7. Negotiate effectively.
8. Embrace constructive criticism.
9. Respect diversity.
10. Keep confidential information confidential.
11. Cope with change.

5. Describe how to display ethical behavior in the workplace.

Every office professional must display ethical behavior to be viewed as a professional.

6. List the human relations questions you should ask yourself before considering international employment.

- What general traits are expected of an overseas worker?
- What type of adaptation and coping skills must I possess?
- What intercultural communication skills must I possess?
- What traits and skills must I possess personally to be effective in an office?

Key Terms

Backstabber. Difficult coworker who tries to discredit colleagues by sharing and embellishing information he or she sought in private.

Basic knowledge skills. Reading, writing, performing mathematical operations, listening, and speaking.

Blamer. Difficult coworker who never solves his or her own problems; when faced with a problem, they think someone else should handle it—the supervisor, a group member, or you.

Bully. Difficult coworker who uses emotional manipulation to try to gain control by making others feel angry or afraid.

Constructive criticism. Process of offering one's opinion about the work of another in a friendly positive way.

Creative thinking. Thinking that generates new ideas.

Decision making. Thinking necessary to specify goals and constraints, generate alternatives, consider risks, and evaluate and choose best alternatives.

Dependability. Being consistent and reliable in your behavior.

Diversity. Variety of experiences and perspectives that arise from differences in race, culture, religion, mental or physical abilities, heritage, age, gender, sexual orientation, and other characteristics.

Downsizing. Reducing staff by eliminating jobs and sometimes whole departments and divisions.

Employability. Possessing the qualities and skills necessary to maintain employment.

Employment. Having a job.

Ethical behavior. Behavior that conforms to accepted professional standards of conduct.

Exceptional customer service. Helping customers, clients, or coworkers with a willingness to put their needs first to help resolve their problems.

Gossip. Difficult coworker who spreads negative rumors about others and tries to set one person against another.

Hard skills. Technical skills an office professional must possess to be successful in the workplace.

High self-esteem. A positive image of yourself; you need to be confident, to be sure of yourself, and to have a good attitude toward your ability to succeed.

Individual differences. Differences in personality types that office professionals must understand to help build a better working relationship or establish rapport with others.

Information. The many types of data office professionals must acquire, evaluate, organize, maintain, interpret, and communicate.

Integrity. Being honest, trustworthy, and sincere.

Interpersonal skills. Skills needed to interact effectively with others, including participating as a team member, interacting with customers, demonstrating leadership ability, negotiating agreements, and working with diversity.

Know-it-alls. Difficult coworkers who believe they are the experts on everything; they have opinions about everything, but when they are found to be wrong, they pass the buck or become defensive.

Knowing how to learn. Using efficient learning techniques to acquire and apply new knowledge and skills.

Leadership. Communicating clearly, persuading others, and challenging policies or procedures when necessary.

Low self-esteem. A negative view of how others see you, your strengths and weaknesses, your social status, or your ability to be independent, any one of which results in a poor self-image.

Negotiating. Exchanging ideas, information, and opinions with others to work toward agreements to formulate policies and programs and/or arrive jointly at decisions, conclusions, or solutions.

Personal qualities. Critical thinking, problem solving, dependability, responsibility, cooperativeness, and honesty.

Personality. Who you are, the sum of all your mental, physical, and emotional experiences.

Problem solving. Thinking that enables one to recognize problems and devices and implement a plan of action.

Professionalism. Aspiring to meet the highest standards possible your profession expects rather than a set of minimum requirements.

Reasoning. A type of thinking that allows one to discover a rule or principle underlying the relationship between two or more objects and apply it to solve a problem.

Resources. Examples of resources are time, money, material, facilities, and human resource management.

Responsibility. Being entrusted with or assigned a duty to perform.

Restructuring. Making changes within the organization to meet competition.

Self-esteem. The opinion you have of yourself.

Self-management. Setting personal goals, monitoring your progress, assessing yourself accurately, and exhibiting self-control.

Self-starter Taking the initiative to begin a task for which you are responsible.

Sociability. Demonstrating understanding, friendliness, adaptability, empathy, and politeness in group settings.

Soft skills. Personal qualities such as critical thinking, problem solving, dependability, responsibility, cooperativeness, and honesty and interpersonal skills such as participating as a team member, interacting with customers, demonstrating leadership ability, negotiating agreements, and respecting diversity.

Teamwork. Collaboration with another employee(s) assigned a task or goal which the team must complete by working together to arrive at a solution or recommendation.

Technology. Practical application of knowledge, often used today to refer to automation and electronic devices; office professionals should know how to select procedures, tools, or equipment, including computers and related technologies.

Thinking skills. The degree to which a person can use these skills to arrive at a decision or viable solution.

Visualizing. A type of thinking that enables one to organize and process symbols or other items.

For Your Discussion

Retrieve file C2-DQ from your student data disk. Remember to save your file by keying your last name before the filename to avoid overwriting the original file.

DIRECTIONS

Enter your response after each question or statement.

1. List the five basic workplace skills an office professional needs to be successful, and explain why each is important.

2. List the six basic knowledge skills an office professional needs, and explain why each is important.

3. Explain why soft skills are important to your success in today's office.

4. How does a person acquire responsibility? Dependability? Positive self-esteem?

5. Explain what is meant by the statement, "Remain in control of your reactions."

6. How can you accept constructive criticism?

7. Explain why interpersonal skills are important to your success in today's office.

8. Discuss the various types of diversity and why they are important.

9. What would you do if your manager's business practices seemed unethical to you?

10. Explain what you think would be your greatest barrier to overcome if you chose to work overseas.

Building Your Office Skills

Exploring the Workplace: *Activities*

1. As a group or an individual project, interview a person who works in a human resources department. Your objective is to obtain a list of personal qualities and interpersonal skills the company would expect of an entry-level office assistant. Create a set of questions in advance. Develop your questions carefully. As you ask your questions, be sure to inquire about problems encountered and what skills employees need to resolve each problem. Do not limit your questions to the ideas given here. Key each question followed by the response in your report to the class or to the instructor.

2. Think of someone whose personality you admire. Make a list of this person's personality traits you like, and then select the most outstanding traits and describe them in detail. Decide why these traits appeal to you. Do you think these traits would appeal to others? If instructed, share your list with another class member and compare the traits. Write a memorandum to your instructor or share your ideas with the class.

3. Read three articles on criticism in such periodicals as *Psychology Online Journal* (www.psychjournal.com) or a journal such as *Management Today* concerning the following topics:

   a. How to deal with criticism when you know it is justified

   b. How to deal with criticism when you know it is questionable

   c. How to control your emotions

   d. How to deal with unjust criticism

   Write a memorandum to your instructor or share your ideas with the class. Staple a copy of each article to your memorandum. Be sure to include each URL or journal citation.

4. Read three articles about diversity in the workplace concerning age, religion, gender, etc., where state or federal laws have been violated. Use such sources as *Business Week, Management Today,* or *The Wall Street Journal.*

   a. Write a memorandum to your instructor or share your ideas with the class. Identify for each article the diversity issue, what law was broken, and what were the consequences.

   b. Attach a copy of each article to the memorandum. Be sure to include each URL or journal citation.

Developing Critical Thinking Skills: *Problem Solving on the Job*

Retrieve file C2-OJS from your student data disk.

Directions

Enter your response after each situation.

1. **Keeping information confidential.** You are an administrative assistant in the purchasing department. Another administrative assistant, Joan Lopez, is getting married in three weeks. The purchasing department employs twelve office workers, two of whom are administrative assistants. According to a rumor, Joan is not coming back to work after the wedding, and two of the office workers want to apply for the position. They have come to you to find out if the rumor is true. You have not seen an official announcement about Joan's employment plans after she gets married. However, Joan did tell you that she does not plan to come back to work after the wedding. What should you say to your two coworkers?

2. **Working in teams.** You wanted to take your vacation during the last week in November, but you did not request it because Robert Lawson, who fills in for you when you are absent, had already requested vacation during the same week. Yesterday Robert canceled his vacation for November because his personal plans fell through. The vacation schedule is approved six months in advance, but you still would like to take vacation during the last week of November. Today is November 15. Your team is working on a huge project that must be completed by November 30. Someone would have to finish your part of the project and the staff is short. Are you justified in making this request now? Explain why you think you are or are not justified in making this request.

3. **Working with a difficult coworker.** You work with Dillan. Dillan is difficult to work with because of his negative attitude toward everything—his personal life, his relationships, his job, and his supervisor. Dillan rarely makes a positive statement about anything or anyone. You are beginning to have negative feelings too. You like your work and your supervisor, and you

can see there will be opportunities for advancement in this position. Analyze the situation. Your objective is to overcome your negative feelings toward Dillan. Outline a specific plan for working with Dillan using the following steps given to resolve the problem. Key each step followed by your response.

a. Gather all the information about the problem.

b. Determine what you know about the problem already that might be helpful in forming a solution.

c. Determine if more information is needed and where to get it.

d. Outline all possible solutions without regard to cost or practicality at this point.

e. Analyze each solution, discarding those you know are unworkable and narrow your choices to two or three solutions.

f. Identify the pros and cons for each solution.

g. Select the best solution among the choices.

4. **Discrimination.** You have been selected to serve on the interview committee to narrow the list of applicants down to five for the vacant office manager position. You and your committee members have reviewed twenty applicant files. During the discussion to select the five finalists to be interviewed further, Aida, one of the committee members, made the comment that even though older applicants often have lots of experience, they are usually difficult to work with and have their way of doing things, not to mention that they might not be with the company very long because of their age. Aida suggested the committee might discuss an age limit for the applicants to help eliminate the ones everyone thought would fall in this category. Everyone laughed but you. No one took Aida seriously; therefore, the subject was dropped. What harm does a comment such as this do? Discuss what you think the committee should have done about this comment, if anything.

Using the Web: *Research Activities*

A. You are to search the Internet to locate information on personality assessment for a presentation you must make at your local Association of Administrative Professionals (IAAP) meeting next month. You are to create an outline of your presentation using word processing. You will not be asked to create the presentation using presentation software.

1. In your browser's search box, enter *personal+ assessment*.

2. Refine your search if needed by using the following key search words: *personality+types*.

3. Print any articles you believe will help you prepare your outline.

4. Develop an outline of your presentation.

5. Make certain you give credit to your sources by identifying the URLs used. Attach the printed copies from the sources you used to your outline.

B. Go to the National Association for Self-Esteem Web site and take the "Self-Guided Tour" (www.self-esteem-nas.org.) Be sure to read the instructions. Make sure you read the "Self-Esteem Enhancers," shown to the right of each question. Write a memo to your instructor explain the pros and cons of taking this tour. Identify the most important thing you learned from this experience.

Get Tech Wise: *Inserting Accent Marks in Languages*

Follow these steps to use Microsoft® Word Symbols to enter the accent mark:

1. Open to a blank document screen and type the word *Espanol* (meaning Spanish).

2. Position your cursor where you need the accented character. Position the cursor in front of the *n*. Delete the *n*.

3. Click on the Insert menu and select Symbol.

4. On the Symbols tab, select (normal text) in the Font text box.

5. Using the scroll bar, scroll through the symbols until you find the accented character you need. Locate the character *n* with the tilde over it: *ñ*.

6. Click on the Insert button, and then click on the Close button.

7. The accented letter should be inserted into your word.

If you plan to use the accented word many times, you can save the name with the accent and omit having to repeat the steps each time you want to use the word.

1. Select the word you just typed that contains the accented letter.

2. Click on the Edit menu and select Copy.

3. Click on the Tools menu and select AutoCorrect Options.

4. On the AutoCorrect tab, in the Replace text box type the name using plain text.

5. Press the Tab key to jump to the With text box.

6. Press the Ctrl+V keys to insert the "accented" name if it is not already there.

7. Click on the Add button, and then click on OK.

The next time you type *Jose,* for instance, it will automatically change to José. Practice entering accent marks in the following names:

José (Spanish for Joseph)

Estéban (Spanish for Stephen)

Adélaïde (French for Adelaide)

'Aziz (Arabic for powerful or beloved)

Dàibhidh (Scottish for David)

Niño (Spanish for child)

Improving Your Writing Skills: *Punctuation Workshop*

Retrieve file C2-WRKS from your student data disk.

Simulation: *In the Office at Supreme Appliances*

Application 2-A

Remember to save your file by keying your last name before the filename to avoid overwriting the original file.

Diversity Self-Assessment

Supplies needed: E-mail from Human Resources Department (see following); Form 2-A, Diversity Self-Assessment. This form is in your working papers.

Directions

Ms. Quevedo supports employees learning about diversity and has asked you to attend this workshop. Please complete the Diversity Self-Assessment as requested by Human Resources.

Supreme Appliances Memorandum

To: All Employees

From: Human Resource Department

Subject: Diversity Self-Assessment

Date: (Current)

To continue our ongoing Employee Training Program, we are offering you the opportunity to attend a workshop on "Diversity in the Workplace." The workshop will be held November 30 in Room 116 from 4 to 5 p.m. Please complete the following self-assessment and bring it with you to the workshop.

Application 2-B

Interpersonal Skills Self-Assessment

Supplies needed: E-mail from Human Resources Department (see following); Form 2-B, Interpersonal Skills Self-Assessment. This form is in your forms packet.

Directions

Your manager has supported you through your internship. She believes you will benefit from attending this workshop and has asked you to complete the Interpersonal Skills Self-Assessment. Evaluate each statement and then enter an S (strong), an A (average), or an I (needs improvement) in the Assessment column. As your manager and mentor, Ms. Quevedo would like to discuss the results of the self-assessment with you before the workshop.

Supreme Appliances Memorandum

To: All Employees

From: Human Resource Department

Subject: Self-Assessment Inventory

Date: (Current)

You are invited to attend our Employee Training Workshop entitled "Improving your Interpersonal Skills." These particular interpersonal traits and skills you will learn about are emphasized as critical for success in a technological environment. We will discuss them at our next meeting.

Application 2-C

Measuring Your Soft Skills IQ

Supplies needed: Form 2-C, Measuring Your Soft Skills IQ. This form is in your working papers.

Directions

To continue your on-the-job training as an intern for Supreme Appliances, complete the Measuring Your Soft Skills IQ self-assessment.

Application 2-D

Risk-Taking Self-Assessment

Supplies needed: Form 2-D, Risking-Taking Assessment. This form is in your working papers.

Directions

While working as an intern, you have learned about the many individual differences based on different personality types. People who are risk takers desire situations that involve thrill seeking. The decisions they make because of this propensity can affect their performance on the job. This assessment stresses the importance of individual differences on the job and helps you identify your comfort level with risk taking. Some examples are death-defying, others are only slightly risky. Let's see how close or far you are from death-defying.

Building Your Portfolio

With the help of a team member or your instructor's help, select the following documents: Diversity Self-Assessment, Interpersonal Skills Self-Assessment, Measuring Your Soft Skills IQ, and the Risk-Taking Assessment. Remember these documents must be error-free. If instructed, place the documents in plastic protection sheets and add to your portfolio.

3 Preparing for Your Job Search

chapter **outline**

learning **outcomes**

When you have completed this chapter, you should be able to:

- Identify sources for locating employment opportunities.
- Complete a self-assessment inventory.
- Describe the significance of practicing ethical behavior during the job search.
- Prepare a resume.
- Prepare a cover letter.
- Complete an employment application form.
- Prepare for an interview.
- Compose the following letters: thank-you, reminder, inquiry, acceptance, and refusal.
- Apply decision-making skills to the job search process.

Few office support positions are protected from corporate restructuring, downsizing, and layoffs. Therefore, it is important to plan an effective job campaign.

Search for a position that matches your qualifications, personality, and interests. Your administrative career should be rewarding both monetarily and in terms of job satisfaction and opportunities for promotion.

The first part of your job search should be your decision about where you want to work—the geographic area and the type of business. Unless you have specialized in the legal or medical field, do not limit yourself to seeking a position in a specific department, such as marketing, human resources, accounting, or sales. Remain open to opportunities; often, getting your foot in the door is the first step to gaining experience and eventually getting the position you really want.

Your office skills are transferable. Often the same basic skills are required in different departments; therefore, never limit your opportunities by expressing interest in working only for one department. Instead, express interest in working for the organization. Let the interviewer know you are flexible and willing to adjust to the needs of the position. The interviewer will strive to match you to a position that will meet the needs of the company and maximize your talents.

Start your job campaign several months before graduation or keep alert to any reorganization plans in your company. As soon as you decide where you want to work, make a job prospect list, using the sources listed in this chapter. Next, prepare your self-appraisal inventory and your resume, write your cover letter, and make a list of the qualifications you plan to emphasize during job interviews. After you launch your campaign, keep searching until you find the right position for you.

Locating Job Prospects

Some of the sources for prospects are the Internet, the college placement office, the yellow pages, private and public employment agencies, government service announcements, chambers of commerce, newspapers, and your network of friends and associates.

Use all of these sources, not just one, to locate job leads. Once you begin your campaign, continue the process. Be persistent in checking up and following through on what is available for someone with your qualifications and interests.

NETWORKS

In planning an approach to meeting and connecting with others for mutual benefit, consider networking. Put in simple terms, **networking** means exchanging information. The more information you give, the more information you usually get back. If you have information and are willing to share it, you will be viewed as a valuable person to have on staff.

During the job hunt, networking is an essential step toward gaining successful employment. Sharing employment information with a network of people is probably one of the most effective methods of obtaining employment.

- You can begin to build your network by discussing your employment goal with your instructors and with businesspeople among your friends and family. Keep in touch with these people as you move through your course work; they may provide employment opportunities.

- Attend functions such as job/career fairs, where prospective employers will be available to meet students.

- Attend and participate in seminars and other functions where office administrators and assistants will be present. By expressing your keen desire for employment and by leaving a positive impression, you will be increasing your opportunity to learn about possible employment opportunities.

When your contacts give you job leads, follow through on them. Then let the person who told you about the lead know the results. This is a simple courtesy and a way of thanking the person for his or her assistance.

To be a good networker, you must be a good listener. By applying your best listening skills you will collect accurate information. This, in the long run, may save you time and effort in your job search. By listening to the needs of other networkers, you will be able to offer them greater assistance. In this way, you will be viewed as a valuable network partner. As previously stated, the more information you provide others, the more people will reciprocate.

Networking is a developed skill that will help enhance your life and your career. It will increase your ability to be employed and to advance in your career.

The following are suggestions for improving your networking skills.

- If you are employed or have recently been employed, choose a corporate mentor. A corporate **mentor** usually holds a position at a higher level than yours. This person can offer you information and advice about the organization and give you career direction.

- Never limit your contacts by missing an opportunity to meet new people. Your network may include business associates, friends, neighbors, past graduates from your college, relatives, and many other groups of people. A network should become a vast chain of information. The more effort you put into networking, the more the network will expand, and the greater your chances of career success.

- Make yourself visible. Becoming a leader of a professional organization or volunteering to serve on a committee will open networking doors.

- Increase your reading of business materials. Remember that information is power and reading will build your information base.

CAMPUS CAREER DEVELOPMENT CENTERS

Most colleges maintain a career development office to assist their students in making contacts for jobs. At the beginning of your job campaign, register with the career office. Complete the information required, placing your name on the active file with the center.

The center staff keeps up-to-date on employment opportunities. They arrange for company representatives to conduct interviews on campus and to offer job fairs. The center maintains a list of job openings prepared from the requests of companies, searching for prospective employees.

Watch for the announcement of forthcoming campus interviews; call the center to schedule interviews if needed. Be sure to prepare for the interview and to keep the appointment. The campus interview is discussed later in this chapter. Your career advisor will be able to help direct you in locating the most recent information regarding your career search, industry profiles, and a directory of employers interested in hiring college graduates.

JOB FAIRS

Job fairs, sometimes called *career fairs*, are held on college campuses for entry-level positions or internships, in hotels and auditoriums for others who are seeking a position, and online. Their purpose is to attract your attention and "sell" you on the companies as potential employers. Most fairs are offered free of charge to job seekers; however, in some cases, where career sessions, such as setting goals and time management, are held, a small fee may be required.

Job fairs provide excellent opportunities for you to network with other people who may be interested in finding a new or different position or exploring options in other areas. Fairs at your campus career development centers are open to current students, alumni, and anyone in the community. Many of the companies that participate in job fairs are interested in visiting with you as they probably have job openings or anticipate job openings in the near future.

BUSINESS NEWS ITEMS

Read the business news in the newspaper in the area where you plan to seek employment for at least a month before you apply for a job. Search for news about established companies that are relocating their offices to your area or opening a branch; established businesses that are moving their offices to new buildings or expanding at their present sites; newly formed companies; and companies that are merging. Any changes within companies may indicate career opportunities.

When you find a news item of interest to you, clip it and save it. It should provide you with the complete name, type of business, location, and possibly the opening date of a new office.

The number of office professionals who move to another city when a company relocates is small compared to the number of executives who transfer to the new location. Therefore, you can expect that any organization that has relocated its offices to another city will be hiring office staff.

A local organization often adds new personnel when it moves its offices to a new location. Such a move often happens because more space is needed to conduct current operations and the company cannot add personnel until it can provide space for them. A company that is expanding its operations often needs additional office personnel. A new organization will need someone in the office as soon as it opens and will add personnel to keep pace with the organization's growth.

DIRECT APPLICATION

Often, the best jobs are not advertised. Many organizations prefer to select their employees from applicants who take the initiative to come to them seeking employment. Do not wait for a job to come to you; it probably will not. Take the initiative to search for a position. Decide where you want to work, and apply. Call the organization and arrange for an appointment with the person in charge of hiring office staff.

Be optimistic. Some of the organizations on your prospective list may not be seeking administrative assistants at this time, but an impressive contact may put you in line for a future opportunity. If an opening for the position you are seeking does not exist, ask the human resources representative to place your resume on file.

If you decide to work in a particular business but do not have a specific company in mind, refer to the yellow pages, which provide local business listings. For example, if you are interested in working for an advertising company, look up *Advertising*; there you will find the names and addresses of the local advertising companies.

STAFFING SERVICES

Openings for positions as office workers are listed with both public and private employment agencies. The state-supported employment offices and the United States Employment Service list openings for all kinds of work—industrial, commercial, and professional. The services are free to the job seeker and the employer. However, the number of jobs listed with a public employment office sometimes is not representative of the openings in the community.

State employment offices generally give a proficiency test in keyboarding and frequently a spelling and vocabulary test to office support applicants. To register with a state employment office, go to the office and fill out an application form. Most likely you will be able to take the tests and be interviewed during your initial trip to the office. If an opening is listed for someone with your skills and work experience, you will be sent to the prospective employer for an interview. After you have registered with a state employment office, check regularly to find out about openings.

Many private staffing agencies do not charge the applicant a fee for their service. In a number of circumstances, however, the prospective employer pays these fees. You can ask private staffing agencies, such as OfficeTeam (www.officeteam.com) and Manpower (www.manpower.com), about the services they offer without being obligated to sign a contract. If you do register with a private staffing agency, study the contract thoroughly and ask questions before you sign.

Most private staffing agencies give excellent service. They administer tests, advise applicants on their appearance, conduct thorough interviews, and carry out a complete job hunt for each applicant. A staffing agency charges a company a placement fee only if the applicant accepts a job obtained through the agency's effort. Therefore, private staffing agencies make a real effort to refer applicants to jobs for which they are qualified and which they are likely to accept.

FEDERAL GOVERNMENT EMPLOYMENT

If you are interested in securing employment with the federal government or in transferring from one federal job to another, you will find many, many opportunities.

Visit or call the Federal Employment Information Center (FEIC) in the area you are seeking employment. Also check the Web site (www.usajobs.opm.gov) for updated job vacancy listings. Request the following information:

- announcements of specific types of jobs
- a list of local government agencies
- application forms

In contacting regional and local agency personnel offices, take the following steps:

1. Request agency career opportunities brochures.
2. Talk with the agency human resources office and request job announcements and information on special hiring programs.
3. Obtain local government field office phone numbers from your telephone directory. Look under "U.S. Government," generally found in the blue pages. Visit your local library and review these publications:

   The Federal Career Directory. If your library doesn't have this publication, check with a local college placement office. This directory provides an agency description and lists typical entry-level positions, agency contacts, student employment programs, and so on.

   The Occupational Outlook Quarterly. This book, published by the U.S. Department of Labor, Bureau of Labor Statistics, is a highly informational quarterly publication that highlights employment trends and features interesting career articles.

Tests are required for specific groups, including office professional workers and air traffic control personnel, and for certain entry-level jobs. The majority, approximately 80 percent, of government jobs are filled through a competitive examination of your background, work experience, and education, not through a written test.

NEWSPAPER ADVERTISEMENTS

The career sections and help-wanted columns of newspapers are valuable sources for job openings. The jobs will be listed under a variety of headings, such as administrative assistant, office assistant, administrative secretary, executive assistant, and information specialist.

- By studying career sections and help-wanted ads, you will gain valuable information about trends in employment opportunities, salary ranges, and qualifications required. Study the ads in newspapers early in your job campaign.

- When you answer a help-wanted ad, be prompt. Reply the same day, if possible, or at least by the next day. Remember that newspapers are widely read and that looking in them for available jobs requires less effort than other search techniques. It follows that the competition will be very high for jobs posted in newspapers.

- Follow instructions. If a telephone number is given, call for an appointment. If a post office box number is given, submit your resume. Many advertisements request that applicants submit resumes by mail, fax, or e-mail and clearly state they do not want applicants to call. If this is the case, follow the instructions. You risk irritating the employer if you ignore the request for no telephone calls. Of course, it's always more proactive and shows a sense of initiative to telephone the employer and to drop off your resume in person. These techniques should be part of your strategy unless the employer has requested otherwise.

Office Support Help Wanted

Executive Assistant to the City Engineer

Engineering is one of the city's major departments. As Department Head, the City Engineer requires an administrative assistant who has excellent communication and critical thinking skills, is a team player, and who can give support by performing technical and administrative tasks quickly and accurately.

Duties include preparing for and arranging meetings, taking meeting notes, composing correspondence, and assisting the City Engineer with administrative tasks. The ability to train junior office staff and to be an office team leader are desirable. There is frequent contact with private executives, professionals, and senior government officials. The diverse duties and responsibilities of this position allow considerable latitude for personal initiative and growth.

The successful applicant will have achieved a post-secondary certificate or degree in office administration and will have superior skills in word processing, database management, spreadsheet, presentation, and desktop publishing.

Salary will be commensurate with training and experience. A full benefit package is offered.

For an appointment, call 506-363-1893.

Receptionist/Bookkeeper

We need an enthusiastic, energetic, and organized assistant to perform general office duties. Experience and training in bookkeeping is required. Bring your resume to 1609 Northfield Road.

CPA Firm

Small CPA firm requires an enthusiastic graduate of an office administration program to create correspondence and financial statements using word processing and spreadsheet skills. Candidate must be able to assume general office duties and work well on a team. Salary negotiable. To apply, call L. Rossin at 506-444-7894.

Office Assistant

Required by small sales office. Responsibilities include bookkeeping and payroll. Applicants must have Microsoft Office skills, organizational skills, and initiative. Reply to Box AM654.

Word Processing

Trained and experienced in word processing; need temp. and perm. positions. Contact J. Johnson, 315-598-2306.

FIGURE 3-1 • Sample newspaper ads.

- Always study the advertisement carefully to determine all the stated qualifications and then submit a cover letter and resume showing that you meet all the qualifications for the job. Follow the suggestions for writing a solicited cover letter discussed in the section on cover letters later in this chapter. See Figure 3-1 for sample newspaper ads.

Blind Advertisements

Newspaper recruitment advertisements either give the name and address of a company or person to contact or are **blind advertisements** giving a post office box number or a telephone number. When blind ads are used in a legitimate fashion, it is generally because the organization wishes to avoid having to interview a large number of unqualified applicants. For example, say the local National Hockey League team requires an administrative assistant. If the team advertises its name in the newspaper, it will receive a flood of applicants, many of whom are unqualified but apply because of their desire to work for celebrities. A simple advertisement that lists the responsibilities of the position, the desired qualifications, and a post office box number is more likely to attract those who are legitimately interested in performing the advertised responsibilities.

Scrutinize blind advertisements carefully. Sometimes they are used for purposes other than recruitment for employment, such as preparing a mailing list of prospective purchasers. If you receive a telephone call in response to a reply to a blind advertisement, ask for the name of the company and ask some questions about the job during the telephone conversation to be sure the job advertised is legitimate.

PROSPECTS IN OTHER GEOGRAPHIC AREAS

To begin your search for job opportunities in other geographic areas, do the following:

1. Conduct research on the Web by entering www.companyname.com. Examples are www.microsoft.com or www.jcpenney.com.
2. Inquire at the local public library for the telephone directory and the newspapers for the city in which you are seeking employment.
3. Write, e-mail, or fax the chamber of commerce in the desired geographic area.
4. Visit the campus career development center. Ask a staff member to help you identify prospects in the city where you will be relocating.

The telephone directory for the city where you want to relocate will be an excellent source of information. Many telephone directories can be found online; however, you may have to subscribe to those directories. Your public library has telephone directories for a number of cities, and large public libraries have telephone directories from all the major U.S. cities. Public libraries have the directories either in paper version or online. Public libraries also subscribe to many newspapers from other cities.

To find what your public library has on file that will be helpful to you, call the library and ask for Information Service. The librarian can answer your specific questions concerning what telephone directories and newspapers are available. You may be able to obtain the addresses of a few companies from the librarian by telephone.

When you write to a chamber of commerce, state your employment goal and ask about opportunities in your field in the geographic area. If the

Stop 'n Check

1. If you were interested in looking for a new position, which three sources cited in this section would you use? Why?

   a. _____

   b. _____

   c. _____

2. How could a blind advertisement work to your disadvantage?

   _____

3. Suppose you and your family were moving to another city within your state. Identify at least two sources you may use to locate potential employment opportunities in the new city.

   a. _____

   b. _____

chamber of commerce sends you a list of prospective employers, realize that the list is limited to chamber of commerce members.

Ethical Issues in the Job Search

ETHICAL☆ISSUES

As you learned in Chapter 1, businesses define their rules or principles in a formal document called the code of ethics that states the primary values and ethical rules they expect employees to follow. Their rules and principles define right or wrong conduct.

Suppose you read an employment ad and you believe you have all the qualifications advertised. However, the ad mentions the need for specific experience. Although you do not have experience in the area mentioned in the ad, you feel you can do the job. After all, you believe you are a quick learner. The action you choose will determine your success. Based on your values and beliefs, study the following options:

- **Option 1:** Move to the next employment ad. Because you don't have the required experience, you don't qualify for the position.
- **Option 2:** Create false experiences and apply for the position. You can just make something up. After all, the last company you worked for isn't in business anymore.
- **Option 3:** Take a chance and apply for the position. In the interview process, you can emphasize you have related skills and share how you can apply those skills to the position.

Let's consider the options above. In the first option, you may be missing a great opportunity. Although you lack the specified experience, you may have related skills. Be prepared to assess your skills and share how you can apply related skills to the experience needed. You can proceed as Option 3 shows. The worst that can happen is that your resume would be rejected. The best that can happen is the prospective employer will see your potential and decide experience is not as important as initiative.

In Option 2, you are the loser. Adding false or misrepresenting information is never a good idea. Misrepresentation of information has a way of "snowballing."

Stop 'n Check

1. What are some consequences of "stretching" the truth or falsifying or misrepresenting information about your skills? Experience? Education?

   a. _____

   b. _____

2. If employers verify employment, education, and duties performed, why would a candidate misrepresent information?

   a. _____

   b. _____

Preparing Employment Documents

The resume, cover letter, and job interview are the applicant's direct contacts with prospective employers. The following discussion will provide you with methods of making all three more persuasive and effective.

RESUMES

A **resume** sometimes called *vitae,* is a summary of an applicant's qualifications for the position being sought. Your resume should answer key questions:

- who you are
- what type of job you are seeking
- what qualifications you offer
- what experience you offer

Using Resume Software

Resume software companies advertise their products in magazines and in computer stores and on the Web. If you access the Web and enter key search words such as *resume software* or *resume maker*, you will find several resume products. Most of these software products are designed to:

- guide you through the entire writing process from beginning to end, providing tips, examples, and action words
- format your information into a professional resume style
- provide help in writing cover letter and follow-up communications, such as thank-you and acceptance letters
- submit your resume to major career Web sites in a clear and readable format, rather than garbled or in an e-mail attachment that can't be opened

You may want to practice using one of the software programs. If so, be certain that your finished documents are grammatically correct and free of errors in spelling, punctuation, and capitalization. In lieu of using a resume software program, you can learn how to write an effective resume in the following paragraphs.

Resume Styles

All resumes should be personalized; however, a few formats offer an attractive and easy-to-read document for potential employers. The style and benefits of these resumes follow. Because the chronological resume is usually the style preferred by employers, it is featured in Figure 3-2.

Chronological Resume. The **chronological resume** format arranges your work experience and education so the most recent information is presented first. The chronological resume has many advantages: it is the preferred resume for employers because it is easy to follow and shows exactly what the applicant has done, not what the applicant thinks he or she can do. This format is especially important when the applicant has an impressive work or educational history. This format works well for recent graduates because it emphasizes their education and also identifies previous work experience responsibilities that relate to the position being sought.

Joseph McIntyre
61 Dorset Drive
Fairport, NY 14450
(518) 586-3372
jmcintyre@yahoo.com

Efficient office assistant with five years' experience; proven ability to demonstrate organizational skills; accomplished as a problem solver with interpersonal skills.

Experience

January 2002–present Office Assistant, William Construction Corporation, Pittsford, NY

Conduct training for telephone system with 8 lines and handle telephone with 2 lines; follow mail procedures; maintain records; handle correspondence; use Microsoft Office software applications; support two project managers.

December 1999–2001 Office Assistant, Robbins-Smith Engineering Company, Rochester, NY

Handled correspondence; used Microsoft Office software applications; billed customers; handled bank transactions; ordered and maintained office supplies inventory; created desk manual for position

Education

Associate in Applied Science degree, Office Administration, Monroe Community College

Special Skills

Microsoft Office Specialist (MOS) certified in Word and Excel
Proficient in Access and PowerPoint
Intermediate user in Microsoft Project
Proficient in Spanish
Coordinator of office staff monthly seminars
Designer of brochures and newsletters

May 1996—May 1999
Administrative Assistant
Image Publishers
Portland
Supervisor of reception desk
Coordinator of media
Coordinator of annual company picnic

FIGURE 3-2 • Chronological resume.

Annette M. Jacobson
1565 Ponderosa Street
Dallas, TX 75244 (214) 620-7238
amjacobs@comcast.com

Administrative assistant with seven years' experience; supervised office functions and directed office support staff.

Skills

Keyboarding speed: 80 words per minute.

Word processing: Both on-the-job and classroom experience in using Microsoft Word and WordPerfect; designing newsletters and brochures; labels and posters

Communications: Three years' experience in customer service via telephone; ability to compose letters and reports; take meeting notes

Organizational ability: Organized eight seminars for in-house training within a two-year period; set up a new records management system

Supervision: Supervised office support staff for three years

Other: Proficient in Microsoft Word, Excel, Access, and PowerPoint

Work Experience

April 2000–present Administrative Assistant, Wilson Products, Dallas, TX
January 1997–March 2000 Executive Secretary, Fairfield Oil Company, Oklahoma City, OK

Education

Bachelor of Science degree, Administrative Management, University of Oklahoma

FIGURE 3-3 • Functional resume.

Functional Resume. The **functional resume** is designed to point to the applicant's skills, abilities, and accomplishments. Refer to Figure 3-3. If you have never been employed, the functional resume works well. A functional resume gives you an opportunity to emphasize leadership and organizational experience indicating that you will be a productive employee. A person who has not been employed but has acquired comparable work experience through volunteering and day-to-day living can also prepare a functional resume. In this style of resume, the experience section is organized by functions, without reference to the time of the performance or to a specific organization.

Targeted Resume. The **targeted resume** format focuses on the applicant's achievements and abilities that relate only to a specific position. The disadvantage of this style is applicants need new resumes for every job application.

Purpose of the Resume

A resume is intended to obtain an interview. It should be mailed, e-mailed, faxed, or personally delivered with a one-page cover letter. As soon as your resume opens the door for a job interview, it has served its purpose. Whether you are offered the position will depend on your qualifications and how well you project your knowledge, abilities, and personality during the interview.

Office professionals, including administrative assistants, executive assistants, and office assistants, with excellent skills in interpersonal communication as well as written communications and software applications such as word processing, spreadsheets, and databases are in demand in many areas of the United States. According to many employers of office staff, the most highly desired attribute is excellent communication skills, including verbal and written communications. An attractive, informative, and accurate resume that accents these skills will help you get the position you desire.

Self-Appraisal Inventory

As a preliminary step to preparing a resume, decide exactly what your qualifications are. Prepare a detailed **self-appraisal inventory** of your educational background, work experience, and personal qualities and interests so you will know exactly what assets you have to offer an employer.

To prepare your inventory chart, record all the data you think might help you in your job search. Use separate sheets of paper to list your education and training, work history, personal qualities, and interests. Include everything as you make your list; record items in any order and rearrange them later, deleting any items that may not be relevant to the position you seek.

Under *Education*, list the following:

1. the highest degree, license, or certificate (list first)
2. any special courses that may support your employment hunt
3. your technical skills, including computer and software training, and the ability to operate any additional equipment
4. school activities that suggest organizational, team, and leadership skills

Under Work History, list all your jobs, including part-time, summer, and volunteer work. Be sure to include work experience that was unrelated to office work. For each job, give the name and address of the organization, your job title, the details of your duties, the dates of your employment, and accomplishments.

Under Personal Qualities, list your strengths, such as initiative, leadership, ability to organize, and willingness to learn and participate in a team. Discuss these qualities when you write your cover letter.

Under Interests, list your hobbies and special talents and the ways you spend your leisure time.

Points of Emphasis

Organize your resume so that the interviewer will grasp your most important qualifications if he or she reads only the first line of each section of your resume. Prepare a one-page resume, or put the most essential data on the first page. Here are tips to follow:

- Many employment consultants emphasize preparing a brief resume. Although some advocate a one-page resume, this is rarely enough space to include the critical facts. As your experience and education expand, so must your resume. Most applicants for office administrative work should have resumes no longer than two pages.
- Indicate the type of position you are seeking in the Objective section.
- Decide whether your work experience or your education will be most persuasive and then place that section immediately after the Objective section.
- To highlight your education, list your most recent experience first. It is often helpful to list key courses that relate to the employment opportunity. For the office professional, this often means software or skills-oriented courses.
- Be consistent; just as you listed your education, arrange your work experience by listing the most recent employment first, followed by other employment.

Suggested Outline for a Chronological Resume

The resumes of two applicants should not be identical, but effective resumes tend to follow a recognizable pattern. Plan your resume so it presents all your qualifications and highlights your strongest points. Review the format shown in Figure 3-2.

A resume is a list; it is not necessary to write complete sentences. Use lists to describe duties, skills, or accomplishments. A common error in listing items in resumes is the use of inconsistent verb forms. In writing bullet items, use parallel construction. For example:

Unparallel Construction of Items
- Keying documents
- Manage electronic databases
- Plan meetings and conferences

Parallel Construction of Items
- *Keying* documents
- *Managing* databases
- *Planning* meetings and conferences

Avoid using "I" statements, such as "I created the monthly department's newsletter." The statement should be written as "Created monthly department's newsletter." A resume contains facts only. Statements that reveal philosophy or opinion may be used in the cover letter but not in the resume.

Heading. In the heading, include your name, address, telephone number, fax number, and e-mail address. If you have a temporary address, provide a permanent mailing address to ensure that you receive any documentation sent to you. Use a telephone number with an answering system so you will not miss any important calls from potential employers.

Job Objective. In the Objective section, state the type of position you are seeking and the name of the company with which you are seeking employment. Write the full name of the organization. Using the name of the company in the resume shows that the resume was specially prepared. Here is an example of an effective objective:

> To work as an administrative assistant with Cabott Industries.

Some authorities agree that the strongest points may be summarized under a category called Skills Summary. For example,

> Efficient administrative assistant with four years' experience. Proven ability to train and direct staff. Successful record in management of three six-month projects, development of training programs, and installation of records management program. Problem solver with interpersonal skills.

Education. Keep in mind the following tips when listing your educational credentials:

1. In one entry indicate your degree (certificate or license), your major, and the name of the college conferring your most recent degree. The date the degree will be (or was) conferred is not required. If you are still attending school, write "Expected Graduation Date: May 15, 200X."

2. List any other degree, certificate, or license granted and the name of the institution. If you took courses but did not complete the requirements for a degree or certificate, list the name of the institution and a summary of the courses taken.

3. List your skills. For instance, if you are bilingual, indicate "Proficient in Spanish." Indicate those skills that are applicable and impressive, such as "effective customer service skills" or "excellent telephone skills."

4. List the different types of software you have experience in using.

5. List courses you took that you believe will be helpful on the job. List them by name, not number.

6. Add school activities that reflect organizational, leadership, and team skills.

Experience. Beginning with your most recent position, list your employment experience. If your work experience has been limited, include part-time, summer, and volunteer work, even when the work was unrelated to office work. Employers place value on experience that is common to all jobs, such as carrying out instructions, being prompt and dependable, working cooperatively with others, and accepting responsibility.

Use a separate entry for each job, and list your current or most recent position first. Give the beginning and ending dates (months and years), the name of the employer, the city in which the organization is located, the position held, the specific duties performed, and accomplishments. If the job was part time or voluntary, place this information under the date. To indicate that you are currently working, leave the date blank following the hyphen after the beginning date.

Interests and Activities. Because the human rights codes relating to equal opportunity employment make it illegal for an employer to discriminate on the basis of age, gender, race, marital status, religion, national origin, or sexual orientation, you are not required to include personal data. However, where you believe certain personal data may be to your benefit, you should include them.

In this section, you may add whatever you believe will support your application, such as honors received, extracurricular activities, and professional associations to which you belong.

References. The question of whether to include references is often raised, because employers know applicants list as references those persons who will provide favorable recommendations. To keep your resume to one page, provide a separate list of your references to be used on your application form, which will be discussed later in this chapter.

Appearance of the Resume

Remember the resume is a specimen of your work. If you use the appropriate word processing or desktop publishing software features, your resume will be a higher quality document.

1. Create your resume with careful thought and attention to detail. Your resume may not get a second chance; you must get it right the first time.

2. Do not use abbreviations or acronyms. You and others within your industry may be familiar with acronyms and abbreviations, but they can confuse those outside your industry. However, it is appropriate to abbreviate "A.A.S." for Associate of Applied Science.

3. Print the resume with a laser printer on bond paper, measuring $8\frac{1}{2} \times 11$ inches. Some authorities suggest soft gray or ecru colors.

4. Give the resume plenty of white space, using 1-inch margins. The size of the margins will actually depend on the setup and on the usual requirement to fit the resume on two pages. To avoid a crowded look, use ample white space before and after headings and between entries. Too much white space, however, will suggest inefficient planning.

5. Print the main heading at the top of the first page. It should be centered and highlighted in such a way that it is eye-catching and easy to read. Suggestions would be to use bold, enlarged, or italic print. Boxes or lines used in this area will enhance the appearance. Apply the "be conservative" rule. Using too many enhancements will detract from the qualifications your resume is intended to present.

6. Use side headings for emphasis but they should not detract from the main titles. To this end, use a combination of capital letters, underlining, and bold or italic print. However, be moderate; you do not want to reduce the importance of the main heading. The font size should be smaller than the main heading.

7. The second page will require a heading. Place your name and the page number at the left margin.

You must get your resume noticed in the stack on the desk of the human resources (HR) representative or recruiter. An HR staff member sorts the resumes that do not meet the job requirements or that appear unsuitable. These unsuitable resumes will never reach the desk of the recruiter or department head. To ensure your resume is not filtered out, follow these simple rules:

1. State clearly your skills that meet the key requirements of the job.
2. Follow carefully the instructions. Give precisely what is requested. If the ad states that the company wishes to have resumes dropped off in person, or if it asks for a handwritten cover letter, do exactly that. Not following instructions demonstrates poor judgment and can be frustrating for the HR staff to eliminate your resume.
3. Concentrate on every detail. An office professional will catch the smallest error when scrutinizing the resumes. Any typographical or spelling error may mean immediate rejection. No employer wants to interview an applicant for an office professional's position who allows errors in a document as important as a resume. For that reason, don't rely only on spell checking your document with your word processing software. Manually proofread the document as well.
4. Respect the prospective employer's preferences. Many ads request that applicants not telephone the company. If you telephone the employer, you leave the impression that you cannot follow instructions, and you may annoy the receptionist or the HR staff.

Put yourself in the position of the person who must sort through and filter out the resumes and then in the position of the department head. Make their jobs easier by making your resume attractive, applicable, easy to understand, and flawless. If you follow these suggestions, your chances of receiving an interview will improve.

Distributing Your Resume

You may distribute your resume in a number of ways: sending it as a fax, attaching it to an e-mail, or uploading it so the organization can scan it.

Fax Your Resume. If you have spent hours printing your resume on bond paper of perfect quality and color, and perhaps have even used colored ink for just the right amount of accent, the fruits of those labors will be lost in faxing it. However, faxing does have the advantage of expediency. Employers will often request that resumes be faxed to save time. Consider the following if you are asked to fax your resume or if you simply determine that faxing is appropriate:

- A faxed resume will probably not be confidential. In fact, several people may see it before the designated receiver. You may be able to avoid this disclosure by telephoning the recipient just prior to sending the fax and asking him or her to collect the faxed document.
- A faxed resume should always include a cover letter, just like the resume you mail or deliver.
- If your resume is attractive enough to earn you points, mail an original in addition to sending the fax.

E-Mail Your Resume. E-mailing your resume and cover letter might be preferable to faxing it. E-mailing has the advantage of keeping the document relatively confidential. However, it does not guarantee that the document will look more attractive. Although the document may look perfect on your screen, it may not have exactly the same format on the recipient's screen or printer. An alternative is to paste the resume and cover letter directly into the e-mail message area. If you are called for an interview, you can take the resume with you.

Scan Your Resume. A growing number of companies are using electronic scanning systems to digitally scan, store, and track resumes and cover letters, which will be discussed in the following section. In fact, hundreds of resumes can be scanned in only a few minutes. A **scannable resume** has a plain format that allows companies to scan it as pure text. When recruiters wish to retrieve a group of candidates, they supply key words that are essential for the right applicant. These key words will identify expertise, experience, and education. For example, they might include such words as *bilingual, desktop publishing, database management,* and *teams.* The computer software scans the database, and within minutes a list of applicants whose resumes match the stated criteria is brought to the screen.

Refer to Figure 3-4 for an example of a partial resume that has been prepared for electronic scanning.

Scanned resumes save the recruiter a lot of time. However, even a resume with extensive credentials may go unnoticed if the scanner cannot identify them. Scanning can dramatically change the appearance of your resume. Many scanning programs make mistakes when reading words or special characters. To be sure all the information on your resume is collected by the electronic system, follow these tips to be sure your resume is scanner friendly.

1. Describe your personal traits in nouns, not verbs.
2. Use the key words found in the job ad.
3. Use straightforward words to describe your experience. Embellished terms will not be on the list of skills for which the recruiter is searching.
4. Use multiple pages if necessary. Unlike humans, computers do not tire of reading.
5. Increase your lists of key words. Include specific software names such as *Microsoft Word.*
6. Use common resume headings such as Objective, Education, Experience, and Interests.

To keep your resume clean and simple, steer clear of these practices:

1. Don't use italics. Instead, use a standard typeface.
2. Don't use bullets. Instead, use asterisks and hyphens.
3. Don't bold any text.
4. Don't underline or use graphic lines.
5. Don't use indents or centering.
6. Don't print your resume on colored paper.

One advantage of an electronic scanning system is that electronic storage takes so much less space than paper storage. This means resumes may be kept on file for an extended period.

If applicants are not aware of the electronic scanning process and submit attractive yet traditionally formatted resumes, they may not be identified by

Kimberly Wong
10507 53rd Avenue NW
Portland, OR 97204-0066
Tel (503) 478-1320
Tel (502) 478-2398
E-mail: kimwong@aol.com

OBJECTIVE
To earn the position of administrative assistant with a company that has a progressive team spirit.

EDUCATION
Portland Community College
Associate of Applied Science
Office Administration Program
Keying 70 words per minute
Microsoft Word
Microsoft PowerPoint
Microsoft Excel
Microsoft Access
Microsoft Project
Microsoft Publisher
President Office Management Society
Team Leader Graduation Planning Committee
Leader Charity Fundraising

EXPERIENCE
May 1999–Current
Administrative Assistant
Coron Industries
Portland
Supervisor of junior staff
Coordinator of budget

FIGURE 3-4 • Example of partial resume that has been prepared for electronic scanning.

the computer, no matter how outstanding. The best approach when you do not know whether electronic or human screening will be used is to submit two resumes. The resume intended for human scrutiny should be printed on attractive paper, using highlighting features, graphic lines, and other design elements. Place a removable note on the nicely formatted resume that states "Visual Resume." Place another removable note on the resume destined for scanning that says "Scannable Resume." The reason you have included two resumes should be briefly explained in your cover letter.

Resume Checklist

Appearance
- ✔ Use attractive spacing.
- ✔ Use plenty of white space.
- ✔ Use quality paper that is white or a conservative color.
- ✔ Avoid excessive enhancements.
- ✔ Use consistent format.
- ✔ Emphasize headings.
- ✔ Bullet items.
- ✔ Follow current format.

Content
- ✔ Use resume headings.
- ✔ Emphasize skills and mastery of software.

- ✔ Emphasize accomplishments.
- ✔ Show most recent education first.
- ✔ Show most recent experience first.

Accuracy
- ✔ Be certain resume is error free.
- ✔ Use spell check function to ensure resume is free of spelling errors.
- ✔ Check your resume for spelling errors the spell check function would not detect.
- ✔ Use parallel construction in wording of bulleted items.

Other
- ✔ Deliver in an appropriate way.

Stop 'n Check

1. List at least two questions your resume should address.

   a. _____

   b. _____

2. Given the descriptions in this section, which resume would be the most appropriate for you?

   _____

Resume Checklist

Before submitting your resume, use the above checklist to ensure your document will appeal to an interviewer. Resumes with spelling and grammatical errors are routinely discarded by employers because of the carelessness such errors demonstrate.

COVER LETTERS

The main purpose of a cover letter, also called *application letter*, is to introduce your resume in the hope of obtaining an interview. Therefore, you should always write a cover letter to accompany your resume. Cover letters are either prospecting or solicited.

Prospecting Cover Letter

A **prospecting cover letter** is written by an applicant who does not know a job opening exists. It is written to express the applicant's interest in working for a particular company, to call attention to the applicant's qualifications, and to inquire about the possibility of a job opening. Understand, however, prospecting letters may not be read as many organizations only review letters and resumes when they have openings.

A prospecting cover letter is a sales letter, and the product is *you*. It represents your initial effort at locating an employer seeking the qualifications you have to offer and at convincing the employer to consider your qualifications. You increase your cover letter's chances of gaining attention when you submit a resume along with it. Let the reader know what qualifications you possess so he or she can compare them with the requirements of the positions available within the organization.

Organize your cover letter around the steps of a sales presentation:

1. Use an opening that gets the reader's attention and arouses interest in knowing more about your qualifications.
2. Focus on facts that convince the prospective employer you possess qualifications matching the requirements of a position he or she must fill.
3. Make a brief reference to the resume you are enclosing.
4. Use a closing that requests action, which in most cover letters is a request for an interview. These points are illustrated in the cover letter in Figure 3-5.

Solicited Cover Letter

A **solicited cover letter** is written in response to an announcement that a job opening exists. The announcement might be made through an ad in the newspaper, placed with a private employment agency, sent to the campus career development center, or disseminated through other sources. When you hear or read about a job opening, write a solicited (invited) letter. A solicited cover letter can be more specific than a prospecting letter because the applicant knows a job opening exists.

Use the first paragraph to refer to the job and to reveal how you found out about it. Include a reference to the source. Request in the opening paragraph that you be considered for the job. Figure 3-6 presents a partial sample solicited cover letter.

The **qualifications cover letter** is a version of the solicited cover letter. It includes only the job requirements that your qualifications meet or exceed, or soon will. In this letter, paraphrase the employer's job requirements, but don't change them to match your qualifications. The sample qualifications letter is shown in Figure 3-7.

Write a persuasive letter in such a way that you discuss every requirement mentioned in the announcement and show how you meet these qualifications. This style differs from a prospecting letter in that you include only the key qualifications you choose to emphasize.

Enclose a resume and refer to it in the letter. In the resume highlight all the qualifications and key words mentioned in the announcement, and include others that may contribute to your getting the job.

Close the letter by requesting action, which usually is a request for an interview in which to discuss your qualifications for the job.

Appearance of the Cover Letter

Print your cover letter on good $8\frac{1}{2} \times 11$ inch bond paper that matches the quality and shade of the paper used for your resume. Include your personal information above the date. Because your letter could get separated from your resume, place your complete mailing address on both the letter and the resume.

2410 Anderson Trail Drive
Dallas, TX 75245
susanchung@hotmail.com
April 5, 200X

Ms. Gloria Redmond
Human Resources Manager
Moore Electronics, Inc.
21 Metro Park
Dallas, TX 75234

Dear Ms. Redmond:

Recently I moved to Dallas, and I am seeking employment as an administrative assistant. From the research I have done on companies in Dallas, I learned that Moore Electronics, Inc. is a young company that is growing rapidly. My 12 years of experience in offices and my recent studies in office administration and business would enable me to contribute to your growth.

Because of the skills I possess, as listed on the enclosed resume, I can perform a variety of office tasks with ease. I enjoy contact with people, and I adapt readily to change. I plan to continue my education by enrolling in online courses.

I have a keen interest in working for Moore Electronics, Inc. I am available for an interview any afternoon after 1 p.m. My home telephone number is 972-555-7238.

Sincerely,

Susan Chung

Enclosure

FIGURE 3-5 • Prospecting cover letter.

Address the letter to a specific person, if possible. Make an effort to locate the name of the employer to whom the letter should be addressed. This information can be obtained with a single telephone call to the company. It is acceptable to address the cover letter to Human Resources Representative.

Limit your letter to one page. Because you have organized all your facts in the accompanying resume, you should limit your cover letter to three or four well-written paragraphs. Most letter styles are acceptable. Follow these recommendations to achieve a simple, readable, and attractive presentation:

- Keep the font and format conservative.
- Keep the appearance professional.
- Keep the information balanced on the page.

253 South 300 West
Salt Lake City, UT 84101
(801) 555-1269
shawn.becker@hotmail.com
April 17, 200X

Mr. Harris Broussard
Jamison Consultants
101 Levoy Drive
Salt Lake City, UT 84123

Dear Mr. Broussard:

Please consider the attached resume for the position of administrative assistant Level III as advertised in the April 16 issue of *The Tribune*. I recently earned an honors certificate for office professionals in Office Technology.

Through my studies I mastered numerous office skills, including the use of word processing, desktop publishing, and database software programs—those skills mentioned in your employment ad. Because I am an energetic graduate who is willing to learn, I am confident I could contribute to your team.

I am available for interviews Monday through Friday after 12:30 p.m. You may contact me using the information at the top of the letter. I look forward to hearing from you.

FIGURE 3-6 • Solicited cover letter.

Time the arrival of your letter for the most attention. If your letter arrives on Monday, it arrives with the weekend delivery. If your letter arrives on Friday, it may get ignored among the week's backlog. Some authorities agree that your letter should arrive on a Tuesday, Wednesday, or Thursday.

Cover Letter Checklist

A cover letter is the window to your resume, so it is critical that your letter gives the best view of your skills. Consider your cover letter as one of your marketing tools. Refer to the checklist on page 93 to help create a cover letter that will gain attention.

APPLICATION FORMS

Throughout your job campaign, you will be asked to complete application forms. Because your resume does not substitute for a completed application form, you will be asked to complete one. If you wish, you may attach your resume to the completed application form, but be sure to complete each section of the application. If a question on the application form does not apply to you, write "Not Applicable" or "Does Not Apply" in the blank. If a question calls for salary expected and you do not want to state a figure, write

Sarah McDonald
5620 Loop Central, #25
Houston, TX 77081
Home (713) 866-4554; Cell (832) 432-1234
srmcdonald@yahoo.com

Human Resources
Kennedy Engineering, Inc.
38720 Wildfern Drive
Houston, TX 77041

Reference Code: 063451BBAC

Dear HR Representative:

I saw your employment ad for a bilingual administrative assistant at Monster.com. In response, I am submitting my qualifications.

Your Requirements	My Qualifications
1. Bilingual—Spanish	1. Proficient in oral and written skills
2. Associate of Applied Sciences	2. Associate of Applied Sciences in business and office administration
3. Minimum of 3 years office experience	3. Five years office experience
4. Working knowledge of Excel, Access, and PowerPoint	4. Microsoft Certified in Word, Excel, Access, and PowerPoint
5. Good communication skills	5. Excellent oral and written communication skills as well as interpersonal skills

Along with my interest, my qualifications match your requirements. I have enclosed my resume and would appreciate an interview. You may contact me using the information above. The best time to reach me is Monday through Friday after 12:30 p.m. I look forward to hearing from you.
Sincerely,

Sarah McDonald

FIGURE 3-7 • Qualifications cover letter.

"Open to Negotiation," which means you would prefer to discuss salary once an offer of employment is made. If you leave the answer blank, the employer may assume (1) you were careless and missed the question or (2) you did not understand the question. Either of these assumptions may eliminate you from the potential pool of candidates.

Regarding references, list three or more former employers and teachers who can provide a specific evaluation of your competence, work habits, and attitude toward work. If you include a character reference, do not give the name of a relative. Ask permission of each person before including his or her name as a reference. For each reference, give the full name, position held, telephone number, and complete address, including the zip code. Use a courtesy

Cover Letter Checklist

Appearance

✔ You have used high-quality bond paper.

✔ Your paper and font match those of the resume.

✔ The documents have been placed in an envelope large enough that they may lie flat without folding.

Content

✔ You have opened with an attention-getting statement.

✔ You have demonstrated knowledge of the company.

✔ You have included key words that were used in the job posting.

✔ You have clearly stated how you would be valuable to the company.

✔ You have summarized your background.

✔ You have closed with a call to action.

✔ The letter is short in length and concise.

Accuracy

✔ You have proofread the letter several times for grammar, spelling, punctuation, and content.

✔ Another person has proofread it and given you feedback.

✔ The letter contains the correct information (full address, telephone and fax numbers, and e-mail address).

Stop 'n Check

Describe the difference between a prospecting cover letter and a solicited cover letter.

_____

_____

title before each name. The position held is significant because it indicates the person's association with you.

Each company designs its own form for employee recruitment in order to include the specific questions it wants applicants to answer. Nevertheless, most application forms are similar.

Supplying information on the application forms you are requested to complete is a significant part of your job search. Follow the instructions carefully and supply the information exactly as it is called for. If the instruction reads "Please print," do so. Your printing and handwriting must be legible. After all, you want the application form to stand out.

Prepare your answers before you write on or key the application form. When you do this, your form will appear neat and organized. A completed application form becomes part of the permanent record of the applicant who is hired.

Many organizations follow the procedure of handing the applicant an application form as the first step of an interview taking place on the organization's premises. (For campus interviews, the interviewer may use the application form you gave the career development center staff.). Here are some suggestions to follow when completing an application form.

- Have a pen, preferably black ink.
- Know the current date.

Stop 'n Check

Identify at least four tips to follow when completing an application form.

a. _____

b. _____

c. _____

d. _____

- Have the names, titles, addresses, telephone and fax numbers, and e-mail addresses for your references.
- Have the dates of previous employment.
- Have a list of your volunteer activities and the associations to which you belong.
- Know your social security number.
- Know the exact title of the position for which you are applying.

Complete the form as requested even if you have your resume with you. If it is acceptable, staple a copy of your resume to the back of the application form.

Interviewing for a Position

An interview gives you an opportunity to convince a prospective employer that you can make a real contribution to the organization. An interviewer can judge your basic qualifications by studying your transcript, cover letter, resume, test results, and completed application form. During the interview, the interviewer will evaluate your personality, attitudes, professional appearance, and ability to communicate (Figure 3-8). An impressive school record and evidence that you possess the necessary office technology skills are pluses, but your success in landing the position you want will depend upon the way you project yourself during the interview.

The purpose of the interview is to give the:

- interviewer an opportunity to evaluate the applicant in terms of the needs of the company.
- applicant a chance to appraise the job and company.

Sometimes getting an interview is extremely difficult. If getting an interview seems impossible, don't get discouraged. This difficulty may reflect the competition for jobs in your specific area or geographic location.

Attempt to schedule several interviews with organizations you believe will offer the type of work you are seeking. Don't set your expectations on one particular position. Becoming overly anxious about getting a particular position can create unnecessary tension. Nevertheless, you should enter each

FIGURE 3-8 • Interviewer and applicant.

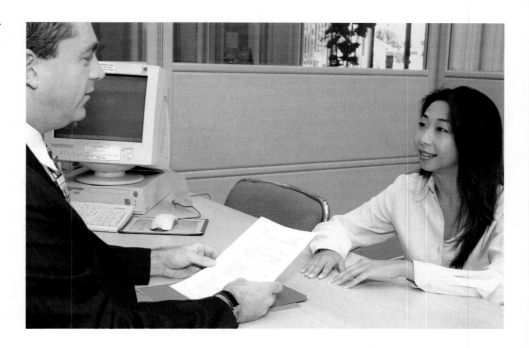

interview with the attitude the job you are applying for is precisely the one you want. As you learn more about the job, it may *become* the position you want.

BEFORE THE INTERVIEW

Prepare thoroughly for each interview.

- Research the organization with which you have scheduled the interview.
- Learn what the current salaries are for office professionals (including administrative assistants, executive assistants, and information specialists) in the community, region, or state.
- Summarize your qualifications.
- Decide on the qualifications to emphasize.
- Anticipate the interviewer's questions.
- Formulate your answers to the interviewer's questions.
- Choose clothes appropriate for the interview.
- Schedule ample time for getting ready and arriving for the interview.
- Travel to the location of the interview.

Do Research

Researching the organization is crucial. The following are effective research methods:

- conducting research on the Internet to study the organization and its products or services
- exploring the organization in the reference section of the library
- reading the organization's most recent annual report
- phoning the organization's receptionist to request information

- analyzing the organization's profitability from its most recent annual report
- identifying the number of employees the organization has
- determining how long the organization has been operating
- locating the extent of the company's operations
- finding any recent expansion the company may have experienced
- locating any mergers or name changes the company has undergone
- finding the company's competitive standing in the industry
- determining the organization's hiring practices

Many applicants fall short during an interview because they lack knowledge about the organization to which they are applying. The interviewer may tell you about the organization and its employment opportunities, but you will be able to converse with more ease and ask pertinent questions if you have researched the organization. Lack of knowledge could be viewed as lack of interest in the organization. Prepare thoroughly; show your interest in the organization through your knowledge about it.

Anticipate Questions

Think about what you have to offer and the qualifications you want to emphasize. Review your resume before you go to the interview. The interviewer may ask you to discuss your job objective and why you feel qualified for it. You should be prepared to talk about yourself in an organized way without hesitation.

Anticipate questions the interviewer will ask and know what your answers will be. Realize, too, that you cannot anticipate all the questions the interviewer will ask, but you can expect questions such as the following:

1. What do you know about this company?
2. What do you know about the position you are applying for?
3. We are looking for someone with extensive experience. Your resume indicates limited experience as an administrative assistant (or whatever the title). How do you expect to compensate for your lack of experience?
4. What made you decide you would like to work for this company?
5. What do you expect to be doing three years from now? Five years from now?
6. Why did you choose a career as an office professional (or administrative assistant, etc.)?
7. Relating to the responsibilities described in the advertisement for this position, what strengths will you bring to our office (or company)?
8. Relating to the responsibilities described in the advertisement for this position, what responsibilities do you believe will be your greatest challenges?
9. Tell me about yourself.
10. How do you rate the education you have received?
11. Throughout your training to be an administrative assistant, what courses did you enjoy the most? Least? Why?
12. Describe the qualities of a good leader. Have you encountered a person like this? Where and when?

13. Describe the characteristics of a poor leader. Have you encountered a person like this? Where and when?
14. Do you plan to continue your education? How? What field? Why is this important to you?
15. Why have you decided to leave your present employer?
16. What are your feelings about working overtime?

At the beginning of the interview you may be asked some general questions relating to your personal interests, or you may be asked to give your opinion about the latest current events. Some interviewers begin with questions they think will put the applicant at ease. Answer all questions thoroughly but without rambling. Seriously consider your answers to all questions; the interviewer is searching for a qualified employee who will stay with the organization if he or she is hired.

To gain insight into your personality and to check on your attitude, the interviewer may ask questions such as these:

• Give an example of how you have displayed initiative.
• How do you spend your leisure time?
• What personality characteristics do you think are essential for the position you are seeking?
• How do you accept criticism?
• Provide an example of a situation in which you were criticized.
• Describe the best/worst employer/teacher you have ever had.
• Explain a stressful situation you encountered and describe how you handled it.

Behavioral Descriptive Questions. An applicant can prepare thoroughly for an interview; however, it is impossible to anticipate all possible interview scenarios. Behavioral descriptive questions are commonly used by interviewers to sort facts from exaggerations. These interviews use a "demo" questioning technique, in which each question leads to the next and probes deeper into an experience or scenario described by the applicant. A typical set of behavioral interview questions is:

1. Describe a situation where you were a team member and conflict arose within the team.
2. What did you do to resolve this conflict?
3. What did you learn from this experience?
4. Since the conflict, how have you applied what you learned?
5. Who has benefited from your ability to resolve conflict?

Some applicants feel intimidated by the probing nature of these questions. However, these questions, if presented in a diplomatic manner, are highly successful in determining the best candidate. Because many people embellish their resumes and then perform well at exaggerating their talents during the interview, the best candidate is not always selected for the job.

Behavioral descriptive questions are not difficult to answer if the candidate has the experience the recruiter is seeking. If you are asked a behavioral descriptive question and simply don't have the experience necessary to answer the question, be honest. The best policy is to tell the interviewer that you have no experience in this particular area. If you have related experience, ask the interviewer if you might refer to a similar situation in a different type of environment.

Unethical Questions. If interviewers ask personal questions, they must phrase them carefully. Many questions relating to topics, such as marital status, age, smoking habits, or race, are unethical. Basing employment decisions on these factors is illegal. For example, an interviewer cannot ask an older person if he or she would be considering retirement in the next few years. If the candidate's response is "yes," the interviewer cannot base the employment decision on this response.

No questions should be asked about national origin. The interviewer can ask what languages you speak and write fluently but should not ask what your native tongue is. You should not be asked questions about your ethnic background or race. Although the interviewer can ask "Are you a citizen of the United States?" he or she cannot ask, "Of what country are you a citizen?"

The interviewer can ask if you have a valid driver's license and if you have ever been convicted of a crime, but he or she cannot ask if you have ever been arrested.

To avoid potential unethical questions being asked during interviews, employers are advised how to conduct job interviews without violating the law.

Ask Questions

An interviewer will expect you to ask questions, too. Some interviews lend themselves to the applicant asking questions periodically throughout the interview, whereas other interviews give the applicant an opportunity at the end of the interview to ask questions. Your research prior to the interview should help you generate a list of appropriate questions. Mention that you have researched the company Web site and that you prepared a few questions. Select appropriate questions, take the sheet to the interview, and refer to it. The following is a list of questions to ask during an interview.

- To whom would I report? To how many people would I report?
- What are opportunities for advancement from this position?
- Why is this position open? Did the person who held the position previously leave? Is it a newly created position?
- What personal qualities improve the likelihood for success in this position?
- How would you describe the corporate culture of this organization?

Make a Statement with Your Appearance

Your appearance—your clothes, hair, and shoes—can certainly cost you the job before you ever open your mouth. Your goal is to look the part of a professional, one who would represent the organization in positive ways. Your appearance should make the statement that you are a professional and that you want to be taken seriously. This is true even in companies that have a casual dress policy. Companies that encourage their employees to dress casually still expect applicants to dress and act professionally in the interview.

Interview Preparation Checklist

- ✔ Your hair should be neat and away from your face.
- ✔ Your nails should be well manicured and clean.
- ✔ Shoes should be clean, polished, and conventional.
- ✔ Body odor should be eliminated.
- ✔ The most appropriate choice of color is a variation of black, navy, brown, or gray.
- ✔ Acceptable business clothing for women can be more colorful than that of their male counterparts, although clothing still must be conservative.

- ✔ Cosmetics should be used sparingly.
- ✔ Jewelry should be simple, minimal, and yet complimentary.
- ✔ Professional attire should include a suit jacket.
- ✔ Clothing should not be revealing; skirts should be a comfortable length and blouses should never reveal cleavage or camisole.
- ✔ Cologne or perfume and hand lotion should be avoided. A fragrance that is attractive to you could be offensive to another person.

Once they are successful and join the staff, they may adopt the company's dress code.

Spend the extra time it takes to look well groomed. Dress conservatively because you want the interviewer to focus on your answers without being distracted by your appearance. By applying the above checklist to your interview preparation, you may be able to convey the proper message.

Whatever you decide will be your image for an interview, consider the strong nonverbal message that your image sends.

Be Punctual

Be sure you know the exact location of the interview. Plan to arrive ten to fifteen minutes early. Avoid rushing before the interview. You can undermine yourself before the interview by becoming stressed because you did not allow yourself enough time. A few days before the interview, travel to the office and note the time it takes to arrive. On the actual day of the interview, allow more time than is needed to get to the location.

Do not schedule two interviews in the same morning or afternoon. You have no control over the length of an interview, and you will not feel at ease if you are concerned about time.

Know What to Take to the Interview

For the interview, you will want to have important materials on hand, but you will not want to be encumbered with items you do not need.

Avoid bringing the following items to an interview. Although it seems like common sense not to bring them, many employers report that applicants often do.

- Never bring packages. Avoid shopping immediately before an interview, unless you can leave all the packages in a locker or in your car.
- Women should never carry a large purse. A small handbag with only necessary items will not distract from a professional appearance. Instead of carrying a backpack, men should carry a folder or small portfolio folder.

Men and women should never carry a briefcase that is oversized or resembles a schoolbag. Keep everything neat and simple and nondistracting.

- Never enter the interview with a cell phone turned on. So that you will not be distracted, turn off *all* signals that alert you of an incoming call or message.

- Most important of all, never bring another person. Naturally you wouldn't bring another person into the interview, but a number of applicants make plans to meet friends or relatives immediately after the interview. You need to concentrate on the interview, not on your friends or relatives waiting in the lobby or reception area. In particular, don't bring children because their behavior may cause you to worry. Demonstrate that you are an independent person; arrive alone and leave alone.

Here's what you *should* take to the interview.

- Your portfolio, if prepared to a professional standard, will be one of the best sales tools you have. Bring it to the interview and look for the perfect opportunity to walk through it with the interviewer.

- Always bring a pen and paper to write down important facts you learn during the interview. Your pen should be attractive and in good condition. One that has been chewed or runs out of ink will not leave the interviewer with the best impression.

- Bring extra copies of your resume. Offer copies to the interviewer just as the interview is ready to begin. Doing so demonstrates your preparation. You will also need a copy for yourself to refer to throughout the interview.

- Bring a list of three or more references that includes names, titles, company names, addresses, telephone and fax numbers, and e-mail addresses. The list should be attractively keyed on a single sheet.

- Bring a version of the advertisement if one was posted or appeared in the newspaper. Highlight the key responsibilities listed. Don't be afraid to bring out the ad and refer to it during the interview. Doing so shows you know exactly what type of position you are applying for and that you are prepared for the interview.

- Bring along your list of questions; you can list the responsibilities of the position and, for each, identify specific examples of how you have demonstrated competence. Don't be afraid to refer to this sheet during the interview. The sheet should appear neat and organized and, of course, should be keyed.

- With desktop publishing, you can prepare personal business cards that are professional looking by printing them on cardstock. Or, for a nominal charge, you can have a professional printer produce a small number of business cards with your name and contact information. The applicant who leaves a business card leaves a professional image. Remember the card is a great marketing tool when you are networking.

DURING THE INTERVIEW

Be courteous, confident, and composed. As you approach the interviewer, smile, greet the interviewer by name, and introduce yourself. For example, "Hello, Mr. Schichili. My name is Courtney Littrell." If the interviewer

Stop 'n Check

To prepare thoroughly for an interview, list at least five tips to follow.

a. _____

b. _____

c. _____

d. _____

e. _____

extends a hand, give a firm handshake. This gesture will express your confidence. Try to relax. You will probably feel a little nervous because the interview is important to you. If you feel nervous, don't call attention to your nervousness by twisting your hair, tapping your foot, thumping on the table, sitting on the edge of the chair, talking too rapidly, or showing other outward nervous signs.

Although one-to-one interviews are most common, you should be prepared to face a group or a panel of interviewers, especially common among companies that are driven by a consensus or team concept. The interviewers have a job to perform; they must match an applicant to the requirements of the position to be filled. The initial interview probably will last about twenty to thirty minutes. An effective interviewer will allow the applicant to talk throughout most of the interview. The interviewer may be an HR representative who will ask more general questions. If the company representative is the hiring manager, his or her questions will be more specific and job-related.

Some interviewers, but not all, break the interview into the following segments:

1. getting acquainted
2. presenting the organization's opportunities
3. evaluating the applicant
4. answering the applicant's questions

Others begin the interview with one or more broad, open-ended questions, such as "Tell me about yourself," turning the discussion over to the interviewee at once. The interviewer controls the interview by telling the interviewee to discuss specific topics. When this interviewing technique is used, the conversation seems spontaneous rather than structured. While the interviewer is talking, listen intently. Give the interviewer an opportunity to talk; show that you are an active listener.

When you are asked a question, give a full answer, not simply a "yes" or "no." The interviewer will ask a question or a comment to introduce a topic you are expected to discuss. Look the interviewer in the eye and answer all questions frankly. Be deliberate; do not start talking before the interviewer completes the question. Avoid talking too much; keep to the point. Do not attempt to answer a question you do not understand. Either restate the question as you understand it or ask the interviewer to clarify it.

While you are talking, keep your goal in mind, which is to promote yourself. Use every opportunity to emphasize your good points and to relate them to what you can do for the organization. To sound sincere, present facts, not your opinion, about yourself. Don't criticize yourself and never make derogatory remarks about an instructor or a former supervisor or employer.

As you are talking, the interviewer will evaluate your mental and physical alertness, your ability to communicate, your attitude toward life and toward the organization, and your enthusiasm for work. Some interviewers will give tests in order to evaluate your skill level.

As discussed in the section "Before the Interview," you should prepare questions to ask at the interview. Every interviewer likes to be asked questions. The questions you prepare must be relevant to the organization or to the job opportunity. If all your prepared questions have been discussed during the interview and you are left without questions to ask, ask the interviewer to elaborate further on a statement or on details given earlier in the interview.

Discussion on Salary

At the initial interview, your questions should not concern salary or benefits. Reserve these questions until you are offered the position. However, if the interviewer asks you about your expected salary, be prepared to state a range. Remember that the figure the interviewer is likely to remember and focus on is the low end of your range.

If you have prepared a personal budget and have researched office salaries in your area, you will know an appropriate starting salary for this employment opportunity.

The *best time* to negotiate salary is *after the job offer has been made*. However, the interviewer is in control of the interview; if the interviewer asks you a salary question during the interview, you must answer it.

Remember that although salary is often a negotiable item, these negotiations must be handled with diplomacy. Although job satisfaction will be achieved mostly through obtaining a challenging and responsible position, don't sell yourself short when salary is discussed. If you have earned a postsecondary certificate and degree and have experience in the field, you have gained bargaining power.

Close the Interview Confidently

Watch for cues that the interview is coming to an end. The interviewer may thank you for coming, suggest you schedule a time to take employment tests, invite you to arrange for a second interview, stand up and say you will hear by a certain date if the organization is interested in you, or offer you the position.

A good closure to an interview would include the following actions:

- If offered a hand, shake hands firmly.
- Restate your interest in the position. For example, "Please consider me for the position. I feel confident I would make a positive contribution to your organization."
- Check the follow-up procedure that will be employed by the organization. Example: "When might I expect to hear from you? If I don't hear from you by that date, may I contact you?"

Stop 'n Check

1. When is the best time to discuss your salary?

   _____

   _____

2. What are two ways you can promote a positive closure to your interview?

   a. _____

   b. _____

If you are offered the position, you are not expected to accept it on the spot. You are making a long-term commitment, and you should be sure it is the position you want. The interviewer would prefer you give it enough thought to be absolutely certain. You may accept at once if you have no doubt about it. Otherwise, tactfully say you would like time to consider it. Ask if you can let the interviewer know in a day or two or at some definite, mutually agreed-upon time.

You cannot always accurately judge how you are being rated. Interviewers who rely on the second interview for making a decision are noncommittal during the initial interview. Appear interested and confident as the interview draws to a close. Express appreciation to the interviewer before leaving.

AFTER THE INTERVIEW

Make each interview a learning experience. Ask yourself the following questions to improve your self-promotion techniques:

1. What points did I make that seemed to interest the interviewer?
2. Did I present my qualifications well?
3. Did I overlook any qualifications that are pertinent to the position?
4. Did I learn all I need to know about the position, or did I forget or hesitate to ask about factors that are important to me?
5. Did I talk too much? Not enough?
6. Did I interview the employer rather than permit the employer to interview me?
7. Was I too tense?
8. Was I too aggressive? Not assertive enough?
9. How can I improve my next interview?

THE CAMPUS INTERVIEW

Your career development center will set up appointments for students nearing graduation to be interviewed by representatives from various companies. These interviews often occur on campus.

Stop 'n Check

After the interview, what three questions will you ask to improve your self-promotion?

a. _____

b. _____

c. _____

As with all job interviews, stress your strong points, and listen attentively. In response to the interviewer's questions, relate how you meet the qualifications for the job. Project your personality, and ask relevant questions.

Don't expect that because the interview is held on campus you should dress casually. Give the interviewer a chance to see how you would look on the job if the interviewer hired you. You will look capable of accepting responsibility if you dress accordingly. The interviewer will be comparing your appearance with that of office professionals who already work for the organization, not with the appearance of other college students.

If, as a result of the campus interview, you are invited for a second interview or to take tests, be sure to get the exact address. Write down the date, time, address, and name of the person who will meet with you.

Testing for a Job

The career development center staff and your instructors may know which companies in your area give tests. If you apply for a job with an organization that administers tests, be prepared to take a word processing production test, a basic math test, a keyboarding test, and a spelling test. The organization could test your skill on any software application or test your ability to compose correspondence.

If you apply for a position at a staffing agency, you will probably be asked to take tests at its location. Be prepared for similar tests, such as basic math, keyboarding, and spelling tests. In addition, you will probably be asked to take computerized tests in word processing, spreadsheets, and databases. The computerized tests generally direct you to perform a function using specific software. Your score will likely be based on your responses to using the software menus, icons, and keystrokes.

Many tests have time limits. Listen carefully to the instructions you receive. If you do not clearly understand what you are expected to do, ask questions. You will be expected to perform at speed levels determined by the organization administering the tests. Test results are usually evaluated by degree of accuracy.

Personality tests and mental ability tests are popular. It is not possible to prepare for these tests. The goal of these examinations is to determine which applicants will work well with existing staff members, which applicants will most likely share the company's goals, and which applicants have potential leadership skills.

Composing Follow-up Letters

The letters essential for continuing and finalizing a job search fall into five categories:

1. thank-you
2. reminder
3. inquiry
4. acceptance
5. refusal

Compose follow-up letters on the same quality paper you used for the resume, and be sure to include your return address, telephone and fax numbers, and e-mail address. Check them carefully for accuracy. Be sure that the company's name and the interviewer's name are spelled correctly.

THANK-YOU

Writing a thank-you letter following an interview is not a requirement but a courtesy. Always write a thank-you letter and send it immediately after the interview. If you want the position for which you were interviewed, you can use a thank-you letter to do far more than express appreciation to the interviewer. Not everyone writes thank-you letters; consequently, when your thank-you letter arrives at the interviewer's desk, it will single you out from other applicants and call attention once more to your application.

Say that you definitely are interested in the position and that you want to be considered seriously for it. When interviewers are considering several applicants with apparently equal qualifications, one question they are trying to answer is, "Which applicant has the keenest interest in working for our organization?"

Keep your letter brief. In the opening paragraph, thank the interviewer, mentioning either the day or the date of the interview and the specific position discussed. Use the remainder of the letter to refer to something specific about the interview and to express interest in the job. Close with a statement to let the interviewer know you are waiting for a reply. Here is an example of how one applicant expressed interest:

> Talking with you last Wednesday afternoon about the duties of an administrative assistant with Midwestern Products convinced me that this is exactly the position I am seeking.
>
> I appreciate the time you spent with me, discussing employment opportunities with your company and describing the requirements for an administrative assistant's position. I feel confident I can meet these requirements, and I am waiting to hear that you also feel I can.

REMINDER

When you do not receive a response to an application or are told that your application has been placed on file, write another letter after a few weeks have elapsed to remind the interviewer that you still are interested. You will find reminder letters especially helpful when you plan to move from one geographic section of the United States to another and make inquiries about positions months in advance of your availability for employment.

Do not assume your resume has been kept on file. Send another copy of your resume with your reminder letter. In the opening paragraph, mention the position you applied for and when. In the body of the letter, briefly state your interest in working for that particular organization, express confidence about what you can do for the organization, and ask if an opening for the type of position you are seeking exists. You may be successful with composing a letter similar to this example:

> In January, I inquired about employment opportunities for office support with your company and sent you a resume detailing my qualifications. Modern Plastics is a company that has enjoyed rapid growth, and I would like to be a member of its dynamic team.
>
> Next week I am moving to Denver. May I please schedule an appointment during the week of May 25 to discuss my qualifications for employment as an assistant with Modern Plastics? Please reply to my Denver mailing address.
>
> For your convenience, I am enclosing a copy of the cover letter and resume I sent to you in January. I look forward to receiving a positive response. Thank you for your assistance.

INQUIRY

Following a job interview, you can write a letter of inquiry or make a telephone call if you have not heard anything by the time the interviewer said you would receive a reply. Be patient. Wait a day or two beyond the time you are expecting a reply and, if you do not hear, telephone or write to inquire. If you are told the position has not been filled, indicate that you definitely are interested.

JOB ACCEPTANCE

Follow up with a letter even when you accept a job offer during an interview or over the telephone. You may receive a letter offering you a position and suggesting you call to accept. Respond by telephone, but also send a letter to leave no doubt about your acceptance.

In the opening, accept the job enthusiastically. Mention the specific position being accepted. If you have received a form for supplying additional information, complete it, enclose it, and refer to it in your letter. Repeat the report-to-work instructions, giving the date, time, and place. In either the opening or the closing, express appreciation. Keep a copy of the letter of offer and your reply. Here is an example of an acceptance response.

> As I expressed over the telephone, I am delighted to accept the position of administrative assistant in the International Markets Division of Midwestern Products. Enclosed are the forms you requested I complete after my interview last week.
>
> I appreciate the opportunity to join your team and am eager to report to work on Monday, June 16, at 8 a.m. Thank you for selecting me for the position.

JOB REFUSAL

If you conduct a thorough job campaign, you may be offered more than one job and will have to refuse all but one of them. Be as prompt in refusing as

Stop 'n Check

Identify five categories of follow-up letters.

a. _____   d. _____

b. _____   e. _____

c. _____

possible. If you have already accepted a position, refuse the second offer at once. This is a courtesy you owe the person who must search elsewhere to fill the position offered you.

If your letter will be disappointing to the reader, you should organize it in the same way you organize other letters of disappointment. Begin by making a favorable statement concerning your contact with the interviewer or about the organization. Express appreciation for the job offer at either the beginning or the end of the letter. Include at least one reason for refusing the offer. State the refusal tactfully, but make it clear you are refusing. By making a definite statement about already having accepted a position or about your continuing to search for a particular job, you will be refusing the offer without making a negative statement. Close with a positive comment.

Don't burn your bridges—you may want to work for the organization at some point in the future. Check your letter to make sure the attitude reflected by your statements does not close the door for you. In the following example, the writer shows appreciation and says he would be interested in a more senior position.

Thank you for the offer to become an information specialist in the Research Department of Renfro Corporation. However, as I mentioned at the time of the interview, I am seeking a position as an executive assistant. Another company in the city has offered me a position at this level of employment, and I have accepted it.

Mr. Davis, I appreciate the offer to work for your company and the interest you have shown me. In the future, if a more senior position becomes available, I would be very interested in working for Renfro Corporation.

Conducting an Electronic Job Search

Computers and telecommunications have changed almost every facet of the way we work. In fact, they have played a part in how we *search* for work. The Internet has become a popular tool for searching for available employment and for posting resumes for potential employers to view.

Searching the Web for employment opportunities will not eliminate the need to practice traditional job-hunting techniques, but it does add another dimension to your job search. Not only will you be able to find positions available, but you can also locate names of companies within a specific zip code in your area.

Job announcement databases are available for browsing. By browsing through Web sites, you will reach many online job search facilities. Here are two popular Web locations:

- www.monster.com
- www.careerbuilder.com

In the highly competitive search for work, the Internet has become a new job market. The Web may be used for job searching, but it is also useful for sending your resume to one of the online career services. The online career service will ask you to either complete the online resume builder form, or send a copy of your resume. Your resume information now becomes part of a database that is accessible to employers looking for employees with specific qualifications.

Any reputable online career service keeps confidential the personal portion of your resume (name, addresses, and contact numbers). When an employer believes your credentials match a job opportunity available, the employer will offer to purchase your name and contact numbers. With your permission, the online career service will release the information to the paying customer—a potential employer. As always, be aware of identity theft. After a job offer, confirm the legitimacy of the company and be cautious of someone who calls or e-mails you to obtain additional information such as your bank account number to set up your payroll deductions.

Making Decisions Regarding Employment Opportunities

Decisions, decisions, decisions! As a job searcher, what happens if you are offered several positions of which any one would be ideal for you? Which one do you choose? How do you learn to make good decisions?

Chapter 2 discussed the need for thinking skills, including decision making and problem solving. The same steps to solve a problem that were described in Chapter 2 can be applied to the following situation.

After a number of interviews, Chandra has been offered two similar exciting, challenging positions to work as an administrative assistant in two different companies. Chandra doesn't know which position to accept. She can't decide. How many people have accepted a position to work in a particular environment only to learn months later they had made the wrong decision? Before Chandra makes a decision, let's help her work through the decision-making process.

Step 1 entails gathering all the information you need to decide. What additional information does Chandra need to learn about the companies who have offered her the positions? For example, Chandra might contact a few people "who know someone who knows someone in these companies." She might research salaries in the San Francisco Bay area where the companies are located. She might also increase her span of knowledge about the companies. At this point, she might do more in-depth research about the companies' products and services and their position in their industry. What are the transportation issues?

Stop 'n Check

What additional job announcement databases are you familiar with? List them here:

_____

_____

Chandra has completed Step 2 (determine what you know) and Step 3 (determine if additional information is needed) by studying all the information she had gathered prior to her interviews, during her interviews, and since she had been offered these positions. In Step 3, Chandra learned one company would reimburse 100 percent tuition while the second company would reimburse tuition up to 50 percent.

Chandra's next step—Step 4 (outline all possible solutions)—is to develop alternatives or possible solutions. The more alternatives she can develop, the better her final decision will be. What alternatives has Chandra been able to develop? Her list includes:

- Accept the position where her friend works and with whom she can carpool.
- Accept the position with the smaller company as she had a good feeling about this employer.
- Continue to look for other potential employment.

At Step 5 (analyze each solution) and Step 6 (identify pros and cons), she begins to consider the alternatives and implications. In other words, she must consider all the good points, or *pros*, and the bad points, or *cons*, of each alternative. Here are a few of her considerations.

- She must ride the Metro to reach one company while she can carpool to another.
- From a friend who is employed by one of the companies, Chandra has learned the company has great benefits and shows a progressive working team concept.
- Chandra had a great feeling about the other company and its environment.
- Being reimbursed for 100 percent of tuition appeals to Chandra, who is interested in continuing her education.
- Benefits are important; however, Chandra's husband has health insurance coverage through his employer.

As Chandra evaluates each alternative, she must consider the following:

- What will each choice cost her?
- What is the most favorable outcome she can expect from each?
- What is the most unfavorable outcome?

Stop 'n Check

Of the steps described in the decision-making process, which one would you consider to be the most difficult to complete? Why?

_____

_____

At this point, Chandra may begin discarding one or more alternatives, or she may discover that she needs more information, which means returning to Step 3 in the process.

In Step 7, Chandra must decide on the best alternative and take action on it. What's "best" depends on things such as the comprehensiveness and accuracy of the information gathered in Steps 1, 2, and 3, her ingenuity in developing alternatives in Step 4, the degree of risk she is willing to take, and the quality of analysis in Step 5. Sometimes people cannot decide; therefore, they more or less make their decisions like throwing darts at a board! After considering all the alternatives and implications, Chandra consciously decided to accept the position with the company where her friend worked, where she could carpool, and receive up to 50 percent on her tuition.

Once a decision is made, evaluate the results of implementing a decision. To complete this step, ask yourself the following question: Did my choice accomplish the desired result? For Chandra, her decision was a good one as in six months she received a promotion and a salary increase.

If the follow-up and evaluation indicate the desired outcome wasn't achieved, you will want to review the decision process to see where you went wrong. Doing so provides additional opportunities to consider other alternatives as circumstances may have changed and allows you to approach your decision again with a fresh perspective.

Considering a CV for International Employment

Working overseas can be an exciting option. The potential benefits to working abroad are many, including lucrative salaries, tax exemptions, overseas service premiums, free housing, completion bonuses, forty days or more of annual vacation time, international travel, and education allowances for dependents.

The range of international employment opportunities available is broader than most Americans expect. The overseas job market is as diverse as the domestic U.S. market.

Individuals with backgrounds in private business, nonprofit organizations, government work, international agencies, teaching, construction, telecommunications, computer specialties, and management information systems may find opportunities that will satisfy their interests and pay them better than comparative positions in the United States.

The **curriculum vitae (CV)** or international-style resume is used in overseas job hunting. The standard CV is between four and eight pages long and may contain a personal information section, references, detailed information on all former positions held, a list of memberships in professional organizations, overseas living and working experience, publication credits, and detailed education information. It should also include a recent picture. Based on the next steps to be taken by an interested potential employer, you may be asked to forward a CV, including copies of all diplomas, certificates, and transcripts, and a copy of your passport.

You should be aware that companies and organizations outside the United States are under no legal constraints as to what information they may require from a potential job candidate.

Quick Tips

PRELIMINARY WORK COMPLETED BEFORE SUBMITTING A RESUME

- Take advantage of the Internet.
  - Visit the company's Web site.
  - Learn as much as possible about the company.
- Remember, a good resume doesn't always mean it will fit job openings with *all* companies.
  - Tailor your resume to focus on the company's specific job opening.

- Editing your resume can be a *minor* task for you but can make a *major* impact on the person reading it!
- Keep a list of the cover letters and resumes you sent, when you sent them, and to whom.

Concept Review and Reinforcement

Review of Key Concepts

OUTCOME	CONCEPT
1. Identify sources for locating employment opportunities.	Sources of job prospects include: network, campus career development centers, offices, job fairs, business sections of newspapers and newsletters, direct application, staffing agencies, the federal government, and newspaper advertisements.
2. Complete a self-assessment inventory.	A self-appraisal inventory helps organize information about educational background, work experience, and personal qualities.
3. Describe the significance of practicing ethical behavior during the job search.	Employers have a zero tolerance for misrepresenting or falsifying information regarding employment, education, or experience.
4. Prepare a resume.	A resume emphasizes employment history, educational background, and special skills and abilities. 　The purpose of a resume is to obtain an interview. • Chronological resume: Lists employment history with most recent position first and identifies specific employers and positions. • Functional resume: Itemizes duties and skills, rather than specific employers and positions.
5. Prepare a cover letter.	Primary purpose of cover letter is to obtain an interview. 　Reasons to write a cover letter: When job you are seeking is located in another city; when you are answering an ad; and when you mail or fax a resume. • An applicant who does not know that a job opening exists writes a prospecting cover letter. • A solicited cover letter is written in response to an announcement that a job opening exists.
6. Complete an employment application form.	Application form may be the first impression a company has of you. • Be prepared to complete an application: have a black ink pen, information for references, dates of previous employment, social security number, and exact title of position for which you are applying.
7. Prepare for an interview.	Purpose of the job interview is twofold: Give interviewer opportunity to evaluate applicant in terms of needs of organization, and give applicant a chance to appraise job and organization. • Before the interview, prepare thoroughly by researching the organization, anticipating questions, planning appearance, and organizing important materials to take to the interview. • During the interview, remain courteous, confident, and composed. Listen intently and answer interviewer's questions by giving full answers. • Discussion about salary is appropriate only after job offer has been made, unless the interviewer brings up the subject. • Watch for cues that interview is closing. Remember to firmly shake hands, restate interest in position, and check follow-up procedure that the organization will use. • Make each interview a learning experience. 　Ask yourself questions to improve your self-promotion.

8. Compose the following letters: thank-you, reminder, inquiry, acceptance, and refusal.

Letters essential for continuing and finalizing a job campaign fall into these five categories.

9. Apply decision-making skills to the job search process.

The decision-making process is composed of seven steps:
Steps 1, 2, and 3. Gather information.
Step 4. Outline all possible alternatives.
Step 5. Analyze each alternative.
Step 6. Identify pros and cons for each alternative.
Step 7. Select the best decision or solution and at some point, evaluate your decision.

Key Terms

Blind advertisement. An anonymous listing of a post office box number or a telephone number but not a company name; used to eliminate interviewing a large number of unqualified applicants.

Chronological resume. Lists employment history with most recent position first.

Curriculum vitae (CV). An international-style resume, between four and eight pages long, that may contain a personal information section, references, detailed information on all former positions held, a list of memberships in professional organizations, overseas living and working experience, publication credits, and detailed education information.

Functional resume. Itemizes your duties and skills rather than specific employers and positions.

Mentor. A more experienced colleague who offers information and advice about the organization and provides career direction.

Networking. The interactions of people who meet and exchange information.

Prospecting cover letter. Expresses the applicant's interest in working for a particular organization, calls attention to the applicant's qualifications, and inquires about the possibility of a job opening.

Qualifications cover letter. Includes only the position requirements your qualifications meet or exceed.

Resume. A summary of an applicant's employment history and educational background.

Scannable resume. A resume that is plain in its format so that companies can scan it as pure text into their resume management systems.

Self-appraisal inventory. A detailed explanation of your educational background, work experience, and personal qualities and interests.

Solicited cover letter. Written in response to an announcement of a job opening.

Targeted resume. Focuses on the applicant's achievements and abilities that relate only to a specific job.

For Your Discussion

Retrieve file C3-DQ from your student data disk.

DIRECTIONS

Enter your response after each question or statement.

1. Explain how business news items can prove to be a valuable source of job prospects.

2. What is the advantage of searching for job openings that are not advertised?

3. How does answering a newspaper employment advertisement differ from using other sources for employment?

4. What is the main purpose of the resume? In what other way can it be used?

5. Why should every job applicant prepare a self-appraisal inventory?

6. How does a chronological resume differ from a functional resume?

7. What is the purpose of the cover letter?

8. How does a solicited cover letter differ from a prospecting cover letter?

9. What guidelines should be followed to organize an effective cover letter?

10. Why would an organization request that an applicant fill out its application form when the applicant has already submitted a resume?

Building Your Office Skills

Exploring the Workplace: *Activities*

1. Research the employment ads for positions for which you qualify or would like to qualify eventually. Make a list of your top three choices. Include the position titles, duties, and types of industries in which these jobs are found—for example, medical, legal, or insurance. Describe why you would like to obtain these positions. Think about the size of the company and its products or services. List your knowledge, skills, and abilities that can be applied to your choices. Evaluate your choices. Consider if one company is closer to you in location. Do you have transportation, or must you consider additional costs in getting to a particular location as one of your choices? As you evaluate your alternatives, consider the size of the company. Does it make a difference to you in benefits and/or advancement? Report your summary in table format in memo form to your instructor.

2. Visit a private staffing service or public office employment agency in your area to determine how the agency places its clients in office support positions. During your visit, gather information about its employment testing program. For instance, ask the agency to share information with you about the kinds of employment tests it gives for at least three different office support positions. Report your findings in a memo to your instructor.

3. Visit your campus career development center to gather the following information: specific career information about your chosen occupation, employment opportunities in your local area, upcoming local job fairs, and interest surveys or assessments that will help direct you in your chosen occupation. Report your findings in a memo to your instructor.

4. In your team, develop items for a Do/Don't checklist, not to exceed a total of ten items. The items represent qualities that make a resume acceptable or unacceptable. Include a rating scale with a range from 1 to 4, with 1 representing unacceptable (U) and 4 being acceptable (A). Each team member prepares a resume. When everyone's resume is complete, review each other's resume and check off items on the form, as you believe they have been accomplished, satisfactorily or unsatisfactorily. Here is an example of a Do/Don't checklist:

DO LIST	UNACCEPTABLE		ACCEPTABLE	
SELF-INVENTORY	1	2	3	4
DON'T LIST	UNACCEPTABLE		ACCEPTABLE	
MISSPELLINGS	1	2	3	4

Developing Critical Thinking Skills: *Problem Solving on the Job*

Retrieve file C3-OJS from your student data disk.

Directions

Enter your response after each situation.

1. **Stretching the truth.** Ismael, your best friend, has been offered a position at your company. Both of you are excited about his job because it is a great opportunity, and you will be able to share a ride to work. Once you learn about the position he has accepted, you are concerned. You are aware of the qualifications for the position, and you know that Ismael doesn't have some of these qualifications. You suspect that Ismael may have "stretched" the truth about his qualifications. What should you do?

2. **Becoming informed.** A job announcement posted on the office technology bulletin board appeals to you. A variety of responsibilities are listed. You believe you have the qualifications required for the position. The salary is excellent. The address of the company is local, but you have never heard of the company. You would like to know more about the company before you apply. When you go to the library to find out about the company, neither you nor the staff can find any information. Using the information in this chapter and other information that may be provided, what can you do next to become informed about the company?

3. **Decision making.** You have received two job offers. One is from a small metal-building manufacturer who employs a total of 100 employees with only one fabrication facility. The second offer is from a national insurance company with thousands of employees and regional offices covering the United States. The smaller of the two companies offers a starting salary that is $1,000 per year more than the national insurance company, but it has no retirement or profit-sharing plan. The larger company offers $1,000 less in direct compensation but provides a liberal benefits package that includes sick leave, profit sharing, and retirement plans. As you consider these two options, consider the following questions:

a. Compare the companies to determine which one offers the greatest potential opportunities for personal and professional growth, the greatest monetary gain, and the best benefits package?

b. Are you looking for immediate financial gain with limited career growth?

c. Are you looking for possible long-term financial gain with possible long-term security?

4. **Identifying unacceptable features in resumes.** You have been an administrative assistant for three years. Because the company is rapidly growing, three new office support positions have been created in your department. Your manager asked you to review the resumes that applicants have sent. After reviewing the resumes, you find that only five of twenty-five resumes look acceptable. List items or features that would not be acceptable in a resume.

Using the Web: *Research Activities*

A. Compare salaries for three position titles in your zip code area.

1. Enter http://salary.com.

2. Using the Salary Wizard shown at the left side of your screen, enter the job title.

3. Click in box for zip code and enter your zip code.

4. Click on Search.

5. Read through the descriptions and select any one that says View Basic Range (free), which means it's free of charge.

6. If the screen asks you to sign up for anything, skip down the screen until you find "Not now . . ." and click on Continue.

7. In a few seconds, a basic report appears. Make a note of the salary information so you can summarize it later.

8. At the top of salary.com, find the Search box and enter another position title and continue with the next search. Be sure to note the salary information for your summary.

9. Repeat Steps 2 through 7 again to create the search. Note the salary information to be included in your summary.

10. Compare the results of the three searches in a memo to your instructor. How important are salary and benefits to you in considering a position? Does any of this information change your mind about the position in which you are currently employed or would like to be employed in the future? Summarize your findings showing the highest salary first. Using a memo format, list the position titles and salaries in a table. Be prepared to share your memo with your instructor and class members.

B. Complete the following Web searches:

1. In your browser's search box, enter *fastest growing occupations requiring postsecondary degree*.

a. List the top 10 occupations.

b. Identify the Web site.

2. In your browser's address box, enter www.acinet.org. This site provides a wealth of career information. On the right side of your screen, locate Career Tools. Find and review the Skills Profiler and Resume Tutorial. Identify at least three things on this site you found interesting. Identify two areas where you would like to spend additional time.

3. Summarize all your findings from Steps 1 and 2 and compose a memo to your instructor reporting the results of your searches. Be certain to identify the Web sites.

C. Determine if you are an expert at job hunting by completing this online quiz.

1. Do a general search for Quintessential Careers Job Skills Quiz.

2. As you read each statement, indicate your answer on a sheet of paper.

3. Before you move to the next question, check your answer.

4. Submit your answer sheet to your instructor.

5. In a memo to your instructor, explain your rating, along with strengths and areas for improvement.

Get Tech Wise: *Using Resume Wizard*

Follow these steps to use the Resume Wizard.

1. Open Microsoft® Word and make sure a blank document screen displays.

2. Click on the File menu and select New.

3. On the New Document task pane, click On My Computer. On the Template screen, click the tab— Other Documents. Double-click on Resume Wizard.

4. Click on the Next button.

5. Select the style you want: Professional, Contemporary, or Elegant. Then click on Next.

6. Click on the type of resume you want to create: Entry level, Chronological, Functional, or Professional. Then click on Next.

7. Enter your personal data. Then click on Next.

8. Accept or add standard headings for the resume style. Then click on Next.

9. Accept or add optional headings for the resume style. Then click on Next.

10. Accept or change the order for the resume headings. Then click on Next.

11. Click on Finish to view your resume.

12. Click the mouse in each bracketed area [ ] and type the requested information.

13. Proofread your data, save, and print.

Improving Your Writing Skills: *Capitalization Workshop*

Retrieve file C3-WRKS from your student data disk.

Simulation: *In the Office at Supreme Appliances*

Supreme Appliances

In Chapters 1 and 2, you had already completed an orientation for interns and had worked for Ms. Quevedo, vice president of marketing for Supreme Appliances, Inc., for several weeks. She has been aware that you would be completing your internship requirements in a few weeks. During the time you have worked for Ms. Quevedo, she has had an opportunity to evaluate your qualifications. She has already determined her staffing needs and knows a position for an administrative assistant will be needed by the time you complete your internship. Because you have demonstrated skills and abilities needed for the position and have put forth a special effort to learn more about the company and division, Ms. Quevedo is interested in your applying for the position. Based on the concepts presented in this chapter, prepare the appropriate documents for HR.

Application 3-A

Preparing for an Interview

Supplies needed: Form 3-A, Self-Appraisal Inventory; use the employment ad from Supreme Appliances or an ad from your local newspaper.

Retrieve file C3-AP-A from your student data disk.

Directions

Attach a copy of the ad to the following documents to be submitted to your instructor.
　Prepare the following:

1. self-appraisal inventory
2. resume
3. cover letter
4. three responses to questions that might be asked of you during the interview (If you have already responded to questions in the Stop 'n Check in this chapter, be sure to select different questions for this application.)
4. questions you might like to ask the interviewer

Application 3-B

Completing an Interview

Supplies needed: Resume, set of questions from Application 3-A, list of questions you may ask the interviewer.

Directions

Schedule an appointment with an interviewer. You may ask someone other than a friend or relative to interview you, or your instructor may set up an appointment for you. Your instructor may arrange for a video to be made of your interview so you can review it. From the review of the video, your instructor or the interviewer may suggest ways to improve your interviewing skills.

Application 3-C

Writing a Thank-You Letter

Supplies needed: Plain bond paper.

Directions

Write a thank-you letter to the interviewer from Application 3-B. If you did not complete an interview, provide a copy of an employment ad (or use the ad from Application 3-A) and address to whom you will write a thank-you letter.

Application 3-D

Writing a Job Acceptance Letter

Supplies needed: Plain bond paper.

Directions

Assume that you have accepted the job from the interview conducted in Application 3-B. Write a job acceptance letter. If you did not complete an interview, provide an employment ad (or use the one from Application 3-A) and address to whom you will write a job acceptance letter.

Application 3-E

Completing an Application Form

Supplies needed: Form 3-B, Application for
Employment.
Retrieve file C3-AP-E from your student data disk.

Directions

Before you begin this application, check with your instructor to see if you are to use a pen or keyboard information on the application form. Follow your instructor's
directions and complete the application form.

Application 3-F

Writing a Job Refusal Letter

Supplies needed: Plain bond paper.

Directions

Assume you have refused the job from the interview conducted in Application 3-B. Write a job refusal letter.

Application 3-G

Completing a Job Search Checklist

Supplies needed: Form 3-C, Checklist for Your Job
Campaign; a folder with multiple pockets in which
to keep your job-campaign materials until they are
ready to be placed in your portfolio.
Retrieve file C3-AP-G from your student data disk.

Directions

Guidelines are provided in Form 3-C for conducting your
own job search. Complete the activities on the checklist,
filling in due dates and completion dates.

Building Your Portfolio

With the help of a team member or your instructor, select the following documents: resume, follow-up letters (thank-you, job acceptance, and job refusal). Remember these documents must be error-free. If instructed, place documents in plastic protection sheets and add to your portfolio.

4

Managing Your Work, Time, and Other Resources

chapter **outline**

learning **outcomes**

When you have completed this chapter, you
should be able to:

- Manage resources, applying the self-
management concept.

- Explain the difference between working
efficiently and working effectively.

- Describe at least eight tools and
strategies to follow to establish your
own work habits.

- Describe at least five ways to organize
the office supplies and your
workstation.

- Identify at least five ways to cope with
stress.

- Discuss the principles of ethical conduct
regarding your work, time, and other
resources.

Organizing work and managing time and other resources are essential for measurable accomplishments day after day, year after year, throughout a lifetime, regardless of the goals a person endeavors to reach. Chapter 2 introduced five basic workplace skills that are necessary to be successful in the workplace. Those skills include *resources*, which involves identifying, organizing, planning, and allocating resources. Examples of resources are workplace facilities, material, people, and time. To manage your work, time, and other resources, you must demonstrate self-management. This chapter focuses on managing resources applying the concept of self-management, which requires you to cultivate attitudes and traits that will contribute to your success.

Continuous Improvement

A quality revolution continues to take place in both the private and public sectors. The generic term that has evolved to describe this revolution is **continuous improvement**. The revolution was inspired by a small group of quality experts—individuals such as Joseph Juran and the late W. Edwards Deming. Today, many of these individuals' original beliefs have been expanded into a philosophy of organizational life that is driven by customer needs and expectations; that is, continuous improvement strategies have expanded the term *customer* beyond the traditional definition to include everyone involved with the organization, either internally or externally—encompassing employees and suppliers as well as the people who buy the organization's products or services.

Many organizations have adopted a sound and effective continuous improvement approach for achieving success. It is fundamental and practiced through these basic principles, such as:

- customer focus
- continuous improvement and learning
- strategic planning and leadership
- teamwork

Companies that adopt continuous improvement programs not only plan for strategic business improvement but also encourage learning and new leadership ideas from their employees. As authors Stephen Robbins and David DeCenzo note in *Supervision Today* (2007, Prentice Hall), "The foundation of continuous improvement is built on the participation of the people closest to the work. As such, continuous improvement can help eliminate many of the bottlenecks that have hampered work efforts in the past and can help create more-satisfying jobs" (p. 47).

As an office professional in a company that embraces a continuous improvement approach to business, you are likely to become a member of a problem-solving team, or a team working to improve a business process somewhere within the organization. Most certainly you will be empowered to make broader decisions within your area regarding ways in which you manage your work, time, and other resources.

WHAT IS A CONTINUOUS IMPROVEMENT APPROACH?

The continuous improvement approach—making the customer the number one priority—does not, at first glance, seem to be significantly different from other customer-focused strategies. However, an all-out quality commitment requires companies to eliminate wasteful practices, redesign business methods, and adopt a focused approach to managing quality for customers, employees, and leaders.

HOW DOES CONTINUOUS IMPROVEMENT WORK?

Continuous improvement provides no single formula that works for every organization. Instead, this approach makes all employees responsible for strengthening the competitive position of their company by improving its products and services. The best use of labor (your work), time, and resources is seen as the key to the success of the continuous improvement approach. Anything less simply increases the expense to the customer, which results in loss of market share, profits, jobs, and ultimately the business itself.

In the office, continuous improvement means that each employee is involved with office teamwork and focused on customer (internal and external) satisfaction. Employees at every level are encouraged to find new and innovative ways of doing their jobs more effectively and to be flexible enough to assist others. You may be empowered—that is, given more autonomy and broader responsibilities—with the goal of simplifying office operations. You will be given responsibility for making decisions that affect your own effectiveness and performance.

You will be judged on your team contribution and on your innovation: If the filing system does not correspond to the operation—change it! If your colleague is having difficulty completing a project—help out! If a customer has a complaint—resolve it! If steps in a procedure need to be refined, share your ideas with your supervisor and your immediate work group. If you see resources being wasted, report it to your manager or work group.

Stop 'n Check

Describe the role of an office professional in a company that adopts a continuous improvement approach to business.

_____

_____

Effectiveness and Efficiency

For the office professional, being effective and efficient are equally important. However, these two qualities are often confused with each other. Although interrelated, these terms have very different meanings.

Stop 'n Check

The need for efficiency has a profound effect on the level of effectiveness. Why is that?

_____

_____

WHAT'S THE DIFFERENCE?

Effectiveness means producing a definite or desired result. For example, an effective professional completes the right task correctly. **Efficiency** means producing the desired result with a minimum of effort, expense, and waste. Whereas it is possible to be effective without being efficient, the cost of inefficiency is usually too great for profit-making organizations; they must combine efficiency with effectiveness.

Office professionals are hired to perform a variety of tasks, being responsible to one or several managers. Yet they continually must do three things to organize their work so they can perform efficiently:

- Divide large projects into manageable segments of work.
- Group related isolated tasks to reduce the time consumed in changing from one unrelated task to another.
- Match the work to the time frame in which it must be performed by classifying it as work that must be done today, work that must be done this week, or work that has no specific deadline.

Time Management Tools and Strategies

Organizational skills are a requirement for success in today's workplace. Office professionals work with a constant and rapid flow of information. To contribute to the processing of information, professionals must be able to organize their work and manage their time and other resources. They also must be able to evaluate their effectiveness and efficiency and to look for ways to increase their contributions to the organization, keeping in mind the goal of continuous improvement. **Time management** is defined as organizing and sequencing tasks so they are accomplished in an efficient manner.

The need for effective time management tools and strategies becomes clear when office professionals answer the following questions:

- Do I ever seem to get everything done that I had hoped to accomplish?
- Is my desk cluttered with papers that I am constantly reshuffling but never processing?
- Do I often work overtime at the office? Do I often take work home to complete?
- Am I continually being interrupted by telephone calls, visitors, and others who monopolize my time or coworkers who want to socialize?
- By failing to set priorities, do I spend most of my time on trivial details without enough time remaining to work on the important jobs?

Office professionals who answer "yes" to all or most of these questions probably spend a lot of time on tasks that produce only minimal benefits.

Time management involves:

- Developing work habits that result in maximum efficiency
- Acquiring knowledge and skills to extend performance beyond present capabilities
- Controlling attitudes and emotions that have a tendency to steal time
- Developing an effective reminder method for following through on each task at the appropriate time

There is no single "right way" for managing time on the job. The rules are often job specific and change from organization to organization. Exactly what constitutes successful time management is hard to define without using specific examples from the workplace.

Effective employees establish efficient work *patterns,* but no two employees necessarily follow the *same* pattern. Nevertheless, the ideas presented in this chapter can be used as a guide to establish your own work habits and time management techniques.

It is important to remember this is only a guide. You will have to work hard and think about how best to adapt these tools and strategies to your own situation. For example, balancing family responsibilities and work responsibilities is a significant challenge to many office professionals. Organizations are developing employee-friendly policies and support systems that provide flexible work schedules and permit more work-at-home and telecommuting options.

In a type of schedule redesign known as **flextime,** employees work a set number of hours each day but vary the starting and ending times. Flextime allows management to relax some of the traditional "time clock" control of employees' time. Similarly, working from home and telecommuting present an extraordinary opportunity to manage your own work, time, and other resources.

Finally, time management involves self-management, which was introduced in Chapter 2. To manage your resources (time, tasks, materials, and people), you must be able to practice self-management. *Self*-management means you focus on achieving specified goals and objectives by a given deadline and in order of priority.

Stop 'n Check

1. Complete the following sentences by filling in the appropriate words. Time management involves:

   a. developing _____ habits that result in maximum efficiency.

   b. acquiring knowledge and skills to extend _____ beyond present capabilities.

   c. controlling _____ and _____ that have a tendency to steal time.

   d. developing an effective _____ method for following through on each task at the appropriate time.

2. Define self-management.

   _____

   _____

LEARN THE JOB

The organization expresses its objectives—the tasks to be accomplished—in terms of long-range, intermediate, and short-range goals. Management focuses its attention on achieving organizational objectives by accomplishing those goals. In any given week, your manager or supervisor will devote time to both dealing with the work at hand and addressing longer-range goals. As you join this dynamic environment, be as flexible, adaptable, and tolerant as you can in order to provide real value-added assistance.

In a new job, you must understand how your manager works. Organize your day's work so that it coincides with that of your manager; do not expect your manager to adjust to your work schedule. At first you should concentrate on learning and learn what is expected of you before taking initiative.

Before you can organize work, you must know what the position or job entails. In most cases, someone will explain your new position and duties to you. This might be the office assistant you are replacing, an administrative assistant in your department, a mentor, an office manager, or your manager. During this orientation, you should:

1. Listen.
2. Take notes.
3. Ask questions that will increase your understanding of what is being explained. Be alert to what are considered priority items.
4. Learn your manager's preferences.
5. Write down the names of people you meet, note their department, and learn quickly what they do (Figure 4-1).

Every day make an effort to learn more about your job and efficient ways to perform the tasks to be done. Learn the job not just for the current week and the next but also for three months to a year in advance. Become familiar with the information in your office. For instance:

FIGURE 4-1 • Office assistant taking notes.

- Carefully study all the instructions left for you by the previous office professional.
- Check on the different kinds of stationery and forms in your desk or office supply cabinet and determine when each is to be used.
- Read instruction sheets that have been prepared for certain tasks you are to perform.
- Find out what is in the active files.
- Study the organization of electronic folders either in the word processing directory or in the electronic mail system.
- Refer to the organization directory or chart to learn the names of the executives and other employees and their titles.

When you report to work, the former employee may not be available to train you. You may not find a procedures or desk manual describing your duties or tasks. In this situation, your manager may be able to direct you. However, if your manager cannot help you with the procedures, you must rely heavily on your resourcefulness and judgment in finding answers. Keep in mind you cannot perform at maximum value to the organization until you fully understand the scope and responsibilities of your position.

ASSIGN PRIORITIES

Setting priorities is the most difficult part of organizing your work and assigning your time. Although you are guided by general policies about priorities, you need to make judgments concerning performing the work in the most beneficial way for your manager and for the organization. Performing the work in the order in which it is submitted to you is not always feasible because some tasks have more pressing deadlines than others. An example of a low-priority item is a memorandum written only as a matter of record. It can be keyboarded and filed at any time.

Some time management consultants suggest assigning priorities to work tasks in four categories:

1. (1 or A). Must be done immediately; cannot be delayed
2. (2 or B). Must be done today
3. (3 or C). Less important—may be done as soon as time allows, perhaps the following week, if necessary
4. (4 or D). Least important—may be completed within the next week or two, if necessary

As time passes, tasks that are in category 4 will move to categories 3 and 2. Other consultants suggest three categories. What is important is that you establish your categories with your manager.

If you are unsure how to determine priorities, ask yourself the following questions about each task:

- Is this task or project a priority of my immediate supervisor or manager?
- Is this work needed immediately? Is this a daily task or a long-range task?
- How much time is required to complete this task?

- Are others involved in the completion of this task?
- Is there a specific deadline for this task?

You can determine the order of priorities in at least four ways:

1. Ask questions of those involved in the process.
2. Study documentation, such as the office manual.
3. Listen to your manager's requests to determine a "pattern."
4. Keep a record of how work flows in and out of the office.

For example, know when routine reports are due and how much in advance to request work from other departments, learn mail pickup and postal schedules, and be aware of the most convenient times to reach executives by telephone.

WORK WITH MULTIPLE MANAGERS

The demands of managers and others for whom you work will be the over-riding factor in how you divide your time. When you are working for two managers, one may have lots of work for you and the other very little. Or perhaps you work for a group of salespeople who are out of the office much of the time; each one may have very little work for you, but every salesperson expects you to do it on the day he or she returns to the office. Under this arrangement, you can prepare a schedule a week in advance showing who will be in the office on which days of the week. This information may not be easy to obtain, but it will be helpful when it comes to answering the telephone and anticipating your own workload.

Over time you will learn how much time you need to devote to performing each person's work. For your own use, keep a record of how you spend your time. Prepare a time distribution chart, as shown in Figure 4-2. The **time distribution chart** is designed to show how work and time are allocated for several workers performing related office tasks; however, with minor changes it can be used to show the distribution of time and duties performed by one worker for several others. To complete the chart, follow these steps:

1. At the top of the columns, write the names of those for whom you perform work.
2. Enter the time used and a brief description of the task performed in the columns below the names.
3. After keeping the charts for several weeks, total the time used on behalf of each person and compute percentages.

After reviewing your results, answer the following questions:

- Were there any surprises? What was the biggest surprise?
- How many of the tasks you performed were planned?
- How much of what you did was unplanned?

Your analysis will give you some estimate of how much work to expect from each person, and it may suggest what you are doing that could be channeled elsewhere. When you have so much work to be done that some of

Susan Clark TIME DISTRIBUTION CHART April 16, 20 — —

MAJOR ACTIVITIES	James	Hrs.	Chung	Hrs.	Rodriquez	Hrs.	Parker	Hrs.	Ramos	Hrs.	For Group	Hrs.	TOTAL
Incoming Mail											Open and distribute	1-1/2	1-1/2
Telephone	Handle calls	1-1/2			Handle calls	1/2							2
Transcribing	Letters	1/2	Report	1/2			Letters	1/4	Memos	1/4			1-1/2
Appointments	By telephone	1/2					Telephone and in person	1/2					1
Payroll											Time sheets, distribute checks	1/2	1/2
Misc.											Replenish supplies	1/2	1/2
TOTAL		2-1/2		1/2		1/2		3/4		1/4		2-1/2	7

FIGURE 4-2 • Time distribution chart.

it must be reassigned, your chart will be especially helpful to you and your manager in deciding which duties or activities might be handled by someone else.

Most office professionals who work for groups comprising employees of different ranks give highest priority to the work of the top-ranked person in the group, second priority to the next in rank, and so on. This arrangement may ensure a good relationship with your manager, but it may also create problems, particularly if some employees at the lower ranks feel they can never get their work done on time or at all. Eventually they will complain. Avoid this situation by learning how to assess the urgency of the work of the senior managers or supervisors in the group. You will discover that some of their work can wait. Make your own judgment without discussing it with others and proceed with completing the tasks. However, when your work is backed up to the extent it must be discussed formally, the most senior manager has the responsibility of assessing the total workload and determining the need for additional help.

Some employees, in an effort to gain priority for their requests, label all requests "ASAP" (as soon as possible) or "Rush." In each case you must judge what is "rush" and what is not. When you sense these employees are under a lot of pressure, you might occasionally prevent a disruption by giving priority to their work; however, this practice must not become the norm. By giving priority to managers who mark all items "Rush," you are encouraging this behavior at the expense of other managers' work. Those managers who decrease stress in the office by practicing effective time management should not be penalized. Dealing with this issue requires diplomacy. The best advice is to collect facts before you approach the problem. For example:

- How many rush items are you receiving?
- Which managers are giving you the rush items?
- What are the rush items?
- On what dates are you being given the rush items?
- When are the deadlines?

The time distribution chart will assist with collection of this information.

You can maintain more control over your work schedule by relying on your own judgment about the order in which work should be done, instead of trying to follow rigid rules. Your judgment must be good, and you need to be as concerned about your rapport with the members of the group as you are about the quality of the work you perform.

Some office professionals aspire to work for only one manager. Advantages and disadvantages to such a situation include the following:

Advantages of Working with Only One Manager:

1. You are often viewed as having more status within the company.
2. You do not have to adjust to conflicting management styles.
3. Your manager has a clearer idea of your time constraints. Where several managers share the same office professional, the managers often are not aware of pressures being placed on him or her by their colleagues.

Disadvantages of Working with Only One Manager:

1. Your responsibilities may be routine. When an office professional works for more than one manager, the worker often receives a greater variety of projects to complete. Remember, the more experience you receive, the more marketable you become.
2. An office professional working for only one manager gains business contacts from only that source. If you work for a number of managers, your chances of networking are improved; this, of course, could improve your future employment opportunities.
3. Working for only one manager may not allow you to practice your organizational skills to the same degree that working for multiple managers would.

The preference is a personal one. Both positions may require equal challenges. If the challenges do not present themselves, find them!

ADOPT A FLEXIBLE PLAN

Management consultants recommend planning work and then following the plan. This is good advice; however, planning may present disadvantages. Consider these issues:

- Planning may create rigidity.
- Plans are difficult to create in a dynamic environment, one in which the environment changes frequently.
- Plans tend to focus on what works today and not how to deal with the issues of tomorrow.

In the end, you must plan for the ideal distribution of your time, but your plan must be flexible. Use your plan as an overall guide, but do not become discouraged when you cannot follow it closely. Your reputation for being flexible, adaptable, and tolerant with your plan will serve you well for the rest of your career.

One of your major responsibilities is to save your manager time. To accomplish this,

- perform as much of your manager's work as you can. For example, ask which telephone calls or e-mail messages you can handle.

- decrease interruptions or at least schedule them. Keep a list of questions you may have or someone else has and present them at a scheduled moment or during a particular block of time that is convenient for your manager.

- collect and verify facts and assemble materials he or she will need to perform the task.

To enable your manager to perform with maximum efficiency, tackle the most pressing or important job first and keep adjusting your plan so you can meet the corresponding deadlines.

You must recognize your work schedule is not truly your own. Your work schedule is governed not only by your manager's objectives and deadlines but also by the inherent schedule of the organization's information. For example:

- You may plan to devote the morning hours to starting a lengthy assignment only to discover your manager wants you to process a new expense summary in order to meet a scheduled payroll run.

- A telephone call from the corporate home office requesting critical information may take precedence over everything else.

- The deadline for sending the department's weekly and monthly revenue report is based on a routine and defined schedule.

- Whenever an interrelated department with which you work changes its schedule, you may have to adjust your schedule to accommodate that department.

MANAGE DETAILS

Keep an ongoing list of the tasks you have grouped and add miscellaneous items by completing a daily **to-do list**. This list must be updated daily, preferably at the end of the day. To keep your to-do list current, use Microsoft® Word or Outlook. If you prefer, write your to-do list in a notebook or create a form.

Figure 4-3 shows a sample format for a daily plan or to-do list. Numbering or ranking priorities according to the 1, 2, 3, or 4 categories discussed earlier will help you to constantly update and reassess your list.

Like every other office professional, you will be faced with the problem of keeping up with a myriad of details. In fact, you will be forced to devise methods for managing them. Not only must you record these details immediately, but you also must put them in a form that will enable you to locate and use them later.

To capture details, use spiral-bound notebooks, notepads, or your computer to help you manage details and reminders. The advantage of an electronic format is that the detail is easily changed or modified and that its distribution to other staff is simple (see Figure 4-4). Forms bring related

DAILY PLAN CHART

Date _____

Rank	Calls to	Phone No.	Notes	Rank	Reminders

Rank	Letters and Memos to	Notes	Rank	Other Tasks

Priority Rank: 1, urgent; 2, today; 3, as soon as time allows

FIGURE 4-3 ● Daily plan.

FIGURE 4-4 • Gantt chart.

GANTT CHART

Name of project: Keying analysis   Name of team leader: <u>Ilka Stiles</u>

ESSENTIAL TASKS		CRITICAL DATES													
		May 01	May 03	May 05	May 07	May 09	May 11	May 13	May 15	May 17	May 19	May 21	May 23	May 25	
1. Design a questionnaire to examine the keying equipment used in offices.	S	▓													
	A														
2. Make appointments with admin. assistants to collect answers for questionnaires.	S		▓	▓											
	A														
3. Prepare and mail confirmation letters with attached questionnaires to admin. assistants.	S				▓										
	A														
4. Interview admin. assistants to collect info. and questionnaires.	S							▓	▓						
	A														
5. Send each admin. assistant a thank-you letter for his/her contribution.	S								▓						
	A														
6. Collate, calculate, and analyze the results of the questionnaires.	S								▓	▓					
	A														
7. Prepare graphs to indicate results of information collected on questionnaires.	S										▓				
	A														
8. Compose and edit report to describe the finding of the data.	S											▓	▓		
	A														
9. Key, assemble, and bind report.	S												▓		
	A														
10. Submit report to general manager.	S													▓	
	A														
	S														
	A														

S = Scheduled time   A = Actual time

information together in one place and prompt the user to record all the essential facts. For example, a Gantt Chart, named for Gantt, a pioneer of project management techniques, provide graphical visualization of a project that displays each task as a horizontal bar. The primary purpose of the Gantt Chart is to graphically display project schedule information by listing project tasks and their corresponding start and finish date in a calendar format.

Recording facts as soon as they become available to you is an important aspect of managing details. You will discover the practice of "do it now" is in conflict with the concept of grouping tasks to save time and energy; nevertheless, you need to capture details at the precise moment they arise in order to keep up with them.

Actually, the means you devise for keeping up with details can vary from task to task according to the work involved and your personal preferences. That being said, recognize in all your work:

- the importance of having some method for capturing details
- the need to be consistent in following your method

You can use check marks, initials, codes, and symbols to indicate the status of each detail you want to capture. For instance:

- The date stamp you place on a piece of incoming mail tells you have already seen it.
- The check mark by the enclosure notation on the file copy of a letter reminds you that you did include the enclosure.
- The electronic date and time notation attached to a computer file (located under File, Properties) indicates when the file was last modified.

In addition, if you are consistent in using each type of notation to convey its respective meaning, the absence of an appropriate notation will alert you to give attention to that item.

When you encounter a new task, spend a little time deciding how you are going to keep up with the details and then be consistent in doing so.

Details arranged in the chronological order in which they were originally recorded usually are not in their most usable form. Details must be arranged so they can be located quickly. The organization can range from indexing on cards to computer information search tools.

Organizing the details you need to keep, such as the names of new contacts, telephone numbers, changes of address, and schedule changes, can be done with great efficiency with a computer because you need to record it only once. Not everything you write down needs to be transferred; this is especially true of reminders of things to do or other temporary items. Cross out the reminders as you complete the tasks, but go over your list carefully and transfer the reminders of tasks yet to be done to your to-do list for the following day. You may also want to transcribe detailed instructions you have in your notebook and place them in your office manual.

As more managers become familiar with their personal digital assistants (PDAs), some office professionals are giving up traditional personal organizer notebooks, in favor of a palm-sized personal digital assistant, such as a Palm. The personal digital assistants (PDAs) retain the essential phone book, calendar, memo pad, and to-do lists. The wireless models enable you to access the Internet to send and receive electronic mail. Having a computer backup of your calendar, action list, and names and telephone numbers is a lifesaver. If you lose or misplace your traditional personal organizer notebook, you've lost it all.

GROUP SIMILAR TASKS

You can save time and energy by not shifting from one task to another. For example, replenish your office supplies once a week or less often. Avoid making a trip to the supply area every day. If supplies are delivered to you, complete one requisition for all the supplies you will need for several weeks.

Stop 'n Check

1. Identify at least one tip you can recall from the following tools and strategies:
   a. Learn the job _____
   b. Assign priorities _____
   c. Work with multiple managers _____
   d. Adopt a flexible plan _____
   e. Manage details _____
2. Of these items above, which tip could you use in the next week or so?
   _____

Different work requires different degrees of concentration and, in turn, a different pace. Therefore, to control your pace, group the tasks that require the same degree of concentration. Letters to confirm information and to make routine requests are favorable in tone, usually short, and easy to write. Group these letters and compose them rapidly; then use a slower pace to compose a letter requiring a long explanation that may require input from your manager.

In addition, group tasks to increase effectiveness. For instance, making a telephone call should not be a routine task to be sandwiched between other assignments in an offhand way. A telephone call conveys an impression of the organization to the receiver. By grouping your telephone calls, you can give them your complete attention and project your personality in a thoughtful, businesslike manner.

WORK AT ONE TASK AT A TIME

Schedule your work so you can keep at one task until you finish it or until you come to a logical stopping place, such as a new subheading. If a stopping place does not exist, try to work at one task at the very least, one hour or longer—even if you have interruptions. Jumping from one task to another is confusing. Furthermore, reviewing work to figure out where to begin and recalling what has and has not been done results in wasted time and energy. You will be rewarded threefold when you stay with a task until it is completed:

- You will be motivated by the satisfaction of having finished the task.
- You will save time you otherwise would lose locating where you left off.
- You will decrease the risk of forgetting to perform a part of the task.

As you work, thoughts about other tasks will flash across your mind. Write down each usable thought on your to-do list and continue to concentrate on the work at hand. Learn how to handle interruptions and shift back quickly to the immediate task; coping with interruptions is discussed later in this chapter.

Form the habit of working at an uncluttered desk. On the immediate work area of your desk, place only the materials you need for the task on which you are working. Because you can give attention to only one main task at a time, put the other work aside, carefully organized and labeled. Stacking work on top of work in a disorganized way leads to confusion; it is how papers get lost and nerves become frayed. The time you spend organizing work in progress will not be wasted. When you put aside everything except the task on which you are working, you will feel more relaxed and be able to focus it. Additional discussion about your workstation is provided later in this chapter.

START THE DAY WITH A DIFFICULT TASK

Begin your day in an unhurried way so you will not need the first thirty minutes at the office to "pull yourself together." If you commute and frequently worry about your bus or other transportation being late, try to improve your day by taking an earlier bus (or train or subway). If you drive, allow an extra five or ten minutes to get a head start on the morning traffic rush. Arrive early, go over your plans for the day (which you prepared the day before), and then tackle a task that requires concentration and effort on your part. Tackle either a task that is difficult or one that you dislike. It will seem easier when you are more energetic and your mind is clear.

Make the first hour one of accomplishment, not one in which you simply *get ready to work*. Perhaps your first tasks will be to listen to the voice mail, take messages and direct them to the person who is to receive them, and read your electronic mail. As soon as you finish these regular duties, start a challenging task. Of course, there will be times when you use the first hour to complete unfinished work from the day before.

Some workers claim that they perform best early in the day, others, in the afternoon, and still others that they concentrate best very late in the day. Psychologists have confirmed that every person has his or her own preferred work cycle. If you consider yourself an afternoon performer, use your afternoon hours for your most creative and challenging work, but force yourself to make the first hour a brisk one. Workers who waste time getting started are putting themselves under unnecessary pressure to accomplish their work in what remains of the day. At any rate, do not use the beginning of the day to perform those easy tasks that can provide relaxation at intervals during the day.

AVOID PROCRASTINATION

Procrastination is an unproductive behavior pattern that causes you to delay working on your most important assignments and to focus on tasks that aren't priorities. We all procrastinate to some degree at certain times, but to some people it is a habit. To break the habit of procrastination, you must first gain an understanding of your behavior and then work to overcome it. You can gain a better understanding of this behavior by taking these steps:

1. Admit that you are procrastinating.
2. Ask yourself what type of projects or tasks causes you to procrastinate. Some office workers might see a major project as a horrendous task, whereas others might find daily routine tasks too much to face.
3. Ask yourself why you avoid these projects or tasks. Are you bored with the routine or afraid of the challenge? Are you avoiding interaction with certain office workers or authority figures? Do you fear failing at greater responsibility?

After answering these questions, you will be better prepared to overcome this unproductive behavior. The following tips will help you avoid procrastination and become more productive:

1. Ask yourself what is the worst thing that can happen while you perform this task. Once you think it through, you will find that the risk created by the project or task is not that great; in fact, the benefits of completing the project or individual tasks will far outweigh the difficulties.
2. If the project is large, divide it into smaller sections. Several small tasks always appear to be easier to accomplish than one large task. For more suggestions, refer to the "Manage a Large Project" section presented later in this chapter.
3. Reward yourself often. Allow yourself a break or a more pleasant task once you have completed a portion of the work. Small and frequent

rewards work better for procrastinators than one large reward after completion of a very strenuous task.

4. Ask yourself what is the downside of not completing the task on time—or worse, not completing the task at all. Does not doing the task mean the loss of your job, a demotion, or the loss of respect from your peers and managers?

5. If you are a perfectionist, you may be avoiding a simple task because of your working style. Remember not all work must be flawless. Working *smarter* instead of *harder* means recognizing the difference between work that must be perfect and work that can contain minor flaws and acting on it.

COPE WITH INTERRUPTIONS

Every challenging office job that demands a variety of duties will be punctuated by interruptions. To avoid some interruptions:

- Practice avoidance by organizing your work area so that it is less accessible to coworkers who wish to socialize during work hours. Try moving extra chairs away from your desk, or moving or angling your desk so that it cannot easily be seen by passersby. Remove the candy dish that encourages your coworkers to drop by to grab one or two pieces and interrupt your work.

- To avoid interruptions caused by noise, relocate noisy equipment away from your desk.

- When you are working on a project or an individual task that requires your full attention, ask another worker to handle your telephone calls; explain the urgency of your task to coworkers and then move to a location away from your desk. Be careful not to overextend your requests for help as your coworkers may grow tired of covering for you during these times.

Your success in coping with interruptions will depend on your attitude toward them and your ability to handle them. You know that interruptions will occur—the telephone will ring, a visitor will walk in, a coworker will ask you a question, your manager will need assistance. What you do not know is the precise moment when the interruption will occur.

Recognize that interruptions are part of the job and allow time for them in your planning. Keep a record of the number of telephone calls you receive in a typical day, the number of visitors you receive, and the number of times you assist your manager and coworkers. Estimate the time consumed by these interruptions and determine how much time you have left for other tasks. Do not create your own frustrations by planning to accomplish more than you can get done. For a review of a time distribution chart, refer to Figure 4-2.

Do not resent interruptions. Keep calm; do not allow yourself to become upset. You will feel less frustrated if you know how much time you need to perform each of your normal tasks. For example, keep a record of how long it takes to key a two-page letter, to compose a one-page schedule, to develop a twelve-page formal report, and to process the daily mail. This is useful information for future planning and scheduling. If you discover you are running out of time to meet a deadline, decide for yourself which work can be postponed. Use your time for the priority items.

Give adequate time to handling each interruption. Do not appear to be rushed. Be courteous, but do not waste time because of an interruption. To reduce the time used for each interruption, proceed in the following ways:

1. Mark your place as soon as you are interrupted—a light, erasable check mark in the margin with a soft-lead pencil will suffice.

2. Once you are interrupted, handle the interruption immediately if it can be dealt with in only a few minutes. If a coworker asks for information, look it up and supply the information while the coworker is at your desk. In response to a telephone call you can handle, follow through on the caller's request, even looking up information if you can do so without keeping the caller waiting a noticeable length of time. However, if the interruption requires prolonged attention, you may have to postpone action on it. Realize, however, that each time you must postpone following through on a request, you are creating a new item for your to-do list.

3. Quickly resume work where you left off at the time of the interruption. Do not encourage coworkers to linger in your office. Be courteous, but do not continue a telephone conversation beyond the time necessary to handle the call.

4. Avoid interrupting yourself because of lack of planning.

5. Keep a pencil in your hand, or keep your hands on the keyboard. These actions inform the visitor that you are eager to continue your work.

6. Do not get involved in office gossip. Small talk creates big interruptions.

7. When a coworker drops by your office for a visit, stand up. Often a person feels invited to sit if you are sitting. If the coworker sits down and you feel the need to sit, do so on the edge of your desk. This does not invite the coworker to become too comfortable.

8. When possible, hold meetings in another person's office. This allows you to leave as soon as the business is complete. Meeting with visitors in reception areas or conference rooms helps to keep the meeting short because these areas often do not provide the privacy of an office.

When You Must Interrupt Others, Be Considerate

✓ Wait until the other person is at a break in his or her work.

✓ Direct your questions to the correct person, and do not interrupt others unnecessarily.

✓ Do not ask others to answer questions to which you can find the answers by looking them up.

✓ Accumulate the questions you must ask your manager; then ask several at one time to cut down on interrupting her or him.

✓ Write an electronic message enumerating your questions. This is an excellent way to avoid a direct interruption and to obtain a quick response.

Stop 'n Check

1. Identify at least one tip you can recall from the following tools and strategies:
   a. Group similar tasks _____
   b. Work at one task at a time _____
   c. Start the day with a difficult task _____
   d. Avoid procrastination _____
   e. Cope with interruptions _____

2. Of the items above, which tip could you use in the next week or so?
   _____

GET IT RIGHT THE FIRST TIME

To produce acceptable work on the first try, plan each task before you begin, focus on the exactness of the details as you perform, and then check each finished task for correctness and completeness before you release it. Remember waste results when work that could have been completed correctly on the first try must be redone.

Before you start performing a task, make sure you understand the instructions. Then review the facts, visualize the work in its finished form, and make a plan.

The speed with which business information flows, especially with the advent of computer networks, has placed a premium on accuracy. An error that has been released is difficult to retrieve. Problems created by errors that are released into the channels of information are not only time consuming to correct but can also result in losses to the organization. For example, a keyboarding error in a budget can be duplicated to other departments within an organization and go undetected until after decisions are made to purchase new equipment. The consequence may be some departments may not be able to purchase the equipment as planned for in a particular quarter and may be delayed in ordering the equipment for some later time or may be forced to delay the purchase for a year. Check your work carefully. Proofreading techniques are provided in Chapter 6.

Evaluate Your Workload

Most organizations provide a lunch hour and short morning and afternoon breaks during a regular workday. With these exceptions, employees are expected to perform efficiently and effectively through the day.

To maintain your best performance throughout the day and the week, experiment with alternating difficult and easy tasks to establish the best combination for conserving your energy. Observe which tasks consume a great deal of energy and which ones seem to require little energy. Rotate tasks that require more concentration and effort with tasks that require less thought and energy. Whether a task is difficult or easy for you to perform will depend on your ability, your experience in performing the given task, and your attitude toward it.

Performing an undesirable task requires an extra expenditure of energy. Repetitive tasks are often disliked because of their repetitious nature rather than for the work itself. Fortunately, the computer and its various peripherals have introduced new and interesting methods of accomplishing routine tasks.

Here are a few more tips to follow:

- Once you discover which tasks are easy for you, save them to perform between difficult tasks.
  - Use them to provide relaxation as you work.
  - Throughout the day, alternate difficult tasks with easy ones.
  - When possible, also alternate sitting with standing tasks.
  - When you cannot change the task, change your pace. After lunch and after your morning and afternoon breaks, tackle difficult tasks.

- When you are estimating the time needed for performing a long, complicated task, allow for a decrease in production as you continue working. You cannot expect to perform at your maximum rate for six or seven hours. Your productivity will be highest when you can keep fatigue to a minimum. Discover and maintain a pace that will make it possible for you to do your best work.

Because of the pressure of work, you may sometime find it necessary to forgo your morning or afternoon break and shorten your lunch hour. A particular due date or deadline may require you to stick to the difficult task and postpone other work. During these heavy peak work times, you may be asked to work overtime, and others in the office may be asked to assist you. All of these pressures may make you feel you have no control over your work schedule. When you face these situations, reevaluate your workload.

How to Balance Your Workload

✔ Establish the duration of peak workload, how often it will occur, and what you can do about it, if anything.

✔ Determine what preparation you can make in advance to lessen the peak workload. To avoid crises and to prepare for the "peaks and valleys," set your own personal deadlines a few hours or days before others set deadlines for you (Figure 4-5).

✔ If there is no let-up in the work, either you are not approaching your job in an efficient way or you need assistance. Discuss the situation with your manager and be prepared to offer viable solutions.

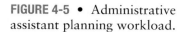

FIGURE 4-5 • Administrative assistant planning workload.

MAKE A DAILY PLAN

Many management consultants agree that if you use the last ten to twenty minutes of your day to get organized, you will notice there is far less clutter after a week or so. This activity can help you wind down at the end of a hectic day and ease your transition from work to home.

At the end of the day, review the work you must do the next day. Estimate the time each of your tasks will take and fit them one by one into time slots. Go through the same steps daily, and then leave your office with the satisfaction of knowing your work is well organized for the next day. To prepare a systematic daily plan, you could proceed as follows:

1. Whether you use an electronic calendar or a desk calendar pad, make sure that the appointment entries in your manager's calendar and yours are identical.

2. Go over your to-do list. Refer to Figure 4-3 as an example of a form. If something on the list must be carried out the following day, enter it in your to-do list. As you are planning your work, you will think of tasks that must be done sometime later. Put notes about these on your to-do list.

3. Locate the reports, correspondence, and other items to which you know your manager will need to refer during meetings or conferences or before he or she places a telephone call, writes a report, or carries out other responsibilities. Flag these with colored stickers so you can retrieve them quickly the following day. Likewise, locate the information you will need in order to proceed with your own work.

4. Complete your paper filing and lock the files. As a part of your filing routine, transfer copies of completed work and the related data from your work-in-progress folder to the file.

5. Clear your desk, putting everything in place.

The next morning, review the entries in your daily appointment calendar and your to-do list. By using this system, you will be well prepared to start your work immediately. You will enjoy the satisfaction of having a plan for your tasks and priorities.

PLAN ASSIGNMENTS IN ADVANCE

With the exception of routine duties, office work requires planning. The amount of planning time needed depends on how complicated the job is, how long it takes, and whether or not the person doing the work has ever performed similar tasks.

Executives in successful organizations plan three to five years in advance. Managers at all levels plan at least one year in advance. Observe how your manager and others in your organization think ahead, and then apply some of their techniques to your own assignments. The time you spend thinking through what needs to be done will save you minutes and hours of redoing work.

Take time to study a job until you can visualize it to its completion, regardless of how complicated or lengthy it is. People who work aimlessly seldom reach the goals toward which they should have been working. If necessary, ask yourself and others what the expected outcome of the specific assignment is. Do not hesitate to ask about the purpose of an assignment. When an assignment is new to you, you may find it difficult, if not impossible, to visualize it to its completion. If necessary, ask your manager to guide you. As you learned in Chapter 1, your contribution to the organization is through the assignments you complete that help the organization achieve its goals.

Don't let thoughts of complicated tasks and deadlines interfere with getting today's work finished. Do one job at a time. Schedule "thinking" time in the same way you schedule time for word processing. Start by writing down your thoughts at random. Organize them later. As you study the job, estimate the time needed to complete each part of it. Start with the completion date and work backward to the current date.

The most critical parts of an assignment are the ones that require other people, either to supply information or to perform certain tasks. Begin your preparation with the segments of the work that involves others.

Assume you are compiling data for a report. Make a checklist of your needs. For instance, will you need special information or materials, such as the most recent figures from the accounting department, a comparative analysis from the data center, photographs to be taken by the audiovisual department, charts that must be reduced in size by the printing department, or the public relations department's approval for the illustrations to be included in the report? Make each of these requests as soon as you are certain of your needs.

As you prepare an assignment in advance, plan it so carefully that you can put it aside and not think about it until you are ready to start it. This is important because thinking about an endless stream of work has a negative effect on performance. Label a folder for the assignment and put everything pertaining to it in that folder. Plan your time. Allow some time for delays. Keep careful notes on what you have and have not done. Once you actually start performing the assignment, make a daily check of the work completed against the projected time schedule.

Review the Gantt chart in Figure 4-4. This chart is an excellent tool for comparing your planned work schedule against the actual time required to complete a task.

MANAGE A LARGE PROJECT

When you start a large project, you will need to allocate some time each day for planning and controlling. The following suggestions should help you manage a large project.

1. Determine the desired goal. Know exactly what you are to accomplish. Being unsure about the goal is a real time waster.
2. Write down the target date.
3. Divide the project into manageable segments and then, as far as it is possible to do so, work with one segment at a time.
4. Set completion dates for each segment; as you progress, check the dates to ensure you are on schedule.
5. Check for the supplies you will need; have a few extras on hand of those that are quickly used.
6. Delegate some of your regular duties, if needed, to make time for working on the project.
7. If you will need the services of others, either within or outside the organization, contact them at the planning stage of the project to find out about scheduling. Determine what you will have to do to meet their schedules.
8. Determine what data you will need, how to obtain it, and when.
9. As soon as you begin the project, make detailed notes in an electronic document or a large bound notebook.
10. Divide the document into subdocuments or divide the notebook into segments, matching the segments of the project.
11. As you plan for each segment or part of a segment, list everything that must be done. Keep adding to your list at random.
12. As you complete each item, mark an X or draw a line through it. Circle in a different color the items still to be done. Do this carefully because the most helpful part of your notes will be the notations about unfinished items.
13. When you have completed an entire segment, write "Completed" at the top of the corresponding page in your document, file, or notebook.
14. When you make a change, be sure to make it everywhere the change occurs.
15. Separate the in-progress segments so you can add to them or reorganize them with ease.
16. Carefully recheck all the circled items to be sure nothing has been left undone.

Creating a detailed project plan and keeping it up-to-date for most nontrivial projects can be a time-consuming process if completed manually. Today, thanks to the use of the computer, automated solutions enable everyone to benefit from using project management methods, such as the one provided by Microsoft® Project, an application software.

Stop 'n Check

1. Identify at least one tip you can recall from the following tools and strategies:

   a. Get it right the first time _____

   b. Evaluate your workload _____

   c. Make a daily plan _____

   d. Prepare in advance _____

   e. Manage a large project _____

2. Of these five items, which one could you use in the next week or so?

   _____

Office Organization

By organizing office supplies and the workstation, an office professional can save a great deal of time and save the company money. Following are suggestions for organizing the office supplies and your workstation.

ORGANIZE THE OFFICE SUPPLIES

1. Label the shelves where supplies are kept. This way other workers who use the supplies will know where to look without interrupting you. This procedure also helps you keep track of supplies on hand.

2. Make sure one person is responsible for controlling inventory and ordering supplies. This is a task that you or a senior office professional will often delegate.

3. Develop your own requisition form, if necessary. Keep these forms in the supply area. Staff will be expected to complete the form if they notice a product is running low. Be sure the form has room for a full description. Encourage the staff to fill in as much information as possible (descriptions, quantities, colors, sizes, and so on). This will simplify your work when it comes to completing the requisition for ordering. In some organizations, the form may be in an electronic format.

4. Compose a list of all items you use on a regular basis. Include the item unit numbers, unit prices, descriptions, colors available, and so on. Post this list in the supply area along with a stack of the requisition forms, which is necessary if you expect staff members to partially complete the requisition forms.

5. Discourage staff members from placing verbal orders with you. This type of interruption can be time consuming: You must stop your work, listen to the request, write down the information, check the supplies, and perhaps get back to the staff members for further clarification.

6. When staff members have rush orders, request they either send you an e-mail request or complete a requisition, and send it to you electronically.

Stop 'n Check

Either in your office or home office, identify at least three tips you can follow to organize office supplies. (If you aren't working, ask a friend who is to share tips on organizing supplies.)

_____

_____

_____

7. Take inventory on a regular basis. Taking inventory once or twice a month on a designated day works well for most offices.

8. Before placing an order, compare prices between the office supply catalogs and advertisements sent to you. Be sure you know your company's procedures for placing orders. Follow designated procedures with accuracy as you will save time and money by getting the order right the first time.

9. Do not over-order supplies, unless you are ordering supplies in standard-sized packages. Too many supplies will cause confusion. Because space is often at a premium, excess supplies tend to create a storage problem. As well, some supplies have a shelf life: if not used before a certain date, they become less useful.

10. When you place an order, be prepared with all the required information. Having requisition forms returned or needing to make a follow-up telephone call to clarify an order will delay delivery.

ORGANIZE YOUR WORKSTATION

A cluttered desk gives clients, coworkers, and managers the impression that you are disorganized. A cluttered desk is not necessarily a sign you are busy; in fact, a cluttered desk simply adds to your workload. It is essential you purge any extraneous materials and then organize the materials you intend to keep.

Place Work in Easy Reach

An unorganized desk area accounts for one of the greatest time wasters in the office. Normal and maximum working areas at a desk have been established through time and motion studies. Materials and supplies should be positioned within the normal working area if the worker is to attain maximum efficiency. You can determine the normal working area of the desk for either the right or left hand by swinging the extended hand and forearm across the desk.

Before you begin a task at a desk or a table, place the supplies, tools, and equipment you will need in the normal working area. Use the space in your desk to store supplies, stationery, and work-in-progress. Materials should pass across the top of your desk but should not be stored on it. Keep a minimum number of items on top of your desk.

File all your work-in-progress in one drawer unless your manager is working on a project that generates so much paperwork the materials have to be subdivided into several folders. Allocate separate space in a vertical file drawer for a project of this magnitude. Never put a single folder of pending material in an unusual place—relocation of this material can lead to confusion and wasted time.

In case you might be absent, let your manager know where you keep important project folders and other work in progress. If the work-in-progress is highly confidential, you may have to store it in file cabinets with special locks at night.

If you have a drawer that is not deep enough to hold file folders in a vertical position, keep it empty. Use it as temporary storage when you want to clear your desk to store the papers on which you are currently working—for instance, while you sort the mail or go to lunch.

Do not use sections of your desk for permanent storage. File completed items immediately after completing a task so you will not be searching in two places to locate one item. Furthermore, you will need the desk space to store the data for the new project or assignment.

Purge Unnecessary Items

One of the first steps to take in organizing your desk is to eliminate all that you don't need. Each time you pick up a document from your desk and wonder where to file it, ask yourself whether there's a law that says you must keep it. If not, consider the recycling box or the garbage bin.

If any of the following applies to a document, you have just cause to purge yourself of paper:

1. Another coworker has filed it where you can access it if needed.
2. The document is duplication. Once you get organized, one copy is all you need of any document.
3. The document is out of date. Newer information is usually better information. You can always get current information from the Internet or from the reference section of the library.
4. Chances are you will never find the time to read the information. If the information is "nice to know" rather than essential, rid yourself of it until you are organized.

You will find that you work much more efficiently after you have organized your desk.

Federal privacy laws require companies to dispose of confidential information properly so it cannot be stolen and misused. If you are disposing of records with private information about customers or coworkers, which might include social security numbers or account data, for instance, follow proper archival or disposal procedures.

Organize Necessary Items

Ridding your workstation of excess paper is only the first step in getting organized. The importance of a highly organized workstation cannot be emphasized enough.

One of the most frustrating time wasters is searching for information that has been filed incorrectly or has simply disappeared. Of course, employing the correct Association of Records Managers and Administrators (ARMA) filing rules is imperative; these rules are discussed in Chapter 8. However,

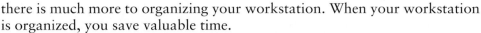

there is much more to organizing your workstation. When your workstation is organized, you save valuable time.

The following suggestions will help you get started:

1. Consider how and where you want incoming work to be placed. Select a system you can use to avoid your manager and coworkers from "dumping" materials on your chair, under your mouse, or on your keyboard. Here is one suggestion:

    • Place all the new mail and paperwork that arrive during the day in the IN box. Once you have processed everything, invariably there are papers and pieces of mail that need to go out; place these in the OUT box. IN and OUT boxes should be clearly labeled and should be either wood or wire because these boxes are the roomiest.

2. If your workstation is currently in a cluttered condition, plan several uninterrupted breaks to attack the problem.

3. Once you have organized the workstation, take a mental snapshot of it and vow you will never leave it disorganized at the end of the day. Start the day with a clear mind and a clear desk. Many offices now practice a clean desk policy, which stipulates that each evening employees must leave their desks in either a totally clear or tidy condition.

4. If your office does not have a paper shredder, approach your manager about purchasing one. Employees are often reluctant to discard confidential material, so they let it accumulate in what eventually becomes a thick folder tucked into a corner of the desk or on top of the desk. Compact shredders can be placed on top of wastebaskets.

5. A basket placed in your workstation to hold work that is pending often becomes a storage bin. If you do not intend to work on a document immediately, file it in its appropriately labeled folder. Then place the folder in the file cabinet and make a comment in your calendar on the day this document must be dealt with. This way the phrase "out of sight—out of mind" will not apply.

6. Use one calendar for all your appointments. Referring to several calendars—personal and business—is a waste of time and will result in disorganization.

7. Wherever you store information—drawers, cabinets, folders, baskets, and so on—affix a label that describes the type of information that should be stored in this location. While you are getting organized, you will have stacks of paper. Organize them by placing a temporary label on top of the pile. Not only will the labels assist you in locating information, but they will also assist others in your absence.

8. Attempt to follow this rule: *Never handle a piece of paper more than once.* At times this rule may be unrealistic, but it will force you to make a decision rather than procrastinate, then handle and reread a document.

9. Never use the surface of your desk as storage space. Your desk is a work area; you need all of it available to remain organized while you conduct your work.

10. Keep your computer reference information current. If names, addresses, and telephone numbers are indexed on your computer system, consider it a priority to update the system as often as possible. You cannot enjoy the efficiency of using a computer system unless it provides correct information.

11. Create a reference for frequently called telephone or fax numbers. Place this reference list nearby or code the numbers into the memory of the telephone or fax machine.

12. Place reference books at an arm's length from your work area. These references should include a dictionary, a thesaurus, an office reference manual, your own desk manual, telephone directories, and the like. When you need these books, you need them *now;* you should never have to look for any of them.

13. Do you really know what is in your desk and cabinets? Schedule fifteen to thirty minutes every month to purge your current bookshelves, desk drawers, and cabinets. You must keep current with the contents of your workstation. Keep the wastebasket and recycling box handy; you should constantly purge your workstation of unwanted materials.

14. If there is a bulletin board in your workstation, be sure the information is current and well organized. If the bulletin board is not easy to use, it is just occupying space and adding to the office clutter. A bulletin board is sometimes an invitation to clutter; if not in use, you may consider removing the bulletin board.

15. After you take a telephone message, place the message in a designated location, off your desk or send the message electronically to the appropriate individual. In this way, you have dismissed the task immediately. You are then free to continue with your other tasks, and your desk is less cluttered.

16. Use colored paper to coordinate your tasks as it draws attention. Using color will assist you in locating categories of information. For example, you will be able to quickly spot blue telephone messages in a pile of white documents. Not only will the colored paper help you get organized but it will also draw the attention of others to requests for action or information you place on their desks. Try using fluorescent-colored paper when you want to get immediate attention.

17. Your workstation will require drawer space for office supplies. Store only a limited supply at your desk; store larger amounts away from your workstation in a supply area or cabinet. The small supplies you keep at your desk such as a stapler, tape, pens, clips, and the like can be stored with drawer organizers. Letterhead, envelopes, forms, and other major paper supplies should be placed in drawer trays, not left out in visible stacks.

18. Your personal items need a place too, but do not crowd your desk surface with family photos. Leave the desk surface as clear as possible and place the photos on top of your credenza or filing cabinet. For personal photos, using the same picture frames will help to avoid a cluttered look.

Use Follow-up Organizers

Follow-up organizers aid office professionals in remembering details and meeting deadlines. In addition to the daily appointment calendar, which you will study in Chapter 10, and the to-do list, office professionals must have a foolproof method of following up on work that will be pending for a week, a month, or longer. The tickler file, which provides reminders according to dates, is the most widely used. A pending file, which is defined in a following

FIGURE 4-6 • Tickler folder.

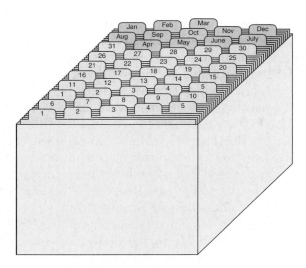

paragraph, can be used for actual documents-in-progress to be processed by specific dates.

Tickler File. Folders can be used to organize a tickler file, depending on the work to be followed up. A **tickler file** is a paper time-management system that can be used for reminders of (1) work to be done at a specified time and (2) incoming information that is anticipated at a specified time. A tickler file set, available at office suppliers, consists of twelve folders with the names of the months printed on the tabs and thirty-one folders with 1 through 31 printed on the tabs to indicate the days of the month. To set up a tickler folder file, place the folders for days of the month, followed by the guides for the months as shown in Figure 4-6.

Do not put original correspondence in the follow-up folders. Make a copy of the original or prepare a memo referring to it for the tickler file; note the location of the original paper on the memo. When you put memos in the folder, use either $8\frac{1}{2} \times 11$-inch sheets of paper or staple small notes to a large sheet. All your notations for the tickler file do not have to be printed. If you recorded the information in longhand as instructions were given or a request was made, you may file these notes as a reminder.

Place a reminder in the file for the date you must begin a task, not the date you must complete it. Follow the same plan concerning reminders for your manager. For instance, if you estimate that it will take you three days to type a periodic report due on Friday, June 30, file the reminder in the folder labeled 27.

A tickler file cannot jog your memory unless you use it. Each morning, without fail, remove the reminders for the day from the tickler file. Place that folder at the end of the numbered folders. As a result, the current folder will always be at the front of the file.

The reminders will fall into three categories:

- those that have already been taken care of
- reminders of work you must carry out that day
- items that must be postponed

Discard any copies or notes pertaining to items completed. Return to the file an item that is still pending. For instance, if you received an acknowledgment saying that a catalog you requested will be sent as soon as the new catalog is reprinted, probably within two weeks, put the reminder back in the file at a date approximately two weeks later.

Near the end of each week as you are planning your work for the following week, review the reminders in the tickler file for the entire week. Estimate the time you will need to complete each task. Remember to coordinate the items to be completed in your tickler file with your to-do list.

On the first day of each month, arrange any reminders for the current month by dates. For example, on the first day of April remove the papers in the April folder and sort and file them by date into the numbered files. Place the folder labeled *April* behind the March folder. As you transfer the items from the month file to the daily files, turn folders representing dates for Saturdays and Sundays backward, and then you will be less likely to inadvertently file a reminder in a folder with a weekend date.

You can accomplish the same thing as a tickler file by adding notes to your calendar. However, if you have bits of notes posted to your computer monitor or on the wall in your work area, you can eliminate these notes by placing them in the tickler folders.

Pending File. A **pending file** supports your regular calendars and holds the actual documents to be completed by specific dates. You should check the pending file regularly to be sure nothing has been overlooked. A pending file is a booklet, made of sturdy card stock, and has dividers labeled 1 through 31.

Stop 'n Check

1. Identify at least three ways you can better organize your workstation, either in your office or at home.

   a. _____

   b. _____

   c. _____

2. Describe the two follow-up organizers mentioned in this section.

   a. _____

   b. _____

Learn to Cope with Stress

Stress happens because of our physical and psychological response or reaction to events, people, and environment. Work can be stressful, yet some people seem to thrive on stress whereas others crumble under the strain. The difference is that those who cope with stress best have control of their jobs and themselves. They are meeting deadlines, but they are setting their own deadlines to the extent that it is possible to do so and working at their own pace. Furthermore, they have a positive attitude toward their work.

A person who has a lot of responsibility outside his or her job often suffers from stress because he or she is trying to do too much—accepting responsibility for family and home, volunteering for community work, going to school, and trying to satisfy many different demands.

To cope with stress, analyze what is happening to you. Frequently, it is not the situation that causes stress but how you react to it and what you do about it. Also, the longer the duration of the problem, the more likely it is to produce stress. A certain amount of stress helps us to be alert, efficient, and creative, but it is important to learn to cope with stress before it becomes too great.

How to Cope with Stress

✔ Recognize that anger and frustration are energy wasters. Handle conflicts calmly, as they occur, rather than letting things build up. For example, if arriving at work late causes you stress, can you get up earlier in the morning? Can you decide what to wear in the evening rather than waiting until the next morning? Can you ask your children to help prepare their lunch in the evening or the next morning? By recognizing the event that triggers your stress, learn to take control.

✔ Organize your work and your time for the entire day. Prioritize your tasks. Do not plan more than is possible to do in a day.

✔ Analyze an overload of work and discuss it with your supervisor. Offer solutions. You will relieve stress when you face a situation rather than allow yourself to be overwhelmed by it.

✔ Do not be overly critical of your work and yourself; do not expect too much of others. Strive for excellence, not perfection, but at times be pleased with an acceptable performance.

✔ Slow down! Work at a comfortable pace that will enable you to keep mistakes to a minimum, to relate well with others, and to avoid backtracking and revising.

✔ Avoid taking on too much. Learn to say "no," but say it tactfully.

✔ Talk about your stressful problems. Find someone in whom you can confide—someone away from the company, who is an effective listener.

✔ Eat nourishing food regularly and in moderate amounts.

✔ Schedule relaxation. During a break on the job, be quiet and practice relaxing techniques. Allow yourself a quiet hour at home. Schedule some time for a hobby.

✔ Get regular exercise of the right kind for you.

✔ Escape to a movie, to your favorite TV program to spend time with others, or do something for someone in need. Escaping from your daily problems will give you fresh energy to cope with them.

Stop 'n Check

1. When does your stress occur?

   _____

   _____

2. Identify one event, person, and particular environment that stresses you.

   _____

   _____

3. Identify a way to cope with the stress described in Step 2.

   _____

   _____

Ethics Regarding Your Work, Time, and Other Resources

ETHICAL ☆ ISSUES

As you learned in Chapter 1, ethical concepts have a far-reaching effect on today's business offices. The ethical office is an extension of the ethical organization, an organization that acts with integrity and lives up to its responsibilities and obligations. It encourages employees to assume their responsibilities by authorizing and entrusting people to complete their job or task ethically and to the best of their ability.

Our ethical responsibilities need to be reviewed with this level of trust. If you find yourself considering any of the following, your organization's policies and trust are likely to be compromised.

With regard to Work

The examples show how employees have demonstrated unethical behavior regarding their work.

- practicing **plagiarism,** using the words or ideas of someone else as your own without permission or reference to the original source
- harassing coworkers
- making false claims of illness
- exaggerating accomplishments
- endangering others with unreasonable conduct or deception
- providing negative public statements about the organization

With regard to Time

Here are a few ways employees have shown disregard for their company's values.

- going home early—consistently
- taking extended breaks (lunch, morning, and afternoon)
- taking frequent smoking breaks
- getting to work late—consistently
- gossiping in the office
- taking personal telephone calls—consistently
- talking too long on personal telephone calls

With regard to Other Resources

Some organizations have noted the following unethical behavior in their employees regarding other resources.

- playing computer games
- conducting personal research on the Internet
- exaggerating time devoted to a task or project
- taking paper, paper clips, binders, stamps, and other office supplies

Stop 'n Check

Discussed in previous chapters, when you face ethical situations, you face a decision. To justify questionable conduct, people have developed some common rationalizations. In *Supervision Today,* authors Stephen Robbins and David DeCenzo identify common rationalizations (2007, Prentice Hall). Below are two examples of common rationalizations. Answer these questions: What does it mean? What are examples of this situation or issue?

1. "It's not really illegal."

   _____

   _____

2. "No one will find out."

   _____

   _____

Consider your company's code of ethics as well as your own standards. Ask yourself if you would feel comfortable if the results of your decision or action were to be published on the front page of a national newspaper or discussed on local television tomorrow. You'll know the difference between right and wrong!

The Environmental Office

In Chapter 1, you learned about your workstation and its environmental importance to you and your health. This section lists environmental suggestions that affect resource management. If your office has not yet committed itself to becoming environmentally conscious, with your team, initiate this change.

- When you must discard paper, ask yourself if the paper can be recycled. Special paper baskets, boxes, trays, and bins for the collection of recyclable paper should be set around the office in convenient locations.

- Fax cover sheets are often a waste of paper; they almost always end up in the wastebasket. Temporary adhesive fax-transmittal labels will often suffice. These small adhesive notes can be adhered to the first page of the fax and are adequate when a lot of cover information is not necessary. The adhesive notes can be purchased in office supply stores.

- Although a little more expensive, recycled paper may be purchased.

Ask the office staff to contribute additional ideas about environmental issues that might pertain to your office that will help everyone to manage their resources. Continue to explore options.

Stop 'n Check

How does an environmental office contribute to the concept of managing your resources?

_____

_____

How Do Different Cultures Understand Time?

The essence of time management is organizing and sequencing tasks—a notion that may seem different to other cultures. This section describes how two employees from different cultures may perceive time management in different ways.

Suppose you were an employee from the home office in Venezuela, and a new employee from Canada came by your cubicle for her 2 p.m. appointment. She arrived on time and as you began to help her, you also handled a telephone call, answered a coworker's question, and sent a fax to someone else. Do you think the new employee would think you were efficient, perhaps a little disorganized, or not very people oriented?

Everyone has his or her personal style and preference for getting work done; that is, some people know at the start of the day what they will do during segments of the day: morning, lunch, afternoon, and evening. When unexpected tasks arise, others that had been scheduled are rescheduled. These workers are interested in performing their tasks or activities.

In contrast, although other workers know in general what the tasks in a given day will be, they allow fluidity in their day. This means they allow for more and less important tasks that take more or less time and assume many tasks will be handled simultaneously. Simultaneous tasking is extremely useful when people and the relationships between people are valued highly. This means these workers can spend all the time they want or need with a person when at the same time they are giving some attention to other (valued) people or tasks. These simultaneous-task workers are interested in achieving their results through their relationships.

From your point of view, you feel you are efficient because in effect you are accomplishing several other tasks in addition to dealing with the visitor. From your visitor's point of view, however, he or she may feel the unfocused activity is not nearly as efficient as it could be. In other words, the visitor may believe that if you were to work exclusively with him or her during the appointed time, the time spent would have been much more efficient.

Learn to understand other cultures' personal styles and preferences for getting work done by discussing these issues with people who are members of the culture you want to understand.

Stop 'n Check

1. What is your preferred style in managing tasks while helping a colleague at the same time?

   _____

   _____

2. In you were a visitor in another office, how would you feel if the person attended to other tasks in addition to helping you?

   _____

   _____

Quicktips

LACK OF COMMUNICATION OR MISUNDERSTOOD INSTRUCTIONS CAN CAUSE A WASTE OF TIME

- If you receive e-mail instructing you to do something:
  - Print the message and keep it as a reference while you work.
- If you are verbally given information:
  - As soon as you can, return to your office and read through your notes.
  - Send a message to the requesting person and list what you understood the task to entail.
    - If there is a problem, it is resolved quickly before you waste a lot of time.

Concept Review and Reinforcement

Review of Key Concepts

OUTCOME	CONCEPT
1. Manage resources, applying the self-management concept.	To manage your work, time, and other resources you must demonstrate self-management, which requires you to cultivate attitudes and traits that will contribute to your success.
2. Explain the difference between working efficiently and working effectively.	*Effectiveness* means producing a definite a or desired result, whereas *efficiency* means producing a desired result with minimum of effort, expense, and waste.
3. Describe at least eight tools and strategies to follow to establish your own work habits.	Tools and strategies include: learn job, assign priorities, work with multiple managers, adopt flexible plan, manage details, group similar tasks, work at one task at a time, start day with difficult task, avoid procrastination, cope with interruptions, get it right first time, evaluate workload, make daily plan, prepare in advance, and manage large projects.
4. Describe at least five ways to organize the office supplies and your workstation.	Organizing office supplies saves resources. Be sure someone is responsible for controlling inventory and ordering supplies. Organize your workstation; designate necessary items to be placed on top of desk, and establish a location for projects in progress.
5. Identify at least five ways to cope with stress.	To cope with stress, analyze what is happening to you. Ways to cope with stress include: • Handle conflicts calmly as they occur, rather than letting things build up. • Organize work; prioritize tasks. • Recognize and analyze an overload of work and discuss it with your supervisor. • Strive for excellence, not perfection. • Work at a comfortable pace. • Learn to say "no" tactfully. • Talk about stressful situations. • Eat nourishing food regularly and in moderate amounts. • Allow relaxation to be part of your schedule. • Get regular exercise. • Escape to a movie, spend time with others, or do something for someone in need.
6. Discuss the principles of ethical conduct regarding your work, time, and other resources.	Complete tasks ethically and do tasks to best of your ability. Your company's policies and trust are likely to be compromised if you engage in unethical situations regarding your work, time, and other resources.

Key Terms

Continuous improvement. Business philosophy that emphasizes customer focus, continuous performance improvement and learning, strategic planning and leadership, and teamwork.

Effectiveness. Producing a definite or a desired result.

Efficiency. Producing the desired result with a minimum of effort, expense, and waste.

Flextime. Permitting employees to work a set number of hours each day at varied starting and ending times.

Pending file. Used for actual documents in progress to be processed by specific dates.

Plagiarism. Use of words and ideas of someone else as your own without permission or reference to the original source.

Procrastination. Unproductive behavior pattern that causes you to delay working on your most important assignments and to focus on tasks that aren't priorities.

Stress. Physical and psychological response or reaction to tense events, people, and environment.

Tickler file. Used for reminders of (1) work to be done at a specified time and (2) incoming information anticipated at a specified time.

Time distribution chart. Displays the distribution of time and duties performed by one worker.

Time management. Organizing and sequencing tasks so they are accomplished in an efficient manner.

To-do list. A summary of priority items to be accomplished during a day.

For Your Discussion

Retrieve file C4-DQ from your student data disk.

DIRECTIONS

Enter your response after each question or statement.

1. Describe the effect that a company's continuous improvement approach would have on an office assistant's work, time, and other resources.

2. Distinguish between effectiveness and efficiency and include examples in your response.

3. Describe at least eight tools and strategies to follow to establish your own work habits.

4. What effect will a manager's work preferences have on the way the office professional's work is organized?

5. Why should an office professional who works for several managers ask them to resolve assignment conflicts among themselves?

6. Describe how to organize yourself at the end of the day.

7. Suggest at least five ways to organize the office supplies and your workstation.

8. Distinguish between a tickler file and a pending file; include examples in your discussion.

9. Explain why a situation that seems stressful to one person is not stressful to another, and identify at least five ways to cope with stress.

10. Identify at least five unethical concepts regarding work, time, and other resources.

Building Your Office Skills

Exploring the Workplace: *Activities*

1. How many unfinished projects do you have? Are you burdened with the thought that "everything is started and nothing is finished"? Make a list of your unfinished projects and tasks. Select the one you can finish in the least amount of time and complete it. Select another task you can complete in a few minutes and then complete it. Notice how you lighten your load by finishing tasks. Use what you have discovered to remind yourself to finish tasks as soon as possible, leaving your mind free to tackle new assignments. Write a memorandum to your instructor describing your list of unfinished projects and tasks and the tasks you completed in the least amount of time. Also, describe what you have learned from completing this activity and how it will help you to list and prioritize future projects and tasks.

2. Are you using bits and pieces of time? To find out, keep a record (a spreadsheet is an excellent tool to set up your record). Begin by keeping a to-do list. In the left column, jot down at random everything you think you must do other than the major tasks. Leave space to the right of each item. As you complete each task, write down the date, the number of minutes used, and when. For example, was it between classes? Were you waiting for your ride? Was it at lunchtime? At the end of one week, determine how much extra time you gained by using bits and pieces of time. Multiply your answer by 52 to estimate the time you could gain in one year. Write a brief summary to your instructor and attach your record. Be prepared to report your results to the class.

3. Keep a time distribution chart for two weeks similar to the one in Figure 4-2. (Using Excel is an excellent tool to set up your chart). Write down what you are doing; what the task involves or refers to; and who else is involved if the task is a meeting or an appointment. Also assign a priority to the task: 1, 2, 3, or 4. Then note whether the activity was planned (P) or involved an interruption (I). At the end of two weeks, analyze your chart for the following:

   a. **Telephone calls.** Add up the calls made or received during the two-week period. How many qualified as legitimate; how many were unwelcome interruptions?

   b. **Drop-in visitors.** Add drop-ins; what percentage of the day do these get-togethers consume? How many were legitimate; how many qualified as unwelcome?

   c. **Paperwork, projects, writing, planning.** How many of these activities qualified as a top priority? As 2s, 3s, or 4s? Averaging more than three or four number 1 priorities per day means ineffective planning or inaccurate rating.

   d. **Other activities.** Consider all remaining entries. Again, ask yourself if the remaining tasks are legitimate or unwelcome, unnecessary, or "firefighting."

   After your analysis, respond to the following questions:

   - Am I complicating tasks, putting more time into them than necessary?
   - Am I using efficient techniques whenever possible?
   - Am I taking on inappropriate work? Being effective? Doing too much for others? Failing to delegate, if possible?

   Summarize the results from your analysis in memorandum format to be shared with another class member. Compare the results and discuss how improvements can be made toward managing your resources. Be prepared to submit your report to your instructor along with your notes from meeting with your team member.

4. Divide into teams and visit an office supply store and look at work and time organizers. Next, compare these organizers with available time organizer software (for example, paper desk calendars versus electronic calendars). As a team, summarize your findings of the manual versus electronic work and time organizers. Be prepared to share the summary with other class teams and to submit the summary to your instructor. If the activity is completed as a team, be certain to identify your team members' names and each person's contribution to the activity.

5. Set up a tickler file system and use it for the quarter or semester. Show your system to your instructor. Once a month, share your progress with your instructor in using the system. At the end of the term, report the results to your instructor. Outline the benefits of using this follow-up system. In the report, include any difficulties you had either in using or maintaining the system.

Developing Critical Thinking Skills: *Problem Solving on the Job*

Retrieve file C4-OJS from your student data disk.

Directions

Enter your response after each situation.

1. **Telephone interruptions.** You have a new job and have been working for three weeks. Each afternoon before leaving work, you carefully plan your work for the next day. You are having difficulty keeping up with your plan because the telephone rings continually. You are becoming frustrated because you must answer so many telephone calls.

   - What problems could be causing this situation?
   - What stress-reducing techniques can you use?
   - What are some solutions to resolve the situation?

2. **Lack of organizational skills.** Jon, one of your team members, has confided in you about the lack of organizational skills shown by his supervisor, Selina. He describes his supervisor as one who focuses on relationships but not on details. In other words, she works well with employees; however, she always seems to be "handling a crisis" rather than planning to avoid one. Selina has difficulty in keeping up with her correspondence, and her office looks like a construction crew has worked in it. Lately, she has missed some major deadlines. Jon has asked you to help him help his supervisor. With another class member, discuss Jon's supervisor's situation and complete the following:

   - What problems can you identify in the supervisor's situation?
   - List as many ways as you can to help Jon approach his supervisor. Discuss the advantages and disadvantages of each item you have listed.
   - Suggest at least three solutions to help Jon help his supervisor to manage her work, time, and other resources.

3. **Stressed out.** You work for five managers, and today one of the managers, Jean Forrester, has sent three reports to you for final completion with a special request to finish this work by this afternoon at 5:30 p.m. However, the other three managers have also assigned work to you and expect you to complete the assignments right away. You have had some difficulty in completing one of the assignments, you have missed lunch, and now you are becoming frustrated due to the pressure of completing all the work.

   - What problems can you identify in this situation?
   - What stress-reducing techniques can you use?
   - What can you do to resolve this situation?

4. **Inefficient performance.** Mickel Rasmussen is a new member on your team. You have noticed that his desk is messy; he cannot find certain telephone directories, supplies, and reference materials. He is constantly asking others for information that he has but doesn't want to or can't locate. Mickel has materials stacked in piles on his desk and on the floor around his desk. He has had trouble determining priorities and has not produced his work in a timely fashion. You realize that Mickel's work is being haphazardly performed. Your manager has come to you to discuss Mickel's inefficient performance.

   - Identify the problems in this situation.
   - Suggest ways that Mickel could improve his efficiency.
   - In your approach to Mickel, consider what you want to achieve and what you want to avoid.

Using the Web: *Research Activities*

A. You have been asked to search the Web to locate various software programs that will improve office productivity. Two of the managers you support are particularly interested in locating the names of software related to financial calendars and law calendars. Complete the following steps.

   1. Enter the following key search words to locate information about productivity software: *prod-* *uctivity management software* or *productivity improvement management (PIM)*.

      a. Summarize your findings, listing at least three Web site addresses.

   2. Enter the following key search words to locate information about financial calendars: *computers, software, calendar, financial.* Summarize your findings, listing at least three Web site addresses.

3. Complete the search for the law calendars. Record at least three findings, listing the site addresses.

4. Complete the search for the recreational sports calendar. Record one finding, listing the site address. Summarize your findings in a memo to be turned in to your instructor.

B. You are to search the Web to locate information on stress management tips for a presentation you must give to your local student organization next month.

1. Print any articles or information you believe will help you prepare your presentation.

2. Write a memo to your instructor outlining tips or techniques to reduce stress. Be certain to include the Web site addresses.

C. You are to research the Web to locate information regarding an effective time management system.

1. Visit http://office.microsoft.com. Click on Work Essentials shown on the left side of your screen. Under Work Essentials, locate Work Essentials for Time Management—Developing an effective time-management system.

2. Research at least three articles that will help you create a time management system.

3. Summarize each article. Explain any additional concepts found in the articles that would be beneficial to you if you were to create a time management system beyond the concepts presented in this chapter. Be specific in your explanation in a memorandum to your instructor.

D. Find out how organized you are by completing the following online organization quiz (it's free!).

1. Enter the website at www.testcafe.com/org/.

2. Respond to each multiple-choice question. Submit your responses.

3. Once you review your results, print the page if directed.

4. In a memo to your instructor, summarize the results and describe ways you will enhance your strengths and improve areas defined by the results of the quiz.

Get Tech Wise: *Microsoft® Outlook*

Get in the habit of using the Task feature of Microsoft® Outlook; Post-it notes placed on your desk or stuck to your monitor can be misplaced or lost easily.

Creating New Tasks

1. Open Microsoft® Outlook and make sure a blank document screen displays.

2. On the File menu, point to New, and then click Task or click on the New Task icon on the Standard toolbar.

3. In the Subject box, type a task name, such as "Proof-read quarterly report."

4. Complete any other boxes on the Task and Details tabs for information you want to record for the task.

   a. If you have received a task assignment via an e-mail message (from another e-mail system using Outlook), simply drag that message to the Task folder. Doing so will insert the subject and body information automatically into a new task.

   b. Edit any field information for more clarity.

5. Make the task recur at regular intervals, and then change to make the task recur based on completion date.

6. If you want, set start and end dates for the task.

7. Click OK, and then click Save and Close.

8. View your tasks each day to see what tasks you have pending and the deadline for each.

   a. Click on the View menu and point to Current View.

   b. Click on Detailed List.

      1. Each task is displayed on separate rows with field headings.

      2. Double-click on any task you want to view and/or edit.

      3. It is up to you to keep the Status field up-to-date, change the deadline date, insert additional information in the body part, and so on.

      4. Save and close.

      5. If you mark it complete, a line will be drawn across the row.

Improving Your Writing Skills: *Capitalization Workshop*

Retrieve file C4-WRKS from your student data disk.

Supreme Appliances

Simulation: *In the Office at Supreme Appliances*

Application 4-A

Setting Priorities

> **Supplies needed:** Form 4-A, Daily Plan Chart.
>
> Retrieve file C4-AP-A from your student data disk.

Directions

Complete Form 4-A by indicating the work to be done and assigning priorities to the items.

It is 9 a.m. on Monday, June 2, and you have enough tasks to keep you busy for one week. Your manager, Amanda Quevedo, is leaving on a business trip at noon today. At 7 a.m., before you arrived, she dictated three letters, and at 8 a.m. she discussed tasks with you to be done in her absence. Here are the notes you took during your conference with her.

1. Send copies of the combined sales report for the week of May 19 to the four regional managers.

2. Call J. R. Rush, assistant vice president of marketing, Eastern Region, and ask him to see David Walters, an out-of-town supplier, who has an appointment with Amanda for Wednesday, June 4, at 10 a.m.

3. Compose a letter to Allen Fitzgerald. Amanda emphasized it must be mailed today. The letters to Nancy Evans and Robert Berger may be mailed tomorrow.

4. Make a daily log of the important incoming mail. Hold all mail for your manager to answer. Contact her if something is urgent.

5. Send an e-mail to Nancy Cromwell, Dallas, telling her that Ms. Quevedo will accept her invitation to speak at the National Sales Conference in Dallas on November 28 at 2:30 p.m.

6. Keyboard the last two pages of the speech that Amanda gave at the chamber of commerce and send a copy of the speech to Art Winfield. He needs a copy by Friday afternoon.

7. Call Mr. Levine, assistant vice president of marketing, Northwestern Region, to remind him Amanda will be out of town for the week and she is confirming his agreement to represent her at the Executive Committee meeting, held every Wednesday at 10 a.m.

8. Make copies of the article on stress management and distribute the copies to the four assistant vice presidents.

9. Call Lakeside Restaurant at (953) 555-0871 and schedule a luncheon meeting for Monday, June 9, at 12:30 p.m. Plan the luncheon for 12 members of the planning committee for the November Sales Seminar.

10. Call American Airlines at (953) 555-5200 to cancel your manager's reservation to New York City on Wednesday, June 4.

Here are additional items from the assistant vice president:

1. A six-page report prepared by Mr. Strickland to be proofed and formatted in final form by Wednesday afternoon.

2. An e-mail message from Mr. Rush asking you to obtain the sales figures for the four regions for the week of May 26. He wrote, "Please create presentation slides showing the sales figures by region so I may refer to them in a staff meeting at 10 a.m. on Tuesday."

3. An e-mail from Mr. Levine asking you add the figures he has circled in red on the 30-page computer printout to the report he sent earlier to you. He wrote, "I need this information by 2 p.m. today (Monday)."

4. A revised 12-page report prepared by Miss Baxter. She needs to receive the final report on Friday to review it before she presents it to your manager on Monday, June 9. You have previously keyboarded this document and have saved it on your computer.

Application 4-B

Evaluation Form

    Supplies needed: Form 4-B, Evaluation Form.

    Retrieve file C4-AP-B from your student data disk.

Directions

You have completed a time management workshop, and the trainer has sent you an evaluation form. He has requested that you complete the form as a follow-up to the training class.

    Complete Form 4-B.

Application 4-C

Stress Assessment

    Supplies needed: Form 4-C, Stress Assessment.

    Retrieve C4-AP-C from your student data disk.
    The HR Department sent the following e-mail and asked you to respond to the questionnaire.

SUPREME APPLIANCES MEMORANDUM

TO: All Employees

FROM: Human Resources Department

SUBJECT: Consideration for Employee Assistance and Wellness Programs

DATE: June 3, 200X

We are requesting that you complete this form on a voluntary basis for the purpose of determining the need for employee assistance and wellness programs.

Understanding that many of you have been subjected to internal stresses with our recent company restructuring, we ask you to be candid with your responses because we do not *require* you to identify your responses with a signature. The results of this survey will be compiled and published for your review once an independent consulting firm has analyzed the results.

Thank you for your assistance.

Building Your Portfolio

With the help of a team member or your instructor, select the best work representative (suggestions include Time Analysis, Daily Plan Chart, Time Management Evaluation Form, results from the organization quiz) of your work from Chapter 4. Follow your instructor's directions for formatting, assembling, and turning in the portfolio.

chapter outline

learning outcomes

When you have completed this chapter, you should be able to:

- Demonstrate the communication skills needed for effective use of the telephone.
- Identify ways to make productive telephone calls.
- Describe ways to demonstrate professionalism when receiving telephone calls.
- List six effective telephone techniques.
- Identify ways for making best use of voice mail.
- Explain ethical issues regarding the telephone.
- Explain how to troubleshoot problems when making international calls.

Today, the telephone is an essential office tool that every employee has, and it rings and rings and rings. Couple the volume of telephone calls with a virtual deluge of faxes and e-mail, and we begin to recognize our dependence on telecommunication services in the office.

Businesses rely heavily on technology to conduct their day-to-day operations and communicate with their customers internally and externally. However, the value of using technology depends largely on how effectively employees are trained to use the technology. Through office professionals who are trained in telephone techniques and in the use of technology, companies can achieve one of their continuous improvement goals—customer focus.

In Chapter 2, you learned about the personal and interpersonal skills you need in today's workplace. To provide effective customer service using the telephone, you will use the same personal and interpersonal skills as well as the communication skills discussed in that chapter.

When you use the telephone to communicate with people inside and outside the company, you are the voice of your organization. In each conversation, you are creating an impression, and the caller does not know whether your office is "under construction or under control." Whatever the situation may be, the caller forms an opinion of the department, organization, its management and employees, and its products and services by the way you answer and handle a telephone call.

Next to face-to-face communication, the telephone is one of the most important links to customer service. Suppose your company has just spent thousands of dollars to update its telephone system but ignores the manner in which its employees use the telephone. Think about the small company that cannot afford to promote its image in the mass media but must rely on the image created by its employees who answer the telephones and make calls to customers and clients. Think for a minute about the image you project on the telephone. Is your voice pleasant? Are you positive? Are you sincere in helping to resolve a situation? It is easy to understand why employees who become proficient in their telephone skills will increase their value to any organization. Your success depends on your communication skills and knowledge of the tips and techniques presented in this chapter to make and receive telephone calls.

Using Your Communication Skills

To be successful in communicating with customers (internal and external), you must be able to speak clearly, listen actively, and use correct grammar.

SPEAK CLEARLY

The following discussion is related to the use of the telephone. Additional topics about communication skills are covered in Chapter 6.

Above all, speak clearly and in a positive tone. If you do not speak clearly, the customer can become frustrated with the conversation and be left with an unprofessional image of your company. Because we cannot rely on nonverbal expressions when speaking on the telephone, our tone and words must be especially clear to communicate effectively. Make your voice an asset at all times and under all circumstances. The better you sound, the better you and your company are perceived. The voice you project is determined by how well you can demonstrate the following elements:

Volume

Speak as though you were talking to someone across the desk from you. Of course, if the caller is having difficulty hearing you, you may have to adjust your speech volume to accommodate the caller.

Rate of Speed

If you speak too quickly, you may run one word into the next. Speak distinctly at a rate that is neither too fast nor too slow. Speaking at the proper rate will enable you to appear confident and poised. Furthermore, the caller will not be able to understand you if you talk too rapidly and may ask you to repeat information. Avoid speaking rapidly in greeting your caller. Because you have to repeat the introduction so often, you may have a tendency to say the greeting rapidly.

Inflection

The term **inflection** means to vary the tone of your voice to bring out the meaning of what you say and add emphasis to what is said. Emphasizing a person's name by varying your tone can leave a positive impression.

Quality

Let your voice show that you have a smile on your face, that you are courteous and enthusiastic, and that you are ready and willing to help the caller. If you need help with adding a smile while talking on the telephone, add a small mirror to your desk area or stick a smiley face on your telephone.

Pronunciation

Pronunciation means saying each word correctly, clearly, and distinctly by moving your lips, tongue, and jaw freely. For example, how often have you heard:

"wouldja" for "would you"	"wanna" for "want to"
"gimme" for "give me"	"innerview" for "interview"

A more extensive list of incorrect pronunciation is given in Chapter 6. Common errors in pronunciation include the following:

Distort sounds. In particular dialects of English, some people will transpose letters in certain words to distort sounds. For example, someone may say, "May I *ax* you a question?" Of course, the correct word is *ask*, not *aks*.

Omit sounds. For instance, the *r* in *February* has been dropped so the month is almost always pronounced as *Febuary*.

Add sounds. While the previous two errors involve distorting sounds or omitting sounds from a word sometimes, a sound (or syllable) gets added. For example, the correct pronunciation is *disastrous*, not *disasterous*.

LISTEN ACTIVELY

Effective listening is active rather than passive. In passive listening, you absorb the information given. If the caller provides a clear message and makes it interesting enough to keep your attention, you will probably get most of what the caller intended to communicate. **Active listening** requires you to understand the message from the caller's point of view. Hearing is easy; but active listening is hard work. To be an active listener, you must focus on the following elements: concentration, empathy, acceptance, and responsibility. In *Supervision Today*, authors Stephen Robbins and David De Cenzo offer these recommendations:

Concentration

You must be engaged in active listening—that is, really concentrating and asking questions of the caller. If you are not engaged in the listening process, the mind tends to wander because it does not have enough to keep it busy. To help you focus on what the caller is saying, ask open-ended questions, ones that cannot be answered with a "yes" or "no." Obtaining responses to open-ended questions helps you to gather more information, clarify intent or feelings, and expand the content of the message. To remember important information that might be relevant later, concentrate on what the caller is saying, not on what your next response will be. You can increase your ability to listen actively by eliminating distractions, such as someone talking to you while you are on the telephone or continuing to keyboard while you are talking to the caller.

Empathy

You must demonstrate **empathy**, which means you must try to understand what the caller wants to communicate rather than what you want to understand. Empathy means that you put yourself in the caller's shoes. If you hold your thoughts and feelings while the caller is explaining, chances are you will increase the likelihood you will interpret the message being communicated in the way the caller intended.

Acceptance

To demonstrate **acceptance**, you must listen objectively without judging content until the caller is finished. It's natural to be distracted by the content of what a caller says, especially when you disagree with it. When you hear something you disagree with, you have a tendency to begin formulating mental arguments to counter what is being said. In doing so, you often miss the rest of the message. Listening objectively is a challenge; be alert to demonstrating acceptance.

Responsibility

As an active listener, take responsibility for completeness. That is, ask questions to gather information to determine the intended meaning from the caller. Take notes to help you with details of the conversation.

To focus on the importance of listening actively, additional information is provided in Chapter 6.

USE CORRECT GRAMMAR

Along with speaking clearly and listening actively, correct grammar helps project a professional image. When you use incorrect grammar, your image, and that of your organization, is at stake. That is, your use of poor grammar reflects negatively on your professionalism. As you recall in Chapter 2, your

Stop 'n Check

1. Identify three skills that contribute to your success in communicating with your customers.

   a. _____

   b. _____

   c. _____

2. Think about a person whom you encountered who did not demonstrate these skills. What impact did the lack of these skills have on your interaction?

   a. _____

   b. _____

   c. _____

image cannot rely solely on your technical skills. You must strengthen your grammar skills, including subject and verb agreement and sentence structure. The following examples represent common errors in grammar:

Grammar

Grammar errors occur when the *subject* in a sentence does not agree with the *verb*. For instance, "Our projections have steadily declined," not ". . . has steadily declined." In sentence structure, the following example would be written as "My manager and his assistant are flying to both Seattle and San Francisco," not ". . . both to Seattle and San Francisco."

Jargon, Technical Terms, or Local Sayings

Use caution in choosing words to convey your meaning. People outside your company, culture, and geographic location may not have the same level of understanding that you have regarding the following phrases:

Phrases	Translation
"*Last week he was up a creek without a paddle.*"	He is in deep trouble.
"*Run of the mill.*"	Common or ordinary
"*As you know, it takes two to tango.*"	It takes at least two people to create the situation.
"*Oh, that happens once in a blue moon.*"	It will never happen.
"*They fouled up.*"	They made a mistake.

Making Productive Telephone Calls

Suppose you need to make a telephone call to Energy Resources. To do this, you pick up the telephone and begin dialing the company. After dialing the number, you begin thinking about the conversation you are about to have with the company representative. Now you realize you should have referred to a folder that contained information related to your call. You also realize you should have written down a few questions related to the information contained in the folder. During the conversation you feel frustrated because you seem to be shuffling papers within the folder and do not appear to be organized with your thoughts. Although you obtained the needed information, you feel you could have been much more productive in handling the call.

The key to making productive telephone calls is to establish a system for managing your time and resources. This section provides ideas for helping you to establish an effective system.

BE PREPARED

Before you place a call, assemble the materials you may need to refer to during the conversation. Write down the questions you want to ask and comments you want to make. Be sure you have the correct number and name of the person with whom you wish to speak.

Use Telephone Directories

A local telephone directory is available for every telephone. Directories for other geographic areas may be obtained, for a nominal fee, by contacting the telephone company that publishes the directory or by using some free Web sites where you can look up telephone numbers. However, the numbers provided online may not be as complete and as up to date as those from phone companies.

Organizations provide their employees with a staff directory for calling other employees within the organization. Organization or staff directories are usually provided as a list available from the office computer. Alternatively, some offices provide hard-copy office directories. Both computer-based and hard-copy office directories can be easily updated as staff and telephone assignments change. The company directory may be updated by the human resources department or by the public information office. Depending on the situation, you may be called upon to update the directory information for your department.

Refer to the introductory pages of your organization's directory for policies concerning telephone use and procedures to follow when placing calls. In addition to local numbers, an organization's directory will include the telephone numbers of its branch offices, plants, distribution centers, and other facilities located outside the local area.

An office professional should become skilled at using the alphabetic and classified sections of public telephone directories and should be thoroughly familiar with the telephone procedures described in the introductory section of the local directory. If you frequently call government offices, become familiar with their listings. Government offices are listed in the alphabetic directory according to political divisions—federal, state, county, and city offices, respectively. Government listings are sometimes found in a special colored section in some directories.

The alphabetic directory, which may be a separate volume or may be bound with the classified directory, contains the name, address, and telephone number of every subscriber in the local calling area, except for those with unlisted numbers. Names of individuals and organizations are listed in alphabetical order.

For the sake of speed, circle new numbers in the alphabetic directory as you look them up. If you do not complete a call on the first attempt, enter the number in your electronic file or write the number in your notebook so that you won't have to look it up again. If you anticipate that you will be using a number often, transfer the name and number to your telephone card file or computer telephone list. When you are given an unlisted number, be sure to record it. You will not be able to look up the number elsewhere. Indicate on your telephone record that the number is unlisted.

The classified directory, called the *yellow pages,* is arranged by subject for products and services. Listings under each subject are then arranged in alphabetical order. To use the yellow pages, think of all the possible ways the reference you are seeking may be listed, and search first for the most likely classification. Some yellow pages directories offer a *Special Guide* section or a *Quick Reference* section at the beginning of the book; these sections can save a lot of time. An alternative to the traditional yellow pages is the *talking yellow pages,* a supplemental publication. This service is provided by the local telephone company and small businesses; its purpose is to help the general public locate business information. It is similar to voice mail in two ways:

- It has business information stored in voice mailboxes.
- Users access those voice mailboxes through numeric instructions.

A company may list its telephone number in a directory as an 800 number. Companies using 800 numbers are automatically billed for charges. If you do not know if a company has an 800 listing, dial 1-800-555-1212 and give the operator the name of the company. A directory of 800 numbers is also available for those who use such numbers frequently.

You can locate telephone information about a company by accessing the Internet. For example, you can locate 800 numbers by using key search words such as *1-800 telephone directory*. The search will provide a listing of different references that will help you locate a 1-800 telephone directory.

Many companies offer free access to yellow pages online directories. Search the Web using key search words such as *yellow pages directories*. In some cases, once you have the information, you will be able to select a map to help you locate a particular company.

Here are two examples of Web sites you may use to find telephone numbers:

www.people.yahoo.com

www.superpages.com

Your organizational skills are evident when you can handle telephone calls in the most efficient manner. Be mindful of the receiver of your call, who is busy and probably on "information overload" as well. Being prepared sends the message that you are time-conscious.

INTRODUCE YOURSELF

If the first person you reach by telephone is the receptionist, give the extension number of the person you are calling (Figure 5-1). If you do not know the extension number, give the receptionist the person's name and department. Receptionists will often say the person's extension number as they look it up; others will give you a number if you request it. Write down

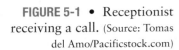

extension numbers and add them to your telephone card file or computer address book.

Give the person ample time to answer. Let the telephone ring at least five or six times. If the person who answers is not the one with whom you wish to speak, ask for the person and identify yourself: "May I speak to Miss Wetherby? This is Sonja Alvarez of Delta Manufacturing." When you do not need to speak to a particular person, make your request of the person who answers. Although some people prefer to add a "good morning" or "good afternoon" to their identification, others feel it is time consuming.

CONCLUDE CALLS EFFICIENTLY

Be mindful of the receiver of your call by concluding calls efficiently. To maintain your professional image, end the call on a positive note. Here are a few tips to use when concluding your calls:

- Use the receiver's name.
- Summarize comments, agreements, actions, and responsibilities.
- Get agreement on the summary.
- Thank the person for his or her time.

For example, "Mr. Slaton, I understand the report will be completed by Monday, June 27, and you will send it to me by e-mail. I will review it and add my supervisor's attachments and return the report to you by this Thursday. Is that correct?"

By using these tips to conclude your calls efficiently, your receiver will appreciate your professional attitude.

LEAVE MESSAGES

So many times people leave messages with only their name and telephone number. Sometimes, a person leaves a message with just his or her first name,

Stop 'n Check

1. Why is it important to establish a system for making productive calls?

_____

_____

_____

2. Of the ideas presented in this section, which one do you feel you could improve?

_____

_____

_____

believing he or she is the only Juan, Shondra, or Almas. If you cannot reach the person called, leave a complete message that includes the following:

- your first and last name
- company name
- reason for call
- telephone number including area code
- best time to return the call

Receiving Telephone Calls

Every time you answer the telephone, you are projecting the image of your organization. To the caller, you are the organization. You must depend on your voice to project a pleasant, businesslike attitude and to give the caller your full attention. This section provides you with some specific tips for receiving telephone calls.

ANSWER PROMPTLY

Answer the telephone no later than the third or fourth ring. An unanswered telephone conveys an image of inefficiency. However, do not lift the receiver and let the caller wait while you finish a conversation with someone in the office—this is discourteous. To be clearly understood, ensure that the mouthpiece or microphone is close to your lips, no more than one inch away, and speak directly into it in a normal, conversational tone; use just enough volume for your voice to be pleasant to the listener.

IDENTIFY YOURSELF

Let the caller know that the right office has been reached. If the incoming calls are answered by a receptionist, he or she will say, "Good morning (or Good afternoon), Delta Manufacturing." When the receptionist rings your telephone, you can say, "Sales Department, this is Sonja Alvarez."

Your manager may tell you specifically how the telephone should be answered. If your manager does not tell you, ask. Never answer a business telephone with "Hello." "Hello" is considered to be too casual for the business office. It is courteous to let the caller know who you are. To identify yourself, use both your first and last names.

When telephone calls come directly to your office, first let the callers know they have reached the right organization; then add the identification for the particular telephone you are answering, and give your name. Example: "Delta Manufacturing, Sales Department, this is Sonja."

When you answer the telephone for many managers, code each station on your telephone, so you can give proper identification for each person whose telephone you are answering.

TAKE COMPLETE MESSAGES

You have several options when taking telephone messages; you may use your computer system's e-mail message form for telephone messages or keep a small notebook, pen, and pad of message forms by the telephone. Spare yourself the embarrassment of asking a caller to wait while you look for a pen or pencil. Many people think taking telephone messages is a simple task. It is simple enough, but handling this task inefficiently wastes time and may cause loss of customer goodwill and business.

There are seven essential elements in a complete telephone message:

1. The date and time of call. The time of the call is important; for instance, if your manager talked with the caller at lunch, the manager needs to know if the call was made before or after lunch.

2. The complete name of the caller, spelled correctly. Remember that your manager does not know every Lawrence or José who calls. If you do not know how to spell the caller's name, ask him or her to spell it for you.

3. The telephone number with area code. Some callers will say your manager or the person for whom this call is intended has the number. You can simply explain you would like to save your manager the time it would take to look up the number. Larger cities have more than one area code. For example, the Dallas/Fort Worth metropolitan area has 214, 972, 817, and 469.

4. The business name of the caller.

5. All pertinent information to help the person for whom the call was intended know what to expect when returning the call.

6. Your initials. If you are the only person taking messages, initialing the form is not necessary. If several people are taking messages, it is helpful to the person receiving the messages to know who took the message should there be any questions regarding the call.

7. Always restate the message to ensure both yourself and the caller that you have recorded it accurately and entirely.

When you must record the name and the number so someone can return the call, write it on a telephone message form as the caller gives you the information. A typical message form is illustrated in Figure 5-2. All of the information on the message form is important; do not skip any part. Telephone message books are available from office supply stores. In some companies, message books are filed for three to six months. If there is no office policy for filing your message books, consider keeping your book for three months and then discarding it. During that time if you need proof of a message taken or a person's telephone number, you can find it in your message book.

FIGURE 5-2 • A completed telephone message form.

Message For:		Urgent ☐
For *K. Macri*		
Date *2/24/0x*	**Time** *2:15*	
Message From:		
Mr. *Fred Dahl*		
Of *Inkwell*		
Phone *845-555-9518*		
AREA CODE	NUMBER	EXTENSION

Called while you were out ☑	Please call ☑
Stopped to see you ☐	Will call you back ☐
Returned your call ☐	Wishes to see you ☐

Message

Follow-up on estimate

Signed _____

BE CAREFUL WHEN ANSWERING CALLS FOR OTHERS

Be careful how you explain your manager's and other coworkers' absence from the office. Here are some tips to follow when answering calls for your manager:

- Simply say "He is away from his desk at the moment. May I ask him to call you?" or "He is not here at the moment. How may I help you?"
- Avoid statements such as:

  "He is in Denver."

  "He's still at lunch."

  "He is in the hospital."

  "He hasn't come in yet."

  "He is in a conference."

In some companies, office professionals use their company's communication system to record telephone messages. They take messages by entering the information using the keyboard. When the person for whom the calls are intended returns to his or her workstation, the telephone messages can be retrieved via the computer. As offices provide workers with training on their integrated information systems, recording messages via the computer will become more popular.

The conference explanation has been overused and will be perceived as an excuse or even as untrue. When it is true, you should state in a sincere way that Mr. Berstein is in a meeting and suggest what time you expect him to return to the office.

If your manager is out of town for a week or so, he or she may choose to access his or her own calls by dialing the telephone number and using a private code. However, if you are responsible for answering your manager's calls, you might say, "Mr. Berstein is not in the office this week. How may I help you?" or "Mr. Berstein is not in the office this week. Nelva Kirkpatrick is assisting while Mr. Berstein is away. May I transfer your call?" Wait for a response. Give the caller the extension should there be other questions while your manager is away from the office.

In most organizations, managers answer their own telephones when they are in the office. Alternatively, you may be expected to take all telephone calls and immediately put them through to your manager. Here are some tips to follow:

- Know exactly whose telephones you are responsible for answering and when.

- Determine how you are to interrupt your manager with a telephone message when he or she is in a meeting.

- Tell the caller that your manager is not available to answer a telephone call before you ask who is calling. If you ask who is calling before you let the caller know your manager is not available, the caller may think he or she personally is being screened. Refer to Chapter 10 for a discussion of how to interrupt your manager when you think that a call is urgent enough to do so.

If you are answering the telephone for a coworker who has stepped away from his or her workstation, let the caller know immediately. For instance, you may begin by saying, "Good afternoon, I am answering Manny's line. This is Sondra. How may I help you?" As you have learned about the importance of being careful when explaining the absence of your manager, the same basics apply to your coworkers. How does it sound to a customer if you say, "Manny went to lunch at 11:30, and I'm not sure when he will return"? And, it is now 1:15 p.m. What impression does the customer have of your organization?

TRANSFER CALLS PROPERLY

Nothing is more frustrating than to be transferred from one department to another or two to three times within a department. Transferring calls properly not only involves knowing how to use the transfer feature on your telephone but also knowing who performs various functions within your company. Your reputation is enhanced as an office professional if you can demonstrate your proficiency in using the transfer feature on your telephone as well as your knowledge about "who does what" in your organization. Here are some suggestions that can help you to increase your efficiency in transferring calls.

- Explain to the caller that you are going to transfer the call to someone else who will handle the call. For example, you might say, "Mr. Jenkins in our accounting department will be able to help you rather than Miss Truong in our department. May I transfer your call to him?"

- Be sure you transfer the call to the right person. Knowing "who does what" can provide you with the information as to the appropriate person to handle a transfer call. Never transfer a call on the speculation that the person to whom you are transferring the call might be helpful.

- Before you transfer the call, invite the caller to call you back if you have not referred him or her to the right person. If the caller does call back, offer to locate the right person and refer the request to that person.

- Never say, "I will transfer you; if I should lose you, Mr. Brighton's number is 531-6088." Say, "For your reference, Mr. Brighton's number is 531-6088. I will transfer you now." Give the caller the name and the telephone number of the person to whom he or she is being transferred, so the caller can place the call again if he or she is disconnected as you transfer the call.

- If your department cannot handle the request and you do not know who should handle it, tell the caller so. For example, you might say, "I don't know the answer to your question; I will be happy to make some inquiries. May I call you back in half an hour?" Another approach is to say, "I need to find out who has that information. May I call you back in half an hour?" Be sure to follow through on your promise. Doing so creates work for you, but it may result in increased business for your organization as it creates a positive image. Be sure to make a note about the action to be taken and the time to help remind you to handle this situation without delay. If your organization has an electronic communication system, such as Groupwise or Microsoft Outlook, create a reminder to help you remember to handle this situation.

- Limit transfers as much as possible. Callers often find themselves being transferred three or four times. Imagine how frustrating this must be for them each time they must repeat their story. In addition, three or four people will have been interrupted by calls they cannot handle. When these callers reach you, stop the runaround. Offer to locate someone who *can* help.

ANSWER A SECOND LINE

Many managers have two or more telephone lines into their offices. If two telephones ring at the same time, answer one and ask the caller if you may be excused to answer the other telephone. For example, "Law firm, this is Shandra. I have another call coming in. May I put you on hold?" Do not leave the line until the caller consents. Press the hold button and answer the second call. Then you might say: "Law firm. This is Shandra. I am on another line. May I put you on hold?" When you return to the line of the first caller, say,

"Thank you for holding, How may I direct your call?" or

"Thank you for holding. How may I help you?"

What you need to do to answer multiple calls depends on whether the calls are local or long distance.

If the call is local, offer to call the second person back, after you have explained why and return to the first caller. As soon as this conversation ends, dial the second caller.

When the second call is a long-distance call, do not offer to call back. Either ask someone else to take the call or explain to the long-distance caller that you interrupted a local call on another line in order to answer. Excuse yourself long enough to get back to the first caller to say, "I will be with you in a minute." Complete the long-distance call as quickly as possible. Try not to keep the first caller waiting more than a minute. When you get back to the first caller, apologize for the delay and thank the caller for waiting. Use these same methods if you are talking on the telephone when the second telephone rings.

Office professionals who are handling multiple lines must learn how to handle calls efficiently and maintain the overall image as their goal. You will experience frustrating times when handling multiple telephone lines, but it is critical to business and customer goodwill to keep a positive, helpful attitude during these times.

DISTRIBUTE MESSAGES PROMPTLY

Delaying the delivery of telephone messages to the appropriate people can cause costly and perhaps embarrassing situations for your manager and coworkers. If you are taking messages for your manager or covering someone else's phone, place the messages in a designated location in such a way that they will not be covered by papers and overlooked. Avoid entering your manager's work area to deliver messages when he or she is trying to work without interruptions. The plan that your manager uses for returning his or her calls depends on the daily schedule, the pace of work, and his or her preferences.

If you receive calls from people who have previously called and left messages with your manager but their calls haven't been returned, simply say, "I will be sure the message is delivered." That's all you can guarantee. Do not say your manager will return the calls. It is up to your manager to decide which calls are of high (or low) priority.

When your manager is unavailable, don't just take messages—take the initiative. Many telephone requests can be satisfied by you or by other coworkers within your department or the company.

If your manager is away and telephones the office to check on the office activities, never say, "Nothing is happening" or "The usual." By this comment you are admitting that you are unaware of office activity. You should always be able to provide a brief summary of activities and incoming telephone calls. Remember, the office professional is an information worker. Your job is to collect, use, and provide information.

SCREEN CALLS

Some managers have such heavy demands on their time that their calls must be screened, and many of those calls must by handled by someone else. If you must screen calls, probe courteously for information. Respond to the caller yourself or determine what the caller's request is and refer the call to someone who can help him or her.

When screening calls, you are attempting to find out who is calling and what the caller wants. You might say, "May I tell Mr. Morton who is calling, please?" You should never ask a caller bluntly, "Who is calling?" or "Who is this?" To find out what the caller wants, you might say, "May I tell Mr. Morton what you are calling about, please?"

You may experience situations when a caller does not give his or her name for one reason or another. Remember that when screening calls, you

Stop 'n Check

1. Think of a situation in which you were the caller and the person receiving your call didn't handle your transfer call properly. What impact did this situation have on you?

   _____

   _____

   _____

2. When answering calls for others, what is one tip you want to remember to use?

   _____

   _____

   _____

want to determine what the caller wants. Your manager is better prepared to help the caller if he or she knows the nature of the call. If you cannot obtain the name of the caller and the nature of business, you have several options, including the following: (1) ask your manager for his or her preference as to how to handle this type of call or (2) tell the caller your manager is not available.

Screening calls (1) saves your manager time and (2) assists the caller. The more you know about your company, the easier your job of screening calls will be. Never tell a caller, "I don't know" and leave the caller wondering what to do next. As mentioned previously, you might say "I don't know the answer to your question, but I will ask Ms. Blanco," or "I will need to find out that information. May I call you back in about ten minutes?" If you really don't know, it's your responsibility to find out or to ask for assistance from someone who does know.

Placing Long-Distance Calls

DOMESTIC LONG-DISTANCE CALLING

As an office professional, you may be required to make long-distance calls within the United States. If so, you may be given an authorization code for tracking purposes to use when dialing long distance from your office telephone. **Long-distance calls** are any calls placed outside the local calling area. The United States and Canada are divided into more than 100 telephone areas. Each of these areas is identified by a three-digit area code, such as 903. As you know, the area code must be used to place all long-distance calls, even within your own area code range. More than likley, your long-distance calls will be placed as a **point-to-point call,** which means you will talk to anyone who answers the called telephone number. For example, suppose you were asked to call a pharmaceutical company in Seattle, Washington. The charges for your call begin when the called telephone is answered.

Types of Point-to-Point Long-Distance Calls

The two types of point-to-point calls are:

1. **Direct-distance dialing (DDD)**—the caller dials the number directly, and no special assistance is needed from an operator.

2. **Operator-assisted calls**—the caller needs the assistance from an operator for a call, such as collect calls.

Because operator-assisted calls cost more, it is more common for you to place DDD calls. From your telephone, dial a number—for example, 9—to get an outside line. Dial the access code "1," the area code of the geographic location you are calling, and the seven-digit local number. Before the number connects you to the person you are calling, you may have to enter a long-distance access code provided by your company's administrative services coordinator. In most areas the number from which you are calling will be recorded automatically; however, in some areas the operator will intercept to ask for your number.

As mentioned previously, rates for operator-assisted calls are generally higher than rates for comparable DDD calls. **Person-to-person calls** require assistance from the operator. For such calls, dial outside your company telephone system (usually 9 or some designated digit) and use the zero-plus method. Dial "0," the area code and the seven-digit number. When the operator answers, give the name of the person you are calling. Charges begin when that person answers.

If the person called is not available and you wish your call to be returned, indicate this to the operator. The operator will ask you for the number to which you wish the call to be returned, and then will say something like this: "Will you have Tom Hankins call Dallas, Texas, area code 972-123-4567."

Before you place a person-to-person call, be certain to check your company policy regarding the types of long-distance calls permitted.

CALLING CARD CALLS

As an office professional, you may be required to travel. If so, you will probably be issued a calling card to place long-distance business calls when traveling on company business. However, your company may issue you a portable telephone to use when making your telephone calls. The **calling card** is an extension of the long-distance authorization code you received to place long-distance calls and enables you to place domestic and international long-distance calls from most touchtone telephones located in the United States and Canada.

Telephone calling cards may or may not require the assistance of an operator. Many pay phones are now equipped with a magnetic strip reader to accommodate telephone calling cards. When you use this method of placing a call, operator assistance is not required and the charge is automatically billed to your personal or business account. The information stored on the card includes a coded account number. To use the card, you will be required to create a personal identification number (PIN). The PIN adds to the security of your authorization code and is required whenever you place a long-distance call. Here are some helpful tips to follow:

- Keep your calling card, authorization code, and PIN secure and hidden from others, especially in public locations and at pay phones. Do not share your card, authorization code, or PIN with others.
- Do not use your calling card for identification purposes.
- Remember, you are responsible for all calls placed with your card (authorization code and PIN).
- Report lost or stolen cards and codes immediately.

Prepaid calling cards provide an option for you if you are traveling on company business. **Prepaid calling cards,** the equivalent of a direct debit card, provide telephone time you pay for before you make your calls. They may be purchased in a number of dollar or minute increments. Prepaid calling cards contain a toll-free access telephone number and a PIN. A magnetic stripe on the back of a prepaid card stores the original purchase value of the card and updates (debits) that amount each time a call is made. Pay telephone equipment can read and update a prepaid calling card as the call progresses. Businesses are finding that calling cards and prepaid calling cards are both convenient and cost effective. If your organization issues you a telephone calling card, treat it as your own.

DIRECTORY ASSISTANCE CALLS

Depending on your company telecommunication policy, calls to directory assistance may be restricted for cost control reasons. In some companies, directory assistance calls are not allowed unless authorized by the administrative services manager or the telecommunication manager. Normally telephone number information is accessed by dialing outside your company's telephone system to get an outside line and then dialing 411 or 1411.

If you need the telephone number of a business to place a long-distance call and know the area code of the business being called, get an outside line and dial "1," the area code of the geographic location you want, and 555-1212. You will reach the information operator, or the automated directory system for the area you are calling. First provide the name of the city or town you want and then the name of the person. Write down the number provided, hang up, and dial "1," the area code, and the seven-digit number. This same procedure is used whether you are dialing inside or outside your area code.

This service is called long-distance directory assistance. Your department may be charged for this service whether you request a number inside or outside your area code. (Refer to the introductory pages of your telephone directory to determine how to request local directory assistance.)

You should note that of all the services offered by telephone companies today, those requiring the intervention of a live telephone operator are the most costly. The office professional is advised to become familiar with automated services and to avoid operator assistance wherever possible.

You don't need to call for directory assistance to locate a telephone area code. You can access the Internet by doing a general search using *telephone area codes*. This search produces a number of options from which to choose; however, be aware of any listing that charges a fee.

TELEPHONE CONFERENCE CALLS

A telephone **conference call** is a call taking place when three or more telephone stations are connected across a network that supports the conversation (Figure 5-3). Telephone conference calls can be initiated by:

1. prearranging a call through a telephone operator
2. using the special "conference" feature on a telephone

Before arranging for a conference call, be certain you are familiar with your company's procedures for setting up this type of call. Additional information regarding meetings and conferencing is provided in Chapter 12.

FIGURE 5-3 • Team on a conference call.

U.S. TIME ZONES

When you are placing a long-distance call, know the time zone of the city you are calling. For instance, when it is 4:30 p.m. in Kansas City, you can anticipate offices in New York City will be closed. When it is 5 p.m. in Kansas City, offices on the West Coast will still be open.

The United States and Canada are divided into five time zones: Atlantic, Eastern, Central, Mountain, and Pacific. From east to west, the time in each zone is one hour earlier than the time in the adjacent time zone. For area codes and time zones, use a time chart or access the Internet and search for *U.S.* (or *Canada*) *time zones.*

Stop 'n Check

1. Describe the two types of point-to-point long-distance calls.

    a. _____

    b. _____

2. Identify at least two tips to follow to secure your authorization code and your calling card number.

    a. _____

    b. _____

    c. _____

3. Name the U.S. and Canada time zones.

    a. _____

    b. _____

    c. _____

    d. _____

    e. _____

INTERNATIONAL CALLING

Although the process may vary from country to country and from city to city within a country, there are generally two ways to make international calls. You may dial directly or use an international operator.

- If you choose to *dial directly*, simply dial:

  011 + country code + city code + phone number

  For example, to call Tokyo, Japan you would dial the following number:

  011 + 81 + 3 + XXXX-XXXX

  Note: The actual number of digits for each category can vary by country or city. **Country code** is the *national prefix* to be used when dialing to that particular country from another country. In some cases you will also need to dial a *city* or *area code*.

- If you *use an* international *operator,* dial:

  01 + country code + city code + phone number

  As you have learned, operator-assisted calls are generally *much* more expensive than calls dialed directly.

Placing International Calls without Realizing It

It's not always easy to tell if you're dialing an international telephone number. In most cases, you have to dial "011" to begin a call to a foreign country. But there are locations outside the United States where telephone numbers may look like domestic long-distance calls but are actually international calls charged at international rates. For example, calls placed to Canada and the Caribbean countries are charged at international rates, even though it may seem that you are making a domestic long-distance call by dialing 1 + the area code + the phone number.

Long-distance international telephone country codes are listed in most telephone directories but are subject to change without notice. Using the Internet, you can search for current *international telephone country codes.* Here is a small sampling of country codes:

Code	Country	Code	Country
93	Afghanistan	376	Andorra
355	Albania	244	Angola
213	Algeria	54	Argentina
684	American Samoa	61	Australia

Time Zones around the World

The world is divided into twenty-four **time zones,** which are based on degrees of longitude. The zones are one hour apart in time. Greenwich, England, is recognized as the prime meridian of longitude; in other words, standard time is calculated from Greenwich, England. The **Greenwich zone** is called the *zero zone* because the difference between standard time and Greenwich mean time is zero. Each of the zones in turn is designated by a number representing

Stop 'n Check

1. Describe the two ways to make international calls.

   a. _____

   b. _____

2. What is the consequence of placing a call without realizing you are dialing an international telephone number?

   _____

   _____

   _____

3. What is meant by the Greenwich zone?

   _____

   _____

   _____

4. Identify the time zone in which you live or work.

   _____

the number of hours by which the standard time of the zone differs from Greenwich mean time. The United States and its possessions are divided into eight standard time zones, established by Congress with the adoption of the Uniform Time Act of 1966. The time zones are Atlantic, Eastern, Central, Mountain, Pacific, Yukon, Alaska-Hawaii, and Bering. The time in these zones is earlier than Greenwich by four, five, six, seven, eight, nine, ten, and eleven hours, respectively.

If you need to determine time in cities around the globe, obtain and use a time chart or access the Internet and search for *international time zones*.

Developing Effective Telephone Techniques

The purpose of this section is to enhance telephone communication between you and the customer. You have probably experienced poor etiquette on the telephone and know this can be a frustrating experience. The following techniques should assist you in serving your callers in appropriate, positive ways.

BE COURTEOUS

Can you think of a time when someone was rude, short, or indifferent to you on the telephone? How did you feel? What impact did it make on you? What impression do you have now of that person? Product or service? Company? Leaders of companies expect their employees to be courteous so they will not irritate or even lose customers. Being courteous means you demonstrate good manners, politeness, and diplomacy. Here are some suggestions to follow to demonstrate courteousness.

- Authorities do not agree on whether a greeting such as "Good morning" and "Good afternoon" should be used when answering the telephone. Nevertheless, a greeting is a courtesy. As well, many callers do not hear the name of the organization if it is the first word spoken when a telephone is answered. Use the most appropriate greeting for your organization.

- Listen actively. As you have learned earlier in this chapter, listening is an essential element in effective telephone use. If the caller interrupts you, permit the caller to talk. Do not, however, permit the caller to complete a long explanation if the caller has reached the wrong office. You should interrupt by saying, "Excuse me, I believe you should speak to someone in the _____ Department. The number for that department is _____. Would you like me to transfer you?"

- When you must leave the line to obtain information, explain why and how long it will take. Give the caller a choice: Ask whether the caller would prefer (1) to wait or (2) to be called back. If the caller chooses to wait, avoid a wait of more than two minutes. When you return to the caller who is holding, offer your thanks for waiting.

    When searching for information takes longer than one minute, check with the caller and let him or her know you are still looking for the information.

- During telephone conversations, use "please," "thank you," and other courteous phrases. At appropriate times, use the caller's name.

- When the caller has dialed the wrong number, be especially courteous. Callers often reach a wrong number because they have looked at the wrong number on a list of frequently called numbers. The caller may be one of your current or future customers.

- The person who initiates a telephone call should terminate it. However, you can bring the call to an end by thanking the person for calling or suggesting that you will give the message to your manager, or whatever is appropriate. When you initiate the call, let the other person know that you are going to leave the line. Do not end abruptly. You may close with "Good-bye" or "Bye." "Bye-bye" is too familiar, so avoid it.

BE CONSIDERATE WHEN USING SPEAKERPHONES

The speakerphone feature on many telephone systems allows hands-free phone conversations, eliminating the risk of any discomfort or injury associated with improper phone use. While using this feature offers an advantage, it has practical limitations: the speakerphone generally does not work well in a noisy environment or for confidential conversations, and can sometimes reduce the sound quality of the conversation. When using the speakerphone, use the following suggestions:

- Let the other person or group of people know you are using your speakerphone feature.

- Ask the person if the reception is clear before you begin any conversation.

- Let the person know who else is in the room.

- Avoid shuffling papers or moving items on your desk because the speakerphone is sensitive to noise.

HANDLE ANGRY CALLERS

When handling angry callers, it is important to know and remember that anger is a *secondary emotion*. This means that when the caller is angry, he or she is usually not mad at you—so don't take it personally. Some other emotion, called a *primary emotion,* always precedes anger, even though you may not be aware of it. Specifically, before the caller feels angry, he or she perceives a threat of a loss or an actual loss of something that is important.

People often cover up primary emotions in order to defend or protect themselves. The negative primary emotions (e.g., disappointment, confusion, pressure) do not feel good, so to relieve the discomfort, people use secondary emotions (like irritation and anger) to shift the focus from themselves to others, usually blaming or criticizing them.

As an office professional, you must respond in a professional manner regardless of the caller's behavior. No matter what happens, avoid the following:

- hastily and/or unnecessarily transferring an angry caller to an unsuspecting coworker
- ignoring an angry customer while he or she "talks it out and calms down"
- telling an angry caller, "Calm down" or "Don't be upset"
- Promising to call back and then either failing to do so or allowing three or four days to pass without returning the call.

Here are some tips to use when handling an angry caller:

1. Deal with the feelings first.
   a. Show understanding.
   b. Provide feedback.
   c. Summarize the situation.
2. Deal with the situation.
   a. Find out what the caller wants.
   b. If it is not possible to do what the person wants, suggest alternatives.
   c. Share information.
   d. Agree on a solution.
   e. Follow up.

RETURN TELEPHONE CALLS PROMPTLY

Become the person who has a reputation for returning telephone calls in a timely manner. Establish a procedure for returning calls. In Chapter 4, you learned a technique for grouping tasks. Remember to apply that technique when returning calls. For example, you may want to group returning several calls at one time prior to lunch and again before you leave work in the evening. Become aware of your routine callers' habits, so you can determine the best times in which to return calls. To return your calls promptly, you must check your messages frequently.

CHECK YOUR MESSAGES FREQUENTLY

People may be trying to contact you or your manager to provide information or ask questions so they can resolve a situation. If you are away from your office on a regular basis, develop a routine for checking your messages frequently. For instance, when you arrive in the morning, check your system for telephone messages. If you have attended several meetings during the morning, check your messages prior to lunch. Be certain to check your messages

Stop 'n Check

1. List the six telephone techniques mentioned in this section.

   a. _____

   b. _____

   c. _____

   d. _____

   e. _____

   f. _____

2. Of these techniques, which one would you like to practice? Why?

   _____

   _____

   _____

again in the afternoon so you will be able to return the calls prior to your leaving for the day or early the next morning.

AVOID TELEPHONE TAG

Although the use of e-mail has increased, people still continue to use the telephone and should do so, depending on the situation. However, people play **telephone tag,** phoning back and forth trying to reach each other without success. Reduce time spent missing each other and increase your productivity by following these suggestions:

1. If possible, gain enough information from your manager to learn of his or her availability. For example, if you and your manager can view each other's electronic calendar, you can check his or her availability.

2. Consider other options: If the telephone tag continues, try sending an e-mail or fax.

3. Determine if you can locate information for another person or from another source rather than waiting on the person you have been trying to call for the past two or three days.

Using Telephone Services, Equipment, and Systems

To be efficient and effective in handling telephone calls, you must be aware of the techniques as well as the telephone services and technologies. If you are unfamiliar with or feel awkward about the support technologies in your office, you can easily project a poor image to your caller.

AUTOMATIC ANSWERING SERVICES

Many offices are equipped with sophisticated telephone systems to handle incoming calls and to monitor outgoing calls. Incoming calls are often intercepted by automatic answering services known as auto announcements, or interactive voice response (IVR). **Auto announcements** are similar to answering machines but are activated only when all incoming lines are busy, or after hours when the caller is prompted to leave a message or to call back during business hours. **Interactive voice response (IVR)** services can be programmed to:

- respond after a predefined number of rings
- respond at specific times of day
- play a variety of announcements
- prompt the caller through a menu of options to acquire information or leave messages
- repeat messages based on the length of time the caller has been on hold.

Office professionals are often called on to help optimize their office's IVR system. When they are, they should involve their local service provider or IVR manufacturer in designing scripts and procedures that appropriately represent the company.

Answering Service

A **telephone answering service** is attended by an operator who answers subscribers' telephones at designated hours. The operator takes messages, records numbers to be called, and judges whether or not to reach the subscriber during after-business hours. For example, the telephones of many doctors are answered after regular hours by telephone answering services.

INTERCONNECT EQUIPMENT

Interconnect equipment refers to telephone equipment that organizations purchase or lease from suppliers other than from telephone companies.

The manufacturers of telephone interconnect equipment have placed new switchboards and other equipment with hundreds of features on the market. Most of the new features of the telephone systems are controlled at the central office. At the central office (which used to be known as the telephone exchange), most mechanical exchanges have been replaced by electronic digital switches. These digital switches are program-controlled and offer users a variety of services. These services are known as **call management services.** They include:

- **caller identification (ID),** which allows the caller's number to be displayed on your telephone.
- **call forwarding,** which allows your call to be forwarded to another number when you are busy or away from your desk.
- Having the telephone system monitor a busy number and inform you when that number becomes free.

Other call management features can enhance your telephone effectiveness. For example:

- By touching a predefined button, the office assistant may speed-dial a number.
- By pressing a key, a previously dialed number may be redialed.
- Most telephone systems provide electronic memory where names and numbers are stored. With the electronic memory feature, frequently used numbers may be recorded and reused for dialing automatically and accurately.

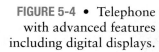

FIGURE 5-4 • Telephone with advanced features including digital displays.

Many more telephone features are gaining popularity as enhancements to productivity such as bilingual displays and voice communication over the Internet. New developments include bilingual alphanumeric displays and the provision to check e-mail via the telephone. Refer to Figure 5-4.

We make no attempt here to discuss all the new features that have been introduced by the interconnect industry; instead, we discuss the basic concepts of telephone equipment and telephone message systems. If you are using interconnect equipment, study the operator's manual to learn how to operate the special features or perhaps attend a training session.

COMMON TELEPHONE EQUIPMENT

The following discussion provides basic information on touch-tone telephones and key telephones.

Touch-Tone Telephones

Most regular telephones are touch-tone activated. The touch-tone telephone provides both regular telephone service and tone transmission of data through a twelve-button keypad. Ten buttons represent the numbers 0 through 9 and the alphabet. The other two buttons, showing the # and the * symbols, generate unique tones that may be connected to special telephone company services. An example of such a service is *repeat dial*, which will redial the last number used.

The touch-tone telephone provides tone transmission of data, which can be received and converted by the central office. In this way, you communicate with the central office and access the call management services mentioned in the previous section on "Interconnect Equipment."

Key Telephones

Key telephones, or *keysets*, provide flexibility in making and receiving multiple calls simultaneously. Key telephones have multiple buttons, and the buttons on one phone set are the same as those on the other sets in an office. A number of calls from both inside and outside the office may be made or received simultaneously.

The basic key telephone is a regular telephone with push-button keys corresponding to the number of telephone lines terminating in the telephone.

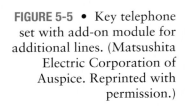

FIGURE 5-5 • Key telephone set with add-on module for additional lines. (Matsushita Electric Corporation of Auspice. Reprinted with permission.)

The push buttons flash on and off to indicate incoming calls on the lines. To answer a call, push the key that is flashing and lift the receiver. If a second call comes in while the first is in progress, suspend the conversation properly, push the hold button, then push the flashing key of the incoming call and answer the call. To suspend this call and get back to the first call, push the hold button again, push the key of the first incoming call. When a push-button key glows steadily, it indicates that the line is in use. Figure 5-5 shows a key telephone with an add-on module that allows more telephone lines to be used.

TELEPHONE MESSAGE SYSTEMS

Organizations often make arrangements for the telephone to be answered after regular business hours or when it is inconvenient for employees to answer their telephones. Commonly used systems are automatic recording machines and voice mail.

Automatic Recording Machines

With this system, a user can turn on a recorded message at the end of the business day. The message might tell callers when the office will be open and invite them to leave their number or a message. Sometimes, customers are encouraged to place orders at night by leaving their requests on the automatic recording machine.

Voice Mail

Voice mail is a computer-based system that processes both incoming and outgoing telephone calls. Special computer chips and software convert the human voice into a digital recording that can be stored in the computer. The recording can then be retrieved at any time for playback. Today, voice mail is a common method of messaging. Depending on the system, voice mail can help in the following ways:

• Voice mail ensures that no calls are missed.

• Messages can be sent regardless of time zones or work schedules.

- Office professionals can leave messages for anyone who has an access code. For example, if you are out of the office and want to leave details of a scheduled meeting, you can give those invited your access code and leave a descriptive voice mail message.
- Voice mail allows messages to be recorded and saved in a mailbox. A voice mail system can also forward messages to another location or to other coworkers.
- Voice mail messages can be sent to a number of people simultaneously.
- Voice mail can also serve as an automated telephone operator by answering calls with a standard recording.

Voice mail also handles telephone messages quickly and efficiently and, if used correctly, may eliminate the annoying practice of telephone tag. However, voice mail has some disadvantages.

- Callers forced to listen to long messages can find the system annoying.
- Voice mail also delivers the implicit message that the caller's time is less valuable than the recipient's.
- Some users do not access their mailboxes regularly.
- The recipient does not know when a message comes in unless the system has a signaling feature.

Because voice mail can be delivered as a public telephone network service, telephone companies provide many sophisticated voice mail features as a service. For example, voice mail can help employers deal with diversity in the workforce. The local telephone company can provide voice mail services in several different languages. A company's voice mail language of choice will provide access for employees and customers to the company's voice mail without encountering a language barrier.

Although voice mail lacks the richness of direct communications, here are some fundamental practices that should be considered to improve voice mail interactions:

1. Consider stating and changing the date of your greeting message on a daily basis. Doing so provides the caller with information that you are, in fact, in touch with your voice mail system.
2. Record an appropriate announcement on your greeting message when leaving for vacation or other extended periods when you will not be checking your voice mail for incoming messages.
3. When leaving messages for others, state your name and phone number clearly and at a slow enough pace for note taking.
4. State your message clearly and concisely.
5. Specify the action you wish to occur.
6. Indicate when you will be available to receive a return call.
7. Consider the tone of voice and impression you are leaving with your message.
8. Avoid leaving lengthy messages.

The features and functions of voice mail systems are improving rapidly. It must be noted that unless used correctly, the voice mail system can annoy

Stop 'n Check

1. Identify at least four services included in call management services.

   a. _____

   b. _____

   c. _____

   d. _____

2. Describe three ways in which voice mail can help your office.

   a. _____

   b. _____

   c. _____

3. Describe three practices that will help minimize caller frustration when interacting with a voice mail system.

   a. _____

   b. _____

   c. _____

4. Explain the difference between a touch-tone and a key telephone.

   _____

   _____

   _____

and frustrate callers, with the result that business suffers. It is essential to put appropriate procedures in place when using voice mail.

The following three practices will help minimize caller frustration:

1. Make it possible for the caller to speak to a representative of the company, in addition to being able to leave a message on the voice mail system.

2. Introduce organizational procedures for responding to voice mail to resolve the problem of messages not being collected or not being answered.

3. Ensure that employees are fully trained to use the voice mail message system. When a system fails to meet its objectives, it is often because of inadequate staff training.

Just as technology is transforming office procedures, it is having a similar impact on telephone messaging. Voice mail and electronic meetings offer office professionals tools for conducting more productive conversations and meetings. You will learn more about electronic conferencing in Chapter 12.

Ethical Issues Regarding the Telephone

ETHICAL★ISSUES

As you have learned, workplace ethics is partly based on core values, such as honesty, respect, and trust, but can be learned directly from the actions of others. For example, what people see their company executives, managers, and coworkers do in the workplace can influence their own views of what is acceptable or unacceptable behavior.

Let's consider an example. Ahn works for a small company that doesn't have a formal ethics program; however, she sees the company's leaders and supervisors modeling ethical behavior and sees the core values applied frequently at work. In the past few months, she has recognized questionable behavior by her immediate team leader. For example, her team leader called her today and asked her to cover for her while she finished her golf game. Ahn was aware the team leader had reported she had doctor appointments that morning and wouldn't be in the office until later in the afternoon. The team leader has called Ahn before to cover for her during an absence that wasn't business related. Ahn is concerned because her team leader has continued to involve her in these situations. Ahn feels uncomfortable about reporting this misconduct.

Another example of misconduct is when Roberto, an employee, uses the company's telephone long-distance code to call his friends and family. In Roberto's situation, telephone reports revealed a list of nonbusiness numbers frequently called. How did this employee harm his reputation through his frequent decisions to demonstrate misconduct?

Employees do not raise ethical concerns or report misconduct they observe at work for many reasons. Over the last decade, studies have consistently shown that one of the main reasons is employees' fear of retaliation for speaking up. Employees often know what is right but feel they will be penalized for reporting it. This is not news to many managers as they already see the value of reducing such fears in the workplace. Whether employees report their observations of misconduct depends on a number of factors, including:

- their belief that management and coworkers will not see them as "informers"
- satisfaction with their company's response to the misconduct reported.

Handling International Telephone Calls

Telephones are easy to use, but some people tend to panic when an international call does not go through immediately. When something goes wrong, you may find yourself asking questions such as the following:

- Why did a fax sound come on when I expected to hear a person answering the phone? Perhaps you have a number that is intended for a fax line or the destination receiver has the telephone connected to the fax line.
- What do I do now that an unexpected person is answering the phone in a language I don't understand? Perhaps you should hang up and dial using an international operator who is trained in the language. Perhaps you can ask to speak to someone who speaks English.
- Why did someone in Minnesota answer the phone when I was dialing Sydney, Australia? Perhaps the area code is incorrect, or perhaps the country code wasn't dialed.

When you are having difficulty making international calls, be sure to consider the following:

- your own office phone system
- the correct format for dialing international numbers
- international holidays
- time zone differences
- language barriers.

Quick Tips

TELEPHONE TIP

When answering the phone:

- Don't use acronyms for your company's name—unless it's a very well-known company like AT&T or IBM.

- Avoid other "shorthand," such as "IS, this is Sue, may I help you." This greeting may not be clear if the caller doesn't know *IS* stands for Information Systems.

Concept Review and Reinforcement

Review of Concepts

OUTCOME	CONCEPT
1. Demonstrate the communication skills needed for effective use of the telephone.	To be successful in communicating with your customer, speak clearly, listen actively, and use correct grammar.
2. Identify ways to make productive telephone calls.	Tips for making productive telephone calls include: • Be prepared. • Introduce yourself. • Conclude calls efficiently. • Leave messages.
3. Describe ways to demonstrate professionalism when receiving telephone calls.	To demonstrate professionalism, follow these tips. • Answer promptly. • Identify yourself. • Take complete messages. • Be careful when answering calls for others. • Transfer calls properly. • Answer a second line. • Distribute messages promptly. • Screen calls.
4. List six effective telephone techniques.	Six effective telephone techniques are: • Be courteous. • Be considerate when using speakerphones. • Handle angry callers. • Return telephone calls promptly. • Check your messages frequently. • Avoid telephone tag.
5. Identify ways for making the best use of voice mail.	The following practices will help you to make best use of voice mail: • Make it possible for the caller to speak to a representative of the company, in addition to being able to leave a message. • Introduce organizational procedures for responding to voice mail to resolve problems or messages not being collected or not being answered. • Ensure employees are fully trained to use voice mail message system.
6. Explain ethical issues regarding the telephone.	• Examples of issues include covering for someone's nonbusiness absence and using the long-distance code for nonbusiness calls. • Whether employees report their observations of misconduct depends on such factors as their belief that management and coworkers will not see them as "informers" and satisfaction with their company's response to misconduct reported.

7. Explain how to troubleshoot problems when making international calls.

To avoid problems when making international telephone calls, follow these tips:

- Be certain the telephone number is correct.
- Use the correct format for dialing international numbers.
- Be aware of the caller's international holidays.
- Know time zone differences.
- Have a plan to adapt to language barriers.

Key Terms

Acceptance. An element of active listening that entails listening objectively without judging content until the caller is finished.

Active listening. An effective communication skill that requires you to understand the message from the caller's point of view.

Auto announcements. Similar to answering machines, but activated only when all incoming lines are busy or after hours when the caller is prompted to leave a message or to call back during business hours.

Caller identification (ID). A telephone service that displays the caller's number on your telephone.

Calling card. Card equipped with a magnetic strip to accommodate placing a call; the charge is automatically billed to your personal or business account.

Call forwarding. A telephone service that allows the telephone system to forward a call to another number when you are busy or away from your desk.

Call management services. Phone services such as displaying caller's number on your telephone and forwarding your call to another number when you are busy or away from your desk.

Conference call. Phone conversation between three or more parties in different geographical locations.

Country code. The national prefix to be used when dialing to one country from another country.

Direct-distance dialing (DDD). A method of making long-distance calls that allows the caller to dial the number directly with no special assistance from an operator.

Empathy. Seeking to understand what the caller wants to communicate rather than what you want to understand.

Greenwich zone. The starting point of standard time, or *zero zone*.

Inflection. Varying the tone of your voice to stress meaning and add emphasis to what is said.

Interactive voice response (IVR). Programmable system that allows a response after a predetermined number of rings; response at specific times of day; a variety of announcements; prompts to lead the caller through a menu of options to acquire information or leave messages; and repeating messages based on the length of time the caller has been on hold.

Interconnect equipment. Telephone equipment purchased or leased from suppliers other than from telephone companies; equipment is digitally controlled from a central office and provides a variety of services.

Key telephone. Equipment that provides flexibility in making and receiving multiple calls simultaneously by using multiple buttons.

Long-distance call. Any calls placed outside the local calling area.

Operator-assisted call. Unlike a direct call you make yourself, a call that requires special attention.

Person-to-person call. Phone calls in which you call a specific individual by dialing "0," the area code, and the telephone number, and have the operator assist you.

Point-to-point call. Telephone call made to any individual who answers the telephone.

Prepaid calling card. The equivalent of a direct debit card, a card with a magnetic strip on the back that stores the original purchase value of the card and updates that amount each time a call is made.

Pronunciation. Saying each word correctly, clearly, and distinctly by moving your lips, tongue, and jaw freely.

Telephone answering service. A switchboard attended by an operator who answers subscribers' telephones at designated hours.

Telephone tag. Nonproductive method of telephoning back and forth by parties trying to reach each other without success.

Time zone. Standardized boundaries to establish time of day based on the degree of longitude.

Voice mail. Telephone answering system that stores messages digitally.

For Your Discussion

Retrieve file C5-DQ from your student data disk.

DIRECTIONS

Enter your response after each question or statement.

1. Explain the importance of demonstrating the communication skills needed for effective use of the telephone.

2. Discuss how preparedness when placing a call demonstrates an office professional's organizational skills.

3. What should you consider when answering your manager's phone?

4. Describe how to handle a transferred call when the caller has been transferred several times.

5. Which two questions are you attempting to answer when screening calls?

6. What guidelines should you consider when using a speakerphone?

7. Distinguish between primary and secondary emotion when handling an angry caller.

8. What are three advantages and three disadvantages of using voice mail?

9. Identify fundamental practices that should be considered to improve voice mail interactions.

10. What should you consider if you are having difficulty in making an international call?

Building Your Office Skills

Exploring the Workplace: *Activities*

1. Use the yellow pages of your local telephone directory to determine how the following are classified: educational services (public schools, private schools, colleges and universities), food catering services, medical doctors (general practitioners), furniture for an office, office stationery, office computers, and airlines. Prepare a list in memo form and submit it to your instructor.

2. With your team, review the following comments regarding messages that have been provided to callers. Read the response, discuss possible interpretations, and determine an alternative response. Prepare your results in a table form and submit it to your instructor.

   "I don't know anything about *that*."

   "I don't know where he is . . ."

   "No one told me where she is . . ."

   "She left early today."

   "He took the afternoon off."

3. Make multiple telephone calls this coming week and evaluate how well individuals receive the calls by answering these questions.

   a. Did the person answer the telephone within five or six rings?

   b. Did the person identify himself or herself by using a greeting, company name or department name, and own name?

   c. If leaving a message, did the person ask for enough information to record a complete message?

   d. If a transfer call was necessary, was the transfer completed efficiently? Were you given a telephone number of the office where the call was being transferred?

   e. If needed, did the person screen the call properly?

   f. Was the person helpful in concluding the call efficiently?

   Prepare your responses along with the questions and submit your report to your instructor.

4. Interview an office professional who handles international calls. Ask the person to share tips to help you effectively handle international calls that involve people who are not fluent in the English language. Report your findings in a memo to your instructor. Be prepared to share your findings with the class.

Developing Critical Thinking Skills: *Problem Solving on the Job*

Retrieve file C5-OJS from your student data disk.

Directions

Enter your response after each situation.

1. **Improving rapport.** During your first job performance review, you were criticized for the way you answered the telephone. You had been asking the caller to state the purpose of the call before you said whether your manager was in the office. After you found out who the caller was and the purpose of the call, you sometimes said, "Mrs. Burke is not in her office," or "Mrs. Burke is in a meeting." It was true Mrs. Burke was not in her office when you said this, but apparently the callers were not convinced. What can you do to improve rapport with callers?

2. **Delivering a message.** You know your manager, Mr. Perkins, is expecting an important long-distance call. He called Mike Williams at 9:30 a.m., and he is expecting Mr. Williams to return his call. At 4:30 p.m. Mr. Perkins was called to the president's office. A few minutes after Mr. Perkins left his office, Mr. Williams called. You feel you should not interrupt Mr. Perkins. You do not know whether Mr. Perkins will return to his desk before 5 p.m. What should you do? List several alternatives and then select the best one.

3. **Answering calls for others.** Robert started working in your department one week ago. His job includes answering the telephone at his workstation. As you are the assistant to the department manager and the person responsible for telephone training, you have noticed Robert has made the following comments: "Who is this?" "Call back later," "She is still at lunch," and "Hold on." What should you do? What suggestions should you make? What additional training do you think is needed?

4. **Receiving personal calls.** You have noticed that Lauren spends a great deal of time on the telephone for personal calls. She leaves her desk frequently and transfers her calls to your workstation. You really do not mind taking her calls, but a majority of her incoming calls have been personal ones. What should you do? List several alternatives for handling the situation and then select the best one.

Using the Web: *Research Activities*

A. Your manager has asked you to locate fax and telephone directories listing names and telephone numbers of businesses in Mexico. You are aware of a number of resources on the Internet.

   1. Locate resources by entering the following search words: *business, fax, telephone directory, Mexico*.

   2. List at least three directories and summarize your findings to submit to your instructor.

   3. Prepare to share your findings with your class.

B. You have been asked to telephone several companies in Europe and Mexico.

   1. Obtain the international telephone codes for three Eastern European countries and two Mexican states.

   2. List the source you used to obtain the codes and the codes in a memo to be submitted to your instructor. Be prepared to share this information with your class.

C. You and your coworkers have decided to improve your pronunciation. In your team,

   1. Research the Internet for English pronunciation software.

   2. List the Web sites and briefly summarize each result in a memo for your instructor.

D. Enter the Web site www.triviaqueen.com/quiz-whiz.htm for a telephone trivia quiz.

Get Tech Wise: *Microsoft® Get Contacts Detail Tab*

Use Microsoft® Outlook Contacts feature to capture all the information you want for the person or company. Retrieve your electronic Contacts file rather than your paper Rolodex.

1. Open Microsoft® Outlook and then click on Contacts in the Folder List.

2. Open an existing card or create a new card by clicking on New Contact from the Standard toolbar.

3. Fill in the information on the General tab.

4. Click on the Details tab.

5. Fill in as much information as you can.

6. Click on Save and Close.

Using the Contact Card When Placing a Call

1. Have the contact card open when you call that person.

   a. Click on the Details tab to display a contact card.

   b. If the person you normally talk with isn't available, you can quickly ask for another person or ask for the supervisor.

   c. If another person can provide help, then update the contact card with this additional information.

2. Click on Save and Close.

Improving Your Writing Skills: *Capitalization Workshop*

Retrieve file C5-WRKS from your student data disk.

Supreme Appliances

Simulation: *In the Office at Supreme Appliances*

Application 5-A

Receiving Telephone Calls

Supplies needed: Forms 5-A-1 through 5-A-4, Telephone Message Forms.

Directions

When your manager is in her office, she answers her own telephone. However, today, August 11, Ms. Quevedo is not in her office. Using the telephone message forms, record messages for the following telephone calls:

- 9:15 a.m. from Mr. Rush. He has heard the quarterly budget meeting is to be postponed. He wants to know if the meeting will be postponed so he can schedule another meeting. He will follow up with an e-mail.

- 10:30 a.m. from Mr. Levine regarding the new product brochure. He will discuss this with Ms. Quevedo on their next conference call.

- 11 a.m. for Ms. Quevedo from Mr. Arnett, 366-8184, a speaker for the November Sales Seminar. He has a business conflict and cannot attend the seminar on Wednesday. Please call.

- 11:15 a.m. for Ms. Quevedo from Human Resources, Extension 5738, asking, "When can Ms. Quevedo see an applicant?" Please call.

After you have recorded the messages, answer the following questions and prepare your responses in a memo to be submitted to your instructor along with the message forms.

1. Did the caller provide sufficient information so you could successfully complete the message form?

2. Did you have to ask additional questions so you would have enough information to correctly complete the form? If so, what kinds of questions did you have to ask to complete the form?

Application 5-B

Placing Telephone Calls

Supplies needed: Forms 5-B-1 and 5-B-2, pages for Notes.

Directions

Ms. Quevedo asked you to place some telephone calls. Here is Ms. Quevedo's conversation with you:

"Mr. Arnett, 303-366-8184, who was scheduled to speak at the November Sales Seminar on Wednesday, November 12, at 10 a.m., cannot attend on Wednesday. He is handling his manager's work as his manager has had a heart attack and will not return to work for at least six months. Mr. Arnett must be in the office on November 12. He can, however, attend the seminar on Monday and Tuesday.

"Find a speaker who can trade times with Mr. Arnett. Call James Yates, 674-8609, who is

scheduled to talk at 2 p.m. Monday. If he can't do it, ask Ruth Agway, 608-547-3232, who is scheduled to speak at 11 a.m. Monday. Another possibility is Ray Morris, 638-1456, who is on a panel on Tuesday afternoon.

"Be sure to call Mr. Arnett and tell him what arrangements you have made.

"Be sure to make the proper notations in the official copy of the program. It would be a good idea to write a confirmation letter to the person whose time has changed."

Note: When you called Mr. Yates, he said he could not attend the seminar on Wednesday.

Before you place any calls, make notes on what you need to say. Record all essential information, such as names, telephone numbers, dates, and time of day. Also write down reminders about what you need to do after you have found someone who can fill in for Mr. Arnett.

Application 5-C

Telephone Services

Supplies needed: Form 5-C, Telephone Services; a local telephone directory or online telephone directory.

Directions

Use a local telephone directory to complete the questions on Form 5-C.

Application 5-D

Telephone Dialogues

Supplies needed: Form 5-D, Telephone Dialogues.

Retrieve C5-AP-D from your student data disk.

Directions

With your team member, read through the dialogues and write comments about the positive and negative aspects of the conversations.

Building Your Portfolio

With the help of a team member or your instructor, select the best papers (Recorded Telephone Messages, Research Activity 1 and 3, and Telephone Dialogue comments), representative of your work from Chapter 5. Follow your instructor's directions about formatting, assembling, and turning in the portfolio.

chapter

6 Building Communications Skills

chapter **outline**

Examining the Communication Process
  Communication Methods
  Overcoming Barriers to Communication
  Communicating across Cultures

Writing Effective Business Messages
  The Writing Process

Preparing Written Communications
  Writing Letters for Your Manager's
    Signature
  Routine Letters
  Letter Formats
  E-Mail Memorandums
  Standard Memorandums
  Informational Reports

Preparing Documents for Distribution
  Proofreading
  Submitting Letters for Signature
  Assembling Enclosures
  Addressing Envelopes

Demonstrating Ethics in Writing

International Correspondence
  Addressing Envelopes
  Writing Letters

learning **outcomes**

When you have completed this chapter, you should be able to:

- Discuss the communication process and explain the importance of communication.

- Discuss various communication methods and explain how to overcome barriers to the communication process.

- Discuss the various types of written communications for which an office professional should develop excellent writing skills.

- Discuss how to prepare routine communications for distribution.

- Discuss the importance of demonstrating ethics through your writing.

- Explain how to address international envelopes and write letters.

Effective communication is the responsibility of every person in the organization. Your ability to communicate with coworkers, supervisors, customers, or clients can enhance your effectiveness or damage it. As an office professional, you will be expected to have excellent verbal, nonverbal, and written communication skills in both the electronic and personal realm.

Examining the Communication Process

Because employees spend the greater part of their time in some type of interpersonal situation, estimated to be as much as 75 percent of the time, effective communication is an essential component of the company's success. The function of communication is to ensure that every employee knows what he or she is expected to do, that the right person receives the correct information, and that all activities within the organization are coordinated. Effective communication ensures that the company's plans and procedures as well as manager's instructions are understood. When this process works smoothly, group and team cooperation is assured and stress is reduced.

COMMUNICATION METHODS

Experts say communication is composed of different methods: verbal (by words and voice); interactive, mobile, and instant (by computer and telephone); written (by letter, e-mail memo, or report); and nonverbal (by body language). Of these, some are more effective in delivering a message than others. Various studies tell us that in a conversation or verbal exchange:

Words are 7–10% effective.

Tone of voice is 38–40% effective.

Nonverbal clues are 45–50% effective.

How effective your communication is depends as much on how you say it as on what you say. Also, whether your message is understood depends on the method of communication you choose to use to deliver it.

Verbal Communication

Verbal communication can mean a telephone conversation, a voice mail message, a formal meeting, or even an informal chat with a coworker at lunch (see Figure 6-1). Much of the communication in an office is verbal. The most effective verbal communication takes place in a comfortable atmosphere on a one-to-one basis. A person can inspire, energize, or even convince others by helping them grasp exciting mental pictures of the topic being discussed. Effective verbal skills can be learned. You should strive to continually improve these skills.

When communicating verbally with another person, follow these guidelines to speak with confidence:

- **Listen and watch for verbal and nonverbal feedback.** Many factors affect how someone reacts to what you are saying. Among them is past experience—what happened to that person in a similar situation.

FIGURE 6-1 • Coworkers visiting at an office luncheon.

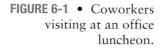

FIGURE 6-1 • Coworkers visiting at an office luncheon.

- **Choose your words carefully when the topic you are discussing is sensitive or controversial.** You may wish to withhold your opinion entirely if you know your view will offend the listener, put the listener on the defensive, or force the listener to disagree with you.

- **Encourage the other person to talk; communication should be a two-way street.** Communication will be open and honest if the person trusts you; it will be restricted if the person does not.

- **Give the other person your undivided attention.** Performing another task while you are talking is distracting and rude. Chapter 5 emphasized the importance of concentrating when listening to a phone caller. Paying attention to what is said applies to anyone you talk to face-to-face as well.

- **Avoid talking incessantly.** Pause often to give your listener an opportunity to respond.

- **Summarize the important points in logical order and give the listener a chance to ask questions at the end of a conversation.** Communication does not take place until the listener truly understands what you are saying.

The words you use when you speak tell others about your verbal skills. Your speech should show you have carefully developed a general aptitude and accumulated knowledge of word meanings and relationships. The best way to build your vocabulary is to read widely and work steadily to improve these skills. In chapter 5 you learned about pronunciation. Figure 6-2 identifies some common mispronounced words and phrases in English. You can avoid making such errors simply by being aware of the correct pronunciation of words and practicing each time you speak.

Interactive, Mobile, and Instant Communication

Speeding up the flow of information is becoming more and more important in business. Technologies that provide instant communication such as e-mail, instant messaging (IM), text messaging, voice mail, cell phones, and wireless networks are common. Even though an office professional might not use many of these communication technologies on the job, they are having a profound effect on how quickly information is sent. For instance, your supervisor may use his or her cell phone, laptop, or handheld device to send and receive messages. You will learn more about other types of interactive

Mispronounced Words and Phrases in English

Errors in pronunciation or misuse occur from hearing words mispronounced or misused by others so often we begin to mispronounce them as well. We also speak so rapidly we run our syllables together or eliminate a syllable. Take your time and pronounce or use each word correctly. Here are some errors commonly made.

Don't Say	Do Say	Explanation
acrossed	across	Don't get them confused.
affidavid	affidavit	It ends in a *t* not a *d*.
athelete	athlete	Two syllables, not three.
bidness	business	Watch substituting the *d* for the first *s*.
cannidate	candidate	It isn't "can I date."
card shark	cardsharp	Sharp, not shark!
Carpool tunnel syndrome	Carpal tunnel Syndrome	It sounds like "car pool," but it is "pal"
close	clothes	I am wearing clothes, not close (near).
duck tape	duct tape	It ends in a *t*, not a *k*.
excape	escape	Watch substituting the *x* for the *s*.
excetera	et cetera	Watch substituting the *x* for the *t*.
expecially	especially	Watch substituting the *x* for the *s*.
fedral	federal	Three syllables, instead of two.
Heineken remover	Heimlich maneuver	His name was not the name of a beer.
heighth	height	Don't confuse the *th* in *width* with the *th* in *height*.
in parenthesis	in parentheses	Remember, *see* in plural—two parantheses.
idn't	isn't	Don't substitute the *d* for the *s*.
jist or dis	just	There is a *uh* sound, not an *i* sound.
libary	library	Don't forget the first *r*.
mannaise	mayonnaise	It is "mayo," not "man."
miniture	miniature	Don't forget the *a*.
off ten	often	Don't pronounce the *t*.
perscription	prescription	It begins with *pre,* not *per.*
prespire	perspire	It begins with *per,* not *pre.*
plute	pollute	Rapid speech makes this one syllable.
probly	probably	Three syllables, not two.
revelant	relevant	No such word as *revelant*.
reoccur	recur	Omit the *o*.
silicone	silicon	No "cone" to it.
suit	suite	You wear a suit but rent a suite (sweet) of rooms.
upmost	utmost	Don't substitute a *p* for the *t*.
wadn't	wasn't	Don't substitute a *d* for the *s*.
ways	way	Don't say "I have a ways to go."

FIGURE 6-2 • Mispronounced words and phrases in English.

communications such as intranets (company versions of the Internet), Web sites, video transmission, and videoconferencing in Chapter 12.

Written Communication

Written communication is just as important today as it ever has been. The rules that apply to letters and reports also apply to e-mail and instant messages. You will learn more about written communications later in this chapter.

Ten Ways to Improve Your Verbal Communications

✔ **Avoid saying "uh," or "You know?" or some such repetitious phrase.** Some people use "uh" when they are stopping to think what they will say next. This pause gives them time to think. A person once said, "I counted 104 'uhs' in another person's message." I doubt if they heard any of what the person was saying otherwise. "Know what I mean?" is a habit and an example of another common ineffective repetitious phrase. Be careful not to pick up the habit of using these phrases.

✔ **Slow your speech.** When you talk fast, you may appear to be nervous and unsure of yourself.

✔ **Don't talk in a monotone.** Inflection helps convey meaning. When you want to make a point or emphasize something, put a dip in your voice by lowering it briefly. Raising your voice slightly at the end of a statement makes it a question.

✔ **Don't speak loudly.** If you are standing close to someone, keep your volume down. Increase your volume depending on the distance from the person. Don't, however, speak so softly your listener has to ask you to repeat what you are saying.

✔ **Speak clearly.** Don't mumble. When you hear "huh?," that is a warning you are not speaking clearly.

✔ **Use the correct word.** Archie Bunker from the TV series "All in the Family" was a master of misusing words. Archie might say about a speaker, "The speaker spoke in a *monochrome* voice," when he meant "The speaker spoke in a *monotone* voice." Others will question your competence if you incorrectly use words.

✔ **Use the right word.** If you aren't sure of a word's meaning, don't use it.

✔ **Always use eye contact.** When you don't look the person in the eye as you speak, the other person may view you as appearing to be shy, unsure of yourself, or incompetent. Remember, though, eye contact is considered disrespectful from subordinates in some cultures.

✔ **Use gestures.** Your body language should show the listener you are interested in speaking with him or her. Be careful not to overdo it; but do show a little animation when speaking with someone.

✔ **Smile occasionally.** A smile shows that you are interested in what is being said and that you are a friendly enjoyable person. Of course, some circumstances do not call for a smile, such as when the speaker is upset or when the occasion is a sad one.

Stop 'n Check

1. Identify three ways you will try to improve your verbal communications.

   a. _____

   b. _____

   c. _____

2. Explain why you chose these three items.

   _____

   _____

   _____

Nonverbal Communication

Most people are skilled at communicating a message without speaking even one word. Using **nonverbal communications**, our facial expressions, body gestures, and the way we dress often express our feelings and opinions better than our spoken words. Make certain the receiver doesn't misinterpret what is often seen as subtle nonverbal cues. It is imperative that your actions convey a clear meaning—that is, the meaning you intend. Verbal communication can be completely discredited by its nonverbal counterpart. The following are ways people use to interpret nonverbal meanings:

- **Image.** It is no surprise that the way you dress creates an **image** to others and sends a message to customers and colleagues. Conservative dress conveys the message that you are a professional and want to be taken seriously. Make sure you are dressed presentably even on "casual Fridays" that many companies allow.

- **Personal space.** Everyone has expectations about personal space. **Personal space** refers to the distance at which one person feels comfortable talking to another. People who stand too close are viewed as aggressive or perhaps overfriendly; people who stand too far away may be seen as aloof. Always be considerate and do not violate another's personal space.

- **Eye contact.** In American culture, a person shows confidence and interest with **eye contact** by looking directly into someone else's eyes when speaking with him or her. Eyes are one of the most important nonverbal language tools. We use our eyes to read the other person's body language and, in turn, our eyes convey nonverbal messages. In other cultures, direct eye contact can make a person feel uncomfortable or even threatened; in such situations, avoid prolonged direct eye contact.

- **Posture.** Your **posture**, the way you stand, sit, and walk, tells others a story and can convey your level of confidence. By leaning toward someone you show attentiveness; likewise, leaning away can show lack of interest and some level of reserve. When you hunch your shoulders and keep your head down, it appears you have low self-confidence. When you puff yourself up, you may be showing aggression. Remember your posture may not be telling the story you intend to tell, so be cautious about how your posture is perceived. A relaxed body posture will help you appear and feel more relaxed and confident.

- **Facial expressions.** The face is the most expressive part of the body. It is capable of many expressions that reflect our attitudes and emotions. In fact, the face speaks a universal language. Many cultures share the same expressions of happiness, fear, anger, or sadness. Others interpret your meanings from your facial expressions. You can break a misrepresentation of appearing aloof, disapproving, or disinterested, by simply smiling. Your smile is the strongest tool you have. It can help you appear warm, open, friendly, and confident. Be aware of the impact this powerful nonverbal tool can have.

Because nonverbal language is far more powerful than verbal communication, it is imperative that you pay attention to the messages your body language sends. It gives signals about your interest in someone or something, your openness, and attentiveness. Nonverbal language tells others what

Crazy Phrases and Sayings Related to Body Language

Have you ever heard someone say, "I don't trust those beady eyes," or "He is so standoffish"? Have you ever wondered what these crazy phrases mean? Here are some interpretations without any scientific basis for each meaning.

Phrase	Meaning
"Beady little eyes"	The pupils unconsciously constrict when we are lying or being deceitful.
"Gets under my skin"	You feel your hair slightly raise; for instance, when you are uncomfortable around a certain person, or conversational topic or tone.
"Opening up to you"	When someone displays open gestures (e.g., uncrossed arms and legs) talking more freely with you and showing a feeling of trust. Open gestures demonstrate trust.
"Pain in the neck"	When something is not to our liking.
"Pushy"	When someone keeps on insisting about a matter or thing and continues to talk about it even when we have asked the person not to do so.
"Shifty eyes"	When the person looks away and avoids meeting the other person's eyes, they may be lying.
"Sparkle in the eyes"	The pupils unconsciously dilate when we see something we like; this action allows more light to be reflected off the back of the eye.
"Standoffish"	When a person stands a little too far away from us and makes us uncomfortable because they are outside our personal zone. Or, when a person does not connect with the group, he or she is considered to be standoffish.
"Stand on your own two feet"	When we need to stop expecting the other person to help us or bail us out when we are in trouble. We must take responsibility for our own actions.
"Under the thumb"	When a person thinks he or she is controlled by another person.

FIGURE 6-3 • Crazy phrases and sayings related to body language.

is going on inside of us. Smiling, making eye contact, using open gestures, and using good posture can project self-confidence. Being aware of your body language can help you send a consistent message. Figure 6-3 identifies some crazy phrases and sayings related to body language that have slipped into our vocabulary.

OVERCOMING BARRIERS TO COMMUNICATION

Anything that prevents understanding of a message is a barrier to communication. Figure 6-4 lists some barriers you will need to avoid.

Missing the Meaning

This is one of the most common barriers to effective communication. One thing is said and another is understood. What might cause the lack of

FIGURE 6-4 • Barriers to communication.

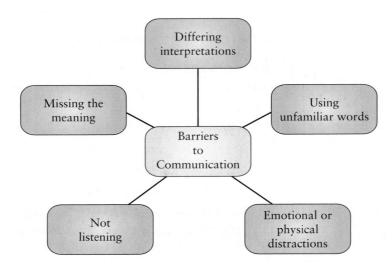

understanding? Some of the reasons might be: Too much information was sent, so the receiver missed key points; perhaps the language was too difficult; the method used to send the message was flawed; or the recipient, for whatever reason, failed to listen carefully or perhaps had bias against the sender. Reasons for the breakdown in communications are often many. What is important is that you recognize barriers and attempt to remove them.

Let's say your supervisor told you to remind him to call a client "about 2 p.m." To you that meant 2 p.m., but the supervisor really meant 1:45 p.m. The supervisor assumed you thoroughly understood his meaning. Remember the sender and receiver of the message must make the same assumptions. To avoid a misunderstanding, the receiver could ask for clarification ("Do you mean right at 2 p.m.?") or the sender could be more specific ("Remind me a little before 2, say at 1:45"). When in doubt, explain what is meant in detail to avoid missing the meaning.

Differing Interpretations

Interpreting a person's meaning differently than he or she meant it is another common barrier. Each person is unique. No other person in the world is exactly like you. You are unique in that your experiences, education, culture, expectations, personality, and many other elements make up who you are. How you interpret something, such as an upcoming project that will require a lot of work, may be different from how another person interprets it. You may be positive, excited, or eager. A coworker who will be working on the project with you may approach it with dread, anxiety, and as too much work to handle. Because you must work together, these differences can cause a barrier to communication. You must seek to understand each other's views to avoid this barrier.

Using Unfamiliar Words

Another barrier to communication is being unfamiliar with the meaning of certain words. Using words unfamiliar to the other person prevents him or her from understanding your message. You must make sure you consider the receiver's level of language skills. Speaking or writing using the appropriate level of language skills for your audience can help avoid this barrier.

Emotional or Physical Distractions

Emotional and physical distractions can affect effective communications. How one feels or physical distractions such as faulty acoustics, poor lighting, or bright colors can affect a person's mood. Make sure there are no distracting sounds, you have a well-lit work area, and the office décor is in cool, restful colors. Soft music will also affect your mood positively. Careless formatting, typing errors, spelling errors, and printing smudges can all be distractions to understanding messages. Paying attention to detail can easily correct these errors.

Not Listening

As mentioned in chapter 5, not listening is perhaps the greatest barrier to effective communication. Few people listen as attentively as they are capable of listening, and those who do have trained themselves to listen. Real listening is an active process. You should listen so intently and identify so closely that you experience the other person's situation. When you are an active listener:

- You show the other person you care and want to understand.
- You show the other person you accept and welcome him or her to talk to you.
- It fosters more meaningful, more helpful, closer relationships.
- It may reduce prejudice or negative assumptions about others because you get to know them better.
- Others will enjoy talking to you and will open up more.

Recognize that good listening skills can be learned, and adopt a plan for improving your listening skills. In addition to the topic presented on listening to telephone callers in Chapter 5, here are other tips to improve your listening skills.

- Concentrate on what is being said and on grasping the meaning of what is said. Give your full attention to the person who is speaking. Avoid saying you understand when you do not.
- Become aware of your listening barriers, such as allowing your mind to wander, planning on what you are going to say next, or being close-minded about what is being said.
- Let the speaker finish before you begin to speak. Remember you cannot listen if you are thinking about the next thing you want to say.
- Repeat information to ensure complete understanding. Ask questions if you are not sure you understand what the speaker has said.
- Take notes and confirm what you understand is what was meant. Listen for key ideas.
- Don't judge until you fully comprehend what the other person is saying.
- Give feedback. Sit up straight and have good eye contact with the speaker. Nod your head now and then to show you understand. When appropriate, smile, frown, laugh, or be silent. These clues help the speaker know you are listening.

Stop 'n Check

1. List three ways to improve your listening skills.

   a. _____

   b. _____

   c. _____

2. Explain why you chose these three ways to improve your listening.

   _____

   _____

   _____

3. List the barriers to communication.

   a. _____

   b. _____

   c. _____

   d. _____

   e. _____

COMMUNICATING ACROSS CULTURES

The U.S. workforce has become a destination for many cultures to immigrate to find peace, prosperity, education, or simply an opportunity to better themselves. Our workforce, as you learned in Chapter 1, is becoming more and more diverse (Figure 6-5). This influx of immigrants means that you may work in an office with coworkers from several cultures. When communicating with various cultures, you will find you must make some adjustments in your communication. Here are some suggestions to improve your communications with those of other cultures.

FIGURE 6-5 • A mix of cultures is common in the workplace.

Oral Messages:

1. **Learn common greetings and responses.** Here are some that will be helpful to you:

Word/Phrase	Spanish:	French:
Hello	hola	hallo
	[OH-la]	[Ah-lo]
Good morning	Buenos dias	Bonjour
	[BWEH-nos DEE-ahs]	[bohnzhour]
Good afternoon	Buenos tardes	bon après-midi
	[BWEH-nos TAR-dahs]	
Thank you	gracias	merci
	[GRAH-seeahs]	[Mere-see]
Goodbye	adios	au revoir
	[AH-dee-ous]	[Ara-vwah]
Please	Por favor	S'il vous plaît
	[Pohr fah-VOHR]	[see voo pleh]
Yes	si	oui
	[See]	[weeh]
No	no	Non
	[no]	[nonh]

2. **Use simple English.** It has been said that English is one of the most difficult languages to learn. Use simple words in short sentences. For example, use *little* rather than *petite*, *like* rather than *resemblance*. Avoid using puns, slang, jargon, and sports or military references.

3. **Speak slowly and enunciate clearly.** Use pauses and full stops to give the listener time to translate.

4. **Watch for blank stares.** Blank stares or a glazed expression tells you the listener may not comprehend your message.

5. **Ask the listener to paraphrase.** When the listener can repeat your message, there is a better chance it is being understood. Paraphrasing will give you an opportunity to correct any misunderstanding.

6. **Accept blame for misunderstanding.** Accepting blame will make the listener feel less embarrassed about not understanding your message. Doing so will also allow him or her to "save face" or show respect.

7. **Listen without interrupting.** Don't help the speaker finish his or her sentences. Finishing sentences only points out what a poor command the speaker has of the language; it also indicates the impatience on the part of the listener.

8. **Follow up in writing when negotiating.** A follow-up message that summarizes an agreement will confirm the results and avoid misunderstandings. A person with limited English speaking skills may read with more understanding than he or she speaks. In some countries, reading is taught and learned well, but the opportunity to practice speaking English is often limited.

9. **Observe nonverbal messages.** Examples of nonverbal messages are personal space and eye contact, as mentioned earlier in this chapter.

Written Messages:

1. **Use familiar formats.** Learn the format for keyboarding documents and addressing envelopes for the country with which you are communicating.

2. **Respect titles and ranks.** Send documents to the highest ranking person in an office and avoid sending copies to subordinates.

3. **Use short sentences and short paragraphs.** Just as you learned earlier in this chapter, keep your words simple and sentences and paragraphs short.

4. **Use correct spelling, grammar, and punctuation.** Always spell-check, then read over for words that might not have been caught by the spell checker. Correct any grammar or punctuation errors. Removing these barriers will help the receiver to understand your message.

5. **Follow all the guidelines for writing effective business messages.** You will learn more about these guidelines in the next part of this chapter.

Stop 'n Check

1. List two ways you can improve oral communications with people of other cultures.

   a. _____

   b. _____

2. List two ways you can improve written communications with people of other cultures.

   a. _____

   b. _____

Writing Effective Business Messages

Excellent writing skills are among the most important skills you can possess. The business letter is one of the main vehicles for transmitting messages between the organization and its customers or clients. You need to develop techniques that enable you to write well, just as you would use affective techniques in developing communication skills.

THE WRITING PROCESS

Letters, reports, e-mail memorandums, and sometimes regular memos (mostly used as a record) are the types of documents the office professional writes. The writing process applies to each of these written communications. However, the office professional will most often be required to write letters; therefore, our discussion here will emphasize writing letters. Letters fall into three categories: (1) those written as an assistant to the manager, (2) those written for the manager's signature, and (3) those written as a correspondent for the organization. Most office professionals today write letters in one or more of these categories. Writing letters is a manager's responsibility he or she may do or delegate the task; consequently, an office professional composes only those letters the manager asks him or her to write.

FIGURE 6-6 • Composing a letter at the computer.

Writing business letters is a significant endeavor. Think of the business letter as your organization's representative, going out alone to do a job. Keep in mind that communication does not take place until the reader comprehends and responds to the message. Realize the effectiveness of each letter you write depends on how well you have written the letter to accomplish its task. Although you may learn many guidelines for writing letters, recognize the significance of giving more thought to anticipated reaction and results than to rigid procedures for writing letters (Figure 6-6).

The person who writes outstanding business letters works at it continually, weighing each word, anticipating reader reaction, and carefully organizing the contents to accomplish its purpose.

An effective business letter:

- focuses on a single purpose.
- is written from the reader's viewpoint.
- conveys a meaningful message through completeness, correctness, coherence, conciseness, clearness, and courtesy.
- reflects a positive, sincere, and appropriate tone.
- is expressed in an interesting style through the use of natural, vivid, and varied language.

Know Your Purpose

The purpose of a letter may be to inform, to create understanding and acceptance of an idea, to stimulate thought, or to cause action.

Isolate the main purpose of the letter you are writing and develop your message around it. Make other points secondary to the main purpose; give the secondary points a subordinate position. Use one letter to do the job when you possibly can, but do not overwork your letter. Sometimes you will need a series of letters to accomplish one purpose. Unrelated topics that require answers should be presented in separate letters.

When you have composed a letter, consider these issues: "After the receiver reads this letter, I want him or her to. . . ." or "The purpose of this letter is to. . . ." or "Will this letter get the results I am seeking?" These considerations will help you clearly define the letter's purpose.

Focus on the Reader's Viewpoint

Keep the reader in mind at all times. Make an effort to write all the sentences in a letter from the reader's point of view. Years ago when this writing technique was developed, it was called the **you-attitude.** You-attitude techniques do not mean the words "you" or "your" is used in every sentence. Using the you-attitude means to show consideration for the reader—to explain what benefit the reader will enjoy, to put the reader's needs first, to emphasize the reader's interests, and to use words that are meaningful to the reader.

Try to put yourself in the reader's place. Get to know the reader through the letters in your letter files and try to visualize the reader in his or her type of business. Be aware that self-interest is crucial in motivating readers to accept ideas or to carry out suggested actions. Reflect the same interest in a reader's needs in a letter that you would if you were talking with him or her in your office or over the telephone. Here is an example of writing from the reader's point of view:

Reader's Point of View:	Your Point of View:
You will receive all future orders by express mail.	We will ship all future orders by express mail.
You will enjoy a 30% savings when you purchase one of our new thin-line cell phones.	We are offering 30% off our new thin-line cell phones.
Free checking, free printed checks, and free online banking are yours for the asking at Central Bank.	Central Bank offers free checking, free printed checks, and free online bill-paying.

Convey a Meaningful Message

To determine that your message will be meaningful to the reader, check it for completeness, correctness, coherence, conciseness, clearness, and courtesy. These requirements are sometimes called the **six Cs of business writing** (Figure 6-7).

FIGURE 6-7 • The six Cs of business writing.

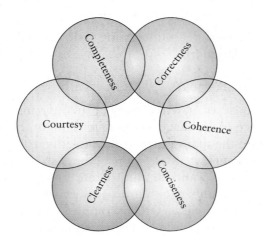

Completeness. When you are responding to a letter, you must answer all the questions the reader asked or include a discussion concerning all the topics mentioned in the reader's letter. Often you can use bullets to list the items or number the items to make each point clear for the reader. When you are making a request, ask all the questions to which you need answers. Always anticipate the background information you must supply so the reader can grasp the full meaning of your message. Also, anticipate the questions the reader will have when reading your letter; inject the response to those anticipated questions. Be certain to include enclosures.

Correctness. Correctness denotes accuracy in every detail: accurate facts and figures in the content, perfect spelling of every word, flawless grammar and punctuation in every sentence, and an absence of keyboarding errors. Appearance is important too: The letter should be centered on the page so it is pleasing to the eye. Inaccurate information will confuse and even irritate the reader and delay response. Therefore, try to eliminate the confusion and additional communication generated by inaccurate, incomplete, or vague information.

Coherence. Coherence refers to the arrangement of words and ideas in logical order. Words and ideas must be arranged so they fit together naturally within each sentence, within each main paragraph, and in the remaining paragraphs that hold the communication together. A coherent communication is woven together so carefully the reader is always sure of the relationship of words and ideas.

Conciseness. To write concise messages, use all the necessary words, but not more. Send the reader a complete message, but avoid obscuring the thought with needless words. To distinguish between completeness and a profusion of words, watch for irrelevant details, obvious information, and unnecessary repetition of words and ideas. Eliminate them.

To be concise does not mean to be brief. When you concentrate solely on brevity, you run the risk of writing a message that is incomplete or curt or both. Instead, write the full message and stop.

Wordiness also results from the inclusion of expressions, often called *trite expressions* that convey no meaning. Here are some examples of wordiness:

Wordy	Concise
A check in the amount of	A check for
Made the announcement that	Announced
For the purpose of providing	To provide
At the present time	Now

Wordiness is an obstacle to concise writing because long phrases are used in place of one or a few meaningful words.

Clearness. Clearness in writing cannot be isolated entirely from correctness, completeness, coherence, and conciseness, but clearness does involve an added dimension: choice of words. Words have different meanings to different people. Nevertheless, as much as possible you must choose words that have the same meaning for the reader as they do for you.

To write a message that can be understood is not enough. You must write a message that cannot be misunderstood. Use familiar words, explain technical words, and avoid colloquialisms, slang, and coined phrases. Words are symbols, tools of thought. Your purpose is to choose a word that will penetrate the reader's mind and create the image you want the reader to associate with the word. To do this, you need a vocabulary large enough to enable you to select a word that conveys the precise shade of meaning you want to express. You must understand both the denotation and connotation of the words you use. **Denotation** is the explicit dictionary meaning of the word. The suggested idea or overtone that a word acquires through association, in addition to its explicit meaning, is called **connotation**. Avoid any word with a connotation that would be distasteful to the reader.

Courtesy. Your attitude toward the reader will have a noticeable effect on the tone of the letter. Even though your attitude is not described in the letter, it has a way of creeping in. Therefore, to set the appropriate tone, examine your feelings toward the reader. Show consideration for the reader and reflect a sincere attitude by using words such as *please* and *thank you*. Notice how different the following sentences might appear to the receiver.

> You must tear along the above perforation and keep this portion for your records.
> Please tear along the above perforation and keep this portion for your records.

Reflect a Positive, Sincere, and Appropriate Tone

The tone of each letter must be appropriate for the given situation. Whenever it is appropriate, write informally and radiate a warm, friendly tone. Be courteous and tactful. Do not write sentences or include words that later you would regret having said.

One way to achieve tact in writing business letters is to replace negative words and phrases with words and phrases that are positive in tone. Compare the tone in the following phrases. The italicized words in the left column are negative in tone. They have been omitted from the phrases in the right column.

Negative	Positive
We are *disappointed* at your *failure* to include your report.	We had hoped to receive your report.
If you would *take the trouble* . . .	Please send (commit, let, do) . . .
You are probably *ignorant* of the fact that . . .	Perhaps you did not know . . .
It is *not possible* for us . . .	We can, however, . . .
We *must* ask that you send us . . .	Please send us . . .

How to Make Your Writing Interesting

When a reader receives a letter that is well written and interesting, it holds his or her attention. Often the reader has received so many pieces of communication that your letter is competing for attention. One way to get and keep that attention is to make the writing interesting. Follow these guidelines to help you create an interesting style of writing through using natural, vivid, and varied language:

- Use active verbs, except when you want the statement to be impersonal. The subject of the sentence should do the action.
- Make the subject of the sentence a person, idea, or thing.
- Use specific, meaningful words. Use general or abstract words only when a concept has not yet been reduced to specific terms.
- Use familiar words and phrases in place of the unfamiliar.
- Use a phrase or a clause to describe rather than an adjective or an adverb.
- Use short words instead of long words.

Stop 'n Check

List five rules to follow in writing an effective letter.

a. _____

b. _____

c. _____

d. _____

e. _____

Preparing Written Communications

To carry out your daily work, you may find yourself writing messages concerning appointments, requests, orders, routine replies, acknowledgments, transmittals, delays, follow-ups, and other business situations. For letters you sign, use the title "Assistant to" followed by your manager's name.

WRITING LETTERS FOR YOUR MANAGER'S SIGNATURE

In some instances you will be asked to write letters for your manager's signature. Writing letters for a manager's signature requires a special skill. It is not an easy assignment because the letter must sound as though the person signing the letter actually wrote it. The reader should not be able to detect that an assistant wrote the letter.

The easiest letter to write for another person's signature is the letter report presenting a series of facts. The personality of the writer is not so apparent in factual reports. If the message is lengthy, the assistant could write an informal report to be accompanied by a cover letter actually written by the manager.

When you are asked to write letters for your manager's signature, study your manager's letters to become thoroughly familiar with his or her vocabulary and style. Use phrases your manager uses, use the same salutation and complimentary close, and organize the letters in the same way your manager does. You may want to use paragraphs, making appropriate changes, from letters your manager has written previously if similar paragraphs are available. When it is feasible, prepare a draft of the letter and ask your manager to review it and make changes before you finalize the letter. Remain anonymous. Do not reveal you are writing letters for your manager's signature.

ROUTINE LETTERS

Following are some types of routine letters you may write either for your signature or for your manager's signature.

Appointments

Appointments are requested, granted, confirmed, changed, canceled, and sometimes refused as part of regular business procedure. An appointment can be handled entirely by letter, by telephone, by e-mail, or by a combination of telephone and e-mail. You will learn more about e-mail later in this chapter. This section covers the specifics of what should be included when writing an e-mail message about appointments.

E-mails concerning appointments should follow the same guidelines used when appointments are arranged by telephone: (1) refer to the purpose of the appointment; (2) clearly set forth the date, day, time, and place; and (3) request a confirmation of the appointment when it is applicable. You will learn more about appointments in Chapter 10.

When you are postponing or canceling an appointment for an indefinite period, always express regret and suggest some provision for a future appointment. When you are postponing the appointment, suggest another specific date and ask for a confirmation.

Routine Requests, Inquiries, and Orders

When writing routine requests and inquiries, anticipate that the reply to your message will be favorable. State the request or inquiry directly, include only essential information, and create a pleasant tone. These messages will be short. If the message seems curt because it is too brief, add a sentence or two to improve the tone. For example:

> Will you please send me a copy of your booklet, "21 Ideas: Tested Methods to Improve Packing, Shipping, and Mail Room Operations." We are continually searching for methods to improve our mailing operations and are looking forward to receiving this booklet.

Routine Replies

When a reply is favorable, state it in the opening sentence. The message of a favorable reply carries a favorable tone; therefore, even a brief message is effective. In a disappointing reply, add a sentence or a paragraph to cushion or soften the message. When declining a request, give at least one reason before you state the refusal.

Acknowledgments

Most acknowledgments either state or imply that another communication will follow. Frequently, the office professional has the responsibility of writing acknowledgments when the manager is away from the office for an extended period.

Acknowledge messages promptly, preferably the same day they are received. Be cautious about giving away business secrets; make statements about your manager's absence in general terms. Avoid making promises or commitments your manager cannot keep or would prefer not to keep. Make copies of the messages you refer to others and of the messages you forward to your manager.

What you say in an acknowledgment depends on what you are doing about the message. You can acknowledge the message without answering it, supply the answer yourself, say you are referring the message to someone else for reply, or let the reader know you are forwarding the message to your manager for reply.

Other uses of acknowledgments are to let the sender know that important documents have arrived and to confirm an order when the recipient is not expecting immediate shipment.

Cover Letters

Chapter 3 discussed cover letters used in a search for employment. Brief cover letters are also written to accompany transmission of other materials and identify the source. Here is an example of a short cover letter:

> Here is your copy of the report "Ten Years Ahead." Mr. Whitehall asked me to send each member of the Goals Committee a copy of the completed report.

Follow-up Letters

You may need to write a follow-up letter when you have not received something promised or due or when you have not received a reply to a letter after a certain period. Keep a careful record of missing enclosures and other items promised and write follow-up letters to obtain them. For information concerning assembling enclosures see the heading "Assembling Enclosures" later in the chapter. Follow-up letters can also serve as reminders.

Be specific about what is being requested. If you are referring to an unanswered letter, send a duplicate of it. Avoid making the reader feel at fault.

Appreciation Letters

Numerous situations arise in business for expressing appreciation. Do not neglect writing thank-you letters. Be prompt in sending a thank-you letter, for the letter loses its effectiveness if it is delayed.

To let the reader know that the letter was written especially for the reader, be specific. For example:

> Thank you for sending your proposal for needed changes in the contract with dealers.

LETTER FORMATS

With the efficiency of e-mail messages, fewer formal letters are being prepared. Further, unless the letter is formal, contemporary letters usually adopt a basic style. The most popular and recognized formats are the full-block and modified-block letter styles. However, there are many acceptable letter styles. When you are new to the office position, begin by following the letter style already used in the office. Once you have established your credibility, you may want to introduce one of the following styles.

Full-Block Letter Style

Figure 6-8 illustrates a **full-block letter style**. Note that:

- Every line from the date to the reference initials begins at the left margin.
- Paragraphs are single-spaced and not indented.
- A double space separates paragraphs.
- Four blank lines are left after the complimentary close to leave room for a signature.

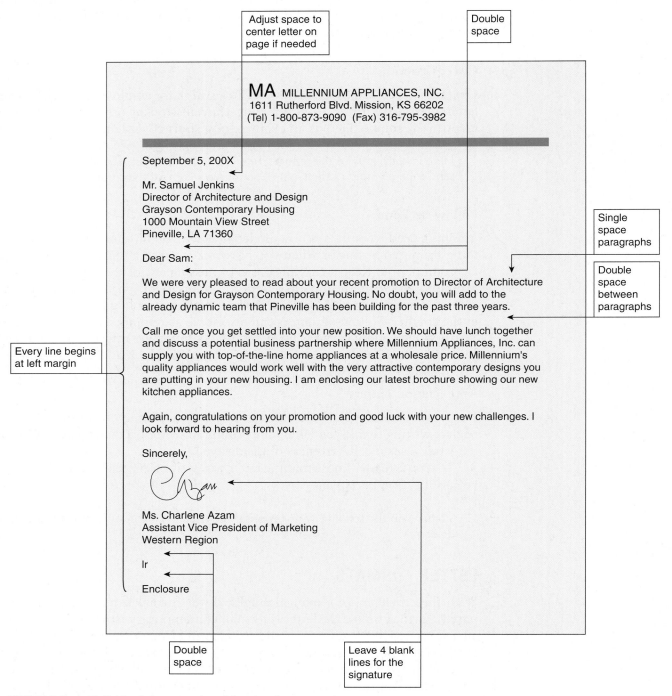

FIGURE 6-8 • Full-block letter style with mixed punctuation.

Notice that Figure 6-8 also shows an example of **mixed punctuation**: A colon is used after the salutation and a comma is used after the complimentary close.

Modified-Block Letter Style

Figure 6-9 illustrates a **modified-block letter style.** Note the format is the same as the full-block style with the following exceptions:

- The date, complimentary close, and signature lines begin *at the center of the page* and are keyed to the right of center (not centered).

- Although not shown in Figure 6-9, the paragraphs are sometimes indented. However, the preference is to block them at the left.

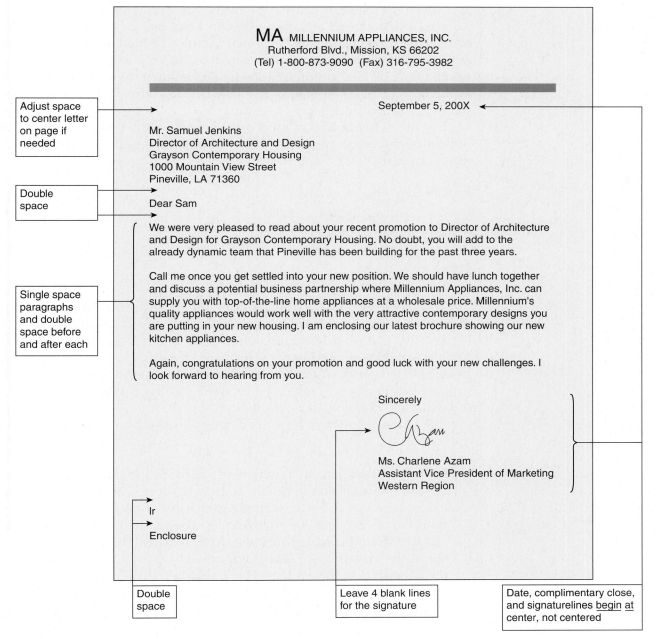

FIGURE 6-9 • Modified-block letter style with open punctuation.

Notice that Figure 6-9 also shows **open punctuation.** This punctuation style uses no punctuation after the salutation or after the complimentary close.

E-MAIL MEMORANDUMS

No Internet tool has such global use as e-mail. It is the most common form of communication, surpassing the letter both within and outside an organization. E-mails are used to transmit, confirm, request, inform, persuade, and report. You will learn more about e-mail in Chapter 7.

There are effective and ineffective ways to use e-mail to convey information in today's office. A major downside is that e-mail has become the most overused communication tool available because it is so easy to use. One manager told us he regularly fields 150 e-mails each day. What a time-consuming, wasteful way to spend an entire morning when half or more of the e-mails could have been eliminated! As an example, he said he had sent some requested information to another employee, and the employee sent him an e-mail thanking him for information he was required to provide! The key to avoiding unnecessary e-mail is to think before you create the e-mail. Ask yourself, "Is this e-mail really necessary?"

E-mail is frequently written quickly and often poorly. The writing principles discussed previously for letters also apply to writing e-mail memorandums:

- Use the "you" approach.
- Use positive language.
- Know your purpose.
- Be coherent, concise, correct, complete, clear, and courteous.
- Make your writing interesting.

You should also take a close look at your e-mail screen. You will see a lot of technical jargon. Knowing what this jargon means can be valuable. In Figure 6-10 is an e-mail message sent using Internet Explorer and Yahoo Mail, a popular e-mail software. This figure identifies the parts of an e-mail message. Each e-mail software screen is different, but the basic e-mail service is the same. Be sure you take time to investigate your screen to fully understand all that your e-mail can do for you.

The following tips will help you to write e-mails that will be well received every time:

- **Include a salutation.** It is preferable to always use the person's name in the salutation. If you normally address the recipient by his or her first name, however, you may omit the salutation or you may include something like "Dear Ann" or just "Ann." If you normally address the person as Miss/Mrs./Ms./ Mr. Brown, that is the way you should address him or her in the salutation—"Dear Ms. Brown" or just "Ms. Brown." When the e-mail has been sent to a group, always respond to a specific person rather than to everyone in the group, and address the person by name.
- **Create a descriptive subject line.** Your subject line must be meaningful. For example, which one would you consider more descriptive: Change in Policy or Change in Vacation Policy? Recipients scan the subject to

① Date: Fri, Apr 7, 200X 1:13:43 -0700 (PDT)

② From: "Lisa Riley" <lisar3000@hotmail.com>

③ Subject: Tips for an E-mail Policy

④ To: "Datona Edwards" <datonae777@hotmail.com>

Lisa:

The following points are to be considered when setting up our E-mail Policy. Please review this list and e-mail me your comments:

⑤
- Minimize the forwarding of e-mails that contain nonbusiness material.
- Check receipt of important messages with a telephone call.
- Be aware that messages can easily be misunderstood and sound as if you meant sarcasm, humor, abuse, or negative tone.
- Ignore and delete chain e-mails.
- Keep the number of e-mails in your mailbox to a minimum.
- Check your personal address book regularly and remove unwanted and incorrect entries.
- Always log out of systems when they are not in use.
- Do not send e-mail messages from another user's mailbox.

Please feel free to add any points to the list. We can finalize our E-mail Policy at our next meeting.

⑥
Datona Riley
3622 Valley View Lane
Dallas, TX 75244
(O) 972.222.5555
(F) 972.222.4444

① Date and time message was sent.

② Source of the message with the sender's name and e-mail address.

③ Subject of the message.

④ Recipient of the message (also the person to reply to).

⑤ Body of the message where the real correspondence happens.

⑥ The sender's signature. Notice more information has been added. Your e-mail software will allow you to create a custom signature for your message.

FIGURE 6-10 • Format of an e-mail message.

determine whether or not to open, forward, file, or trash the message. Your message is competing quite often with many, many other e-mails.

- **Write an attention-getting opening.** Your first sentence or two will determine whether the reader will continue reading on or delete the message. Get to the point, be specific, and indicate a benefit to the reader, as in "How would you like a raise this year? We need volunteers for the Salary Committee."

- **Use short sentences and simple words.** Just as you learned in writing letters, you must write on your audience's level. Keep your e-mail messages simple and easy to read and understand so the recipient will know exactly what you want him or her to do. Try to keep your messages no longer than one screen.

- **Focus on the "you attitude."** Identify what is in it for the recipient for doing what you want him or her to do. List the benefits, use numbering or bullets, and be specific.

- **Keep each e-mail to one subject.** If you want to express two concerns, do so in two different e-mails. Often e-mails are filed by subject and two subjects in one e-mail may mean one is lost, misfiled, or ignored. When possible, send short messages as the subject line so recipients don't have to open the e-mail to read a single line.

- **Add a sense of urgency.** Many times readers will respond faster when they know you are working under a deadline.

- **Avoid flaming. Flaming** is expressing strong opinion or anger. Keying your e-mail message in capital letters means you are yelling at the recipient. If you find yourself writing in anger, take a break. Avoid hitting the "Send" button too quickly. Take time to get your anger under control. Especially avoid flaming in all caps.

- **Don't assume privacy.** Remember you can praise in public, and criticize in private. Don't send anything by e-mail that you wouldn't want posted—with your name attached—on the company bulletin board. E-mail messages are not secure. In some companies the e-mail administrator is assigned the responsibility of checking all e-mails. You could be terminated if you write anything inappropriate.

- **Respond promptly.** Answering as soon as possible supports your reputation for being professional and courteous. When you are too busy, send a short response explaining you will respond at a specific time in the future.

- **Show respect and restraint when sending sensitive information.** Show respect to those receiving sensitive information by not sharing it with everyone. For instance, if you need to reprimand certain individuals for taking too long at break time, don't send a general message to everyone. Target only those who are breaking the rule and don't alienate those who are in compliance.

- **Proofread all messages.** No message should contain misspelled words. Most e-mail programs have a spell checker—use it! Read over the message carefully to catch those words that are spelled correctly but used improperly. Also, use correct punctuation, grammar, and capitalization. Messages with these errors present a poor impression of the sender and the organization.

- **Don't send unsolicited attachments.** Copy and paste all important points in the message rather than sending an attachment. Often attachments take time to download, or recipients fail to have the software such as Adobe Acrobat Reader to open .pdf files. **PDF (portable document format)** is a universal file format developed by Adobe® that preserves all the fonts, formatting, graphics, and color of any source document, regardless of the application and platform used to create it. To view pdf files, you need Adobe

Acrobat Reader, which you can download free on the Internet. Should the recipient need the entire file for some reason, then, of course, it should be attached. When you must send files, be aware of the size of the file to avoid sending attachments that take a long time to download.

- **Carbon copy (CC) only people who really need the information.** Don't reply to all. Reply to only the individual(s) who should receive the information, especially if the information should be kept private.

- **Make sure your PC is protected against viruses.** A **virus** is a program that attaches itself to a file, reproduces, and spreads from one file to another from one computer to another. Viruses can be harmful, annoying, or damaging to your files and computer. Unless you take precautions, such as regularly downloading the latest files from your antivirus software, you run the risk of your computer getting infected with a virus and unknowingly sending virus-infected e-mail messages to everyone in your address book.

- **Do not open suspicious e-mail.** If the e-mail message looks suspicious, don't open it. Many viruses do damage when the message or an attached file is opened. If it says in all caps that "YOU HAVE WON THE SPANISH LOTTERY!" ignore the message. Remember, if it sounds too good to be true, it probably is.

- **Include the e-mail signature in your closing.** Since it is not possible to sign your e-mail, you should include the same information, minus the signature, at the bottom of the e-mail message. Often companies will assign abbreviated names or numbers for employee e-mail addresses, and those abbreviations and numbers mean nothing to someone else. E-mail software such as Microsoft® Outlook or GroupWise will automatically add your signature information below your e-mail message. In the signature line, you should include your name, title, company name, e-mail address, fax number, and company phone number. Keep the number of lines for your signature to five or less.

- **Don't break the e-mail threads.** When an e-mail is sent the first time, the person responding should reply to this e-mail; when the originator of the first e-mail receives this first reply and needs to respond, he or she should do so in the same e-mail. When this thread is followed and not broken, either the sender or receiver can follow the comments each has made throughout all the e-mails. If the thread is broken, it is often difficult to follow what has been said previously.

- **Format your messages simply.** Avoid using colorful backgrounds, fancy fonts, and animated images. When the messages are formatted using these extras, sometimes the message will be sent as gibberish or even could crash the e-mail system. Those fancy formats are for your personal use—not for the office. Formatting e-mail messages should be plain text so any e-mail client can handle the format.

- **Send company e-mails from the company and personal e-mails from home.** Remember if it is sent from the company, it comes from the company. Personal e-mails sent from the office are regarded as official company business regardless of the content. This practice could place you and the company in a situation involving legal risk. Personal e-mail has no place being sent or received in the office.

Stop 'n Check

1. List at least five tips to follow when writing e-mails.

   a. _____

   b. _____

   c. _____

   d. _____

   e. _____

2. Why should personal e-mail not be sent on company computers?

   _____

   _____

   _____

A last comment needs to be made about e-mail. People read their e-mail at different times. Don't expect that you will receive an immediate response from every e-mail. Assume that if you send a message, most people will read it and respond within 24 hours; however, this is not a guarantee. If your message is urgent, pick up the telephone.

STANDARD MEMORANDUMS

You may be called upon occasionally to write a memorandum, also called a memo, rather than send the information as an e-mail message. You should continually strive to improve your writing skills whether writing letters or memos. Keep a reference manual handy for resolving questions about grammar, punctuation, capitalization, and number use. When asked to write a memo, use the following guidelines:

- Use a standard format (most word processing software programs have memo templates from which to choose).
- Write informally.
- Keep the memo to one page.
- Make sure the memo covers only one topic.
- Use lists whenever possible to itemize for easier reading.

Microsoft® Word offers templates for several memorandum forms. You can edit the templates to suit your company's needs. See Figure 6-11 for an example of the Microsoft® Professional memo template from Word. To access Word templates on your computer, click on File, New, On my computer, Memos tab.

INFORMATIONAL REPORTS

An **informational report** tells the reader about a topic, idea, issue, or event, and the information is presented without analysis or recommendation. The purpose of an informational report is to select and emphasize the relevant

FIGURE 6-11 • Microsoft® Word Professional memorandum template.

Memo

COMPANY NAME HERE

To: [Click **here** and type name]

From: [Click **here** and type name]

CC: [Click **here** and type name]

Date: April 15, 2006

Re: [Click **here** and type subject]

How to Use This Memo Template

Select the text you would like to replace, and type your memo. Use styles such as Heading 1-3 and Body Text from the Styles and Formatting work pane from the Format menu. To save changes to this template for future use, on the File menu, click **Save As**. In the **Save As Type** box, choose **Document Template** (the filename extensions should change form *.doc* to *.dot*) and save the template. Next time you want to use the updated template, on the **File** menu, click **New**. In the **New Document** task pane, under **Templates**, click **On my computer**. In the **Templates** dialog, your updated template will appear on the General tab.

facts clearly and concisely. Examples of information reports are trip reports, progress reports, periodic reports, and investigative reports. Because information reports do not contain sensitive or controversial information, they are organized in a direct manner that presents the information in an objective, organized way. Usually the reader is somewhat familiar with the information; therefore, background information is often omitted (see Figure 6-12).

How do you begin? First, ask yourself some key questions such as:

- What kind of report am I writing?
- What is the purpose of the report?
- Who will read it?
- What are the key points of information the reader should know?

Once you have answered these questions, you can gather the information and begin writing the report.

Trip Reports

Should you or your supervisor be sent on a trip, conference, or convention, you may have to submit a report when you return. These **trip reports** are often summarized in an e-mail memorandum or standard memorandum identifying the event (date, time, location), outlining three to five key points (how the trip benefited the company), and itemizing expenses incurred as required (may be on a separate sheet or travel expense form). Close by expressing appreciation for the opportunity to make the trip.

Progress Reports

Progress reports, also called *interim reports*, describe for internal or external readers ongoing projects to bring them up-to-date on the status of a project, plan, or some activity. The basic format for trip reports is used where you include information in an e-mail memorandum or standard memorandum

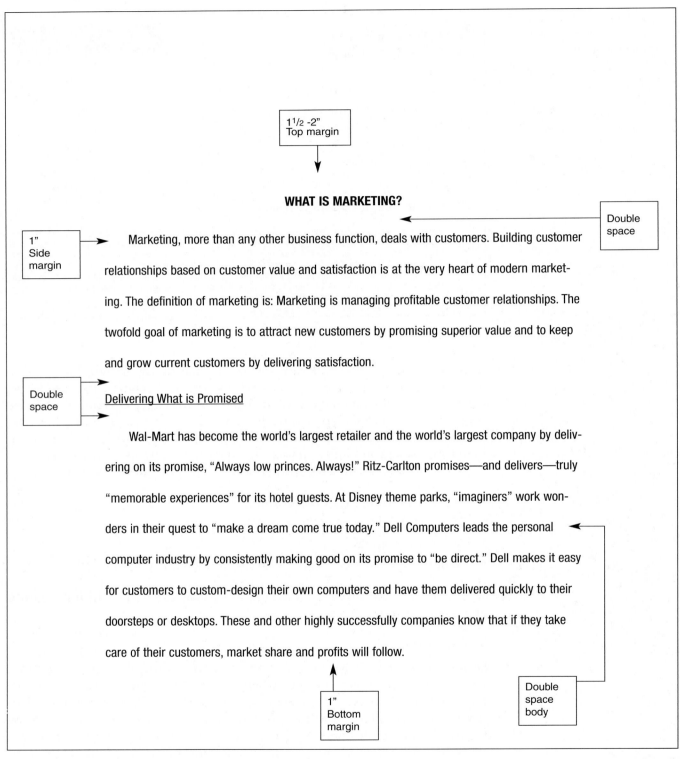

(continued)

identifying the project, plan, or activity; summarizing three to five main points that brings the reader up-to-date; itemizing expenses incurred as required; and expressing appreciation or action to be taken or a statement of the value the reader will receive.

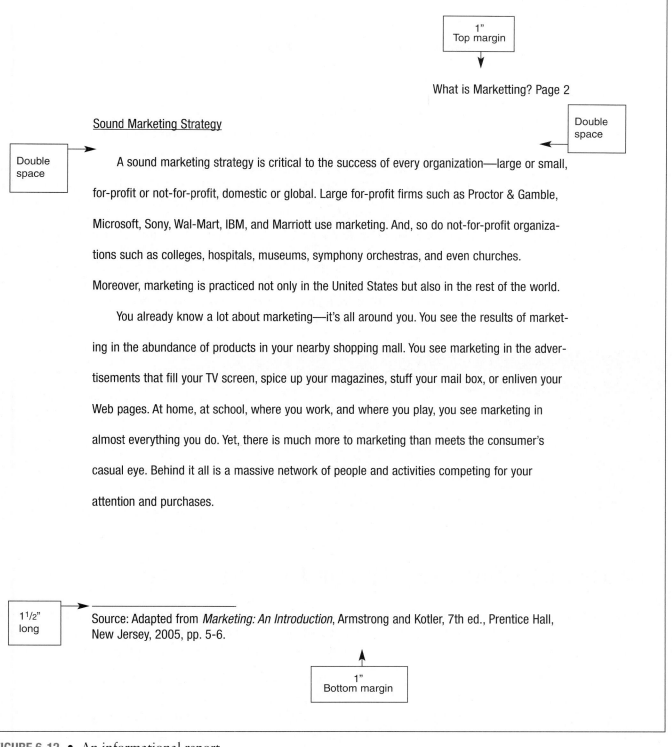

FIGURE 6-12 • An informational report.

Periodic Reports

Periodic reports, sometimes called *activity reports,* help management keep up with company operations. Examples are reports on sales figures, inventory levels, profit figures, employee numbers, and many other bits of information that help management make decisions. Periodic reports use the same format as the previous reports—the e-mail memorandum or standard memorandum. They include summarizing the activities that occurred during the reporting period, which may be weekly, monthly, or annually; identifying problems; noting changes in progress; and making requests as necessary. The main use of periodic reports is to keep management informed about progress within the company, whether positive or negative.

Investigative Reports

Investigative reports are created about a specific topic, situation, or event based on research, without including interpretation or recommendation. The format used for these reports are an e-mail memorandum or standard memorandum that includes an introduction (presents the subject, purpose, and action to date), the body (includes the facts, findings, or discussion) and a short summary (identifies the main points of the report). These reports save the reader time. The information needed is provided in a short report that can be quickly read instead of having to complete the research. The research is delegated to the office professional.

In writing reports, the office professional must have excellent writing, grammar, spelling, punctuation, capitalization, number use skills. The workshops at the end of each chapter in the text are designed for you to review the rules for each of these areas.

Stop 'n Check

Identify the four types of informational reports.

a. _____

b. _____

c. _____

d. _____

Preparing Documents for Distribution

An effective business document is a package of information containing essential facts, knowledge of business procedures and policies, and a specific message. All of these ingredients are carefully woven together and sent to a specific destination.

Once the task of creating a final draft is completed, several steps must be taken to ensure that the information package is accurate and complete. This section discusses the procedures necessary to complete the preparation process: proofreading, submitting letters for signature, assembling enclosures, and addressing envelopes.

PROOFREADING

All communication must be proofread and, if necessary, corrected. An office worker's mistakes easily could cost an organization goodwill, not to mention time and money. It is essential that all documents are correct in grammar, punctuation, content, format, and style. You can use proofreader's symbols

FIGURE 6-13 • Commonly used proofreading symbols.

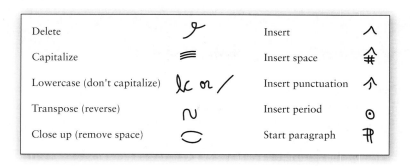

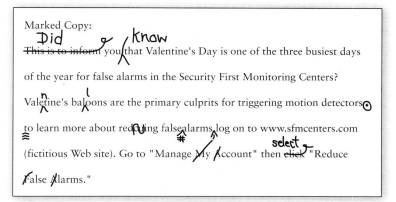

Proofreading at the Computer

✔ Always consider your first version as a rough draft.

✔ Don't depend on your computer's spell checker to catch grammar errors such as words that sound alike but have different meanings such as *you're* for *your*, *cite* for *site*, *their* for *there*, or misused words such as *loose* for *lose* or *then* for *than*.

✔ Be sure to turn on widow/orphan protection when using word processing, so a single line will not be left stranded at the top or bottom of a page.

✔ Print a hard copy to double-check for spacing errors.

✔ Do a thorough job of editing before you begin making your corrections.

✔ Check cross-references to other pages to make certain the information to which you are referring is still on those pages after editing.

✔ After you finish making your editing corrections, proofread each change carefully.

✔ Do a spell/grammar check again of the corrected version.

when editing hard copy. Refer to the proofreading symbols in Figure 6-13, which shows the most common symbols and their use. A complete list of proofreader's symbols is on the back inside cover of this text. Remember people will judge the competence of your organization, your manager, and you by the quality of work they receive.

You can proofread using your word processing software's spell checker. Most word processing software automatically checks grammar and style. Remember, however, word processing software cannot detect every possible error, such as *then* for *than*, and should not replace your own proofreading and checking of a document.

How to Double-Check Outgoing Documents

✔ **Check facts and figures.** Verify specific information, such as dates (verify dates with days of the week), time, amounts of money (verify both figure and written amounts), columns of data, proper names, and locations.

✔ **Check format.** Make sure the date line, enumerations (verify correct numbering, especially where corrections have been made), centering (check spacing before and after centered lines), salutation and closing lines, signature line, and enclosures have the correct placement and spacing. (See Figures 6-8 and 6-9 for correct letter formats.)

✔ **Check for completeness and meaning.** Make sure information is complete (verify substitutions and omissions). Proofread for meaning.

✔ **Check mechanics.** Grammar, punctuation, spelling, capitalization, and number use must be perfect.

FIGURE 6-14 • FOR SIGNATURE folder.

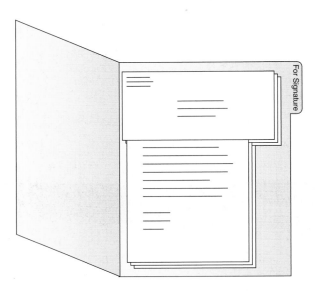

SUBMITTING LETTERS FOR SIGNATURE

To save time and to decrease interruptions, group letters and submit them for signature. Submit as many letters as you can complete, allowing time for your manager or others to sign them and for you to insert them in the envelopes before mail pickup. The most appropriate time or the number of times each day to submit letters will depend on the mail pickup schedule in your organization and what is convenient for your manager. Written communication is most manageable when nothing is in the FOR SIGNATURE folder (see Figure 6-14) but the material to be sent. Place the addressed envelope over each letter and its accompanying enclosures to separate each item from the others in the stack. If a copy of a letter is to be mailed, place the matching envelope over it and put it in the stack immediately after the original.

When the same letter is sent to two or more persons, all these letters must be signed and should be arranged in the FOR SIGNATURE folder in the same order in which the addresses appear on the letter.

Some managers want to see the letters being answered. If your manager wants to see the letters, submit them in a second folder, arranged in the identical order of the items to be signed.

Some office professionals have the responsibility of writing letters for their manager's signature, as mentioned earlier. Submit separately any letters you or someone else has written for your manager's signature. Your manager may want to read the letter before signing it. Before you put a letter in an envelope:

1. Glance at the signature to ensure it has been signed.
2. Verify the enclosures and at the same time make a check mark on the file copy by the enclosure notation to indicate the enclosures were sent.
3. Make certain the addressee on the envelope and on the letter are the same.
4. If your manager has written a note on a letter, photocopy it for the file.

Staple the file copy to the front of the letter being answered, and put these items in the to-be-filed location. When your manager initiates a letter of two or more pages long, staple the pages of the file copy before placing it in the to-be-filed location.

Sometimes all parts of a letter are not answered at one time. You should keep track of this. Never file a letter that is only partially answered. Mark the unanswered part and give it back to your manager. If your manager asks you to sign a letter for him or her, sign it, and place your initials below it.

ASSEMBLING ENCLOSURES

An enclosure notation is typed on a letter to provide a checklist both at the time the letter is being sent and at the time it is received. Therefore, choose the type of notation that will be most helpful to you. Here are some tips to follow:

- You have the responsibility, whenever an enclosure is mentioned, of obtaining or preparing it and attaching it to the document. When you submit documents for signature, you should include all the enclosures with them. If you do submit a document for signature without its enclosure, attach a note to inform your manager and serve as a reminder to yourself to include it.

- Remember copies being mailed also require enclosures. You can make the copies after the documents are signed. The recipient of the copy may need the enclosures that accompany the original document, plus additional ones, to be brought up to date on the transaction.

- If the item to be enclosed is on your desk, put the enclosure with the document. Make a list of the enclosures needed on your to-do list and collect all the enclosures at one time. Check off the enclosures as you obtain them. On this same list, jot down reminders of all the tasks you must complete later pertaining to the processed documents. For instance, you may need to register a letter and request a return receipt or to ask another department to package material for mailing separately.

- Keep a record of the persons receiving the copies and the date of distribution. You can write this information on the original near the top of the page.

- Letter-sized enclosures are placed behind the document and folded simultaneously; small enclosures are placed in the fold of the document. Enclosures that have been prefolded mechanically should be placed in the fold of the document.

- To hold small enclosures temporarily in place until you are ready to insert the document and the enclosures in the envelope, put them in the envelope or fasten them to the document with a paper clip. Paper clips make imprints and will sometimes catch and tear. To prevent this, fold a small sheet of paper over the assembled items before you fasten them with the paper clip. Do not put a paper clip in an envelope to be mailed.

- Do not staple enclosures to the document. Today, mail must go through four or five high-speed machines at the post office. When you use a staple, you run the risk of having the document torn up in a machine and of damaging several other pieces of mail.

- When typing an e-mail message and sending an attachment, make certain the receiver will be able to open and read the attachment. Remember that higher versions of word processing software can read lower versions, but lower versions cannot always read higher versions, and not all word processing software can convert files from other software. You can send files as text files (files saved with a *.txt* extension) and any word processing software can read them.

- When you must mail large items, you are responsible for preparing the labels, even if the items will be wrapped and sent by someone in another department. When you forward an item to another department for handling, it probably will be processed immediately. However, it is your responsibility to see the item is mailed. If follow-up is necessary, place a note to do so in your tickler file (refer to Chapter 4 for tickler file).

ADDRESSING ENVELOPES

The information in the inside address on an external letter and the address on the envelope should be identical; the form could differ. The U.S. Postal Service recommends all envelopes be addressed in all-capital letters and no punctuation appear in the entire address as shown in the following example.

MR HAROLD MARTIN
1515 REGAL ROW
DALLAS TX 75225

The inside address is usually typed with uppercase and lowercase letters. If window envelopes are used, the scanners used by the U.S. Postal Service can sort the all-caps, no-punctuation style more rapidly. Also, if your equipment will store the address to be automatically printed on the envelope and you want the address on the envelope to be in all-caps style, you can accomplish this by using all caps for the inside address. Address the envelope and place it face up over the top of the letter.

Stop 'n Check

List four tips for assembling enclosures.

a. _____

b. _____

c. _____

d. _____

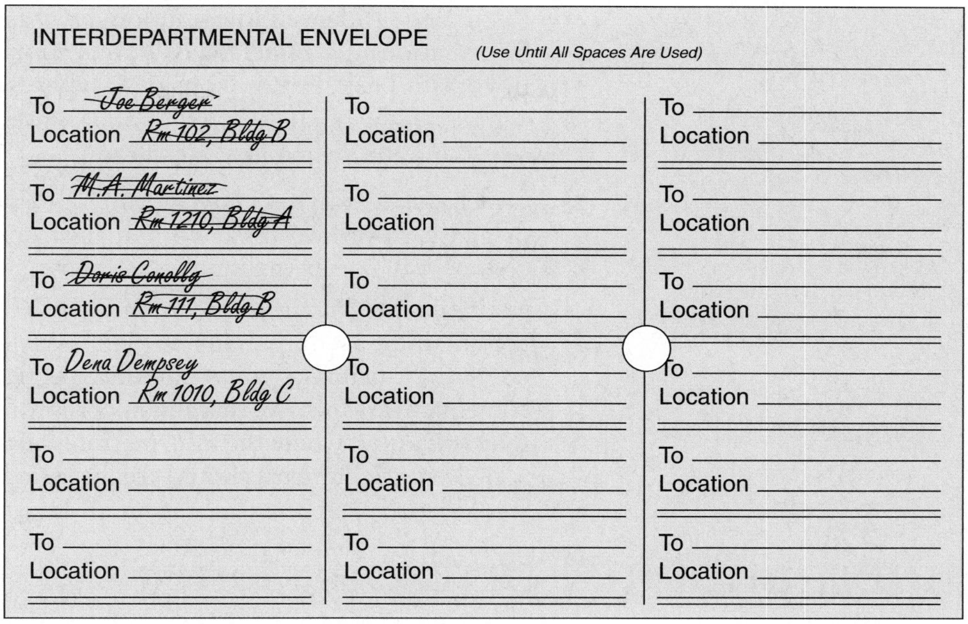

INTERDEPARTMENTAL ENVELOPE *(Use Until All Spaces Are Used)*

To ~~Joe Berger~~ Location ~~Rm 102, Bldg B~~	To Location	To Location
To ~~M.A. Martinez~~ Location ~~Rm 1210, Bldg A~~	To Location	To Location
To ~~Doris Conolly~~ Location ~~Rm 111, Bldg B~~	To Location	To Location
To Dena Dempsey Location Rm 1010, Bldg C	To Location	To Location
To Location	To Location	To Location
To Location	To Location	To Location

FIGURE 6-15 • A reusable interoffice envelope.

If your organization uses window envelopes for external letters, key the inside address at a position on the letters that will ensure all the lines of the address are clearly visible through the window. Fold the letter so it cannot shift in the envelope, obscuring part of the address. According to the U.S. Postal Service, there should be at least one-fourth inch between the address and the left, right, and bottom edges of the window when the insert moves to its full limits in the envelope. If the address contains more than five lines, do not use a window envelope because the entire address will not show.

For interoffice communications at your location and for packet mail, use a reusable interoffice or interdepartmental envelope (Figure 6-15). Be sure the name of the last addressee is crossed out. Write the name of the addressee and an address that is complete enough for the communication to be delivered without delay. Seal an interoffice envelope if the enclosure is confidential. Some organizations do not use interoffice envelopes except for confidential information. When envelopes are not provided for nonconfidential interoffice mail, staple a routing slip with the appropriate information on it near the top left edge of the communication. Do not fold the communication.

Demonstrating Ethics in Writing

ETHICAL ☆ ISSUES

Many businesses today have a written code of ethics that encompasses everything from ethics in business practices to ethics in receiving and writing e-mail. Use the following guidelines:

- Make certain the information included in your writing is correct. Document your writing with source information where necessary or make a note on your file copy of the source you used. If you are asked later where you obtained your information, you will have a ready reference.

- Keep all confidential information away from prying eyes. Place sensitive information in a folder when you are not working on it rather than just in your in-basket or on your desk where others might read it.

- Make certain the information you write is your own. Always give credit where credit is due when you use others' work.

- Never violate copyright laws. A **copyright** identifies the legal right of authors or artists to protect their work against unauthorized reproduction. Make certain you have permission to use copyrighted material before you copy it.

- Maintain integrity in your communications. Much has been reported in the media about accountability at high levels in corporations. Everyone is accountable, including you as an office professional. Never agree to cover for someone else's mistake that might compromise your position. Make certain that you know where the information you work with comes from and keep supporting documents should you be asked to justify or verify information.

International Correspondence

You cannot assume that the rules you have learned about business writing in the United States apply to other countries. Just as you must recognize the differences in cultures, you must recognize and adjust to the differences in rules for writing in those cultures. With the globalization of our economy, your learning must include international information to build your skills in this area.

ADDRESSING ENVELOPES

When addressing envelopes to countries outside the United States, type the entire address in all capital letters. The postal delivery zone should be included with the city, when required. The country name must be typed in English, in all capital letters, and as the only information on the last line. Do not abbreviate the name of the country. For example:

MR THOMAS CLARK
117 RUSSELL DRIVE
LONDON W1P6HQ
ENGLAND

There is a new addressing standard for Canadian destinations. When the postal address delivery zone is included in the address, use the standard abbreviation for provinces and territories. Leave two spaces between the province abbreviation and the postal code, as is shown in the following example between ON for Ontario and K1A 0B1 for the postal code (replaces our zip code). Notice the entire address is in all caps, as you use in the United States.

MS MARGARET LEWOSKI
2121 CLEAR STREET
OTTAWA ON K1A 0BI
CANADA

International postcards have specific maximum and minimum dimensions: Maximum 4 $1/4 \times 6$, Minimum 3 $1/2 \times 5$ $1/2$.

If you are writing from outside the United States to someone in the United States, type *UNITED STATES OF AMERICA* as the last line of the address.

WRITING LETTERS

Because so many U.S. companies have offices or plants outside the United States or do business with international companies, it is highly likely you will encounter letters from outside the country. Letters from abroad may need translation. Therefore, they will come to you in English. The wording may differ greatly from what you have learned in this chapter or in a Business Communications class. For instance, the usual format for a letter written in the United States that gives bad news to the reader would begin by creating a neutral first paragraph that softens the blow by reviewing the facts leading to the bad news, express the bad news, then include a polite closing to maintain rapport with the reader. In Germany, however, the buffer might be omitted, going right to the bad news. In Latin America, the letter might avoid the bad news altogether. In Japan the letter may present the bad news so politely that someone from the United States wouldn't even recognize it. All of this is to say misunderstandings are possible.

The more opportunities you have to read and analyze business letters from abroad, the more you will become familiar with the differences in style and wording. Here is a beginning sentence from the translation of a Spanish letter into English.

"I am grateful for the opportunity to write to you to offer you my catalog. . . ."

If you received this business letter from someone in the United States, you might consider the language flowerly and overly wordy." Instead of saying "I am grateful for the opportunity to write to you to offer," we would say "Thank you for requesting our catalog. . . ." Your acceptance of cultural diversity should extend to business letters from abroad. Be patient, tolerant, and understanding, and remember the sender's culture is different from your own. This difference may be reflected in both the writing and formatting of the correspondence.

Quick Tips

Use this list of 67 often misspelled words to test your spelling IQ. Have someone read them to you and spell them verbally to see if you need to brush up your spelling skills. When you finish, divide the number you spelled correctly by 67 to determine your average spelling ability.

acceptable	accidentally	accommodate	amateur	apparent	believe	calendar
changeable	column	committed	conscience	conscious	consensus	daiquiri
discipline	embarrass	exhilarate	exceed	existence	experience	foreign
gauge	guarantee	hierarchy	humorous	indispensable	inoculate	intelligence
interpret	judgment	leisure	liaison	library	license	medieval
maneuver	millennium	miniature	minuscule	mischievous	misspell	occasionally
noticeable	occurrence	pastime	perseverance	precede	privilege	questionnaire
publicly	receive	receipt	recommend	referred	reference	restaurant
relevant	rhyme	rhythm	separate	sergeant	supersede	tyranny
twelfth	vacuum	weather	weird			

Concept Review and Reinforcement

Review of Key Concepts

OUTCOME	CONCEPT
1. Discuss the communication process and explain the importance of communication.	Employees spend the greater part of their time in some type of interpersonal situation. The function of communication is to ensure all employees know what is expected of them, the right person receives the correct information, and activities within the organization are coordinated. Effective communication ensures management the plans, procedures, and instructions are understood. When this process works smoothly, group and team cooperation is assured and stress is reduced.
2. Discuss various communication methods and explain how to overcome barriers to the communication process.	The various communication methods are: • Verbal communications • Nonverbal communications • Written communications • Writing business letters is a significant endeavor. Keep in mind communication does not take place until the reader comprehends and responds to the message. The effectiveness of each letter you write depends on how well you have written the letter to accomplish its task. Give more thought to anticipated reaction and results than to rigid procedures for writing letters. • Overcome barriers to communications such as missing the meaning, differing interpretations using unfamiliar words, not listening, and emotional or physical distractions.
3. Discuss the various types of written communications for which an office professional should develop excellent writing skills.	Develop skills to write letters for the manager's signature and letters requesting information. Know various letter formats, and write and manage e-mail messages, standard memorandums, and reports such as trip, informational, progress, and investigative reports.
4. Discuss how to prepare routine communications for distribution.	To prepare routine communications for distribution: • Proofread carefully at the computer and the hard copies; double-check outgoing documents for facts and figures, format, completeness, meaning, grammar, punctuation, spelling, capitalization, and number use. • Submitting letters for signature requires verifying that everything is signed, enclosures are included, addresses on the envelopes and letter are the same, and any written note on the letter is photocopied for the file. Staple the file copy to the front of the letter being answered and put it in the to-be-filed folder. Keep track if a part of the letter is not answered. • If an enclosure notation is typed on a letter, make sure the enclosure is included, keep the enclosure with the document being sent, and keep a record of the persons receiving the enclosure and the date of distribution. Letter-sized enclosures should be placed behind the document being sent and folded simultaneously. Hold small enclosures temporarily in place with a paper clip until they are mailed. Do not include a paper clip or staple enclosures in envelopes to be mailed. When typing an e-mail message and sending an attachment, make

certain the receiver will be able to open and read the attachment. When you mail large items, you are responsible for the labels.

- Follow U.S. Postal Service recommended rules for addressing envelopes—all caps and no punctuation. Make sure if you use window envelopes the address is keyed so it will show properly in the window. For interoffice communications, use reusable interoffice envelopes with the last addressee's name crossed out.

---

5. Discuss the importance of demonstrating ethics through your writing.

- Make certain the information included in your writing is correct. Document your writing with source information where necessary or make a note on your file copy of the source you used.
- Keep all confidential information away from prying eyes. Place sensitive information in a folder.
- Make certain the information you write is your own. Always give credit where credit is due.
- Never violate copyright laws.

---

6. Explain how to address international envelopes and write letters.

Type the entire address in all capital letters. The postal delivery zone should be included with the city, when required. Key the country name as the only information on the last line. Do not abbreviate the name of the country.

If you are writing from outside the country to someone in the United States, type *UNITED STATES OF AMERICA* as the last line of the address.

Key Terms

Connotation. The suggested idea or overtone a word acquires through association, in addition to its explicit meaning.

Copyright. Identifies the legal right of authors or artists to protect their work against unauthorized reproduction.

Denotation. Explicit dictionary meaning of a word.

Eye contact. Looking directly into someone's eyes.

Flaming. Expressing a strong opinion or anger via e-mail.

Full-block letter style. Every line begins at the left margin; single space paragraph; double space between paragraphs.

Image. Created by the clothes you wear.

Informational report. Tells the reader about a topic, idea, issue, or event presented without analysis or recommendation.

Investigative report. Created about a specific topic, situation, or event based on research, without including interpretation or recommendation.

Mixed punctuation. Punctuation style that requires a colon after the salutation and a comma after the complimentary close.

Modified-block letter style. The date, complimentary close, and signature begin at the center of the page; single space paragraph; double space between paragraphs. Paragraphs are sometimes indented.

Nonverbal communications. Facial expressions, body gestures, and the way we dress, which often express our feelings and opinions better than our spoken words.

Open punctuation. Punctuation style that requires no punctuation after the salutation or complimentary close.

PDF (portable document format). Universal file format developed by Adobe® that preserves all the fonts, formatting, graphics, and color of any source document, regardless of the application and platform used to create it.

Periodic report. Sometimes called an *activity report*, a document that helps management keep up with company operations such as reports on sales figures or inventory levels.

Personal space. The distance at which one person feels comfortable when talking to another.

Posture. The way you stand, sit, and walk.

Progress report. Also called interim reports, a document that describes for internal or external readers ongoing projects to bring them up-to-date on the status of a project, plan, or some activity.

Six Cs of business writing.
Completeness, correctness, coherence, conciseness, clearness, and courtesy.

Trip report. Often summarized in an e-mail memorandum or standard memorandum identifying the event, outlining three to five key points, itemizing expenses incurred as required, and closing by expressing appreciation.

Verbal communications. A telephone conversation, voice mail message, formal meeting, or even informal chat.

Virus. A program that attaches itself to a file, reproduces, and spreads from one file to another, from one computer to another.

You-attitude. A letter-writing technique in which the writer shows consideration for the reader by putting the reader's needs first, emphasizing the reader's interest, and using words the reader can understand.

For Your Discussion

Retrieve file C6-DQ from your student data disk.

DIRECTIONS

Enter your response after each question or statement.

1. Discuss the importance of communications in the office.

2. Identify ten ways to improve your verbal communication and explain each.

3. List four barriers to communication and explain how each barrier blocks communication.

4. What are three ways you can help improve your communication with a coworker from another culture?

5. Explain what is meant by the "you-attitude" in writing letters.

6. What are ten tips to follow when writing effective e-mails; include an explanation of each?

7. What are the four types of informational reports an office professional might be asked to write? Include an example of each.

8. Discuss how to prepare routine communications for distribution.

9. When letters are to be signed, how should they be arranged in the FOR SIGNATURE folder?

10. Discuss the importance of demonstrating ethics through your writing.

Building Your Office Skills

Exploring the Workplace: *Activities*

1. Interview a person from another culture who was not born in the United States. Create a list of ten questions to ask before the interview. Include questions about birth country; differences in food, dress, and language; problems encountered when the person arrived and thereafter; and obtaining permission to work and/or go to school. What importance does the U. S. Immigration Service play in their lives, if any.

2. As a group, create a business letter collection. Use your office (with permission only) or ask individuals you know who are presently working in an office to share examples. You may include business letters you personally receive. Make copies of the originals and use a black marker and mark out any personal information. Include as many examples of each of the following letters as you can find: appointment letter, routine request letter, inquiry letter, order letter, routine reply letter, acknowledgement letter, cover letter, follow-up letter, appreciation letter. As a group, proofread and explain any error you find. Analyze each letter to see if you can identify its purpose. Does it focus on the reader, convey a meaningful message, and meet the six Cs of writing? Place your letters with corresponding analyses in plastic sheet protectors and in a notebook. Identify each type of letter.

3. In a group, create a checklist for writing letters. Include such tasks as checking grammar, punctuation, and format. Be prepared to share your final product with the class.

4. Research the library or the Internet for books and articles on nonverbal communication and make a list of the various nonverbal expressions and their meanings. Be prepared to share your findings with the class.

Developing Critical Thinking Skills: *Problem Solving on the Job*

Retrieve file C6-OJS from your student data disk.

Directions

Enter your response after each situation.

1. **Poor language skills.** You have just been promoted to office manager, which left an opening for the position you vacated. A temporary has been working in your office, a dedicated hard-working office assistant with excellent technical skills. She is on the job every day, gets along well with the office staff, and is excited about her job. She has two problems. (1) Her language skills are not polished; frequently mispronounces words and often uses words incorrectly. (2) She dresses inappropriately for the office in your opinion. She has applied for the position, and you feel she is the person best qualified for the job, especially with her experience in the job already. If you hire her full-time, what would you do to help her improve her language skills and her dress? Be specific; write a complete step-by-step plan.

2. **E-mail error.** You sent a confirmation e-mail of an informal meeting called by your manager. In the e-mail message, you referred to the information reports your manager asked participants to review before the meeting. You sent the message without attaching the reports. What do you do now?

3. **Writing revisions.** The office manager's assistant reviews all the writing you do, which is mostly letters and reports. Your documents are constantly changed to suit the assistant's personal writing style; many changes are simply another way of saying the same thing. You think these changes are not errors on your part but preferences on the assistant's part. Because you have to do so much editing, you are often not able to complete all your work. Also, the assistant seems to enjoy pointing out your errors, and he is really getting under your skin. What should you do? Identify three ways to handle the situation, assuming each time that the previous attempt didn't work.

4. **E-mail abuse.** You received a scathing e-mail from the e-mail administrator reprimanding everyone using the e-mail system for personal use. Some employees have been abusing the system by sending and receiving personal e-mails. You have not been a part of this group. You feel the administrator was wrong to send the e-mail to everyone and should have addressed the issue with each individual who was abusing the system. How would you have handled this situation?

Using the Web: *Research Activities*

A. Your manager wants to provide those who do research in the office more information on ethics in writing. He has asked you to gather information for him to talk about this topic at his next staff meeting.

1. Locate resources by entering the following search words: *ethics in writing.*

2. Locate at least three articles you think he might reference on this subject.

3. Summarize each article in a short informational report. Be sure to include the source information for each article.

B. You and another coworker work in an office where the workforce is diverse and the two of you want to improve your writing to another culture. Each of you has decided to search the Internet to locate tips for writing internationally and to share the information with one another. Hopefully you can open a dialog with someone in your work area from that culture.

1. Locate resources by entering the following search words: writing internationally, international writing, international business writing.

2. Write a short one- or two-page informational report on what you found. Be sure to include the Web sources for your information.

Get Tech Wise: *Using USB Flash Drives*

You are an office assistant working full-time. In two weeks you will have knee surgery and be in the hospital for one week, then home taking therapy for six weeks. During the six-week period, you believe you can keep up with most of your office work, so you decide to request permission to work at home. Your husband has agreed to courier your working papers and files back and forth to the office twice per week—Mondays and Fridays. Since you will need to have access to several files on your office computer, you need to check out a laptop from the office. Several laptops are available, so access to one will not be a problem. However, you want a flash drive to easily save and move files between your laptop and your desktop computer in the office. Research the Internet or call your local computer stores about flash drives, and write an e-mail memorandum to your instructor who is your manager, requesting the following:

1. Permission to work at home with your husband acting as your courier. Identify the exact dates you will work at home, how you may be reached by phone for assignments, and when your work will be sent to the office.

2. Request permission to check out a laptop.

3. Request the purchase of a flash drive. Explain what a flash drive is and its advantages and cost. Be sure to include all the information necessary to order the drive.

4. Include any other information you feel is necessary.

Improving Your Writing Skills: *Number Use Workshop*

Retrieve file C6-WRKS from your student data disk.

Simulation: *In the Office at Supreme Appliances*

Application 6-A

Practice Your Writing Skills

Supplies needed: Plain paper.

Directions

Ms. Quevedo wants you to broaden your knowledge about marketing since you are working in the marketing department. You are to research online: *marketing trends.* Look for information about selling online, e-mail marketing, effects of television advertising, and so on. Summarize the information you find into a two-page informational report. Be sure to include your sources.

Application 6-B

Inserting Proofreader's Marks

Supplies needed: Form 6-A, progress report about seminar.

Retrieve file C6-AP-B from your student data disk.

Directions

Using the proofreading symbols on the inside back cover of this text, mark the progress report on Form 6-A ready for processing. Check your copy to be sure you have marked all the corrections needed. Key all your marked corrections in file C6-AP-B. Attach your marked copy to the corrected copy for your instructor.

Application 6-C

Presenting Letters for Signature

Supplies needed: Form 6-C-1, Letter Copy; letterhead for Supreme Appliances, Inc. (Forms 6-C-2, 6-C-3, 6-C-4); two No. 10 envelopes.

Retrieve files C6-AP-C2, C6-AP-C3, and C6-AP-C4 from your student data disk.

Directions

You may use the letterhead Forms 6-C-2, 6-C-3, and 6-C-4 in your form packet or files C6-AP-C2 through C6-AP-C4 on your student data disk; you may make copies of the letterhead in case you need extra copies; you may scan the forms into your word processing software if a scanner is available; or you may use plain paper. Put the letterhead forms in your printer tray when you get ready to print. Follow your instructor's directions.

Type the three letters shown on Form 6-C-1, using a correct letter and memo format. Make one copy of each letter. Address an envelope for each letter to be mailed. Arrange the letters and envelopes in a folder for Ms. Quevedo's signature. Because Ms. Quevedo frequently makes notations on file copies, include the file copies in a folder.

Building Your Portfolio

With help from a team member or from your instructor, select the following documents: the informational report and the three letters with envelopes. If instructed, place the documents in plastic protection sheets and add to your portfolio.

chapter

7 Processing Mail

chapter **outline**

Handling E-Mail

Tips for Handling E-Mail
E-Mail Etiquette
Ethical Issues Regarding E-Mail

Handling Traditional Incoming Mail

Sorting Mail
Opening Mail
Inspecting Contents
Registering Special Mail
Date-Time Stamping Mail
Reading and Annotating Mail
Presenting Mail to the Manager
Handling Packages, Publications, and
  Advertising by Mail
Distributing Mail
Answering Mail in the Manager's
  Absence

Handling Traditional Outgoing Mail

Zip + 4 Code
Classes of Domestic Mail
Extra Services
Special Situations
Basic Bulk Mail
Dangerous Goods
Domestic Mail Addressing Tips
Other Domestic Delivery Services
Mail Software Programs
Postal Information on the Internet

International Mail

Special International Services
International Postage

Related Equipment

Metered Mail
Facsimile (Fax) Machine
Photocopiers

International Holidays

learning **outcomes**

When you have completed this chapter, you
should be able to:

- Explain employers' concern for
  misconduct in using e-mail.

- Identify at least five e-mail "netiquette"
  rules to follow.

- Discuss the impact systems knowledge
  related to mail operations has on a
  company.

- Identify ten steps in handling traditional
  incoming mail.

- Describe four steps in preparing items
  to be mailed.

- Distinguish among classes of domestic
  mail.

- Distinguish among the various
  international mail services.

- Describe the basic procedures to follow
  when using a postage meter.

- Describe the general procedures for
  sending a fax message.

- Describe at least five tips for making the
  copy process efficient and economical.

Handling E-Mail

One of the most exciting developments in office communication has been the rise of e-mail. As you learned in Chapter 6, organizations use e-mail among their own departments and to send messages to distant branch offices or to other companies. Just as office professionals are responsible for handling telephone traffic, they are also likely to be first choice when it comes to sorting through the e-mail traffic awaiting their managers' reply. Both managers and office professionals often become overwhelmed by the volume of messages they must sort through daily. Making this task easier for your supervisor often becomes the responsibility of the office professional.

Although electronic mail, courier services, and other mail alternatives have been introduced to the business world, traditional mail services remain the primary means of moving information from one location to another. Whether you are an executive assistant in a large organization or an accounting assistant in a small office, both traditional and electronic mail will arrive daily.

TIPS FOR HANDLING E-MAIL

Telecommunications involves the transmission of information from one location to another by electronic devices. The information is transmitted in a variety of formats, such as voice, data, image, and text. Electronic mail systems are popular because of the high speed with which information can be sent within or outside an organization. A second big advantage is that information can be distributed to a specific location and stored in electronic form until the recipient is ready to receive it. A third advantage is cost. The expense of mailing supplies is reduced. In Chapter 6, you learned how to write effective e-mail messages. This chapter discusses e-mail transmissions and etiquette.

E-mail involves using a computer, a modem or high-speed connection, and communications software. Each e-mail user has a mailbox protected by a special code or password. The user checks routinely for incoming messages. When the user accesses the mailbox, messages appear on the computer screen. If necessary, the user can save or print messages.

E-mail has some drawbacks. Not all messages sent are deemed as important to the recipient as they are by the sender. Messages can also be lost or delayed if there are problems with the host computer that handles the e-mail service. Another growing problem is junk e-mail, called **spam.** With more businesses going online, e-mail is another outlet for direct-mail solicitation. Despite these drawbacks, it is reported that more than 50 million people use e-mail. Because e-mail is fast, cheap, efficient, and convenient, it has become one of the primary forms of business communication.

E-mail can be an effective, convenient way to communicate with your manager, team members, and customers, but only if you manage your mail efficiently. Without careful management, e-mail can bring frustration and confusion to even the most organized employees. Here are a few tips to help you get the real benefits of this service:

1. Check your messages frequently throughout the day. E-mail messages are like pieces of paper on your desk. The messages must be treated with the same importance as you give to traditional incoming mail. You might want to check your messages first thing in the morning, at noon, and

again late in the afternoon. If you schedule regular times throughout the day to check e-mail, you'll be able to better manage your correspondence. Users don't agree whether they should set a signal on their computers to let them know the arrival of new e-mail messages. Some users view the signal as an interruption, while other users simply designate periodic times to check their messages.

2. Respond to messages immediately. Get in the habit of answering messages when you check your e-mail. Answering the messages promptly lets everyone know you are on top of things and can be relied on for prompt response. If you need more time to gather information before responding, let the receiver know you received the message and are working on gathering the requested information.

3. Sort and delete messages regularly. Doing so will save you from having to read through old ones. If you want to keep some messages, you can save them to electronic folders. Try to have no more than one screen of e-mails sitting in your in-box.

E-MAIL ETIQUETTE

It is a fact that e-mail is increasingly replacing standard letters, memos, and faxes as a form of fast, easy, inexpensive, and effective communication. However, many people have not yet learned the basic e-mail etiquette for sending concise and courteous electronic messages.

Based on the importance of e-mail etiquette rules, or **netiquette** as it is sometimes called, the following information is provided as a review.

- Never send anything through e-mail that you don't want made public. E-mail messages travel to many readers—some of whom you may never meet. Remember coworkers, managers, and others may have opportunities to read your e-mail. There's no way of knowing who will eventually read your messages, so make sure whatever you enter in your message cannot return to haunt you later.

- Address the receiver by name in the opening sentence. E-mail etiquette dictates that you simply include the receiver's name in the first sentence. For example, "Marilyn, thank you for your quick response."

- Always reread messages before sending them. Use your spell checker. Even if the receiver knows you were rushed in sending the message, misspelled words show carelessness and make an unfavorable impression. Double-check all facts and figures. Sending incorrect information can cause delays in signing contracts, loss of sales, and so on.

- Keep your message as concise as possible. Unless you are passing along information that has been specifically requested by your receiver, try to keep your message to a maximum of two screens. With the increase in use of electronic mail, some office professionals receive forty messages or more daily. Just as clear and concise writing is important in other business writing, it is equally important in writing electronic messages. Most people do not have the time or inclination to read lengthy postings.

- In Chapter 6 you learned to use capital letters sparingly. In the e-mail world, a message or phrase written in all caps is called "shouting." Not only is shouting impolite, but messages written in uppercase are difficult to read. Use capital letters only for emphasis. Some users recommend that if you want to emphasize certain words or phrases, such as "confidential", highlight them.

- Most e-mail applications will automatically display the original messages in "replies" and "forwarded" messages. When replying to another person and the original message isn't displayed, quote excerpts of the original message. This eliminates the need for you to summarize what the other person has written. Furthermore, you will remind the receiver of his or her original request and save the person time from pulling up the original message for review. Your browser can be set to repeat the sender's message each time you reply.

- Always get a writer's permission before forwarding or posting an e-mail message. When someone sends you a message, the person may assume that the message will be kept confidential. If you forward the message without the writer's permission, you may cause problems for that writer. If the writer knew the message was to be forwarded, he or she may have written the message in a different style, made a telephone call, or not written the message at all. In reality, many people don't obtain the writer's permission before forwarding or posting it in another location. Be careful of what you write. It may be passed on without your consent or knowledge.

- When posting a message to a group, make sure your message is pertinent to all members of the group. People dislike having to take the time to weed out messages that are not appropriate or important to their specific work-related activities.

- When attaching a file to your e-mail, be certain you have actually attached the file. Time is wasted for all who receive an e-mail that is supposed to include an attachment and doesn't. Double-check for attachments before you click the Send button.

ETHICAL ISSUES REGARDING E-MAIL

ETHICAL★ISSUES

What every office employee should realize by now is how public their office e-mail is. In a recent survey of 840 U.S. companies by the American Management Association, 60 percent said they now use some type of software to monitor their employees' incoming and outgoing e-mail. Other workplace privacy experts place the current percentage even higher.

According to the 2005 Electronic Monitoring & Surveillance Survey by the American Management Association and the ePolicy Institute, 55 percent of surveyed employers retain and review employee e-mail messages. With constant efforts by today's businesses to improve their employees' productivity, they are using the most current technology to achieve these goals. Employers have many legitimate reasons for monitoring their employees' computer use, including e-mail, such as:

- maintaining the company's professional reputation and image
- improving employee productivity
- increasing security
- preventing employee disclosure of trade secrets and other confidential information

Few laws regulate employee monitoring, and courts have allowed employers a great deal of leeway in watching employees' e-mails and other Internet activity on company-owned computers. Although employers do have valid reasons for monitoring certain situations, many employers are attempting to reduce employee anxiety regarding privacy issues. More and more companies are establishing policies governing business and personal e-mail and at the same time providing ways to show their employees respect for their personal e-mail needs.

A major consideration is for employees to understand their company's expectation regarding monitoring e-mail and other computer activity, such as Web browsing. Because the company is trying to establish a balance between security and privacy, it is best to check with your company regarding its descriptions of acceptable and unacceptable behavior regarding e-mail.

Stop 'n Check

1. Describe three tips to help you manage your e-mail.
   a. _____
   b. _____
   c. _____

2. Describe at least three legitimate reasons why employers monitor e-mail activities.
   a. _____
   b. _____
   c. _____

3. As an employee, do you agree employers should monitor their employees' e-mail activity? Provide your reasons.
   _____
   _____
   _____

Handling Traditional Incoming Mail

Traditional incoming mail is different than it was even a few years ago. With the priority of the Internet and electronic mail, the office professional is seeing, reading, and controlling less traditional mail now than ever before. Even so, every office still receives paper mail, and handling the mail remains a high priority for an office professional.

When the mail is handled accurately and expeditiously, other office employees can respond more efficiently to the needs addressed in the mail items. What if a check from a customer is delivered to the wrong office and sits on a coworker's desk for three extra days because the coworker is on vacation or has misplaced the check? What is the impact on the office and the company? The accounting department cannot issue credit to the customer's account. The payroll department cannot issue company funds to pay the commission earned by the salesperson and so on. What about the company's focus on the customer—internal and external? The promptness with which you and your manager handle the mail is an important factor in building goodwill and increasing profits for your organization. It is in your and the company's best interest to choose the most efficient means of handling incoming and outgoing mail. Although far from comprehensive, this chapter introduces alternatives and suggestions for working with mail services.

As an office professional, you may or may not have direct contact with the post office, depending on whether your organization has a central mailing department. Nonetheless, as an information worker, you should become knowledgeable about handling incoming mail in your office.

You must keep up with every piece of mail that arrives, and you must be able to distinguish between important and less important mail. As you will be handling mail daily, establish a plan for handling it and follow your plan consistently. As soon as the mail arrives, stop what you are doing, unless it is a rush job, and handle the mail. The information provided in this section on incoming mail is comprehensive. For an office professional to perform all these steps would be too time consuming. Although it is not expected that every office will handle mail with this degree of care, the office professional is certain to perform at least some of these steps:

1. sorting mail
2. opening mail
3. inspecting contents
4. registering special mail
5. date-time stamping mail
6. reading and annotating mail
7. presenting mail to the manager
8. handling packages, publications, and advertising by mail
9. distributing mail
10. answering mail in the manager's absence

Although with the decreased volume of paper mail, some large organizations still have central mail departments. Such departments are responsible for receiving all of the organization's mail and for routing it to the correct departments or individuals. Usually, the mail department provides at least one pickup and delivery to each department every day. At one time, central mailing departments opened, date-time stamped, and distributed the mail. They rarely do so now; instead, recipients open their own mail, or the office professional performs this task for the managers or department.

When the mail is delivered to one location, someone must sort the mail and deliver it to the appropriate workstations. If this task should be assigned to you, sort and make the deliveries at once so the other office support professionals may start processing their own mail.

SORTING MAIL

When mail comes to your desk unopened, begin sorting it into the following groups:

- mail sent with urgency (express, special delivery, certified, and courier)
- letters, including bills and statements

FIGURE 7-1 • Office professional signing for mail.

- interoffice mail (printed copies of budgets, and monthly or quarterly reports)
- personal mail
- newspapers and periodicals
- booklets, catalogs, and other advertising materials
- packages

The office professional may have to sign for courier mail and other insured, registered, or expedited pieces of mail before they can be received. Keep the priority mail separate from the rest of the mail, open it as soon as it arrives, and then put it on the addressee's desk in a way that calls attention to it. Priority mail refers to courier mail that is delivered via an expedited service (Figure 7-1).

In the stack of mail to be opened immediately, assemble letters and other important documents. All interoffice mail is important. Each item either requires a reply or provides your manager with information he or she needs.

You must decide whether mail addressed to an employee who is no longer with the organization is personal or business related. If the mail is personal, clearly write the forwarding address on the envelope and put it in the outgoing mail. Letters, including bills and statements, can be forwarded without additional postage. On the other hand, if mail is addressed by title to someone no longer with the organization, you can assume it is a business letter. When you distribute the mail, deliver it unopened to the person who has the title or is responsible for the work implied by the title. If this person is your manager, put the document with the mail to be opened.

As you sort, put aside all circulars, booklets, advertisements, newspapers, and periodicals until you have opened and processed the more urgent mail.

OPENING MAIL

Before you begin opening the mail, assemble the supplies you will need: opener, date stamp, stapler, paper clips, tickler file, to-do list (or daily chart plan), and pencils (for notations).

Should you open an envelope by mistake, seal it with transparent tape, write "Opened by mistake" and your initials, and distribute or forward the envelope to the addressee.

You can establish "Personal and Confidential" mail procedures with your manager when you first start working. Some high-level executive assistants open personal and confidential mail for their managers. Either way, don't assume—ask.

INSPECTING CONTENTS

Here are some tips for removing and inspecting the contents:

- Keep the envelopes until you are certain all the enclosures and addresses are accounted for.

- Inspect each document for the address and signature of the sender, the date, and enclosures. When a document is not dated, write the postmark date on the document and staple the envelope to the back of the letter. Also, if you notice a major discrepancy between the date on the document and the date of arrival, staple the envelope to the document.

- Check the enclosures received against the enclosure notations. If enclosures are missing, make a note in the margin of the document. Follow up by requesting the missing enclosure. Make a note on your to-do list at once.

- Staple an enclosure that is the same size as a letter or larger to the back of it. Use paper clips to temporarily fasten an item that a staple would damage, such as a check or legal document.

REGISTERING SPECIAL MAIL

A **mail register** provides a record of special (or priority) mail, including insured and registered mail and packages. If you are not provided with a mail register, you can easily design your own form. The form should include:

- date and time received
- sender's name
- recipient's name
- description of type of mail
- distribution (who within the company will receive the mail)

In some offices, the receptionist maintains the mail register. A mail register may be kept in a loose-leaf notebook or in a computer file. Figure 7-2 shows an example of a mail register you can create.

DATE-TIME STAMPING MAIL

The time of arrival of certain correspondence has legal significance. For example, the date a payment is received can be a factor in allowing a cash discount, or a specific time of day can be set for opening bids. When

FIGURE 7-2 • Example of a mail register.

MAIL REGISTER

Date/Time Received	Sender's Name	Recipient's Name	Description/ Type
6/3	Abbot Industries	W. Steele	Fed Express
6/4	Nelson & Nelson	B. Caldwell	Insured pkg.

correspondence is received too late for the recipient to comply with a request, the date received is protection for the addressee.

Organizations do not prejudge which correspondence should be date-time stamped. With the exception of a few documents that should not be marred in any way, organizations stamp all incoming mail either with the date or with both the date and the hour of arrival. The date-time stamp should have the name of the person's office as well as a date and time indicator. Because it may be important to know the exact date an item was received, do not skip this step.

Stamp the date received on each piece of correspondence in the white space at the upper left, right, or top edge. The same pieces of correspondence may come to your desk several times while they are being processed. If you date-time stamp all the mail as you read it, you will know as soon as you see that stamp you have already seen and read a particular piece of correspondence. Consistently stamp booklets, catalogs, and periodicals on either the front or the back cover.

Stop 'n Check

1. List the first five steps in handling traditional incoming mail.

   a. _____

   b. _____

   c. _____

   d. _____

   e. _____

2. Why is a mail register important?

   _____

   _____

   _____

READING AND ANNOTATING MAIL

If your manager receives an extra heavy load of correspondence, the following information can save time for you and your manager by marking and grouping correspondence according to the next step to be taken for each piece. You do this by reading the correspondence in search of the important facts, underlining key words and dates, and writing marginal notes. In some cases, you will not know what the next step should be; in other cases your manager will not agree with your notations. Even so, by using good judgment you can organize the correspondence so your manager can spend his or her time on the correspondence or documents that truly need attention.

Some managers prefer that nothing be underlined or written in the margins of incoming letters. For this reason, get approval before you underline and annotate.

Read the correspondence rapidly, concentrating on the content and using a systematic method of making notes on which you can rely for following through. Develop a questioning attitude—one that will ensure you pick out significant facts and decide what the next step should be. For instance, keep your eyes open for correspondence that:

1. contains the date of an appointment that must be entered in the calendar.
2. mentions a report is being mailed separately.
3. confirms a telephone conversation.
4. requests a decision that cannot be made until additional information is obtained.

Use a pencil to underline and make marginal notes. Underline sparingly; otherwise, your attempt to emphasize will lose its effectiveness. Underline any information that reveals who, what, when, and where.

Provide your manager with additional information in the margins. This is called **annotating**. Use small handwriting and make your notations brief.

Jot down what you would remind your manager of if you were talking to him or her about it. For example, if the letter is a reminder to send a booklet that was requested earlier and it has been mailed, write "Mailed" and the date of mailing. If an item referred to in a letter arrived separately, write "Received." See Figure 7-3 for an example of an annotated letter.

Annotating is preferable to verbally reminding your manager. The use of marginal notes eliminates interruptions, and your manager is able to refer to those notes as he or she answers the correspondence. Remember to ask your manager about preferences in annotating. Marginal notes can confuse readers, and underlining can irritate the readers to whom a letter or report is circulated.

As you read correspondence, pay close attention to the items that require following up. Make the entries in the proper places in your reminder system. Your follow-up plan needs to be foolproof; do not rely on your memory. Enter the date of a meeting or the time of an appointment in both your manager's appointment calendar and your own.

Locate any additional related materials and attach them to the back of the respective incoming correspondence. However, do not delay getting the

MA MILLENNIUM APPLIANCES, INC.
3431 Bloor Street, Toronto, ON M8X IG4
(Tel) 416-795-2893 (Fax) 416-795-3982

September 6, 200X

Mr. Kyle Rhodes
Manager, Sales Office
Millennium Appliances, Inc.
3152–45th Avenue
Vancouver, BC V6N 3M1

Dear Mr. Rhodes:

One of the speakers for the November Sales Seminar is in the hospital. Therefore, he will be unable to present his program for the seminar.

speak at sales
Seminar Tues, 11/11
Honorarium 45 min
Q/A 15-20 min
50-audience
Hilton Hotel

Based on your expertise and many contributions to the industry, you have been recommended as our guest speaker for our sales seminar, scheduled for Tuesday, November 11. In addition to our organization covering your expenses, you will receive an honorarium. The length of your presentation should be approximately 45 minutes, and a question-comment time would be appropriate for about 15 to 20 minutes. The audience will include about 50 sales professionals. If you agree to speak at our sales seminar, we will be happy to arrange for your accommodations at the Hilton Hotel, where our seminar will be held.

May we suggest that your topic relate to the successful methods of team building. I am enclosing a list of topics which will be used by other speakers at the seminar.

Your acceptance of this invitation would be greatly appreciated.
Sincerely,

W. Wilson, Chair
Sales Seminar
enc

FIGURE 7-3 • Example of an annotated letter.

mail to your manager. You can obtain previous correspondence, locate information, and verify figures while your manager is reading the mail.

Keep a record of any special items, such as checks and important forms, forwarded to another person.

PRESENTING MAIL TO THE MANAGER

When placing mail on your manager's desk or in-box, follow these simple rules:

1. Remember the mail is a priority; act on it as quickly as possible.
2. Place the most urgent items on top and the least urgent items on the bottom. When items are delivered by courier or faxed, they may be

urgent; however, you will need to determine this by reading the content. The longer you have worked for a particular organization or manager, the better your judgment will be in separating urgent mail from routine mail.

3. Mail should be placed in such a way it is not visible to people visiting your manager's office in his or her absence. Often, you can protect the confidentiality of the mail by placing it in a large envelope or a folder.

HANDLING PACKAGES, PUBLICATIONS, AND ADVERTISING BY MAIL

Packages should receive priority over newspapers, periodicals, and advertising materials. Expedited parcels should receive the same priority as letters. In some cases, you will be watching for the arrival of packages.

When handling these items, follow these procedures:

- Packages that have letters attached or that are marked "Letter Enclosed" should be processed with the important mail. However, do not open a package or separate a letter from it until you have time to check the contents carefully against the packing slip or invoice. Always avoid opening a package with the intention of checking the contents later.

- Your manager will want to know if certain items have arrived but will be interested in seeing new items, not routine ones. For instance, if a shipment of a recently revised form arrives, your manager will want to know if what has been received is what was specified. Place one of the forms on your manager's desk to see if the new shipment is indeed what was ordered.

Follow these simple procedures when handling publications:

- Unwrap newspapers and try to flatten them. On the front cover of newspapers and periodicals, attach a circulation list, which is a type of routing slip. The **routing slip** is a small sheet of paper on which are listed the names of the people to whom a item is to be distributed. Each recipient should initial and date the slip after he or she has seen the material, and then forward it to the next person. See Figure 7-4.

- If the manager wishes to see the newspapers and periodicals before they are circulated to the rest of the staff, key his or her name at the top of each list. Otherwise, names are commonly arranged in alphabetical order or according to the staff hierarchy.

- As people route the newspaper or periodical to the next person on the list, they should draw a line through their name on the circulation list.

When handling advertising materials, follow these procedures:

- Do not throw away advertising materials until your manager has had a chance to glance at them. Managers want to know about new products in their fields; perusing advertising materials is one way to become aware of what is new. If your manager tells you to screen advertising materials, be sure you clearly understand which items to toss and which to keep.

- After your manager has seen the advertising materials, booklets, and catalogs, you must decide what to do with them. For instance:

FIGURE 7-4 • Routing slip or circulation list.

```
                    ROUTING SLIP

                                   DATE _____

From:          Paul V. Compton

Periodical:    Internet World

Please read, initial, and pass this around.

                     Office No.

Denton, H. V.      672  _____

Barlow, C.         605  _____

Winton, R. M.      616  _____

Peebles, L. M.     682  _____

Donnell, W.        561  _____

FILE:  Return to Paul V. Compton
```

- Which ones should you keep?
- Which ones should you route to someone who has an interest in a particular subject?
- Which ones should you discard?

Ask your manager to initial anything that might be looked at again.

- Do not clutter your correspondence files with advertising materials. Throw away most ads. For those you save, set up a separate file you can go through quickly and update periodically. Advertising materials are usually not dated. However, if you date-stamp them, you can separate the old from the new by looking at the Date Received stamp. Replace old catalogs with new ones. If you keep many catalogs, work out a satisfactory filing system for them. Pamphlet and magazine storage containers are available from manufacturers of filing supplies and are an attractive and organized way to file your catalogs, booklets, and magazines.

DISTRIBUTING MAIL

A manager has mail distributed to others to:

- obtain information so that he or she can reply.
- ask someone else to reply directly.
- keep others informed.

Important mail can be delayed and can even get "lost" on someone's desk. Nevertheless, top management expects mail to be answered. Your manager is still responsible for the reply to a letter or the response to a report even when the actual writing of the correspondence has been delegated to someone else.

As a general rule, your manager will make notations on letters or send memoranda or e-mails asking others to provide information or to reply directly. Some managers attach "Action Requested" or routing slips as they read the mail so they don't have to handle the same pieces of correspondence again. However, an office professional can handle much of this responsibility. When given the responsibility for making requests, realize a considerate tone will play a significant part in getting someone to comply. In contrast, a demanding tone will detract from your efforts and sometimes will result in the letter getting lost.

For informal requests for action, use an Action Requested slip similar to the one shown in Figure 7-5. For example, attach an Action Requested slip to a piece of correspondence that has been misdirected to your manager and obviously should be handled in another department. Write the recipient's name, and check "Please handle."

Sometimes a piece of correspondence requires two types of action, one of which your manager can handle and another someone in another department must handle. When this situation arises, let the other person know precisely which part he or she is to answer. In the margin of the correspondence, indicate the part on which your manager will follow through.

Decide whether the person who is to reply will require earlier correspondence. If you think he or she will need it, attach it to the correspondence being distributed.

To obtain information, you will be communicating with people in numerous departments throughout the organization. Make an effort to get

FIGURE 7-5 • Action Requested slip.

```
                                          DATE _____

TO _____

_____   For your information; do not return.

_____   Let's discuss.

_____   Note and file.

_____   Please note and return to me.

_____   Please handle.

_____   RUSH — Immediate action necessary.

_____   Please answer.

_____   Your comments, please.

_____   Other

COMMENTS:




FROM _____
```

acquainted with them, at least by telephone or e-mail. When you must obtain information from a service department, for example, you should be aware of the department's work schedule. Find out how much time must elapse between the time you request information and the time the material will be ready. Often you will be pressed by a time line, and you must communicate this. You may have to request special service in order to meet your time line. Be cautious of appearing always to request special service as other personnel may not continue to honor your requests.

When you ask someone who is not following a predetermined schedule to assemble facts for you, request the information be ready by a designated time. Suggest a realistic due date. Often, work that can be done when it is convenient to do it gets relegated to the bottom of the stack. Here are some procedures to follow when circulating materials:

- Attach a routing slip to mail that is to be distributed to more than one person.

- When mail is often circulated to the same people, the names can be preprinted. On a preprinted slip, you can change the order in which material is to be circulated by writing numbers in front of the names on the list. Be sure to include "Return to" near the bottom of a routing slip.

- When you distribute a letter, memo, or report to inform others, you will have to decide whether to attach to the original a routing slip listing the names of the recipients, make a copy and attach a routing slip, or make a copy for each person on the list. When deciding, consider factors such as the number of pages, whether each person on the list must be informed at the same time, your immediate need for the original, and the risk that the original will be lost in circulation. Also consider paper waste in deciding how many copies are necessary.

- Your records should show what information has been disseminated. When a circulated item is returned, staple the routing slip to the document. This makes a permanent record of who saw the item and the date he or she saw it. When you do not use a circulation list or routing slip and must make separate copies for each individual, write on your file copy the names of the people to whom you sent the item.

ANSWERING MAIL IN THE MANAGER'S ABSENCE

What happens to the mail when your manager is away from the office depends on his or her preferences and length of absence, and on the time and attention your manager can give—or chooses to give—to what is going on during his or her absence.

While your manager is away from the office, he or she will usually either call or e-mail. With electronic capabilities of telephones, hotels, and airlines, managers can quickly access their e-mail and keep up with their own messages.

If your manager is away from the office for only a day or two, his or her preference probably will be for you to put aside all the mail you cannot answer. However, never put aside correspondence that must be handled immediately. If there is no one in the office who is authorized to reply to an urgent message, you may choose to call or e-mail your manager.

Send letters or e-mails that require immediate action to the person designated to answer them; make copies of the letters and write the name of the person receiving each one on the letter itself. Put the copies in a folder for your manager marked "Correspondence To Be Read."

Answer the letters you can answer. Acknowledge the e-mails not being answered immediately, indicating your manager will return to the office on a specific date and the sender can expect a reply soon after he or she returns. Note and reply to the e-mail address on the incoming e-mail. This form of response is expedient and can provide a concise record of your actions. Most browsers can be set to send an automatic reply to all e-mail messages received when the person is away from the office for several days.

Organize all the business mail in folders that accumulates during your manager's absence. Place the folders, along with your summary of the mail, on your manager's desk in the order listed below. Keep personal mail in a separate folder (perhaps use a different color) and put it on your manager's desk in a separate place. The folders might be labeled as follows:

- "Correspondence for Signature"—for letters you prepared for his or her signature and any other documents ready for signatures. You may consider a red folder for signatures.

- "Correspondence Requiring Attention"—for all correspondence, including any e-mails left unanswered, your manager must answer. A yellow folder will work for this type of correspondence.

- "Correspondence To Be Read"—for copies of letters you and others have answered, and copies of your replies. Again, you would need to clarify your manager's preference for handling the e-mails. For this folder, consider a blue folder.

- "Reports and Other Informational Correspondence"—for all informational items. A green folder is suggested for this type of correspondence.

- "Advertisements"—for advertising brochures and other literature for your manager's perusal. You may consider an orange folder for advertisements.

Stop 'n Check

1. List the last five steps in handling traditional incoming mail.

    a. _____

    b. _____

    c. _____

    d. _____

    e. _____

2. Of these, which do you believe to be the most important? Why?

    _____

    _____

    _____

Handling Traditional Outgoing Mail

Traditional outgoing mail is handled by mailroom personnel in large organizations or by office professionals in smaller organizations. Regardless of who processes the outgoing mail, you should be familiar with basic procedures, such as special mail services and international mail. The more familiar you are with these procedures, the more efficiently you can process the outgoing mail without delays or additional costs incurred in mailing items.

The following steps will help you in preparing items to be mailed:

1. Review all documents for signatures and enclosures.
2. Verify the inside address with the envelope address.
3. Determine the most accurate way of mailing an item if needed.
4. Presort mail for speedier handling by the post office. Separate mail into categories, such as local, out-of-town, and metered.

Outgoing mail is divided into two classes: domestic and international. **Domestic mail** is transmitted within, among, and between the United States and its territories and possessions; Army–Air Force post offices (APO) and Navy post offices (FPO); and to the United Nations, New York City. To learn more about domestic mail, contact your local post office and request the U.S. *Domestic Mail Manual (DMM)* or access the United States Postal Service (USPS) Web site at http://usps.com.

Mail sent within the United States and its possessions should always be addressed using approved two-letter postal abbreviations for state and possession names and the five-digit **zip code** (for zone improvement plan, a number that identifies postal delivery areas) or zip + 4 code for the area. You can locate a zip code at the USPS Web site.

ZIP + 4 CODE

The expanded zip code, called the **zip + 4 code**, is composed of the original five-digit code plus a four-digit add-on. Use of the four-digit add-on number is voluntary for most mail. However, this add-on number helps the USPS direct mail efficiently and accurately. Even if you prefer not to use the four-digit add-on number, using the correct five-digit zip code helps prevent delays.

The zip + 4 identifies a geographic segment within the five-digit delivery area such as a city block, an office building, an individual high-volume receiver of mail, or any other unit that would aid efficient mail sorting and delivery. Using zip + 4 reduces the number of handlings and significantly decreases the potential for human error and the possibility of nondelivery.

The following list shows the standard state abbreviations.

Stop 'n Check

Why is it important to use a zip + 4 code?

_____

_____

_____

State	Abbrev.	State	Abbrev.
A		Montana	MT
Alabama	AL	**N**	
Alaska	AK	Nebraska	NE
Arizona	AZ	Nevada	NV
Arkansas	AR	New Hampshire	NH
American Samoa	AS	New Jersey	NJ
C		New Mexico	NM
California	CA	New York	NY
Colorado	CO	North Carolina	NC
Connecticut	CT	North Dakota	ND
D		No. Mariana Islands	CM
Delaware	DE	**O**	
District of Columbia	DC	Ohio	OH
F		Oklahoma	OK
Florida	FL	Oregon	OR
G		**P**	
Georgia	GA	Pennsylvania	PA
Guam	GU	Puerto Rico	PR
H		**R**	
Hawaii	HI	Rhode Island	RI
I		**S**	
Idaho	ID	South Carolina	SC
Illinois	IL	South Dakota	SD
Indiana	IN	**T**	
Iowa	IA	Tennessee	TN
K		Texas	TX
Kansas	KS	Trust Territory	TT
Kentucky	KY	**U**	
L		Utah	UT
Louisiana	LA	**V**	
M		Vermont	VT
Maine	ME	Virginia	VA
Maryland	MD	Virgin Islands	VI
Massachusetts	MA	**W**	
Michigan	MI	Washington	WA
Minnesota	MN	West Virginia	WV
Mississippi	MS	Wisconsin	WI
Missouri	MO	Wyoming	WY

CLASSES OF DOMESTIC MAIL

The following are basic classifications of domestic mail:

- First Class Mail®
- Priority Mail®
- Express Mail®
- Parcel Post®
- Bound Printed Matter®
- Media Mail® (Book Rate)

The class you choose depends on (1) what you are mailing and (2) how rapidly you would like the mail delivered. Because the rates and weights are subject to change, access the Internet, contact your local post office, or call the USPS 800 number to obtain current information for the following classes of domestic mail.

First Class Mail®

Includes all personal and business correspondence (all bills and statements of accounts, all matter sealed or otherwise closed against inspection, and matter wholly or partly in writing or keyboarded). Any mailable item may be sent as First Class Mail. Each piece must weigh 13 ounces or less. Pieces over 13 ounces can be sent as Priority Mail.

Priority Mail®

Offers two- or three-day service to most domestic destinations. Priority Mail is used for documents, gifts, and merchandise. Any mailable item may be sent as Priority Mail. The maximum weight is 70 pounds, and the maximum size is 108 inches or less in combined length and distance around the thickest part. Mark each package "Priority Mail" in the postage area or use a USPS-provided Priority Mail envelope or box, which is available at many post offices and can be ordered online. Free Carrier Pickup® is available when your carrier delivers your regular mail. You can schedule Pickup on Demand® service at a charge per stop for a specific date and time. Flat rates are available based on weight or destination using a flat rate envelope or box provided by the Postal Service.

Express Mail®

Offers the fastest service, with next-day delivery by noon or by 3 p.m. to most destinations. Express mail is delivered 365 days a year, with no extra charge for Saturday, Sunday, or holiday delivery. Features include tracking, proof of delivery, and insurance up to $100. Additional insurance up to $5,000 may be purchased for merchandise. Pickup service is available for a fee. Express Mail Flat-Rate envelope service is also provided for matter sent in a flat-rate envelope provided by the USPS. All packages must use an Express Mail label. The maximum weight is 70 pounds.

Parcel Post®

Used for mailing certain items—gifts and general merchandise, including books and other printed matter. Maximum weight is 70 pounds. The maximum size is 130 inches in combined length and distance around the thickest part. Rates are based on the weight of the piece and the zone (distance from origin to destination zip code).

Bound Printed Matter®

Identified as advertising, promotional, directory, or editorial that is securely bound (not loose-leaf binders); consists of sheets of which at least 90 percent are imprinted by a process other than handwriting or typewriting; contains no personal correspondence; and is not stationery, such as pads of blank printer forms. The maximum weight is 15 pounds. Rates are based on weight, shape, and distance. The maximum size is 108 inches in combined length and distance around the thickest part. Each piece should be marked "Bound Printed Matter" in the postage area. For special mailing conditions, contact your local post office.

Media Mail® (Book Rate)

Generally used for books (at least eight pages), film, manuscripts, printed music, printed test materials, sound recordings, play scripts, printed educational charts, loose-leaf pages and binders consisting of medical information, videotapes, and computer-recorded media such as CD-ROMS and diskettes. Media Mail cannot contain advertising. The maximum size is 108 inches in combined length and distance around the thickest part. Mark each package "Media Mail" in the postage area.

Stop 'n Check

Identify the six basic classifications of domestic mail.

a. _____

b. _____

c. _____

d. _____

e. _____

f. _____

EXTRA SERVICES

As an office professional preparing traditional outgoing mail, you should know what special services are available from the USPS and when to apply them.

Certificate of Mailing

This evidence of mailing must be purchased at the time of mailing. It is available for First Class Mail, Priority Mail, Parcel Post, Bound Printed Matter, and Media Mail. Items with a certificate of mailing must be presented at a post office or to a rural carrier. A fee is charged in addition to postage.

Certified Mail

This service provides proof of mailing at the time of mailing and date and time of delivery or attempted delivery. A record is maintained by the USPS.

This service is available only with First Class Mail and Priority Mail. A fee is charged for certified mail plus the postage. For an additional fee, Certified Mail may be combined with restricted delivery or return receipt.

Collect on Delivery (COD)

COD allows the mailer to collect the postage and price of an item from the recipient. The goods must be ordered by the addressee. COD service can be used for merchandise sent by First Class Mail, Express Mail, Priority Mail, Parcel Post, Bound Printed Matter, and Media Mail. The amount to be collected from the recipient may not exceed $1,000. The USPS maintains a delivery record. This service is not available for international mail or for mail addressed to APO and FPO addresses, which are explained later in this chapter. COD mail must be presented to a retail employee at a post office or to a rural carrier.

Delivery Confirmation™

This service provides the date and time of delivery or attempted delivery and must be purchased at the time of mailing only. Mailers may retrieve Delivery Confirmation information at the http://usps.com Track and Confirm Web site or by calling 800-222-1811. This option is available for Priority Mail and parcels sent as First Class Mail, Parcel Post, Bound Printed Matter, or Media Mail.

Insured Mail—Purchased at a Post Office

This insurance provides coverage against loss or damage up to $5,000 for Parcel Post, Bound Printed Matter, and Media Mail matter as well as merchandise mailed at Priority Mail or First Class Mail rates. Items must not be insured for more than their value. Insured mail must be presented to a post office or to a rural carrier.

Insured Mail—Purchased Online

This option provides for up to $500 coverage and has the same fees as insurance purchased at a post office, based on the amount of coverage needed up to $500. It may not be combined with insurance purchased at a post office.

Money Orders

This service provides safe transmission of money. The special color blend, Benjamin Franklin watermark, metal security thread, and double imprinting of the dollar amount are incorporated security features. You can buy domestic and international money orders at all post offices in amounts up to $1,000. If your money order is lost or stolen, you must present your customer receipt to apply for a replacement. For a small fee, you can obtain a copy of a paid money order up to two years after the date it is paid. You can also obtain a money order from providers, such as local grocery stores or banks.

Registered Mail

This registration provides maximum protection and security for valuables and provides the sender with a mailing receipt and delivery record maintained by the USPS. The service is available for items paid at Priority Mail and First Class Mail rates and may be combined with COD, Delivery Confirmation, restricted delivery, return receipt, or Signature Confirmation. Postal insurance is provided for articles with a declared value up to a maximum of $25,000. Only items with no declared value may use registry service without insurance. Registered Mail must be presented to a post office or a rural carrier.

Restricted Delivery

A mailer using this option can direct delivery only to the addressee or addressee's authorized agent. The addressee must be an individual specified by name. The service may be combined with Delivery Confirmation, return receipt, Signature Confirmation, or special handling. The service is available only for First Class Mail, Priority Mail, Parcel Post, Bound Printed Matter, and Media Mail that is sent Certified Mail, mail insured for more than $50, or Registered Mail. A fee is charged in addition to the postage.

Return Receipt

The sender receives a postcard or electronic notification, via fax or e-mail, with the date of delivery and recipient's signature. A return receipt may be requested at time of mailing or after mailing. When requested at the time of mailing, it also provides the recipient's actual delivery address, if different from the address used by the sender. Customers purchasing a Return Receipt at the time of mailing may choose to receive it by mail or electronically. Return Receipts are available only for Express Mail (by mail only), First Class Mail, Priority Mail, Parcel Post, Bound Printed Matter, or Media Mail when purchased with one of the following: Certified Mail, COD, mail insured for more than $50, and Registered Mail. A fee is applied in addition to the postage as well as the fee paid if the receipt is requested at the time of mailing or requested after mailing.

Return Receipt for Merchandise

This option provides the sender with a mailing receipt and a return receipt. The return receipt supplies the recipient's actual address, if different from the address used by the sender. A delivery record is maintained by the USPS.

Signature Confirmation™

The sender is notified of the date and time of delivery or attempted delivery and the name of the person who signed for the item. This service must be purchased at the time of mailing only. Mailers may retrieve Signature Confirmation information at the http://usps.com Track and Confirm Web site or by calling 800-222-1811. A delivery record, including the recipient's signature, is maintained by the USPS and is available, via fax or mail, upon request. No acceptance record is kept at the office of mailing. The service is available for Priority Mail and parcels mailed as First Class Mail, Parcel Post, Bound Printed Matter, or Media Mail rates. A fee is applied in addition to postage.

Special Handling

Senders may pay extra for preferential handling for items such as perishables, insects, or poultry. The service does not insure the article against loss or damage. Special Handling is available for First Class Mail, Priority Mail, Parcel Post, Bound Printed Matter, and Media Mail. The charge is based on weight, and a fee is applied in addition to postage.

Stop 'n Check

Of the extra services, which ones maintain a record by USPS?

_____

_____

_____

SPECIAL SITUATIONS

The mail does not always go through without problems. Can all classes of mail be forwarded? What happens to undelivered mail? Is it possible to recall a piece of mail or to refuse mail? As an office professional, you will encounter these questions, and you will have to decide what to do when there is a change in procedure.

Changing an Address

When the organization for which you work changes its address, someone within the organization must notify the post office of the change. If doing this is your responsibility, follow these steps:

1. Access the USPS Web site.
2. Search the information for "Change of Address."
3. Once the Official Change of Address Form is displayed, you can complete it directly on your computer screen. Be sure to print it for your files.
4. You will then need to sign the form and either give it to your mail carrier to mail or mail it to your local post office.

Additionally, you can use the entered information to print Address Change Notification Letters and mail them to business associates to let them know of your new location.

Recalling Mail

If you make an error in mailing that is serious enough to warrant recalling a piece of mail, you may be able to do so *if* you act quickly. Call the post office branch in your mailing zone if the document is for local delivery; call the central post office if the document is for out-of-town delivery. Request that the document be held. For identification, type an address identical to the address on the envelope being recalled. Go to the post office, complete a Sender's Application for Withdrawal of Mail, and present it and the duplicate address to the postal clerk or representative.

Returning Undelivered Mail

Keep mailing lists up-to-date and address envelopes and labels with absolute accuracy to avoid the cost and delay involved when mail is returned. A returned letter must be placed in a fresh envelope correctly addressed with new postage.

If the addressee has moved or simply refuses to accept mail, if there is insufficient postage or an incorrect or incomplete address, or if for other reasons the mail cannot be delivered, the post office will return the item to the sender.

BASIC BULK MAIL

The term **bulk mail** is generally used to describe presorting mail, including Presorted First Class Mail and Standard Mail. Business Mail 101 at the USPS Web site provides basic information for preparing bulk mail, including questions that will assist you in determining the type of bulk mail that is right for you. To answer questions such as "Is bulk mail right for your business?" and "How do you sort bulk mail?" visit the USPS Web site and locate information regarding bulk mail.

DANGEROUS GOODS

Articles or substances that could be dangerous to postal workers and postal equipment, or that could damage other mail, are prohibited from being mailed both domestically and to points outside the United States. It is illegal to use the domestic service to deliver:

- explosives
- flammable solids and flammable liquids
- radioactive materials
- gases, oxidizers, and organic peroxides
- corrosives
- toxic and infectious substances
- miscellaneous dangerous goods, such as asbestos, air bags, and dry ice

A list of restricted items is available for international mail as well. If you are in doubt about any item you wish to mail, call your local post office.

DOMESTIC MAIL ADDRESSING TIPS

The USPS uses computerized systems that scan a wide range of addressing styles; this includes both handwritten and typed addresses. To increase the speed and efficiency of mail handling, the USPS has designed a consistent format for users. USPS requests the use of this optimum format whenever possible, but recognizes other formats as acceptable for computerized scanning. To review guidelines for addressing envelopes, see "Addressing Envelopes" in Chapter 6.

OTHER DOMESTIC DELIVERY SERVICES

Other delivery services are available through companies, such as DHL, Emery Air Freight Corporation, United Parcel Service (UPS), Federal Express Corporation (FedEx), and Purolator Courier Corporation. These companies provide pickup services as well as drop-off locations. They offer online services that allow you to electronically complete the necessary forms and to track a shipment through to its destination.

Messenger or courier services can save you money and ensure immediate delivery within the city. They are useful if you have a constant flow of local deliveries and pickups. You can arrange to have pickups and deliveries made at a set time of the day, or you can ask the service to be on call for your varying needs. Check your telephone directory for local messenger services.

In addition, private companies such as Eagle Mail and Pak Mail provide packing and shipping to anywhere in the world. Additional services include mail boxes, mailing label preparation, and meter mail. They will also insure your mail, accept COD, sell money orders, and send and receive faxes. Many of these companies are drop-off locations for UPS and FedEx. For example, Kinko's is a drop-off location for FedEx.

To select the best provider, compare the services, rates, and regulations of these companies as well as those of the U.S. Postal Service.

MAIL SOFTWARE PROGRAMS

Ensuring that your mailing operations are working in an optimal manner is crucial for maximizing efficiency and cost savings. It's also critical for managing the impact from any postal regulation changes made by the USPS. Maximizing the efficiency of your organization's mailing operations involves optimizing every component of the mail preparation process: standardizing address format, presorting, identifying customer moves, and updating the information in your customer files.

Any organization wants its mailing to reach its destination as quickly as possible at the best possible price. However, three major problems can surface in an organization's mail operations: too much returned mail, unreliable delivery, and excessive mailing costs. To solve these problems, organizations may choose to use mailing software. The advantages of using a mail software program include the following:

- reads files in different formats, such as Access
- validates addresses
- standardizes addresses to USPS requirements
- produces postal reports and forms to track costs
- produces bar-coded labels to qualify for automation postage discounts
- presorts mail according to classes of mail and prints labels in presorted order
- saves time and money

POSTAL INFORMATION ON THE INTERNET

A wealth of information is available at the U.S. Postal Service Web site (http://usps.com). You can look up zip + 4 codes, track your Express Mail, get information on the latest postal rates, and find answers to frequently asked questions. If you are interested in stamps and stamp collecting, you will find information on stamps and stamp releases and can view images of the recent stamp issues.

If you keep exploring, you can find postal news releases and learn about the history of the Postal Service. The Inspection Service has included information on consumer fraud and other crimes as well as information about the history of the Inspection Service. The Web site is continually changing; visit often for new postal information. You also have an opportunity via the Web to make inquiries and request additional information.

Additional mail delivery sites are available for DHL (http://dhl-usa.com), Federal Express (www.fedex.com), United Parcel Service, (www.ups.com), and Purolator Courier (www.purolator.com).

International Mail

International mail is mail that is distributed beyond the United States and its territories or possessions. The *International Mail Manual (IMM)* sets forth the policies, regulations, and procedures governing international mail services provided to the public by the USPS. The *IMM* is distributed to all postal facilities and is available to the public on a subscription basis from the Superintendent of Documents, Government Printing Office.

SPECIAL INTERNATIONAL SERVICES

For basic information regarding USPS international mail services, access the USPS Web site. Because the prices and descriptions may vary, this information is not included in the following list of USPS's special international services:

- Expedited Services—faster services, such as Global Express and Global Priority
- Standard Services—lower cost, such as Global Airmail and Global Economy
- Volume Mailing Service—volume and presort mailing, such as International Priority Airmail, International Surface, International Business Reply Service, and Publishers' Periodicals.

Certified Mail and COD services are not available for international mail, but most other special services, money orders, insurance, Delivery Confirmation, Registered Mail, Return Receipt, insurance, and special handling are provided with certain restrictions. USPS's current services, rates, and regulations are posted on the Internet.

In addition to USPS global delivery, other international providers include DHL, UPS, and FedEx. When you need international delivery, explore different options and compare their services, rates, and regulations. Visit their Web sites for current information.

INTERNATIONAL POSTAGE

It is essential to have some foolproof way of ensuring that correct postage is put on international airmail. Nothing is more frustrating to your manager

Stop 'n Check

1. What is the purpose of the *IMM?*

_____

_____

_____

2. Identify at least three international delivery carriers.

a. _____

b. _____

c. _____

than to learn an urgent package was mailed by the slowest method because the postage was insufficient or because you did not select the most appropriate service to use in the situation. As the office professional supporting your manager, you should see that the mailroom has current postage information for all countries with which you communicate. Make sure the information is clearly posted, so that even the casual user, like your manager, can calculate the correct postage if he or she should need to work over the weekend when no office support staff is available.

Related Equipment

METERED MAIL

Many companies use in-house postage meters. Metered mail need not be canceled or postmarked when it reaches the post office; however, it must be turned in at a postal outlet counter and not simply dropped into a mailbox. Metered mail is sent directly for sorting because it does not need canceling by the USPS. **Canceling mail** refers to the process of printing bars over the stamps, as well as printing the date and time where mail processing has occurred. This process prevents a person from reusing the postage; more importantly, it also allows the receiver to track the actual time, date, and place where processing occurred.

Because properly prepared metered mail can go directly to the sorting machine in the postal center, it may be dispatched slightly sooner than mail that must be canceled. However, the real advantage to the user is the convenience of not using stamps, not waiting in line at the post office, and being able to apply whatever amount of postage is needed.

Postage meters vary in size from lightweight desk models to fully automatic models that feed, seal, and stack envelopes in addition to printing the postage, the postmark, and the date of mailing (see Figure 7-6). The machine itself is purchased, but the meter is leased from the manufacturer (one of several authorized by the USPS) and is licensed without charge by the post office. If you have questions about postage meters, contact a postage meter company, such as Pitney Bowes or Mail Technology, Inc., or the USPS.

The user of a basic postage meter must take the meter to the post office and pay for a specified amount of postage. The postal agent then sets the

FIGURE 7-6 • Postage meter.

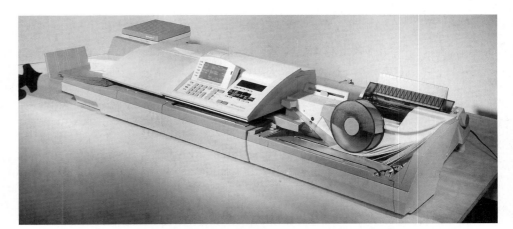

meter dials for this amount. Each time an envelope is imprinted with an amount of postage, the unused balance on the meter is decreased by that amount. When the unused balance runs low, the meter must be taken to the post office to be reset.

Here are some basic procedures to follow when using a postage meter.

1. Check the manual dials or electronic readout to make sure the correct postage will be printed on the mail.
2. Check the meter date to be certain it is the correct date of mailing, not the previous day's date.
3. To work efficiently, group your mail and stamp all mail requiring the same denomination in one batch.
4. Set aside pieces of mail requiring irregular amounts of postage until the rest of the mail is stamped.
5. After you have processed all the mail, reset the machine so the next user will not waste postage because the meter was set for the wrong amount.
6. Bundle metered mail with addresses facing one direction, and group the pieces by the class of mail.

Avoid making mistakes when stamping mail, but if you do make an error, you can request credit from the leasing agent. When complete and legible meter stamps cannot be used because of misprints, spoiled envelopes or cards, and the like, the agent will credit the postage. You should note that in order to receive a credit, you must supply the complete envelope as proof, not just the meter impression.

Stop 'n Check

Why should an organization choose to use meter mail?

_____

_____

_____

FACSIMILE (FAX) MACHINE

The *facsimile,* commonly known as the **fax machine,** is a device that will copy and transmit graphics (charts, photographs, drawings, and handwritten messages) and text messages as electronic signals via the telephone lines or from a personal computer equipped with a modem. The document will be reproduced on paper at the destination fax machine or as a file stored in a computer.

Although sending an e-mail may be quick, sometimes you may not have certain files, such as charts and photographs, in an electronic format to send as attachments. Sending a message via a fax machine may be the quickest way to get documents in several different formats across the city, country, or even the world. Using the fax machine to send a document is less expensive than using most courier services. The speed of fax transmission varies with the size of the page, the density of the image to be faxed, and the levels of technology of the fax machine sending and receiving documents. However, the sender can be sure that regardless of the distance, the document will reach its destination within seconds of being sent.

Fax transmission uses telephone lines to send documents; in fact, sending a fax is as easy as making a telephone call. Fax machines operate automatically, allowing you to send documents without first notifying the recipient. The general procedures are very simple:

1. Complete an adhesive note or use a transmittal form to show contact information of sender and recipient.
2. Place the document to be transmitted in the sending fax unit. Check the instructions to know whether the document must be placed face up or down.
3. Dial the fax number of the receiver. Check to see if you need to dial a long-distance access code for transmission outside the local area code.
4. Once the connection is made, press the send button.

Most offices purchase both a **stand-alone fax machine,** which is self-contained as shown in Figure 7-7, and computer software because it gives them the versatility to send and receive documents using either the stand-alone machine or the computer. Some small offices are purchasing a combined unit, which functions as a fax machine as well as a scanner, copier, and printer (Figure 7-8).

To send a fax from your computer, you need special fax software that comes with a variety of features. Some software programs allow you to send a "broadcast" fax to many other computers; other fax programs allow you to receive incoming faxes in the screen background so you can continue

FIGURE 7-7 • Stand-alone fax machine.

FIGURE 7-8 • A combination fax, copier, and scanner.

working on the computer while the fax is being sent. Remember, a fax sent via a modem is only a picture of the document, not the document itself, so it cannot be edited.

In an office where fax machines are connected to a network, polling may be required. **Polling** allows one fax machine to test others on the network for information. Users can store their messages on the fax network. The person waiting to receive the messages instructs his or her fax station to poll the other machines for faxes with the correct poll code. When the correct code is found, the message is transferred to the polling fax machine. A head office wishing to pick up orders or check inventory from its stores, for example, may require the polling feature.

Establishing clear, simple guidelines for using the fax can reduce unnecessary transmissions and save both time and money. Follow these tips to help establish your guidelines.

1. Determine if the message should be faxed or distributed using another method.

2. If a document is delivered by fax, type an appropriate notation on the line below the reference initials or on the line below the enclosure notation, if used. A notation such as "By fax" is appropriate.

3. Decide which type of cover sheet will be used. WordPerfect and Microsoft Word offer fax transmittal forms, such as the example shown in Figure 7-9.

4. Determine guidelines regarding confidentiality. Confidentiality is perhaps the highest concern facing businesses using fax machines. Consider arranging for only authorized staff members to transmit and receive confidential fax transmissions.

5. Determine how you will report misdirected messages. Nothing is more frustrating than to have sent a message and then find out it was misdirected and no one made an effort to let the sender know about the error.

FIGURE 7-9 • An example of a fax transmittal memo.

Fax Transmission
<Organization>
<Address>
<City, State Zip>
<Telephone>
Fax: <Fax>

To: [Name of Recipient]   **Date:**   July 9, 200X

Fax #:   [Fax Number]   **Pages:**   [Pages (including cover sheet),

From: <Name>   including this cover sheet.]

Subject: [Regarding]

COMMENTS:

Stop 'n Check

1. List three tips to help you establish guidelines for sending fax messages.

   a. _____

   b. _____

   c. _____

2. What is the biggest concern for businesses using fax machines?

   _____

   _____

   _____

PHOTOCOPIERS

With the convergence of printers, scanners, photocopiers, and fax machines into a single device, you can now find multifunction printers, all-in-one, or multifunction devices. Today's printer/copier provides networked printing, scanning, copying, digital sending, and even faxing, with the full finishing capabilities of a traditional photocopier. Although it makes sense from a technology standpoint, it can be confusing to choose from the wide selection of products and decide which product is best for your company.

To gain a better understanding of which types of multifunction products are appropriate, it will help to distinguish between a copier-based device and a printer-based device. A *copier-based device*, running 55 to more than 85 pages per minute, has finishing capabilities, such as stacking, stapling, and hole-punching. Because this equipment is built for high volume and production-level usage, the average cost per page can be lower than the printer-based devices. Copier-based devices are often leased on a usage basis, rather than purchased for a flat fee. A *printer-based device* can cost much less than a copier-based device and does not offer the finishing capabilities.

The following categories provide a general framework in which to demonstrate how both copier-based and printer-based devices may be used in various workgroups:

Personal

- Low-volume; used in individual areas; placed on desktops to print word processing documents, spreadsheets, and other daily work; are usually printer-based devices; may be networked for very small work groups of two to four users
- Easy to use
- Print approximately 15–25 pages per minute

Small to Mid-Size Workgroup

- Mid-volume; provide high-speed networked printing, copying, digital sending, and faxing for small workgroups of five to twenty users
- Need skills to scan and to perform digital sending task
- Accommodate more paper sizes and paper weights; operate through touch control screens; perform features such as front and back printing; stacking, stapling, hole-punching, binding documents into book style, and enlarging and decreasing size of text or images
- Print approximately 25–50 pages per minute

Department

- High-volume
- Multifunction device; floor-console models; provide networked printing, photocopying, scanning, and digital sending for groups of twenty or more users
- Need skills to scan and to perform digital sending task
- Perform same features as mid-volume
- Print up to 65 pages per minute

Production

- High-volume
- Floor-console models; may or may not be attached to the office network; produce documents in book format; hold large supplies of paper; insert tabs and coversheets where programmed to do so; produce high quality color
- Usually require additional training because of extended features

Some high-volume copiers can create images according to programmed instructions and are called **digital intelligent copiers.** They contain microprocessors that enable the copier to produce copies from instructions transmitted by computers as well as by remote equipment by means of telephone wires.

Which Photocopier Do I Use?

As an office professional, you may be asked to serve on your company's technology team to determine the most appropriate device to meet your workgroup's needs. Knowledge of printers/copiers helps you to make an efficient decision. The decision depends on a number of considerations. Here are a few questions to consider:

1. How many copies are needed?
2. How quickly are the copies needed?
3. How important is the appearance of the final copy?
4. Is the original document usable as is?
5. Are the copies to be stacked, stapled, or hole-punched?
6. Is an enlargement or reduction of text or photo required?

Considerations Regarding Photocopying

It is important to consider areas of photocopying that can raise costs. Consider the following scenario:

> Juan, assistant to the regional sales manager, was asked to study the department's rising copying costs. After investigating the procedures and copying habits of the department staff for three weeks, Juan reported the following problems to his manager:
>
> 1. Additional copies were made—more than needed.
> 2. Individuals were copying documents that the in-house copy center should have handled.
> 3. Individuals were making copies for personal use.

Organizations have different options available to them. One popular method of controlling the use of a copier is to provide the appropriate people with individual copy cards or keys. When the card or key is used, the copier registers the number of copies made. This method discourages people from making too many copies and making personal copies. Often the copy cards can be purchased in advance, thus allowing the department to prepay for copying privileges.

Another important consideration is that of copying materials that infringe on the U.S. copyright law. Materials that are protected contain a notice of copyright. In many organizations in areas where copying is done, a notice of the copyright law is posted at the copier to ensure employees are aware of their responsibilities.

A third consideration is that of setting guidelines, if necessary, for your work group to follow when determining the most efficient copier use. It may be necessary for you to establish a range of number of originals to be copied and the type of copier to use in your department. For example, if fewer than 50 originals are to be copied, use a desktop copier; if more than 50 originals are to be copied, use the in-house copy center. If 500 or more copies are needed, consider using a high-volume copier. This may sometimes mean contracting with an outside printing company.

Here are some tips to make the copying process efficient and economical:

- Copy when you have several items.
- Determine the best times to use the copier. Avoid high-traffic times.
- Keep track of the monitoring device assigned to you for copying purposes.

Stop 'n Check

1. What is one advantage for using a personal printer/copier?

   _____

   _____

   _____

2. What two to three factors would distinguish the difference between small to mid-size workgroup and department copiers?

   _____

   _____

   _____

- Plan ahead for large copying needs.
- Make sure you comply with the Copyright Act. As a rule of thumb, you can photocopy from a published edition of more than ten pages, 10 percent of the total number pages OR one chapter. If you are photocopying from a serial, then you are allowed to photocopy one article from a single issue.
- Turn on the "power down" or "standby" mode when you have finished copying.
- Do not photocopy with the lid up. Doing so isn't good for your eyes.
- "Fan" the paper properly and place it correctly within the paper tray to prevent jams.
- Keep all staples and paper clips away from your copier to avoid damage.
- Use the Lighter/Darker control on the display panel to adjust the tone of your copies.

International Holidays

People who conduct international business know how important holiday information can be when mailing or faxing important documents. Did you know that more than 70 percent of holidays celebrated each year change from year to year? Some countries have such diverse ethnic populations that they observe religious holidays for ten or more major religions. How does this knowledge affect the way you and your manager conduct your business communications?

A surprisingly common reason for getting no answer from an international number is that you are faxing a document on a country's national or local holiday. Conducting business may be difficult if people take extra days off from work in order to take advantage of the long holiday. Before you try to mail or fax an important document or package to a country outside the United States, check out that country's schedule of holidays. For a current list, access a search tool such as Google, and search under the key words *international holidays*.

Quick Tips

TIPS FOR SENDING ATTACHMENTS WITH YOUR E-MAIL MESSAGE

If you want to send a file or photo, make an attachment. An attachment is a file you include with an e-mail. For example, let's say you have a document created in Word or WordPerfect you want to share with someone. You can "attach" this document to an e-mail and send it off to the person. How do you attach it?

- Locate a little paper clip icon in your e-mail software. Click it and you should see a dialog box that lets you navigate to (may use the term *browse* to signal you to locate the file to be attached from your hard drive or disk) and either add or attach the file of your choice. The attached file doesn't disappear from your computer; it only sends a copy of it.

- Mention in the e-mail message area the application the file was created in and the number of documents being sent as attachments. For example, "Attachments include three documents created in Microsoft® Excel 2003." This information helps the recipient know how many attachments were sent and if he or she has the software that will open the file without any difficulty.

- Don't attach too many documents in the same e-mail. Large files can overwhelm the system. Your recipient may not appreciate downloading a large file that takes down the e-mail system.

Concept Review and Reinforcement

Review of Key Concepts

OUTCOME	CONCEPT
1. Explain employers' concern for misconduct in using e-mail.	Employers' concerns include: • company's professional reputation and image • employee productivity • security • employees' disclosure of trade secrets and other confidential information
2. Identify at least five e-mail "netiquette" rules to follow.	Netiquette rules include the following: • Never send anything through e-mail you don't want made public. • Address receiver by name in opening sentence. • Always reread messages before sending them. • Keep message as concise as possible. • Use capital letters sparingly. • If possible, set e-mail applications to automatically display original messages in "replies"and "forwarded" messages. When replying to another person and original message isn't displayed, quote excerpts of original message. • Always get a writer's permission before forwarding or posting e-mail. • When posting message to group, make sure message is pertinent to all members of group. • When attaching file, be certain to attach file.
3. Discuss the impact systems knowledge related to mail operations has on a company.	Understanding impact of systems knowledge as it relates to mail operations is critical to company's success. When mail is delivered to your desk, accept responsibility for handling each important piece because internal and external customers depend on you to process it in timely manner.
4. Identify ten steps in handling traditional incoming mail.	The steps, in sequence, for handling incoming mail are: 1. sorting mail 2. opening mail 3. inspecting the contents 4. registering special mail 5. date-time stamping mail 6. reading and annotating mail 7. presenting mail to manager 8. handling packages, publications, and advertising by mail 9. distributing mail 10. answering mail in the manager's absence

5. Describe four steps in preparing items to be mailed.

The steps are:

1. Review all documents for signatures and enclosures.
2. Verify correspondence address with envelope address.
3. Determine most accurate way of mailing item if needed.
4. Presort mail for speedier handling by post office.

---

6. Distinguish among classes of domestic mail.

Classes of domestic mail are

- First Class Mail®
- Priority Mail®
- Express Mail®
- Parcel Post®
- Bound Printed Matter®
- Media Mail® (Book Rate)

---

7. Distinguish among the various international mail services.

In addition to USPS global delivery, other international providers include DHL, UPS, and FedEx.

---

8. Describe the basic procedures to follow when using a postage meter.

When using a postage meter, keep the following procedures in mind:

- Check manual dials or electronic readout to make sure correct postage will be printed on mail.
- Check meter date to be certain it is correct date of mailing, not previous day's date.
- To work efficiently, group mail and stamp all mail requiring same denomination in one batch.
- Set aside pieces of mail requiring irregular amounts of postage until rest of mail is stamped.
- After you have processed all mail, reset machine so next user will not waste postage because meter was set for wrong amount.
- Bundle metered mail with addresses facing one direction, and group pieces by class of mail.

---

9. Describe the general procedures for sending a fax message.

General procedures include the following:

- Complete an adhesive note or use transmittal form to show contact information of sender and recipient.
- Place document to be transmitted in sending fax unit. Check instructions to know whether document must be placed face up or down.
- Dial fax number of receiver. Check to see if you need to dial a long-distance access code for transmission outside local area code.
- Once connection is made, press send button.

10. Describe at least five tips for making the copy process efficient and economical.

Here are some tips for making copying process efficient and economical.

- Copy when you have several items.
- Determine best times to use copier. Avoid high-traffic times.
- Keep track of monitoring device assigned to you for copying purposes.
- Plan ahead for large copying needs.
- Make sure you comply with Copyright Act. As a rule of thumb you can photocopy from published edition of more than ten pages, 10 percent of total number of pages, or one chapter. If you are photocopying from a serial, then you are allowed to photocopy one article from a single issue.
- Turn on "power down" or "standby" mode when you have finished copying.
- Do not photocopy with lid up.
- Fan paper properly, and place it correctly within the paper tray to prevent jams.
- Keep all staples and paper clips away from copier to avoid damage.
- Use Lighter/Darker control on display panel to adjust tone of copies.

Key Terms

Annotating. The practice of making notes in the margin.

Bound Printed Matter®. A U.S. Postal Service mail classification that describes a package weighing at least 1 pound but not more than 15 pounds. Rates are based on the weight of the piece and the zone. Packages must measure 108 inches or less in combined length and girth.

Bulk mail. Generally used to describe presorting mail, including Presorted First Class Mail and Standard Mail.

Canceling mail. Process of printing bars over the stamps, as well as printing the date and time when mail processing has occurred.

Certificate of Mailing. Receipt that provides evidence of mailing. It must be purchased at the time of mailing; no record is kept by the post office. A fee is charged in addition to the postage.

Certified Mail. A mailing receipt provided to the sender, with a record kept at the post office of delivery.

Collect on Delivery (COD). Allows the mailer to collect the price of goods and/or postage on merchandise ordered by addressee when it is delivered.

Delivery Confirmation™. Provides date and time of delivery or attempted delivery; the confirmation must be purchased at the time of mailing.

Digital intelligent copier. Contains microprocessors that enable the copier to produce copies from instructions transmitted by computers as well as by remote equipment by means of telephone wires.

Domestic mail. Distributed within, among, and between the United States and its territories and possessions; Army–Air Force and Navy post offices; and the United Nations in New York City.

Domestic Mail Manual (DMM). Manual that sets forth the policies, regulations, and procedures governing domestic mail services of the U.S. Postal Service.

Express Mail. The fastest USPS service, with next-day delivery by noon to most destinations. Express mail is delivered 365 days a year— no extra charge for Saturday, Sunday, or holiday delivery.

Fax machine. Office machine that copies and transmits over telephone lines graphical (charts, photographs, drawings, and handwritten messages) or textual documents to a corresponding remote fax machine.

First Class Mail®. Classification that includes all personal correspondence, bills and statements of accounts, all matter sealed or otherwise closed against inspection, and matter wholly or partly in writing or typewriting.

Insured Mail—Purchased at a Post Office. Provides coverage against loss or damage up to $5,000 Parcel Post, Bound Printed Matter, and Media Mail matter as well as merchandise mailed at Priority Mail or First Class Mail rates. Items must not be insured for more than their value.

Insured Mail—Purchased Online. Provides for up to $500 coverage and has the same fees as insurance purchased at a post office and is based on the amount of coverage needed up to $500.

International mail. Mail distributed beyond the United States and its territories or possessions.

International Mail Manual (IMM). Manual that sets forth the policies, regulations, and procedures governing international mail services of the U.S. Postal Service.

Mail register. A record of special incoming mail for quick review.

Media Mail (book rate). A U.S. Postal Service classification used for books, film, printed music, printed test materials, sound recordings, play scripts, printed educational charts, loose-leaf pages and binders consisting of medical information, and computer-readable media.

Money orders. Provide a safe way to send money through the mail; can be used in place of a personal check.

Netiquette. Term that describes rules governing e-mail etiquette.

Parcel Post®. A U.S. Postal Service classification used for mailing certain items—books, circulars, catalogs, other printed matter, and merchandise—weighing 1 to 70 pounds.

Polling. Function that allows one fax machine to test others on the network for information.

Postage meter. Machine used to feed, seal, and stack envelopes in addition to printing the postage, postmark, and date of mailing.

Priority Mail®. A U.S. Postal Service classification used to offer two-day service to most domestic destinations. Items must weigh 70 pounds or less and measure 108 inches or less in combined length and girth.

Recalling mail. Service permitting requests to have mail containing errors returned—if sender acts quickly.

Registered Mail. A U.S. Postal Service classification used to provide maximum protection and security for valuables. The service is available only for items paid at Priority and First Class mail rates.

Restricted Delivery. Permits a mailer to direct delivery only to the addressee or addressee's authorized agent.

Return Receipt. Provides a mailer with evidence of delivery and supplies the recipient's actual delivery address if it is different from the address used by the sender.

Return Receipt for Merchandise. Provides the sender with a mailing receipt and a return receipt. A delivery record, for an additional fee, is kept by the post office of address, but no record is kept at the office of mailing.

Returning undelivered mail. Keep mailing lists up-to-date and address envelopes and labels with absolute accuracy to avoid the cost and delay involved when mail is returned.

Routing slip. Form used to route or circulate correspondence, documents, and magazines to other team members or staff within a department, also called a *circulation list.*

Signature Confirmation™. Provides the date and time of delivery or attempted delivery and the name of the person who signed for the item.

Spam. Junk e-mail.

Special Handling. Provides preferential handling for items such as perishables, insects, or poultry. The service does not insure the article against loss or damage.

Stand-alone fax machine. Self-contained unit that uses scanning and printing technology.

Zip code. Stands for Zone Improvement Plan, a five-digit number that identifies postal delivery areas in the United States.

Zip + 4 code. An expanded zip code, composed of the original five-digit code plus a four-digit add-on. The expanded code identifies a geographic segment within the five-digit delivery area such as a city block, an office building, an individual high-volume receiver of mail, or any other unit that would aid efficient mail sorting and delivery.

For Your Discussion

Retrieve file C7-DQ from your student data disk.

DIRECTIONS

Enter your response after each question or statement.

1. Identify at least five e-mail netiquette rules to follow.

2. Discuss the impact of systems knowledge related to mail operations on a company.

3. List the steps, in sequence, for processing traditional incoming mail.

4. Identify the four steps in preparing traditional outgoing mail.

5. Use two to three sentences to describe the basic classes of domestic mail.

6. Distinguish among the following: Certificate of Mailing and Certified Mail; Delivery Confirmation and Return Receipt; Delivery Confirmation and Signature Confirmation.

7. What are three special situations you might encounter in handling outgoing mail that would require your attention?

8. List the basic procedures to follow when using a postage meter.

9. List the general procedures for sending a fax message.

10. Describe at least five tips for making the copying process efficient and economical.

Building Your Office Skills

Exploring the Workplace: *Activities*

1. If you are using e-mail in your organization, complete the following (if not, interview someone who is using e-mail):

   a. How frequently during the day do you check your e-mails?

   b. What are at least three netiquette tips you believe could be used in your organization?

   c. What tips do you have to help others manage their e-mails?

   d. What e-mail system is being used? Microsoft Outlook? GroupWise? ProCom?

2. As a team, obtain a copy of your (or a friend's company) organization's policies and procedures for monitoring employees' e-mail activity. Compose a memo to your instructor summarizing your findings regarding the information provided to employees and attach the copy to the memo. Be prepared to share the information with other class members.

3. Either individually or in your team, obtain a schedule of current rates and fees for the following:

   a. Certified Mail

   b. Return Receipt requested at the time of mailing

   c. Return Receipt requested after an item has been mailed

   d. Special Handling of an item weighing more than 10 pounds

   e. Special Delivery of first class mail weighing less than 2 pounds

   f. Money order for $200

   g. Insurance for a package valued at $60

   h. Registration for an item with a declared value of $300

   i. Mailing a 16-pound parcel within your own local postal zone

Report your findings in a memo to be submitted to your instructor.

4. Interview an office professional who can answer the following questions:

   a. How is the mail delivered in your office? Do you pick up the mail from a centralized mailroom in your company? Is the mail distributed by mail personnel?

   b. How often is the mail delivered to your work area?

   c. How often is the mail picked up from your work area?

   d. How many people do you handle mail for in your work area?

   e. Describe the steps you use to handle the incoming mail for the people you support.

   f. Describe the steps you follow to handle the outgoing mail.

   Organize the responses in a report memo and be prepared to share the information with the class.

5. It has been more than two years since your office has studied different domestic delivery companies, and your supervisor has asked you to gather information regarding the following three domestic (or select international) delivery services: Federal Express, UPS, and DHL. Your supervisor wants you to compare the rates and services provided by each of these companies. Research the information, create a table to present your findings, and summarize the results in a memo prepared for your instructor. Based on your instructor's directions, either individually or in your team, complete this project.

Developing Critical Thinking Skills: *Problem Solving on the Job*

Retrieve file C7-OJS from your student data disk.

Directions

Enter your response after each situation.

1. **Handling publications and advertising materials.** James told you his manager was furious when he admitted he had been throwing away over half of the advertising material at the time it arrived, never giving his manager an opportunity to see it. His manager discovered this through conversations with different callers who asked about the mailed advertisements. James seems confused about what to do with booklets, advertising material, and other standard mail, and has asked for your advice. Knowing his manager wants to see all the mail, what guidelines can you suggest?

2. **Increased mailing costs.** You and three other office assistants in a management consulting firm have the responsibility for reviewing certain cost areas, one of which is the mail operation. For the past three months your team has noticed an increase in mailing costs. After your team reviewed the mail-related expenses, the following were discovered: an increase in Express and Priority Mail to meet deadlines; letters returned with incorrect and insufficient addresses; and several items sent using incorrect mail classifications. Among team members, discuss possible solutions, advantages and disadvantages of each solution, and recommend at least three changes to reduce mailing costs.

3. **Handling traditional incoming mail.** As an office professional to your new office manager who receives a heavy correspondence load, you would like to suggest that she let you review and preview her mail each day before you distribute it to her. Knowing your previous manager never delegated this task, how can you propose this suggestion, giving sound reasons for it, and indicating how it would assist her by saving time?

4. **Handling traditional incoming mail for multiple managers.** You support six managers. Every day each manager receives at least twenty pieces of mail in addition to the following: *The Wall Street Journal*, two or three newsletters, two or three trade journals, and advertisements. Three of the managers want you to log in their important mail ("important mail" has not been defined), and the other three managers need all the help you can give them in handling their incoming mail. They are not well organized in handling their paperwork, much less handling the incoming mail in an efficient way. What actions can you take to handle your managers' mail efficiently and avoid mixing up their mail?

Using the Web: *Research Activities*

A. The operations manager has asked you to locate information about postal services. Rather than calling or visiting the post office, you want to search the Web.

1. Enter the following key search words: *United States Postal Service*, or go directly to the Web site http://usps.com.

2. Research information from the international section. Select the Business section. Search the following three areas: international, business publications, and postage rates.

3. Summarize the most important information from the international section. Print the page, if possible, and attach it to your summary.

B. As a team, you have been asked to research postal software or mailing list software.

1. Summarize at least three different software products.

2. Print each page, if possible, and attach each to the appropriate summary. If you cannot print the pages, be sure to include the Web site source.

C. Enter the following address: www.uspsglobal.com.

1. List at least three services or products that are displayed.

2. Summarize your findings in a report memo to be submitted to your instructor.

D. Go to the Web site of United Parcel Service (UPS) at www.ups.com.

1. Review the products and services. Locate information about tracking a package.

2. Write a memo to your instructor summarizing your findings. If you can print the information, attach a copy to the memo.

E. Your office is interested in ordering postage online, and your team has volunteered to research this topic.

1. In your search, locate at least three sources.

2. Summarize your findings in a memo to be submitted to your instructor. Be certain to include the Web sites in your report.

3. Be prepared to share your team's results with other teams in your class.

Get Tech Wise: *Microsoft® Outlook*

Situation: You frequently send information to a group of people, with limited *added* or *changed* contacts.

Solution: Create the basic message with the recipients' names in it and save it as a template. Each time you need to send a message, you can quickly open the template and add your information.

A. Creating the Template

1. Open Microsoft® Outlook and click on the New Mail Message button on the Standard toolbar.

2. Enter the recipients' names in the To text box, separated by commas.

3. Type the subject in the Subject text box.

4. Type the
   - leading paragraph(s)
   - closing paragraph
   - signature information

5. Click on File and select Save As.

6. By default your message's subject is the file name. You have the option to change the name.

7. Change the Save As type field to: Outlook Template (*.oft).

   This causes the *file location* to change; accept this. This will place a *.dot* extension on the file name.

8. Click on Save to save the message as a template.

9. You are returned to your e-mail message. Assume at this time you do not want to send it out because you are just creating a template.

10. Close the message without saving it. Your original message is already saved as a template.

B. Using the Template

1. Click on the File menu, point to New, and then select Choose Form.

2. The Choose Form dialog box opens.

3. Click on the down-pointing arrow next to the Look In text box.

4. Select User Templates in File System.

5. All Outlook templates created by you display on the screen.

6. Click on the template you need and then click on the Open button.

7. The message is opened with the standard information you need.

8. Place the cursor above the closing information in the body section and type the updated information.

9. Proof your message and click on Send.

Improving Your Writing: *Number Workshop*

Retrieve C7-WRKS from your student data disk to complete the workshop.

 Simulation: *In the Office at Supreme Appliances*

Application 7-A

Processing Incoming Mail

Supplies needed: Forms 7-A-1 through 7-A-7 (Notes, Daily Mail Register, To Do List, and Routing Forms); letter-size folder, plain bond paper.

Retrieve files C7-AP-A1 through A7 from your student data disk.

Directions

Amanda Quevedo is out of the office during the week of July 14. You are processing the mail on Monday morning, July 14.

1. Read Form 7-A-1, Notes on Incoming Mail for Monday, July 14.

2. Your manager always wants mail from a regional office routed to the respective assistant vice president

for the region. However, she expects you to open the letters and to keep a record of the mail forwarded to the assistant vice presidents. Using the notes, complete Form 7-A-2, Daily Mail Register.

3. Using the notes, complete Form 7-A-3, To-Do List; add reminders to yourself and notes about items that require your follow-up.

4. Route magazines and advertising letters from other organizations to the assistant vice presidents.

According to the notes, complete Forms 7-A-4 through 7-A-7, Routing Forms. In a real office situation, each form would be attached to individual magazines and sales and advertising letters.

5. For your instructor, make a list of the items, such as the specific letters, e-mails, and other important items (mentioned in the notes), you will place in a folder for Ms. Quevedo. Label the list "Items for A. Quevedo's Mail Folder."

Application 7-B

Classes of Mail

Supplies needed: Form 7-B, List of Outgoing Mail.

Retrieve file C7-AP-B from your student data disk.

Directions

While your manager is away, you have been asked to assist with training regarding outgoing mail activities. You and your team trainer created a list of outgoing mail items to be used in your training. Before you distribute it to your trainee, you want to reinforce your knowledge of classes of mail by indicating the class of mail for each item listed.

Application 7-C

Extra Outgoing Mail Services

Supplies needed: Form 7-C, List of Extra Outgoing Mail Services.

Retrieve file C7-AP-C from your student data disk.

Directions

While your manager is away, you are continuing with the training regarding outgoing mail activities. You and your team trainer created a list of extra outgoing mail services to be used in your training. Before you distribute it to your trainee, you want to be certain the answers are correct by completing the list. Based on your instructor's directions, either individually complete Form 7-C or complete it with your team members. To receive maximum credit, be sure to answer each question. Be prepared to share your findings with other class members. Submit your final report to your instructor for evaluation.

Application 7-D

Mail Operations—Field Trip

Supplies needed: Form 7-D, Mail Operations—
Field Trip Activity; plain bond paper.

Retrieve file C7-AP-D from your student data disk.

Directions

With approval from your manager, you are continuing with the training regarding mail operations. A trip to a local company has been approved to gain additional information regarding their mail operations. You and your team trainer have created a set of interview questions. Based on your instructor's directions, either individually complete Form 7-D or complete it with your team members. To receive maximum points, be sure to answer each question. Be prepared to share your findings with other class members. Submit your final report to your instructor for evaluation.

Building Your Portfolio

With the help of a team member or your instructor, select the best activity representative of your work (Activity report comparing three mail delivery services, Mail Register, List of Extra Outgoing Mail Services, and Field Trip Results) from Chapter 7. Follow your instructor's directions about formatting, assembling, and submitting the portfolio.

chapter

8

Records Management

chapter **outline**

learning **outcomes**

When you have completed this chapter, you should be able to:

- Discuss how records management works as a system.
- Define the categories of records.
- Distinguish among the filing systems.
- Describe filing supplies and equipment needed.
- Index and alphabetize personal, business names, and governmental and political designations.
- Explain the steps in preparing paper records for filing.
- Discuss methods for tracking paper files.
- List tips for organizing electronic files.
- Identify storage media for backing up electronic files.
- Describe the guidelines for records retention and transfer.
- Describe ethical issues in records.

Records Management

Information is at the center of everything an organization does; it's the heartbeat of an organization. How an organization manages its information can directly affect its ability to compete, operate efficiently, comply with government regulations, and recover from disaster.

OVERVIEW OF A SYSTEM

An **information system** details how an organization plans, develops, and organizes its information. Because information is recorded in many different ways, think about how organizations must handle the following: customer records, invoices, students' transcripts, meeting notes from a board meeting, e-mail, inventory, personnel information, and patient information. Maintaining this information in an organized and secured manner is essential to organizations so it is useful and immediately available to the person requesting the information at the right time.

The purpose of this chapter is to provide basic guidelines for establishing and maintaining the records of your office by the most efficient and economical means available.

You have very likely discovered, through the processing of your own school papers, that if you allow your documents to accumulate haphazardly, you find yourself wasting precious time, frantically sorting stacks of paper, or searching electronic files in a last-minute effort to prepare for your final exams. The same thing may be true in handling your personal business records when it comes time for taxes. Similar panic can happen in an office when a letter, report, or form is needed in a hurry and cannot be located or has been destroyed.

Part of today's record problem is that federal, state, and municipal governments demand so much data from each business. Apart from the growing need for businesses to supply government agencies with data and to maintain enormous quantities of records to meet the government's varying regulations, business records have become increasingly more complex with the information explosion of our world.

One way large organizations and businesses have reacted to the need to cope with so many records has been for them to apply a "systems" approach. **Records and information management** is the application of systematic control to recorded information. It is a logical and practical approach to the creation, maintenance, use, and disposition of records and, therefore, to the information those records contain.

WHY IS RECORDS MANAGEMENT IMPORTANT?

An organization has a responsibility to manage its records, also called *information assets*, effectively to maximize profit, control cost, and ensure the vitality of the organization. Effective records management ensures that the information needed is retrievable, authentic, and accurate. An effective records management system requires an organization to:

- set and follow policies.
- identify who is responsible and accountable for managing records.
- create, communicate, and follow procedures consistently throughout all departments.

WHO IS RESPONSIBLE FOR MANAGING RECORDS AND INFORMATION?

Every employee is responsible. Everyone plays an important role in protecting the organization's records and information by following its established policies and executing its procedures.

Many large businesses find it productive and cost-effective to designate one employee to supervise the management of records for the entire organization. In these large organizations, the **records manager** supervises all the organization's files. He or she also determines how the files will be maintained and who will maintain them, how long each record is to be kept, and when a record is to be removed to an inactive area or made ready for more permanent storage or destruction.

The rapid expansion of information in many fields has created a need for more specialization in records and information management careers, such as records manager or records coordinator. The opportunity for a career path depends on the size of the business, industry, or organization and whether a company maintains its own records or engages in outsourcing. Regardless, positions exist for professionals, ranging from the highest level position of a records and information supervisor (manager or director) to the lowest level position of a records center clerk. As businesses, industries, and organizations have become more aware of how the records and information management system contributes to the success and productivity of a business, they have become more aware of the importance of their records professionals.

If your company does not have a records manager or does not contract with a records consultant, you may be called upon to complete one or all of these tasks.

1. Revise or create a filing system.
2. Select filing supplies and equipment.
3. Standardize filing procedures.
4. Develop the arrangement of records in a sequence so they can be retrieved quickly.

WHAT ARE RECORDS?

Records are the evidence of what the organization does. They represent its business activities and decisions or transactions, such as correspondence and financial statements. Records appear in many formats:

- physical paper such as college transcripts, letters, and contracts
- electronic mail
- databases

When there is a lawsuit, all of these records, including copies that employees have retained and any items deleted from the system, could be used against the organization. For example, Philip Morris USA/Altria Group in July 2004 deleted e-mail that was over sixty days old for more than two years after a legal order was issued to preserve all documents relating to litigation. The company failed to follow its own internal procedures for document and e-mail preservation and was fined $2.75 million.

CATEGORIES OF RECORDS

Determining the categories of records helps an office professional know whether a record is to be kept, where it is to be stored, how it will be stored, and how long it will be retained. For example, paper or electronic advertisements, requests, and inquiries have little or no future use or value to an organization and should not be kept. Many of these documents are taking up space in office filing cabinets. Stop and think about the time it takes you to file this type of material, the supplies and equipment needed, and the expensive space it requires. However, think about a company's contracts, personnel records, and formal meeting minutes from board meetings. These records are evidence of transactions and decisions made for and by the company and are of value.

Categorizing records as to their current and future usefulness and legal implications is necessary to save your organization money in terms of employee time, supplies, equipment, and expensive space. To be effective in managing records, the first step is to consider how records are categorized so you will know what is to be kept short-term, permanently, or discarded. Four common categories are vital, important, useful, and nonessential.

Vital Records

Vital records include records that are essential to the operation of the organization or to the continuation or resumption of operations; the re-creation of the legal or financial status of the organization; or the fulfillment of its obligations to stockholders and employees in the event of a disaster. Vital records may pertain to property, patents, copyrights, insurance, tax, and accounts receivable. Vital records should be identified and stored in a separate location for safekeeping. Vital records may include backup or copying essential computer databases and files (both paper and electronic).

Important Records

Important records, such as customer and inventory records, are meaningful to the business operation but must be limited as to the length of time they are retained.

Useful Records

Useful records are documents, such as correspondence and reports that are needed to conduct the daily business operations. Important and useful paper records are maintained in fire-resistant file cabinets and are kept on-site; any electronic important and useful records are backed up or copied using the appropriate storage media.

Nonessential Records

Nonessential records are not needed beyond their current use and should be discarded after their use because they cost money in space, equipment, and employee time. Examples of nonessential records are requests, acknowledgments, notices of staff meetings, and duplicate copies of correspondence.

FILES MANAGEMENT

Files management is integral to records management. **Files management** applies records management principles to both paper and electronic records created and used by a single office. Files management ensures that records can be retrieved efficiently when needed. A well-designed filing system can produce time savings in faster filing and information retrieval, fewer misfiles, and higher staff efficiency and productivity.

An ideal filing system is comprised exclusively of records but only the ones that provide value to the organization. Although almost every bit of information you create or receive, regardless of its paper or electronic format, is considered a **document**. Unlike records, some documents should not be filed. A number of documents are created or kept for convenience or reference and can be destroyed at any time. Common examples of documents include:

- duplicates such as completed forms, extra copies of reports, and bulletins
- versions of reports that have been through several rounds of editing or preliminary drafts
- miscellaneous notices, such as announcements of meetings, confirmations, and acknowledgements
- requests for information or responses to requests (discarded after the information has been sent or received).

To ensure faster retrieval and filing of information, eliminate these documents from your filing system. Eliminating these documents also reduces the need for extra computer memory, filing cabinet space, and filing supplies. For purposes in this chapter, the term record and document are used interchangeably.

Stop 'n Check

1. Define records and information management.

   _____

2. What is a record? Give at least three examples.

   a. _____

   b. _____

   c. _____

3. Explain the difference between a record and a document.

   _____

   _____

Managing Paper Records

DEVELOPING A FILING SYSTEM

In Chapters 5 and 7, you learned about incoming information, such as e-mail, USPS mail, and other mail from special delivery services, fax, and voice mail messages (written or keyboarded), and copies of documents. In Chapter 6, you learned tips for writing documents that either would be distributed within the company or sent outside the company. When handling both incoming and outgoing information, you must determine a system for filing these records.

The major arrangements, also called *classifications* and *systems*, are alphabetic, numeric, geographic, and subject. In Chapter 4, you were introduced to another arrangement called *chronological (tickler* and *pending)*. The arrangements are often used in combination with one another.

Before deciding on a particular filing system, consider the following questions:

- How will the records be requested? By name, number, geographic location, or subject or a combination? For instance, will you search your system for your customer by name or number, or will you search for your customer by geographic location?
- How will the records be retrieved? Paper or electronically?

Alphabetic

The **alphabetic filing system** is one of the most commonly used systems to retrieve records by name or topic and uses the alphabet to sequence personal, business, and government names. Figure 8-1 shows an alphabetic arrangement for a small office.

The alphabetic system has the following advantages:

- Alphabetic filing is direct because you can go to the file and locate an item without having to first refer to an index. An **index** is a listing of the filed items.
- All other arrangements are directly or indirectly combined with the alphabetic system.

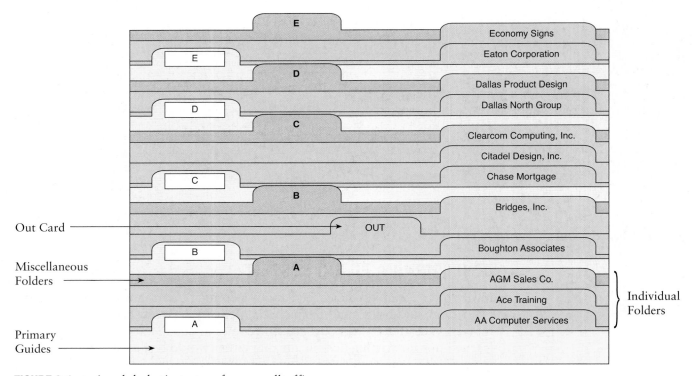

FIGURE 8-1 • An alphabetic system for a small office.

Some of the disadvantages include:

- Because the record is filed alphabetically by name, each individual using the arrangement files records according to the alphabetic scheme he or she believes appropriate. If everyone doesn't strictly follow a uniform set of rules for alphabetizing records, individuals could place files in many possible locations, making retrieval inefficient.
- Expansion may create problems when the expansion takes place in a section of paper files where there is no space to insert additional folders.
- Confidentiality of the files cannot be guaranteed because the file folder labels can be seen by anyone retrieving a file.

Numeric

In the **numeric filing system,** material is filed in some logical numerical order. Examples of users include insurance companies that keep records according to policy numbers, medical offices that assign a number to each patient, and legal firms that assign a case number to each client. See an example of numeric filing in Figure 8-2. A numeric filing system requires a separate alphabetic listing of names in case an assigned number has been lost or forgotten. See Figure 8-3.

FIGURE 8-2 • Example of numeric filing.

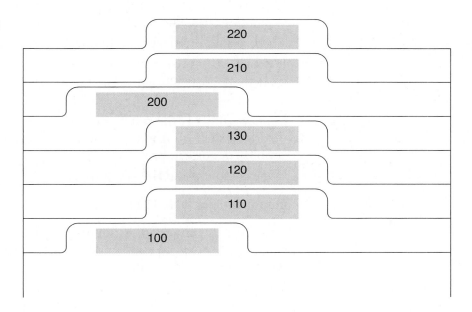

FIGURE 8-3 • Alphabetic listing of names.

100—Insurance
    110—Health & Disability
    120—Home & Property
    130—Insurance Life & Annuity

200—Investments
    210—Brokerage Accounts
    220—Mutual Funds

Numbers are assigned in two ways: terminal-digit and decimal-numeric. **Terminal-digit filing** divides numbers into groups of digits that point to the location of the records. For example, the first group of digits identifies the sequence of the folder behind the filing guide, the next group of digits indicates the guide number in the drawer, and the last group identifies the drawer number. This system is advantageous because it reduces "misfile." **Decimal-numeric filing**, also known as the *Dewey decimal system*, works with subject filing to permit more expansion than a basic numeric system. For instance, you might assign number 500 to Office Equipment. The following example shows the numeric assignment to the main heading, major divisions, and first division for Office Equipment.

500	Office Equipment
500.1	Computers
500.1.1	Laptops
500.2	Fax Machines
500.3	Paper Shredders
500.4	Copiers

The numeric filing system has the following advantages:

- It is well suited for records with identification numbers, for rapidly expanding files, and in conjunction with data processing systems.
- There are no duplicates of numbers as there can be with names.
- It is easier to notice a filing error with numbers.
- Security is greater because the file name does not reveal anything about its contents.
- Numeric filing is the fastest to use and results in the fewest errors. Coupled with shelf filing equipment and color-coding, numeric filing systems simplify document processing.
- It is easy to expand the system.

Disadvantages include the following:

- You must use an index, listing the name of the person, organization, or subject to which the number is assigned. For this reason, a numeric system is called **indirect filing**.
- You must use a register, often called an **accession register,** to show the next number available for assignment.

Geographic

The **geographic filing system** is commonly used by sales and marketing personnel and others who are concerned with the location of companies and individuals. Using this arrangement, you file material alphabetically in some logical pattern, such as by city, state, or region or territory. An example of a geographic filing system is shown in Figure 8-4.

The geographical filing system has the following advantages:

- It allows for direct filing if the location is known.
- It provides easy access because groups of records are filed together.

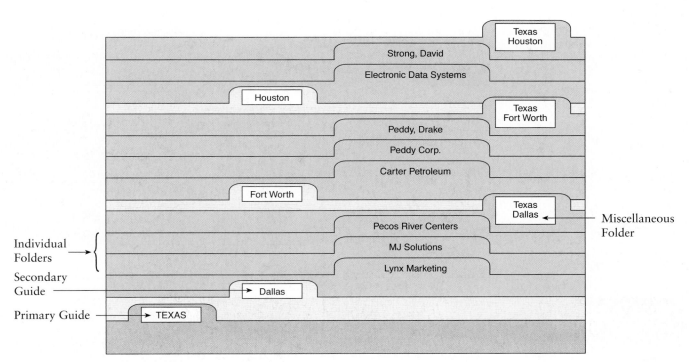

FIGURE 8-4 • Example of geographic filing system.

Some disadvantages include:

- An index is required if the location is not known.
- Sorting the records by city, state, territory, or region increases the possibility of error.

Subject

The **subject filing system** allows you to file records alphabetically according to the main subject because the subject is considered to be more important than the individual or business name. Companies that deal with products, supplies, advertising, and so forth use subject arrangements. Subject files are popular with travel agencies for filing brochures by destination, such as Las Vegas, San Francisco, or Seattle. An example of a subject file is shown in Figure 8-5.

Among the advantages of the subject filing system:

- Access is easy because subject filing relates to groups of records.
- Subdivisions easily expand the system.

The subject filing system has the following disadvantages:

- It requires an index to file or retrieve files by firm name when the subject is unknown.
- It is difficult to classify records by subject; therefore, time is lost while someone searches for a file under a number of subject choices.

As mentioned earlier, filing systems may be combined. For example, for a department with a large number of records, you may combine subject and numeric to reflect a subject such as insurance. It may be assigned a label of 34. Insurance with all other folders shown as 34.1 Auto Insurance, 34.2 Health Insurance, and so on.

FIGURE 8-5 • Example of subject filing.

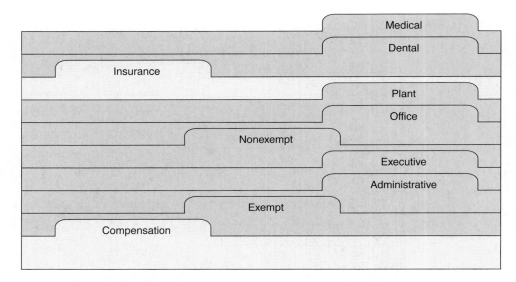

Stop 'n Check

1. Identify four main filing systems.

    a. _____

    b. _____

    c. _____

    d. _____

2. Name two advantages of a numeric filing system compared with an alphabetic system?

    a. _____

    b. _____

Which is the best system to use? An organization must decide on the method that best suits the type of business, the type of paper records being filed, the way in which they are used, and the method that ensures the fastest storing and retrieval.

LOCATION OF PAPER RECORDS

Suppose your records manager resigned last week, and you were asked to join a team charged with the responsibility of merging three workgroups' records. Your team's main task is to determine if all the paper records should be kept in one area or in individual offices. In other words, should the records be centralized, decentralized, or perhaps use a combination of both?

In considering location, your team should answer the following:

- Who needs to have access to the records?
- What types of records are stored?
- How frequently will the records need to be accessed?
- What procedures are needed to protect the files from loss, damage, theft, and unauthorized use?

Centralization

In a **centralized filing system**, records are placed in one central location that is convenient for a group of people who must work with the same information. In a centralized filing system, an individual must be designated as the one responsible for the system. To use this system effectively, establish procedures for **retrieval**, or obtaining filed records for use. The electronic equivalent to centralized filing would be a shared directory, also called a *folder*, that is part of a local area network (LAN) or wide area network (WAN). Advantages include the following:

- greater control over the records.
- storage of records with less equipment and space.
- more readily achieved uniformity and consistency.

Decentralization

In a **decentralized filing system**, individuals or very small groups of employees maintain files at their workstations. An example would be a small department where several assistants maintain correspondence and project records at their workstations. Advantages include the following:

- Records are more accessible.
- Limited access to a record provides greater security and confidentiality.

The main disadvantage is that more copying is required to allow others access to materials, and if the filing task is not done on a regular basis, the information requested may not be readily available.

It is possible for an office to have both a centralized and decentralized filing system. The majority of the records may be filed centrally, while a specific group of records, such as for a project, is located near its primary user.

Stop 'n Check

Describe the advantages of a decentralizing filing system compared with a centralized system.

_____

_____

FILING SUPPLIES

After determining a filing system for managing your paper records, it is important to select appropriate supplies.

Basic Folder Designs

Folders, also referred to as *manila folders*, are the containers for holding the paper. Because folders tend to take a lot of abuse, they are produced using many different weights of paper. Folders come with **tabs,** which are the extensions at the top of the folders. A tab holds a label to identify the folder's contents and is available in different widths called **tab cuts;** for example, if

FIGURE 8-6 • Examples of tab cuts.

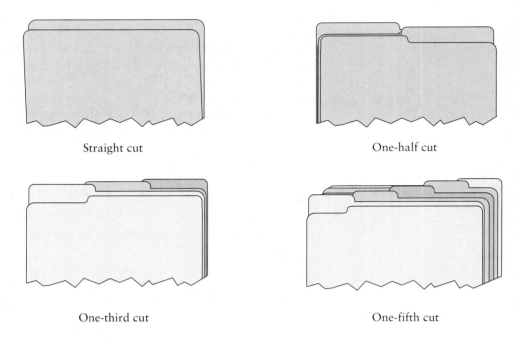

Straight cut

One-half cut

One-third cut

One-fifth cut

the tab is one-fifth as wide as the folder, it is called *one-fifth*. Figure 8-6 shows some of the possible tab cuts.

Hanging folders are suspended by extensions at their top edges across a metal frame within the file drawer, which means they don't rest on the bottom of the cabinet. Records filed in hanging folders are easily accessible because the folders open wide and slide smoothly on the hanger rail. Attachable tabs are inserted into slots at the top of the folders and are used in place of conventional guides with tabs.

Guides

Dividers in traditional filing drawers or compartments are called **guides**. They serve as signposts, separating the filing space into labeled sections. Guides also support the folders in an upright position.

Guides have a tab projecting from the edge, which is available in a variety of sizes and colors. Whereas you can purchase blank tabs in order to customize your system, you can also purchase tabs that list the days of the week, the names of months, or numbers.

Guides for open-shelf filing differ from guides for vertical file drawers. Note the tabs on the guides are along the side and not on the top, as they would be on vertical files.

PLACEMENT OF GUIDES AND FOLDERS

The supplies you need to set up the simplest system in strict sequential order for filing records in regular folders are:

- primary guides—at least one for each letter of the alphabet
- individual name folders
- miscellaneous folders
- special guides

Primary Guides

A **primary guide** divides a file into alphabetic sections and is placed at the beginning of each section. Guides direct the eye to the section of the file in which the folder being sought is located.

Guides are not needed with hanging folders, as the folders are supported from a metal frame, and the guide tabs are attached directly to the folders. When guides are used, a record is filed in either individual or miscellaneous folders placed behind the guides.

Individual Folder

An **individual name folder** is used when you accumulate at least five records for one customer, for example, or when you determine from the current letter or report that much communication will take place between the individual and your manager. In this case, prepare an individual folder with the name typed in indexed order in the caption.

Arrange individual folders in order immediately following the appropriate primary guide, as shown in Figure 8-7. File records within individual folders in chronological order, so the correspondence bearing the most recent date is placed at the front of the folder.

FIGURE 8-7 • Individual folders following primary guides.

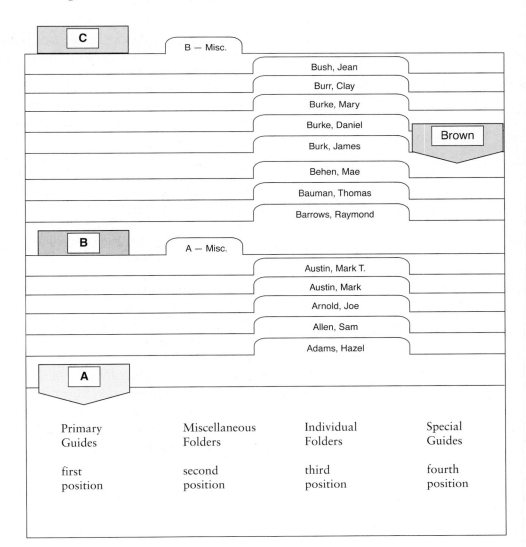

Miscellaneous Folders

For every primary guide in your file, there should be a miscellaneous folder with a caption corresponding to the caption on the primary guide. **Miscellaneous folders** belong *behind* individual folders and contain the papers to and from all correspondents for whom you do not have individual name folders.

Within a miscellaneous folder, arrange the records in alphabetical order by name. When you have two or more records for one individual, arrange them in chronological order, so the one with the most recent date will be in front of the others. Staple related papers together to increase the ease of locating them.

Special Guides

The **special guide** directs the eye to individual folders that are used frequently. Special guides are also used for subdivisions of the alphabet, or to mark the section of a file containing individual folders for several individuals with the same surname.

FILE LABELS

Labels are used to help identify a folder and its contents. Labels come in a variety of sizes, shapes, and colors so you can customize your filing system to meet the needs of your office. Colors should not be used at random. Use colors to represent a topic or the status of a file.

For paper files, identification and labeling allows an office to maintain control over current files and manage growth of new files. Labeling serves as a visual aid by identifying individual folders and groups of folders within the system.

For electronic files, labeling serves as an access tool that allows individual documents to be retrieved in an efficient manner. Electronic files follow many of the same filing identification and labeling guidelines as paper files. Records are organized by directories, also called *folders*. Finally, each folder contains individual records or documents.

When working with paper files, three levels of file identification help simplify filing and retrieval: drawer or shelf labels, file guide labels, and file folder labels.

Key the names on the labels in the indexed order, which will be explained later in this chapter. Capitalize the first letter of each word because words keyed in all-capital letters are sometimes difficult to read. If your labels consist of only one or two words and you use an easy-to-read font, full capitalization will work well. Above all, remember to be consistent with labeling throughout your system. The captions on the labels of the folders should resemble an aligned list of names as shown in Figure 8-8.

Label drawers or sections of files in uppercase with either open or close notations. A typical example of an open notation would be:

CORRESPONDENCE

A **closed notation** indicates the entire span of the contents or either a file drawer or a section of files. A typical example of a closed notation would be

CORRESPONDENCE A–H

FIGURE 8-8 • Captions on labels.

Gunter, Joe

Gray, Thomas

Gray, Marion

Gilbert, William T

Gardiner, Ray M

Gardiner, Ray

Stop 'n Check

1. What is the main purpose of a file guide?
   _____
   _____

2. List the two types of guides.
   a. _____
   b. _____

3. What is the purpose of a miscellaneous folder?
   _____
   _____

FILING EQUIPMENT

When selecting filing equipment, consider the following:

- volume of records requiring storage
- types of records being stored
- space limitations

As you have learned, paper records are usually filed vertically, standing upright and supported by guides and folders in file drawers.

Vertical Drawer Cabinets

Vertical drawer cabinets, often referred to as standard cabinets, are popular in small offices. They have either four- or five-drawers. A typical four-drawer cabinet can store approximately 100 inches of files and requires 5.8 square feet of floor space (with drawer extended). The cabinet can be moved easily and locked for security.

FIGURE 8-9 • Lateral cabinets.

Lateral Cabinets

Lateral cabinets, shown in Figure 8-9, often referred to as horizontal files or open-sided cabinets, also are popular in small offices. They allow files to be accessed horizontally or verticially. A typical five-drawer lateral cabinet can store almost 2.5 times more than a vertical drawer cabinet and requires 6.8 square feet of floor space. Like the vertical filing cabinet, this cabinet can be moved easily and locked for security.

Open Shelves

Open shelving equipment, which resembles open bookshelves, is usually found in large offices and in central file rooms. Refer to Figure 8-10. The advantage of this type of lateral file allows files to be retrieved horizontally and allows full viewing of the folder tabs for rapid retrieval. A 50 percent space savings is estimated when converting from a vertical system to an open shelf system. Open shelves do not offer security for confidential or vital records.

Mobile Aisle Systems

Mobile aisle systems are considered when access to large quantities of files is desired and space is at a premium. These units, which can be automated, work on tracks that move back and forth to conserve floor space. This equipment usually requires professional installation.

Stop 'n Check

Describe the advantages of open shelving compared with vertical drawer?

_____

_____

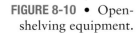

FIGURE 8-10 • Open-shelving equipment.

Indexing and Alphabetizing Rules

Standardization of alphabetic filing rules is essential because it allows filing to be consistent and efficient. The **Association of Records Managers and Administrators,** also known as ARMA International or simply ARMA (www.arma.org), recognized the need for standardization and so published the first rules for alphabetic filing. This not-for-profit, professional organization continues to update and revise the rules. Before you begin learning the rules, study the following terms.

UNIT

File names are arranged in units, and each part of a name used to determine the filing order is called a **unit.** For example, the name *B. R. Grove* has three units: *B., R., Grove.* The business name *Wacky Wig Boutique* has three units: *Wacky, Wig, Boutique.*

INDEXING

Names are not always filed the same way they are written. In preparation for alphabetic filing, the format and order of a name is often altered. The process of arranging units of a name in order for filing purposes is referred to as **indexing,** as defined earlier. An example of indexing is where *B. R. Grove* is indexed as *Grove B R* Indexing always precedes alphabetizing.

ALPHABETIC FILING

Organizing records in a sequence of letters in the alphabet is called *alphabetic filing.* For example, placing the name *Adamson* before the name *Bolton* is

alphabetizing because *A* comes before *B*. When names begin with the same letter, then you must consider the second letter. For example, the names *Barton*, *Belton*, and *Burton* are arranged in alphabetic order because the second letters are in correct alphabetic order.

This process appears relatively simple; however, because the English language is made up of words from other languages, word derivatives, prefixes, suffixes, compound words, and other combinations, the filing process may become complicated and inconsistent unless rules are applied.

Stop 'n Check

1. Define *unit*.

_____

_____

2. Define *indexing*.

_____

_____

3. Define *alphabetic filing*.

_____

_____

GENERAL ALPHABETIC INDEXING PRINCIPLES

Following the four general principles will help you to apply the filing rules.

1. **Alphabetize by comparing names unit by unit and letter by letter.** When first units are identical, move on to compare the second units; when second units are identical, compare third units, and so on. For example, in comparing the following indexed names, you would need to make the distinction in the third unit because the first and second units are identical.

Unit 1	Unit 2	Unit 3
Black	Jeff	Peter
Black	Jeff	Robert

2. **Nothing comes before something.** Thus, in comparing the following indexed names, you would file a folder labeled *Ross William* first because the first two units are identical and the first *Ross William* does not have a third unit. Nothing is filed before something or phrased another way "the least before the most."

Unit 1	Unit 2	Unit 3
Ross	William	
Ross	William	Robert

Another example of this principle would be to compare the following two indexed names:

Unit 1	Unit 2	Unit 3
Chatham	Bus	Depot
Chatham	Business	College

In this case, if you had two folders labeled *Chatham*, Bus would come before Business under the principle that nothing comes before something.

3. **All punctuation marks, special characters, and diacritical marks should be ignored when indexing.** Examples of punctuation marks found in names include periods, commas, apostrophes, hyphens, dashes, etc. **Special characters** include © and ®. **Diacritical marks** include any marks used for pronunciation purposes. Where words have been separated by a hyphen or dash, consider them together as one indexing unit, for example, Ellison-Parker.

4. **Numbers.** *Arabic* (1, 2, 3) and *Roman* (I, II, III) numbers are filed sequentially *before* alphabetic characters. All Arabic numerals precede all Roman numerals.

ALPHABETIC FILING RULES

Learning to apply the following rules will help you to file all your paper records in nearly all situations. ARMA outlines a few exceptions to these rules. If you have a particular situation that requires an exception to a rule, refer to ARMA rules. To simplify this section, all the exceptions have not been included. The following rules have been organized into three categories: personal names, business and organization names, and government and political designations.

A. Specific Filing Rules for Personal Names

Rule A1: Names of Individuals

The surname (last name) is the first filing unit, followed by the first name or initial, and then the middle name or initial. Because nothing comes before something, initials (such as *M*) are filed before a name (such as *Martha*) that begins with the same letter.

As Written	Unit 1	Unit 2	Unit 3
Mary Abbot	Abbot	Mary	
M. Appleton	Appleton	M	
Martha Appleton	Appleton	Martha	
Howard Kimble	Kimble	Howard	
H. A. Kline	Kline	H	A

Rule A2: Personal Names with Prefixes

Surnames that include a prefix are filed as one unit, even if a space or punctuation follows the prefix. Examples of prefixes are *D', da, de, Del, Du, La, Les, Mac, Mc, O', Saint, San, St., Van, Van de,* and *Von der* and are filed with the surname as one unit regardless of whether the surname is written as one word or two. Ignore any apostrophe or space that appears within or after the prefix.

As Written	Unit 1	Unit 2	Unit 3
Agnes Lasalle	Lasalle	Agnes	
Paul R. La Salle	LaSalle	Paul	R
Alice J. MacDaniel	MacDaniel	Alice	J
Susan Saint James	SaintJames	Susan	
Adam Von der Mallie	Vondermallie	Adam	

Rule A3: Titles and Suffixes

Titles and suffixes are not used as filing units except when needed to distinguish between two or more identical names. When needed, the title or suffix is the last filing unit and is filed as written without punctuation.

As Written	Unit 1	Unit 2	Unit 3
Dan Dillan, CPA	Dillan	Dan	CPA
Dan Dillan, Jr.	Dillan	Dan	Jr
Ronald McDerrit, II	McDerrit	Ronald	II
Ronald McDerrit, III	McDerrit	Ronald	III
June Ship, MD	Ship	June	MD
Mrs. June Ship	Ship	June	Mrs

Rule A4: Hyphenated Names

Remove the hyphen, combine the names, and file as one unit.

As Written	Unit 1	Unit 2	Unit 3
Mary-Kaye Cardville	Cardville	MaryKay	
Irene Dale-Scott	DaleScott	Irene	
Helen Ann Dixon-Jones	DixonJones	Helen	Ann
Sara Laura-Lee Wilkes	Wilkes	Sara	LauraLee

Rule A5: Pseudonyms, Royal, or Religious Titles

Pseudonyms (fictitious name assumed by an author) are filed as written. Personal names that begin with royal or religious titles and are followed by only a given name(s) are filed as written.

As Written	Unit 1	Unit 2	Unit 3
Dr. Seuss	Dr	Seuss	
Sister Mary Rebecca	Sister	Mary	Rebecca

Rule A6: Non-English Names

If the surname is identifiable, file the name as any other personal name. If the surname is uncertain, use the last name as the first filing unit and cross-reference (filing a record by a secondary name) the name as written. More in-depth information is provided in a later section in this chapter.

As Written	Unit 1	Unit 2	Unit 3	Cross-Reference
French Favel Caisse	Caisse	French	Favel	
Piccoli Rossi Cimino	Cimino	Piccoli	Rossi	
Adalbaro Garcia Gabindo	Gabindo	Adalbaro	Garcia	Garcia (Gabindo, Adalbaro)

Rule A7: Nicknames

When a person commonly uses a nickname as a first name, file using the nickname. Include a cross-reference to the given name only if necessary.

As Written	Unit 1	Unit 2	Cross-Reference
Bob Browning	Browning	Bob	Browning, Robert
Bill Watson	Watson	Bill	Watson, William
Kitty Williams	Williams	Kitty	Williams, Katherine

B. Specific Filing Rules for Business and Organization Names

Rule B1: Names of Businesses and Organizations

Names of businesses and organizations are indexed in a similar fashion to the names of individuals. However, names of businesses and organizations should be indexed in the order they are written by the business or organization. Therefore, a surname is not necessarily the first unit. If you are unsure of the correct wording or format, refer to the company's letterhead or business card, or make a telephone call to the business or organization's receptionist. For filing business and organizational names with prefixes, see Rule A2.

When the name begins with *The*, place that word at the end as the last indexing unit.

When names of businesses and organizations are identical, indexing order is determined by the address. If the names of cities are identical, indexing order depends on names of states, followed by street names and building numbers. When street names are written as digits (13th Street), the street names are considered in ascending order and filed before alphabetic street names. Street names with compass directions are indexed as written.

As Written	Unit 1	Unit 2	Unit 3	Unit 4	Unit 5
A-1 Bookkeeping Services	A1	Bookkeeping	Services		
AFL-CIO	AFLCIO				
Brookshire Cleaners	Brookshire	Cleaners			
The Central Trust Company	Central	Trust	Company	The	
Columbia Pizza	Columbia	Pizza	2128 13th Street		
Columbia Pizza	Columbia	Pizza	138 15th Street		
General Insurance Company, Amarillo, TX	General	Insurance	Company	Amarillo	TX
General Insurance Company, Rochester, MN	General	Insurance	Company	Rochester	MN

Rule B2: Geographic Names

When filing geographic names, follow the general rules.

As Written	Unit 1	Unit 2	Unit 3	Unit 4
Texas Power and Light	Texas	Power	and	Light
New Mexico Publications	New	Mexico	Publications	

Rule B3: Compass Terms

Each word/unit in a filing segment containing compass terms is considered a separate filing unit. If the term includes more than one compass point, file it as written. Prepare cross-reference as needed:

As Written	Unit 1	Unit 2	Unit 3	Unit 4
South East Paper, Inc.	South	East	Paper	Inc
South Eastern Waste Management	South	Eastern	Waste	Management
South-East Retrieval Systems	Southeast	Retrieval	Systems	

The following rules apply in specific filing circumstances.

Rule B4: Numeric Names

Names containing numbers are filed alphabetically.

As Written	Unit 1	Unit 2	Unit 3	Unit 4
1st Ave Pharmacy	First	Avenue	Pharmacy	
4 J's Barber Shoppe	Four	Js	Barber	Shoppe
Twelve Corners Service Center	Twelve	Corners	Service	Center
12 Corners Sweet Shop	Twelve	Corners	Sweet	Shop

Rule B5: Symbols Used in Business Names

Symbols should be indexed the way they are pronounced. Examples of such symbols include:

As Written	Unit 1	Unit 2	Unit 3	Unit 4
One $ Store	One	Dollar	Store	
Rickman & Hope Intl.	Rickman	and	Hope	Intl

Rule B6: Single Letters in Names

Single letters appearing in company names are filed as separate units, even though they may be written together without spaces.

As Written	Unit 1	Unit 2	Unit 3	Unit 4
ABC Communications	A	B	C	Communications
Triple A Print Shop	Triple	A	Print	Shop

C. Specific Filing Rules for Governmental and Political Designations

When filing governmental or political records, the name of the major entity is filed first and followed by the distinctive name of the department, bureau, and so on. This rule applies to all governmental and political divisions, agencies, departments, and committees from the federal to the county/parish, city district, and ward levels.

Rule C1: Federal Government

For the correct hierarchical order, consult the most current edition of the *United States Government Manual* (USGM). Generally, indexing of the federal government agencies is done first by "United States Government" followed by the most distinctive name, such as Department, Bureau, Agency, and so on.

As Written	Unit 1	Unit 2	Unit 3	Unit 4
Environmental Protection Agency	United States Government	Environmental Protection Agency		

Rule C2: State and Local Governments

Index state, county, town, and city governments or political divisions by their distinctive names. To avoid confusion and to ensure efficient, accurate information retrieval, add the words *State of, County of,* and so on and consider them as filing units. Index the words *State, Department, County,* and *Bureau* after the distinctive name. If "of" is not part of the official name, do not use it for indexing.

As Written	Unit 1	Unit 2	Unit 3	Unit 4	Unit 5	Unit 6
Monroe Community Hospital	Monroe	Community	Hospital			
Monroe County Department of Public Works	Monroe	County	Public	Works	Department	of
New York State Department of Health	New	York	State	Health	Department	of
New York State Human Rights Division	New	York	State	Human	Rights	Division
Rochester Animal Control Center	Rochester	Animal	Control	Center		
Rochester Recreation Bureau	Rochester	Recreation	Bureau			

Rule C3: Non-U.S. Governments

This rule applies to non-U.S. government names filed in U.S.-based filing systems. The distinctive English name is the first filing unit.

As Written	Unit 1	Unit 2	Unit 3
Commonwealth of Australia	Australia	Commonwealth	of
Dublin, Ireland	Dublin	Ireland	

Following the rules explained in this section will ensure consistency in filing. Everyone sharing responsibility for filing and retrieving information must thoroughly understand the system. If you are working and are needing periodic refresher training in proper filing and retrieval, discuss your need with your supervisor. Your supervisor understands the need for efficiency and effectiveness in filing and retrieving information.

PREPARING PAPER RECORDS FOR FILING

Once you have decided which records are to be managed, you must establish a procedure for preparing the records to be filed. The following six steps will help you prepare your records for filing.

1. examine
2. index
3. code
4. cross-reference
5. sort
6. file

Examine

You will want to make certain the item is ready for filing. Follow these guidelines to examine each item.

- Check items that are stapled together and decide if they should be filed together.
- Staple together related papers where one record refers to the other.
- Remove all paper clips and extra staples as these supplies use extra space and can hang on other records.
- Remove small slips of paper that are no longer needed; such as a slip marked "Please file."
- Keep the routing slip with the appropriate documents. You may need to determine later to whom the document was circulated.
- Determine if documents are duplicates and should be deleted/destroyed or filed.

Index

In a previous section, you learned indexing occurs when you determine the order and format of the units in a name when alphabetizing. Careful indexing is the most important part of filing. You have learned a record with a name of *Benjamin Ross* would be indexed as *Ross Benjamin* according to the rules. The most important word for filing is *Ross*.

When you are filing correspondence by name, note the following:

1. Incoming letters are often called for by the name of the organization appearing in the letterhead, so index them by the name of the organization in the letterhead.
2. Outgoing letters are often called for by the name of the organization appearing in the inside address, so index them by the name of the organization in the inside address.

To learn how to index for the variety of names you will encounter, follow the standardized indexing rules presented earlier in this chapter.

Code

After you decide how a record should be filed, mark the indexing caption on it. This process is called **coding**. To code by name, highlight, underscore, circle, or write the indexed name. The code on the record should be complete enough that you can return the record to the same folder each time it has been removed. As you study the indexing rules, you will learn how to determine the order of units within a name.

Cross-Reference

When a record is apt to be called for by two different names at different times, you should be able to locate it by looking under either name. To make this possible, file the record according to the **caption** (the name arranged in index order) by which it is most likely to be requested. Also, file a reference to it by the second name. Handling this task is referred to as **cross-referencing**.

To make a cross-reference for a card file, use a card of the same size as the cards in the file; you may use a different color. Notice in Figure 8-11 the

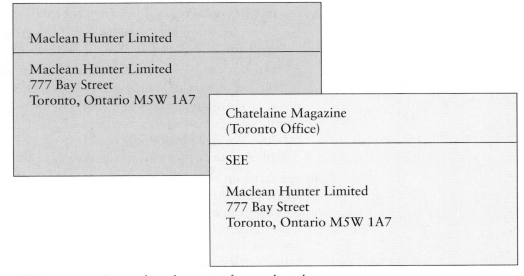

Maclean Hunter Limited

Maclean Hunter Limited
777 Bay Street
Toronto, Ontario M5W 1A7

Chatelaine Magazine
(Toronto Office)

SEE

Maclean Hunter Limited
777 Bay Street
Toronto, Ontario M5W 1A7

FIGURE 8-11 • Original card; cross-referenced card.

two cards prepared for Maclean Hunter Ltd. The information printed below *SEE* on the cross-reference card is the caption on the original card.

To prepare references for correspondence, use preprinted letter-sized cross-reference sheets. Make a large *X* on the actual correspondence in the margin near the name used as a cross-reference; underline the name.

Make two copies of the cross-reference sheet:

1. One copy will be filed in the cross-reference folder. It should be the only piece of paper filed in the folder, because the purpose of the cross-reference sheet is to send you to the correct file. If you have an effective card file system that clearly identifies cross-references, you may eliminate the need for the cross-reference folder and the cross-reference sheet.

2. The second copy will be filed in front of the actual folder where you want all the records to be placed. This cross-reference sheet will serve as a reminder to you that a cross-reference folder exists. If you are missing information, you will need to check the cross-reference folder to see whether someone has inadvertently filed documents in the cross-reference folder.

Avoid preparing unnecessary cross-references, but if you are in doubt, make one. Cross-referencing is necessary in various situations. Consider the following:

1. Correspondence pertaining to individuals may be filed by subject (for example, Temporary Employees) instead of by name.

2. It may be difficult to determine the individual's surname. Consider the name *Kent Ross*. Is the surname *Ross* or *Kent*? If the surname is *Ross*, the correct file will read *Ross, Kent* and the cross-reference file label will read *Kent, Ross*. Inside the folder, the cross-reference sheets will read:

   ### SEE Ross, Kent

3. A married woman may be known by
   a. Her maiden name. For example, in the name *Ms. Heather Ross*, the name is indexed as *Ross, Heather (Ms)*.
   b. Her married name. For example, in the name *Mrs. Heather Whyte*, the name is indexed as *Whyte, Heather (Mrs)*.
   c. Her husband's name. For example, in the name *Mrs. Robert Whyte*, the name would be indexed as *Whyte, Robert (Mrs)*.

      A cross-reference will be necessary for two of the three cases. Most commonly, correspondence would be filed under either *Ross, Heather (Ms)* or *Whyte, Heather (Mrs)*. Only one of these files should contain documents; the other two must serve as cross-references.

4. Subdivisions of a parent company are filed under the name used on their letterhead; they are not filed under the parent company name. To avoid confusion, file correctly under the name of the subdivision, but prepare a cross-reference for the name of the parent company. For example, a subdivision business called *Office Supply Town* with a parent company called *Office Supply Enterprises* would have the correspondence filed as *Office Supply Town*, but a cross-reference sheet would be placed in

the *Office Supply Enterprises* folder to send anyone to the *Office Supply Town* folder.

5. Some organizations are referred to by their acronym because they are better known that way. An example is IAAP (International Association of Administrative Professionals). It is acceptable to file the correspondence under either name; however, it is best to check the organization's letterhead or business card to see how the organization refers to itself. Whether you file by the full name or by the popular abbreviation, *consistency must prevail.* A cross-reference will be necessary to keep all the correspondence or records in the same file.

6. A business name may include several surnames. For *Johnson, Baines, and Strafford,* file the original by *Johnson* and cross-reference *Baines* and *Strafford.*

7. A company may change its name. File by the new name, and record the date of the change. Retain the old name in the files as a cross-reference only.

8. Names of foreign companies and government agencies are often written in both English and the respective foreign language. For a government agency, file the original paper by the English name, and place a cross-reference sheet in the folder with the foreign spelling.

9. For a foreign company, file the original by the name as it is written and the cross-reference sheet in the folder under the English translation.

10. When a department is renamed because of restructuring within the organization, internal correspondence filed by subject is often affected. File the correspondence by the new name; however, retain the old name in the files as a cross-reference.

Sort

Using the code marks mentioned previously as a guide, prearrange the records in the same order in which they will eventually be filed. This preliminary arrangement is called **sorting**. By sorting the records carefully, you will eliminate unnecessary shifting back and forth, from drawer to drawer or from shelf to shelf, as you file them. As a result, you will be working efficiently and saving time.

Horizontal and vertical sorters can expedite the process; these devices, such as trays and booklets, use dividers that are labeled either alphabetically or numerically, to sort records.

File

After records are sorted, they are ready to be filed. **Filing** is the actual placing of records in folders. Here are a few tips to follow to help you in handling your filing task.

- When refiling existing records, the name on the caption in the filing system should be the same as the record being refiled.

- Records should be filed chronologically in the folder, with the latest one in the front.

- New records may require the creation of a new folder. The new folder should agree with the current filing system and the index should be updated to include this file.

In addition, keep the following pointers in mind:

- Keep up with your filing on a daily basis. Allow at least 30 minutes a day to file. When unfiled papers stack up, a simple task becomes a burden. You will spend much more time locating a record when it is in an unarranged stack than when it is properly placed in a folder. Note also that you run the risk of losing papers when they are disorganized.
- Listen carefully, ask questions, and take notes if someone is explaining the filing system to you. In any new office job, you will be placing and locating materials in the files that were maintained by your predecessor. Study the system and learn it quickly so you can file your records efficiently. Do not try to reorganize the files in your office until you are familiar with what they contain.
- If you have suggestions for improving the filing system, jot down your ideas and bring them to the attention of your team members or supervisor at an appropriate time.

Stop 'n Check

List the six steps to prepare paper records for filing.

a. _____

b. _____

c. _____

d. _____

e. _____

f. _____

TRACKING PAPER FILES

When someone removes a file folder, you need a system for tracking the file. **Charge-out methods,** manual and automated, allow you to track files.

A manual system uses special cards, folders, and pressboard guides with the word *OUT* printed on the tabs to substitute for papers and folders taken from a specific location. When only a few sheets of paper are removed from the files, an *OUT* card is used; when the entire folder is removed, either an *OUT* folder or an *OUT* guide is substituted. Review Figure 8-1. Charge-out guides include the following:

- Guides with printed lines for writing a description of the materials removed, the name of the person who has taken the file or the materials, and the date removed.
- Guides with a slot or a pocket to hold a card. The charge-out information is written on the card.

In either case, the guides are placed into the filing system to take the place of the folders that have been removed. The *OUT* card or guide remains in the file until the charged-out material is returned. Both types are reusable.

In large companies, automated tracking systems, with the use of bar code wands, can expedite the check-in and check-out process. **Bar coding** requires software, a label printer, and a scanning device and scans a label and the user and location codes. Bar coding virtually eliminates lost files. The automated systems also can produce reports to show what was requested and by whom.

Regardless of the charge-out system you use, do not hesitate to use it if you have frequent requests to borrow materials from a folder or the folder itself.

Stop 'n Check

Describe two types of charge-out methods.

a. _____

b. _____

Color Coding

Color coding can be applied to any paper filing system. It is popular because it provides easy identification for sorting, filing, and finding; it confirms that the folders have been filed in the right places.
　　Color can:

✔ Code the first two or three digits in numeric filing systems.

✔ Code the first two letters of a name in an alphabetic filing system.

✔ Differentiate similar types of records that belong to various departments.

✔ Identify records that were temporarily removed from files.

✔ Check the filing methods of new employees.

Understanding Electronic File Organization

The dynamics of the electronic environment, also called the *e-environment*, characterized by the empowered end users with a PC on their desk, mean documents can be readily created, easily amended or discarded without a trace, and can be shared much more widely than in the past.

A great concern for organizations is that the majority of the information electronically stored can be a record or act as a record but are not necessarily captured into an organization's formal record-keeping system. What would be the effect if 25 percent of a typical organization's information, much of which again might be in the form of records, is stored on single user storage media such as hard disk drives? What a shock it would be if your company were to do a records survey and learned more than 50 percent of its information was stored on single user PCs and 20 of the 50 percent was identified as vital, important, and useful records. As you have learned earlier, certain records should become part of a formal record-keeping system so they can be managed. Not only are they to be managed, but they may be needed in legal situations.

Understanding the importance of your file management system is critical in the electronic environment. Whether you are new to your organization or have been employed for some time, you must ensure you are following specific naming and saving rules or procedures, if provided, for electronic filing within your organization. If rules or procedures are not available, ask your supervisor if he or she knows a specific individual to contact in your organization.

An **electronic filing system** is a combination of the computer hardware, its operating system, and software. It maintains a list of all files and their location. Understanding your electronic filing system will help in managing:

- files on your local hard drive or a network drive
- files shared through e-mail attachments
- files put on the Web server for your office Web site

FILE

In most ways, an electronic filing system works much like a paper filing system. Put simply, in an electronic filing system you have cabinets that contain file folders that contain files, also called *documents*. In an electronic filing system, a **file** is any document, such as a spreadsheet, database, report, picture, or presentation. In other words, a file is any document created on the computer or received from another computer. Every file has a file name and a **three-letter extension**, assigned by the Windows system, that it associates with a specific program. For example, a WordPerfect file extension is *.wpd*, and a Word file extension is *.doc*. If procedures have not been established for naming your electronic files, be sure to create them. Here are a few suggestions for naming files that are created multiple times, such as letters to the same individual, quarterly budgets, or monthly reports.

- Distinguish correspondence by including name, document type, and date. *Tunnell Margie 03020x Ltr* identifies a letter written to Margie Tunnell on March 2, 200x.
- Identify quarterly budgets by including the quarter number, year, and the label of budget. For example, *Qtr2 200x Budget* represents the file created for the second quarter 200x budget.
- Identify reports by using a subject, such as *Proj10987-03280x* for a project status report dated March 28, 200x.

If you are consistent in naming your files, retrieval will be much more efficient. You won't have to say to anyone, "I know it's here somewhere. Just give me a minute to find it."

FOLDER

A folder, also called a **directory** in an electronic system, contains files. You can create as many folders and subfolders as you need. Folders organize the files in a logical manner, like using manila folders inside hanging folders to organize paper documents in a file cabinet drawer. For example, a human resources department may designate a folder as *Payroll* and create a subfolder as *Payroll Timesheets*.

A good place to place your folders and files is in the My Documents folder on your local hard drive for easy retrieval.

DISK DRIVE

The **disk drive** is the physical location where folders and files can be found. A disk drive name consists of a single letter and a colon. For example,

Drive A is identified as a floppy disk drive.

Drive C is identified as the hard disk drive.

Drive D through Z are designated as optional drives, such as a network drive or CD-ROM or DVD-ROM drive.

MANAGING FILES AND FOLDERS USING WINDOWS EXPLORER

Not to be confused with Internet Explorer (the Internet browser), Windows Explorer is an application program in Windows 98, 2000, and XP. It allows you to view and manage your files, folders, and drives. One way to launch Windows Explorer is to click Start on the taskbar shown at the bottom of your screen, point to All Programs, point to Accessories, and click on Windows Explorer.

The Explorer window is divided into two "panes," with folders on the left and their contents on the right. You can adjust the size of the panes by dragging the dividing line to the left or right.

Display Contents

To display the contents of a drive in the right pane, double-click on a folder on that drive. You'll see a plus sign next to some of the folders; click on the + to reveal other folders and files nested inside. When the folder is open and its contents are displayed, the plus sign turns to a minus sign. To collapse the folders again, click on the minus sign.

You can display files and folders in the right pane in several different views. To change the display of the files and folders, select View from the menu bar. You may choose the manner in which you display drive or folder contents in the right pane.

Copy a File

When you copy a file, you have two copies, one in the new location and one in the original location. To copy a file, click and drag the file to the new location with the right mouse button, release the mouse button, and choose Copy Here.

Move a File

When you move a file, it goes from one location to another; there is still only one copy. To move a file, use the right mouse button to drag the file to the new location. Release the mouse button and choose Move Here.

Delete a File

To delete a file you no longer need, highlight it, and press the Delete key. If you delete a file from your hard drive, you can recover it from the Recycle Bin. The **Recycle Bin** serves as a temporary storage area for files deleted from your hard drive. Deleting a file or folder to the Recycle Bin does not permanently delete the file from your hard drive. The Recycle Bin allows you to restore deleted files. You can recover a file by selecting the Recycle Bin, locating and highlighting the file, and selecting Restore from the File menu. To permanently delete the file, delete the file(s) from the Recycle Bin. To permanently erase files from the Recycle Bin, select the Recycle Bin and choose Empty Recycle Bin from the File menu. If you delete a file from a floppy disk, the file is gone permanently once you delete it.

Find a File

If you cannot find a file, you can search for it. In Windows 2000, NT, and XP, you can select Start, click on Search, and select For Files or Folders. Searching by a file name is the quickest way to find a file. However, if you do not remember the file name, you can also search by date or by text contained within the file. You can only search one drive at a time.

Stop 'n Check

Why is it important to understand the overall picture of filing in an e-environment?

_____

_____

_____

ORGANIZING ELECTRONIC FILES

Use the following tips to help you organize the documents stored in your computer and minimize the time you spend on retrieval.

- Use **My Documents** folder. Take advantage of this feature in Microsoft Windows because the My Documents folder provides an easy way for you to store your documents. For example, you can find files in many places, such as through the Start Menu, the task pane in Windows Explorer, and the common File Open. Windows Explorer displays the structure of files and folders on your computer. To open Windows Explorer, see Get Tech Wise at the end of the chapter.

- Organize your directories and subdirectories logically. As in paper filing, the key to efficiency in electronic filing is in the logical organization of the folders. For example, suppose you were asked to create a new electronic filing system for the training department. Look at your real (paper) file cabinet. Do you have a section for specific training areas? A section for training requests? A section for budgets? Your search of your regular file cabinet reveals a general folder labeled Training Classes/200X and subfolders labeled Microsoft Access I, Microsoft Access II, and so on. To match your paper filing system, create an electronic general folder with the same name and the same subfolders to match your paper filing organization. Whatever major categories you include in your regular paper filing system, include them on your computer and organize them in the same manner. Doing so will enable you to move back and forth from paper to computer files with a minimum of effort.

- Determine the sequence of your files. If one of your files or folders includes customer correspondence, you might use an alphabetical sequence. For example, you might create a general folder labeled Correspondence and create subfolders for each letter of the alphabet. In each subfolder, you can create another level of folders for each customer's name. On the other hand, if you reference your customer correspondence by account number, you might use a numerical sequence.

- Keep names short. Even though Windows allows you to use long file names, long names produce cluttered displays. Be clear and brief.

- Maintain naming consistency with your paper files. The names of your electronic files should be exactly the same as your paper files. Doing so will allow you to move back and forth between the two systems effortlessly.

- Create specialized folders for specific files. If you download information for reports, articles, or pictures for presentations for use later on, create a folder labeled *Download-Articles* or *Download-Reports*.

- Be selective about the files you keep. As in the paper filing system, not all electronic files are to be kept. To determine if the file is to be kept, remember to check for its value to the organization. Can the file serve as evidence of decisions or transactions that have occurred.

- Perform regular maintenance. As in your paper filing system, on some periodic basis, delete or archive files you no longer need. If you have saved paper copies of correspondence, you can delete the electronic files. If your files are saved to your company's network, your files are backed up or saved periodically, usually every evening. However, if your files are saved to your hard drive, you will need to perform a backup or copy of these files on a regular basis. For example, each Friday, you may back up or save copies of your files to an external storage device, which is discussed later in this chapter. On the other hand, if important files are saved to a hard drive and not to the company's server, some office professionals back up these important files at the end of the day. The guiding principle here is to back up your files to prevent any loss or damage of important information.

- Print a list of your filing system. Just as you have a list of your paper filing system, develop one for your computer files. If your computer system were to crash, at least you would have a handy reference of the items in your electronic filing system.

Stop 'n Check

List at least three tips for organizing electronic files.

a. _____

b. _____

c. _____

BACKING UP ELECTRONIC FILES

Storage requirements vary greatly among users. For example, home users who want to back up or copy their files from their hard drive to another device probably have much smaller storage requirements than the la business users. Although your computer's internal hard drive is a type of **storage medium** (the physical material on which data, instructions, and information is saved), other devices are available to users who want to back up their computer files. Other storage media include the following:

Floppy Disks

Floppy disks, an older, portable, inexpensive storage medium, can store up to 500 double-spaced pages of text. Because of their low storage capacity, they have become less popular in the workplace to back up files. You may back up files from your hard disk to floppy disks to transport small files to and from a nonnetworked personal computer, such as to use from work to home.

CD-Rs

A **CD-R** (or *compact disc-recordable*) is a type of optical disc you can use to write only once. Writing or recording on a CD-R requires a CD burner. Determine if your computer has a drive to record files using this medium.

CD-RWs

A **CD-RW** (or *compact disc-rewritable*) is an erasable disc you can write or record over multiple times. However, reliability of the CD-RW is reduced with each successive rewrite. Writing on the CD-RW requires CD-RW software and drive. If you do not know whether you have a CD-RW drive, check with your company's computer technician.

Flash Drives

As you recall from Get Tech Wise in Chapter 6, a flash drive provides portable storage memory that plugs in a port on a computer. You may prefer to use a flash drive to back up your files, especially if you are transporting files from work to home.

This variety of storage media gives you several options for backing up your files from your internal hard drive. However, if you have additional storage needs, be certain to discuss your needs with your company's information technology (IT) representative. You also can learn more about additional types of storage media by searching the Web. The main point is to be certain you have backed up valuable information for safety, especially if this information has not been saved on your company's computer system server. Whatever device you decide to use, store the original and the copy in separate places so the same accident, such as a tornado or hurricane, will not destroy both copies.

Stop 'n Check

Distinguish between: CD-R and CD-RW.

_____

_____

Retention and Transfer

If your organization has a records professional, he or she will be responsible for handling records retention and transfer (or discard). Decisions about retention and transfer are based on a number of factors, including the knowledge that someone must have about the operation of the organization, state and federal laws relating to business functions, cost of keeping records versus the cost of not keeping them, and availability of off-site storage.

Because an entry-level administrative assistant or office assistant is rarely called upon to handle this complex area, the following information is provided to help you understand the importance and impact of retention and transfer in records management.

RETENTION

If there is no retention schedule developed for your organization, seek advice from a records consultant or visit ARMA at www.arma.org for guidelines to follow. Here is an example of areas to consider.

- **Retain two years,** files such as inventory records.
- **Retain three years,** files such as petty cash vouchers.
- **Retain eight years,** files such as expense reports and expired contracts and leases.
- **Retain indefinitely,** files such as correspondence on legal and tax matters and annual reports.

Before putting any guidelines into practice, get legal advice about time limitation statutes in your state. Each state has its own statute of limitations, specifying the time after which a record cannot be used as evidence in the courts. Among the records affected by state statutes of limitations are written contracts, open accounts, injury claims, and accident reports. Determining which records to keep and for how long is a critical function.

Some records must be kept permanently; many records are kept from three to twenty years; others are useful for only a short period and are kept for a year or less; some records are disposed of without being stored. Records that are kept for a year or longer are usually transferred from the active files to a storage area. The records manager prepares a **retention schedule,** which indicates the length of time a record must be kept, the type of storage media, and the schedule for final disposition of records. An office professional should not dispose of any document that has been classified as a record or electronic files that serve as records without written authorization.

If there is no formalized records management in your company, you will have to pay particular attention to your own paper and electronic files. In your position, you will create a lot of documents and handle a lot of paper, but not all documents you create or handle will be identified as records. Whether the documents are official records or not, you need to be diligent about how long you will retain the information you manage. Over the next week or month, become more aware of the length of time you will retain the documents you either handle or create. If you retrieve a file you have not used in several months or over a year, consider if it is important to keep and how long it should be kept. Suppose you believe the file should be deleted (or discarded as in a paper filing system). Before you delete any file of importance (paper or electronic), be certain to obtain authorization from your supervisor.

TRANSFER

The most accessible file space should be used for active files; this means the less-active papers must be moved from time to time to free up the most accessible space for the current files. Organizations use two methods of transfer: perpetual and periodic. Paper storage consumes much more space than electronic storage media. However, the concept of perpetual and periodic transfer is applied to both paper and electronic documents. Paper files may be transferred to a back room, off-site, or processed on microfilm, which reduces files to less than 2 percent of the space they now occupy in paper form.

Perpetual Transfer

The **perpetual transfer method** provides for continually transferring files to inactive storage as a project or case is completed. It is highly applicable for records in construction companies, attorneys' offices, and any organization that handles projects or cases. All the records for one project or case are transferred at the time it is completed. For transferring electronic inactive files, create a folder and label it with the year. Click and drag your inactive files into these subfolders and save these files.

Periodic Transfer

The **periodic transfer method** provides for transferring files to inactive storage at predetermined intervals such as six months, one year, or eighteen months. The inactive paper files are transferred to the storage center, leaving more space to house the active documents, or a company may convert its paper records into an electronic image. The computer files may be moved into a folder labeled with *Archive* and the quarter and year, such as *Archive Qtr1-200X*, or, the files may be moved to one of the electronic storage mediums mentioned in the previous section.

Stop 'n Check

Why should you transfer files?

_____

_____

Ethical Issues in Records Management

ETHICAL★ISSUES

For the past few years, the news has been filled with reports of unethical business practices and growing concerns about unethical behavior in the workplace. Scandals such as Enron/Andersen and records-related mishaps at

Morgan Stanley have renewed interest in corporate records compliance, litigation preparedness, and related issues.

Organizations are expected to be aware of various laws and principles that promote the rights of their employees and customers. The person responsible for managing the company's records must be knowledgeable of laws pertaining to ways to ensure employee and customer records are kept confidential and secure. Some of the issues related to ethical principles of records management are:

- confidentiality of personal information
- security of physical equipment such as desktop and laptop computers as well as paper file cabinets and portable storage media such as a USB flash drive
- validity of information
- disposal of records
- improper use of personal identification numbers (PINs).

As an office professional, you should be aware customer and employee records and e-mails and other correspondence are often used as legal documents and legal actions may be taken if records are not handled in a safe and secure manner.

International Standards for Records Management

Standards create a professional environment of "best practice" procedures. They enable organizations to confidently create systems, policies, and procedures; maintain autonomy from vested interest groups; and ensure high operational quality that leads to exceptional records and information management performance.

The International Organization for Standardization (ISO) is a global network that identifies what international standards are required by businesses and government; develops them in partnership with the sectors that will put them to use; adopts them by procedures based on national input; and delivers them to be implemented worldwide.

ISO 15489:2001, the international records management standard, is recognized worldwide as establishing the baseline for excellence in records management programs. The International Standard states that records management includes:

- setting policies and standards
- assigning responsibilities and authorities
- establishing and sharing procedures and guidelines
- providing a range of services relating to the management and use of records
- designing, implementing, and administering specialized systems for managing records
- integrating records management into business systems and processes

The significance of ISO 15489 is that records managers have a guide that represents standard practices and procedures recognized and accepted all over the world.

Quick Tips

RENAMING AN ELECTRONIC FILE

To rename a file, select a file in any folder view or in Windows Explorer. Right click and select Rename. Enter new file name and press Enter.

Concept Review and Reinforcement

Review of Key Concepts

OUTCOME	CONCEPT
1. Discuss how records management works as a system.	How an organization treats its information will directly affect its ability to compete, operate efficiently, comply with government regulations, and recover from disaster. Applied as a system, an organization can approach control of its recorded information from creation, through use and maintenance, and utlimately to disposition of records.
2. Define the categories of records.	• Vital records are essential to operations or to continuation or resumption of operations; re-creation of legal or financial status of organization; or fulfillment of its obligations to stockholders and employees in the event of a disaster. • Important records are meaningful to business operation but must be limited as to length of time they are retained. • Useful records are documents needed to conduct daily business operations. • Nonessential records are not needed beyond their current use and should be discarded after their use.
3. Distinguish among the filing systems.	• Alphabetic filing identifies records using the A–Z sequence. • Numeric filing uses logical numerical order, such as terminal-digit filing and decimal-numeric filing. • Geographic filing uses locations and A–Z sequence within locations. • Subject filing allows records to be filed alphabetically according to topics.
4. Describe filing supplies and equipment needed.	• Filing supplies include folders, guides, and labels. • Filing equipment includes vertical drawer cabinets, lateral cabinets, open shelves, and mobile aisle systems.
5. Index and alphabetize personal, business names, and governmental and political designations.	• Specific filing rules for personal names include names of individuals, personal names with prefixes, titles and suffixes, hyphenated names, pseudonyms and royal or religions titles, non-English names, and nicknames. • Specific filing rules for business and organizational names include geographic names, compass names, numeric names, and symbols used in business names. • Specific filing rules for governmental and political designations include federal government, state and local governments, and non-U.S. governments.
6. Explain the steps in preparing paper records for filing.	The steps include • examining • indexing • coding • cross-referencing • sorting • filing

7. Discuss methods for tracking paper files.

Charge-out methods include:

- guides with printed lines for writing description of materials removed, name of person who has taken file, and date issued
- guides with slots or pockets to hold cards on which the charge-out information is written

8. List tips for organizing electronic files.

- Use My Documents folder to store and retrieve documents.
- Organize directories and subdirectories logically.
- Determine filing system or sequence of files.
- Keep file names short.
- Maintain naming consistency with paper files.
- Be selective about files you keep.
- Perform regular maintenance.
- Print a list of your filing system.

9. Identify storage media for backing up electronic files.

Storage media includes floppy disks, CD-Rs, CD-RWs, and flash drives.

10. Describe the guidelines for records retention and transfer.

Either use a consultant or visit ARMA's Web site for guidelines to follow. Before putting any guidelines in place, consult your organization's legal department. For retention, consider categories such as inventory records (retain 2 years), petty cash vouchers (retain 3 years), and expense reports (retain for 8 years). For transferring files, consider perpetual and periodic methods.

11. Describe ethical issues in records.

Some issues related to ethical principles of records management are:

- confidentiality of personal information
- security of computer equipment
- validity of information
- disposal of records
- improper use of personal identification numbers (PINs)

Key Terms

Accession register. Shows the next number available for a record.

Alphabetic filing system. Uses the alphabet to sequence personal, business, and government names.

Alphabetizing. Grouping names in A-to-Z sequence.

Association of Records Managers and Administrators (ARMA). Professional organization that focuses on records and information management and standardized the first rules for alphabetic filing.

Bar coding. Type of technology that allows files to be maintained electronically and requires software, a label printer, and a scanning device.

Caption. A key word under which a document is filed.

Centralized filing system. System in which files are placed in one convenient location for a group of people who must work with the same information.

CD-R. Type of optical disc that can be recorded (or written) only once (compact disc-recordable).

CD-RW. Erasable disc you can write or record over multiple times (compact disc-rewritable).

Charge-out method. Used to track paper files that have been borrowed from an area and are to be returned.

Closed notation. Indicates the entire span of the contents of either a file drawer or a section of files.

Coding. Marking the indexing caption on the record.

Cross-referencing. Task of referencing a record by two different names.

Decentralized filing system. Describes a location where individuals or small groups of employees maintain files at their workstations.

Decimal-numeric filing. Also known as the *Dewey decimal system,* a method that works with subject filing to permit more expansion than a basic numeric system.

Diacritical marks. A mark, such as an accent, that indicates pronunciation.

Directory. A section on a company's network system that is allotted to certain people for their files; on a personal computer hard drive, a directory serves as a location for folders.

Disk drive. Physical location where folders and files can be found on a computer.

Document. An electronic or paper representation of information.

Electronic filing system. Includes the computer hardware, its operating system, and software to maintain files.

File. Any document created on the computer or received from another computer.

Files management. Defines the application of records management principles to both paper and electronic records created and used by a single office.

Filing. The task of placing papers in folders.

Flash drive. Data storage device that provides portability and great capacity.

Floppy disk. A portable, inexpensive storage medium for computer files.

Folder. The container for holding material in a paper filing system; in a computer filing system, a folder is also referred to as a *directory*.

Geographic filing system. Allows material to be filed alphabetically in some logical pattern, such as by city, state, region, or territory.

Guides. Dividers used to separate filing space into labeled sections.

Hanging folders. Folders that suspend by extensions of their top edges across a metal frame within the file drawer.

Important records. Documents such as customer and inventory records that are meaningful to the business operation but must be limited as to the length of time they are retained.

Index. A list of filed items.

Indexing. The process of arranging units in order for filing purposes.

Indirect filing. A numeric filing system that uses an index listing the name of the person, organization, or subject to which the number is assigned.

Individual name folder. A folder needed when you accumulate at least five records for one customer.

Information system. A system in which an organization plans, develops, and organizes information.

Label. Identifies the contents of a folder or file drawer.

Lateral cabinet. Often referred to as *horizontal files* or *open-sided cabinets,* a cabinet that allows files to be accessed horizontally or vertically.

Miscellaneous folder. Holds documents for which you do not have individual folders.

Mobile aisle system. A system that can be automated to work on tracks that move back and forth to conserve floor space.

My Documents. An electronic folder designated by Microsoft Windows to store files.

Nonessential records. Documents that are not needed beyond their current use and that should be discarded after their use.

Numeric filing system. Allows material to be filed in some logical numerical order.

Open shelving equipment. Found in large offices and central file rooms, equipment that allows files to be retrieved horizontally and full viewing of the folder tabs for rapid retrieval.

Periodic transfer method. A system in which files are transferred to inactive storage at stated intervals such as six months, one year, or eighteen months.

Perpetual transfer method. A system in which files are continually transferred to inactive storage as a project or case is completed.

Primary guide. Divides files into alphabetic sections and is placed at the beginning of each section.

Record. A written representation of business activities and decisions or transactions.

Records and information management. The logical and practical approach to the creation, maintenance, use, and disposition of records and to the information those records contain.

Records manager. The designated person who supervises all the records in large organizations; he or she also determines how the files will be maintained and who will maintain them, how long each document is to be kept in the file, and when a file is to be removed to an inactive area or made ready for more permanent storage or destruction.

Recycle Bin. Serves as a temporary holding area for files deleted from your hard drive.

Retention schedule. A schedule that indicates the length of time a record must be kept, if additional storage media is required, and when the final disposition of records should occur.

Retrieval. Describes the task of obtaining filed records for use.

Sorting. Prearranging records in the same order in which they will be filed.

Special characters. Marks such as © for copyright and ® for registered.

Special guide. Directs the eye to individual folders that are used frequently.

Storage medium. The physical material on which data, instructions, and information is saved.

Storing. Involves placing paper file folders in cabinets or saving electronic files on a storage medium.

Subject filing system. To file records alphabetically according to main topics.

Tab. The portion of the guide projecting from its edge.

Tab cut. Tabs in different widths.

Terminal-digit filing. Method of dividing numbers into groups of digits that point to the location of records.

Three-letter extension. Suffix to computer file name, such as .wpd or .doc, that distinguishes among the software applications and is assigned by the operating system.

Unit. Refers to parts of a name pertinent in alphabetic filing.

Useful records. Documents, such as correspondence and reports, that are needed to conduct the daily business of the operation.

Vertical drawer cabinet. Usually has four or five drawers and can be moved easily and locked for security.

Vital records. Documents, such as records pertaining to property, patents, copyrights, and insurance, that are essential to operations or to the continuation or resumption of operations; the re-creation of the legal or financial status of the organization; or the fulfillment of its obligations to stockholders and employees in the event of a disaster.

For Your Discussion

Retrieve file C8-DQ from your student data disk.

DIRECTIONS

Enter your response after each question or statement.

1. Discuss how records management works as a system.

2. Define the categories of records.

3. Describe the four main filing systems.

4. Describe the filing supplies and equipment needed for a paper filing system.

5. List the steps necessary to prepare paper records for filing.

6. Explain a tracking method used for paper filing system.

7. Describe the components of an electronic filing system.

8. Distinguish between a CD-R and a CD-RW.

9. Explain the importance of file retention and transfer.

10. Describe at least two ethical issues in records management.

Building Your Office Skills

Exploring the Workplace: *Activities*

1. Save all of your incoming paper mail and copies of your outgoing mail for one week. At the end of the week, complete these steps.

   a. Categorize (e.g., vital, important) each piece.

   b. Of the items to be managed, identify how long each piece will be retained. Suggest how many pieces will be discarded at the end of the retention period.

   c. Prepare a summary of your review in a memo to be submitted to your instructor. As the last paragraph in your summary, explain the points you have learned by doing this activity and include any questions you may have at the end of this activity.

2. Visit an office either at your school or at a local business that uses an alphabetic filing system. Summarize the results of your visit in a memo to be submitted to your instructor. Be prepared to share this information with other class members. Inquire about:

   a. types of folders used

   b. types of labels used

   c. preparation of tabs

   d. use of cross-references

   e. charge-out methods

   f. system for coding the materials before they are filed

   g. types of cabinets or shelves

   h. retention and transfer methods

3. With a team member, visit three Web sites that sell filing supplies and equipment online. Select five items you would need to set up a filing system. Compare the products and the prices among the three Web sites. Be sure to state the Web site address and name. Use an electronic spreadsheet to display your information. Prepare a summary of your findings in a memo format to be submitted to your instructor. Attach a copy of your spreadsheet. Also, be prepared to share the information with other team members.

4. With a team member, visit your school library or a large organization, such as a hospital or insurance company. Interview someone who can explain the following:

   a. how information is stored on their electronic media

   b. what responsibilities are assigned to a records coordinator or records manager

   c. what filing system is used for records

   Prepare a summary of your findings in a memo format to be submitted to your instructor. Also, be prepared to share your findings with the class or other team members.

5. Either revise or create a filing system to keep the home records you need and want. If you currently have a filing system, list your current files. Are you using an appropriate filing system? Why? Why not? If you need to revise your system, summarize what steps you must take to align it with the concepts presented in this chapter.

   If you do not currently have a system, determine either a paper or electronic filing system you want to use. Design your system on paper to be submitted to your instructor. From the design, your instructor should be able to determine the placement of guides and folders with labels.

Developing Critical Thinking Skills: *Problem Solving on the Job*

Retrieve file C8-OJS from your student data disk.

Directions

Enter your response after each situation.

1. **Reorganizing the files.** You are convinced the office assistant who previously worked in your office made up his own filing rules. You have been working for three weeks and have extreme difficulty finding anything the previous office assistant filed. Your manager has told you to reorganize the files and to set up your own system. You are eager to set up a better filing system, but this is the peak season for your department. It will be at least two more months before you have time to reorganize the files. Either individually or with a team member, follow the problem solving steps to determine most appropriate solutions in the meantime.

2. **Misplaced files.** You have set up an electronic filing system for your office, complete with directories and folders. At numerous staff meetings you have asked the managers to file their completed proposals into the correct folders you have set up. However, whenever you have to search for a proposal, you rarely find it in the correct folder or even in the correct directory. How

do you feel about this situation? What do you think is the *real* problem? What solutions do you have for solving this problem? Identify the advantages and disadvantages of each solution. At your next staff meeting, what, if anything, will you suggest to the managers?

3. **Additional filing responsibilities.** The four managers for whom you work have been doing their own paper filing. However, today you were told you are to maintain the files for all four managers. Their paper files will be moved to your area. You are to maintain separate files for each manager. What can you do to make it easier to get the materials to the appropriate manager and to refile the materials?

4. **Centralized filing dilemma.** Your company centralizes paper files for economy and efficiency. Your manager, however, tends to resist releasing materials to the central location, preferring to build up his and your in-office files. The records supervisor has called you several times to remind you to return materials to the central filing area. With your team member, apply the steps in problem solving to help resolve this conflict.

5. **Question of ethics.** You have been asked by your supervisor to destroy files related to an employee in your work group. You are aware the employee has taken legal action against your company for sexual harassment. Describe how you will respond to this situation.

Using the Web: *Research Activities*

A. Your office manager, Charlotte, has just concluded a meeting with the office staff regarding misplaced records. All of you are concerned because the misplaced folders are a source of irritation and are also costly because your company must pay for employees' time while they search for the records. Charlotte has asked you and your team to help her to locate information about records management software.

1. Search for information on records management software by using key words.

2. Summarize the information found on records management software and prepare the summary in a memo to be submitted to your instructor.

B. Either individually or with a team member, research information on the following:

1. Enter the address for ARMA International www.arma.org and locate information about the organization.

2. Locate the code of professional responsibility.

3. Summarize the code and prepare the information in a memo to be submitted to your instructor.

4. Include in your memo ways in which an office professional responsible for records in an office can support the code.

C. You were asked to research information on online training offered by ARMA International.

1. Enter the Web site (www.arma.org) and click on Online Learning under Career Development on the left side of the home page.

2. Locate the online class on E-Mail, Voice Mail, and Instant Messaging: A Legal Perspective.

3. Summarize the topics and general information regarding this online class and submit your findings in a memo to your instructor.

4. Be prepared to discuss these topics with your class members.

Get Tech Wise: *Viewing Folders and Files*

Using Windows Explorer program in Windows 98/2000/XP, you can view and manage your files, folders, and drives.

Directions

1. Click on the Start button and select Programs.

   a. In Windows 98, next click on Windows Explorer to start the program.

   b. In Windows 2000 and XP, click on Accessories. Then click on Windows Explorer.

2. The Explore window has two panes: the Folders pane and the Contents pane.

Folders Pane, on the left, displays all drives (under My Computer) and folders on one drive. To view a drive or folder in the Folders pane in more detail, click on the + symbol.

Contents Pane, on the right, displays the contents in detail of the selected drive or folder.

To see the *Details View,* from the menu bar, click on View; then, click on Details. The sequence is alphabetical by name. The column headings allow you to click to sort the listing in different orders. For instance, click on any column heading once to list the items in ascending order and again to list in descending order.

Improving Your Writing: *Grammar Workshop*

Retrieve C8-WRKS from your student data disk to complete the workshop.

Simulation: *In the Office at Supreme Appliances*

Application 8-A

Indexing Names

> **Supplies needed:** Indexing guidelines; Form 8-A (Indexing List of Names).

Retrieve file C8-AP-A from your student data disk.

Directions

Over the years, someone had dropped cards in a large envelope without any idea of organizing this information. While Ms. Quevedo is away from the office this week, you want to organize the cards that contain names, addresses, and telephone numbers. Before Ms. Quevedo left the office, you mentioned the envelope of cards to her. Because she had been looking for the cards for some time, she is excited you have located them and that you are taking the initiative to organize the cards into a useful system. For this task, you will need to examine the cards and then index them. For the purpose of these assignments, the cards are shown as slips of paper, and you will be working only with the names.

Each name is identified by a number that will be used when you alphabetize the names in the next assignment. For this assignment, ignore the numbers.

1. If you are using the student data file, key the names in indexing order at the top of each slip. As an example, the first slip is already filled in. To navigate within the slips, use your tab or arrow keys. Depending on your instructor's directions, print your answers or submit the electronic file to your instructor.

2. If you are using the working papers, print the names in indexing order at the top of each slip. Submit your answers to your instructor.

Before proceeding to Application 8-B, check with your instructor to see that you are ready.

Application 8-B

Alphabetizing Names

> **Supplies needed:** A printed copy or working paper prepared in Application 8-A; Answer Sheet Form 8-B.

Retrieve file C8-AP-B from your student data disk.

Directions

Today you will alphabetize the names. To make this an easy task, cut the paper into individual slips. Separate the slips into groups, for example, A through D, and so on. Alphabetize the slips. Count the slips to be certain you have a total of 35 slips.

Complete either the electronic file or the Answer Sheet for 8-B provided in the working papers by indicating the card number shown in parentheses before the name, as written in Application 8-A. Do not include the parentheses in your answer. For instance, indicate card number 1 under *L* on the answer sheet. If you have more than one name in a group, list the card number in alphabetical sequence. For example, under *L*, card number 1 would be listed prior to card number 12. To see an example, review the answer sheet and look under *L*.

Because you will need to use the slips in the next assignment, keep them organized and in a safe place. Use a rubber band or a paper clip to keep the slips together and in the correct sequence. After you have entered the card numbers, count the entries. You should have a total of 35. Submit your answer sheet to your instructor. Before proceeding to the next application, check with your instructor to see that you are ready.

Application 8-C

Indexing and Alphabetizing Names

Supplies needed: Form 8-C (List of Names); Answer Sheet Form 8-C1.

Retrieve files C8-AP-C and C8-AP-C1 from your student data disk.

Directions

Today you will index an additional 35 names, alphabetize them, and file these names into your group from Assignment 8-B.

After you index the new names, cut the paper into individual slips. Sort the slips into groups (A through D and so on), as you did in Application 8-B. Alphabetize the slips and file the slips into the correct sequence with the previous slips that were alphabetized in Application 8-B. After you complete this task, be certain you have a total of 70 slips.

Complete either the electronic file or the Answer Sheet for 8-C1 as you did in Application 8-B. Before you submit your answer sheet, count the number of entries. You should have a total of 70 slips. Remember:

1. Enter only the card number; do not include the parentheses in your answer.

2. Indicate the card number under the alphabet on the answer sheet. If you have more than one name in a group, list the card number in alphabetical sequence within the group.

Application 8-D

Retrieving Names

Supplies needed: Form 8-D (Retrieving Assignment 1).

Directions

Before you complete this assignment, be sure all 70 slips are arranged in correct alphabetical order. If you misfiled any slip, be certain you understand why you missed it. Ask your instructor for the Retrieving Assignment 1, which is Form 8-D. On the form, you will find items that are listed and indicate the slip number.

If you are assigned the next application, keep the 70 slips in alphabetical order.

Application 8-E

Indexing and Filing Names

Supplies needed: The slips prepared in Applications 8-B and 8-C; Form 8-E (List of Names); Answer Sheet for 8-E1.

Retrieve files C8-AP-E and C8-AP-E1 from your student data disk.

Directions

Today you will index an additional 40 names, alphabetize them, and file these names with your group from Assignments 8-B and 8-C.

After you index the new names, cut the paper into individual slips. Sort the slips into groups (A through D and so on), as you did in Applications 8-B and 8-C. Alphabetize the slips and file the slips into the correct sequence with the previous slips that were alphabetized in Applications 8-B and 8-C. After you complete this task, be certain you have a total of 110 slips.

Complete either the electronic file or the Answer Sheet for 8-E1 as you did in the previous applications. Before you submit your answer sheet, count the number of entries. You should have a total of 110 slips. Submit your answer sheet to your instructor.

Application 8-F

Cross-Referencing Names

Supplies needed: Form 8-F (Cross-Reference).

Retrieve file C8-AP-F from your student data disk.

Directions

You anticipate that you may have difficulty finding slips 71, 75, 79, and 92 because they could be called for by different names. Therefore, prepare a cross-reference for them. In the upper right corner of each cross-reference slip, enter **71X**, **75X**, **79X**, and **92X** respectively.

After you have completed the cross-references, file the cross-reference slips within the group of 110 slips. Now you should have a total of 115 slips.

Application 8-G

Retrieving Names

Supplies needed: Form 8-G (Retrieving Assignment 2).

Directions

Before you complete this assignment, be sure all 115 slips are arranged in correct alphabetical order. If you misfiled any slip, be certain you understand why you missed it. Ask your instructor for the Retrieving Assignment 2, which is Form 8-G.

Application 8-H

Using Windows Explorer

Supplies needed: Form 8-H (Directions for Using Windows Explorer).

Retrieve file C8-AP-H from your student data disk.

Directions

Because your computer at Supreme Appliances was used by the previous administrative assistant, it has many files and folders that were created on this computer. While Ms. Quevedo is away this week, you would like to spend time browsing Windows Explorer to understand the file organization on your office computer. During this time you would like to perform the common operations in Windows Explorer: (1) expand and collapse drives and folders; (2) display drive and folder contents; (3) copy a file between folders; (4) move a file; (5) delete a file and restore it from the Recycle Bin.

Before you begin this application using Windows Explorer, check with your instructor to see if the steps can be completed on a computer in the classroom or lab. Certain classroom or lab setups may prevent this application from being performed by students on campus.

Building Your Portfolio

With the help of a team member or your instructor, select the best work representative of your work from Chapter 8. Suggestions include Activity 1 or 5, results from one of the Web research activities, or Application 8-D or 8-G. Follow your instructor's directions for formatting, assembling, and turning in the portfolio.

chapter

9 Handling Financial Procedures

chapter **outline**

Banking Procedures
  Nonelectronic Funds Transfer
  Electronic Funds Transfer
  Bank Checks
  Bank Statement Reconciliation

Accounting Procedures
  Petty Cash Fund
  Payroll
  Financial Statements
  Budgeting
  Office Supplies Inventory
  Accounting Department

Ethics in Accounting Procedures

International Currency Exchange

learning **outcomes**

When you have completed this chapter, you should be able to:

- Identify and explain the use of a cashier's check, bank draft, bank money order, and traveler's check.

- Identify the various ways funds are transferred electronically.

- Prepare checks, make stop-payment notification, and endorse checks.

- Reconcile a bank statement.

- Describe what a petty cash fund is and how it is used.

- Calculate a weekly payroll on a payroll register.

- Explain the parts of an income statement and balance sheet.

- Explain the budgeting process.

- Keep an inventory of supplies and order supplies as needed.

- Discuss the importance of demonstrating ethical conduct in financial matters.

- Demonstrate how to change U.S. dollars to foreign money using currency exchange rates.

Larger companies have staff hired specifically to handle their financial functions. These functions include budgeting, accounting, making payments, billing, banking, and other operations, depending on the type of business and the size of the company.

In small companies or professional offices, such as a medical or dental practice, office professionals may handle certain financial tasks in addition to their usual office duties. Regardless of the size of the office, you need to become familiar with some of the basic banking transactions and record-keeping tasks you may need to perform.

Banking Procedures

You may be called upon to handle banking procedures if you work in a small office or if your manager travels abroad. You should, therefore, become familiar with all types of banking procedures.

NONELECTRONIC FUNDS TRANSFER

A depositor establishes a checking account at a bank as a convenient means to transfer funds. The instrument most used for transferring funds is the ordinary **check**, which is defined as a written order of a depositor upon a commercial bank to pay to the order of a designated party or to a bearer a specified sum of money on demand (Figure 9-1).

The parties to a check are the **drawer**, the person who draws the check on his or her account; the **drawee**, the bank upon which the check is drawn; and the **payee**, the person to whom payment is made.

If you are to sign checks for your manager, the organization where you work, or both, you will be asked to complete a signature card, placing your authorized signature on file in addition to your manager's signature with the bank.

FIGURE 9-1 • An administrative professional endorsing a check for deposit.

In addition to the ordinary check, the following are used to transfer funds: cashier's check, bank draft, bank money order, and traveler's check.

Cashier's Check

A **cashier's check**, also called a treasurer's check or official check, is written by an authorized officer of the bank on its own funds. As a result, the drawer's bank guarantees payment to the payee. A depositor may obtain a cashier's check by writing a check on his or her own funds for the amount plus a fee.

In order for the cashier's check to stand as proof of payment, the officer of the bank gives a copy of the check to the person making the payment. The purchaser's name is on the official check. Cashier's checks are suitable for times when a check is not acceptable, such as when it is necessary to guarantee that a certain amount of funds for payment are available. The check may be made payable to whomever you designate and can be for any amount.

Bank Draft

A **bank draft** is a check drawn by a bank on its own funds (or credit) in another bank located either in the same city or another city. The draft is made payable to a third party, which, upon endorsing it, may cash the bank draft at the bank on which it is drawn.

A bank draft can be used to transfer money to another person or organization in another geographical location within the United States or abroad. A bank draft payable in foreign currency may also be purchased.

To obtain a bank draft, an office professional should present to the bank his or her manager's or organization's check made payable to the bank for the desired amount plus the fee. In exchange, the office professional will receive a bank draft made payable to the person or organization specified.

Bank Money Order

A **bank money order**, similar to the postal money order, may be obtained from a bank. Money orders are often used in place of personal checks for transactions such as mail order purchases. Money orders are blank when issued and the purchaser fills in the payee information.

A bank money order requires the endorsement of the payee to transfer the funds. It may be cashed at any bank. The fee for obtaining a bank money order is nominal. The amount for which a single money order may be written is limited, but the number of money orders that may be issued to the same person to be sent to one payee is not restricted.

Traveler's Check

A **traveler's check** (or "cheque," to use the spelling favored by Britain and American Express) is a check that functions as cash but is protected against loss or theft. When the checks are lost or stolen, the owner usually can obtain a refund immediately by contacting a representative office of the company whose checks were purchased. The checks may be purchased at banks or from other sources, such as credit unions. Automated Teller Machines (ATMs) have almost made it unnecessary to carry large sums of cash or cash substitutes. You will learn more about ATMs later in this chapter. However, traveler's checks may still be the best option in some instances. Consider these examples:

> Your manager is visiting another country for only a few hours (e.g., while waiting to change planes). If he or she wants to purchase a snack, newspaper, or magazine and the vendor doesn't take credit cards, using a traveler's check may be his or her only recourse.
>
> Your manager might be low on cash and the ATM network is down. (This seems to happen most often at night or on weekends.)
>
> Your manager's ATM won't accept his or her Personal Identification Number (PIN), or the machine lacks multilingual instructions and the manager can't figure out how to get cash.

One source where you can purchase traveler's checks is American Express. American Express traveler's checks can be purchased at a bank, or at American Express offices throughout the world. American Express traveler's checks are sold in denominations of $20, $50, $100, $500, and $1,000 (U.S.). They may also be purchased in foreign currencies. The cost is usually 1 percent of face value. There is no time limit on their validity. A traveler who plans an extended stay abroad may find it economically advantageous to purchase some traveler's checks in the currency of that country. Your manager can use traveler's checks in shops, hotels, and restaurants without paying multiple commissions or high conversion fees. Unused checks will have to be changed back into U.S. currency unless they are saved for another trip.

The purchaser must obtain traveler's checks in person because the purchaser must sign each one in the presence of the agent from whom the checks are purchased. American Express also has a two-party check. Only one person must sign for the checks. A 2 percent fee is charged for two-party checks. The purchaser's signature on each check is his or her identification and protection. The purchaser can cash a traveler's check at a hotel, bank, other places of business, or an American Express office. In order to cash a traveler's check, the purchaser must sign the check in the presence of the person accepting it.

Traveler's checks are numbered serially. You should prepare a list of the serial numbers of the checks in duplicate, one for your files and the other for your manager to carry, preferably in a place separate from the traveler's checks. Should traveler's checks become lost or stolen, the manager would contact the nearest representative office of the bank or company from which they were purchased and provide them with a list of the serial numbers of the missing checks and the total amount of the checks. The issuer promises to replace them when lost or stolen unless the purchaser has been negligent.

Stop 'n Check

List three nonelectronic transfer ways to obtain funds.

a. _____

b. _____

c. _____

ELECTRONIC FUNDS TRANSFER

As an office professional, you will probably not be required to set up electronic funds transfer; however, you should know about each type and understand how they work. You may already be familiar with some of the way funds are transferred for personal use. You could be required to keep records for your manager related to some of the electronic funds transfer areas.

Electronic funds transfer (EFT) is an electronic delivery system for financial transactions. With the use of computers, financial institutions can perform numerous banking transactions without the use of checks. Advantages include no lost or stolen checks and payments made quickly and on time.

The major EFT services are ATMs, automated clearinghouses (centers for electronic funds transfer between financial institutions and individuals), and payment by telephone.

Automated Teller Machines

Automated teller machines (ATMs), located at banks, in shopping malls, in supermarkets, and many other places, enable customers to obtain cash and make deposits. When a customer activates an automated teller machine with an EFT card and enters a PIN or a secret password, the computer is ready to answer an inquiry about the customer's account, supply balance data, or dispense cash.

Debit Card

Another way funds are electronically transferred is by using a debit card. **Debit cards** are used in the place of checks. Debit cards are obtained through the bank by completing a credit application for a debit card through companies such as VISA or MasterCard. Once the application is approved, the bank issues the debit card, which can be used either as a debit card or a credit card. When using a debit card, a PIN must be entered and then the money is taken directly from the individual's or company's checking account. The only drawback is if the card is lost or stolen, it can still be used as a credit card with no PIN required and money automatically withdrawn.

Direct Payroll Deposit

Direct payroll deposit enables an organization to pay its employees without writing checks. Instead, the organization furnishes the bank with electronic instructions for all payroll disbursements to employees. The bank credits the account of each employee with his or her net pay and withdraws the amount from the account of the employer making payment. The employee receives a statement, often produced by a third party, from his or her employer. The statement shows the gross payment, the type and amount of deductions, and the net payment. Another example of automatic deposits are federal payments, such as social security checks.

Automatic Deposits

Funds can be automatically deposited as well. The company making the **automatic deposit** must be given the account's American Banking Association (ABA) electronic routing number and the account number in which the money is to be deposited. This routing number and bank account number is usually printed on the bottom of all checks.

Automatic Debits

Automatic debits are preauthorized automated transfers of funds for a company from one account to another within the same financial institution. For example, a company might transfer funds from its general checking account to a special account for payroll.

Web Banking

Most banks offer business banking, investing, and insurance services to their customers on the Internet. **Web banking** provides easy management of banking transactions online wherever you have access to the Internet. Primary functions of such services enable business customers to make electronic transfers between accounts and get real-time information on balances and transactions. Accounts may be viewed and manipulated "on screen" just as you might with more traditional methods of banking. Many banks also offer electronic bill payment services.

Access to your Web banking services will depend upon your bank, your company's unique identification, and password. A unique password can be established for each authorized user of the business account. Commercial banking services are comprehensive but varied in design.

Telephone Transfers

Some companies allow payments to be made by phone. **Telephone transfers** can be made by calling the company to whom you wish to make payment, writing a check, giving them the check number and amount, and the company will draft the amount from your checking account and the bank will honor the check. Not all companies provide this service. The advantage is payment does not have to be made until the exact due date and late charges can be avoided.

BANK CHECKS

Businesses use various ways to prepare checks. Checks may be prepared with a check-writing machine, a computer and a printer, or a pen. Some businesses use check-writing machines as a safety measure against possible alteration of checks. Others make use of commercially available software for check writing such as Intuit's Quicken or Simply Accounting.

Stop-Payment Notification

At the request of the drawer, a bank will place **stop-payment notification** on a check for a fee at any time. Stopping payment is a safety measure that

Stop 'n Check

List the ways you have used electronic transfer of funds mentioned in this section.

a. _____

b. _____

c. _____

should be taken when a check has been lost or stolen. This step may also be taken when a check is written for an incorrect amount, when certain conditions of an agreement have not been met, or for other reasons.

Check Endorsement

Banks require **check endorsement** (signing) by the payee when a check is presented for cash or deposit. The payee signs on the reverse side of the check—preferably at the left end. A bank will accept checks for deposit that have been endorsed by a representative of the payee. The endorsement may be made with a rubber stamp, or it may be handwritten in ink.

Endorsements are of three types: blank, restrictive, and full (Figure 9-2).

Blank Endorsement. A **blank endorsement** consists of only the payee's signature. A check endorsed using a blank endorsement is payable to the bearer; therefore, the holder should use a blank endorsement only when he or she is at the bank depositing or cashing the check in case the check is lost or stolen.

Restrictive Endorsement. A **restrictive endorsement** limits the use of a check to the purpose stated in the endorsement. Words such as "For deposit only" or "Pay to the order of" are written before the organization's name or the depositor's signature. As a result, further endorsement of the check is restricted. A restrictive endorsement should be used when deposits are sent to the bank by mail.

Full Endorsement. A **full endorsement**, also called a *two-party check,* transfers a check to a specified person or organization. "Pay to the order of" followed by the name of the person or organization to which the check is being transferred is written on the check preceding the signature of the endorser.

BANK STATEMENT RECONCILIATION

As an office professional, you should know basic information about banking procedures. Although you will probably not have to complete the bank

FIGURE 9-2 • Endorsements.

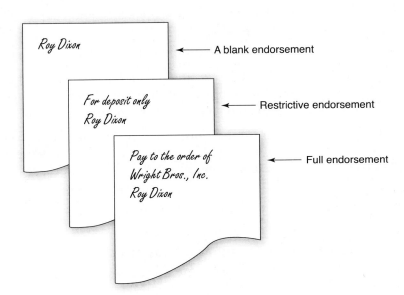

Roy Dixon ← A blank endorsement

For deposit only
Roy Dixon ← Restrictive endorsement

Pay to the order of
Wright Bros., Inc.
Roy Dixon ← Full endorsement

Stop 'n Check

List three types of check endorsements.

a. _____

b. _____

c. _____

Which type endorsement is the safest to use?

_____

reconciliation for the company unless you work for a small company, you should know how to reconcile a bank statement.

Each month the bank issues a current bank statement to the depositor. The bank statement can be mailed to the company or if the company uses Web banking, the account can be viewed from the bank statements online. A comparison of the final bank balance on the bank statement with the company checkbook balance is called **bank reconciliation**.

To balance with the bank statement's figure, checks listed on the bank's statement are checked off in the check register. Some banks return checks that have been paid by the bank with the bank statement each month, other banks return photo copies of each check, and still other banks provide copies of checks upon request. Figure 9-3 shows an example of a bank statement. **Canceled checks** have been paid by the bank. The statement shows the previous month's balance, deposits made, checks paid, bank charges, and the ending balance.

If you are responsible for completing the bank reconciliation with the company's checkbook balance, complete it as soon as you receive the bank statement. Compare the final balance on the bank statement with the balance in the company checkbook and then account for the difference. Usually the two balances do not agree for the following reasons:

- Checks have been written that have not been presented to the bank for payment.
- Deposits may have been made since the statement was sent.
- Automatic credits (deposits) and debits (withdrawals) have been made by the bank.
- Errors in recording checks or deposits may have been made.

Most bank statements have bank reconciliation forms printed on the back of each page of the bank statement for the user's convenience.

To reconcile the bank statement with the company's checkbook:

a. From the bank statement, record in the company's checkbook register all automatic transactions from the statement you have not previously entered, including:
   - + any interest earned
   - + automatic deposits
   - – service charges
   - – automatic payments
   - – telephone transfers and charges

FIGURE 9-3 • Bank statement.

BANK STATEMENT
GILBERT BANK OF ROCHESTER

NAME:	November Sales Seminar C/O Amanda Quevedo 14 Shady Lane Rochester, NY 14623	BRANCH: Rochester Main			
ACCOUNT NO. 3570-810-73-1000	**TRANSIT NO.** 00011-112000	**BEGINNING BALANCE** October 25, 20--	$8,380.25		

CODE	DESCRIPTION	DEBIT	CREDIT	DAY/MO	BALANCE
				10/25	8,380.25
DD	Direct deposit		300.00	10/26	8,680.25
DD	Direct deposit		1,500.00	10/26	10,180.25
DD	Direct deposit		3,000.00	10/29	13,180.25
CK	Check #2009	1,224.00		10/31	11,956.25
CK	Check #2010	510.00		11/03	11,446.25
CK	Check #2015	450.00		11/05	10,996.25
DD	Direct deposit		2,250.00	11/09	13,246.25
CK	Check #2016	1,700.00		11/15	11,546.25
CK	Check #2017	2,000.00		11/18	9,546.25
SC	Service charge	20.00		11/23	9,526.25
CK	Check #2018	2,723.85		11/23	6,802.40
No. of Checks: 6	No. of Credits: 4	Total Debits: $8,627.85	Total Credits: $7,050.00	November 25, 200X	Ending Balance: $6,802.40

b. Enter in the company's checkbook register a check mark for all canceled checks and deposits received by the bank that are listed on the bank statement.

c. Total all **outstanding checks** (checks not paid by the bank) from the company's check register.

d. Total all deposits shown in the company's check register that are not shown on the bank statement, called "deposits in transit."

e. Adjust the bank statement balance.
   • Enter the checking account closing balance shown on the front of your statement.
   • Add any deposits not yet shown on the statement.
   • Subtract the total outstanding checks.

f. The adjusted bank statement balance from your reconciliation should agree with the adjusted checkbook balance.

Stop 'n Check

Place a check mark in the column that represents where each item would appear on a bank reconciliation and indicate if it would be added or substracted.

Bank Transaction	Bank Statement	Checkbook	Added	Subtracted
a. Interest earned				
b. Outstanding checks				
c. Automatic deposits				
d. Service charges				
e. Deposits in transit				
f. Automatic payments				
g. Telephone transfers and charges				

If the adjusted bank statement balance and the adjusted checkbook balance do not agree, follow these steps:

1. Find the difference between the two.
2. Check the bank reconciliation to make certain you have made no errors.
3. Look for omissions of checks or deposits.
4. Check for a math error in the check stubs.

From the bank reconciliation, several journal entries must be made in the company's general ledger. These entries along with the bank reconcialiation are usually made by an accounting assistant or bookkeeper. After these entries have been made and posted to the company books, the cash ledger account should be in balance with the company checkbook as well.

Your part in a company related to the banking procedures is that you may have to verify expenditures and keep invoices and receipts and submit them to the accounting department.

The accounting department will file all canceled checks and bank reconciliations. The retention period for checks and the method of disposing of them will be determined by your company's policy.

Accounting Procedures

Most organizations maintain computerized accounting records. Accounting is a separate business function, performed by accountants, but record keeping occurs wherever a record originates. Consequently, office workers maintain and assist with various financial records. Some office professionals, especially those who work for owners of businesses, help the owners with personal business records.

You may also be responsible for a petty cash fund. In addition, you may be asked to keep a record of office supplies on hand or to assist with payroll records.

PETTY CASH FUND

When the amount of office expenditure is small and payment should be made immediately, it may be more convenient to pay cash rather than write a check. To provide cash to pay for incidental items, such as messenger service, postage due on a package, or emergency purchases of office supplies, organizations establish a **petty cash fund**. The fund can range from $10 to $100 or more, depending on the cash needs for a certain period, usually a month. Even though the fund is used to make miscellaneous payments, the petty cash must be accounted for.

Generally the office professional is responsible for handling the petty cash fund. To keep track of petty cash, observe the following standard procedures:

1. Keep the cash and completed vouchers in a box or an envelope and put them in a safe place. They should be in a locked desk drawer or file or in an office safe. Balance the petty cash record at least once a week. If the cash and vouchers are left unlocked, balance the record at the end of each day.

2. Prepare a petty cash voucher for each expenditure you make. An example is shown in Figure 9-4. The **petty cash voucher**, which is a receipt, should show the amount paid, the voucher number, the date, to whom the payment was made (received by), the purpose of the payment, the expense category to which the payment will be charged, and the signature or initials of the person authorizing payment. Some organizations also require the signature or initials of the person receiving payment.

3. Keep an accurate petty cash record, using either a petty cash book or a distribution sheet or envelope (see Figure 9-5). For each payment from the petty cash funds, enter the date, the amount, the voucher number, and an explanation of the petty cash record. The total of the expenditures plus the cash on hand should equal the original amount of the petty cash fund.

Some petty cash books provide columns for distribution of payments by expense categories; others do not. The columns and the appropriate headings for the petty cash record can be printed on a sheet of paper or

FIGURE 9-4 • Petty cash voucher.

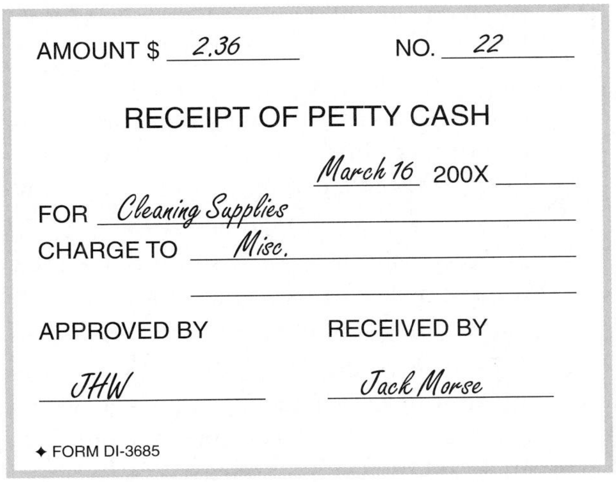

AMOUNT $ _2.36_   NO. _22_

RECEIPT OF PETTY CASH

March 16 200X _____

FOR _Cleaning Supplies_

CHARGE TO _Misc._

APPROVED BY   RECEIVED BY

JHW   _Jack Morse_

✦ FORM DI-3685

FROM _May 3_ 200X__ TO _June 12_ 200X__		**PETTY CASH ENVELOPE** PETTY CASH ENVELOPES PROVIDE A COMPLETE RECORD OF ALL PETTY CASH DISBURSEMENTS. ALL PAYMENTS SHOULD BE SUPPORTED BY A BILL OR VOUCHER SIGNED BY RECIPIENT. EACH VOUCHER SHOULD BE LISTED BELOW AND DISTRIBUTED IN THE COLUMNS HEADED ACCORDING TO YOUR GENERAL LEDGER ACCOUNT NUMBERS OR TITLES.	REIMBURSED BY CHECK NO. _6872_
CASHIER			REFERENCE
AUDITED BY			JOURNAL FOLIO

DATE 200X		VOUCHER NUMBER	PAID TO	DISTRIBUTION											TOTAL	
				Supp	Postage	Misc	Del									
			Petty Cash Fund: $50.00													
5	3	161	Office Supplies	4 08											4	08
5	3	162	Calendar			3 16									3	16
5	3	163	Stamps		3 90										3	90
5	3	164	Reg. Package		3 84										3	84
5	3	165	Cleaning Supplies			2 87									2	87
5	3	166	Carfare				2 50								2	50
5	3	167	Office Supplies	3 64											3	64
5	3	168	Reg. Package		2 79										2	79
5	3	169	Messenger				2 75								2	75
5	3	170	Office Supplies	4 96											4	96
5	3	171	Delivery				3 75								3	75
		TOTAL		12 68	10 53	6 03	9 00								38	24

FIGURE 9-5 • Petty cash envelope.

a manila envelope. Accounting departments frequently supply manila envelopes imprinted with the columns and headings for the petty cash record, including columns for the distribution of payments. Posting the expenditures in the columns provided for each predetermined expense category simplifies preparing the summary of expenditures when you need to replenish the petty cash fund.

4. Replenish the petty cash fund soon enough to keep an adequate supply of cash on hand. In some organizations, petty cash is replenished at a predetermined time, for instance, when only one-fourth of the cash remains. In others, replenishing the petty cash fund is left to the judgment of the person who is responsible for maintaining the fund.

5. To replenish the petty cash fund, balance the petty cash record, formally request a check for the amount needed to bring the fund amount back to its beginning balance, and prepare the petty cash report.

6. Submit the records called for by the accounting department. When the accounting department supplies a petty cash distribution envelope, the usual procedure is to submit the envelope with the supporting vouchers enclosed. Before you release an envelope, copy the record for your files.

FIGURE 9-6 • Petty cash
report.

INTEROFFICE MEMORANDUM

TO: M. Seifert, General Accounting Office   DATE: June 13, 200X

FROM: R. C. Delano

SUBJECT: Petty Cash Report

The following report is a summary of petty cash paid out from

May 3 until June 12, 200X.

<u>Petty Cash Report</u>

June 13, 200X

Opening Balance		$50.00
Expenditures		
Supplies	$12.68	
Postage	10.53	
Delivery	9.00	
Miscellaneous	6.03	38.24
Closing Balance		$11.76

Please issue a check for $38.24 to replenish the petty cash fund

to the original amount of $50. Eleven petty cash vouchers are

attached.

mk

attachments

If you keep a petty cash book, submit a petty cash report similar to the one shown in Figure 9-6. Attach the petty cash vouchers.

7. Cash the check. Enter the beginning amount and the date on the first line of the "paid to" column of the petty cash record each time you replenish the petty cash record (Figure 9-7).

PAYROLL

One of the common accounting procedures an office professional might be required to do is payroll, especially if he or she works for a small company. As with petty cash, a record must be kept that summarizes the payroll for a particular period. This record is called a payroll register. The **payroll register** summarizes for each employee the status of wages earned, payroll deductions,

FIGURE 9-7 • Balancing a petty cash record.

Steps to Replenish Petty Cash

Refer to Figure 9-5 as you read these steps.

1. Count the cash on hand. In the example, you should have $11.76, which is the difference between the amount in the petty cash fund, $50.00, and the amount paid out, $38.24.

2. Total each Distribution column and the Total column of the petty cash envelope.

3. Subtract the total amount paid out ($38.24) from the amount of petty cash ($50.00). The difference should agree with the cash count left in the envelope ($11.76).

4. Total the amount of all the vouchers to see they agree with the Total column ($38.24).

5. Add the totals across the bottom under the Distribution columns to see the sum is equal to the amount shown in the Total column.

6. Write a check or request the amount paid (Total column $38.24) to bring the petty cash fund back to its original amount ($50.00).

and final take-home pay. The summary can be done manually or by computer using a payroll software program, but no matter which method is used, all employers are required by law to create and keep a payroll record for each payroll period. Payroll records usually are prepared weekly, semimonthly, or monthly.

Figure 9-8 shows a typical payroll register. Notice the register shows columns for **employee data** (name, marital status, withholding allowances, hourly rate), **regular hours** worked (first forty hours worked in the payroll period), and the number of **overtime hours** worked (any hours worked over forty hours). Next, **gross earnings** (total regular earnings plus overtime earnings) are calculated.

The deductions begin with the Federal Insurance Contributions Act (FICA). Two taxes are required for all employees: social security and Medicare. Social security, or the **Old Age, Survivors, and Disability Insurance (OASDI)**, as of January 2006 is deducted at the rate of 6.2 percent of the first $94,200

WEEKLY PAYROLL REGISTER

For week ending: June _____ July 31, 200X

Name	Marital Status	Withholding Allowance	Hourly Rate	Reg Hrs	Overtime Hrs	Regular Earnings	Overtime Earnings	Gross Earnings	OASDI	HI	Federal Income Tax	Group Med Ins	Group Dental Ins	Total Deductions	Net Pay
Barton, V. L.	M	3	12.00	40	10	480.00	180.00	660.00	40.92	9.57	36.00	22.00	13.00	121.49	538.51
Carr, S. A.	M	1	12.00	40	9	480.00	162.00	642.00	39.80	9.31	51.00	38.00	8.00	146.11	495.89
Dean, B. B.	M	1	10.00	40	12	400.00	180.00	580.00	35.96	8.41	42.00	41.00	11.00	138.37	441.63
Ellis, R. J.	M	1	11.90	40	8	476.00	142.80	618.80	38.37	8.97	46.00	22.00	5.00	120.34	498.46
Franklin, D. O.	M	3	13.50	40	5	540.00	101.25	641.25	39.76	9.30	33.00	12.00	8.00	102.06	539.19
Gonzalez, P. I.	M	2	12.00	40	13	480.00	234.00	714.00	44.27	10.35	53.00	41.00	10.00	158.62	555.38
Han, T. A.	M	2	12.50	40	11	500.00	206.25	706.25	43.79	10.24	51.00	38.00	11.00	154.03	552.22
Johnson, J. R.	M	0	10.85	40	15	434.00	244.13	678.13	42.04	9.83	64.00	22.00	8.00	145.87	532.26
Kelly, J. S.	M	0	11.00	40	12	440.00	198.00	638.00	39.56	9.25	58.00	38.00	13.00	157.81	480.19
Leamon, D. D.	M	4	13.10	40	10	524.00	196.50	720.50	44.67	10.45	36.00	38.00	10.00	139.12	581.38
Totals						$4,754.00	$1,844.93	$6,598.93	$409.14	$95.68	$470.00	$312.00	$97.00	$1,383.82	$5,215.11

FIGURE 9-8 • Payroll register.

earned, called the *wage base limit*. Federal **health insurance (HI)**, health insurance for older Americans commonly called **Medicare**, has no wage base. All wages earned each year, as of January 2006, are subject to the 1.45 percent set by law. Both of these rates are subject to change by legislation. The combined rate for social security and Medicare is 7.65 percent. **Deductions** are amounts deducted from gross pay, such as social society, Medicare, federal income tax, group medical insurance, dental insurance, union dues, savings bonds, and charitable contributions, as well as federal income tax and FICA. State income taxes must be deducted in some states as well.

Follow these steps to complete a payroll register:

1. Enter each employee's name, marital status (single, married, or head-of-household), number of withholding allowances (the number of exemption allowances claimed on his or her W-4 form), the hourly rate (amount earned per hour), the number of regular hours worked, and the number of overtime hours worked.

2. Calculate regular earnings by multiplying the hourly rate by the regular hours worked.

3. Calculate overtime earnings by multiplying the hourly rate by the overtime hours worked by 1.5 (time and a half).

4. Add regular earnings and overtime earnings to obtain gross earnings.

5. Multiply gross earnings by 6.2 percent to calculate OASDI.

6. Multiply gross earnings by 1.45 percent to calculate HI.

7. The amount of **federal income tax** (money withheld from a paycheck and paid to the federal government as a tax on wages earned) withheld is obtained from *(Circular E) Employer's Tax Guide* federal income tax table booklet. The booklet gives instructions and tables for weekly, biweekly, semimonthly, and monthly payrolls, each showing amounts to be withheld for single, married, or head-of-household deductions for federal income tax. The website for Circular E is www.irs.gov. Enter Circular E in the search box.

8. Enter any other deductions. Examples are group medical insurance, dental insurance, union dues, purchase of savings bonds, contributions to charitable organizations such as United Way, and savings or payments sent to credit unions, to name a few.

9. Total all deductions.

10. Subtract total deductions from gross earnings to calculate **net pay** (total earnings minus deductions).

Stop 'n Check

1. What percent of total wages is withheld for each employee for F.I.C.A.? _____

2. What is the wage base limit for F.I.C.A. each year? _____

3. What percent of total wages is withheld for each employee for Medicare? _____

4. What is the wage base limit for Medicare each year? _____

FINANCIAL STATEMENTS

Most office professionals will not be required to have an extensive knowledge of accounting procedures, but you should be familiar with the two following major financial statements: the income statement and the balance sheet.

An owner or manager of a business must determine the condition of the business he or she owns or manages. Financial reports such as an income statement or a balance sheet, when compared with prior years or with industry averages, can show the owner or manager whether the business is healthy. Reading or interpreting financial statements can tell the owner or manager if a problem exists, to what degree the problem has advanced, and what strengths or weaknesses the company has. As an office professional, you should understand the purpose of the income statement and the balance sheet and recognize what accounting information goes on each (Figure 9-9).

Income Statement

An **income statement** is also referred to as a profit and loss (P & L) statement or operating statement. The income statement shows the results of company operations in terms of money earned (revenue) and expenses incurred. Figure 9-10 shows an income statement.

The income statement covers the results of company operations for a certain period. In Figure 9-10, you will notice the period is for one year. The first part of the income statement summarizes the total amount of sales (revenue) and the cost of the merchandise sold. The difference between the two is called **gross profit on sales**. The gross profit is not the profit the owner can take for personal use because the company has incurred many **expenses** (the cost of operation) that will reduce revenue to a truer picture of what the company made. The income reported after expenses is also not the final income figure. Income tax must be accounted for (estimated and deducted) to arrive at the final income figure for the company.

FIGURE 9-9 • Reviewing financial reports.

FIGURE 9-10 • Income statement.

Rayborn Air Conditioning & Heating Service
Income Statement
For Year Ended December 31, 200X

Revenue		
Sales		$235,000
Cost of goods sold		
Merchandise inventory, January 1	$46,000	
Purchases	19,050	
Merchandise available for sale	$65,050	
Less inventory, December 31	13,000	
Cost of goods sold		52,050
Gross profit on sales		$182,950
Operating expenses		
Wages expense	$25,000	
Depreciation, office equipment	9,000	
Depreciation, trucks	15,000	
Repair expense	4,000	
Advertising expense	1,200	
Oil and gas expense	3,500	
Truck insurance expense	2,900	
Total operating expenses		60,600
Net income before estimated income tax		$122,350
Estimated income tax		34,935
Net income after income tax		$ 87,415

Balance Sheet

The balance sheet summarizes the balances of the **assets** (what the business owns), **liabilities** (what the business owes), and the **owner's equity** (what the business is worth). The **balance sheet** reports what a company is worth on any one given day—usually reported at the end of the month or year. It shows the company's complete financial condition. As an office professional, you should understand its various sections. Figure 9-11 shows a completed balance sheet.

The balance sheet is divided into three parts—assets, liabilities, and owner's equity. The assets are what the company owns and are shown as either current assets or long-term assets. **Current assets** are those assets that can be sold or turned into cash quickly or can be consumed in a short period. **Plant and equipment,** often referred to as **fixed assets,** are those assets with a long life that will be used over many years in the operation of the company such as land and buildings. Liabilities are the debts the company owes. **Current liabilities** are short-term debts—usually debts that can be paid in one year. **Long-term liabilities** are debts due for long periods of time—usually more than one year. Owner's equity is the capital the owner has invested in the company.

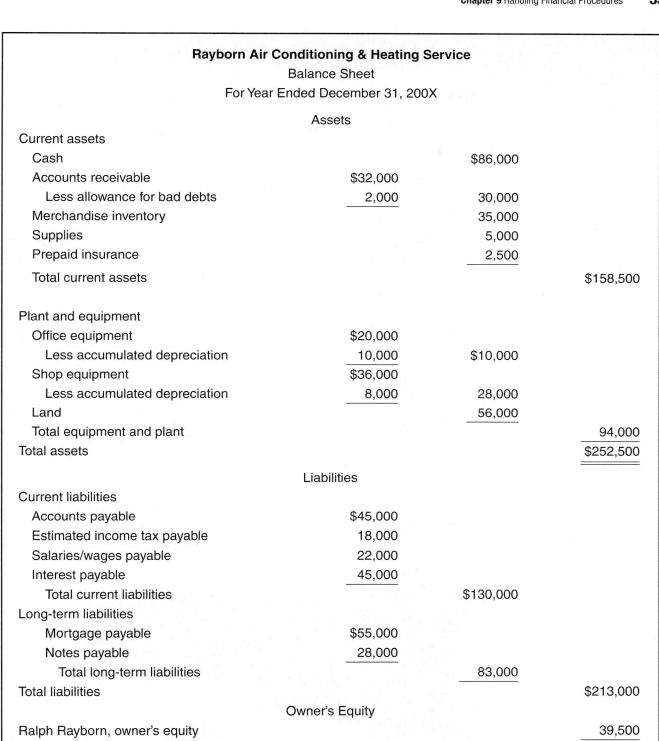

Rayborn Air Conditioning & Heating Service
Balance Sheet
For Year Ended December 31, 200X

Assets

Current assets			
Cash		$86,000	
Accounts receivable	$32,000		
Less allowance for bad debts	2,000	30,000	
Merchandise inventory		35,000	
Supplies		5,000	
Prepaid insurance		2,500	
Total current assets			$158,500
Plant and equipment			
Office equipment	$20,000		
Less accumulated depreciation	10,000	$10,000	
Shop equipment	$36,000		
Less accumulated depreciation	8,000	28,000	
Land		56,000	
Total equipment and plant			94,000
Total assets			$252,500

Liabilities

Current liabilities			
Accounts payable	$45,000		
Estimated income tax payable	18,000		
Salaries/wages payable	22,000		
Interest payable	45,000		
Total current liabilities		$130,000	
Long-term liabilities			
Mortgage payable	$55,000		
Notes payable	28,000		
Total long-term liabilities		83,000	
Total liabilities			$213,000

Owner's Equity

Ralph Rayborn, owner's equity			39,500
Total liabilities and owner's equity			$252,500

FIGURE 9-11 • Balance sheet.

Even though you will probably not create income statements and balance sheets, depending on the size of the company where you work, you may be asked to work with them in some manner. Being familiar with these financial statements will tell you more about your company and its stability.

Stop 'n Check

1. What financial statement lists only revenue and expenses? _____
2. What financial statement shows what the company is worth on any given day? _____

BUDGETING

Budgeting is the process of planning future business operations and defining those plans in a formal report. The report expressed in financial terms is called a **budget**. Budgets may be developed for short periods, such as a month, or long periods, such as a year. Annual budgets are often divided into shorter periods to better evaluate a company's ability to stay within the prescribed budget. Budgetary control is crucial to the successful operation of a business, and as an employee you will be asked to participate in the budget process in some way. You might be asked to serve on the budget committee (see Figure 9-12) that reviews and revises various estimates of income and expenses by other employees. Usually budgeting procedures begin at the department level and move upward, with each area of responsibility combining figures submitted from below them and passing them upward in the company. The ultimate result is the master budget. The **master budget** consists of various budgets that collectively express the company's future activities.

Anytime you or your department wants new equipment, additional personnel, or anything that comes down to costing the company money, you must justify how that spending will benefit the company in some way. It might mean increased productivity or even financial savings if approved. Unless you can paint a clear picture that shows these benefits, however, you are not likely to have your requests approved. When it comes to setting budget figures, everyone is asking for money. The request that most clearly shows justification usually gets approved if the money is available.

FIGURE 9-12 • Budget committee reviewing department budgets.

What if your office really needs an additional part-time person to get all the work done? How would you go about justifying money being spent from next year's budget when you have been asked to cut your budget by 5 percent? You would begin by determining how cost effective that part-time person will be. Study the following scenario:

One Full-Time Office Professional

Salary and benefits	$34,000
Office supplies used	2,500
Telephone line	500
Depreciation expense	2,700
Total annual cost	$39,700

$39,000 divided by 2,080 hours (52 weeks × 40 hours per week = 2,080 hours) worked per year = $19 per hour cost (rounded)

Amount of hours worked overtime last year = 824 × $28.50 rate = $23,484. (1.5 × 19.00 = 28.50)

One Part-Time Office Professional (from Manpower or Kelly Services, for example)

Salary (no benefits) 1,040 hours @ $14/hour	$14,560
Office supplies (1/2 of full time)	1,250
Telephone (shared with another)	0
Depreciation expense (1/2 of full time)	1,350
Total annual cost	$17,160
Savings ($23,484 – 17,160)	$ 6,324

Management could quickly see that by employing a part-time office professional, $6,324 could be saved.

Stop 'n Check

List three important points about budgeting.

a. _____

b. _____

c. _____

OFFICE SUPPLIES INVENTORY

Office professionals should replenish their office supplies during the time of day or week when they are least busy. Yet they need to plan so they are not searching for supplies when they are pressed for time to complete a rush job. Sometimes an office professional is responsible for stocking office supplies for an entire floor or a department. To manage this, you need a record of supplies on hand.

An easy way to determine supplies needed is to keep an inventory of each item. You can do this on your computer, using a spreadsheet program or on a 4 × 6-inch card to create a **perpetual inventory record**. When you check supplies out of the main supply department or order them directly, enter the amount of each item received and then add the amount to the figure in the balance column. When you take supplies from the supply cabinet or shelf, enter the amount in the checked-out column and then subtract the amount to show the new balance. Encourage others who check out supplies to follow the same procedure.

By looking at the perpetual inventory record, you can decide (1) whether or not the item you need is on hand in sufficient quantity and (2) when it is time to check out or order additional supplies.

In most companies, a request for supplies would begin with a purchase requisition that indicates the supplies needed and the amount to be ordered. Combining all requests for supplies from all departments is cost effective. The purchase requisition is used to generate a purchase order, which is sent to the supplier. The supplier fills the order and sends your company an invoice. A bill of lading, listing the goods shipped to you, will accompany the shipment. When the supplies are delivered, the goods received are checked against the purchase order. If all information is correct, authorization to pay the invoice is made.

Often when several supply orders are made, the invoices will be held until a statement is sent at the end of the month. You may pay all or a portion of the amount due depending on the business arrangement with the company. Figure 9-13 shows the forms cycle. In large companies, a computer generates these forms. Using your computer, you would retrieve the purchase order file and enter the request for office supplies. This information could be saved and sent by e-mail to the purchasing department that would process the order.

Electronic procurement of supplies is improving the way businesses buy from and partner with suppliers. Instead of wading through purchase orders and purchase requisitions that may take days or weeks to process, some

FIGURE 9-13 • Forms cycle.

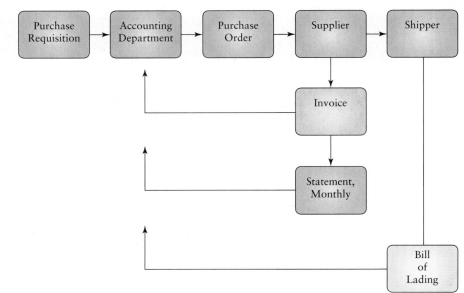

employees go right to their computers and use a Web-based procurement system to summon a virtual shopping cart and order items they need right away over the Internet. These Web-based systems have actually changed employees into strategic buyers by granting them control over a subset of preapproved and budgeted items. They do not have to ask permission to order something. Based on the amount of purchasing power the company grants them, they can order at will and be alerted if their purchase is not allowed or if they've reached their spending limit. The only constraint is they must use approved vendors.

Stop 'n Check

List three tips you learned in this section about replenishing office supplies.

a. _____

b. _____

c. _____

ACCOUNTING DEPARTMENT

The office professional must be familiar with the accounting department. Your company may have a cost center in the accounting department that handles cost control for the company. You must learn the following:

- for which budget account titles and numbers the manager is responsible
- which accounts are used most often
- how the accounts may be used
- what procedures to follow when placing orders or spending money
- how to charge certain expenses and what expenses are allowable
- which department code to use

Often a company hires an outside certified public accountant (CPA) to handle the more complicated aspects of accounting for the company. A bookkeeper is often hired to keep the company's accounting records. The bookkeeper's job involves journalizing (recording each transaction in a journal), calculating payroll and writing checks, paying bills, ordering supplies, and many, many other duties. In a small company, the office professional may be assigned all or part of these tasks. If your job includes bookkeeping, you should have training in this area. The job of an accountant is quite different. Although they know how to keep a set of books, accountants rarely do so. Their job involves creating and interpreting financial statements, advising about financial matters that affect decision making, auditing records, and completing income tax reports. An accountant is required to have a bachelor's degree or higher.

You may find you must provide current accounting information for the CPA. For instance, if you kept the budget information on a spreadsheet, you might be asked to save a copy on disk and send the file to the CPA as an attachment to an e-mail message. If you are using accounting software, such as QuickBooks, to make your entries during the month, you might be asked to make a backup copy of that software, which includes your entries for the period, and send it to the CPA as an attachment to an e-mail message. The CPA would open the software and make the necessary reports from your information, then alert you when you may continue making entries into your software.

Every office professional will be involved in some way with the accounting function in a company. Therefore, as a professional you should know the overall accounting cycle and how it works within the company to efficiently handle the responsibility assigned to your manager.

Ethics in Accounting Procedures

ETHICAL★ISSUES

You probably have read or seen on television news about the financial collapse of many businesses that were ranked among the most admired companies in America—Sunbeam, Enron, WorldCom, Tyco, and HealthSouth. These companies were thought to be among the most stable, profit-making companies in the business world. What went wrong? The inevitable question is, where were the auditors and the accountants as these financial statements of well-being were released? The failure of these companies cost investors millions of dollars. The problem appeared to be one of a lack of ethics, which shook our trust in those involved in accounting practices. Ethics can be taught and learned. In 2003 the Association of Certified Public Accountants incorporated a requirement that to maintain their license to practice, CPAs are required to have an ethics course once every three years.

Because of the high cost of dishonesty, you must be a person others see as having high values. You must be a person who would not compromise those values, especially when working in the accounting area. High ethical standards are required in every phase of the office professional's job.

International Currency Exchange

An office professional might find it necessary to provide his or her manager with the current **currency exchange rate** available when the manager travels abroad. You might also have to exchange money in the United States before the manager leaves or exchange money back into U.S. dollars after the manager returns from a trip abroad.

You can research the current exchange rate for any country's currency in many ways. For instance, you can quickly search on the Internet, call your local bank, or check the newspaper. Or if your airport has international flights, you can usually find a company at the airport that exchanges currency. Exchange rates are quoted per $1 U.S. Once you know the rate, you can multiply the rate times the number of dollars you want exchanged. For example, suppose the Japanese Yen exchange rate is 115.0801. To change $75 U.S. to Yens, multiply $75 \times 115.0801 = 8,631$ Japanese Yen.

When exchanging foreign currency for U.S. dollars, most banks exchange only currency and not coins. When your manager arrives at his or her foreign destination, exchanging currency is often one of the first things to be done. Even if it is a small amount, he or she might need money for transportation to the hotel, tip money, or money on which to eat. To avoid having to do this while traveling, you might be asked to obtain the foreign currency prior to the manager's trip.

Quick Tips

KEEP YOUR COMPUTER WORK AREA CLEAN AND YOUR COMPUTER SAFE!

Keeping your computer clean doesn't take a lot of skill and doesn't need to cost a lot of money. In most cases, just taking a few simple precautions, using common sense, and being ready for the unexpected is all it takes.

Keep a clean work area:

- Don't eat or drink over your keyboard. Crumbs and liquid can damage the unit.
- Don't stack items on top of a large monitor! This will prevent the air vents from working properly.
- Never place magnetic items on your computer processing unit (CPU, also called a tower). Magnets can erase data.

Keep your computer safe:

- Never share your password with others.
- Avoid fancy screensavers, emoticons, smileys, and so on. You may be opening your computer to Adware (software that installs on your hard drive and often causes pop-up ads to appear periodically). You don't need the aggravation.
- Add helpful browser toolbars from well-known companies such as Google or Yahoo. These browsers help you block pop-up screens as well.
- Stay alert to what is happening on your screen and don't be taken in by announcements that something is wrong with your computer. All problems should be checked only by your information systems department.

Remember, prevention is better (and cheaper) than the cure sometimes.

Concept Review and Reinforcement

Review of Key Concepts

OUTCOME	CONCEPT
1. Identify and explain the use of a cashier's check, bank draft, bank money order, and traveler's check.	• A cashier's check, also called a treasurer's check or official check, is written by an authorized officer of the bank on its own funds; it guarantees payment to the payee by the drawer's bank. • A bank draft can be used to transfer money to another person or organization in another geographical location within the United States or abroad. A bank draft payable in foreign currency may also be purchased. • A bank money order similar to a postal money order may be obtained from a bank. • Traveler's checks are used in place of cash with protection against loss or theft.
2. Identify the various ways funds are transferred electronically.	• Automated teller machines (ATMs), located at banks, in shopping malls, in supermarkets, and in many other places, enable customers to obtain cash and make deposits using a personal identification number (PIN). • Debit cards are used in the place of checks. Debit cards are obtained through the bank by completing a credit application for a debit card through companies such as VISA or MasterCard. • Automatic debits are preauthorized automated transfer of funds for an individual or company from one account to another within the same financial institution. • Web banking provides easy management of banking transactions online wherever you have access to the Internet. • Telephone transfers can be made by calling the company to whom you wish to make payment and giving them the check number and amount so the company can draft the amount from your checking account.
3. Prepare checks, make stop-payment notification, and endorse checks.	• At the request of the drawer, a bank will place stop-payment notification on a check for a fee at any time until it has cleared the bank upon which it is drawn. • Banks require check endorsement (signing) by the payee when a check is presented for cash or deposit. • A blank endorsement is writing the signature on the back left of the check the signature to whom the check is written. • A restrictive endorsement limits the use of a check to the purpose stated in the endorsement such as "for deposit only." • A full endorsement also called a two-party check, transfers a check to a specified person or organization.
4. Reconcile a bank statement.	• Reconciling a bank statement makes the checkbook balance agree with the bank's balance by adding to the bank statement any outstanding checks or deposits in transit; by subtracting bank services charges, adding any credits (interest) and subtracting any debits (errors made in the recording of checks) from the checkbook balance.

5. Describe what a petty cash fund is and how it is used.

When the amount of office expenditure is small and payment should be made immediately, it may be more convenient to make the payment by cash rather than by check. To provide cash to pay for incidental items, such as messenger service, postage due on a package, or emergency purchases of office supplies, organizations establish a petty cash fund from $10 to $100 or more, depending on the cash needs for a certain period, usually a month.

6. Calculate a weekly payroll on a payroll register.

- Calculate gross earning by multiplying the hourly rate by 40; then calculate overtime amount by multiplying hours worked times hourly rate times 1.5. Add overtime and regular time to total gross earnings.
- Multiply gross earnings by 6.5 percent to calculate social security.
- Multiply gross earnings by 1.45 percent to calculate Medicare.
- Add all deductions.
- Subtract deductions from gross pay to calculate net pay.

7. Explain the parts of an income statement and balance sheet.

- The parts of an income statement are revenue and expense accounts.
- The parts of a balance sheet are assets, liabilities, and owner's equity accounts. Assets must equal total liabilites and owner's equity amounts.

8. Explain the budgeting process.

Budgeting is the process of planning future business operations and defining those plans in a formal report. The report expressed in financial terms is called a *budget*.

9. Keep an inventory of supplies and order supplies as needed.

Office professionals should replenish their office supplies during the time of day or week when they are least busy. To manage supplies, you need a record of supplies on hand.

10. Discuss the importance of demonstrating ethical conduct in financial matters.

Because of the high cost of dishonesty, as an office professional you must be a person others see as having high values. You must be a person who would not compromise those values, especially when working in the accounting area.

11. Demonstrate how to change U.S. dollars to foreign money using currency exchange rates.

Research in the newspaper or online the exchange rate for the country to be visited. Multiply the exchange rate by U.S. $1. U.S. dollars can be exchanged at most large airports that provide international flights.

Key Terms

Assets. What is owned in accounting, whether paid for or not.

Automatic deposit. Funds that can be automatically deposited using an American Bankers Association (ABA) electronic routing number and the account number in which the money is to be deposited.

Automated teller machines (ATMs). Machines located in banks, shopping malls, or supermarkets that enable bank customers to obtain cash and make deposits.

Automatic debits. Preauthorized automated transfer of funds for an individual or company from one account to another within the same financial institution.

Balance sheet. Summarizes the balances of assets, liabilities, and owner's equity and reports what the business is worth on any given day.

Bank draft. Check drawn by the bank on its own funds.

Bank money order. Similar to a postal money order but obtained from a bank.

Bank reconciliation. Comparison of the final balance on a bank statement with the checkbook balance, then accounting for any difference.

Blank endorsement. The signature of the payee on the back of a check.

Budget. The budgeting process expressed in financial terms.

Budgeting. The process of planning future business operations and defining those plans in a formal report.

Canceled checks. Checks paid by the bank.

Cashier's check. Also called a *treasurer's check* or *official check*, a check written by an authorized officer of the bank on its own funds that guarantees payment to the payee by the drawer's bank.

Check. A written order of a depositor upon a commercial bank to pay to the order of a designated party or to a bearer a specified sum of money on demand.

Check endorsement. The signature on the back of a check presented for cash or deposit.

Circular E, Employer's Tax Guide. Federal income tax table booklet consisting of tables and instructions for federal income tax withholdings.

Currency exchange rate. The ratio at which $1 U.S. may be traded for a foreign currency.

Current assets. Assets that can be sold or turned into cash quickly or can be consumed in a short period.

Current liabilities. Short-term debts usually paid in one year.

Debit cards. Take the place of a check; money is deducted immediately from one's checking account.

Deductions. Amounts deducted from gross pay, such as group medical insurance, dental insurance, union dues, savings bonds, and charitable contributions.

Direct payroll deposit. Payroll money automatically deposited to an account.

Drawee. The bank upon which a check is drawn.

Drawer. The person who draws the check on his or her account.

Electronic funds transfer (EFT). An electronic delivery system for financial transactions.

Employee data. The name, marital status, withholding allowances, and hourly rate information for each employee for payroll purposes.

Expenses. Cost of operation of a company.

Federal income tax. Money withheld from a paycheck and paid to the federal government as a tax on wages earned.

Fixed assets. Assets with a long life that will be used over many years in the operation of the company.

Full endorsement. Also called a two-party check, this signature and instructions on the back of a check, transfer the check to a specified person or organization.

Gross profit on sales. Difference between revenue and the cost of the merchandise sold.

Health insurance (HI). Commonly called *Medicare*, one of the two taxes required for all employees by the federal government.

Income statement. Also called a *profit and loss (P & L) statement* or an *operating statement*; a financial record showing the results of the operation of a company in terms of money earned and expenses incurred.

Liabilities. What a company owes.

Long-term liabilities. Debts due for long periods.

Master budget. Consists of various budgets that collectively express the future activities of the business.

Medicare. Federal health insurance for older Americans.

Net pay. Total earnings minus deductions.

Old Age, Survivors, and Disability Insurance (OASDI). Commonly called *social security*, one of the taxes required for all employees by the federal government.

Outstanding checks. Checks written but not paid by the bank.

Overtime hours. Any hours worked over the first forty hours in a weekly payroll period.

Owner's equity. What a business is worth.

Payee. Person to whom payment is to be made.

Payroll register. A record that summarizes, for each employee, the status of wages earned, payroll deductions, and final take-home pay.

Perpetual inventory record. A record used to keep track of office supplies inventory.

Petty cash fund. A fund used to provide cash for the purchase of incidental office items and services.

Petty cash voucher. A receipt for each expenditure from the petty cash fund.

Plant and equipment. Also called *fixed assets*, assets with a long life that will be used over many years in the company's operation.

Regular hours. The first forty hours worked in a weekly payroll period.

Restrictive endorsement. Limits the use of a check to the purpose stated in the endorsement, such as "Pay to the order of."

Stop-payment notification. Notice to stop payment on a check for a fee

at any time until the check has cleared the bank upon which it is drawn.

Telephone transfers. Payments made by telephone.

Total earnings. Regular earnings plus overtime earnings.

Traveler's checks. Checks used in place of cash.

Web banking. Service that provides easy management of banking transactions online wherever a person has access to the Internet.

For Your Discussion

Retrieve file C9-DQ from your student data disk.

DIRECTIONS

Enter your response after each question or statement.

1. Describe EFT and explain the various ways funds are transferred.

2. Name the various check endorsements and explain how each is used.

3. Summarize the steps for reconciling a bank statement.

4. Summarize the steps for completing a petty cash record.

5. When you replenish the petty cash fund, how do you determine the amount of money to request?

6. Summarize the steps for completing a payroll register.

7. What is included on an income statement, and how do these items help management?

8. What is included on a balance sheet, and how do these items help management?

9. Discuss the importance of demonstrating ethical conduct in financial matters.

10. Summarize the procedures for efficiently keeping up with office supplies.

Building Your Office Skills

Exploring the Workplace: *Activities*

1. Call two local banks, credit unions, or other financial institutions and obtain information about certified checks, official checks, bank drafts, money orders, traveler's checks, ATM charges, and the availability and cost, if any, of online account access and bill payment services. Write a comparison of your findings at the two institutions.

2. If you have a job, ask if someone is in charge of the petty cash fund at your workplace. Interview that person and write a report on the procedures followed. If you do not work, ask someone you know who works to find out this information at his or her company, or call local companies and ask to set up an interview. Explain the purpose of your visit is to gather information for a class project.

3. Interview an office professional and ask him or her about the methods used for setting up a budget each year. Identify the process in a step-by-step approach—what does he or she do first, second, third, and so on. Summarize your findings, including the steps.

4. With your team member locate exchange rates for six countries. Create a table showing the country, the current exchange rate, and the amount of foreign currency you would be able to obtain for $75 U.S. Be prepared to share the results with other class members and your instructor.

Developing Critical Thinking Skills: *Problem Solving on the Job*

Retrieve file C9-OJS from your student data disk.

Directions

Enter your response after each situation.

1. **Lost traveler's checks.** Your boss is out of town and calls to tell you his briefcase was stolen from his hotel room this afternoon. He had locked his remaining traveler's checks in the briefcase. He is frantic and doesn't know what to do. Analyze the situation and outline a plan of action for him, assuming you have followed all the correct procedures concerning traveler's checks.

2. **Petty cash fund.** You are new on the job. Because you keep the petty cash fund, Leah, a coworker, has come to you and asked to borrow $10 until tomorrow. Other employees have told you the manager does not care if they borrow from petty cash. No one has asked you until today. Analyze the situation and explain what you would do and why.

3. **Payroll.** You supervise the payroll department. Several department heads have recently been late in turning in time cards, and your employees have been complaining they are rushed and believe being rushed has caused them to make the careless errors in employees' paychecks that have been reported. It is budget time, and you know your manager wants the department heads to get their budget recommendations in—they are under pressure to finish. Explain how you will handle the situation.

4. **Money missing from petty cash fund.** You have been responsible for handling the petty cash fund in your department. The money and petty cash receipts are kept in a drawer that is locked, and both you and your manager have keys to the drawer. When you attempt to balance your receipts and cash remaining in the drawer, you realize that $50 is missing from the fund. After an employee borrowed from the fund on Monday, you balanced the fund; it is now Thursday. Analyze the situation and explain what you would do and why.

Using the Web: *Research Activities*

A. You may have heard on the news about people being robbed at ATMs and the importance of being safe when withdrawing money. The American Bankers Association offers some consumer tips on the Internet for ATM safety. Follow these procedures to locate the tips:

1. Enter the following: www.aba.com.
2. Locate Consumer Connection at the left of the screen. Click on ATMs under Security, and read the ATM Safety Tips article.
3. Print a copy and summarize your findings in an informational report. Include what you think are the three most important tips.

B. Locate information about the Federal Reserve System by searching the key words *federal reserve bank system*.

1. Browse and read about the Federal Reserve System.
2. Explain how it is structured, what it includes, and how it is governed.
3. Select the reserve district nearest to you and find three points you consider important.
4. Explain how the Federal Reserve System affects you as an employee, consumer, and citizen.
5. Summarize all your information and write an informational report about the Federal Reserve System.

Get Tech Wise: *Microsoft® Office Excel*

Create a Personal Income Statement for You or Your Family

Situation: You are to create an income statement based on one month's earnings and expenses.

Solution: Use an Excel worksheet to create your income statement. This experience would be similar to creating an income statement for a company except income and expenses would be different.

1. Plan an income statement on a sheet of paper. Use your checkbook for last month, if possible. If not, estimate what you spent for each area if you do not have a record. Use these areas: Rent/House payment, car payment, utilities (water, electricity, phone, gas), food, gasoline, clothing, car repair, insurance, entertainment (movies, eating out, sports outings, amusement parks), and any other expenses you incurred.

2. Enter your income statement in Excel. Use your net income figure minus expenses. Use the format for an income statement shown in Figure 9-10.

Enter the following information as your heading in Excel:

Your name

Course Title and Section

Income Statement for Month Ended: (Enter date)

3. Determine how much money you have available over expenses by subtracting expenses from total income. You can enter a formula in Excel. Ask your instructor if you have questions.

4. Key the answer to a-c two rows below your income statement in Excel:

a. Based on the information in your income statement, identify where most of your money is going.

b. In which area could you be more conservative and spend less money?

c. Commit to making one change in your spending habits this next month. What will that change be?

Improving Your Writing Skills: *Grammar Workshop*

Retrieve C9-WRKS from your student data disk.

Supreme Appliances

Simulation: *In the Office at Supreme Appliances*

Application 9-A

Completing a Bank Reconciliation

Supplies Needed: Copy of Figure 9-3, Bank Statement; Form 9-A, Bank Reconciliation Form.

Retrieve file C9-AP-A from your data disk.

Directions

On November 26 you received the bank statement for the November Sales Seminar account for Supreme Appliances, shown in Figure 9-3. On November 23 you received a check from Al's Print Shop for $170.00 as a 10 percent discount for paying promptly. You mailed this check to the bank, but it is not shown on the bank statement. You have checked off all the canceled checks and the following checks are outstanding and have not been paid by the bank:

No. 2111	$386.50
No. 2115	$ 52.40
No. 2120	$110.80
No. 2121	$ 12.15

A service charge of $20.00 has been charged to your account.

Ending balance in the checkbook was $6,430.55. Reconcile the bank statement shown in Figure 9-3 using Form 9-A. Key the bank reconciliation.

Application 9-B

Handling Petty Cash

Supplies needed: Form 9-B, Petty Cash Envelope; Form 9-B-1 through Form 9-B-12, Petty Cash Vouchers.

Retrieve file C9-AP-B from your data disk.

Directions

Mary Higgins, who had been handling petty cash transactions for the marketing division at Supreme Appliances, was transferred to another division, and you were asked to handle petty cash.

You started with the beginning balance of $100.00 in the petty cash envelope. In the "Received" column, write $100.00.

You paid out cash for the following items. Complete each of the voucher forms (Form 9-A-1 through Form 9-A-9) for each of the following transactions.

December 1   Paid Meyers Stationery $3.69 for special drawing pen. (Supplies)

December 3   Paid U.S. Postmaster $29.00 for mailing box priority mail. (Postage)

December 3   Paid U.S. Postmaster $6.85 for postage and insurance on a package. (Postage)

December 4   Paid City Taxi $8.50 to deliver a package to Airlift Shipping office. (Miscellaneous)

December 5   Paid Williams Drugstore $5.25 for two magazines for the reception area. (Supplies)

December 8   Paid B. J. Florist $15.50 for a plant for the reception area. (Miscellaneous)

December 8   Paid Williams Drugstore $6.80 for fertilizer tablets for plants at the office. (Miscellaneous)

December 9   Paid Western Union $15.95 for fax charge. (Miscellaneous)

December 9   Paid Meyers Stationery $4.25 for box of No. 10 plain envelopes. (Supplies)

Your ending balance in the fund is $4.21. On the petty cash envelope, record the totals for the Paid Out and the Distribution of Payments columns. Carry the balance forward to the Received column but label it as "balance." Type a petty cash report in a memo format and ask for enough money to bring the petty cash fund to $100.00. Attach the petty cash vouchers to the report. You are authorized to sign the vouchers.

Application 9-C

Completing a Payroll Register

Supplies needed: Form 9-C, Weekly Payroll Register; or spreadsheet software.

Retrieve file C9-AP-C.xls from your data disk.

Directions

Ms. Quevedo was asked to assign someone to fill in for John Dewhearst, the company payroll clerk, who is on vacation. You and Ms. Quevedo had recently discussed the need for employees to train to be able to do one another's jobs in case of absences. You asked Ms. Quevedo if you could fill in for Mr. Dewhearst to get some training in payroll procedures. She agreed. Follow the steps given in the chapter to complete the following payroll register.

1. Information you will need:
   a. For all hours over forty, employees receive time-and-one-half.
   b. Group medical deduction is $22 for each employee.
   c. Group dental insurance is $12 for each employee.

2. Use a spreadsheet file to complete the payroll register. If you do not have access to spreadsheet software, complete by hand the payroll register shown on Form 9-C-1 in the working papers.

3. Print one copy of the completed payroll if you are using a spreadsheet.

Building Your Portfolio

With a team member or your instructor's help, select the following documents: Bank reconciliation, petty cash envelope, and payroll register of your work from Chapter 9. Remember these documents must be error-free. If instructed, place the documents in plastic protection sheets and add to your notebook. Follow your instructor's directions for formatting, assembling, and turning in the portfolio.

10 Scheduling Appointments and Receiving Visitors

chapter **outline**

Making Appointments

Keeping an Appointment Schedule
Making Appointments by Telephone
  or E-Mail
Using an Electronic Calendar
Using Web-Based Calendars
Using Paper Desk Calendars
Making Entries in Calendars
Canceling Appointments
Preparing a List of Appointments

Receiving Visitors

Greeting Visitors
Attending to the Visitor Who Has
  an Appointment
Attending to Staff Visitors
Terminating Meetings
Interrupting a Meeting
Attending to Unscheduled Visitors
Refusing Appointments

Managing Difficult Visitors

Dealing with Unwanted Visitors

Office Security

Ethics and Visitors

Hosting International Visitors

learning **outcomes**

When you have completed this chapter, you
should be able to:

- Schedule and confirm appointments for
  one or more managers.
- Use appropriate scheduling aids.
- Greet and direct visitors.
- Manage difficult visitors.
- Identify potential ethical implications
  when sharing information.
- Host international visitors.

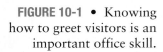

FIGURE 10-1 • Knowing how to greet visitors is an important office skill.

Every time you meet another person, whether a visitor or coworker, you are influencing that person's image of your company, department, or office. You should work toward ensuring that each person you meet believes you sincerely want to help him or her. The impression you leave will make each person want to come back again.

In this chapter you will learn about making appointments, receiving visitors, managing difficult visitors, and hosting international visitors. Using these skills efficiently will offer many opportunities to effect a positive image for your company (Figure 10-1).

Making Appointments

Who makes appointments for managers? The answer is both managers and their assistants. The freedom an office professional is given in making appointments depends on the office professional's ability to schedule the manager's time exactly as he or she wants it scheduled. From the first day on the job, you have two distinct responsibilities concerning your manager's appointments: to keep track of all appointments so one is not overlooked and to keep both your manager's appointment calendar and your calendar up to the minute to avoid conflicts in scheduling.

KEEPING AN APPOINTMENT SCHEDULE

You and your manager will need to keep an appointment schedule. Begin by learning (1) what your manager's preferences are for scheduling appointments, (2) which appointments should be given priority, and (3) how much time appointments should take.

Your best guides for scheduling appointments will be your knowledge of your manager's work habits and your awareness of who his or her business associates and friends are. You will learn this by observing how your manager uses time and works with associates and by being aware of your manager's plans. Remember what your manager tells you about how he or she works best. His or her work habits may vary with the peaks and valleys of the job. Someone once said the busier one is, the more work one manages to get done. Your manager may be a person who speeds up when the workload is heavy, scheduling just as many appointments, but allowing less time for each caller than during a normal workweek.

Before you leave in the evening, check the appointments your manager has for the next day to make certain any information or files are available should they be needed. At some point during the day have a mini-meeting with your manager to update your calendars. Couple your knowledge of how your manager plans work with the previous overall suggestions and use them as guides in setting up appointments.

MAKING APPOINTMENTS BY TELEPHONE OR E-MAIL

When someone requests an appointment by telephone or e-mail, establish immediately whether your manager is the person the caller should see. You will be able to decide this as soon as the caller tells you the reason for requesting an appointment.

If your manager has to approve all appointments, tell the caller you must confirm the appointment, and you will let the caller know if the appointment has been set as soon as you can check with the manager. Be sure to follow through on what you say you will do. Check with your manager and then call the person or send an e-mail message confirming the appointment.

Office professionals who work for executives, doctors, and dentists usually finalize an appointment during the initial telephone conversation. You may be charged with the responsibility for making your manager's appointments, and when you are, you can eliminate almost all follow-up telephone calls. Give the caller a definite appointment. If you have any doubt about your manager confirming it, say, "I will call you back immediately if there should be a conflict I do not know about." This method is the opposite of following through on all appointments to confirm them.

Make sure both you and the person seeking the appointment understand the correct time, date, and location. While you are talking on the telephone, repeat the date, day, and time and write them down or enter them into your calendar immediately to reduce the chance of a mistake. Ask callers if they need directions to your location. Unless you already have it, be sure to get the telephone number and e-mail address of each person who makes an appointment. You will need the information to confirm the appointment, or you may need the information to change the time of a definite appointment.

USING AN ELECTRONIC CALENDAR

The traditional calendar has been turned into something that will stagger the imagination, all because of the personal computer. If your organization has a fully integrated electronic network, you will be able to use an **electronic calendar** (Figure 10-2) on your computer to schedule all of your manager's appointments. Office automation systems are available that enable the user to switch from one function to another with a simple keystroke (Alt+Tab in Microsoft® Office) or movement of the mouse. You can exit an application, such as word processing, to enter appointments, rearrange the schedule to make substitutions, or cancel appointments and then quickly return to the application.

How to Set Up Appointments

✔ Leave Monday mornings free to start on plans for the week and to handle the mail that has accumulated during the weekend.

✔ Schedule no appointments for your manager on his or her first day back after being out of the office for several days.

✔ Avoid crowding your manager's schedule with appointments the day before he or she leaves on a trip. Preparation for the trip has priority.

✔ Schedule appointments so they do not overlap.

✔ Be aware of top-priority meetings and allow plenty of time for them.

✔ Avoid scheduling a top-priority meetings immediately after one of equal significance.

✔ Avoid scheduling an appointment for your manager in another location immediately after a meeting that is likely to run overtime.

✔ Schedule unstructured time frames of ten to fifteen minutes between appointments, giving your manager a chance to make telephone calls, sign letters, think about the next conference, or just take a break.

✔ Schedule appointments with others with whom your manager has a close working relationship late in the afternoon. These appointments are easy to shift when your manager is not keeping to the schedule.

✔ At the time someone is requesting an appointment by telephone, suggest specific times, preferably giving the person a chance to select a time from at least two choices.

✔ Predetermine regularly scheduled times for answering the mail and taking care of other daily activities and consistently reserve the time slots for these activities.

✔ Learn which meeting can be limited to fifteen minutes or less.

✔ When you are arranging an appointment for a short period, let the person know the length of the appointment. If you are setting up the appointment for 2 p.m., say tactfully, "from 2 until 2:15."

✔ When you arrange for an unexpected visitor to see your manager, let the visitor know the next appointment is within ten minutes if it truly is.

✔ Arrange appointments in another part of the city so your manager, if he or she chooses, can go directly from home to an early-morning appointment or not return to the office after a late-afternoon appointment.

FIGURE 10-2 • Microsoft® Outlook electronic calendar displayed on a computer screen.
©Microsoft Corporation. All rights reserved.

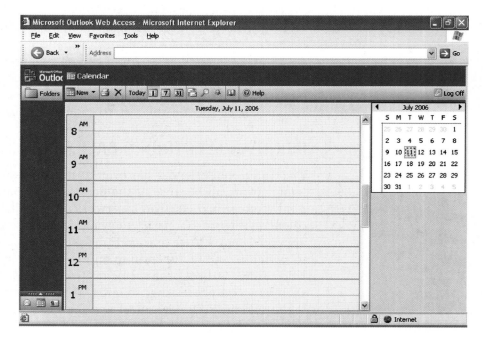

Automated calendaring systems allow you to have an accurate, up-to-the-minute schedule. You can also enter items in the tickler file, add reminders, and note any items that need to be acted on at a definite time of the day. The page on the screen looks the same as the page in a desk calendar. You can select a meeting time by comparing your manager's schedule with that of others on the network, who make their calendars available.

You need to keep only one computerized calendar for your manager because either you or your manager can access the calendar at any time. At the end of the day, you can print or type your manager's schedule for the next business day and place it on his or her desk if preferred.

Certain major software programs combine several functions with the calendar. One of the most popular examples is Microsoft® Outlook. Since many companies use Microsoft® Office, they also use Outlook because of its e-mail capabilities and its calendar. You learned about communicating using e-mail in Chapter 6 and e-mail etiquette in mailing in Chapter 7. Outlook also takes managing your schedule and information a step further than just a calendar. Outlook allows you to juggle everything from electronic mail and calendars to contacts and task lists as you have learned earlier. You can "connect, communicate, and collaborate," according to Microsoft®. You will learn in Chapter 12 about how Outlook allows you to work more efficiently to collaborate with others on planning meetings and conferences.

All previous versions of Outlook offered a calendar for the user, but one of the most popular changes in Outlook 2003 is Outlook's ability to display multiple calendars side by side. For example, if you have created a separate calendar for your personal appointments, you can view both your work and personal calendar side-by-side. With the Delegate Access feature in Outlook, one person can use his or her own copy of Outlook to easily manage another person's calendar. For example, an administrative assistant can manage the calendar of his or her manager. When the manager designates the assistant as a delegate, the assistant can create, move, or delete appointments and can organize meetings on the manager's behalf. Another example is the manager planning a meeting with another person to discuss an issue. You could bring to your display both your manager's calendar and the other person's calendar on the same screen. To share calendars, a person must give you permission. Assuming the person has given you permission to view his or her calendar, you may open it and view it in your window to see when the person is available to meet with your manager. Outlook's calendars are color-coded, making it easy to identify each person's calendar. You can show up to thirteen calendars; however, it would be difficult to manage that many at one time.

Stop 'n Check

1. List at least three tips for scheduling appointments.

   a. _____

   b. _____

   c. _____

2. List Microsoft® Outlook 2003 Calendar's most popular feature.

   _____

USING WEB-BASED CALENDARS

The Internet is taking electronic calendars a step further as well by offering **Web-based calendars** for free. The best part is they *are* free. These calendars are scaled-down versions of the all-in-one scheduling, e-mail, and address-book software that you find on your desktop computer. In the long run, Web calendars will be more useful for the following reasons:

- They store information online; therefore, accessibility is a major advantage.
- They are communal, plugged in, and wired to the world.
- They are available in various languages.
- They are integrated with e-mail, address book, instant messaging, and areas where community groups can publish material.
- Three levels of permission may be offered. Events can be made totally private, totally visible to everyone from anywhere on the Web, or a hybrid in which other people can see which time slots are booked but not for what purpose (see www.calendar.yahoo.com).

The Web-based calendars are becoming important tools in the struggle to attract loyal audiences to commercial sites. Each free calendar asks you to register and become a member; then, a username or sign-on ID and password are established.

USING PAPER DESK CALENDARS

Your manager may use a computer but does not use an electronic calendar and prefers to use a paper desk calendar instead. Perhaps computer capacity is limited, and word processing, database management, and accounting functions are given priority. Your manager may have the responsibility of keeping his or her own calendar and may prefer not to take the time to enter information in the computer because of the number of entries and changes required. As a result, you may need to use desk calendars to keep appointments. Although certainly not necessary, some managers keep both paper and electronic calendars.

Choose appointment calendars and yearbooks that meet both your manager's needs and yours. A wide selection is available, and they are made in a variety of sizes with a choice of a page for each month, a page for each week, or a page for each day. Figure 10-3 shows a monthly calendar.

Executive Appointment Books and Calendars

Managers who make commitments months in advance like a full month displayed on one page with small insert calendars of the preceding and the following months. The monthly calendar enables them to review engagements without flipping through several pages. Managers who make several appointments in one day need a daily appointment calendar.

Many managers prefer pocket calendars or small **electronic organizers** that include a calendar, scheduler, and address area for immediate access. Palm's Treo™ smartphones seamlessly combine a full-featured mobile phone with either a Palm Powered™ or Windows Mobile® organizer with a calendar and personal data assistant (PDA) with wireless communications

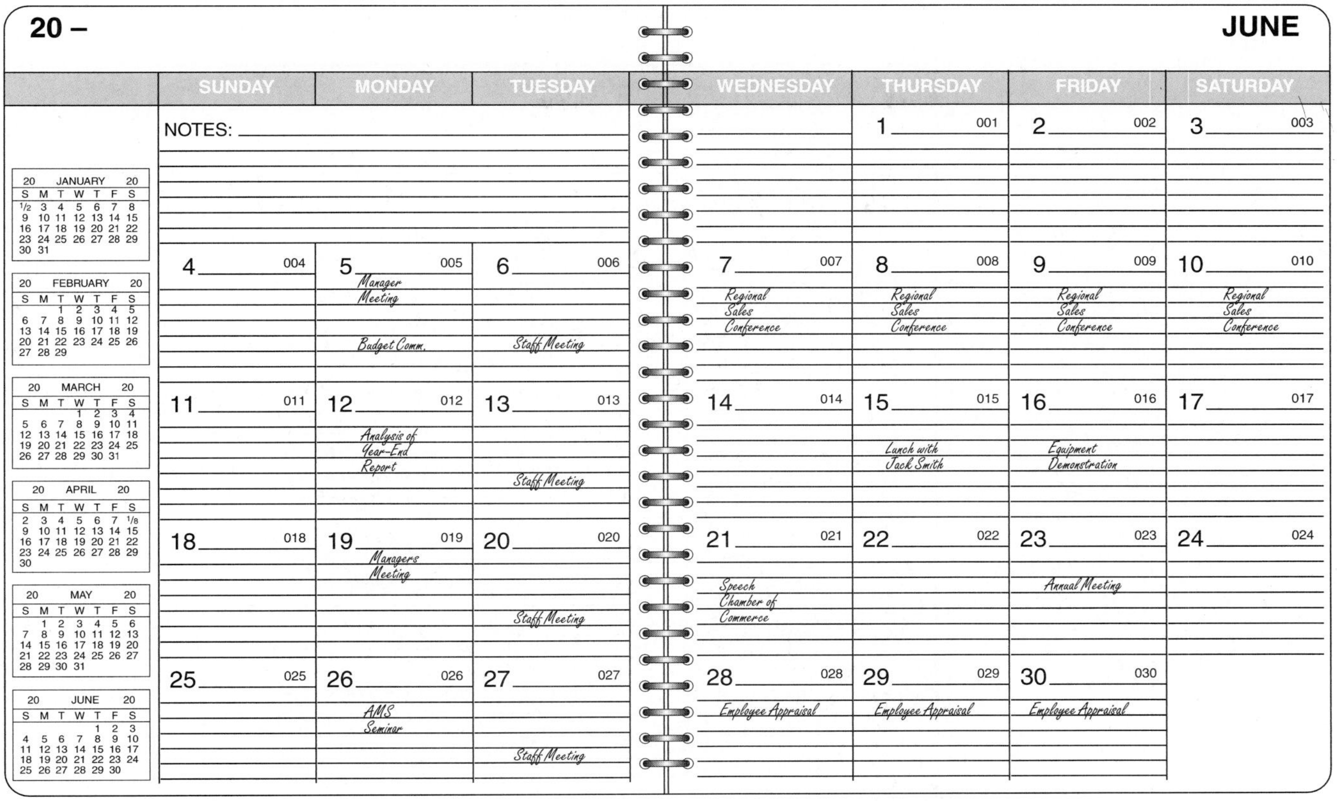

20 –   **JUNE**

SUNDAY	MONDAY	TUESDAY	WEDNESDAY	THURSDAY	FRIDAY	SATURDAY
NOTES:			1 — 001	2 — 002	3 — 003	
4 — 004	5 — 005 *Manager Meeting* / *Budget Comm.*	6 — 006 *Staff Meeting*	7 — 007 *Regional Sales Conference*	8 — 008 *Regional Sales Conference*	9 — 009 *Regional Sales Conference*	10 — 010 *Regional Sales Conference*
11 — 011	12 — 012 *Analysis of Year-End Report*	13 — 013 *Staff Meeting*	14 — 014	15 — 015 *Lunch with Jack Smith*	16 — 016 *Equipment Demonstration*	17 — 017
18 — 018	19 — 019 *Managers Meeting*	20 — 020 *Staff Meeting*	21 — 021 *Speech Chamber of Commerce*	22 — 022	23 — 023 *Annual Meeting*	24 — 024
25 — 025	26 — 026 *AMS Seminar*	27 — 027 *Staff Meeting*	28 — 028 *Employee Appraisal*	29 — 029 *Employee Appraisal*	30 — 030 *Employee Appraisal*	

Mini calendars (left column): JANUARY, FEBRUARY, MARCH, APRIL, MAY, JUNE.

FIGURE 10-3 • Monthly calendar.

including e-mail, messaging, and Web browsing in a small, compact, easy-to-use device.

The Office Professional's Daily Appointment Calendar

If you are not using an electronic calendar, you need a preprinted calendar divided into fifteen- or thirty-minute segments of each day, with the time printed in the left column. See Figure 10-4.

Enter in your calendar all of your manager's appointments, including reminders of tasks that must be taken care of within a given time slot and a list of all the activities that must be followed through by your manager at the end of the day. In addition, prepare a to-do list to remind you of other tasks you must perform at some time during the day. Review Chapter 4 for suggestions about to-do lists.

MAKING ENTRIES IN CALENDARS

All appointments made by telephone, by e-mail, by letter, and in person—including those appointments your manager makes—should be entered in both the manager's and your appointment calendars. Regularly scheduled meetings should also be entered in the appointment calendars.

Be consistent and prompt in recording all appointments and commitments in your manager's calendar. To do this, adopt a systematic plan for making the entries and then do not deviate from your plan.

FIGURE 10-4 • Daily appointment calendar.

DATE		Monday, December 9, 20--
8	00	
	15	
	30	
	45	
9	00	
	15	Call for hotel reservation
	30	R. C. Thompson, ABC Corp.
	45	
10	00	Manager's Staff Meeting
	15	
	30	
	45	
11	00	Explain procedure changes
	15	
	30	Ruth Raines, Adv.
	45	
12	00	
	15	
	30	
	45	
1	00	
	15	
	30	Interview Applicant—
	45	Jane Albright
2	00	Assemble forms
	15	
	30	Len Smith, Forms Design
	45	
3	00	
	15	
	30	Interview Applicant—
	45	Louise Petruzza
4	00	Complete Proposal
	15	
	30	
	45	Meet Jane Hunter – Airport
5	00	
	15	
	30	
	45	
6	00	AMA Meeting
	15	
	30	
	45	

Make tentative entries in pencil and firm commitments in ink. As soon as the appointment is confirmed, write it in ink in both calendars. Write small enough to put complete information in the space provided in the calendar. Draw a diagonal line through each entry once the conference is held or the task is completed; then you will readily know any item not crossed out is yet to be completed.

You may need to request information about appointments your manager makes, especially those made while away from the office. Do this at least once a day. If your manager spends a few minutes each morning discussing the appointments for the day, ask then or suggest that he or she jot down the information and hand it to you soon after the appointment is made.

Once each day, preferably at the end of the day, check your manager's calendar with your calendar to make sure all recorded appointments are identical in both calendars.

At the end of each day, review the items for that day to ensure that all have been crossed out. In fact, never turn the page of your calendar until you have searched for incomplete items. Transfer any item that still needs attention to the page for the following business day.

When you are uncertain whether your manager returned a telephone call or followed through on a promise he or she made, type a separate note concerning each item you think might be incomplete at the time you are clearing your calendar. As you check these notes with your manager, you can throw away the unnecessary notes and give your manager the others as reminders to follow through.

Once each week, either on Friday afternoon or on Monday morning, check your tickler file for the entire week. Make notations, if you have not already done so, in both appointment calendars concerning work that must be completed by a specified time within the week.

CANCELING APPOINTMENTS

When someone calls to cancel an appointment, always offer to schedule another one. Be sure to free both appointment calendars, if you keep two calendars, of the canceled appointment.

When you must cancel an appointment for your manager, let the person whose appointment is being canceled know at once. Get in touch with the person by telephone or e-mail.

Use the following guidelines for canceling an appointment:

- Express regret on your manager's behalf.
- Mention the appointment must be changed.
- State a reason in general terms.
- Offer to schedule another appointment.

Think twice about how you are going to state the reason. You can say your manager was called out of town, if he or she was, but as a general rule, do not say where or why. By doing so you could reveal confidential information. Avoid dwelling on what your manager cannot do. Quickly shift your conversation to a positive comment, such as, "She is expected back in the office on Monday. Shall I set up another appointment for you early next week?"

PREPARING A LIST OF APPOINTMENTS

Some managers prefer to have a separate list of appointments for each day, such as the one shown in Figure 10-5. If so, near the end of each day, prepare your manager's list of appointments for the next business day in a form he or she prefers. Keep a duplicate copy on your desk. If you are using a computer to keep the appointment calendar, a printout may be sufficient.

FIGURE 10-5 • List of appointments.

	APPOINTMENTS FOR MONDAY, MAY 25, 20--
TIME	**APPOINTMENT**
0800	Meet with Dini Corbett to discuss ACCC promotions. Remember to take the F. P. Manufacturing folder.
0930	Interview Linda Nimchuck (applicant for Office Manager).
1100	Meet with Total Management Committee - Room 520. Connie Walters should be contacted prior to meeting for info. on the conference.
1200	Lunch with Sandy Wolfe at the Pasta Place.
100	Pick up Edward Kaye at the Greater Rochester International Airport.
200	Meet with Edward Kaye, Heather Thomas, Ben Ross, and Amelia Taylor in the boardroom on the first floor. Copies of the plan for new equipment purchase are attached. Don't forget to take info. on tax concessions.
300	Speak at IAAP meeting, Rose Room, Ramada Inn. A copy of the program and your speech are attached. Good luck!

When you keyboard the list, arrange it so that it is easy to read. Use an appropriate heading. For example, if you are keyboarding lists for more than one person, include the person's name in the heading. For each appointment, indicate the time, name of the caller, his or her affiliation, and purpose of the visit. Also, include reminders, such as a dinner meeting or a commitment to meet someone at the airport. When an appointment is someplace other than your manager's office, indicate clearly where it will be.

Stop 'n Check

1. When someone cancels an appointment, identify one step you should do.

_____

2. When preparing a list of appointments for your manager, identify one step you should do.

_____

Receiving Visitors

Receiving office visitors is an important part of office work, requiring the office professional to be gracious and diplomatic at all times and courteous to all visitors. In your contact with visitors, put forth a special effort to represent your manager and your organization favorably. Your duties are threefold:

1. To carry out your manager's wishes
2. To present a positive image for yourself, your manager, and the organization
3. To help visitors, within the policy limitations of the organization, to accomplish their purposes for coming to your office

In some organizations the office professional serves as the receptionist and is the first person the visitor meets. Large organizations usually have a reception area in the lobby near the main entrance to the building, and all visitors check in with the receptionist. Sometimes there are receptionists on more than one floor. A visitor tells the receptionist with whom he or she has an appointment, and then the receptionist calls the manager's assistant.

Whether an organization does or does not have a receptionist, the office professional usually receives the visitor before the visitor is admitted to the manager's office. Therefore, regard receiving visitors as a regular part of your job. As you plan your work, allow time for receiving visitors.

Among the visitors who come to see your manager will be visitors from outside the organization. Many will have appointments and some will not. Some may be employees who report directly to your manager; others may be managers and supervisors within the organization, including your manager's superiors; and others will be friends and members of your manager's family.

Learn your manager's policy for seeing visitors. What you need to know most of all is whom your manager will not see and to whom, if anyone, you should direct these visitors. Organizations strive to make friends of all visitors. Therefore, the policy could be to arrange for visitors, with few exceptions, to see someone within the organization for a few minutes at least.

An office professional can easily make the mistake of being too protective of the manager's time, turning away visitors the manager should see. As a result, the office professional could destroy favorable relationships that already exist or that could develop between the manager and others. Guard against being overly protective of your manager's time. When you are uncertain, either make an appointment for the visitor or ask if your manager will see the visitor.

Be especially courteous to visitors you must turn away. Ways to arrange an appointment for a visitor with someone else in the organization and to refuse appointments are discussed later in this chapter.

GREETING VISITORS

Visitors are influenced by their first impressions of the office and the office professional. A favorable first impression and your courteous efforts to make visitors feel welcome create a receptive climate in which your manager can develop and maintain a good rapport with others. The visitor's first impression should be that of an efficient assistant working in a well-organized office.

One of your duties will be to keep your office in order, as you learned in Chapter 4. A busy office does not have to be cluttered. As a reminder, to maintain a well-organized office:

1. Designate and use specific locations for supplies, files, and work-in-progress.

2. Remember that completion of each task includes "putting away."

3. Follow through by clearing your desk of materials you are not using.

If you continually put away items you are not using so nothing accumulates, the few items you have on your desk will enhance the appearance of your office. Remember, visitors notice clutter and may assume business is handled the same way your office appears.

Immediate Attention

Your job is to make all visitors, whether they have appointments or not, feel at ease. When a visitor comes directly to your office, you should greet the visitor the minute he or she arrives. As the visitor approaches your desk, look at the visitor directly, smile graciously, and speak immediately. Nobody likes to be ignored, even for a few seconds. To continue keyboarding until you reach the end of the line or paragraph or to continue reading copy is extremely rude. To continue chatting with another employee is inexcusable. If you are talking on the telephone, the visitor probably will hesitate before approaching your desk. Immediately nod and smile so the visitor knows you are aware of his or her presence.

Manage to put your materials out of sight of glancing eyes without shuffling papers in the visitor's presence. By keeping the materials on which you are working in a folder, you can unobtrusively close a folder as a visitor nears your desk.

Greet an office visitor by saying, "Good morning" or "Good afternoon." Use the visitor's name if you know it. If you are expecting a visitor whom you do not know, but you are sure who he or she is, use the visitor's name. The greeting goes something like: "Good morning, Mr. Slattery, I'm Chris Rogers, Mr. Wilmont's assistant. Mr. Wilmont is expecting you." When you receive visitors for several managers, do not guess who they are. Wait for visitors to introduce themselves.

The atmosphere within many organizations is informal, and employees call their managers by their first names when visitors are not present. However, you should always call your manager by his or her last name when you are speaking of your manager and when you are addressing your manager in the presence of others, particularly international visitors.

Advance Preparation

Your manager may need materials from the files—correspondence and records—to refer to during meetings. Anticipate what materials will be needed and locate them the day before, even though you do not remove them from the files until the next morning. Learn if your manager wants to review the material in advance of the meeting (Figure 10-6). If not, take the materials your manager will use during a meeting to his or her office just before the meeting.

You may have to compile data or collect information from other departments. Get an early start on these tasks so you will have the information ready when it is needed. In fact, present information you compile enough in advance for your manager to review it adequately prior to discussing it with someone else.

Your manager will often need special materials for meetings. Anticipate the needed items and have them ready. They might include notes or minutes

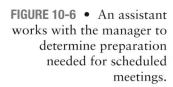

FIGURE 10-6 • An assistant works with the manager to determine preparation needed for scheduled meetings.

taken during a previous committee meeting; printed brochures to be distributed at a department meeting; a PowerPoint presentation set up for a talk your manager is giving as an after-dinner speaker; a list of the names, addresses, and affiliations of new members of a professional group; a copy of shipping procedures and proposed revisions to discuss with your manager's superior; or whatever is related to the purpose of the meeting.

ATTENDING TO THE VISITOR WHO HAS AN APPOINTMENT

Make the Visitor Feel Comfortable

Indicate where to leave his or her coat and escort the visitor to your manager's office. Pronounce both the visitor's name and your manager's name distinctly when you introduce them. The business relationship, not the social rule of introducing the man to the woman or the younger to the older person, is the guide for making introductions in business. A visitor who has a name that is difficult to pronounce will not mind if you ask him or her to pronounce it for you. Mention the visitor's affiliation or the purpose of the visit. Say, "Mr. Wilmont, this is Mrs. Harris of R. C. Products." Stand to one side, not between your manager and the visitor, as you make the introduction. If your manager knows the caller, you can be less formal. As soon as your manager is available, you can invite the caller to go in or you can open the door, if it is closed, and say, "Mr. Wilmont, Mrs. Harris." If appropriate, you may offer the visitor a beverage or ask your manager if anything is needed before you leave.

Invite Visitors Who Must Wait to Take a Seat

Keep current magazines, the morning paper, and other interesting reading material nearby so callers who must wait for any length of time can read. You are not expected to entertain the visitor by carrying on a conversation while he or she is waiting. You can continue with your work.

Attend to Early Arrivals

A visitor who arrives early expects to wait until the time for the appointment. However, when your manager is free, tell him or her immediately the visitor has arrived and ask if he or she is ready to see the visitor. Eventually you will learn your manager's preference about seeing visitors ahead of the appointed time. It will depend on who the visitor is, what the purpose of the visit is, and what tasks your manager must complete between appointments.

Do Not Keep a Visitor Who Has an Appointment Waiting

The visitor's time is valuable, too, and asking the visitor to wait is inconsiderate. Nevertheless, a manager who has numerous appointments in one day may have difficulty keeping to an appointment schedule and, when the manager does have difficulty, visitors will have to wait. Having visitors wait occurs even though the manager and the office professional are making a real effort to usher visitors in and out in the time allotted. When a delay occurs, assure the visitor the wait will not be long. When you say "Mr. Wilmont should be available in a few minutes," you can sound reassuring. Use this statement only when you anticipate the ongoing meeting is almost over.

The real test of how well you receive office visitors lies in what you say and what you do when the wait will be long. First of all, do not let your actions reveal the day is hectic. When emergencies occur or the day is not going smoothly, regardless of the reason, slow down, put some of your own work on tomorrow's list, and approach visitors in a relaxed manner. Give the visitor the impression your only duty at the moment is to meet his or her needs. Your relaxed manner will be contagious.

Be Cautious about How You State the Reasons for a Delay

You can apologize and say all appointments are running behind schedule, but do not explain why. Avoid statements referring to important business, problems, or inefficiency. The visitor is thinking about what is happening to his or her time and wants to know how long the wait will be. If the wait will be very long, tell the visitor approximately how long. The visitor may decide to make an appointment for later in the same day or for another day.

Do not forget about a visitor. Reassure the visitor. If you can judge that a conference is ending, turn to the visitor and indicate that it is. If a visitor whose appointment is delayed cannot wait any longer and tells you he or she must leave, offer to make another appointment and volunteer that your manager will call. Write yourself a note to follow up, for this visitor has been inconvenienced and deserves special attention.

Stop 'n Check

List three tips when receiving visitors.

a. _____

b. _____

c. _____

ATTENDING TO STAFF VISITORS

A critical aspect of every manager's job is maintaining two-way communication with the employees who report directly to him or her. In spite of a manager's effort to establish an easy flow of two-way communication, breakdowns may occur and misunderstandings arise, frequently resulting in personnel problems that should have been avoided. Therefore, many managers announce they have an "open-door" policy for seeing members of their staff.

Arrange for employees who report to your manager to meet in your manager's office or in a conference room designated by your manager. When your manager's supervisor requests a conference with your manager, the implied message is your manager will go to the supervisor's office unless a specific statement is made to the contrary concerning the place of the meeting.

TERMINATING MEETINGS

Arrange with your manager how you are to assist in terminating meetings. Be sure to follow your manager's preference.

On those days when your manager's appointment schedule is crowded, watch the time and tactfully interrupt a meeting, following predetermined guidelines. One appointment that runs overtime on a busy day can throw all the other appointments off schedule, inconveniencing many people and giving the impression of inefficient planning. Find out if your manager wishes you to aid in terminating appointments of visitors who overstay their time.

When a visitor arrives promptly for an appointment and someone is in your manager's office, but you know your manager wants you to interrupt him or her, you can proceed in one of the following ways:

1. Take the visitor's business card or name written or typed on a slip of paper with the notation that the visitor has arrived and hand it to your manager.
2. Enter your manager's office and say, "Excuse me. Your three o'clock appointment is here. May I tell her how soon you can see her?"
3. Call your manager on the interoffice telephone, especially if you think he or she does not want to be interrupted. Suggest a time for the meeting to end, enabling your manager to answer "Yes" or "No" without comment.

If you must remind your manager of an appointment outside his or her own office and, in addition, you are using the reminder as a means of terminating a meeting, do not reveal where your manager's next meeting is or with whom. Your interruption either in person or by telephone may be all that is needed to prompt the visitor to leave. If not, it will be adequate to enable your manager to terminate the conversation.

What can you do when your manager does not have another appointment but the visitor stays and stays, taking up your manager's time unnecessarily? This situation presents a different problem, but it really should not. Most managers are skilled at terminating office visits. They thank the person for coming, stand, and tactfully make statements that let the visitor know the meeting is over. At times, however, managers rely on their office professionals to rescue them from persistent visitors.

Be sure you understand what your manager expects you to do when he or she is having difficulty limiting a visitor's time. In what manner does your manager want to be interrupted? Some assistants pretend the manager has another appointment. You could type a note reminding your manager of work to be done, walk into your manager's office, deliver the note, and say nothing. Another effective tactic is to call on the interoffice telephone, giving your manager an opportunity to say, "We are finishing now" or "Yes, in just a few minutes" or a similar comment that would prompt the visitor to leave. If your manager prefers to continue the meeting, he or she could reply in such a way that you would know the meeting will last awhile longer.

INTERRUPTING A MEETING

Until you know, anticipate your manager does not want to be interrupted while someone is in his or her office. Most managers discourage interruptions while they are conferring with someone. Nevertheless, the interruptions a manager will tolerate are governed by his or her judgment and personality (Figure 10-7).

You must arrive at a definite understanding with your manager concerning what conditions are important enough to justify interrupting during a meeting. At times, your manager may instruct you to interrupt to take a telephone call. At other times, he or she may indicate there should be no interruptions at all. When you are left to your own judgment and do not know what to do, do not interrupt. An intrusion detracts from the tone of a meeting as well as the train of thought. Whether or not you interrupt your manager when an unexpected visitor comes to the office will depend on who the person is and the purpose of the visit.

Clearly establish the method your manager prefers you to follow when you must deliver an urgent message. The following method is frequently used: The assistant types the message, quietly enters the manager's office, delivers the message or places it face down on the desk, and leaves unless an immediate answer is necessary.

FIGURE 10-7 • An administrative assistant interrupts the manager meeting with a visitor.

To keep telephone interruptions to a minimum, offer to take the message or to assist the caller yourself. If you cannot help the caller, ask the person to leave his or her number so your manager can return the call. If your manager has to answer a telephone call when someone is in his or her office, that interruption places the manager in an awkward position. Your manager needs privacy for a telephone conversation and does not want to appear discourteous to the visitor by taking up his or her time with a telephone call.

When you receive an urgent telephone call for your manager while someone is in the office, write the name of the person calling and the purpose of the call, deliver the note to your manager, and wait for instructions. Your manager will either give you a message or take the call.

When you receive a telephone call for a visitor, let the visitor know. As you enter the office or conference room, apologize for the interruption. Address the visitor, tell the visitor who is calling, and ask if the visitor would like to take the call in your office. When several visitors are in the room, type the message, walk in and hand it to the person addressed, and wait for the reply. Instead of taking the call, the visitor may tell you he or she will return the call. Give the message to the person calling, ask for the number, and type it on a telephone message blank for the visitor.

Stop 'n Check

1. List one tip for attending to staff visitors.

   _____

2. List two tips for terminating conferences.

   a. _____

   b. _____

3. List two tips for interrupting a meeting.

   a. _____

   b. _____

ATTENDING TO UNSCHEDULED VISITORS

Be just as pleasant and friendly toward the unexpected visitor as you are toward the visitor who has an appointment. Never judge a visitor by appearance, for appearance is not indicative of the importance of the person to your manager or to the organization.

As soon as you greet the visitor, the visitor probably will tell you his or her name, present a business card, and state the purpose of the visit. Listen carefully and decide what to do. The visitor could be in your office for any one of many reasons. The visitor could be a member of your manager's family, a friend, an important executive, or an aggressive salesperson.

When the visitor is a member of the family, a friend, or an executive, invite the visitor to be seated. If there is someone in your manager's office, you could say, "Someone is in his office, but I will let him know you are here." Either write a note to take to your manager or call him or her on the telephone. Family members may prefer that you not interrupt your manager, but an executive usually does not show up unless he or she has something to say immediately. Do not keep an important executive waiting. Announce his or her arrival.

After you establish a visitor is a friend, offer to let your manager know the friend is waiting. Sometimes salespeople who should not take up your manager's time use this approach. Consequently, keep a conversation going long enough to be sure you should tell your manager about the visitor. When you are uncertain, do not risk turning away someone your manager would want to see.

Someone may come to your office and decide not to wait when he or she discovers it would be inconvenient to see your manager. Always offer to help the visitor yourself. When you know your manager would like to talk with this person, ask if the person would like your manager to call him or her. If the visitor indicates he or she would, write the information on a telephone message blank. Add a note saying the person came to the office. Even when you do not suggest your manager will call, let him or her know who came to the office. Your manager can take the initiative to call.

When a salesperson drops in unexpectedly, ask the purpose of the visit to determine if (1) the salesperson should see someone else, (2) you should offer to make an appointment for the salesperson with your manager, or (3) you should tell the salesperson your manager is not seeking the product or service.

If the salesperson has been calling on your manager, but your manager is no longer involved in purchasing the product or service the salesperson represents, tell the salesperson whom to see. Next, call this person, give the salesperson's name and business affiliation, explain the salesperson is in your office, and ask the person with whom you are talking if he or she will see the salesperson. Write down the name of the person, the person's title, floor, and office number, and hand the note to the salesperson. Be courteous enough to explain to the salesperson how to reach that person's office.

When your manager is too busy to see a salesperson or observes strict guidelines for seeing salespeople, offer to make an appointment. Say you are sorry, but be sure to end the conversation on a positive note. For instance, say "We will expect you at two o'clock on Thursday. Mr. Wilmont will be glad to see you then."

When you know your manager is not seeking the product or service the salesperson represents, graciously tell the salesperson so. Obviously, the salesperson wants an opportunity to convince your manager of the need for the product or service. Invite the salesperson to leave a business card and literature about the product or service. Tell the salesperson you will give it to your manager and offer to contact the salesperson if your manager is interested in learning more about the product. Suggest the salesperson write your manager a letter or send additional information.

Remember your job is to make a favorable impression for the organization as well as run an efficient office. Give a reason, at least in general terms, before you say "No." Visitors who are turned away should feel they have been received courteously.

Occasionally you will encounter visitors who will not state the purpose of their visit. When you ask, the visitor will say it is personal or confidential. Here are some hints to use to screen visitors:

- **Establish clear guidelines with your manager.** If your manager often has visitors who simply drop by without an appointment, have your manager explain how aggressive he or she wants you to be. Establish guidelines for when you should allow the visitor access to your manager.

- **Ask direct questions.** Most visitors who have legitimate reasons for seeing your manager will be willing to state the reason. The visitor who is evasive or refuses to give the reason is often concealing the fact he or she is trying to sell something.

- **Offer to help the visitor.** If the visitor refuses to explain the purpose of the visit, try "I am Mr. Hagerman's assistant. If you explain the nature of your visit, perhaps I can help you." If you are sincere and are willing to help, visitors are more likely to tell you the purpose of the visit.

- **Politely be persistent.** Keep stating "I will be glad to help you if you tell me the nature of your visit," even though the visitor may try to distract you with other information.

- **Have the visitor write a note to the manager.** Another approach when you are in doubt about whether your manager might like to see the visitor is to offer a notepad and an envelope and suggest the person write your manager a note. Then take the note to your manager. Try to do this between visitors rather than interrupting while someone is in your manager's office. Wait for your manager's instructions about what to do.

REFUSING APPOINTMENTS

Managers have much work to do in addition to conferring with callers and talking on the telephone. Some managers plan blocks of time when they hope to work without interruption. At other times, a manager is forced by the pressure of a deadline to devote full time to a task that must be completed.

On those days or half-days when your manager is not seeing anyone, you do not have to pretend he or she is not in the office or in conference. "In conference" has been used as an excuse so much it is regarded as a joke. Furthermore, do not say your manager is solidly booked with appointments except when it is true. Your manager may change plans and confer with a visitor. If your manager does this, the visitor will discover your manager is not solidly booked.

Simply state your manager cannot crowd anything more into today's schedule and then focus the discussion on future arrangements. Handle telephone requests and unexpected office visits in the same way. Say when your manager will have time to see the visitor. Ask questions such as "Shall I ask my manager to call you?" or "Would you like to make an appointment?" What you suggest would vary according to the importance of the request.

Stop 'n Check

1. List three tips for attending to unscheduled visitors.

   a. _____

   b. _____

   c. _____

2. Explain how you would respond for your manager during a time when he or she has designated no appointment.

   _____

   _____

Managing Difficult Visitors

What can you do when a visitor is aggressive or rude? Every office professional experiences difficult visitors or clients from time to time. Although this situation is undesirable, learning how to handle these situations will provide benefits to the company, the visitor, and yourself.

DEALING WITH UNWANTED VISITORS

Remember the bully, the know-it-all, the backstabber, the blamer, and the gossip from Chapter 2. Difficult visitors can act this way as well. How do you deal with a visitor who is obnoxious or one who makes you feel threatened? Dealing with unwanted visitors is something you need to discuss with your office team. Your colleagues may be able to provide names of people who have an abusive history with your office and are, therefore, not welcome in the office. Your company have an organizational policy for handling unwanted callers where security officers can assist you if needed. If there is a company policy, follow it. If no policy exists, your office team should draft a policy and submit it to management for approval. Every organization wants to provide excellent service, but abuse toward employees should never be tolerated.

The following tips can help turn an undesirable situation into one that is satisfactory to both parties:

1. **Use common courtesies.** Immediately learn the visitor's name and use it along with the appropriate courtesy title (*Mrs.*, *Mr.*, *Ms.*, *Dr.*, or some other). Be sure your tone of voice and body language always convey a positive and sincere message.

2. **Listen to the visitor.** Listen to the spoken words, but also listen to the unspoken—that is, to the tone of voice and the body language. Often there is more information in what visitors *don't* say than what they do say. Listen quietly and carefully as the visitor explains the source of distress. Take notes if necessary and ask questions to ensure clarity. Review listening in Chapter 2 and body language in Chapter 6.

3. **Apologize if it is appropriate to do so.** If your company has not performed to the highest of standards, a full apology is in order. Remember to use your tone of voice and body language to reinforce the sincerity of your message.

4. **Show empathy and understanding.** Demonstrate you have listened carefully, and you understand the visitor's reason for distress. Paraphrasing the customer's story may be helpful.

5. **Promise follow-up.** Commit to assisting the visitor yourself or to having someone else take action. Tell the visitor exactly what your action plan will be and when he or she can expect to hear from you.

If you follow these basic rules, a more satisfactory situation should result in maintaining your visitor's goodwill.

Language Barrier

Encounters with visitors can also be challenging if they do not speak your language, and you do not speak theirs. When you do not understand their language, first attempt to determine what language they are speaking. If you recognize the language and know someone in your area who speaks it, ask visitors to take a seat (this may be done with hand motions), then call the person who can speak with them, explain the situation, and ask the person if they would please assist you in helping the visitors. Don't assume the visitors do not understand your language. Many times a person can understand a language but not speak it. Be careful what you say and display a positive attitude toward these visitors. Coming to your office can be a frustrating experience for them.

Because of our diverse culture, today many companies have prepared lists of bilingual employees who can interpret for someone or translate documents. It is quite common for these employees to be paid more for these services. Also, pictures of bilingual employees are often posted so a visitor will know who to go to for assistance and where they are located. Bilingual signs stating available bilingual services are sometimes posted at the company's entrance.

Visitors with Special Needs

Always be prepared to help visitors. Notice if they have special needs and make them as comfortable as possible. Always offer to help; don't wait to be asked, whether it is holding open doors (if the door does not have buttons that automatically open) for someone who uses a wheelchair or simply someone who has difficulty walking. Your helpfulness will show your company is caring and wants to help in any way it can.

Office Security

You should be aware of any procedures established to safeguard your own personal security within the office setting. No one should take security for granted. Many office buildings have security twenty-four hours a day. If this is the case and you feel threatened, you should call security to have an individual removed. Here are some tips to follow:

- Contact the corporate security force if there is one or call the police emergency number (911). Have phone numbers for office security, local police, and ambulance numbers near or taped on your telephone for quick reference.
- Challenge visitors or individuals walking through your office. Try to determine who they are visiting by asking if they need assistance.
- Do not let anyone into your building with your access keys or card as you enter after regular business hours.
- If you have your own office, be sure to lock the door when you leave for lunch or to attend meetings.
- When it gets dark early at certain times of the year, use the "buddy" system when leaving your office building.
- Always keep valuables out of sight, including purses, cash, and stamps. Lock them in a desk drawer or file cabinet if possible.

Stop 'n Check

1. List one tip for handling difficult visitors.

   _____

2. List one tip for observing safety in the office.

   _____

- Place small pocket calculators or recorders in desk drawers when not in use.
- Do not allow unknown or unexpected maintenance personnel free access to your office space without checking to see if they are authorized to be there.

Remember security is everyone's responsibility, and you should use sound preventive measures to safeguard yourself, your property, and the property in the office.

Ethics and Visitors

ETHICAL★ISSUES

You must at all times be careful what information you give to a visitor when the visitor is waiting for your manager or others. Customers will often ask questions of a confidential nature to get ahead of any competition. Here are some areas to avoid when casually chatting with waiting visitors:

- **Avoid sharing confidential information about products, office gossip, company successes, or problems.** You might think this would not be difficult, but what if the person asking is a close friend? A relative? Your manager? The situation then becomes more difficult.
- **Treat each visitor equally.** When two or more visitors appear, use the "first come, first served" rule. Acknowledge both visitors, but invite the second visitor to have a seat while you help the first.
- **Don't ask questions of a personal nature.** A visitor may be offended by questions that appear to be prying into his or her personal life. Don't discuss family, children, religion, or politics. Remember, you have work to do.
- **Never assume based on the color of a person's skin he or she is from a certain country.** For instance, a person from Nepal may look similar to someone from India. You should not ask or make reference to a person's country of birth.

What you must always remember is you choose your behavior, and your behavior should always be to choose what is right or most right in all situations. During times when you are handling visitors, keep in mind your organization's code of ethics as well as your own values.

Hosting International Visitors

If your manager travels to meet international clients, it's very possible those clients will also visit your office (see Figure 10-8). The work of handling international clients requires a completely new set of knowledge and skills.

Being able to build positive relationships with international clients is highly desirable and worth achieving. The best advice is to be flexible, adaptable, and tolerant (FAT). Remember, the experiences and customs of international visitors are different than yours. This is your chance to learn and grow. Here are some tips for your success:

1. **Do your homework!** The comfort of your guests should be your top priority. This means researching their culture and company and incorporating as much of their custom into the visit as possible. Have enough information so you can show an interest and ask intelligent questions.

2. **Learn a few words and phrases in the visitor's language.** Examples might be *hello, how are you, please, thank you, goodbye, and it was a pleasure to meet you*. Even a few words and phrases will demonstrate to the client you are interested in the client and the country. One suggestion is to write the word *welcome*, in the visitor's language, at the top of the meeting agenda.

3. **Locate the client's nearest consulate's office.** As a courtesy to your international clients, have handy the nearest consulate's location, phone number, and ambassador's name for reference should you need them.

4. **Keep an open mind.** Do not judge behavior by your own standards. Attitudes, values, manners, greetings, and gestures may be foreign to you and at times may even seem to be bad manners and in poor taste. They are not! They are simply the product of a different culture.

FIGURE 10-8 • International employees may want to tour your company when visiting.

5. **Listen carefully.** Your international client may speak in broken English. Do not correct his or her pronunciation. Just remember a visitor's English may be a lot better than your Arabic, Japanese, German, or Spanish.

6. **Research cultural attitudes about time.** As you learned earlier, different cultures treat time differently. In North America time is a priority, and we expect people to follow schedules closely, to be on time for meetings, to complete projects before the deadline, and to show up when and where they say they will. This makes it difficult for us to schedule meetings, complete projects, and close deals. Keep this in mind when scheduling meetings and be as flexible as possible.

7. **Learn the preferred eating habits of the country.** Although many international visitors are open to experimenting with new foods, many are not. For example, some cultures do not eat pork. In this case, it would be a gross error to arrange a meal where pork is on the menu. Be certain coffee and lunch breaks include food and beverages the international clients will enjoy.

8. **Determine if gender plays a stronger role in the client's culture than our own.** In certain cultures, women do not hold high-level positions where decisions are made. In this case, conversation is often directed from the international client to the male members at meetings. The gender issue is important for a company to know before deciding whom to send to negotiate in the boardroom or even whom to send abroad as the best company representative.

9. **Identify the proper greetings.** Greeting visitors in the United States is done with a firm handshake, whereas in many other cultures, bowing and kissing are the norms. In some cultures, men and women do not touch. Although women and men in these cultures do not shake hands, members of the same gender may deliver a very warm and physical greeting.

10. **Be aware of body language.** A friendly hand gesture in one country can be obscene in the next and even illegal in another. Pay attention to how others use gestures (movements of the hands, arms, legs, or head) to say what they mean.

11. **Pleasantries come before business.** Unlike in the United States, many cultures do not do business until they have established a relationship with you. This may mean many cups of tea and a lot of social conversation before business topics are ever broached.

12. **Learn to pronounce names correctly.** If needed, find out how to pronounce the visitor's name correctly. In some cultures, such as Chinese and Korean, the family's surname is placed first and then the given name. You will make a lasting impression on your visitor if you use his or her name correctly. Learn the titles of respect that go with others' names and when it is appropriate to use them.

13. **Determine if physical space when talking is different from our culture.** People may feel differently about space or distance in communication than you do. When receiving visitors from outside your culture, pay attention to what is considered an appropriate distance between you and the visitor when talking. With some visitors, standing too far away may be interpreted as being unconcerned, too formal, or too distant. On the other hand, if you stand too close to a visitor, it may be interpreted as your being too casual or too informal. Learn how to use space or distance to your advantage so as not to offend visitors.

The bottom line is you want your international visitors to have a pleasant, positive visit to the United States and a visit that produces a profitable, yet rewarding relationship. With more and more U.S. companies establishing offices outside the United States and more foreign businesses establishing offices here, you are likely to need to develop your skills in this area.

Quick Tips

FACTS ABOUT THE LANGUAGE OF BUSINESS

Studies have shown English is the native tongue of barely a dozen countries; yet, of the world's people, nearly one person in every five can speak English to some level of competence.

More than 80 percent of home pages on the Web are in English, while the next greatest, those in German, represent only 4.5 percent and Japanese, 3.1 percent.

Concept Review and Reinforcement

Review of Key Concepts

OUTCOME	CONCEPT
1. Schedule and confirm appointments for one or more managers.	• Leave Monday mornings free to plan and handle weekend mail. • Schedule no appointments on the first day back from out of the office. • Avoid crowding the calendar the day before a trip. • Schedule appointments so they do not overlap. • Be aware of top-priority meetings and allow plenty of time for them. • Avoid scheduling two top-priority meetings back-to-back. • Avoid scheduling an appointment in another location after one that will run late. • Allow ten to fifteen minutes of free time between appointments. • Schedule appointments with others with whom your manager has a close working relationship late in the afternoon. • For phone appointments, suggest at least two specific times from which to choose. • Predetermine times for answering mail and handling routine daily activities. • Learn which meetings can be limited to fifteen minutes or less. • When arranging a short appointment, set it up by stating the beginning and endng time. • When you arrange for an unexpected visitor to see your manager, the visitor should be advised of the time of the manager's next appointment, if that time is soon. • Arrange outside appointments so the manager can go to the other site directly from home in the morning or from the site to home after a late-afternoon appointment.

2. Use appropriate scheduling aids.	• Both you and your manager will need to keep to an appointment schedule. Begin by learning:
	  • Your manager's preferences for scheduling appointments
	  • Which appointments should be given priority
	  • How much time appointments should take
	 • Use an electronic calendar such as the Microsoft® Outlook calendar.
	 • Check out the Web-based calendars available for use free on the Internet.
	 • Use a paper desk calendar.

3. Greet and direct visitors.	• When canceling appointments:
	  • Express regret on your manager's behalf.
	  • Mention that the appointment must be changed.
	  • State a reason in general terms.
	  • Offer to schedule another appointment.
	 • When receiving visitors, follow your manager's wishes, make friends for your manager and the organization, and help visitors accomplish their purposes.

- Some hints to follow when screening visitors are:
  - Establish clear guidelines with your manager.
  - Ask direct questions.
  - Offer to help the visitor.
  - Politely stick to your guns.
  - Have the visitor write a note to the manager.
- When you must refuse appointments, simply state your manager cannot crowd anything more into today's schedule.

4. Manage difficult visitors.	- Here are the tips for managing difficult visitors:
	  - Use common courtesies.
	  - Listen to the visitor.
	  - Apologize if it is appropriate.
	  - Show empathy and understanding.
	  - Promise to follow up and do so.

5. Identify potential ethical implications when sharing information.	- Your behavior should always be to choose what is right or most right in all situations. During times when you are working with visitors keep in mind your organization's code of ethics as well as your own values.

6. Host international visitors.	- When working with people outside your culture, be concerned about the following:
	  - Know the person's culture.
	  - Learn a few words and phrases in the visitor's language.
	  - Locate the visitor's nearest consulate's office.
	  - Keep an open mind about behavior, attitudes, values, manners, greetings, and gestures.
	  - Listen carefully when the visitor's English is poor.
	  - Learn the preferred eating habits of the country.
	  - Determine if gender plays a stronger role in the visitor's culture.
	  - Identify the proper greetings.
	  - Pay attention to body language.
	  - Learn to pronounce names correctly.
	  - Determine if space is important.

Key Terms

Electronic calendar. A calendar on your computer or network.

Electronic organizers. Pocket calendars that include a calendar, scheduler, and address area for immediate access.

Web-based calendars. Electronic calendars made available for free on the Internet.

For Your Discussion

Retrieve file C10-DQ from your student data file.

DIRECTIONS

Enter your response after each question or statement.

1. Suggest how you can tactfully let a person know his or her appointment is for a short segment of time.

2. To avoid conflicts in scheduling, what is the office professional's first step in granting an appointment when one is requested?

3. Describe how an electronic calendar can be used.

4. Why should you be cautious when you state the reason for canceling an appointment?

5. What are the office professional's main responsibilities concerning receiving office visitors?

6. Explain how to introduce a visitor to your manager.

7. Describe an office professional's role in making a visitor feel at ease when the visitor has an appointment but must wait.

8. While chatting with a visitor, you unintentionally mention a new product that is being developed. By sharing this information, identify possible ethical implications.

9. Suggest two ways to assist a manager in terminating a conference when he or she has another appointment soon.

10. Differentiate between the status of U.S. women in business and the status of women in other cultures. Why is this important to understand in business?

Building Your Office Skills

Exploring the Workplace: *Activities*

1. Go to a computer store and look at the variety of software programs for keeping calendars. Write down the names, costs, features, and hardware requirements. Select the one you prefer and give the reasons for your selection.

2. Go to an office supply store or look at a supply catalog and note the variety of desk appointment calendars available. Write down the name and cost of the one you would select for your own use as an office professional and for your manager. Beside the name of the one you select, jot down the features that appeal to you. Share what you learned with the class.

3. Interview an assistant for the following information about scheduling appointments:

   a. Guidelines in setting up appointments

   b. Ways in which calendars are coordinated between the office professional and manager(s)

   c. Calendar aids

   d. Preferences or procedures for handling visitors—procedures for greeting visitors, refusing appointments, and terminating visits

   Write the interviewee's responses in report form and be prepared to share your findings.

4. If you are currently working or have ever worked in an office, describe the manner in which office visitors are received in the organization. If you have no work experience, interview a friend who is working in an office. Answer the following questions:

   a. Does the organization have a receptionist?

   b. Are the visitors escorted or directed to the offices of the persons with whom they have appointments?

   c. Are the salespeople's visits restricted? If so, how?

   d. What is the visitor's first contact with the assistant?

   Write your responses and share your ideas with the class.

Developing Critical Thinking Skills: *Problem Solving on the Job*

Retrieve file C10-OJS from your student data disk.

1. **Working for multiple managers.** You work for eight managers. You make appointments for all of them and record their appointments in separate appointment books. Today as you were checking your calendar, you discovered that Mr. Yates had requested an appointment with Mrs. Roberts at 10:30 a.m. Wednesday. You had entered the appointment in Mr. Robbins's appointment calendar by mistake. Mrs. Roberts has another appointment at 10:30 a.m. Wednesday, and she will not be in the office on Wednesday afternoon. What should you do?

2. **Managing a difficult visitor.** Recently Mrs. Garson has made three appointments with your manager, Mr. Stoney. Each time she has canceled the appointment the day before—once because she was ill, another time because of bad weather, and the last time because she was too busy to keep the appointment. The last time she canceled the appointment, Mr. Stoney said emphatically, "Do not grant her another appointment!" This morning Mrs. Garson called requesting another appointment. You told her Mr. Stoney could not work in another appointment this week, and he would be

out of town next week. Mrs. Garson is furious and insists on talking with Mr. Stoney. What should you do? What will you say to Mrs. Garson?

3. **Keeping confidential information confidential.** Your manager, Mr. Harper, had a serious heart attack in his office late Tuesday afternoon. Today you are canceling his appointments for Wednesday, Thursday, and Friday of this week. You are explaining that the appointments will be rescheduled with someone else. What should you ask to find out about the urgency of each appointment? How much information should you give about Mr. Harper's illness? What can you say?

4. **Schedule various visitors.** What would you do in each case if each of the following visitors did not have an appointment: (a) your manager's superior, (b) your manager's spouse, (c) your manager's former college roommate who is visiting from out of town, (d) a salesperson with whom your manager wants to keep in touch but cannot see on the day the salesperson calls, (e) a salesperson representing a product your manager does not need and would have no occasion to purchase, (f) a prospective client?

Using the Web: *Research Activities*

A. You have been hired by a manager of a new company. The manager has used Microsoft® Outlook in the past but wants to evaluate other software to see what it offers and how much each one costs. He is particularly interested in e-mail and a calendar, but you are to include any other features as well.

　1. Research the following software: Novell Groupwise, Pegasus Mail, Lotus Notes, and Mozilla.

　2. Identify the basic features of each as well as the cost.

　3. Write a memo to your instructor about your findings.

B. You are an administrative assistant in the IT department for a large manufacturing company. At a weekly staff meeting, several of the supervisors indicate they believe their employees would gain much from some training about Microsoft® Outlook. Your job is to locate companies that provide such training.

　1. Enter the following key search words: Outlook training.

　2. Identify three companies that offer training and print any explanations of their services.

　3. In a memo to your instructor, summarize the information you located.

C. You are a member of a committee that has been asked to gather information to help other administrative professionals become more knowledgeable about greeting visitors who regularly visit your company. You and your team are to research Web sites assistants might visit to take quick self-assessments or sites that list tips on handling visitors including handling international visitors.

　1. Enter the following key search words: *greeting visitor's self-assessments, greeting office visitors,* or *handling international visitors.*

　2. Identify three Web sites that offer information and print a copy of each site's information.

　3. In a memo to your instructor, identify each Web site URL summarizing the information you found.

Get Tech Wise: *Using Microsoft® Outlook to Set Appointment Reminders*

Directions

Use Microsoft® Outlook to set an appointment reminder.

1. Open Outlook.

2. Point to New, and then click on the drop-down box, click on Appointment.

3. Enter your class name as the subject.

4. Enter the room and building number your class is in as the location.

5. Fill in the Start Time and End Time text boxes with dates and times of your choice.

6. Click in the Reminder check box to activate it.

7. Click on the arrow pointing down to select the specific time you want your computer to remind you of your appointment. For example, 15 minutes before your class ends.

8. Save and close your appointment reminder.

9. At the time you specified in step 7 for the reminder, your computer will beep and a dialog box will appear on your screen. (Note: Your computer must be on for you to receive the notice of the upcoming appointment.)

10. Click on Snooze if you want to be reminded again. (You can set the time you want the second reminder to appear if desired.)

11. Click on Dismiss to cancel any further reminders.

Improving Your Writing Skills: *Grammar Workshop*

Retrieve C10-WRKS from your student data disk.

Simulation: *In the Office at Supreme Appliances*

Supreme Appliances

Application 10-A

Scheduling Appointments

Supplies needed: Form 10-A-1, Appointment Calendar, Amanda Quevedo; Form 10-A-2, Appointment Calendar (Student Name); plain paper.

Retrieve file C10-AP-A1 and C10-AP-A2 from your student data disk.

Directions

Ms. Quevedo has been scheduling her own appointments. She uses a monthly calendar and crowds the appointments into the spaces. During a discussion with Ms. Quevedo on Friday, she asks you to schedule her appointments from now on.

You decide to use daily appointment calendars—one for Ms. Quevedo and one for yourself. Ms. Quevedo has no appointments scheduled for Monday and only one for Tuesday. She has the following appointments for Wednesday, August 6, entered in her monthly calendar:

9:00   Agnes Smith, Sales Representative for Small Home Appliances, Inc.

10:00   Pete Rollins, Sales Representative for Home Gadgets, Inc.

11:00   James Hansen, Manager of the Eastern Region of Modern Appliances, Inc., and J. R. Rush, Assistant Vice President of Marketing, Eastern Region

12:00   Lunch with Mr. Hansen and Mr. Rush

3:00   Karen Baxter, Assistant Vice President of Marketing, Western Region, to review marketing plans for fall

You are to transfer these appointments to Ms. Quevedo's daily calendar and yours. On Tuesday, August 5, you receive the following telephone calls concerning appointments. Make these changes on Ms. Quevedo's and your calendar as well.

1. From Thomas Strickland, Assistant Vice President of Marketing, Southwestern Region, saying he must attend a funeral out of town on Wednesday. He has an appointment on Wednesday at 3 p.m. with O. C. Connors, President of Mapledale Homes, Inc. He asks if Ms. Quevedo can see Mr. Connors at 3 p.m.

   Here is your response: "Ms. Quevedo has an appointment with Ms. Baxter at 3 p.m. I'll see if I can move Ms. Baxter's appointment to 2 p.m. I'll call you and let you know."

   Later you call Mr. Strickland and confirm that Ms. Quevedo will see Mr. Connors at 3 p.m.

2. From Pete Rollins's assistant, saying Mr. Rollins had an automobile accident, is hospitalized, and obviously cannot keep his appointment.

3. From Ray Rogers, co-chair of the Eastern Region Sales Seminar, asking for an appointment on Wednesday to review plans for the November seminar. You suggest 10 a.m., and Mr. Rogers accepts.

4. From the Human Resources Department, asking Ms. Quevedo to see a job applicant. You try to postpone this appointment, but the Human Resources Department insists Ms. Quevedo will want to meet this applicant while she is in the building on Wednesday. You schedule an appointment for Bill Boger at 4 p.m.

Before leaving the office on Tuesday, you keyboard Ms. Quevedo's appointment schedule for Wednesday, August 6.

Wednesday at 10:05 a.m. Jason Rhodes, a college friend from out of town, comes to the office for a brief visit with Ms. Quevedo. You say you will schedule him between appointments for a few minutes at 10:45 a.m.

On her way to lunch, Ms. Quevedo asks you to remind her before she leaves at the end of the day to call the Lakeside Restaurant to tell the manager how many will be in her dinner party Wednesday evening. Be sure to enter this in the reminder section of both calendars and include the phone number—(953) 555-1892.

Application 10-B

Receiving Visitors

Supplies needed: Plain paper.

Directions

Waymon Williams, the office professional who has been receiving visitors in the marketing department, is being promoted to an administrative assistant in another department. He is leaving in one week. Ms. Quevedo has asked you to write procedures for receiving visitors in the marketing department. The procedures are to be included in an office procedures desk manual. From your experience in assisting Ms. Quevedo, you have received the following visitors: manufacturers' reps, advertising reps, customers, and field sales reps.

1. Using the information from this chapter as well as suggestions from other sources, create an informational report about receiving visitors in the marketing department.

2. Address the topics of greeting visitors, receiving visitors who do and do not have appointments, terminating meetings, screening visitors, managing difficult visitors, attending to staff visitors, interrupting managers, canceling appointments, and refusing appointments.

3. Proofread the document.

Application 10-C

Writing an Informational Report about Office Security

Ms. Quevedo is on a committee to make recommendations about office security. She asked you and two other office professionals (select two classmates) as a team to gather information about office security. Each of you is to visit or call a company security office to obtain recommended tips or procedures for Ms. Quevedo to take to the committee meeting with her. Your team is to:

1. Identify the companies you will contact or visit.

2. Create several questions in addition to the ones given that each of you will ask. Questions might include: Do you have specific security procedures for office personnel? Do you require badges or other identification? Do all employees have to go through any type of metal detectors? What procedures should employees follow in emergencies?

3. Write one collaborative information report to Ms. Quevedo. Identify each company as a side heading, give information about the company and the person with whom you spoke, and key each question followed by its answer.

Building Your Portfolio

With a team member or your instructor's help, select the following documents: appointment calendar, procedures for receiving visitors, and report on office security.

Remember these documents must be error free. If instructed, place the documents in plastic protection sheets and add to your portfolio.

11 Making Travel Arrangements

chapter **outline**

Planning the Trip
    Internet Travel Services
    Travel Agencies
    Trip Information Needed

Arranging the Travel
    Air Travel
    Car Rental Services
    Hotel Reservations
    Passports
    Visas
    Immunization Requirements
    Security

Following Through
    Prior to the Trip
    During Your Manager's Absence
    After Your Manager Returns

Ethical Issues in Reporting Travel Expenses

International Travel Tips
    Tips for Success

learning **outcomes**

When you have completed this chapter, you should be able to:

- Identify types of services and resources needed to make domestic and international travel arrangements.
- Prepare for a business trip.
- Make air and hotel reservations.
- Make special arrangements for international travel.
- Develop an overall trip plan that includes details to be handled before a trip, during a trip, and at the conclusion of a trip.
- Identify ethical issues in reporting travel expense reports.
- Discuss the importance of understanding cultural differences as they relate to your manager's travel.

You may perform many office tasks and never be called upon to handle someone's travel arrangements. However, anyone who works as an executive or administrative assistant will likely encounter making travel arrangements at some point in their careers. If you work for a manager who travels, you should

- become thoroughly familiar with the organization's travel policies.
- know what travel accommodations are available and how to schedule them to meet the manager's preferences.
- Ensure procedures are followed and office tasks are completed while the manager is away.
- Apply the reimbursement policies.

Planning the Trip

Before you proceed to make travel arrangements, ask questions about the organization's policies and procedures. For example:

- Who is responsible for making travel arrangements?
- Do designated office professionals handle the travel arrangements for all the managers of the organization?
- If the services of a travel agency are used, which agency?
- Which class of flight service do travelers fly?
- What is the policy concerning the use of private cars and car rental services?
- Does the organization have a preference for a particular airline?
- If so, what are the policies for using it?
- How are payments for reservations handled?
- What is the procedure for getting a cash advance for a traveler?
- How is the manager reimbursed for additional travel expenses?

As soon as you have answers to these questions, you will know whether to turn over the arrangements to someone else or to make them yourself. Regardless of who makes the arrangements, try to request all reservations far enough in advance to ensure you obtain the travel arrangements at the best price and accommodations desired.

Stop 'n Check

List five questions you should be able to answer before you make travel arrangements.

a. _____

b. _____

c. _____

d. _____

e. _____

INTERNET TRAVEL SERVICES

The Internet offers an abundance of information that will help the office professional plan business trips. By searching the Internet, the office professional may access the following information:

- hotel pricing and accommodations
- airline travel
- telephone numbers for hotels and airlines
- travel tips
- e-mail, fax, and postal mailing addresses

Because of quick access to the Internet, companies providing travel services have listed their Web sites. Here are the most common sites to visit:

www.americanexpress.com/travel
www.expedia.com
www.hotelstravel.com/services
www.orbitz.com
www.priceline.com
www.travelocity.com

Stop 'n Check

What travel information can you easily access from the Internet?

_____

_____

_____

TRAVEL AGENCIES

Before you call a travel agency, be certain you have already reviewed the travel procedure for using this resource. If your company authorizes the use of a travel agency, you will definitely appreciate their services when you make arrangements for international travel; you may find that working through a travel agent is the easiest and best way to make arrangements for domestic travel as well.

Travel agents receive their commissions from the airlines, hotels, and other organizations whose services they sell and do not charge your organization for services. Local travel agencies are listed in the classified section of the telephone directory. If you are concerned about finding a reputable agency, call the Better Business Bureau to inquire about local travel agencies.

Most travel agents are approved by the International Air Transport Association (IATA). IATA is a conglomerate of international airlines. It allows travel agencies that meet its stringent requirements to use its insignia. An agency seeking IATA's approval must have a solid reputation and the financial backing to ensure its own stability.

Travel agencies use the Internet to maintain up-to-the-minute information on all airline schedules and hotel accommodations. Because of their experience and business connections, travel agents can obtain information quicker and find availability and better prices than most people who do their own bookings.

The travel agent represents *all* the transportation lines, hotels, and motels, not just certain ones. You, of course, must provide the travel agent with all the details needed. When planning a trip, try to work with only one person at the agency and rely on that person to prepare the complete package. The travel agent will create an itinerary, secure tickets, make hotel reservations, arrange for car rental, and perform other services related to the trip.

For international travel, travel agents perform many other services. They provide some information on visas and how you can obtain one, provide information about how much luggage is allowed, furnish guidebooks for the countries being visited, and explain travel restrictions and regulations for bringing foreign purchases through U.S. customs. Travel agents do not give advice on immunizations, however. That advice should be obtained through your local health authority.

TRIP INFORMATION NEEDED

As soon as your manager mentions a trip, start compiling information. Before you contact a travel agent or an airline carrier, compile the details concerning:

1. destination
2. intermediate stops, either going or returning or both
3. date of departure and return
4. date and time of the first business appointment and the time needed between arrival and the appointment
5. preferred time for travel
6. method of travel—air, car, rail
7. class of air service—business class, economy class
8. preferred seat selection—aisle? window? front or back of the plane?
9. hotel preference or the desired location of the hotel within the city
10. need for transportation at the destination or at intermediate stops
11. the need for connecting shuttle service
12. preferred make and size of rental car

For use in planning future trips, maintain a folder labeled "Trip Preferences." When your manager returns from a trip, you should add comments about the transportation and hotel accommodations on a copy of the agenda for the trip. In this folder, keep the manager's comments and all other information that will help you recall preferences when you are planning another trip to the same city or part of the country. If you plan trips for more than one manager, maintain a Trip Preferences folder for each person. Figure 11-1 is an example of a trip-planning checklist.

Arranging the Travel

Making transportation arrangements for international travel is similar to making arrangements for domestic travel. When planning travel, you should consider the effect of a long trip through different time zones. Refer to Chapter 5 for a discussion of time zones around the world. **Jet lag** is a condition that is

Manager's Name _____

PREPARING FOR THE BUSINESS TRIP

Handling preparations:

_____ 1. Get transportation information from your travel agency, company travel department or other sources.
_____ 2. Submit time and route schedule.
_____ 3. Make transportation reservations.
_____ 4. Confirm that airline tickets have been sent or will be available at the ticket counter before departure.
_____ 5. Check travel documents for accuracy (airline/train).
_____ 6. Prepare the travel itinerary and appointment schedule for appropriate people.
_____ 7. Route copies of itinerary/appointment schedule to appropriate people.
_____ 8. Assemble business information, file folders, and supplies to be taken on the trip.
_____ 9. Make financial arrangements for the trip.
_____ 10. Give hotel confirmations and transportation ticket confirmation to your manager.

Transportation:

_____ 1. Destination(s)
_____ 2. Desired departure time
_____ 3. Desired arrival and departure times for stopovers
_____ 4. Airline decisions
_____ 5. Time schedules
_____ 6. Plane/train accommodations (class, seat assignments, and meal specifics if applicable.)
_____ 7. Car-rental arrangements (preferences of rental agencies, vehicle preference, dates and times, method of payment, whether drop-off in another city is desired)
_____ 8. Shuttle/limo arrangements at destination
_____ 9. Baggage identification tags and requirements (if international)

Hotel:

_____ 1. Desired arrival and departure times
_____ 2. Special accommodations (meeting/conference room)
_____ 3. Shuttle/limo arrangements to and from hotel (from airport)
_____ 4. Fax numbers at hotels
_____ 5. Business services available

Business documents:

_____ 1. Summary of file folders taken (or copies made of information)
_____ 2. Passport
_____ 3. Visa
_____ 4. Immunization
_____ 5. Itinerary

FIGURE 11-1 • Checklist for making travel arrangements.

Stop 'n Check

Once you learn your manager will be traveling, what are at least five details you need to address?

a. _____

b. _____

c. _____

d. _____

e. _____

characterized by various physical and psychological effects, such as fatigue and irritability, following a long flight through several time zones. When planning an overseas trip, ask your manager about preferences for an adequate rest period following arrival in the country to be visited and following the return home.

To make travel arrangements with ease, you should know about air travel services and other types of transportation, including how to arrange for car rental services; how to make hotel reservations; how to obtain passports and visas for international travel; and what is involved in meeting immunization requirement if needed.

AIR TRAVEL

Because many managers are required to fly to meetings in different cities, you need to be well informed about air travel services.

Sources of Air Travel Information

You can obtain air travel information about a specific trip by telephoning a local travel agent or specific airline. However, all this information is easily accessible on the Internet.

If you are involved in making extensive air travel arrangements, consult the North American and international editions of the ***Official Airline Guide (OAG)***. The *OAG* contains information on airline travel, from flight itineraries and special fares to baggage allowance. The *OAG Electronic Edition Service (EES)*, available for a fee on the Internet, is an online travel service allowing travelers to compare fares, check seat availability, and book flights from their computers on a twenty-four-hour basis. In addition, it provides information about hotel accommodations, restaurants, weather forecasts, and access to a comprehensive variety of travel-related facts. You can locate this service by accessing www.oag.com/oag/website/com/en/Home/.

Types of Flights

The most desirable flights are those on which the traveler is least likely to be delayed or inconvenienced. Therefore, when making arrangements, consider the flights available in this order:

1. a **nonstop flight**, which is uninterrupted from point of departure to destination
2. a **direct flight**, on which, regardless of the number of stops en route, the passenger remains on the same plane from departure to destination
3. a connecting flight with another flight of the same airline
4. a connecting flight with another flight of another airline

When a passenger changes aircraft without changing airlines, the gate for the connecting flight may be near the deplaning gate. The distance between boarding gates of two different airlines at a major airport may be far, and walking or being shuttled from one gate to another is time consuming. If the first flight is delayed, the passenger may not have enough time to meet the connecting flight.

Because delays cannot be predicted, use wise judgment when making reservations; if the traveler must make a connection, allow adequate time between the flights. Remember that many airports have more than one terminal and that many cities have more than one airport. A connection between two different airports in a large city can often take two hours, or even longer. Think of the activities involved: deplaning, picking up baggage, getting transportation to the second airport, and locating and boarding the next flight.

Commuter flights are short direct flights between two neighboring cities. These neighboring cities need to be close enough that significant numbers of travelers use the service as a convenience. Many business travelers rely on commuter flights to meet with clients or colleagues in neighboring cities and even to go to work each day. These flights leave frequently—often every hour. Although reservations are recommended, they are often not required because of the frequent schedules.

Class of Service

The services passengers receive aboard the plane—especially where they sit and the food and beverages served—are purchased by **class of service**. The basic classes of service that most travelers use are business class and economy class. The priority services for business class traveling include expeditious check-in and boarding as well as additional comfort and service during the flight.

Some organizations allow their executives to fly **business class** because it provides wider seats with more legroom and working room—an important consideration on long flights. Other organizations, for obvious financial reasons, require their executives to fly economy class. Although the **economy class** is the most common way to fly, it has less space between seats and offers little to no service.

Flight Reservations

You can make a flight reservation yourself through the Internet or by simply telephoning the airline reservations office. The tickets can be paid for by providing a credit card number.

A number of airlines no longer print a paper ticket; instead, they prepare **electronic tickets (e-tickets)**. The system now works like this:

- Book the reservation over the telephone or Internet.
- Include the traveler's frequent flier card number, a card that provides extra benefits.
- Use a credit card or charge account to pay for the tickets.
- Receive a faxed or e-mailed itinerary and confirmation from the airline carrier.
- Just prior to departure, the traveler proceeds to the airline ticket counter or baggage check-in, states the flight number for which he or she has reservation, shows identification, and receives a boarding pass. A popular and quick method to check in and receives a boarding pass is to use a kiosk. The traveler approaches the device, scans a credit card, and confirms the reservation by following the easy steps. Once the steps are completed, a boarding pass is printed.

Reconfirmation of airline reservations is required on international flights. The traveler should reconfirm reservations for each part (also called *leg*) of the trip.

Booking the airline reservations online can be efficient for the office assistant. The assistant can access the availability of flights in minutes. Alternative schedules can be printed and then compared and selected by the traveler. Keep in mind that executive travel and flight plans change frequently and rapidly. The office professional can save time by making the reservations, which eliminates calling the travel agent every time a change must be made.

Timetables

No two airline timetables are identical, and airline timetables are different from rail timetables. Timetables are easy to read when you know what to look for. All carriers publish electronic and paper timetables and update them often.

Reading the 24-Hour Clock

For air travel, the times shown are based on the 24-hour clock. This is to eliminate confusion between a.m. and p.m. Under this system, time begins at one minute past midnight (0001) and continues through the next twenty-four hours to midnight (2400). Refer to Figure 11-2.

Ground Transportation

Airports are often located twenty or more miles from cities; for that reason, one or more types of ground transportation—airport limousine, taxi, bus, and car rental—are available at all airports.

The distance and direction of the airport, the travel time needed, the types of ground transportation available, and approximate costs are listed in the *Official Airline Guide* for all destination cities. The transportation services are coded as follows: limousine (L), taxi (T), car rental (R), and air taxi (A). To determine what arrangements to make for ground transportation, ask the airline reservations agent or your travel agent.

Limousines and shuttle bus services operate on a regular basis between the airport and downtown hotels. They leave the designated hotels in time to get the passengers to the airport for departing flights, and they meet incoming flights.

Air taxi is a helicopter service that is available at some airports. Helicopters operate between two airports of a destination city, between an airport and downtown heliport (helicopter landing ports), and between destination

FIGURE 11-2 • Time conversion for the twenty-four-hour clock.

1:00 a.m. =		=
=		=
=		=
=		=
=		=
=		=
=		=
=		=
=		=
=		=
=		=

airport and an airport not served by jet aircraft. Compared to the cost of other types of transportation, air taxi service is expensive; however, it saves time.

A traveler who must make a connecting flight at an airport may need air taxi service in order to make the connection. As stated previously, on domestic flights, avoid scheduling a connecting flight that involves a second airport. When people travel abroad, they may have to make a connection involving two airports because the traveler's incoming flight may arrive at one airport and the next flight may depart at another. Before making a reservation for air taxi service, find out about airport limousine or bus shuttle service between the central terminals serving the airports involved.

In making arrangements, you may want to consider another airport. Many major cities have more than one airport. You may find that you can get a lower fare if your manager will land at one of the "alternative" airports and drive an extra few miles to reach his or her destination. For example, if your manager is traveling to New York City, he or she can land at LaGuardia, Kennedy, or Newark airports. Other metropolitan areas served by two or more airports include Chicago, Los Angeles, and Washington, D.C.

Stop 'n Check

1. What are at least two advantages for using e-tickets?
   a. _____
   b. _____
2. Convert the following times to a 24-hour clock: 2 p.m., 6 p.m., 10 p.m.
   a. _____
   b. _____

CAR RENTAL SERVICES

The best way to arrange for a car rental is either to telephone the local office of the car rental agency or to access the agency online. The largest car-rental agencies offer both domestic and international car-rental services, publish worldwide directories of their services, provide a toll-free number for making reservations, and have a Web site with reservation facilities. Here is a list of car rental agencies:

Hertz
Avis
Enterprise Rent-A-Car
Budget
National Car Rental

When you are making arrangements for car rental, specify the following:

- city, date, and time
- size of car desired, such as small-range or mid-range

- location where the car is to be picked up
- name of the person who will pick up the car
- location where the car is to be returned
- the length of time the car will be used
- method of payment for the charges
- map with directions from car rental center to destination

A car can be picked up at the agency right at the airport or near the airport when the passenger arrives. All the traveler has to do upon arrival is to go to the airport car rental office, present a driver's license, and complete arrangements for payment of charges.

Charges incurred are payable at the completion of the rental, but the arrangements for payment must be made in advance. Major credit cards are accepted. Cash may not be accepted. At the time you are making the reservation, be prepared to give the account number and the expiration date of the credit card to be used for payment. Your company may have arrangements with car rental agencies entitling you to a discount.

HOTEL RESERVATIONS

Many hotels provide a toll-free number for making reservations. You can obtain the toll-free number by calling directory assistance at 1-800-555-1212 or by accessing the Internet.

If you are not familiar with the hotels in the destination city, contact a local travel agent. Most international accommodation information changes so rapidly that agents consult online computer information, which is updated frequently. Because many of the larger hotels and resorts have their own Web sites, you can access this information and make your own reservations.

Here are some ways to save your organization money.

- Search the Internet for Web sites that specialize in offering "best" rates. For example, www.hotel.com and www.expedia.com are sites specializing in travel and hotel rates.
- Book the right kind of room. Some hotel chains offer the option of rooms for business travelers. These rooms cost slightly more per night but can save money in the long run because they do not charge phone access fees. At seventy-five cents or more a call, phone access charges can add up quickly when your manager is calling customers, getting messages from the office, accessing the Internet, and so on. Some hotels offer high-speed Internet access as well, usually for a daily charge. When making hotel reservations, be aware of the additional charges for these rooms, your manager's preferences, and your company's policies about reimbursement rates.
- Check out concierge levels. Some hotels provide concierge-level rooms that include breakfast, newspapers, and an afternoon snack and drink buffet. Although these rooms carry a higher rate, their cost is often less than your manager may spend on purchasing meals and periodicals.
- Avoid large hotel chains. Most major cities have cost-effective alternatives to the major hotel chains, such as independent hotels, short-stay efficiency apartments, or other money-saving alternatives. Again, be certain to ask your manager about his or her preference when it comes to reserving hotels.

Stop 'n Check

Identify at least two ways to consider possible cost savings when making hotel reservations.

a. _____

b. _____

Always ask for a confirmation of a hotel reservation. When the operator gives you a confirmation number or an electronic confirmation note, be sure to attach it to the itinerary so that the traveler will have it should there be any question about the reservation. Hotels require a deposit when you request that a room be held for late arrival. This is called a **guaranteed reservation.** Make the request and arrange for the deposit to guarantee the room. Major credit cards are accepted by hotels to reserve the room for late arrival. Late arrival is usually after 6 p.m. Be aware: if the reservation is not used, someone should cancel the reservation, as the credit card holder will be responsible for charges. Many hotels require 24- to 48-hour notice of cancellation, or the credit cardholder will be charged.

PASSPORTS

A **passport** is an internationally recognized travel document that verifies the identity and nationality of the bearer. A passport allows the bearer free passage within the bearer's borders. It entitles the bearer to the protection of his or her own country and that of the countries visited.

A U.S. citizen who goes abroad must carry a passport. The Intelligence Reform and Terrorism Prevention Act of 2004 requires that by January 1, 2008, travelers to and from the Caribbean, Bermuda, Panama, Mexico, and Canada have a passport or other secure, accepted document to enter or reenter the United States.

To apply for a passport, a person must complete an application form. The application usually is made locally, but the issuance of passports is under the jurisdiction of the U.S. Department of State. The addresses of passport acceptance facilities in your area are available on the Internet at http://travel.state.gov. The application form gives complete details for applying for a passport. A passport is valid for ten years.

VISAS

Many countries require foreign travelers to hold a visa. A **visa** is a stamped permit to travel within a given country for a specified length of time. The visa is usually stamped or attached inside the passport. However, some countries provide loose visa documents so the visa can be removed when traveling to uncooperative countries.

Well in advance of the departure date, the office assistant or the traveler should check passport and visa requirements with the consulates of the countries to be visited. The traveler should obtain the necessary visas before going abroad.

Visa requirements are subject to change, and they can change rapidly. Travelers should apply directly to the embassy or nearest consulate of each country that he or she plans to visit or consult a travel agent. Most foreign consular representatives are located in principal U.S. cities, particularly New York, Chicago, New Orleans, San Francisco, Houston, Dallas, and Washington, D.C. The addresses of foreign consular offices in the United States may be obtained by consulting the *Official Congressional Directory*, available in many public libraries, or city telephone directories or by accessing the Internet at www.state.gov/s/cpr/rls/fco/.

After obtaining a passport, the traveler must send it to each consulate involved to obtain visas. The time and level of patience it takes to process a visa after it reaches a consular office can vary from one day to three weeks. Allow ample time and use prepaid courier services whenever possible to send the documents. Some travel agents are experienced in obtaining visas, but you do not need to rely on travel agents because the process is usually straightforward.

IMMUNIZATION REQUIREMENTS

The International Health Regulations adopted by the World Health Organization (WHO) stipulate that vaccinations may be required as a condition of entry to any country. The WHO sends communications to local health departments advising them of required and recommended immunization for travelers.

For travel to many countries, an International Certificate of Vaccination is not required. If the traveler needs an immunization certificate, he or she can obtain it from the local health department. The form must be stamped by the office where the vaccinations are administered.

SECURITY

As a result of the terrorist attack on the United States in 2001, all travelers, both national and international, should be aware of security issues. As an office professional who makes travel arrangements and who helps the executive prepare for the trip, here are some factors to consider:

- Travel to and through some countries can put Americans at risk. When booking flights, choose reputable flights and, if possible, avoid countries that are unfriendly to Westerners.
- Location is a critical consideration when booking hotels. Be certain you book reputable hotels in safe locations.

Stop 'n Check

1. What change has occurred in the law that will require certain travelers to have a passport to enter and reenter the United States?

_____

_____

2. Is a visa required in every country? Yes _____ No _____

- Security at airports is heavy. Executives who travel should expect to have their notebook computers, digital pocket organizers, pagers, cell telephones, and briefcases thoroughly examined before they board a flight. At different security levels, some of these items may be required to be packed in checked baggage rather than carry-on bags.

- Batteries in the computer and pocket organizer should be charged. With increased airport security, people carrying electronic devices may be asked to start these machines to prove they are truly business tools and not explosive devices.

- Many airports insist on jackets and shoes being removed as travelers pass through security.

- Travelers should expect to answer questions about why they are traveling to certain countries. Is it for business? If so, what business?

- Travelers should carry their passports and their immunization cards (for some countries) on their person because government officials can request these documents at any time.

- When executives are taking gifts to clients, they should not be wrapped prior to boarding the flight. Airport security can insist the parcels be unwrapped for inspection.

- Travelers should expect to be searched by security officers if any level of metal registers as they pass through the metal detection gate.

Following Through

Although you may rely on a travel agent when planning a trip, you are directly responsible for checking the completeness and the accuracy of the final arrangements.

PRIOR TO THE TRIP

Just before your manager leaves on a business trip, your main duties will include checking ticket confirmations; getting a cash advance, if needed, for the trip; preparing the schedule; assembling materials for the trip; perhaps arranging to have new business cards made; and getting instructions about special responsibilities you will have in your manager's absence. Be sure you understand your specific duties in completing this last task. Assumptions can lead to costly and potentially embarrassing situations.

Checking Tickets

Verify ticket information in ample time. Thoroughly check each item on the confirmation with the itinerary. The information on the confirmation and the travel portion of the itinerary should be identical.

Requesting Travel Funds for the Trip

Credit cards, such as American Express, Visa, and MasterCard, make it possible to travel without carrying large sums of money. Although most people rely on credit cards while traveling, everyone who travels needs some cash.

Many organizations provide a cash advance to employees who travel. If this is your organization's policy, complete the required form, and obtain the cash. Figure 11-3 shows a travel fund advance form. Although forms vary, it is important on all forms to complete all appropriate blanks with accurate information. Doing so will help avoid delays in receiving the travel advance.

Occasionally managers prefer to carry **traveler's checks** in addition to cash. However, this is unlikely for business trips. Most business travelers take limited cash and often carry their company credit cards. Cash is readily available to the traveler through automatic teller machines found in hotels and banks.

FIGURE 11-3 • Travel fund advance form.

TRAVEL FUND ADVANCE

Please forward completed forms to: Accounting Department
Millennium Appliances
3431 Bloor Street
Toronto, ON   M8X 1G4

Tel (416) 795-2893   Fax (416) 795-3982

Name of Employee Requesting Advance: *Iain Brown*

Date of Request: *March 25, 200x*

Employee Number: *784244*

Destination: *Vancouver, B.C.*

Reason for Travel: *Meetings with sales staff & clients*

Departure Date: *April 5, 200x*   Return Date: *April 7, 200x*

Date Advance Required: *April 3, 200x*

Amount Requested:

Accommodation	(Refer to Policy 430) $	*370.00*
Meals	(Refer to Policy 431) $	*120.00*
Transportation	(Refer to Policy 432) $	*100.00*
TOTAL REQUESTED	$	*590.00*

Preferred Method of Payment/Distribution _✓_ Company Check _____ Traveler's Check

Balance Outstanding (Includes this request) $ *0*

___*L. Phillips*___   *G.M.I. Marketing*   *March 26, 200x*
Authorization   Date of Authorization
(as per Schedule of Authorities)

Approval Limits

$3000   -Manager
$10 000   -Director
$10 000+   -President

Understanding Per Diem

One of the first things you will need to understand is the per diem rate. **Per diem** is a Latin term meaning "per day" and means an amount of money determined by the company it will pay per day to traveling employees for expenses.

Become familiar with your organization's policies, as they vary among companies. Some companies allow travelers to claim more than the per diem if receipts can be provided, whereas other companies expect their travelers to cover their own expenses beyond the per diems allowed. Be sure to check your company's per diem rates and policies before you make travel arrangements.

Preparing the Itinerary

Usually, an **itinerary** is a combined travel and appointment schedule. Even with the use of personal digital assistants, the travel itinerary and the schedule of confirmed appointments can also be prepared as two separate paper lists. An itinerary shows when, where, and how the traveler will go. It should include the

- day
- date
- local time of departure and arrival
- name of airport
- flight number
- place of departure and arrival
- car rental information
- name of hotel, telephone, and fax numbers

The itinerary should also include details about confirmed appointments. Examples of such details might be:

- names and titles of the people the traveler will see
- personal notes about people the traveler may see to aid conversation and familiarity, including reminders about family members, recent achievements, or personal interests
- Dates and times of appointments
- Purpose of the appointments
- Software and/or documents required for the appointments

These details are illustrated in the itinerary in Figure 11-4.

As soon as the travel and hotel accommodations and the appointments have been confirmed, you can prepare the final itinerary. Make a step-by-step plan that is so complete the manager will know where to go, when, and what materials will be needed by referring to the itinerary.

Preparing an itinerary can be time consuming because you must obtain the information from several different sources. Here are a few tips to follow:

- Arrange the papers relating to hotels and appointments in chronological order.
- Give the itinerary an appropriate heading.

FIGURE 11-4 • Example of an itinerary.

ITINERARY FOR JASON PARKER

Oklahoma City - Tulsa - Dallas

May 3–6, 200x

MONDAY, MAY 3

6:55 a.m.	Leave Rochester Airport on AA Flight 476 to Chicago. AA Flight 406 from Chicago to Oklahoma City.
11:22 a.m.	Arrive in Oklahoma City. (Jack Lewis will meet you at the airport. Lunch with Mr. Lewis.)
	Reservation at Sheraton Hotel. (Confirmation in AA ticket envelope.)
3 p.m.	Appointment with M. J. Young, OC Branch Office.

TUESDAY, MAY 4

10:15 a.m.	Appointment with Ray Berger, Tulsa Office. (Rental car is with Avis.)
1 p.m.	Lunch with R. Berger and J. Caswell.
3 p.m.	Conference with Sales Group, Tulsa Office.
5:15 p.m.	Return to Oklahoma City.

WEDNESDAY, MAY 5

9:25 a.m.	Leave OC airport for Dallas on AA Flight 104.
10:09 a.m.	Arrive Dallas/Forth Worth airport. (Reservation at Americana Inn of the Six Flags.)
11:30 a.m.	Appointment with A. J. Masterson, Manager, Dallas Branch.
1 p.m.	Lunch with A. J. Masterson, Ray Packard, and Larry Jones. (Executive Dining Room.)
3 p.m.	Appointment with Janet Bradlow, Room 216, School of Business, Southern Methodist University.
6:30 p.m.	A. J. Masterson will pick you up at the Americana to join him and Mrs. Masterson for dinner.

THURSDAY, MAY 6

11:25 a.m.	Leave Dallas/Fort Worth airport on AA Flight 261; AA Flight 185 from Chicago to Rochester.
4:11 p.m.	Arrive in Rochester.

Parker Associates
14325 Washington Blvd.
Rochester, NY

- Use the days and dates as the major divisions, and list the entries under each division in order according to time.
- Check the final itinerary more than once to make sure it is 100 percent correct and complete.

You should prepare the itinerary in the style your manager prefers. However, if the travel agent has already prepared a detailed itinerary, instead of rekeying it to add the appointments, prepare a separate schedule of appointments.

Just prior to departure, when all the details have been finalized, make at least four copies of the itinerary and list of scheduled appointments, with one copy for

- the traveler
- the traveler's superior
- your office

File your copy as a permanent record of the trip. If a major change in the manager's itinerary becomes necessary, inform everyone who has a copy.

Assembling Materials for the Trip

Of all the steps involved in travel planning, this one provides the best opportunity to demonstrate your attention to detail. Your manager may express extra appreciation if you complete the task of assembling materials for the trip. Many executive assistants perform the following tasks for their traveling managers.

- As you make arrangements for the trip, compile a complete list of items your manager may need during the trip.
- Place the papers for each appointment in separate envelopes or folders. Number each one in consecutive order to match the order of the appointments. If you use folders, fasten the materials to the folders.
- Make two copies of the list you have compiled of items your manager must take. Staple the list inside Folder #1 or attach it to Envelope #1. Keep one copy for yourself.
- After you have assembled the items, number them in the order in which they will be used and check them off your list as you place them in a designated area.

Receiving Special Instructions

Before your manager travels, determine tasks related to any special incoming mail, expected telephone calls, materials to be sent to meetings your manager cannot attend, and special responsibilities you must handle in the manager's absence.

Ask your manager if he or she wants to post an automatic return e-mail message. For example, Microsoft® Outlook and other electronic mail systems provide features to "auto-forward" e-mail (all or specified) to someone else or to activate the "Out of Office," which notifies the sender with a predefined message.

DURING YOUR MANAGER'S ABSENCE

Most managers use the Internet to access their e-mail while they are away from the office and may telephone the office regularly. Rather than say "Not much is going on," or "The usual is going on," be ready to report any significant events, important mail, and telephone calls. In your notebook, make a summary of what you should discuss. If the manager keeps in touch with the office through e-mail, you can provide this information on a daily basis and get your manager's feedback immediately.

Stop 'n Check

1. Of the tasks to be taken prior to your manager's departure, which one would require the most time?

   _____

   _____

2. Which task would require additional knowledge or training?

   _____

   _____

3. If you have current or prior experience in completing tasks prior to your manager's departure, which one has presented the most difficulty?

   _____

   _____

If possible, plan your schedule so you can spend the first day the manager is back in the office following through on work generated by the trip.

While the manager is away, you have added responsibilities and may need to allow extra time to handle them. For example, you may be asked to review faxes to determine if any of the information is urgent and needs to be handled by either you or the acting manager. Save some time for communicating with the person who has been designated to act in the manager's role. Offer assistance if you can perform certain tasks.

AFTER YOUR MANAGER RETURNS

Your activities on your manager's first day back in the office after a trip will focus on briefing the manager on what happened during the trip, following up with correspondence, assembling receipts for his or her expense report, and filing materials your manager brings back.

Report the most significant happenings first. Put on your manager's desk:

- The digest of the mail and the correspondence that arrived in your manager's absence, arranged in folders as explained in Chapter 7.
- A summary of telephone calls that were directed to you and were not left on his or her voice mail.

Review your list of the materials your manager took on the trip that must be returned to the files. Locate these materials and file them. Also, file materials your manager acquired during the trip. Copies of materials from the files your manager took on the trip can be disposed of. First, however, check carefully for notes that may have been made on them.

Travel Expense Voucher

The manager may want you to prepare a **travel expense voucher** or form, which is to be completed once your manager returns from a trip. The form is completed showing the "reportable" expenses based on the receipts obtained during the trip. If you are not sure about your company's policy with regard to travel expenses, be certain to review the policy to ensure the form is complete and accurate. Completeness and accuracy are the two necessary ingredients for ensuring a quick return of funds owed to the traveler.

Refer to Figure 11-5 for a sample travel expense voucher. Note all expenses must have the approval of a senior manager. Although these forms vary from company to company, most require at least the following information:

- date the expenses were incurred
- location where the expenses were incurred
- cost of transportation (including tips)
- cost of hotels
- cost and explanation of other business expenses related to the trip (including telephone calls, laundry services, or a necessary business item that was purchased)
- cost of company-related entertaining
- cost of meals (including tips)
- amount of any travel fund advance obtained

Remember most claimed expenses must be verified by receipts and must not exceed costs specified by company policy. Either you or your manager can complete the expense forms. If the travel expense voucher is in electronic format, you can retrieve the form and key the information. If not, it is acceptable to submit these documents in handwritten form.

TRAVEL EXPENSE VOUCHER

NAME: *Iain Brown*   PIN: *784244*

CONTROL #: _____   TITLE: *Sales Manager*   DATE: *April 10, 200X*

Date	Location	Work Order	Transport*	Hotel	Other	Entertain	Meals	Total	Explain Other, Entertain & Meals
April 5	Chicago		55.00	185.00		70.00	— — 19.00	329.00	Taxi airport — hotel Lunch with Edwards & Ross
April 6	Chicago			185.00		125.00	11.00 —	321.00	Lunch with Bollen Dinner with Wolfe
April 7	Chicago		55.00				11.00 — —	66.00	Taxi hotel — airport
April 7	St. Paul				45.00			45.00	Airport parking 3 days at $15.00
EXPENSE TOTAL			110.00	370.00	45.00	195.00	41.00	761.00	
LESS: CASH ADVANCES								695.00	
BALANCE CLAIMED OR RETURNED								66.00	

CERTIFICATION OF EXPENSES

I certify that I have incurred these expenses.

I. Brown _____   *April 10, 200X*
Employee's Signature   Date   Checked by   Date

AUDIT

LEGEND

*   Include vehicle from Side 2 (if applicable)

** Enter on Side 2

*** Distribute on Side 2

APPROVAL OF EXPENSES
K. Winters
Payment Approved by
V. P. Sales
Title
April 16, 200X
Date

FIGURE 11-5 • Sample travel expense voucher.

Ethical Issues in Reporting Travel Expenses

ETHICAL★ISSUES

One continuous goal in an organization is its commitment to its stated values and beliefs. Companies develop and maintain their codes of ethics and educate employees about their responsibilities to uphold these codes. Employers expect employees to operate in accordance with the highest attainable standards of ethical business conduct. They ask employees to take action against improper conduct by reporting it if they encounter it.

When an employee demonstrates unethical behavior, it may begin with peer pressure or a superior's direct request to violate the company's code of ethics. Consider the situation of Emily Jo, who routinely assisted in the preparation of travel expense reports. What began as a one-time request from her supervisor to "pad" expenses became a mountain of bogus entries. Once found out, Emily Jo was terminated.

Although companies have their own policies, there may be gray areas in expense regulations that often lead employees to "fudge" the numbers in their favor. What if you were asked to falsify an expense report for your manager? You have several options: (1) inform your manager you feel it is wrong to inflate the numbers and ask for his or her support in your decision; (2) before you do anything, report the request to your ethics officer or a human resources representative; (3) honor the request but inform your superior you will not do it again; and (4) comply with your manager's request.

Employees are expected to follow the travel expense policies to ensure honest and efficient use of company funds. If you prepare travel expense records or represent or certify the accuracy of information in such records, you must be diligent in ensuring their accuracy and integrity.

International Travel Tips

Customs vary widely from one country to another, and understanding and observing these cultural variables is critical to a traveler's success. Taking the time to learn something about the culture of a country before doing business there shows respect and is usually deeply appreciated. It also enhances the chances of a successful outcome. The following tips for success are offered to better understand other cultures so business travelers can develop prosperous, long-term relationships.

The more business executives know about the culture where they are traveling, the better they can interact with associates there. For instance, should business be conducted during breakfast? It depends. If you are traveling to France to conduct your business, the answer is no. Americans like to schedule meetings at the breakfast hour, but many French businesspeople prefer to eat their breakfast and read their papers in peace. What if a gift wrapped in red is offered to the host? If you are conducting business in Denmark, the gift would probably be well received because red is a positive color. However, a host receiving a gift in an African country might be offended as red represents witchcraft and death.

TIPS FOR SUCCESS

The key to success in the traveler's business dealings and personal relationships in a foreign country is thorough preparation in learning about the country and a sincere desire to fit in with the new culture. Here are some tips you may pass on to your manager:

- **Do your homework!** Researching a country's culture and company and incorporating as much of its custom into the visit is advantageous. Have enough information so you can show an interest and ask intelligent questions.

- **Printing business cards.** Print new business cards. One side should contain the usual information in English; the reverse side should be printed in the foreign language. Foreign business contacts will view this as a courteous gesture.

- **Keep an open mind.** You should not judge behavior on your own standards. Attitudes, values, manners, greetings, and gestures are likely to be foreign; you might even consider some to be bad manners and in poor taste. They are not! They are simply the product of a different culture.

- **Listen carefully.** Your international clients may speak in broken English. Just remember their English is a lot better than your Arabic, Japanese, or other native language.

- **Be aware that different cultures may treat time differently.** In the United States, time is a priority, and we expect people to follow schedules closely, to be on time for meetings, to complete projects before the deadline, and to show up when and where they say they will. Time does not have the same priority in all cultures. Some have a much more relaxed view of time. In fact, some cultures do not work in the afternoon and prefer to have only morning and evening meetings. This makes it difficult to schedule meetings, complete projects, and close deals. Keep this in mind when scheduling meetings and be as flexible as possible.

- **Body language is often misinterpreted.** A friendly hand gesture in one country can be considered obscene in the next and maybe even illegal in another.

- **Slow down so you can warm up.** Unlike Americans, people from many other cultures do not do business until they have established a relationship with you and your company representatives. This may mean many cups of coffee or tea and a lot of social conversation before business topics are ever approached.

- **Keep a book on language translation of common terms or use an electronic language translator.**

Quick Tips

MICROSOFT OUTLOOK AND TRIP PLANNING INFORMATION

Did you know you can open one of your contact cards and click on the map icon from the Standard toolbar to automatically display a map of the address?

Concept Review and Reinforcement

Review of Key Concepts

OUTCOME	CONCEPT
1. Identify types of services and resources needed to make domestic and international travel arrangements.	Services and resources include the following: • organization's policies regarding travel expenses • favorite Web sites • travel agency contact information • information about manager's preferences toward air travel, hotel accommodations, and car rentals • *Official Airline Guide (OAG)* • visa requirements • international travel tips
2. Prepare for a business trip.	To be successful in planning a trip for your manager, you must: • ask questions about policies and procedures within organization. • determine preferences for air, hotel, and car accommodations.
3. Make air and hotel reservations.	Gather the necessary details on the following: • date of departure and return • date and time of first business appointment • preferred time for travel • hotel preference • car rental
4. Make special arrangements for international travel.	To arrange for international travel, you must accommodate for your manager's jet lag because it can result in fatigue and irritability. In addition, you must be well informed about visa requirements for the country to be visited. Understand the 24-hour clock and its effect when you are trying to contact your manager. Furthermore, you might suggest a different business card be printed to include the language of the country to be visited. Remember to include your research on the country's business culture and customs.
5. Develop an overall trip plan that includes details to be handled before a trip, during a trip, and at the conclusion of a trip.	Refer to the trip-planning checklist for details to be addressed before your manager travels, while your manager is away, and when your manager returns home.
6. Identify ethical issues in reporting travel expenses.	Ethical issues include your manager "padding" his or her travel expenses or your manager asking you to pad the expenses.

7. Discuss the importance of understanding cultural differences as they relate to your manager's travel.

Business people in other cultures may view time commitments differently. For Americans, time is a priority; however, time does not have the same priority in other cultures. If your manager is traveling to a country for the first time, he or she should be aware of the particular reference to "time" as it relates to scheduling meetings, completing projects, and closing business deals.

Key Terms

Business class. Airline section considered to be more prestigious and providing wider seats with more legroom and working room—an important consideration on long flights.

Class of service. Classification of air travel that specifies type of seating, food and beverages served, degree of service, and price of ticket.

Commuter flight. The type of flight that allows travelers to fly short distances between two neighboring cities.

Direct flight. When a passenger remains on the same plane from departure to destination, regardless of the number of stops en route.

Economy class. In most cases, has less space between seats and limited meal service and is the most common and cheapest way to fly.

Electronic tickets (e-tickets). Airline ticket information sent as an e-mail to customers.

Guaranteed reservation. A hotel reservation held with a credit card or deposit that ensures a reservation in case of late arrival.

Itinerary. A combination of travel and appointment schedules that shows when, where, and how the traveler will go; details about confirmed appointments are also included.

Jet lag. A condition characterized by various physical and psychological effects, such as fatigue and irritability, following a long flight through several time zones.

Nonstop flight. Allows the passenger to travel from point of departure to destination without making intermediate stops.

Official Airline Guide (OAG). The leading reference containing information on airline travel, from flight itineraries and special fares to baggage allowance.

Passport. A form of identification given to a citizen by his or her own government, granting permission to leave the country and to travel in a foreign country and to return to his or her own country.

Per diem. Latin term meaning "per day."

Traveler's checks. Drafts that can be used as cash and redeemed for face value if lost or stolen.

Travel expense voucher. Form that shows the "reportable" expenses based on the receipts obtained during the trip.

Visa. An endorsement or stamp placed in a passport by a foreign government that permits the traveler to visit that country for a specified purpose and limited time.

For Your Discussion

Retrieve file C11-DQ from your student data disk.

DIRECTIONS

Enter your response after each question.

1. Organizations have definite policies and procedures concerning travel. Name at least three areas in which you would expect policies to be clearly stated.

2. What information relating to a trip should an office professional compile before contacting a travel department, travel agent, or airline?

3. What is the official source of information on airlines?

4. Explain the difference between a passport and visa. Who issues passports and visas?

5. What main duties should an office professional perform just prior to the manager's leaving on a business trip?

6. What information should be included in an itinerary?

7. Explain how an office professional's time can be used efficiently during the manager's absence.

8. What are the main duties pertaining to the trip after the manager's return?

9. Describe potential ethical issues in reporting travel expenses. If unethical decisions are made, what impact do these decisions have on your organization?

10. Discuss the differences between priorities of time in different cultures.

Building Your Office Skills

Exploring the Workplace: *Activities*

1. In a memo to your instructor, describe your experience in making travel arrangements.

   a. Outline your responses according to the major topics in this chapter; for example, describe your experiences in planning trips.

   b. For each main topic:

      1. Explain the easiest and most difficult tasks for you to complete.

      2. Describe the most interesting or unique experience you had.

      3. Include one tip that wasn't covered in this chapter.

2. For three locations—New Delhi, India; Beijing, China; and Manila, Philippines—obtain the latest information and prepare a report on one of the following topics:

   a. passport requirements and where passports may be obtained locally

   b. visa regulations and where they can be obtained

   c. immunization requirements

   d. ground transportation to and from the local airport

   e. city transportation

3. Interview an office professional who makes travel arrangements. Ask the following questions:

   a. Is a checklist used to complete the travel function?

   b. Is there a department within this organization to handle the travel arrangements?

   c. What are your specific responsibilities for making travel arrangements?

   d. Is international travel involved? If so, what specific information or steps must be completed for the traveler?

   e. Does the traveler call in while away from the office? If so, what topics does the office professional usually need during these times?

   f. What kinds of activities are completed during the traveler's absence?

   g. What procedures are followed to complete the travel function when the traveler returns?

   h. What advice can the office professional give to help when handling the travel function? Summarize your findings in memo form, and be prepared to share your findings with the class.

4. Your manager is traveling to Cairo, Egypt, for the first time and will be away from the office for three weeks. She is leaving for Cairo in one month. This is the first opportunity you have had to make international travel arrangements, and you want to ensure that all details are complete and accurate. Your manager has asked you to gather all the details and review them with her at the end of the week. Make a trip folder to present to your manager. In sequence, identify what you would do to plan this trip.

Developing Critical Thinking Skills: *Problem Solving on the Job*

Retrieve file C11-OJS from your student data disk.

Directions

Enter your response after each situation.

1. **Communicating with your manager.** Your manager is planning a business trip to Istanbul, Turkey, and she has a passport but says she doesn't need a visa. You are responsible for assisting her with the travel plans. What should you do about the visa in this situation? If she does need a visa, what will you say to your manager?

2. **Missing materials.** When Ms. Orlando, your manager, arrived in New York City, she could not find her luggage. Her notes for the presentation she is to give at the conference are in her suitcase. You have a copy of the notes. Ms. Orlando calls you at home on Saturday morning and asks you to go to the office, find the notes, and call her. She says the notes are brief, and you could read them to her over the telephone. How do you react to this request? What suggestions would you make about packing notes for future talks?

3. **Handling changes in travel.** You work for three executives. Two of them are planning to attend a management conference in San Francisco, and you made travel reservations for them. Now the third executive has decided to attend the conference and has asked you to make travel arrangements for the same time that the other two executives are traveling. You call the airline. A seat is not available at that time. What should you do while you are talking with the reservations clerk?

4. **Preventive measures.** This was the first time you made travel arrangements for your manager, and your manager had the following problems on his trip. How would you prevent these problems from reoccurring on the next trip?

   a. The hotel room was guaranteed for arrival, but a nonsmoking room was not requested. Because of a large convention being held at the hotel, your manager could not get a nonsmoking room when he arrived.

   b. Although you told your manager a car had been rented, the rental agency did not have a reservation. Your manager could not rent his preferred car size.

   c. A schedule of appointments was not included in the travel file given to your manager.

5. **Ethical dilemma.** In your team, respond to the following: Expense "padding" is the same as thievery. Is participating in this behavior the same as stealing? Why or why not? If time is allowed, share your responses with other teams in your class.

Using the Web: *Research Activities*

A. Your manager travels extensively and has asked you to find the cost of subscribing to the electronic version of *OAG*.

   1. Locate cost information on the electronic version of *OAG* by keying in the following search words: *travel, official airline guide*.

   2. Summarize the information in a memo to your instructor.

B. Your manager has asked you to reserve a flight on Southwest Airlines for departure (prior to 10 a.m.) on Monday two weeks away and return on Thursday (after 2 p.m.) of the same week.

   1. Connect to the Internet, and enter the following site: www. southwest.com.

   2. Enter the information and print out a copy of your findings.

   3. Submit your findings in a memo to your instructor.

C. Locate current local times anywhere in the world.

   1. Connect to the Internet, and enter the following site: www. worldtimeserver.com.

   2. Enter at least three major cities in the world and determine current local times.

   3. Submit your findings in a memo to your instructor.

Get Tech Wise: *Categorize Contacts for Travel Information*

Setting Up Contact Cards

1. Open Microsoft® Outlook. Click on Contacts in the Folder List.

2. Click on the New Contacts icon on the Standard toolbar.

3. Create a contact card for each company or person you work with in preparing for travel.

4. While still creating the contact cards, click on the Categories button at the bottom of the screen.

5. Select from the many predefined categories or add a new one (e.g., Travel Agents). Add similar contacts to the same category.

6. Click on OK.

7. Click on Save and Close on the Standard toolbar.

Viewing Contact Cards by Categories

1. In Microsoft® Outlook, click on Contacts in the Folder List.

2. Click on View on the Menu bar.

3. Point to Current View.

4. Select by Category.

5. The data is displayed in rows and columns, similar to an Excel worksheet.

6. Click on the *plus* (+) sign to display all contact cards for a category.

7. Double-click to open a contact card to see more data.

8. Click on the *minus* (−) sign to hide the contact card listings for a category.

Improving Your Writing Skills: *Grammar Workshop*

Retrieve file C11-WRKS from your student data disk.

Simulation: *In the Office at Supreme Appliances*

Application 11-A

Preparing an Itinerary

Supplies needed: Form 11-A, Notes on Ms. Quevedo's trip to the Southwestern Region; plain paper.

Retrieve file C11-AP-A from your student data disk.

Directions

Ms. Quevedo will make a business trip to the Southwestern Region during the week of September 1 through 5. She will visit the regional sales office in Dallas and the manufacturing plant in Fort Worth. She will speak to the Sales Management Club at the University of Houston. From the notes provided in Form 11-A, prepare Ms. Quevedo's itinerary.

Application 11-B

Making an Airline Reservation

Supplies needed: Plain paper or card.

Directions

Ms. Quevedo asked you to make an airline reservation for her from Rochester, New York, to Dallas on Tuesday, October 10. You know that Ms. Quevedo prefers to travel in the morning and prefers nonstop and direct flights.

You call the airlines. A nonstop flight is not available. You make a reservation for her with American Airlines on Flight 716. The flight leaves Rochester at 10:03 a.m., arrives in Chicago at 10:50 a.m., leaves Chicago at 11:27 a.m., and arrives at the DFW International Airport at 1:49 p.m. She will be on the same plane for the entire trip. She has requested an electronic ticket (e-ticket) confirmation.

Compose a memo to Ms. Quevedo giving her complete information about the airline reservation.

Application 11-C

Planning an International Business Trip

Supplies needed: Plain paper.

Directions

Ms. Quevedo has asked you to plan her international business trip. She is making a presentation in Mexico City and Guadalajara one month from today.

1. Ms. Quevedo needs reservations at the Marriott Hotel in both cities for one week each. She has asked you to determine specific information about these two cities. Your findings must include the following:
   a. travel times
   b. time zone changes
   c. travel documents needed
   d. medical requirements
   e. airlines to use

f. approximate cost for transportation and lodging

g. nearest American Embassy location

h. international country and city telephone codes

i. average weather temperatures

j. holidays during her stay

2. To assist her in understanding the hosts' cultural and business practices, Ms. Quevedo asked you to research the following:

   a. greetings, handling of introductions, using appropriate titles, exchange of business cards, and any other important points of business etiquette

   b. gift giving for the hosts

c. the hosts' work hour practices

d. the hosts' attitudes toward time in general

e. nonverbal communication patterns as they relate to the hosts

f. the country's currency exchange

g. letter-writing styles

3. Because you are already working on completing a large project, you have asked one of the assistants in your work group to help gather this information.

4. Summarize your team's findings in a memo to your instructor.

5. Be prepared to present your findings to the class.

Application 11-D

Verifying an Expense Reimbursement Voucher

Supplies needed: Form 11-D, Copy of Expense Reimbursement Voucher; Form 11-D1, Completed Expense Reimbursement Voucher. These forms are located in the working papers.

Directions

In the absence of one of the office assistants, Sheryl Robinson from the Sales Department at Supreme Appliances has asked you to verify her expenses.

Expenses Reimbursement Voucher

Directions

When you have completed an expense report, an important task remains: reading the documents for accuracy and completeness. To complete this task accurately, you must verify information shown on one form that is either transferred or entered from one form to another.

1. Read and verify the expense worksheet (Form 11-D) kept by Sheryl Robinson during her recent business trip.

2. Compare Form 11-D with the completed expense report (Form 11-D1).

3. In the numbered blanks provided on Form 11-D1, indicate if the information on the final form is correct by writing a C, or I if the information is incorrect, by the appropriate number. As an option, your instructor may request you to fill in the blank form (Form 11-D2) to complete this voucher.

4. Ask your self the following questions whe preparing the final expense report:

   a. What must I do to compare and verify the information?

   b. Is the transferred information correct (according to the worksheet)?

   c. Are the figures that were transferred in the appropriate column?

   d. Did the figures get transferred accurately?

   e. Are the calculations correct?

   f. Do I have all the necessary receipts to submit with the completed form?

   g. Did I get my manager's signature on the completed form?

Building Your Portfolio

With the help of a team member or your instructor, select the best papers representative of your work from Chapter 11. Suggestions include Activities 1 through 4, Web Activities A, B, and C, and Applications A, B, C, and D. Follow your instructor's directions about formatting, assembling, and submitting the portfolio.

chapter

12 Planning Meetings and Conferences

chapter **outline**

Before the Meeting
    Scheduling and Organizing
    Reserving a Meeting Room
    Sending Notices
    Preparing the Agenda
    Choosing a Meeting Format
    Assembling Materials
    Ordering Refreshments, Meals,
      and Beverages
    Handling Last-Minute Details

During the Meeting
    Taking Notes
    Recording Minutes

Meeting Follow-up
    Preparing Notes
    Preparing Minutes

Team Meetings
    Preparing for a Team Meeting
    Selecting Participants
    Starting the Meeting
    Ending the Meeting and Follow-up

Virtual Meetings
    Audio Conferencing
    Videoconferencing
    Direct Broadcast Video Conferencing
    Web Conferencing
    Virtual Conferencing

Ethical Behavior in Meetings

International Conferencing

learning **outcomes**

When you have completed this chapter, you should be able to:

- Follow procedures to prepare for a business meeting.
- Prepare a checklist of activities to be completed before, during, and after the meeting.
- Identify the structure and procedures used in team meetings.
- Identify the most common forms of electronic meetings.
- Discuss ethics as it relates to meetings.
- Identify the additional responsibilities required to plan an international meeting.

Informal meetings can vary from a meeting in your manager's office to small committee meetings or staff meetings in a conference room. Formal meetings may consist of meetings for board of directors or large meetings for a professional society. Depending on the formality, you may be responsible for any or all of the following:

- arranging the date and time
- reserving the meeting room
- sending notices
- preparing the agenda
- planning for supplies, equipment, and software
- planning food and refreshments
- assembling materials
- attending the meeting
- handling telephone interruptions
- recording the meeting
- following up after the meeting
- preparing and correcting meeting notes or minutes

An office professional is responsible for arranging meetings—either making the arrangements or seeing they have been made. The office professional may also have responsibilities in connection with meetings conducted by teleconferencing or Web conferencing.

Suppose you are headed into a meeting you have been responsible for planning and someone hands you a note saying the caterer will be late delivering the refreshments for the next break time. Suppose the projector's bulb burns out and everyone looks to you for the extra bulb because you had the responsibility for handling media. Regardless of how well you have planned the arrangements for a meeting, difficult situations (and embarrassing ones) can and do occur. Judgments are made about your organizational skills based on how you handle meeting arrangements. These judgments reflect conscious evaluations of your abilities, skills, and potential for advancement within a company. In fact, how you handle yourself, how well you plan the arrangements, and how you work with others sends a message about your professionalism.

The task of planning meetings gives you one of the very best opportunities to make your manager look good and to secure your relationship as a team member. The guidelines presented in this chapter will help ensure you are successful in organizing and coordinating meetings.

Before the Meeting

There are numerous meeting arrangements to make and different options available to help you get organized. Before you begin, be certain you fully understand your responsibilities for making the meeting or conference arrangements. Begin by clarifying your responsibilities toward planning meetings to help prevent any misunderstandings later.

SCHEDULING AND ORGANIZING

To be successful in planning informal or formal meetings, make a list of the items to be dealt with before the meeting.

The following items should be completed in ample time:

1. Reserve the meeting room.
2. Make and confirm hotel accommodations and transportation available to and from the meeting, if necessary, for any out-of-town participants, or provide participants with several hotel and car rental options so they can make their own reservations.
3. Get a written confirmation or a confirmation number of all reservations.
4. Determine how the meeting will be announced. You may or may not be responsible for this task if a meeting or conference is to be held in a location other than your company. For a meeting held on the company's premises, this task is usually the office professional's responsibility. You will also need to keep track of responses to the announcement and follow up with reminders.
5. Determine audiovisual or any other special equipment needs. If this meeting is a formal conference where speakers or presenters are involved, ask each speaker or presenter for a written request for his or her audiovisual needs.
6. Order or lease audiovisual equipment.
7. Confirm attendance at least twenty-four hours prior to the meeting to confirm food order (if ordering food) or to be able to reproduce copies of documents for distribution.

A sample checklist for an in-house meeting is shown in Figure 12-1. The checklist includes items to complete (1) before a meeting, (2) on the meeting day, and (3) after the meeting. This list can be kept on your computer, or you may want to work from a hard copy. Either way, plan in advance and check and double-check your list.

Using the Computer to Schedule a Meeting

How you handle the tasks before a meeting depends on staff and space availability and the preferred method of communicating meeting plans. Arranging an in-house meeting is easy when the following conditions exist: (1) the managers in your organization use the computer to keep their calendars; (2) both scheduled time and free time can be accessed; (3) the calendars are not classified as private and, therefore, are available to others; (4) the managers use electronic mailboxes; and (5) the conference rooms are scheduled using the computer. When shared electronic calendars are used, you would follow these steps:

1. Check the availability of the facilities.
2. Review the calendars of those who are to attend the meeting.
3. Find a time when all the participants are available.
4. Schedule the meeting and send the information about the meeting to the participants' electronic mailboxes.
5. Send reminders via the e-mail system.

FIGURE 12-1 • Meeting checklist.

	General		letion Date
	Secure names/		
	Reserve meeting		
	Make calendar n		
	Prepare meeting		
	Prepare agenda		
	Send notice/agenc		
	Prepare list of mate equipment needed		
	Order refreshments		
	Prepare meeting eva...ion forms		
	Prepare handouts		
	Make hotel reservation(s)		
	Confirm meeting room(s)		
	Meeting Room(s)		
	Location of electrical outlets		
	Extension cords		
	Audiovisual equipment		
	Audiovisual supplies		
	Name tags/name cards		
	Seating arrangements		
	Arrange for water pitcher/glasses		
	Arrange for pads/pens		
	THE MEETING DAY		
	Final check on meeting room(s)		
	Final check on food		
	Final check on equipment		
	AFTER THE MEETING		
	Prepare/distribute notes/minutes		
	Prepare follow-up correspondence		
	Summarize evaluation forms		

Using the Telephone to Schedule a Meeting

If you and others do not use the computer for planning tasks, then you must make meeting arrangements using traditional methods. Using the telephone to find a room for an in-house meeting and a time when it is convenient for all the participants to meet can become a time-consuming task, so plan ahead when you are using this method.

At the time your manager asks you to schedule an in-house meeting or to find out when the other managers are available, he or she should give you at least first and second choices of meeting dates and times and tell you the purpose of the meeting. Enter the meeting for both date and time choices in your manager's appointment calendar. Contact the other participants and request the meeting for your manager's first choice. Also, inquire whether each person could be available at the second time selected. By doing this, you already will have the information if some of the participants have a conflict and the meeting has to be scheduled for the time of the second choice. Scheduling a meeting of three or four people can become complicated, involving many telephone calls or e-mail messages, because executives and professionals make numerous appointments, and some of them may travel. Consequently, let the participants or their assistants know you will respond immediately if you cannot arrange the meeting as tentatively scheduled. As soon as you schedule the meeting, enter the date and time as a firm commitment in your manager's calendar and yours; clear the calendar of the extra or alternate meeting time.

Using a Schedule Form to Schedule a Meeting

If you have any difficulty setting up a meeting with other managers at your company's facilities because of telephone tag or find some participants are traveling, consider using a schedule form similar to the one shown in Figure 12-2. Certain times which were not available for meetings have been blocked out on this form. The form is routed or electronically distributed and participants are asked to select a specific meeting time indicating their first and

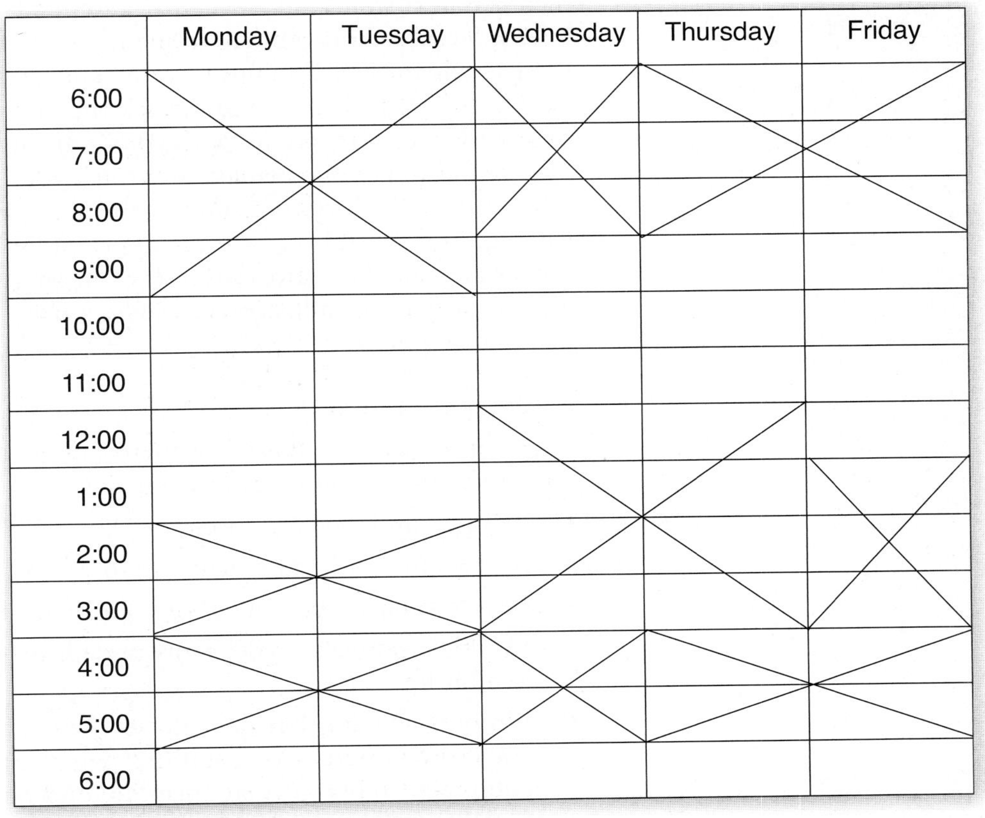

FIGURE 12-2 • A form for scheduling meetings.

Stop 'n Check

List three ways to schedule a meeting discussed in this section.

a. _____

b. _____

c. _____

second choices. When this form is returned to you, you should get an idea of when the participants are available.

Another use of this form is to fill in the time participants are requesting as they call in or send their response by e-mail. If your manager has given you his or her first and second choices, then block out all other times and fill in only the responses from the participants.

Make sure you discuss your options with your manager before making arrangements.

RESERVING A MEETING ROOM

The type of meeting or conference room you will need depends on the purpose of the meeting, the size and needs of the group, and the necessary equipment. For instance, a specially equipped room is needed for a video teleconference. You can determine the size of the room needed by checking the participant list. If minutes were kept for a formal meeting or conference held in the past, then you can check the previous minutes to get an estimate of attendance. Also, confer with your manager about facilities needed. For an off-site meeting, your manager may ask you to reserve a conference room at a hotel near the airport from which most participants will be arriving and leaving. You should confirm the approximate number of participants so the hotel's meeting facilitator can reserve an appropriate-sized room. Hotels provide information online about their services. Some of the services provided by major hotels are:

- equipment rental
- meeting services that coordinate audiovisual services for associations, conventions, and corporate meetings
- banquet and meeting rooms
- room setup and equipment specifications
- on-site supervision and labor coordination
- exhibitor services—a department dedicated to the special requirements of exhibitors
- business centers that provide services such as fax transmission, photocopies, computer workstations with Internet connections and office equipment rental, off-site printing and binding, color copies, and office supplies for purchase

If you must schedule a luncheon or dinner meeting at a hotel or a restaurant, call the banquet manager or the sales/catering manager. Inquire about any costs in addition to the cost of the meal plus gratuity. You may have to guarantee a minimum number of attendees to avoid additional costs. On the other hand, if you are asking a hotel or a restaurant for a meeting room only, establish what the cost of the room will be before you work out other details.

Frequently room reservations at locations other than your company's facilities are made well in advance of a meeting date. Therefore, at the time you make the reservation, enter a notation in your calendar reminding you when to prepare and send out notices. You can enter the reminders at one time for a full year if you are to prepare and send notices for a group whose meetings are regularly scheduled a year in advance. Be alert to any changes in meeting dates and indicate them in your reminder system. You also need a reminder to check the room reservation several days before the meeting (or if appropriate, several weeks).

As you make arrangements for meeting facilities, keep in mind the effect of the room and its furnishings. The atmosphere of the room will contribute significantly to an effective meeting. If the participants are distracted because they are physically uncomfortable, it will detract from the success of the meeting. See Figure 12-3 for an example of an attractive, comfortable meeting room.

Here are some questions to ask when arranging for a room:

- Do the room and its furnishings contribute to an effective meeting?

- Does the arrangement of the room meet the purpose of the meeting? For example, if the purpose of the meeting is to resolve problem-solving situations, then a U-shaped or semicircular furniture arrangement would be most appropriate. On the other hand, if the participants are to review recommendations, then a circular or rectangular arrangement works best.

- Is the room large enough to comfortably accommodate the participants and any planned audiovisual aids?

- What type of media equipment is in the room and is there an audio/video department at the location to assist in case of problems?

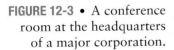

FIGURE 12-3 • A conference room at the headquarters of a major corporation.

Stop 'n Check

List three services provided by major hotels for meetings.

a. ____________________

b. ____________________

c. ____________________

- Is the room free from distractions and interruptions such as telephones and loud noises?
- Is there adequate lighting, heating, and ventilation?
- Does the room accommodate serving refreshments or a meal?

SENDING NOTICES

The type of notice, timing, and details to be included are decisions you must make, depending on the type of meeting and how far in advance planning occurs. For routine meetings you may use your e-mail system to post notes of upcoming meetings, or you may create a form announcement. More formal meetings require drafting a notice for the specific occasion. Business professionals are busy people, so it is important to announce meetings as soon as possible. Microsoft® has several attractive templates you can use to create your meeting announcements to save time. If these are not available on your computer, you may download them from the Microsoft® Web site.

As soon as you have established a date, time, and venue, send out the notices by e-mail. Figure 12-4 provides an example of a meeting notice.

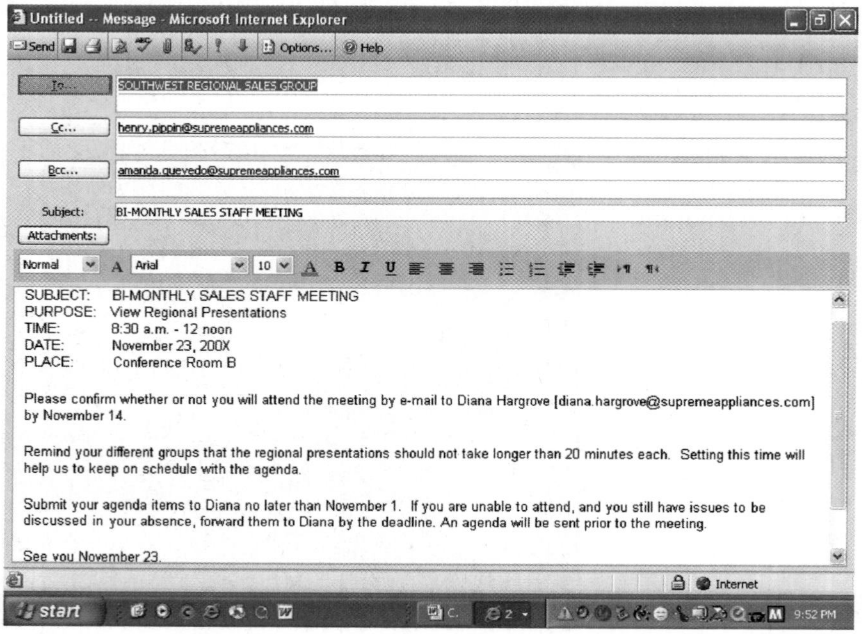
Untitled -- Message - Microsoft Internet Explorer

To... SOUTHWEST REGIONAL SALES GROUP

Cc... henry.pippin@supremeappliances.com

Bcc... amanda.quevedo@supremeappliances.com

Subject: BI-MONTHLY SALES STAFF MEETING

SUBJECT: BI-MONTHLY SALES STAFF MEETING
PURPOSE: View Regional Presentations
TIME: 8:30 a.m. - 12 noon
DATE: November 23, 200X
PLACE: Conference Room B

Please confirm whether or not you will attend the meeting by e-mail to Diana Hargrove [diana.hargrove@supremeappliances.com] by November 14.

Remind your different groups that the regional presentations should not take longer than 20 minutes each. Setting this time will help us to keep on schedule with the agenda.

Submit your agenda items to Diana no later than November 1. If you are unable to attend, and you still have issues to be discussed in your absence, forward them to Diana by the deadline. An agenda will be sent prior to the meeting.

See you November 23.

FIGURE 12-4 • Notice of an informal in-house meeting.

When composing notices, always specify:

- time
- date
- location
- deadline for accepting agenda items
- action to take if member will attend
- action to take if member cannot attend

Participants for a meeting are usually asked to submit topics for the agenda. Requests for items should be made early enough to prepare a final agenda based on the replies received. Clearly state the deadline for the latest time you will accept agenda items.

Time and Type

Determine the best time to send the notices. Consider also that often notices sent too early are ineffective because they can be forgotten. The amount of lead time for sending notices varies according to the formality of the meetings. For example, suppose it is now 10 a.m. and your manager asks you to set up a small informal meeting this afternoon at 2:30 p.m. with five other managers. Obviously, you do not have much lead time to send notices to the participants. What are your options? You may notify everyone using the e-mail system or telephone. In today's electronic world, e-mail is often solely used for all messages—replacing the routed memo entirely.

Some announcements for formal meetings and conferences may be sent to participants as far as one to three months in advance. These announcements may be in the form of specially designed brochures with registration forms, formal letterhead invitations, or printed forms.

For some types of meetings or conferences, enclose an addressed return card with the notice to make it easy for the recipients to reply. If you are not using e-mail to send the notice, add to the file copy the date the notice was mailed.

Details in Notice

Use who, what, when, how long, where, and why as guides for composing notices. Be explicit about when: state the day, date, and hour. Include anything else in the notice that is essential. For instance, if you have a preliminary agenda, enclose it. If the participants need to bring along materials, mention this request in the notice.

Stop 'n Check

List three items of information you should include in meeting notices.

a. _____

b. _____

c. _____

PREPARING THE AGENDA

Whether your manager is conducting an informal meeting or acting as chairperson of a more formal meeting or conference, he or she needs to follow a prepared agenda that has been provided to participants. An **agenda,** also called an *order of business,* is a list of topics to be covered during a meeting or conference, arranged in the order in which the topics will be discussed (Figure 12-5). Preparing the agenda usually means you keyboard, copy, and distribute the agenda. Should your manager ask participants to submit topics

FIGURE 12-5 • Agenda for an informal in-house meeting.

AGENDA

MEETING NO. 4

QUALITY CONFERENCE COMMITTEE

DATE:	Wednesday, June 10, 200X
TIME:	2 p.m.
PLACE:	Conference Room 3
CHAIRPERSON:	Jeffrey Keaton
RECORDER:	Gina Darroch
COMMITTEE MEMBERS:	Jodi Alford, Satvinder Bhardwaj, Gina Darroch, Gordon McLeod, Chris Dennison, Jeffrey Keaton, Allan Kohut, Kenneth Skoye, Benjamin Ross, Brian Van Bij, Donna Welch, Marian Weston, Edward Woods

TIME	TOPICS	MEMBER	DECISIONS AND FOLLOW-UP
2:00-2:10	Adoption of Minutes (Meeting No. 3)		
2:10-2:20	Facilities Report	B. Van Bij	
2:20-2:30	Registration Report	A. Kohut	
2:30-2:40	Awards Report	C. Dennison	
2:40-2:50	Communications Report	G. McLeod	
2:50-3:00	Budget Report	S. Bhardwaj	
3:00-3:10	Public Relations Report	B. Ross	
3:10-3:20	Publications Report	M. Weston	
3:20-3:30	Other Business		
3:30-3:40	Announcements		
3:40-3:45	Adjournment		

How to Prepare an Agenda

✔   Include the names of all participants.

✔   Include the date, time, and place.

✔   Include the topics of issues.

✔   Indicate the level of action, if requested, to be taken by the participants for each topic or issue: discuss, decide, or recommend.

✔   Include time limits, if requested, for each topic or issue.

for the agenda, the request should be made enough in advance to allow time for receiving the replies before preparing the final agenda.

If you are responsible for preparing the agenda, key it and send it as an e-mail attachment. Even for an informal meeting, an agenda should be distributed to all the members. Send the agenda early enough that each member receives it several days before the meeting. They will need time to prepare for the meeting. The more prepared the members are, the more productive the meeting.

CHOOSING A MEETING FORMAT

When the group has not already established the order of business, you can use the following two samples as guidelines.

Formal meeting

1. Call to order by presiding officer
2. Roll call—either oral or checked by the secretary or have a check-in sheet (see Figure 12-6)
3. Approval, amendment, or correction of minutes of previous meeting
4. Reading of correspondence
5. Reports (in this order):
   - Officers
   - Standing committees
   - Special committees
6. Unfinished business from previous meetings
7. New business
8. Appointment of committee
9. Nomination and election of officers—once a year
10. Announcements, including the date of the next meeting
11. Adjournment

Informal meeting

1. Check-ins or warm-ups (optional get-acquainted activities)
2. Review goals of agenda or purpose of meeting
3. Review roles of members (optional)

FIGURE 12-6 • A meeting check-in sheet.

MEETING CHECK-IN SHEET					
Meeting Title:			Date:		
Presenter:			Place/Rm:		

Name	Title	Company	Phone	Fax	E-Mail

4. Review ground rules (optional)
5. Discuss issues listed on agenda
6. Review follow-up actions to which members have committed
7. Closure
8. Determine date and time for next meeting if necessary

Stop 'n Check

Identify the elements of an agenda for an informal meeting.

a. _____
b. _____
c. _____
d. _____

e. _____
f. _____
g. _____
h. _____

ASSEMBLING MATERIALS

As soon as a meeting date has been set, start assembling the necessary materials. Just prior to the meeting, arrange them in a folder in the order in which your manager will refer to them. In addition to the agenda, materials that may be needed include:

- Extra copies of the agenda
- An up-to-date participant list
- Minutes of the previous meeting
- A list of standing and special committees

- A list of action items not yet completed by members
- Letters, memorandums, and reports related to the agenda items
- Copies of material your manager has prepared for distribution
- Materials available from others directly related to the topics or issues to be considered
- Meeting check-in sheet for large conferences to assist with future mailings and to know who attended (include participants' name, title, company, phone, fax, and e-mail address; see Figure 12-6.)

You should consider what supportive materials might be called for during the meeting. Assemble them, but if the meeting is in your manager's office, keep them on your desk. If you attend the meeting, take the folder of supportive materials with you; however, do not put these papers in with the other materials your manager will take to the meeting. Having to shuffle extra papers not only would disrupt your manager's thoughts but also would distract the group.

If the meeting is out of town, put the supportive materials in folders, carefully labeled so your manager can quickly find the papers. As a precaution, never put your file copies with materials to be carried around. Make copies and leave the originals in the files.

ORDERING REFRESHMENTS, MEALS, AND BEVERAGES

If your manager asks you to order refreshments and meals for participants, be sure to confirm the number of participants with the catering staff. A critical concern should be that before deciding on the type of food served, consider the dietary concerns of individuals who prefer certain types of food such as vegetarians and people observing religious conventions or medical restrictions. Keep in mind the following guidelines for ordering:

1. For a morning meeting, coffee, tea, and juice can be served; also, water should be available. For light refreshments, consider fruit and pastries or bagels.
2. For a luncheon meeting, consider a salad or light entree.
3. For an afternoon meeting, coffee, tea, juice, and soft drinks can be served; in addition, cookies or energy snack bars and fruit may be served (Figure 12-7).
4. For a dinner meeting at a location other than your company's facilities, consult with the catering staff for appropriate serving suggestions.

HANDLING LAST-MINUTE DETAILS

Someone once said, "We don't plan to fail, we just fail to plan." So, plan— and be prepared to make changes. Remain flexible. Prior to the meeting or conference, conduct a last-minute check of all details. At this point, a checklist serves as a valuable tool in the planning process. Refer to the sample checklist in Figure 12-1.

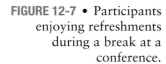

FIGURE 12-7 • Participants enjoying refreshments during a break at a conference.

Stop 'n Check

1. List two types of materials that may be needed in a folder for your manager's meeting.

   a. _____

   b. _____

2. What food is best served for a luncheon meeting?

   _____

3. To avoid missing last-minute details, what form might you use?

   _____

During the Meeting

Whether or not you are required to attend meetings with your manager will depend on the type of organization you work for, your manager's preferences, and the purpose of the meeting. In many instances you may be asked to participate in the meeting, and your role may many times involve taking the meeting notes or recording the meeting proceedings. If you are asked to attend a meeting, arrange for someone to answer your telephone. Do not encourage interruptions, except for the most urgent calls.

TAKING NOTES

Before you take notes of any meeting, clarify the extent to which you are to take notes. For instance, in an informal meeting, you are not expected to record the entire conversation **verbatim** (word for word).

Note taking usually is necessary near the end of a conversation when the participants are summarizing. When you think you have recorded all the essential information, you may read it to the participants, thus checking your notes and perhaps reminding them of something to add. After the meeting, your manager may use the notes to prepare a recommendation, such as a change in procedure or a request for new equipment. A popular way of taking notes today is to use a laptop computer. Regardless of the method, after the meeting you can prepare a draft of your notes that will be meaningful to your manager.

RECORDING MINUTES

As an administrative assistant, you may be assigned the task of recording minutes and transcribing them. **Minutes** are notes recorded for a more formal meeting, such as for a meeting of officers of a corporation. Minutes serve as a record an official meeting was held, discussions took place, and decisions were made during the meeting. Different methods are used for recording minutes, including using a tape recorder and a notepad.

Using a Notebook Computer

Most meetings do not require a verbatim transcript. In this case, the best practice is to key notes onto a notebook computer during the meeting (Figure 12-8). Your job of transcribing your notes will be mostly completed when you leave the meeting. All that will be required is some reformatting and editing.

During the meeting, your computer can be used for more than recording notes. It may operate independently but may also be connected online to the office network. The online connection allows access to information that may be needed to make informed decisions during the meeting.

Using a Tape Recorder

A tape recorder is used to obtain a verbatim record of a meeting for the purpose of (1) preparing a verbatim transcript, (2) assisting the secretary in writing the minutes, and (3) securing a record of discussions on controversial topics.

FIGURE 12-8 • Notebook computer used during a meeting.

When you are recording a meeting on tape, you need to be alert to what is not being recorded and take essential notes. For instance, when a chairperson recognizes a speaker, the chairperson does not always call the speaker's name. Likewise, a chairperson does not always restate a motion as the vote is taking place. When members are following distributed materials, reading as the discussion ensues, the section to which the speaker is referring is not always clearly designated on the tape. Consequently, use notes to supplement the recording.

Record the time, date, and place of the meeting; attendance; reference to corrections and additions to the minutes; who is speaking to introduce reports and make motions; paragraph and page references to distributed materials being discussed; the exact statement of each motion if the chairperson does not state it; who volunteers for follow-up work; time of adjournment; and anything else that will be helpful to you in preparing the minutes. If you indicate in your notebook each time a motion is made, you can organize the minutes quickly as you listen to the tape.

Determine the policy for keeping tapes. Keep each tape until the minutes have been approved or for a much longer period when the topics are controversial or can become controversial. Some groups keep the minutes tapes permanently. Keep a tape until you have approval to erase it.

Put the tapes in their storage containers. Store the tapes being preserved where no one could inadvertently obtain one for recording, for a tape is simultaneously erased as a recording is made. Cassettes have a safety feature, two easy-to-remove knockout tabs at the rear of the cassette, to prevent accidental erasure of a recorded tape. Remove them to prevent the record push button from functioning if the tape is placed in a recorder. If you wish to make the cassette recordable again after removing the knockout tab, place a piece of adhesive tape over the holes.

Using a Notebook

When you take notes to provide a permanent record for a group, your task is similar in meetings conducted formally to those held informally. You are not expected to prepare a verbatim transcript. Only motions and a few other items must be recorded verbatim. Your task is to record the essential information that will serve as a basis for writing the minutes. Minutes provide a record of all the action taken during the meeting, not a detailed review of what was said; consequently, record all action and everything else that seems important.

Meeting Follow-up

Numerous details must be taken care of immediately after a meeting has been held. Prepare a to-do list of all the actions you need to take. Here are some items that might be included:

1. Check the room for orderliness. Pick up extra copies of agendas, proposals, and reports left in the room. Also, check the room for any articles left by the participants and clear away any leftover food and beverages or call the appropriate service department.

Tips for Successful Note Taking

✔ Prior to the meeting, study the minutes of similar meetings to become familiar with the form used.

✔ Prior to the meeting, create a template with as much information as possible. During the meeting, have the template on the screen of your notebook computer where you can add information as the meeting progresses.

✔ Sit near the chairperson so you can assist each other.

✔ Ask the chairperson to see you get a copy of all materials read or discussed. These materials are part of the record and should be attached to the minutes. Do not wait until the end of the meeting to collect them.

✔ Arrange a signal, such as slightly raising your hand, with the chairperson to let him or her know you need assistance in getting statements that must be transcribed verbatim.

✔ Before the meeting begins, record the name of the group and the date, time, and place of the meeting.

✔ At the meeting record the names of those attending and those absent. Using a list of participants you prepared in advance, place a check mark in the appropriate column to indicate attendance and absence.

✔ Write the exact words of anyone who asks his or her view be made part of the record.

✔ Be alert during the informal discussion about the details of a topic. Record each detail as it is discussed. After a detail is agreed on, and this usually is not by vote, write a word such as "Agreed" or "Yes" by it. Each of these items must be followed up. For information not needed, but should be kept until you transcribe, you can use the "strikethrough formatting" command. If using Microsoft® Word, to use the strikethrough formatting command

- Select the text not needed
- Click on Format on the Menu bar.
- Click Font, making sure the Font tab displays.
- Select Strikethrough by placing a check mark in the Effects box.
- Check on OK.

This will place a diagonal line across suggestions made but not accepted if you have entered them in your notes.

✔ Indicate in your notes the name of each person making a motion.

✔ Be sure to take detailed notes on any obligations your manager assumes during the meeting.

✔ While a committee is being appointed, write the name of the committee and the full names of its members, and identify who accepted the position of chairperson.

✔ When officers are elected, record the names of all the officers, incumbent as well as new, and their respective offices.

✔ Make notes on the place, date, and time of the next meeting.

✔ Write down the time of adjournment.

✔ As soon as the meeting adjourns, verify any points about which you have doubts. You may need to ask about a person's title, the full name of a product or place, the correctness of technical terms with which you are not familiar, or any small details you need to prepare complete minutes.

Stop 'n Check

What are the three items you can use to take meeting notes?

a. _____

b. _____

c. _____

2. Make any necessary follow-up entries in the appointment calendars.

3. Send materials through e-mail to people who were absent.

4. Prepare a list to remind your manager of his or her obligations resulting from the meeting.

5. Put a copy of everything—agenda, reports, and so on—in a folder to use as reference at a later date. Be sure to include in your folder any summaries resulting from taking notes during the meeting.

6. Handle any requests that may have resulted from the meeting.

7. See that the audiovisual equipment is returned.

8. Enter the date and time of the next meeting in the calendars.

9. Complete the minutes.

10. Reserve the room and equipment for the next meeting.

To ensure there is clear understanding of what was agreed upon and to provide a complete record of transactions, the chairperson should write a memo to all members involved in follow-up actions. The chairperson should also send letters of congratulations to newly elected officers—even if these members were present at the meeting.

PREPARING NOTES

If you took notes, follow these general guidelines to produce the draft:

1. Produce the draft while the discussions are still fresh in your mind.

2. If an agenda was used, follow the sequence of topics or issues shown.

3. Prepare a concise summary in paragraph form with centered or side headings. Include the date, place of meeting, and the names of the participants. Keyboard the notes in summary form as shown in Figure 12-9.

PREPARING MINUTES

If you took minutes, here are some guidelines to follow to produce the draft:

• If the meeting has been recorded on tape, listen to the tape and take brief notes. Do not waste your time making a verbatim transcript of the tape. When a meeting has been run smoothly, you can listen to a portion of the tape, compose that part of the minutes, listen to the next portion, compose, and continue until you reach the end of the recording. When the proceedings are difficult to follow, listen to the entire recording, taking notes as you listen, and then repeat portions of the tape to verify information as you compose.

• Write the minutes immediately following the meeting. When you work from your manager's notes, it is more than likely you will have to ask questions to elicit additional facts.

• Keyboard a rough draft of the minutes, either double- or triple-spaced, and submit them to your manager for approval before you prepare the minutes in final form.

• Follow a standard arrangement for each group for which you write minutes but not necessarily an identical arrangement for all groups. Your purpose is twofold: (1) to include all the essential information as a record that will be meaningful to others in the future and (2) to make it easy for the reader to locate a single item.

• When a meeting has been conducted so informally that motions were not made and agreement was by consent instead of voting, include the essential facts about the purpose of the meeting, who attended, when, and where and then summarize the action.

FIGURE 12-9 • Minutes of a meeting.

MINUTES OF THE EXECUTIVE TEAM OF CONTINENTAL TECHNOLOGY INC.
Meeting No. 9 — July 8, 200X

The Executive Team of Continental Technology Inc. met in a regular session at 10:30 a.m., Wednesday, June 8, 200X, in Conference Room 3. The following members were

PRESENT:	Verna Chiasson	(Quality Advisor)
	Penny Handfield	(Guidance Team)
	Maurice Ingram	(Team Member)
	Daniel Lawrence	(Team Member)
	Laura Milton	(Team Leader)
	Betty Noble	(Guidance Team)
	Paul Noel	(Team Member)
	Gregory Patrick	(Recorder)
	Dana Rahn	(Facilitator)
	Michelle Savard	(Team Member)
	Gayle Schmitt	(Team Member)
	Mike Sherman	(Team Member)
ABSENT:	Wendy Scarth	(Team Member)

Maurice Ingram moved to approve as read the minutes of meeting No. 8. This motion was seconded by Mike Sherman. The following topics were then discussed:

REDUCTION IN ADMINISTRATIVE COSTS: The ideas presented at the June 10 meeting for cutting administrative costs were revised and the following decisions were made:

Travel. Effective August 1, 200X, all executives of Continental Technology will no longer travel executive class; economy fare only will be paid by the company, with the exception of executive class fares approved by the vice-president. Where Continental executives are taking major clients on business trips, the executive class will automatically be approved by the vice-president.

Sales Incentive Trips. The consensus was that the yearly sales incentive trips, given to sales executives reaching their quotas, should be shortened in length. The trips will be shortened from one week to four days. As well, these trips will no longer be to extremely distant points; they will now be to warm weather North American resorts. It was felt that this would reduce both the air fare and accommodation charges considerably. This will be effective May of next year.

EMPLOYEE EVALUATIONS: Laura Milton circulated copies of a new Employee Performance Evaluation which has been designed to follow ISO 2000 principles. The Executive Team voted unanimously in favor of using the new form beginning September 1.

ANNOUNCEMENTS: **Catalog.** A new product catalog will be available July 25. Copies can be obtained by calling Betty Noble.

New Team Member. Wendy Scarth joined the team as of July 1. However, she is currently taking a training course and absent from meeting No. 9. Wendy works in the Marketing Department and was previously employed by CanTech in Philadelphia.

Next Meeting. The 10th regular meeting will be held in Conference Room 3 at 10:30 a.m. on Thursday, August 15, 200X.

ADJOURNMENT: The meeting was adjourned at 11:45 a.m.

Respectfully submitted,

G. Patrick   *July 10, 200X*

George Patrick, Secretary   Date

Stop 'n Check

1. List two items you must complete to follow-up after a meeting.
   a. _____
   b. _____

2. List one guideline to follow to produce the draft of the notes of a meeting.
   _____

3. List one guideline to follow to produce the draft of the minutes of a meeting.
   _____

Team Meetings

The team concept of meetings focuses on equal participation. Each participant's input is considered to be as significant as all other participants' input, from the maintenance employee to the chief executive officer. The team concept is effective because each member is empowered to participate regardless of his or her organizational status.

Teams make decisions at their level of authority. If a decision must be made at a higher level of authority, the team forwards a recommendation to management. Because team meetings encourage all participants to express their views, conflict and team challenges may occur.

PREPARING FOR A TEAM MEETING

A meeting that follows team techniques requires the same preparation as any other meeting—a convenient time is established, people are invited, and an agenda is prepared and delivered to participants prior to the meeting (Figure 12-10).

When team techniques are followed, careful attention is given to issues that arise even at the preliminary stages. The following techniques will be helpful when preparing for a team meeting.

FIGURE 12-10 • A group team meeting.

- Choosing an appropriate time is important.
- The people who form the team may be from all levels of the organization.
- All team members carry equal status.
- The prepared agenda may be general because the actual topics to be discussed should be decided by the team.

SELECTING PARTICIPANTS

Part of the team philosophy is to get input from people who are actually working within the process. In other words, the people who know the most about a topic should be at the meeting to discuss it and to make wise recommendations and decisions about it.

Each role in the team is equally important. The following briefly discusses the roles of team participants:

1. **Team leader.** The team leader acts as a chairperson, directing the meeting, moving from one topic to the next, and keeping on schedule.
2. **Guidance team.** The guidance team should consist of two or more people who are familiar with the organization. These people usually come from management positions; this enables them to provide information other members may be unaware of and will be helpful when team decisions are made. They should be people who have the authority to make changes and the authority to put decisions into practice.
3. **Project team members.** All members who will take part in the decisions and vote on issues are considered project team members.
4. **Facilitator.** The team leader often carries both the roles of team leader and facilitator. The facilitator's responsibility is to make the meeting process flow with ease and produce results.
5. **Recorder.** The recorder's task is to prepare minutes. This task is often rotated among team members so no one team member always has the additional responsibility of taking notes at each meeting.

STARTING THE MEETING

Here are some suggestions that will make the team meetings productive:

- **Maintain the schedule.** The team leader starts early, and the meeting begins and ends as scheduled.
- **Warm up.** If the team members do not know each other, the team leader should start the meeting by having all members introduce themselves. This activity is considered to be the warm-up.
- **Check in.** Checking in is an opportunity for each team member to express his or her present state of mind to the whole team. An example is "I've had a productive day, and I'm ready to participate."
- **Agree on the goals.** Once the check-in is complete, the team leader should review the agenda.
- **Review the roles of the team.** At the first meeting, the team leader should review the roles of the team leader, guidance team, facilitator, recorder, and project team members.

- **Establish the house rules.** These rules are also referred to as the *ground rules*. The team should suggest and agree on some general rules before the meeting progresses. Here are some examples:
  - Everyone will be given an equal opportunity to speak.
  - Any person wishing to speak must raise his or her hand.
  - Criticize only the issue, not the person with the issue.
  - Side conversations are not allowed.
  - Each person must focus on the speaker.
  - Expect unfinished business.
  - The meeting will begin and end on schedule.
  - Everyone will focus on the topic and will not interrupt the team's work for outside reasons.
  - No negative body language is allowed.
  - The recorder will be given a few minutes to verify information or ask questions.
  - Before ending the meeting, the team will establish a meeting date for the next meeting.

Stop 'n Check

1. List one issue you should give careful attention to when preparing for a team meeting.

   _____

2. What other role does the team leader perform?

   _____

3. List one suggestion that will make a team meeting productive.

   _____

ENDING THE MEETING AND FOLLOW-UP

Just as you learned previously in this chapter, numerous details must be taken care of immediately after a meeting has been held. Review the list of suggestions given in that section.

As a follow-up to the meeting, evaluate each meeting to help improve future meetings. Here are some questions you or the team might answer:

1. Was the purpose of the meeting clear?
2. Did the group work toward a consensus?
3. Was conflict used in a positive way to distinguish between ideas?
4. Did the group insist on what action was to be done, by when, and by whom?

Virtual Meetings

Because managers today have a greater span of control—sometimes locally, nationally, and even internationally—they are constantly seeking ways to spend less time traveling and more time conducting business. **Span of control** is the number of people and functions one manager can supervise. Virtual meetings, also called **teleconferencing,** are a means of holding meetings over communication links connecting two or more locations. The most common types of virtual meetings are audio conferencing, videoconferencing, direct broadcast video conferencing, Web conferencing, and virtual conferencing.

AUDIO CONFERENCING

Placing conference calls by telephone when the participants are located in different geographic areas is called **audio conferencing,** also called *teleconferencing.* Using this method to hold conferences saves travel time and costs and at the same time maintains effective communications. This virtual meeting is the most widely used teleconferencing tool today; it can be used effectively when there is no need for video transmission.

If you are responsible for arranging a conference call, here are some suggestions to follow:

1. Obtain essential information—cities, names, and the date and time of the telephone conference. Pay particular attention to time zone changes.
2. Ask participants to avoid using cell phones or cordless phones because they are likely to get interference such as static.
3. Remind everyone the use of speakerphones can pick up background noises and can sometimes cut off parts of their conversation.

Your telephone must have conference capability, which means the phone will have a conference button. Suppose your organization located in Texas has two branch offices located in New Mexico and Arizona. Your manager has asked you to arrange a telephone conference next week with the two branch managers. You can arrange the conference call yourself by dialing a number and asking the receiver of the call to hold while you conference another person into the call. You simply put the first caller on hold, press the conference button, and dial the second number. When the second caller is connected, you release the hold button to include the first person, who has been waiting on hold. A three-way conversation is now possible.

VIDEOCONFERENCING

Because more and more businesses are allowing employees to work at home, or telecommute, a greater need has arisen for virtual teams to use videoconferencing. Teleconferencing that combines telephone and video is referred to as **videoconferencing.** In a videoconference, two or more persons who are at different geographic locations can conduct business verbally and visually as if they were in the same room (see Figure 12-11). Satellite carriers offer full videoconferencing, which resembles two television sets or two PCs (called *desktop videoconferencing*) talking to each other. Videoconferencing TV-based videophones that use a camera and microphone integrated into the unit are available to simplify the process. Videoconferencing is expensive because it uses numerous pieces of equipment that include cameras, monitors,

FIGURE 12-11 • A video-conference.

microphones, speakers, and PCs. When participating in a videoconference, remember the following:

- Thorough preparation is essential to any conference.
- Make sure the light and sound levels are right for the videoconference. Most microphones can be adjusted. Be sure to check these levels before the meeting.
- Look at the camera when you talk. Once the attention is on you, give the camera a chance to switch to you.
- The other participants can see you, so you must conduct yourself in the same way as in a face-to-face meeting.
- With both audio and videoconferences (see Figure 12-11) that take place over significant distances, there will be a delay in receiving the message. Even a delay of a second can cause confusion as to who should speak next. Slow down. Wait for your message to be received on the other end and wait for the other person's voice to be received on your end.

DIRECT BROADCAST VIDEO CONFERENCING

Direct broadcast video, also called *one-way video,* is video transmission from a single location combined with telephone response from each of the receiving locations. Direct broadcast video is especially helpful for example, in making immediate announcements about new products available through the organization or a corporate-wide announcement by the president. You might be asked to monitor the one-way video and report to your manager important information.

WEB CONFERENCING

A **Web conference** or *Web meeting* occurs when organizations conduct conferences or meetings through computer terminals using Web conferencing services over the Internet. Web conferencing delivers the real-time meeting quality of an audio and video conference without the costs of using a special dedicated room that requires specialized equipment and training. Online services such as Microsoft's LiveMeeting allows a meeting to be run from a Web console rather than downloading software to a PC. Web conferencing services that enable this real-time conferencing offer text chat, audio, video, document sharing, whiteboards, and presentations. They target large organizations that want to achieve significant cost savings by reducing travel and meeting costs.

So you will better understand how a Web conference is handled, let's assume you read on the Internet about a one-hour Microsoft® Excel training seminar to be held online through a Web conference and would like to attend. You go to the designated Web site, view all the possible times the conference is available, and select a session convenient for you to attend. Registration is required. Some training conferences are free and others charge a fee, which you may pay by credit card online. Prior to the meeting time, you will be sent an e-mail outlining the procedures to attend. To attend you go to the Web site and log on using a username and password given to you in the e-mail much as you would log on to a chat room. Once you are logged on, you dial a telephone number on your phone to hear the audio portion. Speakerphones are recommended. You view the training session on your computer screen and hear the instructor who brings up Excel on the screen explaining as he or she moves the cursor around. Questions are either allowed in real time over your telephone during the training session or a question and answer session is set up after the presentation. To end the session, you exit the Web site and hang up your phone. Among the advantages of Web conferencing services are:

- no need for an expensive dedicated room, equipment, training, or software
- unlimited number of meetings for a fee
- unlimited number of participants
- unlimited meeting duration
- meeting from any PC
- password protection so it is secure and firewall friendly

VIRTUAL CONFERENCING

Virtual conferencing can be used for business purposes to provide specific discussion groups the opportunity to share ideas through the use of the Internet. This system acts like a newsgroup, a message board, chat room, or a bulletin board system, in that a space is provided on the Internet where users can post electronic messages to other users. The purpose of the system is to foster a community atmosphere that will allow people to exchange ideas and information. A feature called *virtual reality* can be used to allow the participants to download files that allow them to experience the feeling of "being there." For instance, you might download the file of a museum of fine art. You may elect to allow the computer to take you on a tour of the museum, making you feel as if you are viewing the room from the computer screen. As the camera moves from room to room, you feel as if you were actually turning left or right, and looking up, down, and around the room. You may also elect to take the tour manually by using the mouse or arrow keys on the keyboard to advance through the tour. These experiences allow you to provide input to the discussion group based on realistic experience you have had.

In addition to becoming familiar with one or all of the types of virtual conferencing, you will have the following responsibilities when you make conference arrangements:

- notifying conference participants and arranging a convenient time when all of them are available
- reserving the teleconference facility, if necessary
- requesting any special equipment needed by the participants
- preparing and assembling materials to be distributed
- requesting a person to serve as a technical backup in case the conference leader has difficulty with the equipment
- taking notes during the teleconference
- completing the teleconference follow-up activities, such as summarizing notes and evaluation forms

Stop 'n Check

List the five types of virtual meetings.

a. _____

b. _____

c. _____

d. _____

e. _____

Ethical Behavior in Meetings

ETHICAL★ISSUES

As you learned in Chapter 2, ethics is a system of deciding what is right, or more right, in a given situation. You may find yourself in situations where you might not want to tell the truth to avoid hurting someone's feelings. For instance, what if you were a new participant in a team meeting and after the meeting the facilitator asks you if you enjoyed the meeting and learned a lot of helpful information when you were really bored and already knew everything discussed. It is wrong to say "Oh, yes, I really enjoyed the meeting," to avoid hurting the facilitator's feelings. It would be an outright lie. You may want to learn to sidestep a question or issue without being brutally honest when it is simply a matter of avoiding hurting someone's feelings. Your response to the facilitator could be "I really did find several points you made interesting and helpful."

What if, however, the situation has damaging consequences? For instance while attending your manager's presentation, you notice certain figures in the sales report have been changed to report higher sales. After the meeting you question him about it, and he tells you he increased the figures because the

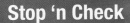

Stop 'n Check

What responsibility might you have when attending a meeting that would display ethical behavior?

_____

department is under pressure to increase sales. If you do not report this behavior and he does it again, he can say you helped him change the figures because you did not report it the first time you noticed it. You have the responsibility to do the right thing based on your own values, and you should report any unethical behavior from the beginning. By doing so, you will be following your company's code of ethics.

Following ethical behavior in meetings, as well as in any personal interaction, is using choices that will build positive qualities—trust and credibility.

International Conferencing

As world communications becomes more and more commonplace, the office professional may find it necessary to help the manager prepare an international meeting or conference (Figure 12-12) or participate in one. You may be required to manage all aspects of the meeting, including:

- advertising
- scheduling
- soliciting papers

FIGURE 12-12 • An international meeting.

- making announcements
- serving as liaison and providing protocol
- supervising staff members
- selecting and negotiating a major hotel, which would involve obtaining information about:
  - conference rooms
  - exhibit and display space
  - banquets
  - meals
  - tours of areas of interest to attendees and spouses
  - registration
  - audiovisual equipment
  - on-site administrative support services
  - refreshments breaks
- tracking and handling finances and payments, including exchange rates
- making travel and lodging arrangements
- making security arrangements
- arranging for transportation
- providing interpreters, if needed

You might be asked to find information about all of the above while maintaining the correct protocol, dealing with cultural differences, and dealing with a different language. Here are some hints:

- Become familiar with the country where the meeting is to be held. What are its religious beliefs, social customs, business philosophy, and family structure?
- Familiarize yourself with the customary formats of business documents used.
- Learn the name of major political leaders, sports figures, and other celebrities.

All of this information will help you know what *not* to do as well as what to do. If you think globally, you can give yourself the edge as you are planning or progressing through your career. Take every opportunity to familiarize yourself with significant communications and cultural barriers that need to be overcome with various cultures. One of your best sources is the United States government. You can get information from the Small Business Administration's Office of International Trade (www.sba.gov), the U.S. Department of Commerce (www.commerce.gov), or the U.S. Department of State (www.state.gov).

Stop 'n Check

List three aspects of an international meeting that might be delegated to you.

a. _____

b. _____

c. _____

Quick Tips

HAVE YOU BLOGGED LATELY?

What is a blog? A **blog** is a shortened term for *Web log*, a Web site that is updated on a regular basis, structured in reverse chronological order so the most recent posted information is listed first, typically with a strong personal perspective. Blogging could be called another way of meeting online at your convenience.

Companies may use blogs to ask questions of their customers about changes in products, announcements about new products, requests for comments or opinions about ideas affecting their business, and so on. If your company has a blog, you might be asked to monitor the blog and report to your manager new comments. Visit www.blog.com and browse the blogs. You will see blogs from businesses to personals.

Concept Review and Reinforcement

Review of Key Concepts

OUTCOME	CONCEPT
1. Follow procedures to prepare for a business meeting.	When scheduling a meeting: • Reserve meeting room. • Make and confirm hotel accommodations and car rentals, if necessary. • Obtain written confirmation or confirmation number for all reservations. • Determine how meeting will be announced. • Determine audiovisual or any other special equipment needs. • Order audiovisual equipment. • Order food or refreshments, confirming number with caterer.
2. Prepare a checklist of activities to be completed before, during, and after the meeting.	Use a checklist of activities to be completed before, during, and after a meeting similar to the checklist shown in Figure 12-1 to avoid missing any details.

3. Identify the structure and procedures used in team meetings.	• Choosing an appropriate time is important.
	• Employees who form the team may be from all levels of organization.
	• All team members carry equal status.
	• Team should prepare very general agenda.
	• Select the following members:
	  • **Team leader** acts as chairperson, directing meeting, moving from one topic to next, and keeping on schedule.
	  • **Guidance team** should consist of two or more people who are familiar with the organization and have authority to make changes and put decisions into practice.
	  • **Project team members** take part in the decisions and vote on issues.
	  • **Facilitator** ensures meeting flows with ease and produces results; team leader may take this role.
	  • **Recorder** takes notes and prepares minutes.

4. Identify the most common forms of electronic meetings.	Most common types of teleconferencing are audio conferencing, videoconferencing, direct broadcast video conferencing, Web conferencing, and virtual conferencing.
5. Discuss ethics as it relates to meetings.	Ethics is a system of deciding what is right, or more right, in a given situation. Following ethical behavior in meetings, as well as in any personal interaction, is using good choices that will build positive habits—trust and credibility.
6. Identify the additional responsibilities required to plan an international meeting.	Here are some tips on preparing for an international meeting. • Become familiar with the country. • Familiarize yourself with the customary formats of business documents. • Learn the name of major political leaders, sports figures, and other celebrities.

Key Terms

Agenda. Also called an *order of business*, a list of topics to be covered during the meeting or conference, arranged in the order in which the topics will be discussed.

Audio conferencing. Conference telephone calls connecting participants in different geographic areas.

Blog. A shortened term for *Web log*, a Web site that is updated on a regular basis, structured in reverse chronological order so the most recent posted information is listed first, typically with a strong personal perspective.

Direct broadcast video conferencing. Also called *one-way video*, is video transmission from a single location combined with telephone response from each of the receiving locations.

Minutes. Written notes that serve as a record of an official meeting.

Span of control. The number of people and functions one manager can supervise.

Teleconferencing. The means by which meetings are held over communication links connecting two or more locations.

Verbatim. When something is stated word for word.

Videoconferencing. System in which two or more persons in different geographic locations can conduct business verbally and visually as if they were in the same room.

Virtual conferencing. System that acts like a newsgroup, message board, chat room, or bulletin board system, in that a space is provided on the Internet where users can post electronic messages to other users.

Web conferencing. Sometimes called *Web meetings*, educational sessions or business meetings conducted over the Internet with remote participants at their computers.

For Your Discussion

Retrieve file C12-DQ from your student data disk.

DIRECTIONS

Enter your response after each question or statement.

1. How can a computer be helpful in arranging business meetings?

2. In arranging meetings, what preliminary activities are the office professional's responsibility?

3. On the meeting day, for which activities can the office professional accept responsibility?

4. After the meeting, for which activities can the office professional accept responsibility?

5. What information should you provide your manager immediately following a meeting he or she has chaired?

6. Identify the structure and procedures used in team meetings.

7. Describe an efficient way of organizing notes for writing minutes when the transactions of the meeting were recorded on tape.

8. Explain the five most common forms of virtual meetings available to today's business.

9. Discuss ethics as it relates to meetings. Give specific examples other than those given in the text.

10. In arranging an international meeting, for which aspects of the meeting might the office professional be responsible?

Building Your Office Skills

Exploring the Workplace: *Activities*

1. Interview an assistant who has handled all the details for a formal or informal meeting. Summarize the assistant's responses to the following questions:

   a. What are the most critical steps taken when you first plan a meeting?

   b. What methods are used to notify people of an upcoming meeting?

   c. Are you responsible for taking notes or minutes in meetings? If so, can you share how you format the notes or minutes?

   d. What types of activities, if any, are you involved in during a meeting?

   e. What types of activities do you complete after a meeting?

   f. Are you involved in making arrangements for teleconferencing?

   g. What are the most common problems that arise when planning meetings or conferences?

2. Research magazines, newspapers, or the Internet for articles relating to electronic conferencing. Summarize the information and be prepared to report your findings to the class.

3. With the use of audio and video electronic technology, public and private educational institutions are using virtual meetings. Interview a school administrator who is responsible for virtual meetings in his or her institution. Report your findings on what technology supports virtual meetings, how questions and answers are handled during the meeting, and what common problems arise when planning virtual meetings.

4. Call the sales or catering department of two hotels in your area. Request the following information:

   a. approximate cost for a room to hold a meeting for 10, 30, and 100 people.

   b. a price list for refreshments

   c. availability and cost of audiovisual equipment

   d. advance notice needed to reserve the room

   e. rules, if any, concerning canceling room reservations

   f. other features offered for companies planning meetings at their hotels

   Summarize your findings in report form for your instructor.

Developing Critical Thinking Skills: *Problem Solving on the Job*

Retrieve file C12-OJS from your student data disk.

Directions

Enter your response after each situation.

1. **Crisis telephone call.** You receive a long-distance call for Mary Ann Cortelli, who is supposed to be attending a meeting chaired by your manager, Allen Bigby. The meeting is being held near your office. About seventy-five participants are in attendance. Ms. Cortelli preregistered for the meeting, but she has not picked up her registration badge or her luncheon ticket. You speculate she is not at the meeting. The telephone call seems urgent. What should you do?

2. **Missing presentation.** Your manager, Ms. Corona, is giving a talk at a national conference in another state at 2 p.m. tomorrow. As soon as she arrives at her destination, she calls you to say she does not have the PowerPoint presentation she needs to illustrate her talk. "Is it on your computer?" she inquires, and sure enough, it is saved on your computer. She brought her laptop with her. She says, "Get the presentation to me. What will you do?

3. **Agenda.** One of the assistants in another department has come to you for advice. Her manager has not been distributing an agenda prior to meetings. On occasion when her manager has used an agenda, it does not include all of the items and no time limits have been indicated for each topic or issue. Participants in the meetings have been complaining to the assistant. They have asked her to get the manager to use an agenda more effectively. What should an agenda include? What would you say to her?

4. **Training instructor unavailable.** You have scheduled a two-day training session for eighteen employees. The meeting is scheduled in three days and all arrangements have been made. You receive a call from the instructor explaining he has become very ill. What should you do? Outline in detail your actions.

Using the Web: *Research Activities*

A. You are constantly involved with scheduling virtual conferences for meetings and training. You heard there is an association especially for employees that use electronic conferencing in the workplace. You mention the association to your manager, and the manager wants to know more about it.

   1. Enter the following: www.imcca.org.

   2. Locate information about the Interactive Multimedia & Collaborative Communications Alliance (IMCCA). Browse the IMCCA Web site and find and print the following information:

      a. history of IMCCA

      b. mission statement

      c. newsletter

      d. membership information

      e. opportunities

      f. resources

   3. Write an informational report to your manager providing the information requested.

B. Research the Internet for tips for taking minutes.

   1. Enter the search words: *taking meeting minutes*

   2. Locate information on available software, recording equipment, and training for taking minutes.

   3. Write a memo to your instructor summarizing the information you found on each of these areas. Be sure to include the product name and URL along with each summary.

C. Research the Internet for various meeting agenda templates.

   1. Enter the search words: *meeting agenda templates*.

   2. Based on the results, write a memo to your instructor summarizing the information. Be sure to include the website in your report.

Get Tech Wise: *Microsoft® Outlook for Meeting Notifications*

Directions

1. Open Microsoft® Outlook and click on Calendar in the Outlook Shortcuts.

2. Click on New, then Appointment. The Untitled Appointment dialog box will appear.

3. Type a subject, location, and comments in the message area:

Type as your subject: Office Procedures Meeting

Type as your location: Room 224

Type as your comments: Discussion will be about using Outlook to set up meetings.

4. Click on the Scheduling tab.

5. Click on "Click here to add a name" and type the name of two of your classmates or friends.

6. Fill in the date and time text boxes under Start Time and End Time.

7. You can send the meeting notice from either the Appointment or Scheduling tab window. You can also decide if the recipient's attendance is required or optional.

8. Click on the Send icon.

9. When the recipients receive your message, they can click on the Accept, Tentative, or Decline buttons on the toolbar.

10. You will receive their "accept, decline, or tentative" reply and any comments they have for you.

11. If you need to edit or delete this message, simply open it to make changes or to delete. You will automatically be prompted to notify attendees.

Improving Your Writing Skills: *Grammar Workshop*

Retrieve file C12-WRKS from your student data disk.

Supreme Appliances

Simulation: *In the Office at Supreme Appliances*

Application 12-A

Sending Notice of Meeting

Supplies needed: Plain paper.

Directions

Ms. Quevedo has called a meeting of the Executive Committee of the November Sales Seminar. She has asked you to send the notices. The meeting will be held in Ms. Quevedo's office at Supreme Appliances, Inc., at 5 p.m. Wednesday, September 10. The purpose of the meeting is to finalize plans for the November Sales Seminar. The Executive Committee members include the assistant vice presidents of each region and the sales managers from Boston and Texas. Create the body of an e-mail to send to the participants.

Ms. Quevedo needs to know (1) if the person can attend the September 10 meeting, (2) if the person has a report to make, and (3) if the person thinks an October meeting of the Executive Committee will be necessary. Phrase your questions carefully in your e-mail. Ms. Quevedo will approve a draft of the body of the e-mail before it is sent.

Submit your draft to your instructor.

Application 12-B

Keyboarding Minutes

Supplies needed: Form 12-A-1, November Sales Meeting Notes; plain paper.

Directions

Ms. Quevedo put her notes from the September 10 meeting of the Executive Committee of the November Sales Seminar in your in-basket with the following note attached "Please key these minutes for me." You are to keyboard Ms. Quevedo's notes from Form 12-A-1.

Application 12-C

Hosting International Visitors— Collaborative Assignment

Supplies needed: Form 12-B, Meeting Checklist; plain paper.

Retrieve file C12-AP-C from your student data disk.

Directions

Ms. Quevedo has asked you to help her with hosting the group she presented to in Guadalajara. She wants to avoid any miscommunication that may interfere with the success of the meeting. Ms. Quevedo has asked you to set up a team to help make arrangements for hosting the seven visitors. Your team has the responsibility for this group of five men and two women from their arrival time at Dallas–Fort Worth Airport on Sunday to their departure time (one week from their arrival).

1. During the group's visit, your team is to make arrangements for two meetings: the first to be held at 10 a.m. Tuesday and the second to be held at noon (a luncheon meeting) Wednesday. In addition to making arrangements for the two meetings, your team has been asked to make arrangements for dinner on Thursday at 7:30 p.m. Complete Form 12-B for the meeting.

   In addition, Ms. Quevedo has asked your team to gather the following information in report format about the visitors:

The Country

- In which state of Mexico is Guadalajara located?

- What are the main industries in Guadalajara?

- What are some historical aspects of Guadalajara?

- What are some political aspects of Guadalajara?

- Who are some sports figures from Guadalajara?

Nonverbal Communication

- You may refer to the information gathered in Application 11-C to complete this section on nonverbal communication.

- Are there any nonverbal communication patterns we use that may be interpreted as offensive in their country?

- Can you anticipate some possible miscommunication problems? If so, identify a few.

- Can you determine the appropriate speaking distance between persons from this culture?

Daily Business Life

- Again, you may refer to Application 11-C.

- How should we greet these visitors?

- Determine if gift giving is appropriate for these visitors. If so, what kind of gift is appropriate?

- What kinds and colors of flowers are appropriate to use for our meetings?

- How are business meetings conducted in the visitors' country compared to our own?

- What business etiquette or manners must we know before these visitors arrive?

Food

- What rules govern dining at our luncheon here at the company and at a restaurant?

- What kinds of food do these visitors prefer?

2. Prepare your findings in informational report form. Be prepared to share the information with your class.

3. Based on your findings from the cross-cultural study, plan the three events incorporating the following. Write a memo to Ms. Quevedo outlining these three meetings.

   a. Morning meeting: Be versed in introductions; plan the seating arrangement (your manager; yourself; Henry Pippen and his assistant, Kirk Lawrence; J. R. Rush; Thomas Strickland; Sid Levine; Karen Baxter; and the seven visitors who will be in attendance); refreshments; and the flower arrangement.

   b. Luncheon meeting: Plan the seating arrangement (your manager; yourself; Henry Pippen and his assistant, Kirk Lawrence; J. R. Rush; and the seven visitors). Select the caterer, the menu, and the flower arrangement.

   c. Dinner: Make the restaurant reservations, confirm the final count, make arrangements for travel from the hotel to the restaurant, and plan the seating arrangement (the group will consist of the seven visitors, you, Ms. Quevedo and her husband, and J. R. Rush and his wife).

4. Be prepared as a team to share your information with the class.

Building Your Portfolio

With the help of a team member or your instructor, select the following documents: Keyboarding minutes, memo to Ms. Quevedo, and informational report on hosting international visitors. If instructed, place the documents in plastic protection sheets and add to your portfolio.

chapter **outline**

Planning a Presentation
  Define Your Purpose
  Consider Your Audience

Organizing the Content
  Gaining the Audience's Attention
    in the Introduction
  Organizing Main Points
  Keeping Your Audience Interested
  Summarizing and Concluding
  Handling Questions/Comments
    from the Audience

Delivering the presentation
  Structuring Your Presentation
  Delivering Your Presentation
  Evaluating Your Presentation

Designing a Multimedia Presentation
  Selecting the Design
  Producing Speaker's Notes and Handouts
  Adding Multimedia Features

Dealing with Nervousness

Ethics and Speaking

Speaking to Diverse Audiences

learning **outcomes**

When you have completed this chapter, you should be able to:

- Explain the importance of identifying your purpose for a presentation.
- List the points necessary to organize the content of your presentation.
- Discuss how to organize the content of your presentation.
- Discuss the various ways you can structure your presentation.
- Discuss delivery techniques before, during, and after your presentation.
- Discuss how to conquer fear when making presentations.
- Discuss the importance of ethics in speaking.
- Identify various areas you should research before speaking to a diverse audience.

Sooner or later in your career, you may be called upon to make a presentation. Public speaking is a set of skills, not a talent. Anyone can develop effective presentation skills. For many people, presenting a topic can be an unpleasant experience. It need not be so.

The key to giving effective presentations is practice. Take advantage of every opportunity you have; for instance, you may be comfortable around your coworkers at staff meetings. When called upon to make a report, apply the techniques of making effective presentations to giving your report in the meeting. The more experience you have at speaking before an audience, the more likely you will become more comfortable at doing so. Where would be a better place to start than around those with whom you feel most comfortable?

Presentations put you on display and allow you to show your audience how skilled you are. First, though, you must learn the techniques of making effective presentations, and that is the purpose of this chapter.

Planning a Presentation

As with any work you do, planning is the first, most important element of an effective presentation. With good planning you can polish your presentation skills, which will allow you to speak with confidence, clarity, and conviction. See Figure 13-1 for the process you must go through to plan an effective presentation.

FIGURE 13-1 • Flowchart for planning a presentation.

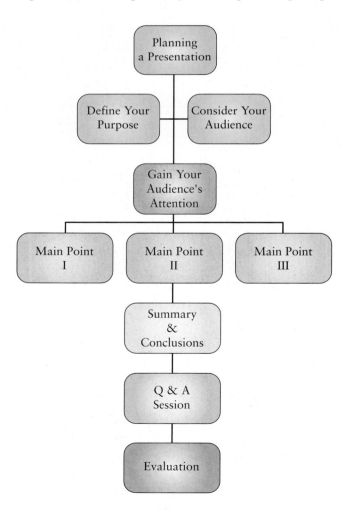

DEFINE YOUR PURPOSE

The first step in planning your presentation is to define the purpose. Identifying the purpose allows you to have a clear understanding of what you want your audience to achieve as a result of listening to your presentation. In this step, begin to ask yourself some important questions, such as:

- Why am I giving this presentation?
- What is it I want my audience to do or leave knowing when my presentation is over?

Limit your purpose to one goal. Most presentations are time limited, and it is better to accomplish one goal than to rush through several goals and get none accomplished. Here are some examples of concise statements of purpose:

The purpose of my presentation is to:

- Explain the new method for submitting travel expenses and mileage.
- Share information on two facilities, one of which will be selected for this year's company picnic.

In the first example, it is clear what you want your audience to do. You want them to leave knowing how to correctly submit the forms for reporting travel expenses and mileage. Think how important it is to accomplish this task in your presentation so you are not faced with having to correct or retrain several members in your audience. In the second example, you want the planning committee to be able to select the facility for this year's picnic based on the information in your presentation. Your planning should be such that all the audience's questions are answered in the presentation.

CONSIDER YOUR AUDIENCE

You need to understand your audience. To reach them, you must understand what they need. They will ask themselves as you speak, "What is in this presentation for me?" If they don't immediately identify with your message during your introduction, they may tune you out and not listen at all. Begin by asking yourself some basic questions about your audience.

- To whom am I speaking?
- What do they already know about the topic?
- What will they want to know about the topic?
- What do they need to know about the topic?

The answer to these questions will help you know what content should be presented and at what level to speak. If the audience consists mainly of experts, you would not present basic information. If the audience consists of those individuals who know very little about your topic, you would begin with the basics. Ideally, if you had the opportunity to survey your audience, you would know what direction to take when planning your presentation.

Stop 'n Check

What are the two areas to consider when planning your presentation?

a. _____

b. _____

Organizing the Content

It is imperative that you organize your content carefully (Figure 13-2). Your talk must be well organized and your points presented logically and clearly. Introductions and background information are boring. Unless it is necessary the audience know the information, avoid giving the basics—give it to them in a handout to be distributed later and get right to the point.

GAINING THE AUDIENCE'S ATTENTION IN THE INTRODUCTION

Many times the first few minutes of a presentation are lost while people find a chair, drift in with coffee, and finish their conversations they were having with the person next to them. Since you have a limited time, it is your responsibility to gain their attention.

Here are some points to remember:

- **Introduce yourself.** If you are not formally introduced, make certain you introduce yourself. Don't assume everyone knows who you are. Describe your position, knowledge, or experience; explain what qualifies you to speak on this topic.

FIGURE 13-2 • Plan your presentation before you begin writing.

- **Handle administrative details.** You should find out ahead of time if there are any administrative details you need to handle with the audience. The audience can become distracted and become worried if details are overlooked.

- **Identify your role.** You should plan exactly how you want to appear to your audience—friend, expert, judge, teacher. Whatever role you choose, you must establish it from the beginning.

- **Plan for questions.** Identify in the beginning how you will handle questions so no one in the audience will interrupt your presentation unless you want them to. You may plan for a ten- to fifteen-minute question-and-answer session at the end. If you say you will have this session, watch your time and be sure you allow time for it.

- **Explain if there are handouts.** If members of the audience know you will give them PowerPoint® copies or notes as a handout, many will relax and listen to your presentation rather than trying to copy each slide as it is presented or take notes vigorously.

- **Give the audience an overview.** In giving the overview, explain each point you will cover. For instance, say something like "I will concentrate on the following four points: First of all. . . . Then . . . This will lead to . . . and finally. . . ." This will explain briefly how your presentation will proceed. The audience will then know what to expect.

Now that you have the preliminaries out of the way, you must gain the audience's attention. You should entice the audience to listen to you. Help them understand why they should listen. In the example given earlier where you would be showing them how to complete the forms for reporting travel expense and mileage correctly, they will listen because you are going to make their job easier. In the second example, when the committee sees each facility's strong points, they will be able to decide where to have the company picnic. They can relax and listen because you have done the work for them.

You want your audience to believe your presentation will be interesting, enjoyable, and above all, worthwhile. Here are a few additional ways in which you may gain their attention (Figure 13-3):

- Ask a poignant question.
- Use a famous quotation.
- Tell an anecdote or story.
- Make a startling comment such as "Did you know . . . statistics show. . . !"
- Give historical background.
- Refer to a current event.
- Explain your purpose.

This opening should lead naturally into your presentation. You should next identify the first main point ("This morning/afternoon/evening I will begin by talking about. . . .")

ORGANIZING MAIN POINTS

Most presentations are twenty or fewer minutes long, so limit your main points to no more than four. Present each main point one by one in a logical

FIGURE 13-3 • How to gain your audience's attention.

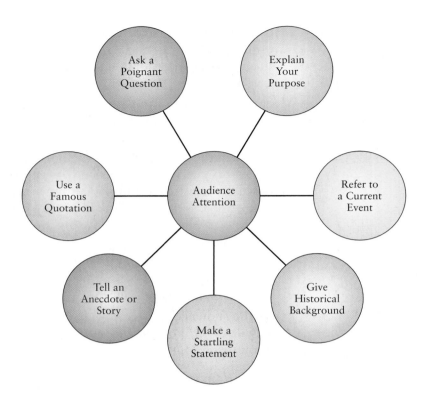

order. Be sure to use clear examples to illustrate each point. Always pause at the end of each point. This gives your audience time to take notes, or to think about what you have said. Make it absolutely clear when you move to the next point. For example, say:

- "The next point I want to make is . . ."
- "I will now talk about . . . "
- "Let's consider my next point . . ."

Extemporaneous speaking (speaking freely and naturally) is the most effective delivery style because it allows you to continuously maintain eye contact with your audience. It is not necessary to write a complete script of what you will say. If you feel you need reminders to jog your memory as you give your presentation, use cue cards. If you do so, the cards should be numbered and should contain only key words for phrases in large enough bold type that you can read the word or phrase at a glance.

KEEPING YOUR AUDIENCE INTERESTED

You should involve your audience whenever possible. The audience enjoys interaction more than just sitting and listening. The uniqueness and novelty of an activity will increase the impact of your presentation. Even with large audiences, you can build into your presentation brief exercises the audience can complete. Some examples are:

- a brief survey or checklist asking for opinions related to the topic
- asking listeners to turn to the person sitting next to them and discuss briefly some point
- brief games that relate to the topic

Here are some additional ideas to add variety to your presentation:

- Alternate moving and standing still, speaking and listening, doing and thinking.
- Add stories, anecdotes, testimonials, analogies, and demonstrations.
- Use humor appropriately and always in good taste.
- Read your audience. If the audience starts making movement sounds, and you begin to hear low talking, you are losing them. This will tell you to move on and even omit part of your presentation. Keep an eye on the audience's body language to know when to move more quickly through your presentation.

Remember your audience members will drift in and out listening to you; thus, they will not give you their complete attention all the time. You can help them by interjecting activity, movement, or involvement to bring their attention back to your presentation.

Stop 'n Check

List three ways you can gain your audience's attention at the beginning of your presentation.

a. _____

b. _____

c. _____

SUMMARIZING AND CONCLUDING

Your closing remarks will leave a final impression on the audience, and these remarks will most likely be the one thing they remember from your presentation. Because of the impact a conclusion has, you need to plan your closing statements with care. Don't run over your time limit. Start on time and quit on time. Although your audience enjoyed your presentation, they will become restless and may even change their opinion of your presentation if you keep them longer than the time limit.

Begin by getting your audience's attention. Don't *tell* them you will end by summarizing even though that is what you might do. This will turn them off because they think they have heard all you have to say before. End with a change of pace. Here are some effective conclusions:

- Give a simple review of the main points and purpose of the meeting. This closing usually will suffice if your presentation is for internal use.
- Demonstrate how all your main points fit together into an idea the audience can take with them. You can also sum up the main points. You might say, "You have learned this . . . this . . . and this. Now that you understand . . . you will be able to . . ." or "Let's look at what we learned today. . . ." or "So, in conclusion . . ." or "Now to recap the main points . . ." or "My final point is . . ."

- Close with a question when you want the audience to continue thinking about what you have said. An example would be, "Now that you know the how-to, will you make the commitment this week to meet the challenge?"

Explain your conclusions by pulling together your opening and overall purpose. Explain how your main points will enable them to achieve your purpose. Encourage or motivate them to action by making a moving statement, telling a moving story, or making a call to action or a challenge.

The main thing to remember is your closing needs to be clear, logical, and strong.

HANDLING QUESTIONS/COMMENTS FROM THE AUDIENCE

Make certain you leave enough time for the audience to ask questions if you told them in the beginning you would do so. Here are some points to remember:

- Don't just ask for questions; guide your audience through the main points. For example, say, "What questions do you have about . . . ?"
- When a question is asked, be sure to listen carefully so you understand what is being asked. If you don't understand the question, ask for clarification. It is often helpful to rephrase the question in your own words to make sure you understood what was asked. Rephrasing questions will allow you to shorten long, rambling questions.
- Don't be afraid to admit you don't know. Tell them you'll find out and get back to them, and then be sure to do so.
- Be sure to repeat each question over the microphone for large audiences so everyone can hear the question before you respond.
- Don't rush an answer. Pause and think about what you are going to say before you respond. When you answer, get to the point; don't digress.
- If no questions are asked, be sure you have one or two questions you can ask of the audience to begin the discussion.

Managing Hecklers

Hecklers are people who shout an uninvited comment or ask deliberate questions meant to interrupt, anger, or upset a speaker. Prepare yourself for the worst questions by anticipating what they will be and planning answers for them. Answering questions is an important part of your presentation skills. No matter what you do, remain calm if a person begins to heckle you. The worst thing you can do is to show anger. If you don't want to answer the heckler, simply say, "Thank you for your opinion" and move on. Don't let yourself get into an argument. An argument only gives the heckler control.

Delivering the Presentation

All presentations should have structure, which allows your audience to follow your meanings. **Structure** means the manner of construction of the presentation and the logical arrangement of its parts.

Stop 'n Check

1. List one way you can deliver your conclusion.

    _____

2. Identify one tip to follow when answering questions.

    _____

3. What can you say to a heckler?

    _____

PRESENTATION STRUCTURE	
General to specific	Allows you to present each main topic followed by a subtopic, which is then followed by a statement that leads to a specific conclusion.
Questioning	Introduces relevant background information followed by possible solutions with advantages and disadvantages given for each solution. Finally, summarize all possible solutions with the preferred solution identified for the audience, asking the audience for approval or discussion.
Specific to general	The reverse of general to specific. Present the details first, which leads to a main point. Each point is treated the same way. All main points are then summarized.
Beginning-middle-end	Provides a brief introduction, followed by all main points, and ending with a brief conclusion. This structure is the simplest, most direct, and most often used method of structuring presentations.

FIGURE 13-4 • Ways to structure your presentation.

STRUCTURING YOUR PRESENTATION

Choose the way you want to deliver your ideas. Your choice will depend on what type of presentation you are making. For instance, you might choose one method if you are in a staff meeting where your presentation is disseminating information, another method when explaining a decision that has already been made, or a formal presentation as guest speaker for a large group. See Figure 13-4 for some other choices.

Once you have identified the purpose of your presentation, you should choose the most appropriate structure to achieve your purpose.

DELIVERING YOUR PRESENTATION

Delivery has to do with how you present yourself to the audience. Audience members will focus their attention on you, and you can make or break the presentation by your actions. As you speak, the audience will be observing eyes, voice, body language, and appearance.

Your Eyes

Your eyes are by far the most important of the four parts of the human body that will influence audience response. Your eyes will convince the audience of your honesty, openness, and confidence. During your presentation you should establish eye contact with each member of the audience. If your audience is large, you can do this by continually looking to the right, to the left, straight ahead in the distance, and then repeat the same procedure down front. Each member will feel as if you are looking at him or her because it is difficult to tell precisely where you are looking. Hold your gaze fixed at each point for five or six seconds before changing. A quick smile before changing positions will convince audience members in that direction you have seen them and acknowledge their presence.

Your Voice

Your voice's projection and variation are its most important aspects. Speak clearly. Don't shout or whisper. Deliberately pause at key points. Slow down and take your time. You should speak slightly louder and slightly slower than when talking normally. How you say it is as important as what you say. Here are some points to remember:

- Speak loud enough for everyone to hear you. It is best to check the acoustics in the room prior to your presentation.
- Vary the volume and pitch of your voice. Use a higher pitch when making a new point.
- Keep your words simple. Don't try to impress the audience with your vocabulary.
- Check the pronunciation of difficult, unusual, or foreign words before your presentation.
- Be careful of verbal ties such as "um," "you know," or "like."
- Drink water before you speak as it will lubricate your vocal chords. Breathe deeply and slowly to project your voice.

Body Language and Appearance

Face your audience. Avoid talking to the screen if using slides, transparencies, white board, or easel tablet. You will lose your audience if you do not focus on them. Here are some dos and don'ts to remember.

Do:

- Stand securely with legs slightly apart, back straight, and body relaxed facing the audience. If you are a female, do not wear high heels unless it is a fashion event.
- Keep your arm and hand gestures under control. Move your arms only above the belt line and slightly outside the chest area.
- Make planned position changes. Walk calmly toward the screen, overhead, tablet, or whiteboard. Make a brief stop on the way and continue your presentation with a few remarks.
- Use body language to convey your message. When you talk in a conversation with friends, you use your hands, facial expressions, and body to enhance understanding. Do the same in your presentation. It will make your presentation more interesting for the audience.

- Dress appropriately for your audience, not for yourself. First impressions influence the audience's attitude toward you. Even though dress is a personal choice, select your clothes carefully and deliberately. It is better to be overdressed than underdressed when making a presentation.

Don't:
- Pace back and forth, rock back and forth, or stand stiffly in one place all the time.
- Play with the pointer, fumble with notes, or rattle change in your pocket.
- Read the presentation from your notes, screen, or tablet.
- Block visual aids from your audience.

Practice, Practice, Practice

Rehearsing could make the difference between an effective and an average presentation. Plan to rehearse your presentation out loud at least four times. Make sure one of your rehearsals is in front of an audience—family, friends, colleagues, or children. They will be brutally honest with you on what you should or should not do or say. Each time you rehearse, time yourself so you can adjust the presentation to fit the time allotted. Another excellent practice is to videotape or record yourself. Either of these practices will give you feedback and help fine-tune your presentation.

Stop 'n Check

1. What is one way to structure your presentation?

   _____

2. What is the most important aspect of the human body that draws the audience's attention?

   _____

EVALUATING YOUR PRESENTATION

Encourage those around you to give you feedback about your presentation. You can also prepare an evaluation form to have the audience complete at the end of your presentation. The feedback you receive from these forms can be invaluable to help you plan your next presentation. One thing to remember is you cannot please everyone, so ignore those evaluations that are low or have negative comments. Focus on the majority of the evaluations and use the comments as a way to improve. Figure 13-5 shows an example of a speaker evaluation checklist you might use.

To help improve your presentation, answer the following questions:

- Was the purpose achieved?
- Was the information relevant?
- Did anything unexpected happen?
- Did I begin and end on time?
- Did all visuals support the presentation effectively?

SPEAKER EVALUATION FORM

Speaker's Name: _____ **Date:** _____

Directions: Place a check mark in the appropriate blank which represents your evaluation of the speaker's skill level with 1 = poor, 2 = fair, 3 = good, and 4=excellent.

Introduction	1=poor	2=fair	3=good	4=excellent
Caught the audience's attention				
Stated the purpose of presentation				
Provided a preview of presentation				
Body				
Each point was well developed				
Each point was clearly supported				
There was internal logic to points				
Conclusion				
Summarized all main points				
Had a clear ending				
Delivery				
No difficulty with pronunciation				
Was articulate				
Used appropriate rate of speech				
Used appropriate volume				
Used appropriate eye contact				
Used appropriate amount of gestures				
No annoying ums/repetitive phrases				
Finished within allotted time				
Appeared comfortable and confident				
Style				
Used appropriate language				
Used vivid language				
Visual Aids				
Could read all visuals				
Visuals were uncluttered and simple				
Visuals were attractive and appealing				
Visual's format was consistent				
Handouts were attractive/adequate				
No disturbing sounds or transitions				
Question/Answer Period				
Allowed allotted time for questions				
Adequately understood each question				
Repeated questions for audience				
Did not rush answers				
Audience				
Delivered to appropriate audience				
Narrowed topic sufficiently enough				
Paid attention to needs of audience				
Technical content was sufficient				
Did you gain helpful information?				
Overall Evaluation				

FIGURE 13-5 • Speaker evaluation checklist.

- Did I allow time for questions?
- What did I learn from this presentation?
- What could I do differently next time?

Designing a Multimedia Presentation

Visuals give presentations clarity and make them interesting. As well as Power-Point slide presentations, you should also consider DVD/CD material, demonstration or role plays, photographs, illustrations, maps, graphs, and diagrams. Remember your presentation does not have to be technical to be effective. Ask yourself these questions about the visuals you choose:

- Can the audience quickly and easily grasp what they see?
- Are they spending more time reading and not listening?

SELECTING THE DESIGN

When using visuals, design can make or break your presentation no matter how important your information is. These important design concepts can help avoid a visual disaster.

Make Your Font Size BIG!

The one thing you want to be sure is that everyone in the audience can see and read each visual you plan to use. A rule of thumb is if it looks right on your computer screen, it is probably too small. Stand about six feet away from your screen. Keep enlarging the font size until you can read it from that distance; then it should be about the right size. There is nothing more frustrating than sitting in a meeting and squinting to read the slide projected on the screen.

If you choose larger text, it will be easier to see from the back of the room, but you will not get much information on one slide (Figure 13-6). Make the font size 24–48 size font. A mixture of upper- and lowercase characters is easier to read.

FIGURE 13-6 • Use 24-point type size or larger for slides.

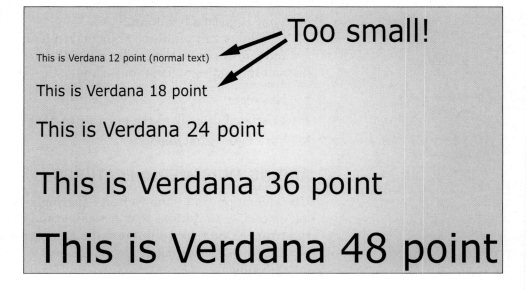

Keep Each Slide Simple

Use only essential elements of the concepts you plan to discuss. Use only single words or phrases on each slide. Use text sparingly. *Never* use complete sentences. The slide should not explain your point; you should explain the point to the audience. Here are some rules to follow when making slides:

- uncluttered and simple
- attractive and visually appealing
- bold and large
- no more than six lines per slide
- no more than seven words per line
- limited number of text slides in a row

Pausing for a few seconds after a new slide appears to give the audience time to view the slide and understand it. Once you have their attention, expand upon the pertinent information related to that slide. Interweave graphics, graphs, or simple tables that present information. Be prepared to explain completely the data and source behind any graph.

Keep Your Format Consistent

Be consistent by using the same format throughout your slides. This means in the use of design, color, font size, and so on. If you use color, use no more than three colors. Change distracts the audience and makes it difficult to follow the logical sequence of your points. A good idea is to use a summary slide at the beginning to introduce the audience to your presentation; then use the same slide as a summary at the end. This gives the audience the feeling your presentation has come full circle.

PRODUCING SPEAKER'S NOTES AND HANDOUTS

Speaker notes and handouts can free the audience from having to make or take copious notes during your presentation and allow them to relax and listen. Let your audience know when the notes or handouts will be distributed. Never hand them out and have the audience reading through your presentation, turning pages and making noise while you are trying to speak. Be sure you get a count of the number attending and provide ample copies so everyone is given a handout.

Handouts can reinforce your main points and can often provide background information that will be helpful to the reader. They should not distract the audience. Handouts should:

- be simple
- be related directly to the purpose of your presentation
- have high visual impact

ADDING MULTIMEDIA FEATURES

Use animation and sound effects sparingly because they can distract the audience. Use transitions that are simple and easily reveal information at the right time. Don't try to impress the audience with your PowerPoint skills. Keeping the slides simple is always the best way to avoid the visuals distracting the audience.

Stop 'n Check

List three design concepts you should follow when creating a multimedia presentation.

a. _____

b. _____

c. _____

Dealing with Nervousness

A certain amount of nervousness, also called **podium panic,** is common for all presenters. You are not alone. In most cases, however, the audience doesn't even know you are afraid (see Figure 13-7). There are several ways to get past the anxiety by relaxing and then focusing only on the presentation. Remember the audience does not know what you are going to say, so if you stumble over a part and skip saying something you planned to say, they will never know the difference! Here are some techniques to help you overcome podium panic:

- Try this example of a relaxation technique to help clear the anxiety:

  Use a relaxation technique. Take a deep breath—as deep as possible and hold it in and slowly count to ten; after counting, completely exhale all the air you can and relax every bone and muscle in your body. Count to ten again; repeat the process ten times. While taking the deep breathing exercises, think only of the number one; see it in your mind. No matter what tries to come into your mind, think only of the number one.

FIGURE 13-7 • Exercise can help relieve nervousness.

- Expect success. Your nervousness and fear may be connected with low self-esteem, as you learned in Chapter 2. Instead of picturing failure, imagine yourself giving a good, strong presentation. Be aware of your internal dialogue and think positive thoughts about your ability to make presentations. Everyone is nervous and does not want to look foolish, but your nervousness can actually improve your presentation. It can give you the energy to make your presentation interesting, exciting, and memorable.

- Prepare thoroughly. Rehearse your presentation a minimum of four times—at least once before a mirror and once before friends or family. They will be honest with you about ways to improve.

- Practice for distractions. Many of your fears may be related to being afraid you will lose concentration. If you do, just tell the audience "Give me a moment to organize my thoughts." Pause, take a deep breath, relax, and begin where you left off, perhaps by repeating the last point. The audience won't mind; they understand how difficult it is to speak before a group. Also, as you practice, have someone deliberately interrupt you by slamming a door, turning on the TV, dropping things, or coming in and out of the room.

- Never memorize a speech. Speak naturally and let the audience feel as if they know you and understand you may be nervous.

- Think of communication, not performance.

- Know that nervousness and its symptoms are not seen. Never call attention to it or apologize for it.

Ethics and Speaking

ETHICAL★ISSUES If your presentation is to be effective, your audience must believe you to be credible, truthful, and qualified. Every statement you make, each figure you show, and each conclusion you draw, must be supported by fact or based on credible information. Not only is your presentation being judged, but your professional reputation is being judged as well. Never say anything you cannot prove should someone question it.

For example, Olivia Venzor presented material at a conference material she had researched. After her presentation, several participants came to her and said they were familiar with the research behind the topic she had presented and were offended she had not given appropriate credit for the materials. Olivia apologized for not identifying the source. Even though this error was not intentional, it may affect her future presentations with this group. An apology may not have been enough to rebuild her credibility.

Always give credit where credit is due.

Speaking to Diverse Audiences

You most likely will not be asked to speak to an international audience as an office professional, but you might be asked to help prepare a presentation for your manager or some other executive (Figure 13-8).

FIGURE 13-8 • Know your audience when people from diverse cultures are present.

U.S. audiences are becoming more diverse. It is the speaker's responsibility to be aware of and acknowledge whether or not a significant portion of the audience comes from different backgrounds. Recognizing cultural differences and adjusting your presentation accordingly means the chances of these cultures achieving the purpose of your presentation is greatly increased. You should research the cultures of your audience.

Here are some tips to help improve your success when facing diverse audiences:

- Consider the pace of presenting information. We have been trained that a presentation should consist of a progression from an introduction, to the body, then to the conclusion. That may not be the case in international circles. You may need to adjust your presentation to quickly present your main points, prove each concisely, and move right to your recommendations.

- Be careful when using humor. It is up to you to research local customs and types of humor that are appreciated in that culture to avoid offending someone.

- Be careful when selecting color in your visuals. Colors carry different suggestions and meanings in different cultures. In Japan, for example, white symbolizes death.

- Know what to expect when it comes to questions. Americans and Canadians are comfortable with questions; most Asian cultures are more likely to respond with silence or perhaps only a few questions.

- Choose your words carefully. Although English is widely spoken around the world, use simple words. Avoid slang, American buzz words, and sports terms. Remember, many English words have different meanings when translated into another language. For instance, *mad* to us means angry, but to the British it means *insane*.

- Pay attention to protocol. You should research the appropriate way to acknowledge your hosts and other key people in the audience so as not to offend.

- Speak slower than normal. Your audience may include non-English-speaking individuals. They often translate mentally from English into their native tongue when listening, and this takes a few seconds to translate. If you speak at a slightly slower pace, your audience will be more comfortable, and they will appreciate your doing so.

- Know what to expect from your audience. Other cultures respond outwardly to presentations in different ways. For example, audience members in Japan may show concentration by closing their eyes and nodding their head up and down slightly. This doesn't mean you are putting your audience to sleep. In Germany and Austria, your audience may rap on the table instead of applauding; if you wave goodbye to Latin Americans and certain cultures in Europe, the audience will remain seated and won't leave. The point is to know how each audience will respond.

You can help your manager by researching how best to structure the presentation to achieve its purpose. Use reference books, travel guides, and Web sites that serve foreign travelers. The U.S. State Department Web site (www.state.gov) has a wealth of information.

Quick Tips

A BASIC PRESENTATION

You may have heard this method of explaining how to deliver a presentation:

- Tell what you are going to tell them,
- then tell them,
- then tell them again what you told them.

This structure follows the beginning-middle-end structure and is quick and easy to remember.

Concept Review and Reinforcement

Review of Key Concepts

OUTCOME	CONCEPT
1. Explain the importance of identifying your purpose for a presentation.	Define the purpose of a presentation as the first step in your planning. Form a clear understanding of what you want the audience to achieve as a result of listening to your presentation.
2. List the points necessary to organize the content of your presentation.	The major elements defining your purpose and considering the audience.
3. Discuss how to organize the content of your presentation.	Organize content by: • Gaining audience's attention by introducing yourself, handling administrative details, presenting presentation's structure, identifying your role, planning for questions, explaining about the use of handouts, and giving an overview. • Organize the main points. • Keep the audience interested. • Summarize and conclude. • Take questions/comments from the audience.
4. Discuss the various ways you can structure your presentation.	• General to specific • Questioning • Specific to general • Beginning-middle-end
5. Discuss delivery techniques before, during, and after your presentation.	• Practice, practice, practice. • Delivery involves your eyes, voice, body language, and appearance. • After your presentation, take time to evaluate and ask for feedback from your audience and those around you.
6. Discuss how to conquer fear when making presentations.	Use these techniques to help you overcome podium panic: • Use relaxation techniques to calm yourself. • Use positive self-talk. • Prepare yourself thoroughly. • Never memorize a speech. • Think of communication, not performance. • Know nervousness and its symptoms are not seen. Never call attention to your nervousness or apologize for it.

7. Discuss the importance of ethics in speaking.

Your audience must believe you to be credible, truthful, and qualified. To accomplish this make sure every statement you make, figure you show, and conclusion you draw is supported by fact or based on credible information with sources identified. Always give credit where credit is due.

8. Identify various areas you should research before speaking to a diverse audience.

Research the following areas:

- Consider the pace of presenting information.
- Be careful using humor.
- Be careful using color in your visuals.
- Know what to expect when it comes to questions.
- Choose your words carefully.
- Be careful when illustrating points.
- Pay attention to protocol.
- Speak slower than normal.
- Know what to expect from your audience.

Key Terms

Extemporaneous speaking. Speaking naturally and freely.

Heckler. People who shout an uninvited comment or ask

questions meant to interrupt, anger, or upset a speaker.

Podium panic. Nervousness about giving a speech or presentation.

Structure. The manner of construction of the presentation and the logical arrangement of its parts.

For Your Discussion

Retrieve file C13-DQ from your student data disk.

DIRECTIONS

Enter your response after each question or statement.

1. Why should you begin preparing your presentation by first identifying its purpose?

2. When considering your audience, what questions might you ask and how would you go about obtaining the answers to each one?

3. Explain three ways to gain your audience's attention at the beginning of your presentation.

4. Discuss how you would organize each of your main points and what statement you would use to introduce each point.

5. Explain three ways you can keep your audience interested in your presentation.

6. Identify five ways you can summarize the conclusion of your presentation.

7. Explain three ways you can handle questions or comments from the audience.

8. Discuss four facets of the human body the audience will observe and what impact they may have on the effectiveness of your presentation.

9. Explain the main tips for designing a multimedia presentation.

10. Discuss how failure to be credible, truthful, and qualified can negatively impact your presentation.

Building Your Office Skills

Exploring the Workplace: *Activities*

1. Interview an individual who holds a position in your career area and gives presentations. Ask the following questions: How important is oral communications in your job? What type of presentations, either formal or informal, do you make and how often do you make them? How do you typically prepare these presentations? How important has the ability to present been to your career advancement? Create an informational report for your instructor. Identify the person's position, typical responsibilities, and company. Type each question followed by his or her response. End your report with an explanation of what you learned from this experience. Be ready to present your information to the class.

2. As a team, visit a business meeting, board meeting, city council meeting, campus club meeting, or any place where oral presentations are being made. Use the speaker evaluation form in Figure 13-5 to evaluate one of the speakers. Write a one-page memo to your instructor explaining the following: where you went, what the meeting was, who you evaluated, and what each person learned from this experience.

3. You learned in this chapter you must gain your audience's attention. You can do this by asking a question, using a quotation, telling an anecdote or story, making a startling comment, giving historical background, or referring to a current event. Choose two of the following situations and prepare an opening for each (select either for or against) that would gain your audience's attention:

   a. Background checks should/should not be mandatory for all employees.

   b. Drug testing should/should not be mandatory for all employees.

   c. All full-time college students should/should not be required to live in dorms.

   d. All forms of smoking should/should not be banned from the workplace.

   e. All students in public schools should/should not be required to wear uniforms.

4. You are to give a presentation to a diverse audience and need to gather information about your audience. Select any two cultures other than your own to research. Go to www.cia.gov/cia/publications/factbook/ and locate information on your chosen cultures. Search elsewhere on the Internet for information about food, customs, and famous people, and so on. Write an information report on what you found on each culture that will help you in your presentation. If directed, be prepared to present your information.

Developing Critical Thinking Skills: *Problem Solving on the Job*

1. **Critiquing a friend.** Your team has agreed that each month a different team member would give a presentation to help develop everyone's presentation skills. At the end of the presentation, the team would orally critique the presentation to give feedback. You are in this month's team meeting and your good friend and coworker, JoElla, has just given a presentation that she spent very little time developing. So much time was wasted at the end of her presentation clarifying the information that other important matters could not be discussed. You are the first person to critique JoElla's presentation. Your honest evaluation is she did a poor job. What oral comments will you make to help JoElla improve? How will you critique her presentation without hurting her feelings?

2. **Handling a heckler.** David Hughes works in your company. You know who he is but do not know or work with him personally. You have noticed at every meeting you are in with him, he tries to heckle the speaker. He interrupts in the middle of a presentation and asks a question even though the presenter has announced that questions will be taken at the end. He criticizes the presentations and generally makes a nuisance of himself in every meeting. You will be presenting next week, and he will be there. How do you plan to handle David and his heckling?

3. **Short on handouts.** You are giving a presentation and have arrived an hour early to check out the room and equipment you have requested. You noticed the room arrangement is set for fifty people. You were told to bring handouts for around twenty people. What can you do to accommodate all of the participants if more than twenty show up?

4. **Diverse audience.** You arrive to give a presentation and are informed that two audience members are visually impaired and two are hearing impaired. What will you do to accommodate these four individuals during your presentation?

Using the Web: *Research Activities*

A. You are interested in improving your speaking skills. Visit the Web site of the well-known speaker Dale Carnegie.

1. Enter the following URL: www.dalecarnegie. com.

2. Browse the site and create a list of ten quick tips for speaking before an audience. Key your information in memo format for your instructor, including the site location.

3. Be prepared to present the results of your research.

B. To continue your interest in improving your speaking skills, visit Toastmasters International's Web site.

1. Enter the following URL: www.toastmasters. org.

2. Browse the Web site and prepare a memo to your instructor about the organization. Include the ten tips for successful public speaking.

3. Be prepared to present the results of your research.

Get Tech Wise: *Importing Word Presentation Outline into a PowerPoint Presentation*

You can create a PowerPoint presentation from an outline you created using Word's Outline feature.

1. Create the outline using Word's Outline feature found on the View menu. To review these procedures click on Help and type *outline feature* then click on Search, select *Five-level outline with instructions*. The instructions to create an outline will appear. Create the outline and save the file.

2. Enter PowerPoint and click Insert on the menu bar, and then click Slides from Outline.

3. Using Windows Explorer find the word file on your hard drive of the outline that is to be imported into

PowerPoint, and then click on Insert. The text from the Word document appears in the PowerPoint presentation.

4. Click the Next Slide button to move from slide to slide in the presentation to read and edit the text.

5. Scroll to the top of the presentation, and then click the Slides tab in the left pane.

6. Save your presentation.

Improving Your Writing Skills: *Grammar Workshop*

Retrieve C13-WRKS from your student data disk to complete the workshop.

Supreme Appliances Simulation: *In the Office at Supreme Appliances*

Application 13-A

Completing a Speech Anxiety Self-Assessment

Supplies needed: Form 13-A, Speech Anxiety Self-Assessment, which is located in the working papers.

Directions

As part of your training, Ms. Quevedo wants you to improve your presentation skills. Complete the self-assessment. Ms. Quevedo wants to discuss the form with you.

Application 13-B

Creating a Presentation Checklist and Evaluating a Presentation

Supplies needed: Plain paper.

Retrieve the file C13-AP-B.ppt from your student data disk.

Directions

Since television news has had so many reports about hurricanes, several of the employees at Supreme Appliances have remarked they knew very little about them. Ms. Quevedo's friend, Luis Gonzalez, a local television meteorologist, gave her a presentation on hurricanes for the employees. Ms. Quevedo has asked you and your team to do the following:

1. Create an evaluation checklist for a presentation based on the concepts taught in this chapter. She does not want to send the presentation to the employees without having it evaluated first. Your checklist should be similar in format to the speaker evaluation form shown in Figure 13-5.

2. From the C13-AP-B.ppt file on your student data disk, evaluate the PowerPoint presentation on hurricanes using the presentation checklist you and your team created.

3. Research further information about hurricanes and make recommendations for adding additional information to the presentation based on your research findings.

4. Write an informational report to Ms. Quevedo addressing your evaluation and recommendations.

5. Be prepared to present your recommendations to your class members.

Application 13-C

Creating a Presentation about Teamwork

> **Supplies needed:** PowerPoint software and plain paper.

Directions

You attend a monthly administrative support team brown bag luncheon. Each month a different member makes a presentation. This is a professional development meeting as well. Ms. Quevedo caters the lunch for everyone from a local sandwich shop. You are to present the topic: The Importance of Teamwork. You are to:

1. Create an outline of your presentation using word processing to be submitted with your presentation.

2. Create a presentation using PowerPoint if it is available. If you are familiar with importing files, you can import your word file into PowerPoint (see Get Tech Wise). The presentation should be between 15 and 20 minutes long.

3. Be prepared to present your topic to your class members.

Application 13-D

Creating a Presentation about United Way

> **Supplied needed:** PowerPoint® software and plain paper.

Directions

You have volunteered to be the chairperson for the United Way committee this year at Supreme Appliances. As chairperson, you are to do the following:

1. Go to the United Way of America's Web site at www.unitedway.org.

2. Browse the Web site and locate information about United Way, its work and partners, and other information you believe will be important to your audience.

3. Create an outline of your presentation in word processing to submit to your instructor.

4. Create an effective presentation that will tell about and motivate Supreme Appliances' employees to give to this charity. If you are familiar with importing files, you can import this file into PowerPoint (see Get Tech Wise). The presentation should be between 15 and 20 minutes long.

5. Be prepared to present your information to your class members.

Building Your Portfolio

With the help of a team member or your instructor, select the following documents: Activities 1, 2, 3, or 4; Web Research 1 or 2, Application 13-C. If instructed, place the documents in plastic protection sheets and add to your portfolio.

14 Preparing to Meet the Challenges

chapter **outline**

Prepare for Advancement

Learn from Your Performance Appraisal
Set Goals
Adapt to Change
Gain Additional Responsibility
Increase Your Effectiveness
Learn from a Mentor
Develop Your Leadership Qualities
Cross Train
Act as an Information Magnet

Commit to Your Values and Ethics

Continue to Develop Professionally

Advance Your Education
Join a Professional Association
Become Technically Certified
Take Action

learning **outcomes**

When you have completed this chapter, you should be able to:

- Identify strategies for advancement.
- Describe leadership qualities.
- Describe how values relate to ethics.
- Identify associations available to office professionals.
- Identify certifications offered to office professionals.
- Develop a strategy for professional development.

What does the future hold for you? With the development and application of technology in the office, there is a greater need for professionally trained office professionals such as office managers, administrative assistants, information specialists, receptionists, record technicians, and mailroom assistants.

The computer, with the development of new software programs, provides the tool that allows today's office professionals to broaden the scope of their jobs. Today's office professionals must be able to implement the systems needed to process information, for no organization can compete in today's global market without having the information it needs when it needs it. Office professionals will be expected to use technology effectively and possess personal qualities and interpersonal skills necessary to become productive members of the team.

This chapter focuses on strategies for advancement and ways to continue to develop professionally.

Prepare for Advancement

An office professional often can take paths leading to other careers, including ones that involve supervision and management. Therefore, office professionals should prepare themselves mentally for advancement and for greater challenges and responsibilities. Following are a number of strategies for preparing for advancement.

LEARN FROM YOUR PERFORMANCE APPRAISAL

As soon as you are employed, your goal will shift from getting a job to holding it. The organization that hired you expects you to be a productive worker and to improve as you gain experience on the job.

Most organizations have policies about evaluating employees' job performance, but the way in which employees are evaluated varies from organization to organization. The review for evaluating employees' past job performance is called a **performance appraisal.** Completing a performance appraisal allows opportunities for you and your supervisor to discuss your past accomplishments and areas for improvement in the future. You can anticipate a performance appraisal within the first three to six months and at least once a year after that. While you may be asked to complete a rating sheet on yourself, your manager may complete a rating sheet as well.

During the meeting about your performance, you are entitled to ask questions and to discuss your contributions to the organization. At some point during the meeting, your manager may suggest specific ways to improve your performance. Listen carefully, for you are being given guidelines concerning what is expected of you. You should be aware that in addition to telling you how you are doing, what is expected of you, and ways to improve your performance, your manager is trying to build mutual confidence and trust and to reinforce the values of the organization.

From the first day on the job, keep notes on your performance, noting particularly how your production has increased and ways in which you are accepting more responsibility. Let your manager know you have a professional development plan, and you are seeking ways in which to grow.

Stop 'n Check

1. Rate yourself on the following two common performance factors. Use the rating scale of 4 (Exceptional), 3 (Commendable), 2 (Improvement Recommended), and 1 (Unsatisfactory).

   a. _____ Quality of work—accuracy, completeness, and orderliness

   b. _____ Punctuality—adheres to work schedule; is prompt in notifying supervisor of tardiness or absence; submits work in a timely manner

2. If you received a Commendable rating on these two factors and believed you should have received an Exceptional rating, how would you respond to your supervisor? What would you say? What documentation or examples do you have to present?

   _____

   _____

   _____

   _____

Maintain an impeccable performance record and refer to your notes when you are evaluating your own performance.

When you are comfortably settled in your first job, your initial reaction may be to take it easy. Don't coast. Many opportunities for advancement are available, but advancement comes only to those who are prepared.

SET GOALS

In Chapter 2, you learned ways to exhibit self-management, which included goal setting. If you haven't already set a professional goal for yourself, do so. For example, do you want to become an executive assistant, a supervisor of office staff, a records manager, or a manager of office administrative services? Once you have decided on your goal, study to provide yourself with the background necessary to achieve that goal. Once you achieve that goal, set another.

To accomplish your goals, you may need support and resources from management. If so, select a person in management on whom you can rely for assistance and with whom you can develop a mentor relationship. To set your goals, keep these steps in mind:

- Write down your goals and review them frequently. Enroll in a management class.

- List your goals in action terms. Answer the question: What do I need to do? Inquire about a management class? Enroll in a class?

- Identify your goals in measurable terms. Ask yourself: How will I know I met this goal? Completed the course? Yes? No?

ADAPT TO CHANGE

As you recall, in Chapter 2 you learned that the challenge of change presents opportunities to grow. When change occurs, identify negative feelings and learn to deal with them by rearranging your priorities and working positively to make adjustments. Keep a positive attitude because it helps you to channel your energies into improving your situation.

Stop 'n Check

1. What goal have you been unable to successfully meet?

   _____
   _____

2. According to what you have learned about goals in Chapter 2 and in this section, why have you not been able to meet this goal?

   _____
   _____

3. If the goal is still important to you, what can you do to take the next step in meeting this goal?

   _____
   _____

Unexpected situations can occur that influence your goals and their achievement. Sometimes situations occur that interfere with your achieving your goals, such as the reorganization of your department. When forces beyond your control interfere with achievement of your goals, take time to reevaluate your plan. Ask yourself: Are my goals realistic? Are my goals appropriate for me? Do my goals need to be changed or even postponed? To handle unexpected situations, you must remain positive and flexible.

Creativity and flexibility are needed in organizations today. Companies require their staff to "do more with less." This means that effective managers realize problems often cannot be solved by using the same old methods. Today's office workers must have an attitude that allows for recognition and acceptance of new ideas and new ways of solving problems and getting results.

It is a fact that people resist change if they perceive the change, such as new procedures, updated equipment, change in management, or a different work schedule, as a threat. Often office workers resist change because management did not effectively communicate the change. Keep in mind that effective communication is the key to introducing change. See Figure 14-1.

FIGURE 14-1 • Effective communication is the key to introducing change.

When you encounter resistance to change, remember that keeping a positive attitude allows you to be more open to taking steps to improve the situation. Look for opportunities that might come your way as a result of the change.

GAIN ADDITIONAL RESPONSIBILITY

To be an effective office professional, you must be clear about what you want from your position and be willing to make it happen. If you have identified your professional goals, then you are well on your way. It is a fact, though, that people need responsibility to be motivated on their jobs. To keep up your enthusiasm, you can be a tremendous help to your manager by taking the initiative to ask for responsibilities that he or she might otherwise have to handle.

When asking for additional responsibility, remind your manager of your success in handling a particular task or project in the past where you required little or no instruction. For instance, Sylvia asked her manager if he would like her to take the lead in organizing the annual company picnic. Although this activity was team-led and Sylvia's manager was the chair of the team, he had a number of tasks to be completed prior to the team's involvement. In asking for additional responsibility, Sylvia reminded her manager she had successfully completed a project similar to this one. By gaining additional responsibility, Sylvia has many opportunities to demonstrate her level of initiative not only to her manager but to other coworkers as well.

INCREASE YOUR EFFECTIVENESS

Make your supervisor look good. This means meeting deadlines, being willing to do "extras," making your work look more professional and polished, and being informed so that your supervisor is never caught off-guard.

- Ask questions to learn the "why" behind what goes on in the daily office routine.
- Ask for frequent feedback on your work, mention special contributions you have made to the team, and inform your manager about any courses you are taking or additional training you would like to have.
- Understand, accept, and respect the chain of command in your organization.
- Remain loyal to your own values, your manager, and the organization. It helps your professional image if you do not make negative remarks about either your manager or the organization—its employees, policies, products, or services.

Stop 'n Check

1. If you are currently working, identify an area in which you could request additional responsibility. If you are not working, in what area in this class could you accept additional responsibility?

_____

_____

_____

Stop 'n Check

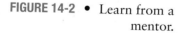

2. Identify at least one area in which you can become more effective in your work or class or at home.

_____

_____

LEARN FROM A MENTOR

As you learned in Chapter 3, mentors are people in your profession who are more senior than you. They understand the organization's policies, procedures, politics, and history, and they are willing to share useful advice with more junior members. They help people who are new to the organization or the profession to become successful. The mentor relationship often involves a new employee and an office veteran (Figure 14-2). The new employee may have strong state-of-the-art technical skills, but the mentor knows the organization's culture.

Meetings with mentors and the information they share is confidential because a mentor's advice is intended to show a junior member shortcuts to success. Mentors welcome the questions of junior staff members and see it as their responsibility to nurture younger people with potential for success.

People often consider their mentor as the most important person in their professional career. A mentor has to be a person with whom you feel comfortable and who is pleased to answer your questions. The mentor has to be someone who has the answers to your questions about:

* how the organization works
* how information flows in the office

FIGURE 14-2 • Learn from a mentor.

- ways to avoid unnecessary conflict
- how the organization selects people for promotion
- who holds the power to decision making
- how to get your ideas noticed and accepted

Before you ask someone to become your mentor, think about the characteristics you would like to see in a mentor. For example, think of the role models in your organization. Who has a strong work ethic, years of experience, job expertise, personal warmth, and respect? Once you have identified the desired characteristics, you may ask someone to become your mentor. Or, you may ask one of the following to help you identify a mentor:

- human resources department representative
- team member
- manager

Stop 'n Check

1. Jot down qualities you would like to see in a mentor.

_____

_____

  a. Identify at least three people in your company (or family) who have these qualities who could serve as a mentor to you.

_____

  b. Of these three people, which one could you approach to discuss the potential of serving as a mentor to you?

_____

2. If you already have a mentor, which qualities do you like best about your mentor?

_____

_____

  a. What has been the best advice your mentor has given you?

_____

_____

DEVELOP YOUR LEADERSHIP QUALITIES

It has been said that in a group of people, a small fraction will be leaders, a larger fraction will be followers, and a substantial proportion just won't want to get involved. Beyond the skill of performance, the small fraction of leaders has developed the skill of *leading* the performance, two entirely different skills. You do not have to be a supervisor or manager to lead; as an office professional, you can learn to be a leader—one who can:

- Influence others to do their very best.
- Help others to accept challenges even when they believe they cannot handle them.
- Inspire confidence.

Beyond competence, which means a person is knowledgeable in the areas relevant to his or her organization's success, here are other qualities to help identify whether you are capable of developing the skill of leading.

- **Integrity**—Show consistency between words and actions; choose the more difficult right over the easier wrong; admit mistakes; consistently support standards.

- **Vision**—Support the vision for your organization, department, or unit; show a strong sense of direction.

- **Effectiveness**—Focus on results versus tasks and techniques; build on strengths, not on weaknesses.

- **Passionate commitment**—Demonstrate high enthusiasm and energy levels, feel the thrill of challenge, persevere from start to finish, create enthusiasm and desire to excel among others, and inspire others to work at their highest level.

- **Communication**—Congratulate, thank, and acknowledge people who are displaying behaviors that support the organization's values, speak positively about policies and procedures, show others they are important by following up with those coworkers who receive promotions, graduate with degrees, are ill, are having children, or are getting married.

This list of qualities may look familiar, as you were introduced to leadership in the section on interpersonal skills in Chapter 2. Because these skills and the personal qualities described in Chapter 2 are critical to developing the skill to lead, it is important for you to focus on them again in this section.

Stop 'n Check

1. What is your strongest leadership quality?

   _____

   _____

2. What is an area for improvement?

   _____

   _____

CROSS TRAIN

Cross training involves learning and performing the responsibilities of your coworkers. It is valuable to the organization. When one employee is absent from work, other employees can simply fill in. However, it has even greater benefits to the person who has the initiative to learn how to perform other people's jobs. The more you know and the more you gain additional skills, the more valuable you will be to the organization.

The office assistant who is preparing for advancement, or who just wants to protect the security of his or her current job, should learn as many skills and gather as much information as possible.

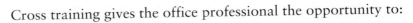

Cross training gives the office professional the opportunity to:

- take on new technical and communication challenges.
- learn more about the organization and the flow of work.
- get more exposure by working with new people.
- get acknowledgment from management.

Cross-trained employees are more challenged, more knowledgeable, more interesting, and generally happier.

Stop 'n Check

1. If you are currently working, in what area would you like to cross train?

   _____

2. In what area is it most realistic for you to cross train?

   _____

3. What steps can you take to discuss cross training—that is, to see if it is possible for you to cross train?

   _____

   _____

ACT AS AN INFORMATION MAGNET

To prepare for advancement, monitor your changing environment by gathering information. Here are a number of suggestions:

- Subscribe to and read professional magazines.
- Listen to motivational or informational tapes while you travel to and from work.
- Read office bulletins and newsletters to remain up-to-date on corporate matters.
- Attend seminars, conventions, conferences, and workshops to keep abreast of new technology and procedures.
- Volunteer to be a committee member or chairperson for special events.
- Apply or offer to work on special task forces.
- Request that you be placed on the office circulation list for all information and professional materials.
- Make a point of meeting new people and listening to their ideas.
- Read the local newspaper to follow community and international events.
- Travel to as many locations as possible.
- Visit libraries and note the many resources available.
- Become aware of your company's policies.
- Make a point to watch documentaries on television and read or study new topics.

Stop 'n Check

Identify two areas in which you can improve your role as an information magnet.

a. _____

b. _____

Commit to Your Values and Ethics

Values and ethics are central to any organization. Throughout the chapters, ethical issues have been discussed. Let's take a closer look at values.

Values can be defined as those things that are important to or valued by someone. That someone can be an individual or, collectively, an organization. When values are shared by all members of an organization, they are extraordinarily important tools for making judgments, assessing probable outcomes of contemplated actions, and choosing among alternatives. Perhaps more importantly, they put all employees on the same level with regard to what all employees as an organization consider important.

Values are what people judge to be right. They are more than words—they are the moral, ethical, and professional attributes of character. These are not the only values that should determine your character, but they are ones that are central to your profession and should guide you as an employee in your organization.

Values are the embodiment of what an organization stands for and should be the basis for the behavior of its employees. However, what if employees of the organization do not share and have not internalized the organization's values? Obviously, a disconnect between individual and organizational values will be dysfunctional. Additionally, an organization may publish one set of values, perhaps in an effort to push forward a positive image, while the values that really guide organizational behavior are very different.

So, there are some disconnects, and these disconnects create problems. However, the central purpose of values remains. They state either an actual or an idealized set of criteria for evaluating options and deciding what is appropriate, based on a number of things, such as experience.

So how do values relate to ethics? Individually or organizationally, values determine what is right and what is wrong, and doing what is right or wrong is what is meant by ethics. To behave ethically is to behave in a manner consistent with what is right or moral. Part of the difficulty in deciding whether or not behavior is ethical is in determining *what* is right or wrong.

What does "generally considered to be right" mean? All one needs to do is to look at the positive values of society and the organizations one belongs to, and what is right or wrong should be evident. Obviously, it's not so easy.

Most of your ethical development occurs before entering an organization. The influence of family, church, community, and school will determine your individual values. The organization, to a large extent, is dealing with individuals whose value base has been established. This might imply that ethical organizations are those fortunate enough to bring in ethical individuals, while unethical organizations brought in unethical people. But it is not that simple. While the internalized values of individuals are important, the organization has a major impact on the behavior of its members and can have a positive or negative influence on their values. Staying committed to your values increases your satisfaction with your decisions and their results.

How can you help to create an ethical climate? Be certain your pattern of behavior aligns with your own values as well as your organization's values. Increase your awareness of how to apply your organization's code of conduct. Through additional training, learn how to deal with situations with an ethical dimension and how to anticipate situations that involve your values and ultimately ethical choices.

Continue to Develop Professionally

As you read this chapter, you may conclude that preparation for a successful career is endless. Your conclusion is right. Professionals who continue to develop their knowledge and skills do so by advancing their education, joining professional associations, and becoming certified in their technical skills.

ADVANCE YOUR EDUCATION

A college degree is useful in advancing to a higher level office position. In fact, any additional education will prove helpful. When you have an efficient and effective performance record, additional education may provide the competitive edge you need to advance (Figure 14-3).

FIGURE 14-3 • Education is essential in advancing your career.

Many organizations offer in-house training. The courses usually are of short duration and do not offer college credit. Talk with your supervisor or training director about what is available. Express an interest in taking courses that will help you perform your job or advance in your career. When you successfully complete enough courses, they will become an impressive part of your employment record and will support your efforts toward advancement.

Most large organizations have educational benefits. Some organizations will pay all or part of the tuition for job-related courses that are successfully completed. Ask your human resources representative about the educational benefits; express your interest in taking job-related courses. Consider courses in these areas:

project management	business administration
team building	conflict resolution
communication	organizational behavior
time management	supervision or management

The emphasis in education today is on continuing education. By committing yourself to lifelong learning, you will be increasing your opportunities for promotion and enriching your personal life. Employees who believe and practice continuous education are more likely to survive during periods of company right-sizing and recession. **Right-sizing** is the process of optimizing company resources to achieve efficiency.

As an office assistant, you choose either to have a job or to have a professional career. If you have a strong desire to advance and to earn a reputation for being a professional who contributes to the organization, you will seek ways to achieve professional recognition.

JOIN A PROFESSIONAL ASSOCIATION

Becoming a member of a professional association is an excellent way to gain educational skills and new credentials in your field. A number of associations promote professionalism, such as Association of Records Managers and Administrators (ARMA), which you learned about in Chapter 8. The following discussion identifies four additional associations that offer credentials to office professionals willing to study and take the challenge.

International Association of Administrative Professionals (IAAP)

The IAAP is an association committed to advancing office professionals by promoting high standards and enhancing the image of the profession. This association provides resources and information to help its members enhance

---

Stop 'n Check

In what ways, other than completing this course, can you advance your education?

_____

_____

their skills so they may contribute to their organizations in an even more effective manner. Not only does it work to improve the professional skills of its members, but it also works to educate the public about the value of the office professional.

The IAAP offers two examinations that lead to professional certifications. For more information about the IAAP and the certifications, visit the Web site at www.iaap-hq.org.

NALS, the Association for Legal Professionals

Formerly called the National Association for Legal Secretaries, NALS remains a leader in the legal services industry, offering professional development by providing continuing legal education, certifications, information, and training to those choosing the legal services industry as their career. NALS members represent every area of this industry from paralegals and legal assistants to legal administrators and office managers.

Legal office professionals who wish to demonstrate their commitment and aptitude for the legal secretarial profession are encouraged to take the NALS's examination leading to certification. For more information, contact NALS through its Web site at http://www.nals.org.

National Virtual Associates Society (NVAS)

This professional organization is committed to the growth and success of people who work outside the traditional office setting in a virtual environment or home-based office. Its membership is open to anyone who works in a virtual environment and is interested in networking, receiving support in the growth and success of their business, and supporting others in the growth and success of their businesses. In this organization, you will find virtual assistants, secretaries, administrative and executive assistants, desktop publishers, graphic designers, and transcriptionists to name a few. NVAS offers an examination to become a certified virtual associate. For more information, contact NVAS at www.nvas.org.

National Association of Educational Office Professionals (NAEOP)

This nonprofit organization is made up of educational office professionals who are dedicated to professional and personal growth through education, certification, and networking. For more information, contact the organization at www.naeop.org.

BECOME TECHNICALLY CERTIFIED

Technical skills are some of the most highly valued skills of office professionals. By continuing to upgrade technical skills, office professionals can

Stop 'n Check

1. List the current organizations in which you are an official member.

   _____

   _____

2. Are you interested in joining any additional professional organizations? If so, which one are you interested in joining?

   _____

improve their resumes and increase their opportunities for employment and advancement. To validate technical skills, office professionals should earn certification from recognized programs. In addition to the certifications offered by many professional organizations, one of the most recognized technical certifications is the Microsoft® Office Specialist (MOS) program.

The MOS certification is available at three levels: Specialist, Expert, and Master. Candidates begin by selecting the Microsoft® Office product for which they want certification and the appropriate level of expertise. For more information, contact Microsoft® at www.microsoft.com/learning/mcp/officespecialist/.

Stop 'n Check

Of the certifications offered by Microsoft®, which one is most appealing to you according to your qualifications?

_____

TAKE ACTION

If your supervisor supports professional development activities, you may be able to take advantage of a number of workshops, seminars, and conferences. To be proactive, consider the results of your performance appraisal, interests, and additional knowledge and skills you would like to develop. Evaluate each of these areas to determine your priorities. Once you have identified your priorities, then rank them as 1, 2, 3, and so on. Focus on your first priority by applying the steps you have learned to meet stated goals. Doing so will help you stay on track to develop your professional image.

As you complete your professional development activities, be sure to keep a log of your activities and keep your completion certificates in a folder or notebook for future use. For instance, you can refer to this information during your next performance appraisal or update your resume using this information.

Professional growth is stimulating; it has a motivating effect. If you continue to apply strategies for advancement and look for professional development opportunities, your reward will be a successful and enjoyable career, not "just" a job.

Stop 'n Check

1. Identify at least one professional development activity you would like to complete within the next three months.

_____

2. What action do you need to take to begin the activity?

_____

3. What resources do you need to take the first step?

_____

Quick Tips

ADMINISTRATIVE PROFESSIONALS WEEK

Why is there an Administrative Professionals Week? Should there be one? Here are some facts that will help you answer these questions.

- Administrative Professionals Week is observed internationally every year in April. During that week a day, usually Wednesday, is always observed as Administrative Professionals Day.

- The International Association of Administrative Professionals (IAAP) is the sole official sponsor of Administrative Professionals Week.

- The observance of this week is designed to educate the public, especially business leaders, about the critical contribution made by office administrators and the need for continuous upgrading and education in this profession.

- Common forms of recognition during this week are gifts, time off, flowers, and complimentary lunches.

- Many administrative professionals report that being sponsored for a professional seminar or course or receiving a subscription to a professional magazine is the recognition they most prefer.

Concept Review and Reinforcement

Review of Key Concepts

OUTCOME	CONCEPT
1. Identify strategies for advancement.	Strategies for advancement include the following: • Learn from your performance appraisal. • Set goals. • Adapt to change. • Gain additional responsibility. • Increase your effectiveness. • Learn from a mentor. • Develop your leadership qualities. • Cross train. • Act as an information magnet.
2. Describe leadership qualities.	Leadership qualities include the following: • integrity • vision • effectiveness • passionate commitment • communication
3. Describe how values relate to ethics.	Values determine what is right and what is wrong, and doing what is right or wrong defines ethics. To behave ethically is to behave in a manner consistent with what is right or moral.
4. Identify associations available to office professionals.	Professional associations include the following: • International Association of Administrative Professionals (IAAP) • NALS, the Association for Legal Professionals • National Virtual Associates Society (NVAS) • National Association of Educational Office Professionals (NAEOP)
5. Identify certifications offered to office professionals.	In addition to the associations listed previously, Microsoft® offers certifications on different software applications.
6. Develop a strategy for professional development.	To develop a strategy, consider results of your performance appraisal, interests, and additional knowledge and skills you would like to develop. Evaluate each of these areas to determine your priorities and rank them. Focus on your first priority by applying steps you have learned to meet stated goals. Keep a log of activities, and keep completion certificates in a folder or notebook for future use.

Key Terms

Cross training. Learning and performing the responsibilities of coworkers.

Performance appraisal. The review of employees' job performance.

Right-sizing. When a company optimizes its resources to achieve efficiency.

Values. Those things that are important to or valued by someone.

For Your Discussion

Retrieve file C14-DQ from your student data disk.

DIRECTIONS

Enter your response after each question or statement.

1. What benefit can an employee derive from a performance appraisal?

2. List steps to follow when setting goals.

3. Discuss the steps to take when handling change.

4. Explain the purpose of having a mentor.

5. Name two associations that provide professional certifications.

6. Explain the process involved in setting goals to ensure you would be more likely to achieve them.

7. Explain the meaning of *cross training*.

8. Discuss the positive aspects when you seek additional responsibility.

9. Discuss the desirable qualities of a leader.

Building Your Office Skills

Exploring the Workplace: *Activities*

1. Interview two office professionals, each from a different company. Consider the following questions:

   a. Do you wish to be promoted in the organization? If so, to what position?

   b. Does the position require any additional training, experience, or college courses? If so, identify the requirements.

   c. Does your company have a mentoring program? Do you have a mentor? If yes, describe your relationship. If no, if you wanted to request a mentor, how would you go about this task?

   d. Prepare your notes in a memo to be submitted to your instructor. Be prepared to share your findings with the class.

2. Identify one goal you want to reach one year from now.

   a. List the steps to be taken within three months, six months, nine months, and twelve months to accomplish this goal.

   b. List the resources you will need to meet your goal.

   c. Submit your plan in a memo to your instructor.

3. Describe an example of a major change in your professional or personal life. Answer the following questions.

   a. Who initiated the change?

   b. How was the change communicated to you?

   c. How did you feel about the change?

   d. How do you feel about the change now?

   e. How did the change affect you?

   f. What opportunities did you seize as a result of the change? If there were none, why do you think you did not take advantage of the change itself or the results of the change?

4. Think of your career as a business.

   a. Create a business plan. Consider the following questions: What business are you in? What is your product? What is the market for your business? Who are your customers? Why should your customers buy your product? What is special and different about your career as a business?

   b. Submit your responses in a memo to your instructor. Be prepared to share your findings with the class.

Developing Critical Thinking Skills: *Problem Solving on the Job*

Retrieve file C14-OJS from your student data disk.

Directions

Enter your response after each situation.

1. **Implement change.** You have just been promoted to a supervisory position in the purchasing department. For the past three years, you have been employed in that department as an administrative secretary, and you have realized that several of the office procedures need to be changed. In preparation for making a major change in an office procedure that will affect others in your department, determine at least five questions you should answer that will help you implement change effectively.

2. **Importance of advance education.** You are sitting at break time with two of your peers, Shannon, a personnel assistant from Human Resources, and Phoung from Accounting, discussing obstacles and opportunities in different career options. Shannon and Phoung have just graduated from the local community college with associate degrees. You ask Shannon and Phoung to respond to the following question: "As an office assistant, how important is it for me to have a college degree?" If you were asked this question, how would you respond?

3. **Meeting the challenge.** On a number of occasions, Kim has complimented you on your successful startup with the company because you have been very thorough, positive, and professional in your area of responsibility. Kim feels that she is not "going anywhere" in her current position. She feels that she doesn't have any direction; she appears dissatisfied with her job, but she would like to continue in the office administration field. She has asked you, "How do you meet the challenge of the position?" In other words, how do you do it? What do you tell her?

4. **Demonstrate leadership.** For several years your company has used a particular software package, and you have been the support person and trainer for the

company employees. Now your department has shared with you that the company will be changing to another software package in eight to ten months. Your company expects everyone to switch to this new software and become proficient in it as soon as possible. Most all employees are grumbling about having to learn another software package. You were told that your number one goal is to become an expert in the software and be able to provide training and support during and after this changeover.

a. List some training methods you feel will help you learn this new software.

b. List ways your training and support can project a positive attitude toward this new software.

c. Identify leadership qualities needed to work with the employees during this transition.

Using the Web: *Research Activities*

A. If you want to advance in your career, you must develop leadership qualities. Do you have these qualities? Evaluate your qualities by completing an online leadership quiz (it's free).

   1. Enter www.testcafe.com/lead/leadfree.cgi.

   2. Answering the questions honestly will result in a more accurate description of your strengths and areas for improvement.

   3. Print the results to submit to your instructor.

   4. In a memo to your instructor, describe what the results mean to you and what steps you will take to enhance your strengths and improve areas of weaknesses.

B. To check your current career satisfaction, complete the following online quiz (it's free).

   1. Enter www.testcafe.com/car/.

   2. Answering the questions honestly will result in a more accurate description of your strengths and areas for improvement.

   3. Print the results to submit to your instructor.

   4. In a memo to your instructor, describe what the results mean to you and what steps you will take to build on the results of this quiz.

Get Tech Wise: *Microsoft® Office Specialist Certification*

You can become certified in any or all of the Microsoft® office products: Access, Excel, Outlook, PowerPoint and Word. Visit the Web site at www.microsoft.com/learning/mcp/officespecialist/.

1. Select the Microsoft® Office application that interests you.

2. View and print the topic information covered in the test.

3. While at the Web site, search for certified testing centers located in your area.

4. Also, view information on ordering learning materials. Microsoft® sells a CD that gives hands-on experience and results similar to the test.

5. Once you learn the topics that will be covered on the test or you order training materials, practice, practice, practice, and practice some more!

6. When ready for the exam, call the certified training site and schedule a test. These tests are timed, usually 45 minutes.

7. Immediate feedback is provided after the test, indicating if you passed or failed. Regardless of whether you pass or fail, you will get a printout showing how you scored in each area. If you passed, Microsoft® will mail a certificate to you.

You decide the level of certification:

- MOS Master Certificate (requires all five applications)
   - ✓ Word Expert
   - ✓ Excel Expert
   - ✓ PowerPoint
   - ✓ Outlook
   - ✓ Access

- MOS Specialist Certificate (requires core level only)
   - ✓ Word
   - ✓ Excel

- Application Certificate (you choose which level for the application)
   - ✓ Any one application

Improving Your Writing Skills: *Grammar Workshop*

Retrieve C14-WRKS from your student data disk to complete the workshop.

 Simulation: *In the Office at Supreme Appliances*

Application 14-A

Earning MOS Certification

Supplies needed: Access to the Internet; plain bond paper.

Directions

On your last performance appraisal, you indicated your interest in pursuing the Microsoft® certification. Because you believe you are proficient in Word, you would like to research Microsoft's certification in this software application. The results of your research regarding Word should include requirements and exam preparation. Indicate the areas in which you are proficient and the areas for additional study. Prepare your information in a memo to submit to your instructor.

Application 14-B

Creating a Presentation

Supplies needed: Plain bond paper.

Directions

Develop an outline in word processing of the information researched in Application 14-A. Prepare a presentation and present this topic to your class members. Before you prepare, review the concepts in Chapter 13 so you will use your planning time and effort wisely.

Application 14-C

Developing a Strategy for Your Professional Development

Supplies needed: Plain bond paper.

Directions

Develop a strategy for your professional development. To do so, design an electronic spreadsheet or use word processing to capture the following information:

1. State your immediate career goal.
2. State your career goal for the end of a five-year period.
3. Identify the gap between the two goals in terms of the experience, training, certification, human relations skills, and interpersonal skills needed.
4. For each of the factors in the gap, describe your plan of how you will achieve the necessary skills to close the gap.
5. Prepare a memo covering the contents of your strategy to submit to your instructor and attach the electronic document.

Application 14-D

Clarifying Your Values

Supplies needed: Form 14-A, Value clarification.

Directions

You have registered for a workshop on Personal Values, which is to be conducted next week. To prepare for the workshop, you have been asked to complete Form 14-A. Follow the steps below:

1. Identify your values. Check the values consist, primarily, of personal characteristics and character traits.

2. Prioritize them in order of importance to you. Place 1, 2, 3 by the checked items.

3. Now answer the questions below:

   a. List the top 5 values.

   b. What patterns can you identify in the top five values you have prioritized? For example, do coworkers compliment you for demonstrating behavior that supports these values? Do these values appear on your performance evaluations?

   c. What pleases you about the list?

4. Summarize the results in a memo to be submitted to your instructor.

Building Your Portfolio

With the help of a team member or your instructor, select the best papers representative of your work from Chapter 14. Here are a few suggestions: Activities 2, 3, and 4; Application 14-A, C, and D. Follow your instructor's directions about formatting, assembling, and placing the documents in the portfolio.

Appendix

Using proper grammar and a consistent, logical approach to punctuation, numbers, and capitalization is the hallmark of a true professional. Some companies may adhere to specific rules or preferred styles in these areas. Check to see if that is the case in your office. Rules apply to the Improving Your Writing Skills workshops, which are located at the end of every chapter.

PUNCTUATION

Perhaps the most misunderstood punctuation mark is the comma. A comma alerts the reader to a rest or a pause between two ideas. An omitted or misplaced comma in documents can lead to significant misunderstandings and embarrassing situations.

Rule 1: Commas Used with Conjunctions (Chapter 1)

Commas are placed before coordinating conjunctions when they separate two independent clauses in a compound sentence. Examples of coordinating conjunctions are *nor, for, yet, neither, or, and*, and *but*.

> Dave is a good programmer, and he has been given the lead programmer's job for a month's trial.

> If clauses are short and related, you may omit the comma before *and*.

> TIP: *Therefore, however*, and *accordingly* are not considered true coordinating conjunctions. Use a semicolon before these words, not a comma.

Rule 2: Commas Used with Nonrestrictive Words, Phrases, and Clauses (Chapter 1)

A word, phrase, or clause that is not absolutely essential to a sentence may be set off in commas. Restrictive words, phrases, and clauses are essential to the meaning of the sentence and are not set off by commas.

Word: The meeting, *however*, ran well into the evening.
Phrase: Mrs. Gonzales, *the data processing coordinator* [nonrestrictive], retired after 25 years with the company.
Data specialist [restrictive] Ernest Johnson will be giving a seminar next week.
Clause: Talk to your manager about it tomorrow, *when she returns to the office* [nonrestrictive].
Write down the message *as soon as you hang up* [restrictive].

Rule 3: Commas Used with a Series (Chapter 2)

When listing a series of words, phrases, or clauses, set them off with commas.

> The will of the Slaton estate was to include Shannon, Joe, and Mark.

It is critical to retain the comma between the last two items in this example to prevent any possible misunderstanding. If this example read ". . . to include Shannon, Joe and Mark," it would make a tremendous difference in sharing a portion of an estate.

Rule 4: Commas Used between Adjectives (Chapter 2)

When a series of adjectives have the same worth and refer to the same noun, they should be separated with commas. If the word *and* can be substituted and be grammatically correct, a comma is required.

> They are bright, young, attractive lawyers. (*Bright, young,* and *attractive* are adjectives of equal value.)

Compare this example to the next one.

> The red modern building is the second to be recognized for its structure. (*Red* and *modern* are not of equal value.)

Rule 5: Commas Used with Introductory and Parenthetic Phrases (Chapter 2)

Place commas after introductory words, phrases, and clauses. Commas are almost always placed after long introductory elements and those containing verb forms.

> As the earthquake intensified, the employees gathered around the radio.

Parenthetical and defining words and phrases are set off in commas unless they have a close relation to the rest of the sentence.

> They can, *I believe,* meet the deadlines.

> They were *definitely* the best presenters for the new products.

CAPITALIZATION

Because capitalization will vary according to the situation, a number of rules must be followed. The main rule to remember is to be consistent when capitalizing. Here are the main rules and examples of capitalization.

Rule 6: Business (Chapter 3)

Capitalize all titles (academic, business, religious, military, as well as titles of respect or honor) in these situations:

a. When they immediately precede a name
   Professor Rochelle, Dr. Todd, Chairperson Stone, President Clinton, Lieutenant Gibbs, Queen Elizabeth, Vice President Louise White, Ambassador Saxton
b. When they are used in mailing, such as titles following the names
   Mrs. Gwen Hilton, President Hilton International Services, Inc. 1231-A International Boulevard Dallas, TX 75244

Do not capitalize the following titles under these circumstances:

a. When following a name or used alone

   Mr. Carlos, the president of Datalife; the secretary of state; the district attorney

b. When a title precedes a name but the name is set off by commas.

   The chairperson, Nick Nelson, arrived yesterday.

Rule 7: Organizations, Institutions, and Education (Chapter 3)

Capitalize official names of organizations.

   Rotary Club, Young Men's Christian Association, United Methodist Women, Phi Beta Kappa, Girl Scouts of America

Capitalize names of schools or colleges and their departments.

   Van High School, Music Department

Capitalize names of classes of a high school, college, or university; official names of courses; and course subjects when they are derived from proper names.

   Senior Class, Computer Science I, Latin, English

Capitalize academic degrees, whether abbreviated or written in full, if the person's full name is given.

   John Rochelle, M.S. (or Master of Science)

Do not capitalize general terms referring to organizations or institutions.

   the chamber of commerce, the parent-teacher association

Do not capitalize course subjects not derived from proper nouns.

   We are studying economics this quarter.

Rule 8: Enumerations (Chapter 4)

Capitalize the first word in each section of an enumeration if the enumerations are in a complete sentence.

   The assistant uses the outguide in the following cases: (1) Someone outside the agency wants the material. (2) The manager takes the material out of the office.

Capitalize itemized listings.

   The technical skills required for the position are

1. accurate keyboarding
2. telephone skills
3. knowledge of filing systems

1. Word processing experience and accurate keyboarding skills (50+ wpm)
2. Extensive customer service experience, both in person and on the phone
3. Ability to reorganize our office filing system

Lowercase an enumerated item not preceded by a colon.

> She listed the technical skills as (1) keyboarding and (2) applications such as Word, Excel, and Access.

Rule 9: Proper Nouns (Chapter 4)
Capitalize nouns or abbreviations used with numbers or letters in a title.

> Division IV, Precinct 4, Act 11

> grade 6, section A

Capitalize *Room, Suite,* etc., when used in addresses.

> Odenwald International Connections, Inc.
> Jefferson Building, Suite 111
> 130266 Forest Lane
> Dallas, TX 75234

Do not capitalize *section, grade,* or *article* when used with letters or numbers.

Rule 10: Money (Chapter 5)
a. In documents:
> Nine Hundred Twenty-Five Dollars ($925.00)

b. In writing checks:
> Three Hundred and No/100
> Do not capitalize amounts of money in general writing.
> They made over two hundred dollars.

Rule 11: Geographical Terms (Chapter 5)
Capitalize the following:

a. Points of the compass when they refer to a specific section of the United States
> the South, the Midwest, the East

b. Popular names of specific localities.
> the Bible Belt, the Cotton Belt, the Corn Belt

c. *Coast* when it refers to a specific locality or stands alone
> East Coast, Gulf Coast

Do not capitalize the following:

a. Points of the compass when they denote simple directions or specific compass points
> moving west, south two blocks, east shore

b. Regional terms that merely localize adjectives
> northern Italy, western Texas

c. *Coast* when used with geographic names
> Texas coast, Florida coast

d. Adjectives derived from political divisions and major parts of the world
> southern United States, tropical Africa

Rule 12: Government and Political Terms (Chapter 5)
Capitalize the following:

a. *Government* and *administration* when part of a title
   United States Government
   The Reagan Administration

b. *Federal* when part of a title
   Federal Register, Federal Reserve System, Federal Reserve Board
   Regulation W

c. *National* when part of a title
   The National Science Foundation, the National Guard

d. *State* when part of a title
   New York State, Washington State, State of the Union Message

e. *County* when part of a name
   Dallas County

f. *District* when part of a name
   Alexandria School District, District of Columbia

g. *Ward, Precinct,* when part of a name
   First Precinct

h. *Legislature* when part of a name of a specific group
   Texas Legislature

i. *Conference* and *Congress* when part of a name
   Judicial Conference of the United States, Tenth Annual Conference of the United Office Workers, Congress of Parents and Teachers

j. Full titles of government departments, commissions, bureaus, boards, and committees
   Houston Police Department, Yale University Department of Economics, Commission on Fine Arts

NUMBER USAGE

Office workers encounter general and specific numbers in documents.

a. References to general numbers are expressed in words.
   Approximately two hundred executives attended today's workshop.

b. References to specific numbers are expressed in figures.
   There were 197 executives attending today's workshop.

   TIP: Remember to be consistent in your number style. Here are some rules to follow when working with numbers.

Rule 13: Numbers One through Ten (Chapter 6)
Use words for:

a. Numbers ten and under
   They ordered five flat-panel computer monitors.

b. Street names ten and under
   4012 Seventh Avenue

c. Units of time ten and under

Her manager stayed in Europe for six months.

d. Numbers appearing consecutively that can be written with fewer letters

Everyone recommends drinking at least six 8-ounce glasses of water daily.

We must approve the fire code in 18 ten-unit buildings today.

Use figures for:

a. References to numbers below and above ten when used together

We ordered 6 computer mice, 11 enhanced keyboards, and 20 scanners.

b. References to numbers above ten

We expected 150 participants to register for the conference.

Rule 14: Dates (Chapter 6)

Use words for formal usage.

The opening invitation read: September ninth, two thousand ten

Use figures for:

a. Dates in business documents

November 10, 200X
10 November 200X (military, foreign, and some government correspondence)

b. A date when it follows the name of the month (never use *th, d, st, rd,* or *nd* when a date follows the name of the month)

The report will be presented at the staff meeting on June 7 (not June 7th).

c. A date including the word *of* (In this case, use *th, nd, rd,* or *st* after the figure, or else spell out the number.)

The report will be presented at the staff meeting on the 7th of June.

Rule 15: Percentages (Chapter 6)

Use the figure:

a. Plus the word *percent*

The report showed 25 percent of the respondents . . .

b. In tabulations with the % symbol

| DVDs | 11% |
| CDs | 89% |

Rule 16: Time (Chapter 7)

Use words for clock time if the word *o'clock* is used or understood.

They arrived at six o'clock.

Use figures for:

a. Clock time if the expression is followed by *a.m.* or *p.m.*

They arrived at 8 a.m.

(Note the colon and zeroes are not used for "on the hour" time. However, use the colon and zeroes in a listing of times to provide consistency.)

b. Exact units of time

Their observations took 1 year and 3 months.

Rule 17: Serial and Similar Numbers (Chapter 7)
Use figures for:

a. Measures and measurements

The cyclists finished the last 30 miles of their trip.

The length of the desk measured 6 feet 3 inches.

b. Serial, model, policy, invoice, and number (No.) references (Capitalize *serial, model, policy,* and so on when used.)

The computer system was listed as Serial WX-01-128-6399 and Model 1401-B.

His Policy No. 32-00789-1 was being reevaluated.

GRAMMAR

Grammar is a system of principles or rules that tells us how to use the parts of speech correctly. Once you know the basic rules, it is easier to communicate. Before you study the following rules and complete the exercises, review the parts of speech and how they are used.

Nouns name people, animals, places, ideas, concepts, activities, qualities, and things.

Pronouns are words that replace nouns, such as *his, her,* and *them.*

Adjectives modify or describe a noun or pronoun, such as "He is a *fast* transcriber."

Verbs show action or link a noun with words that describe the noun, such as "The president *called a* meeting."

Adverbs modify a verb, an adjective, or another adverb, such as "She *quickly* filed the report."

Conjunctions join words or clauses, such as *and, or,* and *but.*

Interjections show surprise or other strong emotion, such as *My!, Oh!,* or *Great!*

Prepositions relate nouns or pronouns to other words in the sentence, such as *in, at,* and *through.*

Rule 18: Subject and Verb Agreement (Chapter 8)
a. Make sure the subject and verb always agree in person and number. A singular person must have a singular verb.

Subject	Verb
Each [singular] of the workers	*completes* [singular] the report.
All [plural] of the workers	*complete* [plural] the report.
The *president* [singular], as well as the other officers,	*has* [singular] arrived.

b. Use a plural verb if two or more singular nouns are linked by *and.*

Helen and Pam [plural] *work* [plural] in the afternoon.

c. Use a singular verb if two or more singular nouns are linked by *nor* or *or.*
Neither Helen *nor* [singular] Pam *works* [singular] in the afternoons.

Rule 19: Noun and Pronoun Agreement (Chapter 9)
A noun and its pronoun must agree in person and number.

Every *one* of the branch offices had *its* own Christmas party.

Note: The pronouns anyone, each, everyone, everything, someone, either, neither, nobody, and another are always singular; therefore, a singular verb should be used.

Rule 20: Parallel Construction (Chapter 10)
Parts of a sentence that are parallel in function should be parallel in form.

Correct: The president *approved* the last three policies, and then the board of directors *rejected* them.

Incorrect: Stephanie enjoys *swimming, hiking,* and *played* basketball.

Rule 21: Make Modifiers Clear (Chapter 11)
Modifiers (words, phrases, and clauses) describe, limit, detail, or in some way change the meaning of the subject. Place the modifier close to the word it is supposed to modify.

Incorrect: *Having been trained on project management software,* the *manager* asked *Yun-Sung* to demonstrate it. (Who had been trained on the software?)

Correct: The manager asked *Yun-Sung,* who had been *trained on project management software,* to demonstrate it.

Rule 22: Use Adjectives and Adverbs Correctly (Chapter 12)
Use adjectives to modify nouns and pronouns and adverbs to modify verbs, adjectives, or other adverbs.

Incorrect: She works *careless* (adjective).
Correct: She works *carelessly* (adverb).
Incorrect: Mary proofs *considerable* (adjective) faster than Jenneth.
Correct: Mary proofs *considerably* (adverb) faster than Jenneth.

Commonly misused words: *good* and *well,* and *real* and *really. Good* (adjective) must modify a noun; *well* is used as an adverb or an adjective.

Incorrect: He did good.
  She doesn't feel good.
Correct: He did a *good* [adjective] job.
  He did well.
  She doesn't feel well.

Real is an adjective; *really* is an adverb.

Incorrect:	They are *real* effective presenters.
Correct:	They are *really* [adverb] effective presenters.
	She is wearing a *real* [adjective] leather jacket.

Rule 23: Choose Active-Voice over Passive-Voice (Chapter 13)

The property of a verb that indicates whether the subject acts or is acted upon is either active or passive voice. In sentences that are written with active-voice verbs, the subject of the sentence is the doer of the action. In sentences written with passive-voice verbs, the subject is acted upon.

Active voice: Lisa managed the apartments for ten years.

Passive voice: The apartments were managed by Lisa for ten years.

Notice in the active voice the emphasis is on Lisa. Active-voice sentences are shorter, more direct, and easier to understand than passive-voice sentences. The reader knows immediately who did the action. Most business writing should use active-voice verbs.

In the passive-voice sentence the emphasis is on apartments. Passive-voice sentences show less emphasis on who did the action. When writing about a sensitive issue such as negative news, the passive voice can be used to soften the blow and avoid directness.

Rule 24: Plural and Possessive Form of Words (Chapter 14)

When you are uncertain about the plural form of a word, consult a dictionary. The plurals of hyphenated or spaced compounds are formed by pluralizing the main element of the compound; for example, the rule for pluralizing *editor* in chief is *editors* in chief, and more than one *letter* of credit would be *letters* of credit.

Capital letters and abbreviations ending with capital letters are pluralized by adding *s* alone. Here are a few examples: three VIPs, HMOs, and PTAs.

When the first element of a compound is a *possessive*, simply pluralize the final element. For instance, proofreader's mark would be written as proofreader's mark*s* and visitor's parking permit would be shown as visitor's parking permit*s*.

Index